OPEN BOUNDARIES
A Canadian Women's Studies Reader

Barbara A. Crow
University of Calgary
Lise Gotell
University of Alberta

Prentice Hall Allyn and Bacon Canada

> **To our feminist foremothers who built the
> Women's Studies programs we now inhabit.**

Canadian Cataloguing in Publication Data

Crow, Barbara A.
  Open boundaries : a Canadian women's studies reader

Includes index.
ISBN 0-13-020568-0

1. Feminism — Canada. I. Gotell, Lise. II. Title.

HQ1181.C3C76 2000   305.42'0971   C99-931526-9

Prentice-Hall, Inc., Upper Saddle River, New Jersey
Prentice-Hall International (UK) Limited, London
Prentice-Hall of Australia, Pty. Limited, Sydney
Prentice-Hall Hispanoamericana, S.A., Mexico City
Prentice-Hall of India Private Limited, New Delhi
Prentice-Hall of Japan, Inc., Tokyo
Simon & Schuster Southeast Asia Private Limited, Singapore
Editora Prentice-Hall do Brasil, Ltda., Rio de Janeiro

ISBN 0-13-020568-0

Vice President, Editorial Director: Michael Young
Acquisitions Editor: Nicole Lukach
Marketing Manager: Christine Cozens
Signing Representative: Andy Wellner
Developmental Editor: Lise Creurer
Production Editor: Cathy Zerbst
Copy Editor: Miriam Walfish
Production Coordinator: Wendy Moran
Art Director: Julia Hall
Cover Design: Liz Harasymczuk
Cover Image: Tony Stone
Page Layout: Gerry Dunn

1 2 3 4 5   04 03 02 01 00

Printed and bound in Canada.

Visit the Prentice Hall Canada Web site! Send us your comments, browse our catalogues,
and more at **www.phcanada.com**.

CONTENTS

Chapter Three: The Gendered Division of Labour and the Family   169

Chapter Four: Sexuality   231

PREFACE

Our challenge as Women's Studies scholars is to continue the feminist work of "asking questions," and to sustain a place where such questions can be posed. While the controversies that mark feminist scholarship are not settled, we believe that Women's Studies is a vital place where questions can be asked, appreciated, and debated. The sense of open boundaries that we believe is integral to Women's Studies made it difficult to determine the content of this volume. We are not trying to define the "discipline" in this reader; Women's Studies is by necessity interdisciplinary and "definitions" are temporary. Our approach has been to bracket some central topics, questions, and contributions.

There were many pieces we wanted to include, but space requirements limited our selections. We debated how to include the pieces. Many of the pieces have been abridged to allow us to capture the main points of a wide variety of feminist authors. We selected six topic areas where we think Canadian feminists have made significant contributions in the social sciences: "Canadian Feminist Theories," "The Canadian Women's Movements," "The Gendered Division of Labour and the Family," "Sexuality," "Reproduction," and "Engendering Violence." These six areas are ones that typically frame the organization of introductory courses.

This collection is shaped by our own individual studies, by our training in eastern Canadian universities (we met as graduate students at York University) and by our work as assistant professors in Women's Studies at the University of Calgary and the University of Alberta. When we put the collection together we recognized that we needed to narrow our representation of Canadian feminism and in some ways, the nature of our representation has been shaped by Canadian feminist scholarship itself. Socialist feminist theory and research have been important to the development of Women's Studies in Canada.

As early as 1969, Margaret Benston argued in "The Political Economy of Women's Liberation" that women's work, women's *unpaid* work, is integral to capitalist societies and that in order for women to be liberated, unpaid work needed to be theorized and politicized. Benston's insights are further developed and refined in the chapters on "Canadian Feminist Theories" and "The Gendered Division of Labour and the Family." One of the critical changes that occurred in the post-war period was the expansion of women's labour force participation and the creation of the double day as a reality for the majority of Canadian women. Socialist feminist scholarship has sought to theorize the importance of the sexual division of labour and to make sense of how family and work are interconnected. With its emphasis on material conditions and social relationships, socialist feminist scholarship has provided rich ground for analyzing the differences between women's experiences of family, and the dominant ideology of the heterosexual family in terms of race and class.

The challenges posed by postmodernism, with its rejection of grand theory and its attention to "women" as a constructed category, are the source of one of the central debates in feminist scholarship and in turn, in Canadian feminist theory. It might seem as though this theoretical challenge represents contemporary Canadian feminism and Canadian Women's Studies. But as this text emphasizes, debates over postmodern ideas occur within an already established tradition, one in which socialist feminism has been extremely influential.

Other chapters of this volume on the "Canadian Women's Movement," "Sexuality," "Reproduction" and "Engendering Violence" reveal how Canadian feminist analysis has developed and established a dialogue around key issues. The work on the Canadian women's movement is quite substantial and extremely important to consider in light of the federal government's recent decision not to fund the National Action Committee on the Status of Women. Historically, the Canadian women's movement has had an engaged relationship with the state, and has lobbied the government to encourage equality through the extension of the welfare state. The embrace of neo-conservative agendas, decreased funding for social programmes and the construction of social movements as "special interest groups" has had an extremely damaging impact on feminist activism. Today, we need new strategies to keep social justice on the government platform. The literature on the Canadian women's movement reveals significant theoretical and activist engagement with race, gender, class and sexuality.

In the chapter on "Sexuality" we seek to highlight the ways in which Canadian feminism has theorized the institution of heterosexuality. Representations of heterosexuality are challenged and contested within the contributions on pornography. The readings in this chapter also undermine heterosexual privilege and compulsory heterosexuality by giving voice to lesbian and transgender identities. Similarly, as we illustrate in the chapter on "Reproduction," once the major battle for abortion rights was won in Canada, issues surrounding reproduction, and more specifically, new reproductive technologies, have been hotly debated. Canadian feminists were successful in demanding and facilitating a Royal Commission on New Reproductive Technologies (1993). The Commission ensured that Canadian women were guaranteed the right to information about the status, the various success rates and the risks of these technologies. Generally, Canadian feminists have opposed reproductive technologies with few dissenting voices (McCormack 1989, Achilles 1993).

Finally, in the chapter on "Engendering Violence," we try to reveal the importance of theorizing violence within Canadian feminism. Oddly, while Canadian feminists still struggle with the issue of funding and are concerned about how shelters have been institutionalized, violence against women has become part of the Canadian public consciousness. Even though Canadian criminal legislation is heralded world-wide,[1] the battles around gender violence are far from won. Recent Canadian analyses of violence illustrates how governments have managed to take over feminist violence discourse, while at the same time, the authority of feminist scholars and activists has been eroded.

As we emphasize in the reader as a whole, the creation and sustenance of feminist knowledge is vitally important. Without the rich spaces offered by Women's Studies programmes, this project would not continue. Women's Studies plays a particular role in the university. Its interdisciplinary approach allows students to look at topics from a broad range of academic disciplines. It takes a problem-based approach to thinking, and encourages this thinking as a development in contemporary higher education. The kind of rigorous critical thinking that Women's Studies promotes is essential if universities are to fulfill their role in helping people find their place in an increasing plural, interdependent, and changing world. Certainly, as Louise Forsyth highlights in her essay in this reader, Women's Studies confronts multiple challenges at the end of the millenium, but this is also a time of exciting possibilities.

---

1 Canada, for example, is unique in including a statutory definition of consent as "voluntary agreement" in Criminal Code provisions in sexual assault. At a 1997 international conference on "Gender, Sexuality and Law" held at Keele University, U.K., participants from many countries expressed surprise upon hearing a paper critical of the interpretation of Canadian sexual assault law. A woman from South Africa indicated that feminist reformers in her country have used the Canadian legislation as a model in their lobbying.

ACKNOWLEDGMENTS

I would like to thank the feminist scholars and activists who have encouraged, facilitated, and challenged my participation in Women's Studies at York University, Rutgers University, Hunter College and the University of Calgary. In particular, I would like to acknowledge Professor Naomi Black for her initial encouragement for me to enroll as a double major in Women's Studies at York University and her guidance during my graduate studies.

I would like to thank my co-editor Lise Gotell for her insightful and critical analytic skills that have shaped this collection. As well, despite the distance and our two small children, child care arrangements, frantic emails in the early morning—our friendship has been strengthened and I look forward to more opportunities to work collaboratively.

I would like to thank Nancy Bennett, Paige Hamilton-Platten, Susan Prentice, Susan Rudy and Melanie Sinclair for their assistance with this project. In particular, I would like to thank my in-laws, Beverly Longford and Sydney Longford, for their long visits to care for Eli while Michael and I managed full time jobs in Montreal and Calgary—I could not have completed the project without them. And finally, thanks to my partner, Michael Longford, for his continued support of my efforts in Women's Studies.

— Barbara Crow

Without the enthusiasm of my friend and colleague, Barbara Crow, this project would not have begun. This reader came into my life at a difficult time and its completion has been a true struggle for me. Barbara's engagement in and commitment to Canadian Women's Studies inspired my participation. Negotiating sometimes differing scholarly perspectives and as well as challenges of distance, childcare and very busy schedules has only strengthened our friendship and our academic partnership.

My work on this collection has been enabled by all of my friends who have helped me care for my son Liam and supported me in so many other ways while I have rushed to meet deadlines—Jane Arscott, Chris Gabriel, Mary Hughes, Brodie Nutbrown, Anna Pellatt, Claudine Potvin, Annis May Timpson and Janice Williamson. These friends and my colleagues in the Women's Studies Program at the University of Alberta, especially Dallas Cullen, have sustained and encouraged me, reminding me of the value of a Canadian Women's Studies reader. Claudine Potvin, through her constant care and countless cups of coffee, has been my anchor in this and in all of my other challenges. My son Liam, as always, reminds me what is truly important in life and helps to put work in its place.

I too would like to thank my academic feminist "foremothers" without whose guidance I would never have been able to begin my journey as a feminist scholar.

— Lise Gotell

We would also like to thank the Faculty of General Studies at the University of Calgary for a small grant that allowed Deidre Martin to secure the preliminary set of permissions and the University of Alberta Faculty of Arts for its support through the Support for the Advancement of Scholarship Fund. Julianna Wiens' research assistance and work on proofreading the collection demonstrates the value and skills obtained through a Women's Studies degree. We are also grateful to the staff at Prentice-Hall, particularly Rebecca Bergasel who started the project, Nicole Lukach, Carina Blåfield and Cathy Zerbst, and to our copy editor Miriam Walfish. Finally, we must acknowledge the many feminist voices that speak through the pages of this volume. The authors of the pieces we include have shaped, nurtured and challenged Canadian Women's Studies.

CREDITS

Nancy Adamson, Linda Briskin, and Margaret McPhail, excerpted from *Feminists Organizing for Social Change: The Contemporary Women's Movement in Canada*. Copyright © Nancy Adamson, Linda Briskin, Margaret McPhail, 1988. Reprinted by permission of Oxford University Press Canada.

Vijay, Agnew, "Race, Class and Feminist Practice" in *Resisting Discrimination: Women from Asia, Africa, and the Caribbean and the Women's Movement in Canada* (Toronto: University of Toronto Press, 1996), pp. 66–92. Reprinted by permission of the University of Toronto Press Incorporated.

Pat Armstrong, excerpted from "Restructuring Public & Private: Women's Paid and Unpaid Work" in Susan Boyd, ed., *Challenging the Public/Private Divide: Feminism, Law, and Public Policy* (Toronto: University of Toronto Press, 1997), pp. 37–61. Reprinted by permission of the University of Toronto Press Incorporated.

Katherine Arnup, excerpted from "Living in the Margins: Lesbian Families and the Law," in Katherine Arnup, ed., *Lesbian Parenting: Living with Pride and Prejudice* (Charlottetown: gynergy books, 1995; 1997), pp. 378–398. Reprinted with the permission of Katherine Arnup.

Himani Bannerji, "Introducing Racism: Notes Towards an Anti-Racist Feminism," *Resources for Feminist Research/Documentation sur la recherche feministe*, Vol. 16, No. 1, March 1987, pp. 10–12.

Shannon Bell, excerpted from "Feminist Ejaculations" in Arthur Kroker and Marilouise Kroker, eds., *The Hysterical Male: New Feminist Theory* (New York: St. Martin's Press, 1991), pp. 151–169.

Margaret Benston, "The Political Economy of Women's Liberation," *Monthly Review*, Vol. 21, September, 1969, pp. 194–205. Copyright © 1969 by Monthly Review Press. Reprinted by permission of Monthly Review Foundation.

Judy Bernstein, Peggy Morton, Linda Seese, and Myrna Wood, "Sisters, Brothers, Lovers...Listen," in *Up from the Kitchen, Up from the Bedroom, Up from Under, Women Unite!: An Anthology of the Canadian Women's Movement* (Toronto: Canadian Women's Educational Press, 1972), pp. 31–39.

Janine Brodie, Shelley Gavigan and Jane Jensen, "The Politics of Abortion" in *The Politics of Abortion* (Toronto: Oxford University Press), pp. 8–13.

Lorenne Clark and Debra Lewis, "The Problem of rape" in *Rape: The Price of Coercive Sexuality* (Toronto: The Women's Press, 1977), pp. 23–30. Reprinted with permission of Lorenne Clark.

Susan G. Cole, excerpted from *Pornography and the Sex Crisis* (Toronto: Second Story Press, 1992), pp. 17–60.

Elly Danica, "Chapter 1," copyright © Elly Danica from *Don't: A Woman's Word* (Charlottetown: gynergy books, 1998), pp. 7–14. Used with permission of the publisher.

Tania Das Gupta, excerpted from "Families of Native Peoples, Immigrants, and People of Colour," in Nancy Mandell and Ann Duffy, eds., *Canadian Families: Diversity, Conflict*

T. Brettel Dawson, "First Person Familiar: Judicial Intervention in Pregnancy, Again: G. (D.F.)," *Canadian Journal of Women and the Law*, Vol. 10, No. 1, 1998, pp. 213–228.

Louise Forsyth, "Women's Studies. What do we need Now? Celebration? Commiseration? Or New Boots For Walking? Intellectual Challenges to Teaching and Research in Women's Studies," University of Alberta, October 23–24, 1998.

Bonnie Fox, ed., excerpted from "Introduction" in *Hidden in the Household: Women's Domestic Labour Under Capitalism* (Toronto: The Women's Press, 1980), pp. 9–15.

Lise Gotell, "A Critical Look at State Discourse on 'Violence Against Women': Some Implications for Feminist Politics and Women's Citizenship" in Caroline Andrew and Manon Tremblay, eds., *Women and Political Representation in Canada* (Ottawa: Ottawa University Press, 1998), pp. 39–84.

Roberta Hamilton, excerpts from "An Examination of the Marxist and Feminist Theories," in *The Liberation of Women* (London: George Allen & Unwin, 1978), pp. 76–105.

Marlee Kline, "Complicating the Ideology of Motherhood: Child Welfare and First Nation Women," *Queen's Law Journal*, No. 18, 1993, pp. 310–319; 338–341.

"List of Recommendations," in *Report on the Royal Commission on the Status of Women in Canada* (Ottawa: Information Canada, 1970), pp. 395–418. Reproduced with the permission of the Minister of Public Works and Government Services Canada, 1999.

"Looking Through a Feminist Lens" in *Canadian Panel on Violence Against Women* (Ottawa: Canadian Panel on Violence Against Women, 1993), pp. 3–22. Reproduced with the permission of the Minister of Public Works and Government Services Canada, 1999.

Eleanor MacDonald, excerpted from "Critical Identities: Rethinking Feminism Through Transgender Politics," *Atlantis*, Vol. 23, No. 1, Fall, 1998, pp. 3–12.

Linda MacLeod, "Wife Battering can happen in your Family" in *Wife Battering in Canada: The Vicious Circle* (Ottawa: Canadian Advisory Council on the Status of Women in Canada, 1980), pp. 5–8. Reproduced with the permission of the Minister of Public Works and Government Services Canada, 1999.

Lee Maracle, "Isn't Love a Given" in *I Am Woman: A Native Perspective on Sociology and Feminism* (Vancouver: Press Gang Publishers, 1988; 1996), pp. 20–30.

Thelma McCormack, excerpted from "Public Policies and Reproductive Technology: A Feminist Critique," *Canadian Public Policy*, Vol. 15, No. 4, 1998, pp. 361–375.

Sheila McIntyre and Jennifer Scott, Submissions to the Committee on Justice and Legal Affairs Review of Bill c-46, 1997, pp. 3–11.

Heather Menzies, excerpted from "The Social Construction of Reproductive Technologies and of Choice" in Gwynne Basen, Margrit Eichler and Abby Lippman, eds., *Misconceptions: The Social Construction of Choice and New Reproductive Technologies*, Vol. 2 (Maple Pond, Ont.: Voyageur Publishing, 1993), pp. 17–32.

Angela Miles, excerpts from "Global Visions," in *Integrative Feminisms: Building Global Visions 1960s–1990s* (New York: Routledge, Copyright © 1996), pp. 131–145. Reproduced by permission of Routledge, Inc.

Roxana Ng, excerpts from "Sexism, Racism and Canadian Nationalism," *Socialist Studies/Etudes Socialitestes: A Canadian Annual,* No. 5, 1989, pp. 12–26.

Mary O'Brien, excerpts from "Production and Reproduction" in *The Politics of Reproduction* (London: Routledge and Kegan Paul, 1981), pp.140–184.

INTRODUCTION: WHAT IS WOMEN'S STUDIES?

Barbara Crow and Lise Gotell

Women's Studies places women at the centre of inquiry. It is a field of study that developed out of a critique of phallocentric knowledge, which treats men's experiences as central and representative of the universal. The academic study of women and gender usually reaches beyond disciplines, partly because of the questions it asks, which initially arose from feminist activism, not from the paradigm of any discipline. In fact, Women's Studies has been described as the institutional arm of the women's movement.

In the 1970s, when many students and faculty became active in social movements, including the students', civil rights, gay rights, antiwar, and women's movements, women started to demand space for themselves within higher education. These activist academics fundamentally challenged prevailing canons by asking critical questions about what constituted knowledge and whose knowledge was legitimated and valued. It was from these political roots that the first Women's Studies programs sprung up in Canadian universities almost 30 years ago. Women's Studies as a field of scholarly endeavour may be marked by deep diversity, and this is something we highlight in this reader, but its common features are its overtly political nature, its commitment to material and social change, and its commitment to breaking down the traditional academic boundaries between the personal and political.

Although feminist practice and Women's Studies scholarship are entwined, academic feminism has often been charged with diverting focus away from feminist political struggles. Feminist academics have been critiqued for producing theory rather than focussing on real life conditions, for being elitist and inaccessible. In this collection, however, we take the view that it is not theorizing and academic practice per se that are problematic, it is instead particular theories and practices. There are exciting possibilities for critical and exploratory thought outside the constraints of the everyday. Indeed, much contemporary feminist debate occurs in academia; the strength of this work is the critical distance academia provides, creating opportunities for theorizing and renegotiating gender relations (Kemp and Squires, 1997, 6). Women's Studies must be viewed as an element of a wider feminist endeavour, and conversations between activists and scholars must be encouraged. This productive relationship between politics and academia has been a vital part of the Canadian Women's Studies project. In 1990, Margrit Eichler found that 93 percent of Women's Studies faculty members combine scholarship with feminist activism (1990, 7). Her study draws attention to Women's Studies as a politically informed activity.

A fundamental shift occurs in the academy when we make women subjects. In *Canadian Women's Studies/Feminist Research*, Caroline Andrew underlines the dramatic influence of Women's Studies: it is engaged in a project of rendering women visible, engendering reality, transferring knowledge and knowing, nurturing feminist pedagogy, and struggling with difference and differences (1993, 4-9). *When Women Ask the Questions: Creating Women's Studies in America*, a recent publication by history professor Marilyn Jacoby Boxer, reveals the profound effect Women's Studies has had in American universities as well. Women's Studies foregrounds feminist language, theory and methodologies. By analyzing gender relations, Women's Studies seeks to make women's subordination visible. At the same time, this field of inquiry reveals the social construction of the category "women" and thereby contests its meaning.

A central shortcoming of early Canadian Women's Studies was its essentialism. In other words, feminist scholars described gender relations as an analytic category separable from race, class, sexuality and ability. The conception of women's experience informing and underpinning this approach reflected the identities and concerns of white middle-class women. In recent years, our understanding of women's experience has widened to include historically marginalized voices. Some of the contributions in this volume, for example the pieces by Bannerji, Ng and Valverde, have propelled this development. In the current context, the category "women" has emerged as a conceptual window for interrogating interlocking systems of power, including race, class and sexuality.

Diversity in Focus: Our Approach in This Reader

Academic feminism at the turn of the millennium is marked by diversity of method, motivation and focus. In its earlier days, feminism, newly institutionalized in Women's Studies programs, adopted a posture of defensiveness by necessity. Attempting to legitimize their place in the university where the study of women had never been seen as scholarly or worthwhile, Women's Studies practitioners emphasized the unity or potential unity of feminism and its challenge to patriarchal scholarship. Almost 30 years after the establishment of the first Canadian Women's Studies program, we are fortunate to be the beneficiaries of that first wave of academic feminist struggle. The development of Women's Studies programs has contributed to the creation of a space in which the differences that constitute feminism can find their fullest expression.

It is our intention in this text to provide an overview of some key debates that have marked the evolution of Women's Studies in Canada. We are second-generation feminist scholars; the struggles and achievements of our academic foremothers have enabled us to inhabit our classrooms as places of respectful debate and challenge. One of the critical insights of feminism has been the claim that knowledge is always situated and engaged. In this way feminism challenges the very claim that knowledge is objective. The "view from nowhere gaze" that has been the centre of post-Enlightenment Western thought has been dethroned and revealed as masking the specific perspective and interests of dominant social groups. With this insight comes the necessary realization that the creation of feminist "Truth" cannot be the aim of Women's Studies scholarship. Instead, as graduate student Eva Karpinski recently emphasized, the notion of community that we create must "accommodate critique and questioning" and the right to "dissent and disagreement"; it must be "specific, situated, self-critical" (1998, 139). The unsettling of foundations that has characterized feminism's relationship with traditional academic disciplines must be brought into the very heart of

Women's Studies. Offering competing answers to an ever-changing set of questions and providing students with the critical tools to assess contending perspectives is how we see the role of academic Women's Studies practitioners.

We compiled this reader with this approach to teaching Women's Studies in mind. While there have been some fine Canadian introductory texts, a text, or even a collection of overview articles, cannot always illuminate the rich contours and distinctive edges that comprise Women's Studies scholarship. It is for this reason that many instructors have supplemented texts with course kits designed to bring a multiplicity of voices to students.

This collection, focussing on the development of Canadian Women's Studies scholarship in English, grew out of our own efforts to map for our students the diverse contributions of Canadian scholars. It is our hope that this reader will reveal the dynamic nature of Canadian feminist debates, the genuine diversity within current feminist theory and some of the central issues at stake in the differing approaches to feminist activism.

The Institutionalization of Canadian Women's Studies

The first undergraduate course in Women's Studies in Canada was offered by Professor Marlene Dixon at McGill University. Since this first course, almost every Canadian university has established an undergraduate program in Women's Studies, beginning with the University of Toronto in 1974. Initial programs borrowed and cross-listed courses from various disciplines. Some of these courses focussed on "women and" or "women in," such as "Woman and Politics" and "Women in Canadian Literature," with an emphasis on making women visible where they had once been absent. More recently, some programs have obtained designated budget lines and core faculty. Courses now interrogate the production of gender and its intersection with race, class, and sexuality, and include such titles as "Queer Theory," "Gender, Race and Class," "From Silence to Song: Voices of Women with a Disability," and "Feminist Culture/Popular Culture." While there has been a dramatic shift from the concerns and emphases of earlier course offerings and there is greater institutional commitment, many programs still rely on unstable funding, the cross-listing of courses and the good will of feminist faculty. Cross-listing courses enables the interdisciplinarity that is a critical dimension of Women's Studies. Nevertheless, many Canadian Women's Studies programs are forced to rely almost exclusively on cross-listed courses. When programs are not able to mount core courses, curricular development is impeded. Programs that rely upon cross-listed courses are at the mercy of the planning priorities of other units.

As the twentieth century draws to a close, some Canadian Women's Studies programs are still struggling to get off the ground, while others are expanding with the hiring of young scholars and the introduction of new courses and graduate study.[1] A special issue of the U.S. journal *differences* entitled "Women's Studies on the Edge" (1997) captures the contradictory state of Women's Studies at the end of the millennium. It points out that Women's Studies' intellectual work remains on the critical "edge," asking new questions and taking theoretical perspectives that enliven its continued challenge to masculinist scholarship; but Women's Studies also remains on the "edge" in the sense that programs remain very much struggling on the institutional margins of the university. As Yee contends, it may be that Women's Studies "occupies an embattled position on campuses" precisely because it makes "women and feminism visible in the academies" (1997, 50).

Accompanying the development of Women's Studies and women's increased participation in post-secondary institutions,[2] there has also been a growth of services designed for and by this constituency. These services include the creation of women's centres and sexual harassment offices, the support of feminist scholarship through various awards, the formation of women's committees as offshoots of larger university representative bodies,[3] the establishment of special library collections,[4] and the implementation of various university policy initiatives, including pay and employment equity. These developments reflect not only the increased presence of women in post-secondary education, but also the political role of Women's Studies faculty who have been at the forefront of struggles for the kinds of institutional changes that are required to make universities more hospitable to all students, staff and faculty.

The phenomenal growth in feminist scholarship that has occurred over the past 25 years is reflected in ongoing Canadian feminist journals, presses, and associations. As Gabriel and Scott highlight, feminist publishing has a crucial role to play:

> Women have struggled long and hard to find a place in public discourse. The lack of access to critical material resources such as printing and publishing has been a significant barrier to efforts to create and disseminate a counter-hegemonic discourse against the dominant patriarchal, racist and homophobic mechanisms of capitalist society. Feminist publishing [has] worked to recover women's history, provided women with alternative political views and generally been part of the organized expression of the movement. (1993, 26)

From its beginnings, Canadian academic feminism has confronted disciplinary journals and other scholarly fora resistant to the insights offered by feminist approaches. This resistance lingers on. For example, Arscott and Tremblay found that in the 30-year history of the *Canadian Journal of Political Science*, only 3.5% of its articles have focussed on women (1999, 128–129). In this context, the proliferation of Canadian feminist journals, associations, and presses has proven essential for the creation of research and theory. Publications such as *Resources for Feminist Research* (1972), *Atlantis* (1974), *Canadian Woman Studies* (1978), *Fireweed* (1979), *Tessera* (1983), and *Canadian Journal of Women and the Law* (1985) have become internationally recognized journals. Feminist presses now include Press Gang (1970), the Toronto Women's Press (1972), Eden Press (1977), gynergy books (1987), and Sister Vision Press (1984). Academic associations fostering feminist scholarship and creating the possibility of conversations among diverse researchers include the Canadian Research Institute for the Advancement of Women (CRIAW) (1976), the Canadian Women's Movement Archives (CWMA) (1976), the Canadian Congress for Learning Opportunities for Women (CCLOW) (1978), the Canadian Women's Studies Association (CWSA) (1982), the National Association of Women and the Law (NAWL) (1980) and most recently, the establishment of five Women's Studies chairs (1985). As well, there are two important documentation centres, the Centre de documentation conseil du statut de la femme in Quebec City and the Women's Educational Resources Centre in Toronto. Finally, there is now a significant literature exploring and analyzing women in Canada (see bibliography) to which this reader contributes.

Canadian Women's Studies: Analytic Tools and Changing Directions

The analytic tools of Women's Studies are feminism, sex, gender, race and class. Definitions of feminism as both a practice and an academic endeavour now proliferate. Most introductory Women's Studies courses present a typology of feminist theories, and these feminisms are modified by other theoretical positions—for example, liberal feminism, Marxist feminism, psychoanalytic feminism, and postmodernist feminism. What many professors and students find in this typology is that feminist theories overlap and that any attempt to define feminism narrowly or categorically, without multiplicity, will inevitably be problematic. Nonetheless, it is important to understand the divergent approaches feminist scholars have employed in their efforts to analyze systems of domination. Much of this reader represents a conversation among competing feminist theories. In keeping with our focus on Women's Studies as a field of academic inquiry marked by diverse voices, we prefer the encompassing approach to feminist theory Elliott and Mandell put forward in *Feminist Issues: Race, Class, and Sexuality* (1998):

> First, feminist theorists seek to understand the gendered nature of virtually all social and institutional relations... Second, gender relations are constructed as problematic and as related to other inequities and contradictions in social life... Third, gender relations are not viewed as either natural or immutable but as historical and sociocultural productions, subject to reconstitution. Fourth, feminist theories tend to be explicitly political in their advocacy for social change. (4)

In advocating for egalitarian social change, feminist scholars have been forced to recognize that, as bell hooks argues, if "feminism is a movement to end sexist oppression, then it must not focus exclusively on any specific group of women, any particular race or class of women" (1997, 26). Attention to the construction, formation and articulation of gender by many of the contributions to this reader reveals that gender is made in specific ways. To understand the content poured into the category "women," we need to recognize the racial construction of that category; we need to recognize that the material conditions of middle-class professional women and women living in poverty differ in fundamental ways; and we need to acknowledge that compulsory heterosexuality and norms of gender conformity have an impact on how lesbians, bisexuals and transgendered people relate to the category "woman." Disentangling the complex relationships, discourses and material structures that intersect on the very bodies of contemporary Canadian women is a preoccupation of contemporary Women's Studies.

It is also important that we interrogate and disrupt the place of "nation" and "Canadian" in Women's Studies, especially in the contemporary global context of the rise of ethnic nationalism. Canada is a country where feminist organizing is divided by national identity and where scholarly conversation is often difficult because of linguistic duality. Given the close association between Quebec feminism, the Quebec state and the project of Quebec nationalism, most scholars now recognize that there is a fundamental division between Quebec feminism and feminism in the "rest of Canada" (Lamoureux, 1987). Our collection does not include any selections in French and therefore does not address the different trajectories and voices that constitute Quebec feminism. However, we chose not to modify "Canadian" with the adjective English in the title of this volume in order to encompass the national identities of First Nations' women, whose scholarship has greatly influenced Canadian feminist thought, and the contributions of immigrant women with diverse ethnic and linguistic identities. Much scholarship by immigrant women, women of colour and native women has been concerned with identifying the racist, classist and sexist dimensions of Canadian nation-building and construction. The feminist anthology *Painting the Maple* provides us with ways to problematize and reveal how "Canada" invokes certain exclusionary assumptions and values (1998).

It is difficult to pin down the distinctive characteristics of Women's Studies in Canada, mainly because of the plurality of voices in this forum and the manner in which these voices contest the meaning of Canadian nationhood. Contemporary Canadian feminism is shaped by the maternal feminist legacy of the "first wave" and by the organizations and activists that struggled on after the vote was won.[5] It has also been shaped by our colonial history and by the cultural and economic dominance of the United States. Nevertheless, some feminist scholars have sought to articulate the specific configuration of Canadian Women's Studies.

Maroney and Luxton emphasize the overwhelming contributions that Canadian socialist feminists have made to academic scholarship. This tradition can be understood as the result of Marxist-influenced social movements in the 1960s and to social democratic traditions that have maintained an openness to socialist politics in Canada (1987, 8). As the reader moves through this volume, she confronts the legacy of this socialist feminist tradition—its careful analysis of work and family and its attention to political economy. It is also the case that most contemporary Women's Studies instructors have been critically influenced by this tradition, both as its creators and students.

Another distinctive feature of Canadian Women's Studies scholarship grows out of the particular character of feminist politics after World War II. Whereas it could be argued that only a minimalist welfare state emerged in the United States, in post-war Canada the state underwent massive expansion, taking on new roles and engaging in the project of ensuring social citizenship. Women's movement activism has thus focussed on the state, and (with the exception of Quebec) on the federal state, given its central role as the initiator of social programs and the guarantor of national standards. This focus has resulted in a rich literature within Canadian Women's Studies that interrogates the role of the state vis-à-vis women. As the threads of the Canadian welfare state have been dismantled over the past 15 years, an equally rich literature has emerged disentangling the impacts of neo-liberalism on feminism (Brodie, 1995).

But it would be a great simplification to define socialist feminism and state theory as the essence of Canadian Women's Studies. Women's Studies everywhere has become the site of multiple inquiries and new kinds of questions. Many initial contributions to Canadian Women's Studies stressed the sociological and the material, and while this rich tradition continues to have a strong presence, some scholars have shifted their attention to the interaction between images and social representation, identity and upholding social order. The critical insights of radical social constructionism are represented most clearly in this volume in some of the pieces dealing with sexuality, reproduction and violence. This literature calls attention to the ways in which masculinity, femininity, race and sexuality are continually produced and reproduced in language and in discourse.

American feminist Judith Butler, for example, calls attention to gender as "performance," to the rigid binary that divides masculine from feminine and to the necessity of deconstruction, that is, the erosion of gender as dichotomy (1990). For Butler, identity always excludes just as it includes, and, given that "women" are constructed, our experience and identity provide no stable ground from which to build theory and politics. Challenging the idea that "woman" represents a fixed category, this literature calls attention to the multiple ways in which women are constructed in language and in discourse, including within feminist theory itself.

Women's Studies is a burgeoning field of intellectual inquiry and insight at almost every Canadian university. Its content, scope and direction continue to be challenged by its foremothers and its descendants. What makes Women's Studies most exciting to us is that it is both a dynamic theoretical framework and practice. Women's Studies keeps "women" on the table as a visible, yet contested and complex, category of analysis that validates the existence of women in society and addresses sexism and racism directly in the production of feminist scholarship. No other theory and practice tries to understand the relationship between systems of domination, explores and makes concrete the interconnected and interdependence of these systems of domination, and makes explicit its work for social change. Sometimes this approach has the effect of making feminism seem "messy." We believe, however, that this appearance is a reflection of the complexity of feminist theories and practices. To paraphrase Audre Lorde, while surely the master's tools cannot dismantle the master's house, such dismantling will involve the simultaneous uses of different kinds of feminist tools. We hope that this reader contributes to that complex project.

ENDNOTES

1. There are Women's Studies M.A. programs at Memorial University, University of Toronto, Simon Fraser University, York University, Carleton University (interdisciplinary M.A. through Canadian Studies), Dalhousie University (joint M.A. with Mount Saint Vincent and Saint Mary's), University of Northern British Columbia (M.A. in Gender Studies), University of Ottawa (collaborative program). The only Ph.D. program is located at York University.

2. Women's participation rates in undergraduate programs have increased from 43% in 1972 to 53% in 1992; in master's programs from 27% in 1972 to 46% in 1992; and in doctoral programs from 19% in 1972 to 35% in 1992 (Normand, 1995).

3. An example is the Canadian Association of University Teachers (CAUT) Status of Women Committee.

4. Special library collections include the Nellie Langford Rowell Library at York University and the housing of the Canadian Women's Movement Archives at Carleton University.

5. The women's movement is often described as having a first and second wave, referring to times of increased women's movement activity and public attention to it. The first wave is considered to have occurred between 1880 to 1920, with a focus on attaining political rights for women, while the second wave, from the 1960s to the present, focussed on women's bodies, specifically reproduction. More recently, young feminists have characterized the nineties as the "third wave," focussing on diversity.

WHAT DO WE NEED NOW: CELEBRATION? COMMISERATION? OR NEW BOOTS FOR WALKING?[1]

by Louise Forsyth

If I Have to Look at Those Decorations One More Time ... !

Let me begin with the admission that I am an incorrigible grinch when it comes to the official celebrations that form the patterns of our social and work calendar, the annual cycle of repetitious cultural practices that serve well a patriarchal and heterosexist agenda: Valentine's Day, St. Patrick's Day, Easter, Mother's Day, Father's Day, weddings in May, Christmas, New Year's, and yes, even Hallowe'en. Each one makes me long to find a hiding place from a relentlessly invasive culture that reinforces itself with every opportunity to buy yet another greeting card, complete with its canned message. Neither feminist and anti-racist movements nor the women's, queer, and cultural studies programs appear to have had much impact on the public forum when it comes to challenging the relentless rhythms of patriarchy's official celebrations.

I mention my personal aversion to these celebrations because, as I was walking across the campus to come to this October Research Day Forum on Women's Studies, I noticed everywhere decorations, graffiti, and posters inviting attendance at various ghoulish happenings planned to celebrate Hallowe'en. Hallowe'en is probably the least noxious of society's rituals; parts of it can even be reclaimed for women's history. Its origins have been sufficiently deformed, however, that this official moment in the life of society must be seen, like all the others, to be serving dominant ideologies by reinforcing prevailing views of women as wicked, dangerous, needing to be controlled, with violence if necessary. Even Hallowe'en then, in today's version of the tradition, fails to create the opportunity for joyful celebration of women's community, knowledge, power, beauty and spirituality.

I find it difficult to simply relax and enjoy the official calendar of collective celebrations. I find it particularly difficult to consider such days as the high spots in the course of my own life's journey. I feel that the entirely predictable annual return of ritualistic celebrations puts pressure on us to live our lives as characters in stories crafted to keep us in places suiting others, rather than us. They are like tunes whose beat keeps us busy dancing with officially designated partners. They pattern our environment uniformly; they put words in our mouths; they costume our bodies and impose a language on them. For all the fun, innocence and congeniality these celebrations appear to offer, they are a powerful, coercive form of social control. No sooner is one high holiday done than family members, colleagues, schools, the media and their advertisers announce the next.

The relentless, rhythmic beat of society's calendar of events surrounds us so completely that no individual can escape entirely from it, whether at work or in private lives. This ritual dance distracts us from shaping our own celebrations, from making our own decisions about what to celebrate, when and with whom. In doing so it produces almost insurmountable impediments to the emergence of a sense of communality on alternative bases. And I believe that this is a serious problem if we wish for an end to injustice, oppression and violence.

I both loathe having reasons for celebration dictated to me by society's fixed calendar and revel in celebrations that we conceive ourselves around shared projects, joys and passions. A sense of community, shared collective memory, vision for the future are possible only when they are represented in our celebratory events. These events may be primarily academic and professional, or they may be social. The main thing about them, though, is that we are taking time for the things that are important in our lives. This is why I'm feeling real excitement about this gathering today and tomorrow. I look forward to sharing our ideas, projects, trials and disappointments as Women's Studies scholars. We'll talk and we'll listen; we'll ask questions and share new insights. At the end of the day we'll chat, laugh, eat and drink together, at Claudine's invitation. Such opportunities to celebrate bold pioneering work in Women's Studies with friends, colleagues and students from several campuses are rare. For this reason they are to be cherished and savoured.

Because Women's Studies, and women, are still marginalized in schools, colleges and universities; because we are able so seldom to come together to share our knowledge, our passions and our frustrations; because we do not often have the time to represent ourselves to ourselves as a community, I see this conference as an exciting event, simultaneously subversive and challenging to the tenacious *status quo* that continues to require we beat to its rhythm in the university, society and our personal lives. No matter how discouraged and cynical we may sometimes feel, it is essential that we not lose the energy to come together in celebration.

What, then, are we here to celebrate during these two days?

The following points are some of the reasons why I believe there is good cause for celebration:

- Women's Studies, like Gay Studies and Native Studies, have a small but significant place in the universities of western Canada. Their existence, however vulnerable, is an acknowledgment of the legitimacy of the pursuit of knowledge by, for, and about women. It is also an implicit acknowledgment that academic and scientific traditions have so far been incomplete and biased because they have excluded or marginalized the majority of people through unexamined assumptions about gender, class, ethnicity and a number of other criteria used to construct hierarchies of privilege and power. Such acknowledgment is good reason for celebration, for Women's Studies departments and programs were unknown just a few decades ago in Canadian universities. I wonder how many undergraduate and graduate Women's Studies programs there are now. Not having had the time to do the necessary research, I can only wonder and marvel at all the activities about which I hear.

- Women's Studies programs in Canada are part of a powerful and richly varied network of Women's Studies initiatives in the west and around the world.

- The Canadian Women's Studies Association has a membership of about 350 scholars and students; the National Women's Studies Association in the United States has a membership that numbers in the several thousands.

- In established disciplines, Women's Studies have caused tired old canons to be challenged and, if not entirely thrown out, at least revised and renewed. Feminist research has been a vital force in curriculum renewal. Our students represent this and the next generation.

- Women's Studies scholars have disseminated their work in many fora and forms of publishing, including creative and insightful research on the field of Women's Studies itself. As the following selected bibliography shows, they have formulated bodies of new knowledge, new methodologies, new technologies and new pedagogies.

- The richly diverse field of Women's Studies has a history that each of us feels on a personal level and enjoys through membership in a community of friends and scholars; we have assumed a unique identity.

- Our teaching and research have produced culturally recognized realities that women knew and lived before but did not have the words to communicate; our work has served to excavate women's stories and memories.

- Our teaching and research have contributed to struggles against oppression, violence and injustice; they have provided tools to many who are working for social change; they have contributed to understanding and collaboration.

- Women's Studies has produced outstanding, innovative research that has gained recognition from community groups, peers, funding agencies and the public; Women's Studies scholars are among the most creative and innovative in their research.

- Through our questions, explorations, analyses, and words, we have collaborated in opening some doors so as to enable resistance to other forms of marginalization, oppression and exploitation based on race, class, sexual orientation, physical ability, age, ethnicity and other excuses for injustice and violence.

As an example of the legitimate celebration of the accomplishments of those involved in Women's Studies, Frances A. Maher was able in 1994 to speak convincingly about how they are transforming social institutions and society. In her examination of the *Feminist Classroom*, she offered an *Inside Look at How Professors and Students Are Transforming Higher Education for a Diverse Society*.

But our celebration cannot afford to be an end in itself. Like rituals and ceremonial events that mark life's transitions or moments of pain, sadness, grief and loss, our celebration here must recognize that the task remains far from over and that disappointments and setbacks are inevitable. Our celebration must nurture us as we look at harsh realities and accept, together, the need to continue.

Moving on to Commiseration Then

Feminist movements have succeeded in bringing about some social change; teaching and research in Women's Studies have challenged old canons and transformed what humanity and its cultures claim to know about themselves and how they represent themselves. We can see that these changes have occurred by looking around us. They are also evident in the hysterical panic shown throughout patriarchal institutions—anguished screams almost always disguising themselves behind the banality of *political correctness*—as they confront the painful need to examine and re-vision themselves. Despite these successes, we have not managed to disrupt in any serious way the implacable parade of human events, whether in their ceremonial manifestations or in their violent and oppressive scenarios of power.

We know that there is still so much that needs to happen before Women's Studies programs and departments achieve the visibility and legitimacy they deserve, and before women are able to take their full place in universities on terms appropriate to them. We want real change in the academy to happen across all disciplines, including the sciences and professions, and on the public forum. The demographic distribution of students, staff and faculty members is still severely skewed in favor of keeping power in the hands of the already privileged. I have recently had occasion to travel to a number of Canadian universities to discuss the place of the humanities and social sciences. Without exception, my impression has been that administrators must make a conscious effort to include Women's Studies in their vision of the academic mainstream. Those who see the university as a whole do not yet appear to see Women's Studies as a significant player in the larger picture nor to see equity issues as central to the strategic planning that is currently underway. The obstacles underlying the apparent loss of momentum in the transformation of schools and universities have recently been studied in books such as Jacqueline Stalker and Susan Prentice's *The Illusion of Inclusion* (1998), Rosanna Tite's *Our Universities' Best-Kept Secret: Women's Studies in Canada* (1990), and Virginia Valian's *Why So Slow? The Advancement of Women* (1998).

An obvious reflection of the marginalized position Women's Studies occupy in Canadian universities, and one of which we are reminded daily, is the inadequate level of funding and other resources made available to Women's Studies departments. I know of no exception to the general stressful situation in which Women's Studies departments survive and thrive thanks only to the energetic commitment of faculty members and staff through their willingness to put in hours of unpaid and unrecognized extra work. The thought quite often crosses my mind that the failure to provide adequate resources to Women's Studies departments and programs serves both to disadvantage their offerings and research and to keep Women's Studies faculty members and staff so busy and under stress that they have no time to celebrate and organize for systemic change.

There is another perspective in which we cannot fail to recognize the challenges we still face. This is the challenge surrounding the image of Women's Studies, the ways in which Women's Studies are represented in the eyes of women generally, particularly young women and men. I still hear people say too often that Women's Studies teachers and scholars have no interest in intellectual rigor or academic excellence; that they just want an excuse to rap/ to tell their personal stories/ to fight for their own special interests/ to indoctrinate or impose a narrow party line of political correctness on everyone. Behind these biased, but unfortunately widespread, views lies the unexamined assumption that everyone in Women's Studies or doing feminist research in other disciplines is a bra-burning feminist as pictured in the stereotypes of the 1960s.

How often do we continue to hear our students say: "I'm in favour of equal rights for girls and women, but I wouldn't call myself a feminist"? How often do students, colleagues, family, and media convey to us the message that they recognize girls and women used to have problems *back in the olden days when my mother (or grandmother) was a girl*, but people of the current generation don't have problems any more? The suggestion is that the disadvantaged alone are responsible for their difficulties. These questions assume that liberal respect of the rights of individuals is sufficient to protect the rights of all. We know that this is a deceptive and dangerous assumption. We know as well that these questions depend for their logic on the belief that the cultural practices of society and its institutions do not need to change, only individuals. All that is necessary is for social institutions to open a few more doors in order to allow in a few more individuals from diverse backgrounds. As bell hooks has so eloquently explored in *Outlaw Culture: Resisting Representations* (1994) and Lee Maracle in *I Am Woman: A Native Perspective on Sociology and Feminism* (1996), it is precisely at this point that feminism confronts its greatest challenge: that of affirming new collectively-held values with enough energy and creativity to force systemic change. It is not enough that a few rise above circumstances of oppression to enter the hierarchies of the privileged. We must, instead, disrupt the direction and order of the implacable parade of "educated men" evoked by Virginia Woolf in *Three Guineas* (1938). We must refuse to participate automatically in the ritual dances imposed by society. Lee Maracle discusses the distances that are encouraged between individual members of oppressed communities, specifically the aboriginal community, and expresses her regret that social practice and discourse call "the majority of Native people to forsake one another":

> The end result is each of us digging our own way out of the hole, filling up the path with dirt as we go. Such things as justice and principles prevent the whole people from becoming dispassionate. Until all of us are free, the few who think they are remain tainted with enslavement. (13)

Maracle's call is addressed specifically to Native people; it has a particular urgency for Native women and men. It has, as well, a powerful application for Women's Studies students and scholars who seek to understand their complicity in the oppression of others and themselves.

Reductionist views that the need for feminist scholarship and Women's Studies no longer exists and the lack of awareness regarding the many forms of injustice, oppression, silencing and violence that still surround us, are widespread throughout universities and society. They stand in the way of opening new public spaces to those who are marginalized. Indeed, they provide all too easy alibis that protect us from seeing the need for radical social change if we are ever to overcome racism, sexism, homophobia, classism, ageism, and ableism and to share alternative forms of knowledge, spirituality, and reality. Those who hold such reductionist views find it convenient to leap upon any perceived weakness in Women's Studies practices and premises, all the better to discredit them.

Indeed, the human fallibilities of those of us who are involved in Women's Studies are easily exaggerated and used by critics to distort and debunk feminist scholarship in ways that delight our enemies. For example, in her book *The Courage to Question: Women's Studies and Student Learning* (1992), Caryn McTighe Musil and her collaborators were able to suggest that Women's Studies are intellectually intolerant, that they closely circumscribe the range of allowable questions. Daphne Patai and Noretta Koertge, in *Professing Feminism: Cautionary Tales from the Strange World of Women's Studies* (1994), speak as feminists yet raise the spectre throughout the book of a narrow ideological conformism that they claim prevails in Women's Studies departments. They state unambiguously in the book that feminist pedagogy and methodology stand in the way of academic rigour and intellectual achievement. As well, they speak strongly against research and teaching involving collaboration with partners in the community.

Women's Studies teachers and scholars must, of course, address the issues and criticism raised by such authors when they appear legitimate. We must do so on the basis of conditions that prevail today. We cannot afford to rest our case on the arguments, no matter how convincing, put forward by the authors of second-wave feminist theoretical texts that have now become classics for us. Time moves on; cultural, material, conceptual and socio-political conditions change. Patriarchy, for example, does not manifest itself today in the same ways and under the same circumstances it did ten or twenty years ago. Our students, colleagues and community partners do not want reflections or answers to questions that were raised a decade or two ago. They have their being in the context of the present historical moment, with all the cultural complexities that implies. At least at the beginning of their studies, our students will find interesting only those gender-related problems that they have encountered or, at least, with which they are able to resonate.

New Boots for Walking

And so I would like to move on to a few thoughts about new boots—boots for walking, dancing, running or slogging. They must be sturdy boots. We find ourselves in new terrains, on new fields, in new streets. The voices of popular culture and oral traditions, media technologies, shifts from text-based to image-based modes of communication must be heard as we determine where we stand and where we will walk, what questions we will ask, with whom we will travel, how we will resolve matters of authority and agency for ourselves and with others, as we chart our various journeys. We must use, carefully, strengths we have already developed, in order to learn how to move on, to think and to know differently. We have the energy and the vision needed to meet the challenges woven into the fabric of the knowledges we have already produced and the new situations women face today. We will study, do research, speak and be—differently—in society and in the university. I quote from Bill Readings' *The University in Ruins* (1997): "Change comes neither from within nor without, but from the difficult space where one is." I also quote from a recent e-mail sent by the co-moderators of the PAR-L listserve congratulating the Women's Studies program at the University of Ottawa on its 15th anniversary:

> The 're-visions' Women's Studies has made are vitally important. The measure of a program's success is the lives we touch, the consciousness we raise, and the climate and culture that we are transforming. As the American poet Adrienne Rich has said, "re-vision ... is for women more than a chapter in cultural history: it is an act of survival." *Ça se fête!* (27 September 1998)

I see Women's Studies as an endlessly present and yet deferred set of imagined and real possibilities, the *not yet* that keeps our vision focussed and our paths open, without fear of the incomplete and the non-closed. I do not know where our boots will take us. I only know that we must put them on if we are to survive. We must invent our trajectories as we go. Despite my inability to see clearly where the paths of the future will take us, there are four exciting things about which I am quite certain:

- The folks with whom we are walking are not the same folks with whom we began the journey a few decades ago. Women's Studies communities are now richly diverse in their cultural spaces: diverse in race, ethnicity, age, sexual orientation, dreams of love, abilities, disciplinary and philosophical preferences, and pragmatic orientations. They often stand in places we are not yet well prepared to study. They are frequently uninterested in the questions we asked with such passion during the 1970s and 1980s. They often resist the messages of the Women's Studies canon which, in spite of our best efforts for openness, we put in place in the academy. We have learned to listen and to learn. We are called upon to change our conceptual, theoretical and discursive models, inventing as we go, challenging ourselves and our students to the greatest possible intellectual and ethical rigour. Of particular urgency for us is the need for Women's Studies to be welcoming and relevant to aboriginal students, scholars and peoples.

- We have learned a lot about feminist pedagogy. What we have learned has enabled us to work with our students using a dialogic model of teaching that respects individual spaces and freedoms, while working through, in real time and in real terms, what and who is *other* to oneself without colonizing, dominating or denying expression and agency in modes of relating and communicating. This journey must continue, for schools and universities continue, in the main, to extinguish the thrust of real curiosity.

- Women's Studies has an opportunity to analyze, use, and control ideological and electronic technologies for its own purposes. Much research is already available on the relation between girls and women and technology. This research highlights our particular responsibility to encourage women students to use technologies for ends defined by themselves and their community. What does it mean to us in our teaching and research to explore all of the many news ways of disseminating knowledge?

- Women's Studies now has a richly diverse history and a collective memory that gives us discursive power and legitimacy. We can expect that colleagues who wish to be on top of their disciplines will have read feminist research and incorporated it into their own teaching and research. Those who are not on top of feminist research reveal themselves as poor scholars and delinquent teachers, ill-prepared to meet the needs of undergraduate and graduate students, and to generate knowledge that is interesting and meaningful for the future. New challenges to our scholarship are emerging in a range of academic areas: neurobiology, behaviour genetics, sociobiology, evolutionary biology, for example. We must be prepared to meet them.

- We must work in the Women's Studies community to disrupt and dissipate the repetitive and ritualistic calendar of events that serves so effectively to keep us all participating in the patriarchal agenda. We need to share perspectives that speak to women's real experiences, desires, imagination, visions. We need to put on our Women's Studies boots and—as often as possible—swing to the rhythms of our shared celebratory events. It is only through working together, passionately, that we will manage to bring about real cultural and systemic change.

---

1 This is a slightly revised version of opening remarks made to the Research Day Forum on "Intellectual Challenges to Teaching and Research in Women's Studies," organised by Dr. Claudine Potvin, University of Alberta, October 23, 1998.

SUGGESTED READING

WOMEN'S STUDIES TODAY: A SELECTED BIBLIOGRAPHY

Prepared by Louise Forsyth

I. Articles and Books

Alcoff, Linda. 1988. "Cultural Feminism versus Post-Structuralism: The Identity Crisis in Feminist Thought," *Signs* 13.3: 405-436.

Andrew, Caroline. 1989. *Getting the Word Out: Communicating Feminist Research*. Ottawa: University of Ottawa Press.

—— 1990. "Laughing Together: Women's Studies in Canada," *International Journal of Canadian Studies* 1.2: 135-148.

Bargad, Adena and Janet Shibley Hyde. 1991. "Women's Studies: A Study of Feminist Identity Development in Women," *Psychology of Women Quarterly* 15: 181-201.

Belenky, Mary Field et al. 1986. *Women's Ways of Knowing: The Development of Self, Voice and Mind*. New York: Basic Books.

Bowles, Gloria and Renate Duelli-Klein. 1983. *Theories of Women's Studies*. London; Boston: Routledge and Kegan Paul.

Boxer, Marilyn Jacoby. 1998. *When Women ask the Questions: Creating Women's Studies in America*. Baltimore, MD: John Hopkins University Press.

Bray, C. 1988. "Women's Studies at a Distance: Experiences of Students and Tutor," *Canadian Journal of University Continuing Education* 14.2: 37-49.

Briskin, Linda. 1990. *Feminist Pedagogy: Teaching and Learning Liberations*. CRIAW Feminist Perspective Series # 19. Ottawa: Canadian Research Institute for the Advancement of Women.

Brodribb, Somer and Micheline de Sève. 1987. *Women's Studies in Canada: A Discussion: A Guide to Women's Studies Programmes and Resources at the University Level*. Toronto: Resources for Feminist Research /Documentation sur la recherche féministe.

Buikema, Rosemarie and Anneke Smelik, eds. 1995. *Women's Studies and Culture: A Feminist Introduction*. London, UK: Atlantic Highlands, NJ: Zed Books.

Bunch, Charlotte and Sandra Pollack, eds. 1983. *Learning Our Way: Essays in Feminist Education*. New York: The Crossing Press.

Canadian Studies Resources Guide and the Canadian Research Institute for the Advancement of Women. 1993. *Canadian Women's Studies/Feminist Research*. Ottawa: Government of Canada.

Caplan, Paula. 1993. *Lifting a Ton of Feathers: A Woman's Guide for Surviving in the Academic World*. Toronto: University of Toronto Press.

Champagne, John. 1995. *The Ethics of Marginality: A New Approach to Gay Studies*. Minneapolis: University of Minnesota Press.

Cherny, Lynn and Elizabeth Reba Weise, eds. 1996. *Wired Women: Gender and New Realities in Cyberspace*. Seattle. Wash.: Seal Press.

Collins, Patricia Hill. 1990. *Black Feminist Thought: Knowledge, Consciousness and the Politics of Empowerment*. Boston: Unwin Hyman.

Cruikshank, Margaret, ed. 1982. *Lesbian Studies: Present and Future*. Old Westbury, NY: Feminist Press.

Culley, M. and C. Portuges, eds. 1985. *Gendered Subjects: The Dynamics of Feminist Teaching*. Boston: Routledge and Kegan Paul.

Eichler, Margrit. 1990. *What's in a Name: Women's Studies or Feminist Studies*. Toronto, ON.: Ontario Institute for Studies in Education, Dept. of Sociology in Education.

—— 1990. *Not Always an Easy Alliance: The Relationship Between Women's Studies and the Women's Movement in Canada*. Toronto, ON: Ontario Institute for Studies in Education, Dept. of Sociology in Education.

—— 1990. *Women's Studies Professors in Canada: A Collective Self-Portrait*. Toronto, ON: Ontario Institute for Studies in Education, Dept. of Sociology in Education.

Evans. Mary. 1997. "Whose Direction? Whose Mainstream? Controlling the Narrative and Identity of Women's Studies," in Ann B. Shteir, ed. *Visions and Realities*. Toronto: Ianna Publications and Education, Inc.

Fonow, Mary Margaret. 1999. *Women, Culture and Society* (student workbook). Ohio State University, Kendall-Hunt. **www.kendallhunt.com**.

Frankenberg, Ruth. 1993. *White Women, Race Matters: The Social Construction of Whiteness*. Minneapolis: University of Minnesota Press.

Garber, Linda. ed. 1994. *Tilting the Tower: Lesbians, Teaching, Queer Subjects*. New York: Routledge.

Grosz, Elizabeth. 1990. "Bodies and Knowledges: Feminism and the Crisis of Reason," in Linda Alcoff and Elizabeth Potter, eds. *Feminist Epistemologies*. New York: Routledge.

Hagen, June Steffensen, ed. 1990. *Gender Matters: Women's Studies for the Christian Community*. Grand Rapids, MI: Academic Books.

Harding, Sandra 1992. *Whose Science? Whose Knowledge? Thinking from Women's Lives*. Ithaca, NY: Cornell University Press.

Hinds, Hilary, Ann Phoenix, and Jackie Stacey, eds. 1992. *Working Out: New Directions for Women's Studies*. London; Washington, DC: Falmer Press.

hooks, bell. 1994. *Outlaw Culture: Resisting Representations*. New York: Routledge.

Jackel, Susan, ed. 1984. *Reaching Out: Canadian Studies, Women's Studies and Adult Education*. Proceedings of the Annual Conference of the Association for Canadian Studies Held at the University of British Columbia, Vancouver, BC, on June 4-6, 1983. Ottawa: Association for Canadian Studies.

Kennedy, Mary, Cathy Lubelska and Val Walsh, eds. 1993. *Making Connections: Women's Studies, Women's Movements, Women's Lives*. London; Washington, DC: Taylor and Francis.

Korenman, Joan Smolin. 1997. *Internet Resources on Women: Using Electronic Media in Curriculum Transformation*. Baltimore, MD: National Center for Curriculum Transformation Resources on Women.

Ladenson. J.R. et al, eds. *Re-Visioning Knowledge and the Curriculum: Feminist Perspectives*. East Lansing: Michigan State University Press.

Lewis, M. 1993. *Without a Word: Teaching Beyond Women's Silence*. New York: Routledge.

Luke, Carmen and Jennifer Gore, eds. 1992. *Feminisms and Critical Pedagogy*. New York: Routledge.

Madoc-Jones, Beryl and Jennifer Coates, eds. 1996. *An Introduction to Women's Studies*. Oxford, UK; Cambridge, Mass: Blackwell Publishers.

Maher, Frances A. 1994. *The Feminist Classroom: An Inside Look at How Professors and Students Are Transforming Higher Education for a Diverse Society*. New York: Basic Books.

Maher, Frances A. and Mary Kay Tetreault. 1996. "Women's Ways of Knowing in Women's Studies, Feminist Pedagogies, and Feminist Theory," in Goldberger, Nancy et al, eds. *Knowledge, Difference, and Power. Essays Inspired by Women's Ways of Knowing*. New York: Basic Books: 148-174.

Maracle, Lee. 1996. *I Am Woman. A Native Perspective on Sociology and Feminism*. Vancouver: Press Gang Publishers.

Maynard, Mary and June Purvis, eds. 1996. *New Frontiers in Women's Studies: Knowledge, Identity, and Nationalism*. London; Bristol, PA: Taylor and Francis.

McLure, Gail Thomas. 1997. *Women's Studies*. Washington: National Education Association.

Montgomery, Fiona and Christine Collette, eds. 1997. *Into the Melting Pot: Teaching Women's Studies in the New Millenium*. Aldershot, Hants, England; Brookfield, VT.: Ashgate.

Musil, Caryn McTighe, ed. 1992. *The Courage to Question: Women's Studies and Student Learning*. Washington: Association of American Colleges.

Nemiroff, Greta H. 1990. "Women's Studies in Canada: How Far Have We Come?" *Women's /Education/ des femmes* 7.2: 21-25.

Overall, Christine. 1998. *A Feminist I: Reflections from Academia*. Peterborough, ON: Broadview Press.

Paludi, Michele A. and Gertrude A. Steuernagel, eds. 1990. *Foundations for a Feminist Restructuring of the Academic Disciplines*. New York: Haworth Press.

Patai, Daphne and Noretta Koertge. 1994. *Professing Feminism: Cautionary Tales from the Strange World of Women's Studies*. New York: Basic Books.

Peck, Elizabeth G. and JoAnna Stephens Mink, eds. 1998. *Common Ground. Feminist Collaboration in the Academy*. Albany: State University of New York Press.

Prentice, Susan. 1994. *The Margaret Laurence Chair Guide to Women's Studies: A Guide to Undergraduate Programmes in Women's Studies in the Prairie Provinces and Graduate Programmes in Women's Studies in Canada*. Winnipeg, MN: Margaret Laurence Chair in Women's Studies, University of Manitoba.

Pruth, Raj and Bela Rani Sharma. 1994. *Trends in Women Studies*. New Delhi: Anmol Publications.

Readings, Bill. 1997. *The University in Ruins*. Cambridge: Harvard University Press.

Rich, Adrienne. 1979. *On Lies, Secrets, and Silences: Selected Prose 1966-1978*. New York: W.W. Norton.

Richardson, Diane and Victoria Robinson, eds. 1993. *Thinking Feminist: Key Concepts in Women's Studies*. New York: Guilford Press.

Ristock, Janice L. and Catherine G. Taylor, eds. 1998. *Inside the Academy and Out. Lesbian/Gay/Queer Studies and Social Action*. Toronto: University of Toronto Press.

Robinson, Victoria and Diane Richardson, eds. 1997. *Introducing Women's Studies: Feminist Theory and Practice*. 2nd ed. Washington Square, NY: New York University Press.

Rosser, Sue V. 1990. *Female Friendly Science: Applying Women's Studies Methods and Theories to Attract Students*. New York: Pergamon Press.

Sandler, B.R., L.A. Silvergerb and R.M. Hall. 1996. *The Chilly Classroom Climate: A Guide to Improve the Education of Women*. Washington, DC: National Association for Women in Education.

Schick, C. 1994. *The University as Text: Women and the University Context*. Halifax: Fernwood Publishing.

Schulman, B.J. 1994. "Implications of Feminist Critiques of Science for the Teaching of Mathematics and Science," *Journal of Women and Minorities in Science and Engineering* 1:1.

Schuster, M. and S. Van Dyne, eds. 1985. *Women's Place in the Academy: Transforming the Liberal Arts Curriculum*. Totowa, NJ: Rowman and Allanheld.

Shteir, Ann B. et al. 1998. "Women's Studies in Focus: Conflict and Community Building in Women's Studies," *Atlantis. A Women's Studies Journal* 22: 136-150.

Smith, E. and Norlen, V. 1994. "Tele-distance Education in Women's Studies: Issues for Feminist Pedagogy," *Canadian Journal for Studies in Adult Education* 8.2: 29-44.

Spender, Dale, ed. 1981. *Men's Studies Modified: The Impact of Feminism on the Academic Disciplines*. Oxford: Pergamon Press.

Stalker, Jacqueline and Susan Prentice, eds. 1998. *The Illusion of Inclusion: Women in Post-Secondary Education*. Halifax: Fernwood.

Stanton, Domna C. and Abigail J. Stewart, eds. 1995. *Feminisms in the Academy*. Ann Arbor: University of Michigan Press.

Tite, Rosanna. 1990. *Our Universities' Best-Kept Secret: Women's Studies in Canada*. Toronto, ON: Ontario Institute for Studies in Education. Dept. of Sociology in Education.

Valian, Virginia. 1998. *Why So Slow? The Advancement of Women*. Cambridge, Mass and London, EN: The MIT Press.

Weiler, K. 1991. "Freire and a Feminist Pedagogy of Difference," *Harvard Educational Review* 61.4: 449-474.

Westfall, B. 1992. "The University, Women's Studies, and Rural Women: Some Thoughts of Feminist Pedagogy and Rural Outreach," *Women's Education* 7.1: 23-26.

Wilton, Tamsin. 1995. *Lesbian Studies: Setting an Agenda*. London and New York: Routledge.

Wine, Jeri D. and Janice L. Ristock, eds. 1991. *Women and Social Change: Feminist Activism in Canada*. Toronto: James Lorimer and Co.

Woolf, Virginia. 1938. *Three Guineas*. London: The Hogarth Press.

Zimmerman, Bonnie and Toni A.H. McNaron, eds. 1996. *The New Lesbian Studies: Into the Twenty-first Century*. New York: Feminist Press at the City University of New York.

II. Journals

Atlantis: A Women's Studies Journal
Canadian Journal of Women and the Law
Canadian Woman Studies/Les cahiers de la femme
Canadian Women's Studies, 1979-1981
differences: A Journal of Feminist Cultural Studies
Feminist Studies
Fireweed
Gender and Education
Gender and Society
Resources for Feminist Research/Documentation sur la recherche feministe
Signs
Tessera
Women's Studies International Quarterly
Women's Studies International Forum

III. Databases, CD-roms, and Websites

Canadian Lesbian and Gay Archives
www.clga.ca/archives

Canadian Research Institute for the Advancement of Women
ww3.sympatico.ca/criaw

Canadian Women's Movement Archives
www.uottawa.ca/library/cwma/cwma.html

Canadian Women's Studies Programmes
www.utoronto.ca/womens/cdnwomen.html

Fonow, Mary Margaret, ed. 1999. *Reading Women's Lives: An Introduction to Women's Studies*. Simon and Schuster Custom Publishing: Department of Women's Studies, Ohio State University (database and CD-rom)
www.sscp.com/womens studies

Discussion of the Growth of Ph.D. Programs in Women's Studies:
chronicle.com/colloquy/98/women/background.html

European Women's Studies Organization:
women-www.uia.ac.be/women/wise

Feminist and Women's Organizations
www.igc.apc.org/women/activist/orgs.html

National Women's Studies Association
www.nwsa.org

U.S. Women's Studies Programmes
www.users.interport.net/~kater

WomenWatch The UN Internet Gateway on the Advancement and Empowerment of Women
www.un.org/womenwatch

CANADIAN FEMINIST THEORIES

At the end of the twentieth century, it is common to hear that feminist theory is at an impasse. Some contend that uncertainty, globalization, proliferating differences and a distrust of theory itself, have pulled the rug out from under the feminist theoretical project just as it was being laid. In this section of the reader, we explore some of the central contributions that Canadian feminists have made to this "rug laying." We would like to dispute the contention that we are at a point of impasse. Our conversations have simply taken new turns and we are placing greater demands on feminist theory in order to take complexity into account. At this moment, we can benefit from a look at past conversations and the directions that they have taken. It is not our intent to present the contributions of Canadian feminist theorizing as a progression; nor is it our intention to present any particular theorist or kind of theory as the last word. Instead, it is our view that students can benefit from reviewing and understanding the fault lines and concerns of existing Canadian feminist theoretical conversations. This kind of understanding is necessary to propel feminist thinking into the next millennium.

Students frequently want to run away at the very mention of "theory." Our students will often tell us that they find feminist theory difficult and detached from the everyday. But theory is simply about constructing informed interpretations of the world in which we live. If our goal as feminists is to promote egalitarian social change, then it necessary for us to critique the status quo; theory-making is essential to this task. Theory itself should not be rejected. Instead, particular kinds of theories need to be interrogated and displaced from their powerful position in shaping how we see the world and how we seek to act within it. As Chris Weedon argues, "To dismiss all theory as an elitist attempt to tell women what their experience really means is not helpful, but it does serve as a reminder of making theory accessible and of the political importance of transforming the material conditions of knowledge production and women's access to knowledge"(1997, 7). Recent feminist theory has emerged as a critique of the patriarchal values and interests embedded within existing social theories. Indeed, as feminists have pointed out from a variety of perspectives, "malestream" theory has not only tended to exclude women and their experiences. It has also been involved in justifying and rationalizing oppression and in privileging the masculine over the feminine.

In their contributions to the production of feminist theory, Canadian feminists begin from diverse starting points. We noted in the introduction how Canadian feminist theory has been greatly influenced by Marxism. Marxism, like feminism, emphasizes power as a fundamental category of analysis and seeks to provide a theory of social change. Indeed as Meg Luxton and Heather Jon Maroney emphasize, Marxism offers feminism powerful conceptual categories and a (usually sex-blind) "macrostructural theory of economic, political and social structures"(1987, 6). Contemporary Canadian feminists have played important roles in the conversation between Marxism and feminism. They have challenged Marxism's sex-blindness, while often advocating for an analysis of women's oppression that analyzes the crucial role of economic forms and class relationships.

Hamilton's influential book, *The Liberation of Women* (1978), critiques Marxist theory because of the emphasis it places on economic production. Like other Marxist feminists, Hamilton is influenced by Engel's early insight that production is actually a twofold process and includes not only the production of food, clothing and tools (as in traditional Marxist thought), but also the production of human beings. As Hamilton illustrates, however, the twofold character of production that is at the basis of society and history has been ignored in the evolution of Marxist thought. The position of women, to the extent that it has been explored within Marxist theory, has been narrowly cast as an analysis of the intersection of domestic labour and wage labour. Marxism has considered women's oppression as being secondary in importance to class, as the "women question." Canvassing the insights of radical feminist theorists, with their emphasis on sexuality and reproduction, Hamilton argues for a conjunction of Marxism and radical feminism. Marxism brings to feminism an attention to historical changes in economic relationships, such as the increasing separation of housework and paid work that occurred in Canada in the nineteenth century. It also draws attention to class differences in women's oppression.

Mary O'Brien's internationally renowned book, *The Politics of Reproduction* (1981), brings a different perspective to bear on the Canadian feminist conversation with Marxism. As both a midwife and a political theorist, O'Brien seeks to return "reproduction" to a place of primacy in history. Marx, she writes, negates reproduction by neglect; but in order for there to be history, as O'Brien astutely observes, we need to be born. Using the Marxist method, but focussing on biological reproduction, she constructs a sweeping theory of the origins of women's oppression. Biological reproduction, O'Brien argues, creates different forms of consciousness for women and men. For women, reproduction is a process that connects them with nature; for men, reproduction is alienation—alienation from the product of their "seed." O'Brien contends that western philosophical thought has been constructed to provide meaning to what men cannot do—reproduce. O'Brien postulates that patriarchy is shaped by men's desire to gain control over the continuity of generations, of which women are more obviously a part. Men's alienated reproductive consciousness has led them to posit a second nature, one that justifies and legitimates their governance of the world of politics and devalues women in the so-called "private."

In contrast to Hamilton's emphasis on the intersections of capitalism and patriarchy,

O'Brien's contribution is focussed on the centrality of reproduction and of patriarchy, specifically, the rule of men as a biological group. As such, it has been labeled radical feminist. But what joins Hamilton and O'Brien together, aside from their common engagement with Marxism, is a failure to account for the importance of racism as a fundamental social relation shaping women's lives. In an attempt to construct a theory explaining the dynamics of women's oppression, feminist thought of the 1970s and 1980s highlighted patriarchy and/or capitalism. Bannerji's piece in this section, "Introducing Racism: Notes Towards an Anti-Racist Feminism," emphasizes the erasure of women of colour from what constituted the mainstream of Canadian feminist theory. Racism becomes invisible, she argues, because it is part of our historically constructed everyday life and way of seeing. Feminist theorizing has most often relied on the specific concerns of middle class, white women, masquerading as the universal women's experience. In this very important, albeit brief, article, Bannerji highlights the exclusions that attend feminist efforts to theorize "women." She calls for feminist theorists to recognize that all women's experiences are shaped by racism. Ng's piece "Sexism, Racism and Canadian Nationalism," stands as an example of the kind of historical, inclusive and intersectional analysis advocated by Bannerji. In this work, Ng reveals the ways in which Canadian nationalism is constructed on racist and sexist policies, practices and beliefs. She argues that we must interrogate what we mean by "Canadian." She describes how the development of Canadian nationhood has required and perpetuated hierarchies that have disadvantaged and marginalized some white women and people of colour.

Smith's article, "The Everyday World as Problematic" (1987), also from a Marxist feminist perspective, shifts our attention away from feminist efforts to theorize women's oppression in all of its complexities and towards a consideration of epistemology—that is the theory of knowledge. She articulates and defends an epistemological position—feminist standpoint theory—that informs what may appear to be quite distinct feminist theoretical views (including the socialist, radical and antiracist perspectives articulated above). According to Smith, women have been excluded from what counts as knowledge. Knowledge, even though it is represented as universal and objective, actually expresses the situated and specific perspective of dominant groups who have had the power to describe and define the world. This knowledge is not merely under-inclusive, but incorrect. Members of dominant groups cannot see how their point of view is dependant upon the essential, yet invisible work of women and the working class.

In arguing for the "everyday world as problematic," Smith insists that it is only from a position of marginality that one can see the true power-infused character of societal relations. This reality becomes visible though struggle, when women collectively realize that their experiences of the world do not coincide with dominant accounts. The feminist standpoint position Smith outlines informs the work of Hamilton, O'Brien and Bannerji, all of whom contend that the experiences of women, even if intersected by class and/or race, provides the foundation of feminist knowledge. The key concept of experience provides this epistemology with a concreteness; it can thus claim a validity that allows it to compete with dominant knowledge.

Standpoint theory has come under attack with the rise of postmodern feminist theory. Standpointism is viewed as a knowledge project that assumes that correctly produced knowledge will add up to an answer to the question "what should we do?" This assumption, some feminists argue, is no longer tenable in an increasingly complex, postmodern world. Theorists such as Judith Butler and Joan Scott contend that experience provides no stable ground for knowledge; experience itself acquires meaning only through construction in discourse (1992). In other words, from a postmodern feminist perspective, there is no stable "I" and no fixed collectivity "women." Subjects and groups are shaped by language and reality does not stand apart for the concepts used to describe it. Differing dramatically from the contributions discussed above, postmodern feminism rejects the project of grand theorizing—efforts to explain history and social life as a single interconnected totality. Grand theorizing erases the intricacies that constitute society, just as it obscures shifting and complex power relations. Consistent with the view that feminist "Truth" is itself constructed, postmodern feminism challenges us to be self-critical about our own knowledge claims. It advocates little narratives, multiple theories, and the celebration of differences.

Postmodern feminist theorist Judith Butler (1990) calls attention to the manner in which the "we" of feminism is built upon exclusions. Butler seeks an erosion or deconstruction of the binary construction of gender—that is, as two discrete, mutually exclusive and hierarchical categories, man and woman. She asks feminists to be self-conscious about the processes that produce identity categories. Butler argues that any assertion of identity, in the case of feminism "women," inevitably produces exclusions and can never serve as a point of departure for a democratic political movement. This anti-foundationalism has been viewed with alarm by some feminist thinkers who contend that we "need to be assured that some systematic knowledge of the world is possible. We need to constitute ourselves as subjects and objects of history. We need a theory of power that recognizes that our practical daily reality contains an understanding of the world" (Hartsock, 1990, 171-172). Weir's piece in this section, "From the Subversion of Identity to the Subversion of Solidarity" (1986), attempts a critical engagement with Butler's postmodern anti-foundationalism. Weir characterizes Butler's concept of "identity as repression" as a kind of "sacrificial logic" that throws the baby out with the bathwater. While agreeing that repressive and exclusionary forms of identity cannot serve as the basis of feminist politics, she rejects the equation of identity with domination or with the erasure of differences among women. In the selection included here, Weir maps an alternative theory of feminist identity based upon the model of solidarity that does not exclude, but instead includes differences.

The debates about identity, differences, truth and knowledge within feminist theory continue on, moving in new directions and engaging new generations as we enter the new millennium. And while we have tried to sketch some of the main contributions of Canadian feminism in this reader, the end of the twentieth century also brings about a necessary engagement with "global feminism." We live in a context of rapid globalization—that is, the intensification of linkages that transcend the nation state. This brings to the fore the necessity of conceptualizing relationships between different national feminisms. Global links have also been highlighted through the networks formed at international women's conferences since the 1970s.

In its earlier years, the concept of "global feminism" assumed the existence of a universal sisterhood facing a homogenous patriarchy. Miles' contribution to this volume, "Global Visions" (1996), is written from a radical feminist viewpoint. But this piece illustrates the ways in which critiques by Third World feminists and by women of colour have led to a renewed emphasis on "diversity" as a basis of global feminism. Miles recognizes how Third World women have been differently inserted within the new international regime of free trade and global production processes. She also challenges first world feminists to look to women of the South for ways to organize against the global economic and military order. In her view, the basis of women's international solidarity lies in their common ties to, and respect for, nature, and their preoccupation with survival. This provides a foundation for challenges to the privileging of profits over ecology and human life. At the same time, as she insists, international feminist organizing needs to be built upon respect for differences.

AN EXAMINATION OF THE MARXIST AND FEMINIST THEORIES

Roberta Hamilton

This debate is an ideological dispute that arose as part of the histories of Marxism and feminism, histories that at times have merged into one, and at other times have appeared to diverge completely. The immediate task is to sort out whether the debate has produced inevitably conflicting accounts of female subordination, or whether both are necessary, and together draw us closer to a convincing explanation of women's oppression and exploitation.

Reviewing a little of the history of the relationship between Marxism and feminism will help to put the substantive issues in perspective, and in fact explain why there has been a debate. While there have been women throughout history who have found ways to decry their lot, it was Marx and then Engels who offered not only an explanation for the origins of female oppression and an analysis of its history, but also a strategy for its resolution. For them, the position of women in society was a serious question that would be resolved with the advent of communism. But succeeding generations of Marxists, particularly after the death of Lenin and the political demise of Trotsky, did not develop their analysis further or indeed pay it more than lip service (Mitchell, 1971, 76)....

For Marxists the analysis of the position of women is often referred to as the "woman question"; for feminists it is *the* question, the issue, the "and-in-the-beginning." Each theory deals with important issues which the other slights. In large part the strengths of each are the weaknesses of the other.

Here I will first summarise the kind of work that has been done in the last few years from a Marxist perspective, and then show two of the main problem areas which arise in the course of the Marxist analysis but are never properly dealt with: biological inequality and sexism. Following this I will outline the feminist account and discuss the problems inherent in it.

The Marxist analysis has extended Engels' analysis of the integral role played by the family in advanced capitalist society. Peggy Morton began by defining the family as "a unit whose function is the maintenance of and reproduction of labour power, i.e. that the structure of the family is: determined by the needs of the economic system, at any given time, for a certain kind of labour power" (1971, 53). She pointed out that the fluctuating needs of the economy for labour power, the requirement of a family for a stable income and the need of husband and children for nurturing are in contradiction even while they act to reinforce the family. Woman in her dual role as housewife and worker is the intersecting point between these increasingly contradictory forces.

Following from this, one of the key questions that Marxists have asked and begun to answer is: what is the relationship between wage labour and domestic labour, and, further, should the time spent in domestic labour be included in determining the value of labour power? Seccombe has contributed to this analysis by "tracing the flow of value right through the reproduction cycle of labour power—as wage goods enter one side of the household unit and renewed labour power bound for market comes out the other" (1975, 87). Housework is defined as that labour needed to convert commodities purchased by wages on the market place into "regenerated labour power" (1974, 9). As such, Seccombe argues that the house-wife produces value by contributing to the production of a commodity, namely, labour power. Seccombe has thus elaborated Marx's formulation that the value of labour power is not only "the value of the means of subsistence necessary for the maintenance of the labourer" but also "must include the means necessary for the labourer's substitutes, i.e., his children" (1906, 190-1).

While Seccombe's argument has met with considerable opposition, this stems from not seeing the doubly deceptive aspect of the wage form. Not only do wages appear as a pay-ment for value produced, rather than as the cost of maintaining the worker, but they also con-ceal the contribution of domestic labour to the production of that labour power. In response to critics, Seccombe also began an analysis of the relationship between the wage labour of women and their domestic labour. He posits that married women are being propelled in greater and greater numbers to the market place, because the wage for their labour power is greater than the value that they can produce through domestic labour. This is a recent occur-rence resulting from the increased productivity of domestic labour due to household tech-nology in conjunction with the even greater increase in productivity in the market place (1975, 92). Seccombe has explained, through the theory of value, what every working mother who is contributing a *second* income knows: economically, it pays to work. This is usually not true for sole-support mothers whose income cannot cover the necessities of life plus the expenses incurred by their working.

This analysis of the role of domestic labour, women's wage labour and the relation-ship between the two in capitalist society has been an important advance in the Marxist theoretical understanding of the woman question. Also important has been the study of women from the Marxist historical perspective. While the paucity of such work is surpris-ing, given the centrality of the historical method in Marxist theory, Eli Zaretsky's major articles have clearly illustrated its rewards. Gone is the static notion of the family, of personal life and of the role of women. Their development as intrinsic elements in the rise of the capitalist mode of production takes its place (1973a and b). Margaret George's beautiful little study "From Goodwife to Mistress" also shows what can be achieved through histor-ical analysis (1973). It could serve as a prototype for the sort of work that is needed.

There are two inter-related questions which a Marxist analysis somehow acknowledges without seriously posing, and which have formed the basis of the radical feminist position. First, there is the issue of the unequal role in procreation between men and women. Second, there is the problem of sexism. Is it, as most Marxists would have it, simply a descriptive term for an attitude that needs to be discarded to allow for working-class solidarity? Or is it more profound than that? Is it a convenient "cover-up" word which masks the need for a real analysis of how men and women see themselves and each other?

Trotsky never asked what biological inequality really meant for a socialist revolution, but he had no doubt that there was an inherent inequality which really mattered: "the boldest revolution, like the 'all-powerful' British Parliament, cannot convert a woman into a man—or rather, cannot divide equally between them the burden of pregnancy, birth, nursing and the rearing of children" (Trostky, 1970, 61). Everyone knows this is true. Whether Trotsky betrayed the revolution, or whether he was a prophet outcast, this is not the point upon which the charges of prophecy or heresy against him were based. Yet, this is the first area, the unequal burden of maternity and paternity, which the Marxist analysis does not tackle, and as a result has had to cultivate a significant blind spot to avoid. Evelyn Reed is the longest-standing continuous contributor to the position that female biology has not been a factor in oppression. To say that biology is destiny, according to Reed, is to reduce humans to the animal level but "humans are above all social beings who have long since separated themselves from their animal origin" (1972, 4). Not only is this an opinion under considerable attack today, but Reed does not even stick to it herself. When it is convenient she treats human beings and animals as if there were no difference. For example, she combats the argument that women could not be hunters because they were "biologically handicapped by their uteruses" by saying that "there is no uterus handicap imposing hunting inferiority upon lionesses and tigresses" (1972, 14). Reed tries to have it both ways and it is difficult to take her seriously.

Margaret Benston made an important early contribution to the analysis of the role of women's work in capitalist society (1969). But on the question of biology she is less credible. "How did it come to pass," write Benston and Davitt "that from a position of equal biologic necessity and importance, women came to occupy a socially inferior status?" This is an amazing assumption from which to begin. Men and women are needed equally for the admittedly inevitable task of conception, but surely bearing, giving birth to and suckling infants (not to mention forty years of menstrual periods and five years of menopause) give women by far the more important biological role. And if, as they postulate, women's position in society has always been linked to the work they do, then *this* work must be included, certainly in any Marxist sense of the word.

They go on to caution that we must not conclude, as have some feminists, that the oppression of women proceeded the more fundamental dividing of society into classes. For while it is true that mothers had to nurse babies, this was a result of the long period of dependence of human infants; it was, therefore, the biology of infants, not of mothers, that tied them down to this task! The point is surely that the effects of biology must be dealt with, not explained away. When these authors continue by passing off the fact that there was no sure way of controlling births, they provide further evidence of their unwillingness to deal with the historical roots of female oppression (Benston, 1975).

Writings in *Marxism Today* on the "woman question" are replete with such statements as "women need no longer be subject to the restraint of their biology" (Hunt, 1975) or "whatever the historical roots of [women's] oppression, the social inferiority of women is increasingly unnatural" (Hunt, 1974). Despite these throwaway lines, it is hard not to conclude that the effect of biological differences on the position of women is an embarrassment to Marxists, that it is more-or-less known information which, like the happenings in a Victorian bedroom, is best left unexplored.

Marlene Dixon's denunciations of feminism and the autonomous women's movement exhibit more than the usual blindness about the difficulties of an unqualified Marxist explanation for the oppression of women. Dixon is clearly torn. Having been a prime target for the left when she first espoused the Women's Liberation movement, she cannot, even now, discount the earlier need for an autonomous women's movement. She cites men and women from the male-dominated left as having been "the most vocal and visible and disruptive enemies of the women's struggle—constantly hounding and harassing the early organizational meetings". Her explanation for their behaviour? "Sexism, a simple mindless rage at 'uppity women' who threatened male supremacy" (unpublished paper). Her castigation of the male-dominated left makes as much sense as decrying individual capitalists for not sharing the wealth with their workers. For Dixon "male chauvinism" is an attitude to be morally condemned; this may be an understandable reaction to a situation, but it is surely no substitute for an analysis. Dixon herself provides poignant evidence of the tenaciousness of sexism when she writes:

> Today we face an old familiar battle, for the newly emerging communist camp in the USA is busy liquidating the woman question in the class question; advocating individualized struggle between individual man and women in monogamous relationships as the proletarian way; refusing to provide any analysis of the exploitation of women and denouncing all struggles around sexism as "bourgeois feminism". In short, we women must begin again. (unpublished paper)

For Peter Pink writing in *Marxism Today*, male chauvinism in the working class is simply part of capitalism's big sell (1973, 285):

> We know to our cost that the ideas of the capitalists can so effectively be made the ideas of the proletarians. If women and children are regarded in the British working class family by the male members of that family in much the same way as the capitalists regard the members of their families, it must be said that the ruling class has convinced a large number of members of the working class of the correctness of that view.

He goes on to state breezily that "in the British working class family, there are no objective grounds on which male domination can be justified". "Justified to whom?," one might ask.

The participants in the *New Left Review* debate agree (without debate) "that sexism within the working class . . . is based ultimately on the solid foundation of the man's control over the wage" (Coulson, 1975, 65). The other half of their own argument, namely, that women are increasingly also working for wages, does not seem to disturb their reasoning, nor does the fact that sexism does not disappear in socialist countries. This facile view of sexism is not an accident but proceeds from Seccombe's analysis of the role of housework in capitalist society. A housewife's labour, he writes, "is compelled directly by the demands placed on her by her husband and children . . . which *only* [my emphasis] reflect the material imperative of the family's needs to keep the total household in the best possible condition given the limits of the wage's purchasing power" (1975, 88). What about the housewife's self-imposed demands, her need to be a good mother and wife?

> Even women who now make an economic contribution to the home retain to a large extent the feeling that it is their work at home which makes them indispensable. Over and over I have heard women describe how they must go on working at home until everything is perfect, even after they have done a full day's employment, and even though their husbands often say, "Leave it, you've done enough". (Rowbotham, 1973, 80)

Further, why don't husband and children feel similar self-imposed demands? This over-sight of Seccombe's is compounded when he raises the question of women going out to work. According to Seccombe, "if the additional goods and services bought with a second wage could not significantly reduce domestic labour time, then the alternative of taking an outside job could never exist for married proletarian women" (1975, 92). That some of her chores might shift to other household members, and the possible effects of that shift, is not considered. Nor is the possibility that a woman's housekeeping standards might drop, or that she will work more hours a day than before.

But the real problem is not that Seccombe did not consider these questions; it is the further omission that his analysis permits. There is no discussion of what happens in a fam-ily when the rational or humane solution might be to distribute domestic duties; that is, there is no discussion of the meaning of "women's work". It is not, as Seccombe seems to imply, that the duties are inherently unshareable. It is that most men do not want to share them, and that the levels of their not wanting to are deeply buried. And it is that women will feel guilty if they do suggest it, or more likely will not even see it as a potential solution.

In the absence of these questions, male privilege and millennia of patriarchy become translated in the *New Left Review* debate into "sectional interests," interests which need only be suppressed to allow the collective interest of the class to assert itself through "rev-olutionary politics" (Coulson, 1975, 67).

If Lenin still lived he would be unhappy but not surprised by some of the substantive issues raised by radical feminism. He had been forewarned. "Clara [Zetkin, a leader of the German socialist and labour movement] … I have been told that at the evenings arranged for reading and discussion with working women, sex and marriage problems come first. They are said to be the main objects of interest in your political instruction and education work. I could not believe my ears when I heard that" (Draper, 1972, 84). In a sense, his attitude is symptomatic of the failure of Marxist analysis to deal with the position of what Marx once described as the "fair sex (the ugly ones included)" (Draper, 1972, 88).

Unlike the recent Marxist analysis of women which could take off from the earlier works of Marx and Engels, radical feminism as an explanatory theory still awaited a mid-wife. The earliest work in the late sixties was primarily descriptive, powerful (as indeed sisterhood seemed to be in those heady days), but none the less descriptive. What it did was give full weight to the *experience* of female oppression.

In 1970, Shulamith Firestone published what is still the most comprehensive statement of radical feminism, and a brilliant book, *The Dialectic of Sex*. She began by asserting what feminists and Marxists had striven so hard to deny: that historically women have borne the greater burden for the perpetuation of the species (1970). Simone de Beauvoir had described this situation in convincing detail in *The Second Sex*: "The enslavement of the female of the species and the limitations of her various powers are extremely important facts; the body of a woman is one of the essential elements in her situation in the world." Yet she had opted ultimately for an existential explanation: "biology is not enough to give an answer to the question that is before us: why is the woman the Other?" (1953, 33). For Firestone it *was* enough. Upon this fundamental biological inequality of the sexes had risen the caste-like system in which men receive ego gratification and enjoy creature comforts from their dom-ination of women. Central to the analysis was the family: the crucible for this intimate but hierarchical relationship. The recent study of the family owes much to this feminist appraisal.

Through this approach the family was simultaneously rescued from both its relative neglect by Marxists and the aura of stuffy boredom inflicted on it by contemporary social scientists.

The biological inequality of man and woman provided the basis for the institutions (in particular the family) which have developed to keep women oppressed. That biological inequality itself became institutionalised and thus protected against the changes that the development of birth control techniques, including abortion, and safer childbirth procedures might have brought about. In this context the radical feminists analysed love, sexual intercourse, the vaginal orgasm (what woman who has read *The Myth of the Vaginal Orgasm* does not owe a debt to Anne Koedt? (1973)), abortion, rape, courtship, marriage, the sex role system and sexuality. Additionally, "since sexism is so basic and pervasive an ideology, feminists are continuously extending their critique into areas hitherto unrecognized as 'political'" (Koedt *et al.*, 1973, vii).

"Love," wrote Firestone, "is the pivot of women's oppression today." The unequal power relationship between men and women corrupts love. Men need women for emotional support (behind every man is a woman), but are unable to reciprocate. "The question that remains for every normal male, is then, how do I get someone to love me without her demanding an equal commitment in return?" (1970, 137). Women need emotional support, too, but are willing to forgo that in order to "have" a man. Having a man matters economically but, more insidiously, without a man a woman does not experience herself as a person. Firestone, like other radical feminists, made the point that Freud had endlessly repeated: people are essentially bisexual. Men must deny the "feminine" in them to be real men; women must repress their "masculinity" in order not to threaten men (Burris, 1973, 356). "But while the male half is termed all culture, men have not forgotten their female 'emotional' half: they live it on the sly. As the result of their battle to reject the female in themselves … they are unable to take love seriously as a cultural matter" (Firestone, 1970, 137). Firestone began a systematic explanation of why this should be so, although it fell short of a comprehensive theory of how women and men are made in social terms.

The extent of female colonization has been shown in the acceptance by women of male definitions of their sexuality. "Women have . . . been defined sexually in terms of what pleases men; our own biology has not been properly analyzed" (Koedt, 1973, 199). There is a further and more crucial point that Koedt did not draw out. It is that nature conspired to ensure orgasm to males but not to females. While the very act of procreation insists on the male orgasm, conception can take place even without female arousal. Males did not create this situation, as the radical feminists seem to imply, any more than they decreed that women should have the babies. But these two biological truths together form the basis of an alternative to Marxist theory that sex inequality stems from the mode of production. Inherent in the biological differences is an inequality which human society can struggle to overcome but which a theoretical treatment of the situation of women can scarcely ignore.

This is not an excuse for refusing to study how the institutionalization of that inequality exaggerated and distorted the ways in which those differences have been played out throughout history. We can assume that the woman at the beginning of the sixteenth century experienced her sexuality differently from her counterpart a century after. And later there was the Victorian woman whose mother told her the night before her wedding: "After you are married something very unpleasant is bound to happen. But pay no attention to it. I can assure you I never did." She was the victim of an organised plot whose goal was nothing less than to cut her off from any sexual pleasure nature might have intended.

The point is rather that all these developments had biologically fertile ground on which to work. It is not that the female orgasm is in any sense "less" than the male orgasm; some would suggest quite the contrary. Rather it is that unlike the male orgasm it is not intimately connected with procreation; it has not been necessary for the survival of the species, and therefore, its fortunes have waxed and waned with the vicissitudes of human society.

For radical feminism, sexism (with its roots in human biology) not capitalism, is the main enemy of women. Again, Firestone (1970, 37):

> the contemporary radical feminist position ... sees feminist issues not only as women"s first priority, but as central to any larger revolutionary analysis. It refuses to accept the existing leftist analysis not because it is too radical, but because it is not radical enough: it sees the current leftist analysis as outdated and superficial, because this analysis does not relate the structure of the economic class system to its origins in the sexual caste system, the model for all other exploitative systems, and thus the tapeworm that must be eliminated first by any true revolution.

There are two major problems with the solely radical feminist account of female oppression as it is presently stated. First there is the rhetorical question put by Morton—Does Lady Astor Oppress Her Garbageman? In other words, the positing of a simple caste system of males and females obscures the class contradictions among women (1971, 49). Marlene Dixon's polemics have thrown these contradictions into stark relief (1972, 229):

> The ethic of sisterhood ... disguises and mystifies the internal class contradictions of the women's movement. Specifically, sisterhood temporarily disguises the fact that all women do not have the same interests, needs, desires: working class women and middle class women, student women and professional women, anglophone and francophone women have more conflicting interests than could ever be overcome by their common experience based on sex discrimination. The illusions of sisterhood are possible because Women's Liberation is a middle class movement—the voices of poor and working class women are only infrequently heard, and anglophone and francophone voices are heard separately.

Radical feminism brought out a very important truth but, as Mitchell put it, "it is a general non-specific truth" (1971, 90). Filtered through class, race and culture it endures, but in so doing it also separates, as does light reflected through a prism. It is not that most radical feminists do not, in some sense, recognise class. Firestone insists that the achievement of "full self-determination including economic independence to both women and children would require fundamental changes in our social and economic structure. That is why we must talk about a feminist socialism" (1970, 207). The problem is rather that the privileges of class have been sufficient to forestall any demand by feminists in the middle and upper class for socialism. This is clearly not a simple trade-off of submission in exchange for a certain lifestyle. It is, rather, that an individual raised consciousness can be useful for the privileged woman and less so, even a liability, for the poor woman.

Second, the lack of a particular analysis of the social relations of production led to an idealistic, and, if executed, possibly dangerous solution, namely, test-tube babies. While Firestone allows that under current conditions "any attempted use of technology to 'free' anybody is suspect" (1970, 206), she still sees it as a first demand for feminist revolution. Any proper analysis of capitalist relations of production and imperialism and how they would deal with test-tube babies, let alone how a fascism of the right or left would use this power, would surely have made the present state of the biological tyranny of childbirth pale by comparison. There is a further problem with a purely technological solution. Firestone asserts correctly that "the natural is not necessarily a human value" (1970, 10). But she extends this to its perhaps logical but alarming conclusion that "humanity has begun to outgrow nature". This resembles the ideology of Western man which began perhaps harmlessly enough when God gave man "dominion over the fish of the sea, and over the fowl of the air, and over every living thing that moveth upon the earth" (Genesis 1:28), but has now, with the development of capitalist technology, reached its most dangerous hour. The opportunity of watching as people wreak havoc with nature will perhaps make feminists more cautious in assuming that radical changes to nature will necessarily bring liberation.

There is a third weakness in radical feminism which exists because the methods of history and psychoanalysis have not been used to extend its theoretical development. The analysis has been couched in an ahistorical framework in terms of both the race and the individual. While biological differences are constant, the institutions which have emerged from them and then turn back to magnify or lessen their effects are not. I hope that the chapter on Protestantism illustrates how the forms of patriarchal ideology do change and can be analysed historically.

The individual history, how a man or woman is made in social terms, how those biological differences are transformed into their social meanings, has also not been analysed. And as Wollheim has put it, "if it is psychoanalytic theory that is looked to as that from which the necessary supplementation will come, it is hostility and not mere negligence that has first to be surmounted" (1976, 61).

The hostility is not hard to find. Kate Millett refers to Freud as "the strongest individual counterrevolutionary force in the ideology of sexual politics" (1969, 241). For Anne Koedt, it was "Freud's feelings about women's secondary and inferior relationship to men that formed the basis for his theories on female sexuality" (1973, 200). Firestone even suggests that clinical Freudianism was imported into the United States to "stem the flow of feminism" (1970, 68). There is good circumstantial evidence for the charges, especially if one looks at the work of Freud's more errant disciples (Marie Bonaparte and her clitoridectomies, God forbid, see Koedt, 1973, 201) and at the clinical work of practitioners.

But Juliet Mitchell, whose earlier work called for the study of psychoanalysis, a theory that attempts to explain "how women become women and men, men" (1971, 167) has undertaken to rescue the science of psychoanalysis for the use of revolutionary feminism from both its practitioners and its feminist detractors. On one basic point Freud and the feminists agree: the essential bisexuality of humanity. The aim of psychoanalysis is, therefore, not discordant with that of feminism. "Psychoanalysis does not try to describe what a woman is— that would be a task it could scarcely perform—but sets about enquiring how she comes into being, how a woman develops out of a child with a bisexual disposition" (Freud, 1964, 116).

Feminists were put off using the tools of psychoanalysis to answer this question; their answers have thus tended to be polemical, shedding more rhetoric than light on the subject. Mitchell has begun to put this right. Her analysis is challenging and exciting. Her restoration of the unconscious to the full place it deserves—for psychoanalysis is the science of the unconscious—helps to explain what people dimly comprehend: that how they feel about being masculine or feminine goes deeper than they care to know. The child becomes what the parent unconsciously wishes it to become; the assurance of those who "brought their children up in the same way regardless of sex" is shattered. This, of course, is not an excuse for despair: "the therapeutic task which psychoanalysis sets itself, 'to repair all the damages to the patient's memories', can be carried out because even the impressions of infancy 'have never really been forgotten' but are 'only inaccessible and latent, having become part of the unconscious'" (Reiff, 1961, 44).

Along with her insistence on the study of the unconscious, Mitchell's introduction into feminist and Marxist literature of the significance of Freud's other great and related discovery, that of infantile sexuality, is long overdue. Her precise formulations on the making of the female and male in social terms, and the relevance of this to the overthrow of patriarchy, however, raise serious questions. She closely follows Freud's formulations on pre-Oedipal sexuality (all babies have their first love-affair with their mothers) and the Oedipus complex in boys and girls (complete with castration complex and penis envy). But as Wollheim has pointed out, she makes the process historically limited. The Oedipus complex necessitated by the incest taboo will pass into history when women need no longer be used as exchange objects among men. The question of biologically induced social differences between men and women is thereby begged. There is no apparent reason why the removal of the taboo from incest will alter the biologically created fact that the girl, realising that she is without the phallus, will proceed to envy it (1974, p. 87). Now if that is the way it is, that is the way it is. But, if so, it is difficult to see how Mitchell can envisage the overthrow of patriarchy.

Wollheim, in his criticism of Mitchell, offers the possibility of an alternative kind of account for the development of the woman in society. He suggests that Freud (and, therefore, Mitchell) got his transferences wrong because of his clinical neglect of the theoretically postulated bisexuality. If it were "done right," so to speak, the findings of psychoanalysis might indicate that "what women have suffered from over the centuries is man's inability to tolerate the feminine side of his nature." This, of course, coincides with the descriptive conclusions of feminists. But Wollheim goes further: "if this is so, the intellectual task that confronts feminism is to try to trace the cultural and institutional devices which have facilitated the projection of this intolerance onto social forms" (1976, 69). Surely the beginning of this task must take us back to the essential postulate of radical feminism: namely that the biological differences between men and women were the first and most binding facilitators. If radical feminism pushes its theoretical development in this direction, to uncover further the implications of biological differences in themselves, and to use psychoanalysis to show how those differences become translated into social meanings, it can produce a forceful explanation of the historical development of patriarchy.

The most thorough attempt at synthesising Marxism and feminism has been made by Sheila Rowbotham. The aim of her most recent work is to show that Marxism is "useful as a revolutionary weapon for women [by] at once … encounter[ing] it in its existing form and fashion[ing] it to fit our particular oppression" (1973, 45). She follows this line of thought to good avail in her analysis of women's work as wage labourers and as houseworkers. While her argument is not as systematically worked out as the *New Left Review* debate, her perceptiveness, her willingness to be personally vulnerable, her often poetical descriptions and her method break through the boundaries of her theoretical framework. By alternately getting close to her subject and then backing off she reveals not only the theoretical dimension of female labour but also its subtleties, the way the system works in its day-to-day operation, the means by which women are in turn defeated and find new ways of railing against their situation.

But her insight from an earlier work that Marxism and feminism cohabit in the same space somewhat uneasily being "at once incompatible and in real need of each other" (1972, 246) is not expanded. Substantively she gives full weight to the viability of patriarchy but she does not attempt to develop any theoretical base for it. This leads her to such statements as capitalism "has still retained the domination of men over women in society" (1973, 122). Aside from endowing capitalism with an almost teleological rationality, this also assumes that ultimately the social relations of production control the fate of patriarchy. Her nod in the direction of biological differences is cursory and speculative: "the physical weakness of women and the need of protection during pregnancy enabled men to gain domination" (1973, 117). While she insists that the relationship between "dreams, fantasy, vision, orgasm, love and revolution" be studied and taken seriously (1973, 44), her framework does not, at this point, provide her with the right questions or concepts; certainly she borrows little, if at all, from radical feminism. At the theoretical level, the synthesis becomes reductionism. It has proceeded out of the *need* of Marxist-feminists for synthesis; it could more properly be called the absorption of feminism by Marxism.

In her interpretation of the findings of Freud, Mitchell developed a theoretical analysis of patriarchy, as a kind of parallel theoretical analysis to her work on women and class. She insisted that the capitalist mode of production and the ideological mode of patriarchy must be analysed *separately* (1974, 412):

> To put the matter schematically, in analyzing contemporary Western society we are (as elsewhere) dealing with two autonomous areas: the economic mode of capitalism and the ideological mode of patriarchy. The interdependence between them is found in the particular expression of patriarchal ideology—in this case the kinship system that defines patriarchy is forced into the straight-jacket of the nuclear family. But if we analyze the economic and the ideological situation only at the point of their interpenetration, we shall never see the means to their transformation.

Both the Marxist and the feminist accounts must be used in the analysis of women in society. The first is rooted in the social relations of production and the emergence of private property; the second is rooted in the study of how biological inequalities and differences are transformed into their social meanings and institutionalised. The first requires a socialist revolution; the second, working on the precondition of developing technology, requires an overturning of that which has been considered "natural" since the beginning of time and the conscious rediscovery for the individual and for the race of the experience of bisexuality….

In analysing the position of women in society, we must draw upon these two equally necessary perspectives. Mitchell came to this conclusion through her analysis of class and her study of psychoanalysis…. It seems to me that there is a major problem with each theoretical position taken on its own.

The feminist assertion that female oppression came first is most assuredly true. But while class exploitation may be an afterthought of human development, it is certainly one with a long and distinguished history. Feminists must take seriously the enormous differences in life-chances between women at different points in the mode of production. Anything else is not only self-delusion but also leads to incorrect strategies for struggling against patriarchy. To prepare for that struggle, we must also become more proficient with the tools at our disposal, in particular the methods of historical and psychoanalytic analysis.

Marxists must consider the consequences for women *in any social system* of bearing the greater burden of perpetuating the species. There is a biological inequality which all the birth control pills and worker-run factories cannot erase. Men have conquered the world because they had nature on their side. The social repercussions of this, how men and women spend their lives, how they experience their sexuality, are translated into privileges not only for rich men but for all men.

Perhaps at some point a marriage between Marxism and feminism may be possible. But a decent period of shacking up, perhaps under the same roof but with separate bed-rooms, seems to me to hold out a good deal more promise for arriving at some real under-standing both of the differences between men and women and of the differences between women and women. A child conceived now of a union between Marxism and feminism would indeed be ill-begotten, brought into the world out of the need for simplicity and dogma rather than understanding.

Different structures are developing for the overthrow of capitalism and the disman-tling of patriarchy. Individually and collectively choices need to be made about where to direct time and energy. But by recognising what is left out of our choices, what we do not select as our own area of work, we will perhaps not only bc more tolerant of those who make other choices, but in fact grateful that there are those working on another front. Paradoxically we are in a situation where more than one revolution is needed, but where each can only suc-ceed with the realization of the other.

PRODUCTION AND REPRODUCTION

Mary O'Brien

…The separation of life from necessity is in the first instance an ideological separation, a yearning and a dream of the sweet sunshine always outside the cave of the contradictions of carnality. The move to transform necessity to ideology, and ideology to social practice, entails tremendous struggles, and can be maintained only by continuous and active vigilance. The social structures which emerge from attempts to separate life from necessity are the *division of classes* in the productive realm and the *division of public and private life*, of family and polity, in the reproductive realm. The grounds of these separations lie in the dialectical structure of the processes of productive labour and biological reproduction, the series of alienations, negations and mediations which structure the way experience is thought about….

The social relations between classes and between men and women are therefore necessarily relations of struggle, the struggle of the upper classes and all men to conserve their freedom from labour. The quality of freedom from labour is of course quite different in terms of reproduction, in which men are forced to be free, and in terms of productive labour, the necessity for which must be forced on others. The struggles in each case are both ideological—the apologetics and rationalizations of private and public power—and practical—collective actions to objectify existential needs. This is so, too, of the struggles to overcome alienation from nature, which becomes a struggle to contain and exploit both nature and her servants, the productive classes and women. In the case of the struggle with women, the ideological creations are the "principles" of patriarchy and potency, which serve to legitimate the realities of the segregation of women in the private realm, the creation of a public, male realm of freedom and control and the objectification of assorted "principles" of continuity, including the public realm itself, which takes on a "constitutional" capacity to transcend the individual lifespan.

The form and strength and visibility of these struggles varies historically, and varies in response to changes in the actual modes of production and reproduction. Clearly, change in modes of production has been more frequent in historical terms. This is partly because productive labour is a generalized human praxis: the whole human race is involved. Everyone eats. Nature, further, is both provident and niggardly in her provision of means of food and shelter. Productive labour is universally a synthesis of mental inventiveness and physical effort. Reproductive labour, on the other hand, is genderically differentiated; maternal labour is material but involuntary, while paternity is voluntary and essentially ideal. Another important factor in the uneven transformation of mode of reproduction is the fact that technological development in a male dominant society gives no priority to contraception. Indeed, there is evidence that contraceptive methods have been suppressed, in much the same way as technological know-how has been withheld from labouring classes and exploited races. The clearest instance of male reactionary reproductive conservatism is the huge legal and religious edifice erected to outlaw abortion, but feminist historians also claim that the distribution of herbal contraceptives was one of the "sins" for which "witches" paid such a brutal price.[1] Today, of course, contraceptive technology is maintained at a murderously primitive level, while reactionary ideologues gear up communications technology in opposition to any change in the oppression of women or the "sanctity" of the private realm....

...The "materiality" of reproductive process, which is the flesh-and-blood reality of the process, has been relegated by male-stream thought to a brute objectivity, shot through with a contingency more absolute than that of nature's providence. It is precisely this brute contingency which places man in active opposition to nature, obsessed with an ambition to control and exploit. When we turn to the modern materialism developed by Marx we find that the brute objectivity of biological reproduction remains relatively intact, though with a distinct tendency to become conflated with the processes of reproduction and production. The term "material" is appropriated for the qualitative "metabolism" of production, while reproduction is left to linger undialectically and a little sadly in the "necessary" realm of biological intransigence....

The impact of capitalism on reproductive consciousness, on reproductive praxis as opposed to abstract family structure, hovered only on the edge of Marx's understanding. Nonetheless, Marx's theory still offers the most promising basis for the critique of male-stream thought, which is the necessary starting point of feminist theory. Making history is something more than the definition of issues and the attempt to solve immediately pressing problems. It is, in the Marxist phrase, praxis, a unity of theory and practice. This is one reason why the development of specifically feminist theory is an urgent task. Yet neither intellectual nor material history can stop and start all over again for women, it is not simply a matter of "catching up" either. Unlike men, women have had no objective basis for a separation of genetic continuity from human history. Now, we do have such a challenge to meet, for the separation of sexuality and reproduction which nature decreed for men technology has now decreed for women. This constitutes a material change in that combination of consciousness and experience which is the process of reproduction.

In this book, which is an anticipation and exploration rather than a promulgation of feminist theory, the process and relations of reproduction have been isolated with a sort of calculated naiveté, designed to rescue biological reproductive process and its material base from historical obscurity and ascribed unimportance. This artificial isolation must be abandoned where praxis overtakes analysis, as it must. Feminism cannot root out economic determinism with the equally blunt trowel of biological determinism. Human oppression emerges from both productive and reproductive dialectics, and Marx's analysis of the former perhaps offers the most promising starting point for a feminist praxis, which must then proceed to extend dialectical materialism to give a synthesized account of both poles of human necessity.

Marx's model is material, historical and dialectical, and an approach to the theoretical comprehension of the material base of the antagonisms within the social relations of reproduction must be all of these things. Further, since Marx, political theory, the dialogue of men with man, has been a puny affair and, indeed, Marx himself has been accused of subsuming politics in political economy. In western society and most particularly in the United States, political theory has acquired rude labels—speculative, normative, traditionalist and so forth—and has shown itself as somewhat cowed in the face of attack by the atheoretical and ahistorical empiricism of a dominant quantitative approach to social science.

Genderic inequality can of course be described and, in limited areas, quantified. Feminist scholars are engaged in doing both of these things, often usefully but increasingly repetitively. Such activity cannot *change* genderic inequality, and therefore shows the distinct tendency to the collapse into utopianism, polemic or mere statistics, which tendency is a direct consequence of an inadequate theoretical ground....

The appeal of Marx to feminism also emerges from the fact that feminist praxis must be, in some sense, revolutionary, and Marx is the revolutionary theorist *par excellence*. The revolutionary implications of feminism create discomfort and discord within the movement: we have observed Millett's struggle with the ambiguities of a doctrine of women as less aggressive than men, and a theory of the need for revolution. The whole question of violence is a difficult one for feminism, but as far as women are concerned, even a modest reformism is perceived as revolutionary, and even the mildest critique of the family incites contempt and angry resistance in both communist and capitalist states. The common ground of both liberalism and socialism, the assertion of human freedom, shrinks and trembles at the logical implications of women's humanity....

[F]eminist praxis is revolutionary in an economic sense which transcends the realities of class struggle. It is also revolutionary in a political sense. Politics as experienced in the contemporary world is the culmination of centuries of man's preoccupation not only with overcoming nature but also with the metaphysical premise of a "natural" dichotomy of ruler and ruled, a dualism articulated in antiquity and still holding ideological sway. It is not claimed here that these dichotomies have been discovered to be wholly genderic, or to proclaim a hollow conceptual victory for Yin and Yang over Eros and Thanatos, or master and slave, or mind and body, or universal and particular. It is claimed that the insistent dualism of man's thought has a material, genderic component which has been inadequately analysed. Political and social institutions objectify specifically masculine needs and mediations, as well as representing the interests of a ruling class. To insist upon the participation of fecund women in the conduct of communal life is to do more than seek strategies of female emancipation: it is to drag the process of reproduction, its objective contradictions and its historical mediations, from the dark corners of historiography and the hidden premises of political philosophy to its true status as a necessarily social and humanly valuable activity. It is also to claim for procreativity the capacity to transcend its natural roots and to "make history" in a significant way. This is revolutionary in both theory and practice....

[T]here are two necessary processes in the experiential matrix of human nature which are both dialectically structured, but which are not identical. These are, of course, the necessities to produce and reproduce. Marx's one-sidedness is the source, too, of the ambiguity in his use of the word "reproduction". In the production/consumption relationship, Marx maintains, people "reproduce" themselves, fuel their own life process. The facts that all animals must eat to stay alive, and that human animals must additionally produce their own subsistence, are rescued by Marx from their status as crude empirical truisms and restored to their proper significance as *a priori* of social life. Marx's problem, like that of Hegel and the state-of-nature theorists of the Enlightenment, is to move from the individual to the social, from the particular to the general. Hegel treats the problem with the philosophical parable of master and slave as a sort of Platonic "noble lie". In this primordial drama of adult male versus adult male, the prior birth and nurture of the protagonists in an already patriarchal society is presumed. Process as such enters human subjectivity in the self-conscious challenge to otherness, and to the power of death as the Great Negation. The annulment of the slave's capacity for self-determination in the fear of death, and the refusal of the master to recognize him as a potent force, is in turn negated in the labour by which the slave remakes his cathexis with the natural world. This is a very elaborate second birth indeed, in which the fear of death, an emotion, is the true parent of biological and conscious life....

Marx wants to historicize the parable without proposing any mythical alienations of man from nature. His strategy is to negate, to deny in theory, the historicism of reproductive process, and this is a negation which is never in turn negated, never transcends its historical non-being. It must, of course, remain a negation only in theory, for the *fact* of reproduction persists in human experience, and there would be no history without it. Marx therefore makes a categorical shift. There is no qualitative transformation possible in reproductive process, there is simply empirical variation in reproductive relations, in the forms of family, imposed by the stage of the historical process of change taking place in modes of production. The necessary sociability, the continuity and creativity of reproductive process, are arbitrarily transferred to the productive process, and man starts off on the task of producing history and producing himself with a force mysteriously appropriated from reproductive process. This theoretical, indeed magical, appropriation of labour power freezes reproductive process in a floe [sic] of impotence, and leaves the social relations of reproduction to tag along behind modes of production as best they may.

Idealism's metaphysical banishment of reproduction to the heavens stands opposed to materialism's metatheoretical banishment of the dialects of reproduction to a prehistorical but eternal sexual division of labour.

The first of these, idealism, then appropriates the creative function and dialectical form of male reproductive consciousness, and awards these to mental processes, to "pure" thought. Materialism appropriates the formal structure of reproduction for production, so that the productive process now includes among its products people and history. All history may indeed be class struggle, but that struggle does not produce its protagonists: it reproduces them; they are born. The necessity of birth is a substructure of human history, but it is not the same as, nor a product of, the necessity to produce the lives with which the process of biological reproduction has peopled history.

In the third of the 1844 Manuscripts Marx introduces the question of sexual relations in the context of his critique of crude communism, which, he says, wishes to destroy everything indiscriminately in a passion to generalize private property.[2] Marriage is "incontestably a form of private property" expressed in "an animal form" and contrasted to the idea (the "open secret" of crude communism) of women as common property, of universal prostitution. Both bourgeois property relations and unreflective communism, according to this young and passionate Marx, crave for universal access to all women. He seems to see however, that this broad castigation needs some further explanation, and development of an alternative, materialist view of generic relations. He proceeds in an attempt to strip the "open secret"— a simple and primitive lust and resentful envy—of its secrecy. The passage must be quoted in full:

> In the relationship with *woman*, as the prey and handmaid of communal lust, is expressed [sic]
> an infinite degradation in which man exists for himself; for the secret of this relationship finds
> its *unequivocal,* incontestable, *open* and revealed expression in the relation of man to woman
> and in the way in which the *direct* and *natural* species relationship is conceived. The imme-
> diate, natural and necessary relation of human being is also the *relation* of *man* to *woman.*
> In this *natural* species relationship man's relation to nature is directly his relation to man, and
> his relation to man is directly his relation to nature, his own *natural* function. Thus, in this
> relation is *sensually revealed*, reduced to an observable *fact*, the extent to which human
> nature has become nature for man and to which nature has become human for him [original
> italics].3

The almost indecent haste in which a relation of man to woman becomes a relation of man
to man is perhaps exacerbated in translation, for English unlike German, does not provide
separate words for masculine man (*man*) and mankind (*mensche*). We do not wish to become
bogged down in the contentious linguistic issue of whether either the English collective
"man" or the German *mensche* in fact really means "everyone". Giving Marx the broadest
possible latitude in this respect we may interpret him as saying: the immediate natural and
necessary human relationship is that of men and women. In this relationship people are
conscious of their own sexual needs and their need, therefore, of other human beings. Sexual
need confirms them as both natural and social beings, and the degree to which they can
create humane conditions for the expression of this relationship is an indicator of how far they
have progressed from mere animality. Such an interpretation proclaims an important truth,
that sexual relations are necessary and necessarily social. They are not, however, perceived
as dialectical, there is no generic struggle, and there are not yet any products, namely,
children, who are merely implied in the term "species relationship". Marx, like Hegel before
him, has in mind the moment of sexuality rather than the reproductive process as a whole.
In fact, he later goes on to deny to birth any real human significance on the existential
grounds that any man who owes his existence to another is a "dependent being" and thus precluded from free expression of his humanity: "But I live completely by another person's
favour when I owe to him [sic] not only the continuance of my life but also *its creation*;
when he is its *source*" [original italics].4

Marx rejects a hankering after creation myths, but he does appear to share Sophocles'
notion that the male is "true parent of" the child, without recognizing that this is an ideological
formulation. He also argues, in the same passage, that popular consciousness cannot reject
the notion of creation, because the fact that "nature and man exist on their own account" posits
an existence which "contradicts all the tangible facts of practical life". To be sure, in the
Manuscripts Marx has not yet parted from Hegelian ways, but it is still surprising that he
seems quite unperturbed by the positing of a "material" view of a fundamental life process
which "contradicts all the facts of practical life". Marx, quite traditionally, is interested here
in the historical constitution of man's second, self-made nature. To this end, he quite specifically negates reproductive continuity, which he sees as infinite regress lurking as progress.
If, like Aristotle, he argues, you say that man is produced by the coitus of two human beings,
you lapse into infinite progression (who engendered my grandfather and his father and so
forth) and do not keep in mind "the *circular movement* which is perceptible in that progression, according to which man, in the act of generation, reproduces himself: thus *man*
always remains the subject"5 [original italics]. Marx sees the essentially social character of
reproduction and appears to be aware of the temporal contradictions within the process,
and it would probably be unfair to read him as implying that, as man always remains the sub-

ject, woman becomes mere object of man's sexual desire. He certainly does not consider the actuality of man as alienated subject, nor does he fully understand that paternity is radically subjective, in that it is present to consciousness as idea to be objectified only by appropriation of the child. He does not see that alienation from time and nature is mediated in reproductive labour, but only by women, for he does not deal with the fact that the production of children needs reproductive labour as well as sexual activity. A stubborn insistence that biological continuity *is* continuity, he says, can only lead to the question of who created man in the first place, a "perverted" and "abstract" question which posits non-existence.

The young Marx, still engaging in "hating all gods," the passion which had informed his doctoral dissertation, and still clearly under the influence of Feuerbach's anthropological determinism, simply takes refuge in polemic at this point. It is, none the less, a significant polemic, for it is shot through with an unarticulated awareness that it might just be the case that paternity is an abstraction, that there just might be problems for male reproductive consciousness in the relation of thinking and existing:

> If you ask a question about the creation of nature and man you abstract from nature and man. You suppose them *non-existent* and you want me to demonstrate that they *exist.* I reply: give up your abstraction and at the same time you abandon your question. Or else, if you want to maintain your abstraction, be consistent, and if you think of man and nature as non-existent think of yourself too as non-existent, for you are also man and nature. Do not think, do not ask me any question, for as soon as you think and ask questions your *abstraction* from the existence of nature and man becomes meaningless. Or are you such an egoist that you conceive everything as non-existent and yet want to exist yourself? [original italics.][6]

Socialist man, on the contrary, takes his proofs of his man-made existence from real experience, even though his existence contradicts his now denatalized autonomy. Marx is overly excited because the question that he raises is not the one which needs to be asked at all. We must ask Marx what is wrong with biological reproduction as a basis of real continuity. Of course people "make themselves" in their interaction with the world and other people, but why can socialist man not be created until birth has been deprived of the capacity to create continuity? Marx could have posited a dynamic dialectic between biological time and historical time without lapsing into the trap of an infinitely regressive and crude causality. He did not do so, and could not do so, first, because of his male perspective and, second, because he did not anticipate the possibility of *rational* control of reproduction.

This is not the mere aberration of a young thinker. The transfer of reproductive power and sociability to productive relations remains constant. In *The German Ideology*, Marx is less confused, but he still insists on the hegemony of productive labour in the formation of human historical consciousness, a position from which he never retreats.[7] In the version of *The German Ideology* he seems at first sight to be presenting us with the remarkable spectacle of people eating and producing and needing before they are born at all—"life involves *before everything else* eating and drinking" [my italics]—while the second determination of life process emerges from the fact that needs produce more needs: "and this production of new needs is the first historical act." Only as the "third circumstance which from the very first enters into historical development" does reproduction appear, a process described as men making other men.[8] Marx backtracks a little from the "before everything else" which I italicized above: these are not to be seen as stages of development, he says, but as aspects of development which exist simultaneously, and production and reproduction appear as a dou-

ble relationship, on the one hand natural, on the other social. But it is a tenuous conces-
sion, for immediately and momentously Marx proceeds to negate by neglect the actual
sociability and historicism of reproductive process: "It follows from this [the double relation,
natural and social, of production and reproduction] that a certain mode of production . . . is
always combined with a certain mode of cooperation."9 It also follows, in history and in
logic, that reproduction also involves a certain mode of co-operation, but Marx does not
say so. The co-operation of men as appropriators of children, and of women as bearers and
nurturers of children, slips out of history. Only production thereafter has the capacity to
make history and inform consciousness. Production also, by an unexplained alchemy, determines the forms of the social relations of reproduction.

In *Capital*, Marx has made up his mind on the question of what constitutes a natural economy, and he has also abandoned the radically liberal individualism which produced the
youthful diatribe against the indignity of having to depend on one's life on the sexual activity of others. In his discussion of commodity fetishism, he defines "the particular and natural form of labour" as that in which the personal interdependence of the members of the
economic unit is present to consciousness in its true social form.10 For an example of this
directly associated labour form, Marx tells us, we do not need to go back to "that spontaneously developed form which we find on the threshold of the history of all civilized races".
We still have examples of this "spontaneous" form close to hand, for we can find it "in the
patriarchal industries of a peasant family" [my italics]. Like Hegel, Marx presumably feels
that the patriarchal family had developed "spontaneously" before the dawn of dialectical
history, that is, without a struggle. This is no doubt due to the fact that it is natural. Male-
stream thought in general seems to live contentedly with the vague notions that women's "special relation" to nature unfits her for activity outside of the private realm, while patriarchy
derives its power from its naturalness, but manages to switch it to the public realm. This
is, of course, because male-stream thought has not analysed the sense in which patriarchy is
a resistance to experienced alienation from nature, a historical move from the ideal of paternity to the concreteness of patriarchy. Marx, indeed, considers alienation from nature to be
specific to capitalism. Not without a touch of nostalgia, he argues that the family, both
ancient and modern, "possesses a spontaneously developed system of division of labour."11
As we saw, the discovery of the ancient matriarchate did not sully, for Marx or Engels, the
naturalness and spontaneity of patriarchy.

One of the reasons for Marx's position, apart from the uncriticized dominance of the
dogma of male supremacy which was specific to his epoch, is that he is preoccupied with the
notion of universality. The notion of integration, which Hegel has yearned for but found
only in the Absolute Idea, is for Marx a worldly possibility. Real history will start from
human equality and rational, co-operative sociability. Sociability and co-operation are the preconditions of classless society. Marx perceives "universality" concretely, as the annulment
of alienation and the restoration of a unity of men with nature, with their products and with
other men. This socialist universality is the goal of history and the condition of human freedom, but Marx has to uncover practical and material universals in which this goal can be
grounded: he needs to find true universals, experiences common to all. In this quest for a concrete universal, he finds, correctly enough, hunger and sexuality. However, he perceives
the latter as immediate, while the former requires the mediation of production. He translates *male* experience of the separation of sexuality and reproduction into *a priori* universal
truth. Thus the labour of reproduction is excluded from the analysis, and children seem to

appear spontaneously or perhaps magically. Productive labour, thus sterilized, does not produce value, does not produce needs and therefore does not make history nor make men. Birth as such is contingent, immediate and uninteresting a "subordinate" relationship....

Marx never perceives the alienation of the seed as a material alienation which sets up an opposition between men and children, men and women and man and other men. The act of appropriation by the non-labourer of both product and "means of production," of the actual child and the mother's reproductive labour power, remains for Marx a natural relationship....

Marxism offers one important clarification of the question of continuity. Marx shows us that continuity is specifically a "need" of a ruling class anxious to perpetuate itself in power; that is to say, continuity is both the principle and practice of class regeneration, political activity to create the ideological conditions for the maintenance of the *status quo*. This limited view of politics as ideological enterprise accounts in part for the curious attenuation of political discussion in this most political of thinkers, though Marx planned to turn to politics had he lived longer. Subsequent Marxists have been largely content with the master's epigrammatic dismissal of the state as the executive committee of the ruling class, and Marxist work on the state is, like that on the family, fairly rudimentary. Yet Marx's other laconic comment—that the political realm is the battleground of opposing ideologies—is of equal importance. Marx did not recognize male supremacy as an ideology with an objective material base in the relations of reproduction. Marxist sociology, tending to study work relations and to neglect family and political relations, attenuates a theory of consciousness which already has problems in accounting for individual as opposed to class consciousness. Ideologies, including that of male supremacy, are developed by political thought in its interpretation of the relation of public and private, and the symbolic and social representation of principles of continuity. These values are then enforced by the family. Certainly, political ideologies serve dominant class interests, but they are eagerly accepted by men who have no property but their uncertain children. They serve the ruling class, but they also serve the brotherhood of man....

Marx knows that capitalism objectifies the relations of production, but he does not comprehend the genderic significance of the objectification of continuity which is itself an essential precondition of a materialist philosophy of history. The continuity of the reproduction of the species is the actual and logical premise of the survival of that species, which distinguishes itself from other species by making history and conserving a historical consciousness. The theoretical comprehension of the reality, of process is possible only under conditions in which an objective and dynamic continuity permits the comprehension of history as well as genetic continuity as objects materially present to consciousness.

De Beauvoir has remarked that the history of man is in a real sense an antiphysis:

> The theory of historical materialism has brought to light some most important truths. Humanity is not an animal species, it is a historical reality. Human society is an antiphysis—in a sense it is against nature; it does not passively submit to the presence of nature but rather takes over the control of nature on its own behalf. This arrogation is not an inward, subjective operation; it is accomplished objectively in practical action.[12]

The bringing to light of history as antiphysis is not so much the achievement of historical materialism, or even of the elated experimentalism of Bacon and founders of modern science. In creating socially recognized paternity, men outwitted nature long ago. Marx aspires to the restoration of a human metabolism with nature, which is to be a humane mediation of the dialectical opposition of man and nature of which women will be passive beneficiaries. What might seem the obvious theoretical route to such an achievement, namely, the positing of a dialectical relation of historical and biological continuity, eludes Marx's theoretical understanding. He turns to productive continuity, basically concerned with the "reproduction" of the individual life, and proclaims it as the necessarily *social* base of co-operative endeavour. By means of some fancy theoretical footwork, reproduction, which is impossible in individual terms, remains particular and ahistorical. In the dialectical sense of particularity as the opposition to universality, both Marx and Hegel give individuality a normative evaluation. For Hegel, the principle of particularity is woman the ethical cripple; for Marx, the bourgeois property owner who is scheduled for burial. This emerges from the fact that at the centre of the prodigious insight that human reality is process lurks the negation of an actual social process, whose product is none other than the individual. Socialism must do better. One understands the puzzlement of Madame Cao, a Vietnamese freedom fighter in conversation with a Western feminist socialist:

> Alice Wolfson explained the lack of leadership in the woman's liberation movement in terms of American individualism and the feeling that collectivity was an important and necessary stage. "Madame Cao thought for a moment and then said, yes, but the collectivity which destroys the potential of the individual is not good collectivity. It is necessary to reach a compromise."[13]

A compromise is impossible in any theory where the individual is constituted abstractly without ever getting born, and the alienation of second nature from first nature is perceived as infinite.

ENDNOTES

1. Barbara Ehrenreich and Deidre English, *Witches, Nurses and Midwives: A History of Women Healers* (Old Westbury, New York, 1973).

2. Cited in Erich Fromm (ed.), *Marx's Concept of Man* (New York, 1970), p. 125

3. Ibid., p. 126.

4. Ibid., p. 138.

5. Ibid., p. 139.

6. Ibid., p. 129.

7. Marx and Engels, *The German Ideology*, Ch. 1.

8. Ibid., pp. 17-18.

9. Ibid., p. 18.

10. Marx, *Capital*, Vol. 1, Bk 1, Ch. 1, Section IV, p. 89.

11. Ibid., pp. 89-90.

12. Simone de Beauvoir, *The Second Sex* (New York, 1953), 47.

13. Alice Wolfson's "Budapest Journal" in *Off Our Backs*, 14 December 1970, quoted by Rowbotham, *Women, Resistance and Revolution*, 219.

INTRODUCING RACISM: NOTES TOWARDS AN ANTI-RACIST FEMINISM

Himani Bannerji

From its very early phase the word "silence" has been important in the vocabulary of feminist writing. It spoke of being *silent* or having been *silenced*—of two distinct but related themes. In a cluster with "silence" there are other words speaking of gaps, absences, being "hidden in history," of being organized *out* of social space or discourse, or *into apathy*, and of "a problem without a name." Not exceptionally, therefore, there also appeared other expressions—signifying women's struggles—about gaining or giving a voice, a direct assumption of our subjectivity, creating a version of the world from "our" own standpoint, and thus speaking from our own "self" or "centre" or experience.

For many years now I have read and taught this literature. I have spoken of it as combatting sexism internally within ourselves and externally in relation to a sexist world. I did this for years and in a way it had a resonance for me, and gave me the feeling that finally I had a way of interpreting what I felt since my early childhood. But very soon I began to develop a discomfort and sometimes even a feeling of antagonism towards this type of feminist writing, for reasons initially unclear to me. Of course, this was accompanied by feelings of guilt and worries that perhaps my politics were not feminist after all. Needless to say, I did not encounter feminists in the university who experienced any basic and fundamental sense of insufficiency with this feminism, which passes as *the* feminism. I had heard of old struggles between feminists on the ground of class, but when I came into the scene the talk of class, if it ever existed in Canada, had ceased to have any serious content. With the exception of isolated instances, class was paid mere lip-service, and the discourse of gender, professionalism and mobility had asserted itself in the university. Lacking colleagues, I spoke to my students and other women in the city who, like me, also happened to be non-white, or so-called "immigrants" from the less industrialized parts of Europe and Latin America. It was speaking with these women that saved my sanity, because this feeling of discomfort that I had with feminist currency or discourse seemed to be something other than paranoia or reactive politics on my part. In editing "Women of Colour," Issue 16 of the feminist magazine *Fireweed*, some of us tried to grope towards a formulation of what felt wrong and of some of the reasons for our entry at a wrong angle into the feminist world of Toronto.

In time I began to understand better what was going on in my classroom. The truth was that neither I nor many of my students with a Third World or southern European background were participating in our own capacities as "persons" in that classroom: rather we were "personas," characters called "students" and "teacher" in a Canadian university, learning the "feminist framework" which in the end turned out to be the story of the European bourgeois family. At the end of some of the books we used a section on "women of colour" was included, but this topic was not integrated into the book's overall perspective. Similarly, in some of the university's courses a section or two was taught on the topic of "women of colour" or "immigrant women," but again the issues were not integrated into the course material as a whole. I began to toy with the idea of designing a course on "Women of Colour" or "Immigrant Women . . . and Racism!"

So this was the issue—that once more there were gaps or silences, that people like us were never present in what we taught and read. In volumes of material produced in the west on women, with all the talk of "herland" and "herstory," our absences have not ceased: our voices, if we have any, are very small ones. I have rarely, while doing work in Women's Studies proper, come across a framework or methodology which addresses or legitimizes the existence and concerns of women like us, or helps give our voices strength and authenticity. How then can we speak of "gaining voices," "shattering silences," of sharing experiences, being empowered, and so on? The great bulk of Canadian literature on women and what passes for Women's Studies curriculum leaves the reader with the impression that women from the Third World and southern Europe are a very negligible part of the living and labouring population in Canada. Furthermore, the silences in this literature would seem to imply that nothing much is to be learned about the nature of economic social and political organization of Canada by studying lives or concerns of women of colour. Not even most of the works of feminist women writers claiming to be interested in "class" in Canada contain full-length chapters on such a population. One might ask what produces this phenomenon which simultaneously expresses a lack of consciousness as well as a false consciousness? And this happens in a country with the history of a settler colonial state and economy, where "reserves" exist in large numbers for the indigenous peoples, where a working class is still being created through racist immigration policies and segmentation of the labour market, and where a U.S. dependent capitalism has long ago entered an imperialist phase?

The full answer to my question of how we got here is complex and not fully visible to me. But I do have these notes towards an answer which offer us a possibility of explanation as well as a basis for moving towards an anti-racist feminism. It is this possibility rather than the urge for sharing experiences which impels me to this writing. The answer begins in the history of colonial and imperialist economic, social and political practices which have in the past and now continue to construct Canada. It also lies in certain habits or ways of thinking and seeing that have emerged in the course of history, as well as clearly developed ideologies and methods for constructing social and political discourse—feminist or any other.

For my exploration I will rely to some extent on Antonio Gramsci's notion of common sense, which, put simply, might be seen as the submerged part of the iceberg which is visible to us as ideology. Writers such as Fredric Jameson have phrased it in terms of the political unconscious. Its efficacy for understanding the situation of non-white people living in the West is clearly demonstrated by a volume produced in Britain about race and racism in the 1970s, entitled *The Empire Strikes Back*. In this volume Errol Lawrence paraphrases Gramsci in a way which is useful for me. He writes:

> The term "common sense" is generally used to denote a down-to-earth "good sense". It is thought to represent the distilled truths of centuries of practical experience: so much so that to say of an idea or practice that it is only common sense, is to appeal over the logic and argu-

mentation of intellectuals to what all reasonable people have known in their "heart of hearts" to be right and proper. Such an appeal can act at one and the same time to foreclose any discussion about certain ideas and practices and to legitimate them. (*Empire Strikes Back*, 48)

What is more, common sense is accretional, and being unthought out it leaves plenty of room for contradictions, myths, guesses, and rumours. It is therefore by no means a unified body of knowledge, and as a form of our everyday way of being it is deeply practical in nature. The general direction of its movement as such comes from common socio-economic and cultural practices which, in turn, common sense helps to organize. From this point of view the history, ontology, and ongoing practice of an imperialist capitalist society appears to me to find its epistemology in the common sense of racism. Whereas clearly stated racism definitely exists, the more problematic aspect for us is this common sense racism which holds the norms and forms thrown up by a few hundred years of pillage, extermination, slavery, colonization and neo-colonization. It is in these diffused normalized sets of assumptions, knowledge, and so-called cultural practices that we come across racism in its most powerful, because pervasive, form.

These norms and forms are so much a daily currency, they have been around for so long in different incarnations, that they are not mostly (even for an anti-racist person) objects of investigation for they are not even visible. They produce silences or absences, creating gaps and fissures through which non-white women, for example, disappear from the social surface. Racism becomes an everyday life and "normal" way of seeing. Its banality and invisibility is such that it is quite likely that there may be entirely "politically correct" white individuals who have a deeply racist perception of the world. It is entirely possible to be critical of racism at the level of ideology, politics and institutions—do Southern Africa solidarity work, or work with "women of colour" for example—and yet possess a great quantity of common sense racism. This may coexist, for example, with a passively racist aesthetic. Outside of the area which is considered to be "political" or workplace—i.e. public life—this same white activist (feminist or solidarity worker) probably associates mainly or solely with white middle class people. That fine line which divides pleasure and comfort from politics is constituted with the desire of being with "people like us."

While white obviously racist individuals are avoided, the elements of everyday life—family forms, food, sport, etc.—are shot through with racism. Non-white people associating with them will/do feel oppressed by their very way of "being" rather than by what they say or do "politically." These white progressive activists may have dealt with the overtly political, ideological dimension of their own racism, but not with their common sense racism. It is perhaps for this reason that the racism of the left feminists is almost always of omission rather than that of commission. They probably truly cannot *see* us or why it is that racism and "ethnicity" are integral to the study of women in Canada—even when they study the area of labour/capital relations, i.e. class. And those feminists who do see us or that racism is an issue very often deal with it in the spirit of Christian humanism, on the ground of morality and doing good, or in the spirit of bourgeois democracy, which "includes" or adds on representatives from the "minority" communities.

The fact of the matter is that it is almost impossible for European societies as they are to eliminate racism in a thoroughgoing way. Racism is not simply a set of attitudes and practices that they level towards us, their socially constructed "other," but it is the very principle of self-definition of European/Western societies. It could be said that what is otherwise known as European civilization—as manifested in the realm of arts and ideas and in daily life—is a sublimated, formalized, or simply a practiced version of racism. In his book *Orientalism*, Edward Said (1979) draws our attention to this as he points out that the "Orient was almost a European invention" and "one of its deepest and most recurring images of the other"—but additionally "...the Orient has helped to define Europe (or the West) as its contrasting image, ideal, personality and experience" (2). What he says of "orientalism" can be said of racism as well, that it is "...a style of thought based upon an ontological and epistemological distinction made between 'the Orient' and (most of the time) the 'occident'" (2).

If we substitute the two terms with black and white, or better still with a comprehensive binary of white and non-white, European (including the U.S. and Canada) and non-European—we get the picture. Europe or America created (and continues to create) myths of imperialism, of barbarism/savagery, a general inferiority of the conquered, enslaved and colonized peoples and also created myths of exoticism at the same instant as it defined itself also as an "other" of these. The negative determinations of Europe's or America's/Canada's racism manifest themselves everywhere. Some of the humblest to the most cerebral/aesthetic dimensions of white people's life are informed with racism. Its notion of female beauty, for example, which is so inextricably meshed with eroticism (sexuality) is fundamentally racist—not only sexist—not to mention some of the obviously "social" practices, such as mothering, "good housekeeping," etc. The racist assumptions about "the black family," as manifested in the works of U.S. sociologists such as Daniel Moynahan, constitute the negative dialectic of a "good American (white) home (family)." This is taken up very clearly in the essays of Pratibha Parmar, Hazel Carby, Errol Lawrence, et. al. in *The Empire Strikes Back*, where the racism of British middle class social assumptions are fully bared by being put next to the white/European "civilized" ideals of the family. As many black writers point out—most importantly Frantz Fanon in *The Wretched of the Earth* and Aime Cesaire in *Discourse on Colonialism*—the colonizer (slaver or imperialist or whatever) not only reorganized the identity and social space of the colonized, but also at the same instant, through the same process, his own. Europe was not only substantively itself, but also non-Africa, non-India.

It is not surprising then that both in its omissions and commissions racism is an essential organizing device of European (white) feminist discourse—as much as of any other type of discourse. If this were to be effectively challenged it would need the turning of every stone of imperialism. White feminists would have to re-examine the very ground of their historical-social identity, their own subjectivity, their ways of being and seeing—every bit of what passes for "culture" or art. In short, it would be a process of re-making themselves, and their society, in totality. This would of course have to take place in the world, not in their heads, since common sense, as I said before, is a very practical matter. In the world, as practices, it would have to be a kind of anti-imperialist, anti-capitalism that tries not only to undo ideologies, institutions, economies and state powers as they presently exist, but also to reconstruct the most mundane aspects of social life, and to re-think class—that well-spring of struggles and changes.

So we have a sense now of what may be some of the reasons for the fact that in the annals of feminist history, or "herstory," in Canada, there are only fleeting glimpses of us. A few allusions to "slavery," a few numbers indicating a statistical state of being in the records of government agencies, some reference to an entity called the "immigrant woman" or the "visible minority" woman, are what we have so far. The result is that for a few years I stood next to a blackboard and in the name of women—*all* women—taught a one-dimensional theory of gender and patriarchy, which primarily reveals the concerns and preoccupations of white middle class women. And I sense among many of my women students a disinterest, a withdrawal and a patient resignation to the irrelevancies of an institutional education. Now I no longer do that kind of teaching, and instead try to raise the issues I raised in the paragraphs above to question those methods of social analysis current among us, which are by and large liberal-empiricist or idealist (ideological) ones. I also try to show how these methods, in the end, serve the interest of the status quo—a white imperialist hegemonic discourse. This cannot but serve the interests of white middle class women.

While reading feminist writing a reader cannot but be aware of the particular connotation the word "woman" takes on which extends way beyond description into the realm of power and politics. Gendered divisions of labour and accompanying relations of power are connotatively inseparable from this word nowadays. But as it gains a political nuance, so it also takes on a quality of universality and an overridingness. As the word becomes in some ways political/actionable on one ground—that of gender and patriarchy—so it also becomes an abstraction. How does this happen? And what does it have to do with not attending to racism?

In this method of operating, the abstraction is created when the different social moments which constitute the "concrete" being of any social organization and existence are pulled apart, and each part assumed to have a substantive, self-regulating structure. This becomes apparent when we see gender, race and class each considered as a separate issue—as ground for separate oppressions. The social whole—albeit fraught with contradictions—is then constructed by an aggregative exercise. According to this, I, as a South Asian woman, then have a double oppression to deal with, first on the count of gender, and second on the count of race. I am thus segmented into different social moments, made a victim of discrete determinations. So it is with the moment of gender, when it is seen as a piece by itself, rupturing its constitutive relationship with race and class. Needless to say, race and class could also be meted the same treatment. What this does is to empty out gender relations of their general social context, content and dynamism. This, along with the primacy that gender gains (since the primary, social determinant is perceived as patriarchy), subsumes all other social relations, indeed renders them often invisible. The particular—i.e. one moment—begins to stand in for the whole.

This process is fully at work in the method and social analysis of much of the feminist literature we read. What seems to happen is that the word "woman" takes on a conceptual/categorical status encoding patriarchal social relations which are viewed as substantive structures. So issues pertaining to "women" would be discussed largely without locating them in a historical, social organization context, such as that of race and class (in the case of Canada). In fact, the notion "women" in plurality is substituted with that of *Woman*—a singular yet universal entity. So it becomes possible for a feminist journal to call itself "*Canadian Woman Studies*." The assumption is, of course, that all women are one, and this is inescapable since the logic of such a method of decontextualizing, or dehistoricizing, can only lead to this conclusion since the aspect of gender is not constitutively related to other social and formative relations.

Having established this pseudo-universality which confers a legitimacy and an interpretive and organizing status to this notion of "woman"—the actual pieces of writing, however, go on to speak of some very concrete existing problems and experiences of particular groups of women, and not to do philosophy. They are in fact specific problems and experiences of the woman who is writing, or of people like herself, that are peculiarly oppressive for her. There is, of course, nothing wrong with that—as long as we know it—and are not presented with it as "Everywoman's problems" and concerns. This is of course not done since to speak in the name of all confers a legitimacy without which such a stand of authority could not have been constructed. Nor are problems of race and class emphasized or seen as related to gender issues, because such a thing would break down the homogeneity and even reveal the class location of the theorist/writer. The result of course is that with which I started at the very beginning—my/our experience—a new political and academic field in which we are marked by absence, subsumption and, if we are noticed at all, we are given an interpreted status by those who are in a position to control and generate forms of discourse. As at the level of method, one moment stands in for others in a controlling, hegemonic relation to the rest, so that in the actual writing, one group of women's interests (however valid for them) is smuggled in, masquerading as the interests of all women.

Both the method and the politics implied in it are old. It is the fact that they are employed in an oppositional political context—namely feminism—that makes it initially hard to recognize them. In *The German Ideology*, Marx talked about this very method of extrapolation, universalization, establishing "mystical" connections and eventually interpretive schema "theories." This is his critique of ideology. In his "introduction" to what has come to be called *The Grundrisse*, he further critiques this ideological method, when he makes an attempt to create a method of social analysis in which the different social moments can retain both their specificity and reveal their implication and constitutive relation to all other specific social relations.

The advantage of this ideological procedure is well brought out in the context of the bourgeoisie's assumption of political power. We see in several texts—beginning with the most explicit *Communist Manifesto* to *The Eighteenth Brumaire of Louis Bonaparte*—Marx speaks of how it benefits a particular class to speak of itself/its interests, etc. as the universal class/interests. It is a way to gaining power and keeping power. As Gramsci put it years later in the context of Italy, to gain and keep leadership one must exert a moral and social hegemony. If the middle class women's interests are those of all of us, then we must drown ourselves in their version of the world and their politics. This gives them a solid base to wage their own hegemonic fractional conflict with bourgeois males, while we intensify our own oppression. If we were actually to advance our own position, we could not but show that organization by race (or racism) is a fundamental way of forming class in Canada, and that this formation of class is a fully gendered one. Far from being our "sisters," these middle class women are complicit in our domination. Being class members of a middle class created on the terrain of imperialism and capitalism—hiding it (even from themselves perhaps) behind ideological methods constructed for ruling—they cannot but be part of our problem, not the solution.

This version that I have offered of the mainstream feminist theories, or even of those socialist feminists who are colour-blind or leave out the determinations of class, is also arrived at by being sensitized by the work of Dorothy E. Smith. In her work on Marx's method, attempts at creating a sociology from a woman's standpoint, and enquiry, into how the work of sociologists (academics in general) in the process of ruling holds an exploitive system in place—Smith gives us an extremely valuable insight into the production and practice of ideology. Also valuable has been the work of Michel Foucault, who bared for us the role of power in constructing/defining what constitutes knowledge and thus in constituting the "other" in the course of, or for the purpose of, domination. It must also be mentioned that the liberal empiricist method of thinking in terms of single issues, so current in North American academia and politics, is also particularly favourable to this ideological way of thinking about (and subsequently acting in) the world. And all this fits right in with the racist common sense of a people, whose self-definition and social organization not to mention economic organization, has been fundamentally based on racism and imperialism.

The ground of discourse as much as the ground of everyday living are contested grounds. Class struggle in Canada goes on—even in the name of extending a helping hand. Class rule solidifies itself in an oppositional guise, where bourgeois men and women wrestle for power but form a solid body vis-à-vis us. Maybe one should re-read Mao Tse-tung—and figure out where the contradictions lie—and where they are genuinely antagonistic or non-antagonistic. The poor in the French Revolution did get to storm the Bastille, but Napoleon came to power. Here we—the other women—haven't even stormed the Bastille, but a Napoleon is already in the wings.

THE EVERYDAY WORLD AS PROBLEMATIC: A FEMINIST METHODOLOGY

Dorothy Smith

I The Standpoint of Women in the Everyday World

…The fulcrum of a sociology for women is the standpoint of the subject. A sociology for women preserves the presence of subjects as knowers and as actors. It does not transform subjects into the objects of study or make use of conceptual devices for eliminating the active presence of subjects. Its methods of thinking and its analytic procedures must preserve the presence of the active and experiencing subject. A sociology is a systematically developed knowledge of society and social relations. The knower who is construed in the sociological texts of a sociology for women is she whose grasp of the world *from where she stands* is enlarged thereby. For actual subjects situated in the actualities of their everyday worlds, a sociology for women offers an understanding of how those worlds are organized and determined by social relations imminent in and extending beyond them.

Methods of thinking could, I suppose, be described as "theories," but to do so is to suggest that I am concerned with formulations that will explain phenomena, when what I am primarily concerned with is how to conceptualize or how to constitute the textuality of social phenomena. I am concerned with how to *write* the social, to make it visible in sociological texts, in ways that will explicate a problematic, the actuality of which is imminent in the everyday world.…

To avoid potential misunderstanding, I should state first what I do not mean by the standpoint of women. A sociology for women should not be mistaken for an ideological position that represents women's oppression as having a determinate character and takes up the analysis of social forms with a view to discovering in them the lineaments of what the ideologist already supposes that she knows. The standpoint of women therefore as I am deploying it here cannot be equated with perspective or worldview. It does not universalize a particular experience. It is rather a method that, at the outset of inquiry, creates the space for an absent subject, and an absent experience that is to be filled with the presence and spoken experience of actual women speaking of and in the actualities of their everyday worlds.

…The exclusion of women is not the only one. The ruling apparatus is an organization of class and as such implicates dominant classes. The working class is excluded from the ruling apparatus. It also excludes the many voices of women and men of color, of native peoples, and of homosexual women and men. From different standpoints different aspects of the ruling apparatus and of class come into view. But, …the standpoint of women is distinctive and has distinctive implications for the practice of sociology as a systematically developed consciousness of society.

I proposed women's standpoint as one situated outside textually mediated discourses in the actualities of our everyday lives. This is a standpoint designed in part by our exclusion from the making of cultural and intellectual discourse and the strategics of resorting to our experience as the ground of a new knowledge, a new culture. But it is also designed by an organization of work that has typically been ours, for women's work, as wives, secretaries, and in other ancillary roles, has been that which anchors the impersonal and objectified forms of action and relations to particular individuals, particular local places, particular relationships. Whatever other part women play in the social division of labor, they have been assigned and confined predominately to work roles mediating the relation of the impersonal and objectified forms of action to the concrete local and particular worlds in which all of us necessarily exist.

The standpoint of women therefore directs us to an "embodied" subject located in a particular actual local historical setting. Her world presents itself to her in its full particularity—the books on her shelves, the Cowichan sweaters she has bought for her sons' birthdays, the Rainforest chair she bought three years ago in a sale, the portable computer she is using to write on, the eighteenth-century chair, made of long-since-exhausted Caribbean mahogany, one of a set of four given her by her mother years ago—each is particularized by insertion into her biography and projects as well as by its immediacy in the now in which she writes. The abstracted constructions of discourse or bureaucracy are accomplishments in and of her everyday world. Her reading and writing are done in actual locations at actual times and under definite material conditions. Though discourse, bureaucracy, and the exchange of money for commodities create forms of social relations that transcend the local and particular, they are constituted, created, and practiced always *within* the local and particular. It is the special magic of the ubiquity of text and its capacity to manifest itself as the same in diverse multiple settings that provide for the local practices of transcendence.

A standpoint in the everyday world is the fundamental grounding of modes of knowing developed in a ruling apparatus. The ruling apparatus is that familiar complex of management, government administration, professions, and intelligentsia, as well as the textually mediated discourses that coordinate and interpenetrate it. Its special capacity is the organization of particular actual places, persons, and events into generalized and abstracted and universalized system of ruling mediated by texts. A mode of ruling has been created that transcends local particularities but at the same time exists only in them. The ruling apparatus of this loosely coordinated collection of varied sites of power has been largely if not exclusively the sphere of men. From within its textual modes the embodied subject and the everyday world as its site are present only as object and never as subject's standpoint. But from the standpoint of women whose work has served to complete the invisibility of the actual as the locus of the subject, from the standpoint of she who stands at the beginning of her work, the grounding of an abstracted conceptual organization of ruling comes into view as a product in and of the everyday world.…

Women's lives have been outside or subordinate to the ruling apparatus. Its conceptual practices do not work for us in the development of a sociological consciousness of our own. The grid of political sociology, the sociology of the family, of organizations, of mental illness, of education, and so forth, does not map the unknown that extends before us as what is to be discovered and explored; it does not fit when we ask how we should organize a sociology beginning from the standpoint of women. We start, as we must, with women's experience (for what other resource do we have?); the available concepts and frameworks do not work because they have already posited a subject situated outside a local and actual experience, a particularized knowledge of the world. Women are readily made the objects of sociological study precisely because they have not been its subjects. Beneath the apparent gender neutrality of the impersonal or absent subject of an objective sociology is the reality of the masculine author of the texts of its tradition and his membership in the circle of men participating in the division of the labor of ruling. The problem confronted here is how to do a sociology that is for women and that takes women as its subjects and its knowers when the methods of thinking, which we have learned as sociologists as the methods of producing recognizably sociological texts, reconstruct us as objects.

If we begin where people are actually located in that independently existing world outside texts, we begin in the particularities of an actual everyday world. As a first step in entering that standpoint into a textually mediated discourse, we constitute the everyday world as our problematic. We do so by interesting ourselves in its opacity for we cannot understand how it is organized or comes about by remaining within it. The concept of problematic transfers this opacity to the level of discourse. It directs attention to a possible set of questions that have yet to be posed or of puzzles that are not yet formulated as such but are "latent" in the actualities of our experienced worlds. The problematic of the everyday world is an explicit discursive formulation of an actual property of the organization of the everyday world. I am talking about a reality as it arises for those who live it—the reality, for example, that effects arise that do not originate in it. Yet I *am talking* (or rather writing) about it. I am entering it into discourse. The term "problematic" enters an actual aspect of the organization of the everyday world (as it is ongoingly produced by actual individuals) into a systematic inquiry. It responds to our practical ignorance of the determinations of our local worlds so long as we look for them within their limits. In this sense the puzzle or puzzles are really there. Hence an inquiry defined by such as problematic addresses a problem of how we are related to the worlds we live in. We may not experience our ignorance as such, but we are nonetheless ignorant....

II Problems in the Relationship of Observer and Observed

Beginning from the standpoint of women implies beginning at a point prior to the moment that organizes the detached scientific consciousness. It means therefore beginning in the world that both sociologist and those she observes and questions inhabit on the same basis. Taking the standpoint of women means recognizing that as inquirers we are thereby brought into determinate relations with those whose experience we intend to express. The concepts and frameworks, our methods of inquiry, of writing texts, and so forth are integral aspects of that relation. Furthermore what has been argued of the everyday world of women in general applies equally to that everyday moment in which we encounter those we will write about in some form or other. The relations with others organized by our inquiry are also shaped by social relations subtending it and entering into the inquiry in unseen ways....

III Sociological Methods of Writing Texts

Established sociology is preoccupied with suppressing the presence of the sociological subject.[1] This points to an underlying contradiction. While objectivity, in the sense of the detached scientific knower, has come to be seen as an essential property of its scientific texts, actuality has continued to resist this discursive production. However flexible her joints and acrobatic her postures, the sociological knower is always and cannot escape being part of the world that goes on outside her head, as well as inside it, and is her object of inquiry. Her head and her inquiry are as much part of it as the object of her investigation. Scientific detachment itself is a product of distinctive and specialized social organization, consisting, on the one hand, of methods of writing and reading the texts of scientific discourse and, on the other, as Schutz has shown us,[2] of the subject's own practices of suppressing and discarding her biographical and local setting and the pragmatic concerns of her world of working to enter the cognitive domain of science as reader of scientific texts. To forget her bodily being is also to forget her own historicity.

The sociologist's methods of writing texts produce a world for her readers such that they too stand outside it. Those of us who have had the experience of being members of a category that is the object of sociological inquiry can recognize the strangeness of finding ourselves as subjects transformed in a course of reading into objects and of the unspoken sociological stipulation instructing us to disregard what we know of ourselves as embodied subjects. The unspoken relationship between sociologist and those she observes is hidden in the conceptual practices that externalize their activities and practices as properties of structures or systems, and reinterprets the daily actualities of their lives into the alienated constructs of sociological discourse, subordinating their experienced worlds to the categories of ruling....

If we forgo the move of objectivity, are there procedures enabling us to determine which among differing versions of the world we can rely on as an account of how it is? What is the status of our version if we forgo our claim to write the "third" and overriding version?

Can we, as Sandra Harding suggests,[3] come to rest in an acceptance of intrinsic many-sidedness of our worlds and therefore of the many stories that may be told of it, of which ours is only one? Post-modernists have celebrated and theorized the overthrow of the transcendental subject, replacing it with a recognition of multiple alternative narratives, none of which can claim a privileged status over others. Harding has described this move as follows:

> Once the Archimedean, transhistorical agent of knowledge is deconstructed into constantly shifting, wavering, recombining, historical groups, then a world that can be understood and navigated with the assistance of Archimedes' map of perfect perspective also disappears. As Flax puts the issue, "Perhaps 'reality' can have 'a' structure only from the falsely universalizing perspective of the master. That is, only to the extent that one person or group can dominate the whole, can 'reality' appear to be governed by one set of rules or be constituted by one privileged set of social relationships?"[4]

Harding concludes that "by giving up the ghost of telling 'one true story,'[5] we embrace instead the permanent partiality of feminist inquiry." The "one true story" is nothing more than a partial perspective claiming generality on the basis of social privilege and power.

But suppose we posed the problem at a more mundane level where we are not grappling with notions of truth, but more simply and rudely with how to write a sociology that will somehow lay out for women, for people, how our everyday worlds are organized and how they are shaped and determined by relations that extend beyond them. Inquiry itself does not make sense unless we suppose that there is something to be found and that that something can be spoken of to another, as we might say "Well, this is the way it is. This is how it works." It would not be enough to be able to say "This is how it looks to me" when that is not just a way station toward something more final, but is all we are going to be able to say. If we want to be able to offer something like a map or diagram of the swarming relations in which our lives are enmeshed so that we can find our ways better among them, then we want to be able to claim that we are describing is actual in the same way as our everyday worlds are actual. We want to be able to say with confidence that we can speak of it truthfully and faithfully.

The problems of multiple perspectives for sociology and the decision rules provided by sociological methods of constituting objectivity arise in the context of a sociology that has built into its methods the assumption that we cannot encounter the world without a concept, that knowing it relies on the ordering procedures already established in the theoretical armamentarium of the discourse. If we move then to a sociology whose business is making out a world that is put together in determinate ways prior to our thinking it and that makes as its enterprise the discovery of just how it is done, then the issues are no longer at the level of "truth" but rather, in assessing the products of inquiry, "Has she got it right? Is this how it really works? Is it accurate? Faithful to the character of the organization and relations investigated?" Such questions can be asked only if there exists the practical possibility of another account that *can* invalidate hers. If it is a power play, as Harding suggests,[6] to claim the veracity of one version, is it not also essential to the most modest possibilities of knowing how things work that a social scientific account can be called into question? And therefore that another version can be on some grounds preferred?…

IV Sociological Inhibitions to Exploring the Everyday World as Problematic

Opening an inquiry from the standpoint of women means accepting our ineluctable embeddedness in the same world as is the object of our inquiry. It means recognizing that our work enters us into relationships with others that are structured by relations not fully present in them and that our textual pretensions to objectivity are betrayed by the secret presence of those relations in the text itself and the conceptual and other devices that we make use of in producing it. To work then from the standpoint of women as a method of thinking and of writing the subject into texts, we must cede from the outset our discursive privilege to substitute our understandings for those whose stories instruct us in their experience of lived actualities. Yet clearly if we move to an investigation of the relations that are not plain either to our interlocutor or ourselves, she cannot be our resource for everything we want to know. We want to know more so that she can also.

Beyond the encounter on the common ground of an everyday world, we have shown dimly the workings of another level of organization. Individuals' accounts of their experience may disclose a level of organization beyond that experience.…

V Exploring the Social Relations Determining the Everyday

Let us explore, in a very preliminary way, such a set of extended relations as they have been crystallized in Mrs. Pember Reeves' book on the household economies of working-class mothers in London in the early twentieth century.[7] We reach back through an account that has transformed an original multivocality into one voice in a complex of relations in which different matrices of consciousness and experience are generated.

In Mrs. Reeves' study, she tells, among others, of the working day of a working-class woman she calls Mrs. T. Here then is Two, telling of One's life in a text intended for others certainly more like herself than like One. In the textual context, One is the stranger, the other whose life must be told because to the implicit "we" of the readerly conspiracy it is not familiar (their own daily routines are not a topic). Mrs. Reeves is at work organizing our relationship to Mrs. T., drawing us imperceptibly into the presuppositions of the relations that are both strangely visible but also silenced in the text. Here then we will not take the text as it appears in "document time,"[8] detached from the social relations in which it was made *and of which it formed an operative part*. It is treated rather as it gives textual presence to the actualities of the lives of working-class women in a definite and historically specific context of reading.

Much of Mrs. Pember Reeves' account of Mrs. T.'s working day is based on Mrs. T.'s own account, though we are not given the latter verbatim. Though Mrs. T. does not speak to us directly, she is present in the text as that subject whose experience is its necessary condition:

> We now come to the day of a mother of six children with two rooms to keep. Mrs. T. … is the wife of a builder's handyman on 25s a week. The two rooms are upstairs in a small house, and, as there is no water above ground floor, Mrs. T. has a good deal of carrying of heavy pails of water both upstairs and down. She is gentle and big and slow, never lifts her voice or gets angry, but seems always tired and dragged. She is very clean and orderly. Her husband is away all day; but he dislikes the noise of a family meal and insists on having both breakfast and tea cooked specially for himself, and eats alone.

6:00	Nurses baby.
6:30	Gets up, calls five children, puts kettle on, washes "necks" and "backs" of all the children, dresses the little ones, does hair of three girls.
7:30	Gets husband's breakfast, cooks bloater, and makes tea.
8:00	Give him breakfast alone, nurses baby while he has it, and cuts slices of bread and dripping for children.
8:30	He goes; gives children breakfast, sends them off to school at 8:50, and has her own.
9:00	Clears away and washes up breakfast things.
9:30	Carries down slops, and carries up water from the yard; makes beds.
10:00	Washes and dresses baby, nurses him, and puts him to bed.
11:00	Sweeps out bedroom, scrubs stairs and passage.
12:00	Goes out and buys food for the day. Children at home.
12:25	Cooks dinner; lays it.
1:00	Gives children dinner and nurses baby.
1:45	Washes hands and faces, and sees children off to school.

2:00	Washes up dinner things, scrubs out kitchen, cleans grate, empties dirty water, and fetches more clean from yard.
3:00	Nurses baby.
3:30	Cleans herself and begins to mend clothes.
4:15	Children all back.
4:30	Gives them tea.
5:00	Clears away and washes up, nurses the baby, and mends clothes till 6:30. Cooks husband's tea.
7:00	Gives husband tea alone.
7:30	Puts younger children to bed.
8:00	Tidies up, washes husband's tea things, sweeps kitchen, mends clothes, nurses baby, puts elder children to bed.
8:45	Gets husband's supper; mends clothes.
10:00	Nurses baby, and makes him comfortable for the night.
10:30	Goes to bed.[9]

The text is the product of a project undertaken by Reeves as a member of the Fabian Women's Group. It reports on a study of whether improving the nutrition of working-class women in late pregnancy and while nursing their babies improved their and the child's overall health. Its very existence is grounded in class relations, and class relations are at work in how the text is constructed as an account of the lives of working-class women *for* an "educated" middle class. The project itself, the need for a *study* rather than hearing from the women themselves; the taken-for-granted entitlement of the visitor to inquire into the family lives and domestic work and routines of working-class women; the unmentioned quid pro quo that adds to Mrs. T.'s daily work the additional task of keeping a record of her daily routines and weekly budget; the work of editing her account into readable English (for the women Mrs. Reeves wrote about practiced, according to her, at best a phonetic spelling), and its entry into the textual discourse of early twentieth-century English socialists: all these are practices articulated to the class relations of the England of that period. This was a time in which women of the dominant classes were active in the management of the working-class family. They were involved in what we have in the past described rather contemptuously as "charities"; they supported women's organization in trade unions; they were concerned with working-class housing, with working-class health and nutrition, with the training of working-class women for motherhood, and so forth. This text is situated in this context of an active organization of class in which women of the dominant classes played a leading role. The interests of the Fabian Women's Group in the nutrition and health of working-class mothers and their newborn children are located in a class-based concern about the health, nutrition, living conditions, and education of the working class, which first arose, in Britain, in the context of recruiting for imperialist wars that exhibited the physical inadequacies of working-class men as military "material."[10] This then is the site of the text and of the relevances that organize it.

Returning to the text, we can see aspects of the structuring of Mrs. T.'s work and experience and how these are organized in relations beyond her narrow domestic world. Her daily routine is powerfully structured by the employment and school schedules of her husband and children. Let us focus on the children and their relationship to school. First, school attendance is required, and the timing of the children's coming and going and its meshing with her husband's employment schedule are primary organizers of mealtimes and bedtimes and hence of how her domestic work has to be allocated to spaces in between the disjunctures created by the timing of their meals and the like. Her work cannot be organized in accordance with its own logic. But more is involved than cooking and scheduling meals to fit these external schedules. Mrs. T. includes in her daily routine washing the children's necks and backs, those parts of their bodies that the children themselves either cannot easily reach or see and might miss or skip. She washes them before school in the morning, and she also washes their hands and faces before they return to school after lunch. We notice that Mrs. T. must fetch water from the yard and carry it upstairs, and then she must carry the slops downstairs to dispose of. At school these children will be inspected by the teacher for their cleanliness. They are going to have the backs of their necks and their hands scrutinized. The children's cleanliness and Mrs. T's care to ensure they go to school clean are enforced by the school, whatever personal pride Mrs. T. may take in her children's appearance. The school's concern, enforced by the teacher, with the cleanliness of working-class children has arisen as part of the same concern as that which motivates Mrs. Reeves' study. The dominant classes have taken steps to manage the health of the working class and the working-class family, and the school is one agent through which these new managerial concerns are implemented. When we make the link between the work organization of Mrs. T.'s day and the school, the way in which the state through the school enters into that organization can be discerned in the background.

We can see thus how Mrs. T. in a curious way comes to act as an agent of this external authority vis-a-vis her children, at least in this matter. She is constrained to enforce in the home the order imposed by the school. But the relaxation does not appear in this way. We begin to see that the working relationships among women and men and parents and children sharing a household cannot be understood as if families formed autonomous systems. While Reeves' orientation and description isolate Mrs. T.'s work process, giving it a self-contained character, ours anchors it in the same complex of social relations in which the study arises and which the text "expresses."

The use of a historical example bars us forever from moving beyond the text or outside it, to talk to Mrs. T. directly. But the explication of experience as such is not the objective of this sociology for women. The use of a historical example places it in any case out of reach. Yet we see that there is a way of addressing the other side of the disseevered relationship between the women sociologist or Fabian socialist who tells the tale and those others mute but for her text who are somehow given presence in it. To take up the exploration and analysis of the social relations in which One's life is embedded is to take up the organization of her experience not as an external system but as a world. The social character of which arises in the constant ongoing intercoordination of actual activities. The reality of the relations that organize the encounter between One and Two and the ways in which Two may represent One in the texts of her discourse are an ongoing accomplishment. All the features of the world that Reeves puts before us exist (are constituted?) in social relations in which these named objects are accomplished in their quiddity.

The work of women such as Mrs. T. enters social relations such as these and is part of their formation. These relations also organize and determine their work. We understand then the reciprocal or dialectical character of social relations, for they arise in the co-ordering of people's work while their specific properties also organize the work process at the local historical level. Mrs. T.'s household and family are organized in determinate ways in the context of school and wage labor. They do not stand suspended as an instance of an abstract family located in an abstracted conceptual space. Rather they are clearly a work organization sustained on a daily basis by its members and continually organized and reorganized by how its members' work practices take up such material exigencies as a capitalist market in real estate and rental properties; as the enforcement of school and the authority of school authorities to examine children's cleanliness; by the specific character of the local organization of retail stores, transportation and the like; by opportunity for additional nutritional support conditional upon allowing Mrs. Reeves and others like her to come into the home, to look about, and to approve or disapprove the housewife's dispositions. Here is the matrix of experience and an everyday world, the problematic of which we have sought to open up (in a very preliminary way). The conjunction in this book of Mrs. T.'s absent but determining experience and Mrs. Reeves' own speaking is not irrelevant. It is precisely here that we can explore the relations in which both are implicated and active and in which the account itself, *Round About a Pound a Week*, is embedded. It is precisely in these relations that we discover class and its actual character as a routine, daily accomplishment....

VI The Sociologist inside the Whale

Mrs. Reeves' study enables us to hold at a historical distance the relations we are concerned with exploring. Reaching through her work, we discover the presence of others who do not speak directly to us; through her work we have discovered the relations at work in it through which those others have been silenced. We see her text as a moment in the organization of those relations. In returning from the past to reflect upon our present, we discover our own sociological texts as moments in the organization of relations within which our work is embedded. Redesigning the relationship between sociologist and those she learns from her investigations is not enough. Any such reconstruction still bears the determinations of the extended relations within which the encounters between sociologist and the subject are embedded. The methodology of its writing structures how it enters into the organization of the social relations that it bears.

Texts are organizers of social relations. Methods of writing them produce their capacity to organize. Sociological methods of writing texts produce accounts relating ourselves as readers to those of whom they speak in a relation of ruling. Of course we do not magically transform those relations by writing our texts in different ways. We have to recognize the real limitations of what our work can do. But a discipline such as sociology has developed powerful methods for producing texts that will operate in the extended relations of ruling. What we have focused upon here is how to produce alternatives that will go beyond the reporting of experience to the development of a knowledge of the social relations within which we work and struggle as subjects. We are seeking methods of inquiry *and* of writing sociology that organize the relation between the text and those of whom the text speaks as "cosubjects" in a world we make—and destroy—together.

The alternative I have been developing here begins with people as subjects active in the same world as we are situated in as bodies. Subject is located at the beginning of her acts—

work and other practical activities; through these she joins with others, known and unknown, in bringing into being a world that they have, but do not necessarily know; in common. The objects of our worlds, whether concrete (cigarettes, tables, horses, or microchips) or relational (commodities, gifts, capital), are accomplishments of ongoing courses of action in which many are implicated. These are actual activities; their concerting or co-ordering is an ongoing process....

ENDNOTES

1.   See Dorothy E. Smith, "The Ideological Practice of Sociology," *Catalyst* 8 (1974): 39-54, for an analysis of the sociological methods that suppress the presence of actual subjects.

2.   Alfred Schutz, "On Multiple Realities," in *Collected Papers*, vol. 1 (The Hague: Martinus Nijhoff, 1962).

3.   Sandra Harding, *The Science Question in Feminism* (Ithaca: Cornell University Press, 1986).

4.   Ibid., p. 193; the reference is to Jane Flax, "Gender As a Social Problem: In and For Feminist Theory," *American Studies/Amerika Studien*, Journal of the German Association for American Studies, 1986.

5.   Harding, *Science Question in Feminism*, 194.

6.   Ibid., 193.

7.   Reeves, *Round About a Pound a Week*.

8.   Cf. Dorothy E Smith, "The Social Construction of Documentary Reality," *Social Inquiry* 44, no. 4 (1974): 257-68.

9.   Reeves, *Round About a Pound a Week*, 167-68.

10. See Anna Davin, "Imperialism and Motherhood," *History Workshop: A Journal of Socialist Historians*, no. 5 (Spring 1978): 9-65.

FROM THE SUBVERSION OF IDENTITY TO THE SUBVERSION OF SOLIDARITY?

JUDITH BUTLER AND THE CRITIQUE OF WOMEN'S IDENTITY

Allison Weir

Judith Butler avoids Luce Irigaray's paradox—the affirmation of a women's identity in the face of a repudiation of identity as a phallogocentric construct—by sticking to a much more consistent deconstruction of identity. For Butler, the subversion of identity must be extended to a subversion of any notion of a women's identity. Butler's critique of gender identity and her theory of gender as performance lead in important directions, but her acceptance of the claim that identity is always a product of a sacrificial logic leads her into new paradoxes.

In her book *Gender Trouble: Feminism and the Subversion of Identity*, Judith Butler offers a compelling political and philosophical analysis of the ways in which fixed gender identities serve to constrain the constitution of subjectivity. To do this, she draws a number of different arguments together. Central to her analysis is the psychoanalytic argument, developed with some ambivalence by Freud and made explicit by Lacan, that gender differences and heterosexual orientation are not simply natural but are rather products of a fixed socio-symbolic order which is fundamentally patriarchal. The psychoanalytic argument is supplemented and criticized by Foucault's argument that gender identities must be understood as the effects of multiple discourses, practices, and institutions, rather than as expressions of a single repressive symbolic order. And both of these arguments are supplemented and called into question by feminist analyses of the ways in which the institutions of gender produce sexed identities: in particular, Butler draws on Monique Wittig's critique of the institution of compulsory heterosexuality and on Luce Irigaray's critique of phallogocentrism.

From these theorists Butler draws the important arguments that, first of all, sex and gender identities are not simply natural and prior to social and linguistic influences, but are discursively and culturally constituted; and that, secondly, this constitution is organized in part through regulative institutions which maintain and reproduce specific power relations by enforcing particular performances of gender. In particular, the institutions of phallogocentrism and compulsory heterosexuality operate to define male and female identities through a binary logic: identity is established in terms of opposition to, exclusion of, and desire for the other.

The analysis of the roles of these repressive institutions in the constitution of gender categories is an important one. But Butler places this analysis in the context of a metatheory of identity and of language which effectively undermines any possibility of the subversion of repressive identities. Butler's fundamental claim is that any identity is always and only the product of a system or logic of power/language which generates identities as functions of binary oppositions, and seeks to conceal its own workings by making those identities appear natural. Ironically, by adopting this single, totalizing theory of the logic of identity, Butler herself represses any possibility of *difference* among different forms of identity. It becomes impossible to differentiate between repressive and nonrepressive, exclusive and inclusive, immediate and mediated, metaphysical and socially constructed forms of identity. The identity of the self, the identity of meaning in language, gender identity, women's identity, lesbian identity, feminist identity, identity as uniqueness and as sameness, identity as and identity with, are all understood to be expressions of a single sacrificial logic of identity. In other words, Butler subverts her own call for a subversion of identity by rendering identity so omnipotent and intransigent that the subversion becomes impossible. Thus, it becomes impossible to see the affirmations of existential and political identities which provide a sense of meaning and solidarity to participants in feminist, gay and lesbian, and black struggles for empowerment as anything other than paradoxical affirmations of the identitary logic of domination and exclusion.

In this chapter, I want to argue that, in order to realize Butler's project—to theorize gender as an "effect of institutions, practices, discourses with multiple and diffuse points of origin"[1]—we need to move beyond the assumption that all of those discourses operate according to a single sacrificial and exclusionary logic of identity. We need, first of all, to recognize differences among different types and forms of identity, and secondly, to reformulate and reconstruct identities which can include, rather than exclude, differences.

To develop these claims, I want to begin by looking at what Butler has to say about the problem of women's identity.

> For the most part, feminist theory has taken the category of women to be foundational to any further political claims without realizing that the category effects a political closure on the kinds of experiences articulable as part of a feminist discourse.[2]

In this formulation, Butler is conflating very different types of identity. I think that she is right to call into question any claim to an *immediate* experiential or metaphysical identity among women, and any claim which reifies and naturalizes male and female gender identities. And she is right to criticize any imposition of an identity shared by members of one privileged group upon others—typically, by white middle- or upper-class heterosexual western feminists upon all women—i.e., the imposition of a *false* claim to identity which *represses* differences.

But what exactly is the basis for Butler's claim that "the category of women" necessarily imposes a "closure on the kinds of experiences *articulable* as part of a feminist discourse"? Here, Butler rejects even the position of Gayatri Spivak, who argues that while we need to reject any claims to metaphysical or ontological identity we should retain the "category of women" for strategic purposes, as a political tool. Butler asks:

> But is it the presumption of ontological integrity that needs to be dispelled, or does the practical redeployment of the category without any ontological commitments also effect a political consolidation of its semantic integrity with serious exclusionary implications?[3]

What Butler is claiming here is that something called "semantic integrity" necessarily excludes difference and closes off the possibility of articulating different experiences; in other words, language operates to impose false identities that prevent and foreclose the possibility of the emergence of different voices....

From the argument that sex and gender are both socio-linguistic constructions, Butler moves to the argument that language always operates by invoking an "illusion of substance,"[4] and that language, by imposing identities, represses difference and nonidentity.[5] Thus, the category of women operates to foreclose the articulation of difference: it "effects a political closure on the kinds of experiences articulable as part of a feminist discourse."[6]...

[S]he argues that "the unproblematic claim to 'be' a woman and to 'be' heterosexual" is symptomatic of a "metaphysics of gender substances" (21). Sex or gender "appears within hegemonic language as a *substance*, as, metaphysically speaking, a self-identical being. This appearance is achieved through a performative twist of language and/or discourse that conceals the fact that 'being' a sex or a gender is fundamentally impossible" (18-19). Once again, language is seen as something which "conceals" a "fact"! But what Butler fails to recognize is that "being" a sex or a gender is impossible only if it is assumed, *a priori*, that "being" necessarily refers to a fixed essence. It is impossible to "be" a woman if we assume that to be a woman is to embody some transcendent and eternal essence of womanhood. It is, however, not impossible to be a woman if we accept that the meanings of "being" and "woman," like all human meanings, are socially and historically mediated, and open to contestation and to change, and can be recognized as such....

From the Subversion of Identity to the Subversion of Solidarity?

I have argued that, because Butler sees language as a force of deception and repression, restriction and exclusion, she is unable to move beyond a conception of the *social* as purely restrictive, and leaves no room for any kind of positive development in the social, discursive constitution of identities.

The conception of language and the social as a violation, as the imposition of *order* on heterogeneity, is what unites Butler's *metaphysical* critique of identity as the repression of nonidentity, as the illusion of being which is the repression of doing, and specific *political* critiques of the imposition of repressive identities upon differences. The metaphysical critique, because it reduces all forms of identity to the same thing, just waters down the political one. There is no basis for differentiation between repressive and non-repressive forms of identity. As Nancy Fraser writes in a critique of Foucault:

> The problem is that Foucault calls too many different sorts of things power and simply leaves it at that. Granted, all cultural practices involve constraints—but these constraints

> are of a variety of different kinds and thus demand a variety of different normative responses. Granted, there can be no social practices without power—but it doesn't follow that all forms of power are normatively equivalent nor that any social practices are as good as any other. … Clearly, what Foucault needs, and needs desperately, are normative criteria for distinguishing acceptable from unacceptable forms of power.[7]

What Butler needs, I would argue, are normative criteria for distinguishing acceptable from unacceptable forms of identity. This is a crucial distinction, because without it, it becomes impossible to grant the importance of affirming *political* identities, and identifications, without lapsing into paradox. It is important to be able to see that it is possible to come out as a lesbian, to identify with women, and to affirm solidarity with feminists, without necessarily repressing difference and nonidentity.

Because her argument rests on the critique of all forms of identity as repressive, Butler reduces the idea of an essential Woman, the socio-linguistic category of women, and the ideal of feminist solidarity, all to the same thing.

As I have argued, Butler conflates the "category of women" with the idea of an essential Woman: it is impossible to be a woman because "being" implies a transcendental essence. But the socio-linguistic category of women, rather than invoking the deceptive illusion of an immediate identity (according to a representation model of language) can instead be understood as a socially mediated form of identity which is inclusive of differences, and which is open to change.

Butler shifts again from her critique of a metaphysical *identity of women* to a rejection of the ideal *of feminist solidarity*. While she can accept, she says, the value of coalitional politics which bring together different interest groups to work on specific goals, there must be no attempt "to assert an ideal form for coalitional structures *in advance*," or to insist "in advance on coalitional 'unity' as a goal."[8] This barred "in advance" signifies, once again, the rejection of the imposition of any immediate or transcendental identity upon the coalition as an agent, any claim to a collective "being" that would precede or restrict the "doing" of individual or group members. For Butler, this translates into an assumption that the ideal of solidarity is a repressive one. "The insistence in advance on coalitional 'unity' as a goal assumes that solidarity, whatever its price, is a prerequisite for social action" (14). And she asks, rhetorically, "Does 'unity' set up an exclusionary norm of solidarity at the level of identity that rules out the possibility of a set of actions which disrupt the very borders of identity concepts . . .?" (15).

Solidarity, then, is rejected as a basis of feminist politics, because it *excludes* the possibility of subversions or disruptions of the group identity, and, presumably, of disruptions of group actions aimed at the achievement of agreed-upon goals. In other words, a coalitional activist group should refrain from affirming any solidarity or common purpose, because it might thereby thwart its own subversion. An interesting notion, in the abstract, but it's difficult to imagine how such a group could actually get anything done. Or why it would want to.

Butler claims that this policy of "no commitments" allows for the spontaneous emergence and dissolution of group identities in the service of achieving particular, specific goals. But this evades the issues of group solidarity, the need for a sense of shared meaning and purpose, and the importance of a capacity for commitment to a future and a consciousness of a past. And it denies the possibility of developing group identities which could include and facilitate differences, which could accommodate change without disintegration, which could sustain enduring commitments to ideals and identifications with others.

Butler is making the false assumption that commitment and solidarity necessarily exclude the possibility of conflict and disruption. Either we have a restrictive and repressive totalizing group identity based on false assumptions of substantive unity which effectively exclude the possibility of change, creativity, questioning, and difference; or we have freedom from restrictions, spontaneous self-cremation, and dissolution. But this, once again, is a false opposition between identity and difference. For of course it is possible to affirm solidarity and allow for conflict and difference. In fact, without an ideal of identity and a commitment to solidarity there will be no conflict. What would produce conflict among people whose guiding principle for political action is "do your own thing"?

The point is that by imposing her own *a priori*, "in advance" rule that there must be no commitment to a feminist solidarity which might restrict our freedom, Butler is approaching the problem from the wrong end. Rather than beginning from the transcendental claim that identity represses difference, we need to begin with the question of how we can do politics. For it's one thing to claim that doing must precede being, but another, in practice, for a group to decide what to do, and which action to take. This, of course, raises the question of collective and individual agency. And Butler argues that too many feminists have wrongly assumed that there must be a "metaphysical locus of agency" (25)—an individual human subject, a collective identity—at the origin of any political action. But the argument Butler anticipates is not the argument I want to make. Rather than join Butler on the terrain of disputes about ontology and origins, I want to approach the question from the other end—from the standpoint of the goals of our actions, and the normative ideals which guide those actions.

Butler argues that there is no need to posit a normative ideal of individual or collective identity as a basis for feminist politics. It is quite enough to define our politics in *terms* of our immediate goals and strategies. But it is not very difficult to show that it is impossible to define our goals without appealing to the normative ideals of individual autonomy and collective solidarity. We need only list some very basic feminist goals.

Feminists are in fact surprisingly united in agreement on many basic political positions: there is little controversy as to the importance of rights to abortion and reproductive freedom, freedom of sexual orientation, equal pay and equitable conditions and relations of work, universal access to childcare, autonomy and solidarity in our personal relationships, and genuine and meaningful participation and representation in political and public spheres. There is also fundamental agreement as to the need for the abolition of all forms of sex, race, and class oppression and exploitation, and hence for the abolition of oppressive and exploitative economic, political, social, familial, and cultural structures. In all of these positions we are appealing, necessarily, to the normative ideals of the integrity and autonomy of the individual, and of the equal rights of all individuals to freedom of choice, thought, and action. At the same time, we are appealing to an ideal of the collective good, of a society where all individuals and social groups have basic rights to self-determination, freedom, and happiness, however these may be defined. Moreover, we are affirming, as feminists, a solidarity in our collective commitment to these goals, as well as a collective capacity to interpret and articulate our collective needs and values in order to establish these goals. Given this unavoidable and perhaps embarrassing consensus in practice, how are we to argue consistently that we can define our goals without reference to the norms of individual autonomy and collective identity? And how are we to argue that the identity (or the autonomy) of the individual, and the collective identity or solidarity of feminists (or of women), are oppressive concepts? One way of dealing with this situation, as we have already seen, is simply to affirm paradox, and learn to live with it. After all, life is complex and full of contradictions. So we have to fight for a woman's right to choose on one hand, and deny the validity of the concepts of rights, choice, and women, on the other. This option is becoming, for me, less and less sustainable.

The problem, I think, lies not in the disjuncture between theory and practice, but within the theory itself. Ultimately, Butler's attempt to eliminate the paradox between the deconstruction and affirmation of identity by consistently deconstructing it has simply produced another paradox. And the paradox is an unnecessary one, for it is produced by the false assumption that identity is necessarily repressive of difference. Rather than equating identity with domination on one hand while we continue to affirm it on the other, we need to reformulate our conceptions of identity. We need conceptions of identity which are not essentialist, not metaphysical, and not repressive. Thus, it becomes possible to formulate self-identity and autonomy not simply in terms of repression, but in terms of a capacity to participate in a social world, to interpret and articulate needs and desires, to act with reference to values and ideals, even given our states of ambivalence and confusion. And our collective identity as feminists can be formulated in terms of a collective capacity to interpret and articulate collective needs, to set collective goals, through a continual process of dialogue based on a commitment to the inclusion of all voices. This, of course, depends upon an ability to understand language as a medium of shared understanding and dialogue, of the articulation of difference, and not only as a force of deception and oppression. We need to understand language, then, as the medium of a social identity which is not simply repressive.

A model of feminist solidarity as something which can *include* difference and conflict is suggested by bell hooks. hooks has argued that feminists need to shift from an affirmation of mutual "support," which would correspond to Butler's conception of immediate and repressive identity, to an ideal of solidarity, which would correspond to a conception of mediated and non-repressive identity. The idea of support, hooks argues, has corresponded to a shallow notion of sisterhood as a sort of direct identification based on shared victimization, which demands an avoidance of conflict and a suspension of critical judgment. The illusion of undivided unity has inevitably been shattered with the emergence of divisions and hostilities. "The fierce negative disagreements that have taken place in feminist circles have led many feminist activists to shun group or individual interaction where there is likely to be disagreement which leads to confrontation. Safety and support have been redefined to mean hanging out in groups where the participants are alike and share similar values."9 In other words, the response to the unavoidable recognition of diversity and division has frequently been an avoidance of conflict through an affirmation of the impossibility of solidarity, and a retreat back into support and safety, in the name of an irreducible nonidentity. Thus, hooks traces the affirmation of nonidentity back to an ideal of undivided identity, an ideal which is ultimately unsustainable, and which always leads to failure. Rather than avoiding confrontation through avoiding participation in a collectivity, she argues, we need to shift from an ideal of undivided unity to a form of identity which will not be shattered by confrontation. We need to affirm an ideal of solidarity: a sustained, ongoing commitment to shared values, which will allow for confrontation without complete destruction. The shift from an ideal of support to an ideal of solidarity is, I think, the political dimension of a theoretical shift from an ideal of immediate identity, which turns out to be repressive, to an ideal of mediated identity, which has the potential to include, rather than exclude, difference and heterogeneity. hooks concludes her discussion with an affirmation of feminist solidarity which is certainly idealistic:

> Women do not need to eradicate difference to feel solidarity. We do not need to share common oppression to fight equally to end oppression. We do not need anti-male sentiments to bond us together, so great is the wealth of experience, culture, and ideas we have to share with one another. We can be sisters united by shared interests and beliefs, united in our appreciation for diversity, united in our struggle to end sexist oppression, united in political solidarity.[10]

Ideals can be discounted as unrealistic and illusory; but they can also give us something to strive for.

ENDNOTES

1. Judith Butler, *Gender Trouble: Feminism and the Subversion of Identity* (New York: Routledge, 1990), xi.

2. Judith Butler, "Gender Trouble, Feminist Theory, and Psychoanalytic Discourse," in Linda Nicholson, ed., *Feminism/Postmodernism* (New York: Routledge, 1990), 325.

3. Butler, "Gender Trouble, Feminist Theory, and Psychoanalytic Discourse," 325.

4. Butler, *Gender Trouble*, 29.

5. In *Gender Trouble*, Butler argues that she is not talking about repression, for, following Foucault, she rejects the "repressive hypothesis"—the claim that there is some pure substance which can be emancipated once power is lifted. On the contrary, she argues, following Foucault, that "sexuality is always situated within matrices of power" [97], that "to be sexed . . . is to be subjected to a set of social regulations, to have the law that directs those regulation reside both as the formative principle of self-interpretation" [96]. This of course would be accepted as a definition of repression by any Lacanian. In arguing that Butler (following Foucault) conceives of language as a form of repression, I am arguing that she understands language in terms of a repression of nonidentity by identity. That nonidentity often does come to be associated with some sort of repressed substance is a problem Butler shares with Foucault and with Derrida.

   In fact, in the very place where she repeats Foucault's critique of the repressive hypothesis, Butler defines the system of power/language as a repression of plurality. Following Foucault, she argues: "The object of repression is not *the desire* it takes to be its ostensible object, but the multiple configurations of power itself, the very plurality of which would displace the seeming universality and necessity of the juridical or repressive law" [75].

   (In *Bodies That Matter: On the Discursive Limits of "Sex"* [New York: Routledge, 1993], Butler acknowledges that repression can be a useful concept.)

6. Butler, "Gender Trouble, Feminist Theory, and Psychoanalytic Discourse," 325.

7. Nancy Fraser, "Foucault on Modern Power: Empirical Insights and Normative Confusions," in *Unruly Practices: Power, Discourse, and Gender in Contemporary Social Theory* (Minneapolis: University of Minnesota Press, 1989), 31-33.

8. Butler, *Gender Trouble*, 14.

9. bell hooks, *Feminist Theory: From Margin to Center* (Boston: South End Press, 1984), 63.

10. hooks, *Feminist Theory*, 65. hooks' argument is echoed by Lisa Kahaleole Chang Hall, who quotes a comment made by one frustrated participant after weeks of infighting in a group that called

itself Sisters in Solidarity: "'Sisters in Solidarity,' shit. Y'all are gonna end up 'Bitches in Solitude.'" Hall argues that "[i]dentity politics at its best is about making connections between people and groups not normally perceived as related. … There's no possibility of solidarity when people assume that identities are singular and fixed, self-evident and mutually exclusive." Lisa Kahaleole Chang Hall, "Bitches in Solitude: Identity Politics and Lesbian Community," in Arlene Stein, ed., *Sisters, Sexperts, Queers; Beyond the Lesbian Nation* (New York: Plume, 1993), 220-21.

GLOBAL
VISIONS

Angela Miles

Global economics, political, and military relationships connect us all through a series of ties that do not bind but rather alienate us from one another. Daily, we in the North deal with and depend on products of the global commodity and labor markets, most of us unaware of our own place or the role of others in these far-flung networks....

The worth of these things needs to be seen in terms of an altogether different value system—one that is holistic (integrative) as opposed to dualistic (separative) and grounded in the value of life rather than profit. Measuring value in terms of what contributes to the sustenance of human and nonhuman life reveals the absurdity, even criminality, of measuring only production for the market and for profit. It makes it possible to see that what is called progress/growth/modernization/development entails a process of relative or absolute deprivation for women, colonies, and marginal groups and communities. Expansion of the market and production for exchange at the expense of production for use (1) removes the means of subsistence from individuals and communities; (2) institutionalizes men's dependence on wages and women's dependence on men; and (3) fuels the concentration of wealth and power in fewer and fewer hands, ultimately in a few nonaccountable transnational corporations and financial institutions.

The alternative vision that undergirds an integrative understanding of the world involves redefining everything from mainstream and radical views of history to wealth, worth, work, progress, growth, and development. It also makes it possible to see the ways in which current separations between production and reproduction, investment and consumption, individual and community and society and nature (and between culture, economics, and politics) are both false ideological constructions that reflect and serve the competitive, individualistic system and, at the same time, actual products of this system. These separations need to be revealed as false even as we resist their actual impact.

Global feminisms hold the seeds of the world they want to create. Their response to alienated and exploitative globalization is not simple withdrawal, refusal, or reaction but the creation of autonomous, democratic, and empowering global relations in the struggle for alternative visions. The global understanding of women's oppression as the product of a long historical process of colonization and control of women, workers, nature, and indigenous, anti-colonized peoples links all oppressions organically, not as add-ons or a litany of separate dominations; expands and integrates the field of struggle; underlines women's central role in resistance and reconstruction; enriches the integrative conception of women's equality, specificity, diversity, and commonality; and reinforces the conviction that what is needed is a paradigm shift of enormous proportions: "Women's voices have moved on from the modest ambition of being heard on public matters to the far more subversive endeavour of plotting a different path to civilization" (Oliviera 1992, 71).[1]

The feminist struggle for transformation rather than assimilation is articulated explicitly by Third World and First World activists; Indian feminist Kamla Bhasin asks, for instance, "[Do] we want to be integrated into the present system and move only faster towards destruction? Or do we women want to challenge it?" And she answers: "I believe that we must challenge it and I know that we *can*. We must look for a new vision, new types of development so that we can transform knowledge and relationships with the poor, with the oppressed, with women, with nature" (1990, 24)....

We have seen that integrative feminists see women's exclusion from all institutionalized power and their customary responsibility for individual and community survival as resources in the struggle to consciously develop alternatives. The analyses and visions of integrative feminists in both North and South selectively and critically incorporate aspects of women's traditional knowledge and concerns.[2] The appreciation of women's work and interests is generally harder won and more fragile in the North, however, than in the South, where women's subcultures and consciousness have not been so thoroughly disrupted....

The articulation of general community concerns by women from women's points of view is not the abandonment of feminist vision but potentially its full realization—a process that requires that autonomous women's and general community struggles be brought together to become one. Mutually enriching interaction between women-focused and communitywide activism thrives in the North as well as in the South (Garland 1988). Nevertheless, it is true that many feminists in the Two-Thirds World are particularly well placed to conceive of this possibility and to understand its importance for developing global feminisms that go beyond pressure for women, to move the whole of society in women-defined directions.

Global feminist dialogue has thus supported integrative-feminist revaluing of the female, confirmed its radical political potential, and strengthened both feminist autonomy and the conceptualization of feminist struggle as women-defined general social change. It has deepened the mutually reinforcing articulation of women's particular interests and feminism's universal relevance and has sustained integrative feminism's dialectical refusal to see these as mutually exclusive possibilities.

The articulation of feminism's ecological politics has also been enhanced by global perspectives. Globally informed challenges to profit-centered rather than life-centered measures of productivity necessarily make visible the value of nature's as well as women's production. Global struggles for a society organized around the cooperative requirements of life rather than competition and profit have to name and resist the destructive dynamics that deny, control, and destroy women, workers, nature, and indigenous peoples: "Feminism as the affirmation of women and women's work allows a redefinition of growth and productivity as categories linked to the production, not destruction, of life. It is thus simultaneously an ecological and a feminist political project which legitimises the ways of knowing and being that create wealth by enhancing life and diversity, and which delegitimises the knowledge and practise of a culture of death as the basis for capital accumulation" (Shiva 1989a, 13)....

Feminists claim women's association with nature as a part of the creative and conscious *political* process of reconstructing femininity, humanity, human society, nature, and their relationships:

> The Feminine is no longer the same nor the opposite of the Masculine. Neither is it an essence linked to an immobile Nature, but rather experience linked to a historical nature, a becoming. In this way, femininity is entering a region of freedom. . . . Femininity's freedom to define itself in due course will relate to nature, not as essence but as experience. It will not deny the body as its original point of departure for living in and thinking about the world, but will integrate this thinking into the world. This plan to integrate the history of female Nature into the design for femininity's future is both feminist and ecological. (Oliviera 1992, 71-72)

The project articulated here aims to claim and create new forms of freedom in remaking history and society as well as the feminine in a conscious and deliberate process of grounding human/female reason in the body (physicality) and nature. It is a spiritual and emotional as well as political and rational project that claims a far broader, more complex, and inclusive field of action and (redefined) freedom than has ever been carved out before.

Third World feminists have played an integral role in supporting a broader, ecological conception of feminism. The destructive environmental and social impacts of "development" occur at a much faster rate there than in the West. Two-Thirds World peoples have experienced in a much more concentrated time span and with more devastating results the social dislocation and environmental destruction that Western Europe suffered over five hundred years of changes in land ownership and agricultural and industrial technologies. Where these changes directly threaten whole ways of life and communities, women's struggle has been a struggle in defense of community against this devastation. The necessary connection between defending and affirming women, workers, nature, and community is more evident in these contexts than in North America, where environmental impacts, though extensive, are generally slower moving, less obvious, and less immediately dangerous to whole communities....

A number of Third World feminists have adopted and are independently defining the term "ecofeminist" which originated in the North (Mies and Shiva 1993; Oliviera 1992; Perpiñan 1993). At the same time, integrative ecofeminists in the First World are being drawn to a more organic conceptualization of their politics (Diamond and Orenstein 1990; Plant 1989). What many used to describe as combining environmental and women's movement concerns is now more frequently conceived as articulating the ecological aspects inherent in feminism itself.[3] Certainly, global economic analyses, analyses of war, militarism, and violence against women, and indigenous feminist analyses[4] all share and reciprocally support a concern for nature and ecology as essential aspects of women-centered and women-defined social transformation.

An awareness of the ecological vision inherent in feminism also enriches our appreciation of diversity as both the means and the end of feminist struggle. Integrative feminists welcome diverse political positions as building blocks of politics that they expect will always be in process: "It is precisely the diversity of thought and action that makes this new politics so promising as a catalyst for change in these troubled times" (Diamond and Orenstein 1990, xii). Sectarian thinking is explicitly rejected (D'Souza 1992, 46) in such a large project, which requires radical departures into uncharted waters and bold new questions rather than closed systems of thought: "Feminism is a developing world-view evolving through practice rather than dogma, and as such our attempt at definitions should be seen as part of an ongoing process. Charges . . . of being a 'partial world-view' and of offering no real alternatives, must be seen against this process" (Gandhi and Kannabiran 1989, 13)....

The global and ecological awareness that reveals the common colonization of women, workers, nature, and indigenous peoples also reveals remarkable parallels between indigenous worldviews and the women-associated values that inform integrative feminisms— parallels that are widely and increasingly recognized in both the First and Two-Thirds Worlds....

[N]ative American writer Paula Gunn Allen sees parallels between integrative feminist principles and basic concepts in many traditional American Indian systems: "Traditional American Indian systems depended on basic concepts that are at present being reformulated and to some extent practiced by western feminists, including cooperation (but by that traditional Indians generally meant something other than noncompetitiveness or passivity), harmony (again, this did not necessarily mean absence of conflict), balance, kinship, and respect" (1986, 206)....

Integrative feminists are envisioning wholly new forms of free yet connected ways of living in harmony, not harking back to or glorifying any golden ages. As we have seen, feminists can be among the fiercest critics of tradition. Holistic knowledge and practice and many of the values that have been hidden, pushed aside, and destroyed by capitalist and patriarchal enforcement of monolithic separative Western science and the Western worldview are prized in this project. But we are not retreating into parochial and patriarchal worlds. We are using the particular to create new universal and shared possibilities. Selected aspects of traditional alternatives are affirmed in the face of their erasure as of the struggle against the current intensification and globalization of commodification and control: "Hope for the future . . . requires that women create new models, allowing for diversity and drawing from the best of the past, but refusing to accept any form of domination in the name of either tradition or modernization" (Bunch 1987, 304).

Feminists in all regions of the world are committed to developing new models. They are consciously and explicitly engaged in defense and reform, not to save the old world, but to build a new one. They are convinced that even major reform of existing structures will not save the world or women. They hold no hope for anything short of fundamental change. Integrative feminists in international networks on health, housing, education, law reform, population, human rights, labor, reproductive and genetic engineering, female sexual slavery and trafficking in women, violence against women, spirituality, peace and militarism, external debt, fundamentalism, environment, development, media, alternative technology, film, art and literature, publishing, and women's studies are forging alternative forms of global relations. Without exception they are generating and working with new paradigms unashamedly informed by utopian goals. The Indian feminist Kamla Bhasin expresses this, using concepts she learned from Japanese activists: "Feminism is showing us the possibility of finding new kinds of space, of searching for new rhythms and of discovering new roots, dreaming new dreams. It seeks to integrate a radically new conception of progress and development in all aspects of our lives. We must all of us work harder to definite [*sic*] our vision of a more human life, more human development, of 'Janakashaba' (this is the word in Minimata dialect for an alternative world, as we learnt during our stay in Japan)" (Bhasin 1990, 24).

The fact that consensus is emerging globally around transformative perspectives among feminists active in all areas of practice was evident at the World Women's Congress for a Healthy Planet in Miami in November 1991. The congress's broad mandate brought together fifteen hundred activists, researchers, and policymakers from eighty-four countries involved in diverse networks in all regions of the world to "develop policy goals and actions, for use in this decade and into the next century" and to guide women's intervention in preparations for and deliberations at The U.N. Conference on Environment and Development (the Earth Summit) in Brazil in June 1993.

Participants heard from women resisting dictatorship, militarism, violence against women, nuclear energy and weapons testing, forced migration and homelessness, the appropriation of tribal lands, poverty, starvation, external debt, biotechnology and biogenetics, toxic dumping, abusive and controlling population programs, and exploitative sexual policies and practices. Because women brought to this exchange prior experience of global dialogue in diverse preexisting networks, shared life-centered values, and women-centered perspectives that recognize class and colonial power, mutual learning was swift and discussion quickly led to unanimity around integrative positions.

Resolutions were passed acknowledging the links between issues and situating them all within the large feminist project of transforming the world—a project in which the Conference Report claimed a central and defining role for women: We come together to pledge our commitment to the empowerment of the Earth and for a balance, between them and the life-support systems that, sustain us all" (World Women's Congress for a Healthy Planet 1992, 16).

Regional caucus statements from Africa, Europe, International Indigenous Women, Latin America and the Caribbean, the Middle East, North America, Pacific, Women of the South, and Women of Color of North America articulate remarkably similar concerns, priorities, and principles, reflecting the influence of intensive exchanges in plenary meetings, hallways, workshops, and drafting sessions on already well-established shared perspectives. They express strong commitment to continued dialogue and solidarity and leave no doubt that Women's Action Agenda 21, the collectively written Conference Report, reflects a genuine and developing consensus of indigenous and nonindigenous participants from all regions of the world.

The "Statement from the Women of the South Caucus" reads in part:

> We, the women of the South, affirm that equity and justice must be the guiding principle between men and women, among communities and among nations, for a healthy people and a healthy planet.
>
> We believe that people have the right to sustainable livelihoods which encompass every aspect of human well being: material, spiritual, cultural, ecological and political. ...
>
> We condemn the alienation of people from land, especially the indigenous peoples, the poor and women. (World Women's Congress for a Healthy Planet 1992, 34)

The women of the South demand an end to overconsumption "which underpins the lifestyles of the North and the elite of the South [and] is a central element of the Western development model" (ibid., 34). They condemn poverty, unequal trade relations, structural adjustment programs, coercive population-control strategies, militarism and nuclear testing, and the dumping of hazardous waste. And they declare that:

> Traditional knowledge and technology, of which women and indigenous people have been the major creators and caretakers, must inform all national and international strategies to promote environmentally sound development.
>
> We urge greater South-South dialogue and cooperation, particularly among the women of our countries, in the search for common solutions to common human and environmental problems.
>
> Long live solidarity of Women of the World! (ibid., 34)

Both the European and North American Caucuses take clear stands against inequality in their own regions and declare their solidarity with their sisters of the South against Northern waste and exploitation as a basis for their participation in global dialogue and the development of a new future. They recognize the value of traditional knowledges and the need to end the hegemony of Western patriarchal science and the Western worldview as well as Western exploitation and domination. The report of the North American Caucus reads in part:

> We North American women are living in nations in which overconsumption by some co-exists with poverty and social deprivation for many and ecological degradation for all; and in which women and children everywhere are threatened physically as well as economically. As a means of deepening our understanding and developing our alternative visions and values we welcome both the North-South dialogue and the dialogue among social movements. . . . We join with our sisters in the South in rejecting the world market economic and social order which is promoted, protected and sustained by both military might and military production. We support reforms that . . . challenge the dualistic and destructive logic of this system. We particularly support changes which contribute to:
>
> 1. An equalizing redefinition and redistribution of power and resources within and between nations and regimes;
>
> 2. A shift in the exploitative and hierarchical relations among and between people and the planet;
>
> 3. A basic redefinition of such concepts as power, human rights, wealth, work and progress, in terms which recognize and reaffirm the value of women, nature, and indigenous peoples;
>
> 4. The demilitarization of our economics and our cultures in order to free our creative genius for a more humane and renewable planet.
>
> We see all these as necessary parts of a process in which the knowledge, values, wisdom and vision of women around the world can shape the priorities and ways of being in the world. (ibid., 32)

The emerging global consensus reflected in the regional caucus statements and the Conference Report as a whole testifies to the fact that the alternative values at the core of integrative feminisms challenge existing social relations at a level deep and radical enough to provide a frame for global solidarity.

Integrative feminists in North America, like those all over the world, recognize that the oppositions at the core of dominant Western culture are destructive and false, and they are committed to creating a world that fosters and celebrates, rather than masks and interrupts, connections. Their visions are of cooperative, egalitarian, life-centered social arrangements wherein the currently devalued, marginalized, and trivialized women-associated responsibilities and values of love and nurturing are the organizing principles or society; wherein differences do not mean inequality and can be celebrated as constitutive of commonality; wherein freedom is found in and won through community; and wherein humanity's embeddedness in nature is not only recognized but welcomed.

As we have seen, many of the diverse North American feminists who seek to transform their own communities and society in these integrative terms have a strong global awareness and presence. Not all integrative feminists in North America understand the global context of their visions, however. Not all yet see that the industrial patriarchy whose destructive logic they criticize in the North is both product and producer of colonizing global processes of "modernization" and development that must be resisted worldwide.

As our global links and learning grow, reinforced by the increasing activism and influence of women of color, and indigenous, immigrant, and working-class women in the North, global knowledge is increasing in North America. It is strengthening the transformative potential of our politics and our ability to participate fully in the worldwide development of feminism. Like feminists everywhere, we need global solidarity/support for our local struggles.

ENDNOTES

1. Early in this phase of feminism in North America, feminists drew powerful parallels between colonialism and women's oppression that served an important function in helping women see patriarchal oppression that was so pervasive and "naturalized" as to be almost invisible: for instance, men's ownership, control, and use of women's bodies and labor. They also used these parallels to counter the prevailing (even monolithic) opinion of the time that women's oppression was trivial and of an entirely different order from serious race, class, and colonial oppression.

    Not surprisingly, the exploration of the parallels and tensions between feminism and nationalism and patriarchy and colonialism was particularly rich in Quebec (Jean 1977, 5). However, the early arguments paralleling patriarchy and colonialism differ from those presented here, because they did not generally extend to an analysis of the common underlying historical dynamics of domination that actually reveals these oppressions and their causes and consequences to be linked aspects of the same process of "development."

2. The fact that the incorporation of women's knowledge and concerns into integrative feminist analysis is selective is very important. For integrative feminisms are not simply glorifying women's traditional knowledge and concerns but are using these as a basis from which to do the hard and challenging political work of constructing conscious feminist values and visions to inform and shape both resistance to dominant patriarchal forms and the struggle to establish new ones (Apthekar 1989, 183; Bhasin 1990, 25).

3. The following quotation from Judith Plant is typical in its implication that ecological concerns are unique to explicitly ecofeminist-defined politics and are, in an sense, an import to feminism from environmentalism: "Historically, women had no real power in the outside world, no place in decision-making and intellectual life. Today, however ecology speaks for the Earth, for the 'other' in human/environmental relationships; and feminism speaks for the 'other' in female/male relations. And ecofeminism, by speaking for *both* the original others, seeks to understand the interconnected roots of all domination as well as ways to resist and change. The ecofeminist's task is one of developing the ability to take the place of the other when considering the consequences of possible actions, and ensuring that we do not forget that we are all part of one another" (1989, 156).

    Anne Cameron refuses to call her politics "ecofeminist" on the ground that "the term 'ecofeminism' suggests that the old 'feminism' was not at all concerned with ecology, could not have cared less about the environment, had no analysis of industrial exploitation, and ignored the need for peace" (1989, 63). The view that ecological concerns are integral to feminism is closer to most Third World, indigenous, and Black integrative-feminist views—and one that ecofeminists are increasingly coming to share.

4. See especially Enloe 1989; FINRRAGE 1989; Harris and King 1989; Kishwar and Vanita 1984; Morgan 1990; Schuler 1992; Women against Fundamentalism 1990; Women Living Under Muslim Laws n.d.

SEXISM, RACISM, AND CANADIAN NATIONALISM

Roxana Ng

My Starting Point

My concern about the dynamic of sexism and racism, and of the interrelation of gender, race/ethnicity and class arose out of my experience as a "visible minority" immigrant woman and a member of the intelligensia living in a white dominated Canada. Working politically in the immigrant community, I and other women of colour frequently feel that our status as women does not have weight equal to our status as members of minority groups. Our interests and experiences are subsumed under the interests of immigrant men, especially those of "community leaders." This situation is analogous to the classic position of the Left: women's issues are secondary to the class struggle. Women are often told that their interests can be taken up only after the revolution.

Working in the women's movement, on the other hand, women of colour also feel silenced from time to time. Our unique experiences as women of colour are frequently overlooked in discussions about women's oppression. At best, we are tokenized; at worst, we are told that our concerns, seen to be less advanced, have to do with a patriarchy characteristic of our indigenous cultures.[1] There is something missing in the women's movement which gives us an increasing sense of discomfort as we continue to participate in struggles in which only a part of our experiences as women of colour is or can be taken up.

Analytically, in standard social science debates (which filters to the Left and to the women's movement through people's multiple roles and locations in society), there is a tendency to treat gender, race and class as different analytic categories designating different domains of life. While I continue to experience gender and race oppression as a totality, when I participate in academic and intellectual work I have to make a theoretical and analytical separation of my experience and translate it into variables of "sex", "ethnicity" and "class" in order for my work to be acceptable and understandable to my colleagues. It is not uncommon, when I present papers in conferences, to receive comments about the lack of definitional clarity in my use of concepts of gender, race/ethnicity and class. I am asked to spell out clearly which category is more important in determining the position of, for example, immigrant women....

[A]s I continue to teach and do research in ethnic and women's studies, and especially since my two-year sojourn in New Brunswick, it became clear to me that we cannot understand gender and ethnic relations in Canada without attending to how these relations have been mediated by the Canadian state historically, and continue to be organized by state processes. (Let me remind the reader that Nova Scotia and New Brunswick are the oldest provinces in the colony of Canada, settled and dominated not only by Irish and Scottish immigrants but also by Loyalists.) Thus I would argue that it is not enough for feminist and ethnic historians to rewrite women's history and ethnic history. In order to understand how Canada came to be a nation with its present configuration, we have to rewrite the history of Canada.

This paper does not address problems of racism and sexism in the Left and of racism in the feminist movement directly. It is a methodological paper which calls for a different conceptualization of gender, race/ethnicity and class by grounding these relations in the development of the Canadian social formation. In so doing, I challenge current theorizations of ethnicity and class, and show the interlocking relations of gender, race and class by means of historical examples. I make use of a method of work informed by Marx's analysis of capitalism in the nineteenth century[2] and feminist interpretations of Marx's method.[3] This method insists on locating the knower in a particular subject position in relation to her inquiry, and on situating contemporary realities in the historical development of nation states in a definite mode of production. It treats historical and contemporary moments and events, not as separate fields or areas of study, but as constituents of a society with its own internal logic and dynamic.

In developing the present analysis I asked myself: How do I account for the silencing I and other women experience in our diverse and different social locations? How do I have to understand history in order to understand my experience as a totality lodged in a particular social formation? I don't claim to put forward a complete or definitive theory or argument. This paper is an attempt to develop a method of thinking which illuminates sexual and racial oppression from the standpoint of women of colour—standpoint in this context referring to the relationship between the knower's experience and the social organization generating her experience. It is also an attempt to develop a praxis for eradicating sexism and racism, not merely in structures and institutions, but more fundamentally in our unconscious thoughts and action....

[I] am using the term "the Canadian state" as a short-hand for the multiplicity of institutions and departments which administer and coordinate activities of ruling. It therefore includes the formal government apparatus and the various policies and programs which come under their jurisdiction, and the functions performed therein. More importantly, I wish to advance the notion of the state as the central constituent in the developing relations of capitalism in Canada (Macintosh 1978). This set of relations didn't appear overnight. As Corrigan correctly points out, it was constructed through time, by complicated and extensive struggles of people grouped together by their differing relationships to the emerging dominant mode of production (Corrigan 1980:xxii). Indeed, as we shall see, the history of ethnic and gender relations *is* the history of Canadian state formation....

Gender usually falls outside the realm of analytical relevance for ethnic theorists. Implicitly, like other areas of sociology, women's experiences are subsumed under those of men. More often, the significance of gender (read woman) is overlooked or is treated as a separate field of investigation. Thus, we find women being included in the study of the family or the domestic labour debate, for example, but political economy remains completely sex blind.[4] While efforts by feminists to incorporate women into the study of ethnicity and class are increasing, these efforts are only at a preliminary stage. Frequently, the similarities between racism and sexism are compared,[5] and parallels between the experience of women and the experience of ethnic minorities are drawn (Juteau-Lee and Roberts 1981:1-23). Recently, feminists such as Roberts and Juteau Lee have attempted to conceptualize the relationship between gender, ethnicity/race, and class by suggesting that they are three different systems of domination which overlap (Juteau-Lee and Roberts 1981:1-23). Their inclusion of gender in ethnic studies is a major breakthrough, but the question of the precise relationship between these three systems of domination remains to be conceptualized and investigated....

[G]ender relations are crucial and fundamental to the division of labour in a given society—any society. In most societies, gender is the basic way of organizing productive and reproductive activities. But gender relations are not the same in all societies. Furthermore, like ethnic and class relations, they change over time in response to changing social, political and economic relations. My investigation of immigrant women's domestic work, for example, reveals the transformation of their domestic labour after immigration to Canada. Whereas in a less industrialized setting women's work is organized organically in relation to farming and other subsistence activities, in Canada it is organized industrially by the husband's waged work outside the home, school schedules, the degree of mechanization of the household (e.g., the use of vacuum cleaner and other appliances), public transportation systems, distances to shopping facilities, and so on. The change in women's domestic labour in turn creates new areas of contestation and conflict between immigrant women and their husbands; as well, it upsets the previous balance of power among all family members (Ng and Ramirez 1981). Smith observes:

> In pre-capitalist societies, gender is basic to the "economic" division of labour and how labour resources are controlled. In other than capitalist forms, we take for granted that gender relations are included. In peasant societies for example, the full cycle of production and subsistence is organized by the household and family and presupposes gender relations. Indeed, we must look to capitalism as a mode of production to find how the notion of the separation of gender relations from economic relations could arise. It is only capitalism that we find an economic process constituted independently from the daily and generational production of the lives of particular individuals and *in which therefore we can think economy apart from gender.* (Smith 1985a, emphasis in original)

Thus, gender as well as ethnicity and race are relations integral to the organization of productive activities. The theoretical and analytical separation of gender from the economy (productive relations) is itself the product of capitalist development, which creates a progressive separation between civil society, politics and the economy in the first place, and renders relations of gender, race and ethnicity more abstract and invisible to productive processes in the second place.[6]

When we treat class, ethnicity and gender as relations arising out of the processes of domination and struggles over the means of production and reproduction over time, a very different picture of their interrelationship emerges. We find that we don't have to develop a set of criteria—be they "economic" or pertaining to descent—for defining gender, ethnicity and class. We see that they are relations which have crystallized over time as Canada developed from a colony of England and France to a nation built on male supremacy. Indeed, we can trace ethnic group formation and gender relations in terms of the development of capitalism in Canada, firstly through its history of colonization, and subsequently through immigration policies which changed over time in response to the demands of nation-build-ing. People were recruited firstly from Ireland, then the Ukraine and Scandinavia to lay an agrarian base for England and Canada; they were imported from China through an indentured labour system to build the railways for Canada's westward expansion; more recently peo-ple from southern Europe were recruited to fill gaps in the construction industry. In the overall framework of immigration, men and women were/are treated differentially. For example, Chinese men were not allowed to bring their wives and families to Canada so they could not propagate and spread the "yellow menace" (Chart 1983). Even today, men and women enter Canada under different terms and conditions. The majority of third world women enter the country either as domestic workers on temporary work permits or as "fam-ily class" immigrants whose livelihood is dependent on the head of the household or on the sponsor (Estable 1986; Djao and Ng 1987:141-158).

Indeed, the emergence of the Native people as a group, not to mention the Métis sub-group, is the result of the colonization process which destroyed, re-organized, fragmented and homogenized the myriad tribal groups across the continent. Until very recently, the dif-ferential and unequal status of Indian women was set down by law—in the *Indian Act* (Jamieson 1978). Ethnicity and gender *are* the essential constituents in the formation of the Canadian class structure.

The treatment of gender and ethnicity as relations constituted through people's activi-ties helps us to observe the differential work carried out by men and women in nation build-ing. Barbara Roberts divides the work of national building during the period between 1880 and 1920 into two aspects. The first aspect had to do with developing the infrastructure of the economy: the building of a nation-wide transportation system, the development of a manufacturing base and a commodity market, and so forth. The development of this aspect of the economy was the domain of men. The second aspect had to do with the building of the human nation: the development of a population base in Canada. Women reformers (whom Roberts calls upper class "ladies") were the active organizers of this aspect of nation build-ing. To ensure the white character and guarantee Christian morality of the nation, upper class women from Britain worked relentlessly to organize the immigration of working-class girls from that country to serve in the new world as domestics and wives (Roberts 1990; Lay 1980:19-42). These "ladies" thus established the first immigration societies in the major cities of Canada, attending to the plight of immigrants.

Similarly, Kari Dehli's research on school reforms in Toronto at the turn of the century shows how middle class mothers of (mainly) British background worked to enforce a par-ticular version of motherhood on working class immigrant women. In the 1920s Toronto expe-rienced a serious depression. Many working class immigrant women were forced to engage in waged work outside the home. Alarmed by the declining state of the family (many work-ing class children attended school hungry and poorly dressed), middle class women worked hard to propagate and enforce "proper" mothering practices in working class families. It was in this period that the notion of "proper motherhood" gained prominence in the orga-nization of family life through the school system.[7]

These examples point to the class-based work done by men and women to preserve Canada as a white nation and to enforce a particular ideology to guarantee white supremacy.

But as ruling class men consolidated their power in the state apparatus, they also began to take over and incorporate women's work into the state. Roberts found that by 1920, con-trol over immigration and the settlement of immigrants had shifted from the hands of the ladies to the hands of state officials: As state power was consolidated, women's work was relegated more and more to the domestic sphere (Roberts 1990; Smith 1985b:156-198). Similarly, community work has been incorporated into the local state—in boards of education. The central role played by middle class women in school reform was supplanted by the rise and development of an increasingly elaborate bureaucracy within different levels of the state. Interestingly, it is also as the state consolidated its power that sexuality became legislated by law. During this time, homosexuality became a crime, and sexual intercourse was legitimized within legal marital relationship only (Kinsmen 1987).

I am not arguing that gender and ethnicity are reducible to class. I maintain that the examination of gender, ethnicity and class must be situated in the relations of a specific social formation, which have to do with struggles, by groups of people, over control of the means of production and reproduction over time. An examination of the history of Canada indicates that class cannot be understood without reference to ethnic and gender relations, similarly, gender and ethnicity cannot be understood without reference to class relations.

On the basis of the foregoing one can see why I maintained, at the beginning of this paper, that gender, ethnic and class relations are inextricably linked to the formation of the Canadian state, if we see the state as the culmination and crystallization of struggles over the dominant—in the case of Canada: capitalist—mode of production. The history of the Native people, from the fur trade period to their entrapment in reserves, is the most blatant example. (The expulsion of the Acadians—a primarily agrarian group with a subsistence economy—by the British colonizers, including the Loyalists, from the richer arable lands of the Atlantic region offers another historical testimony of consolidation of power and control by the Anglo-Saxons and the Scots.) The struggles of groups of Irish, Scottish and English descent in the Maritimes is yet another example (Acheson 1985)....

In sum, I have presented some historical sketches of gender, race/ethnicity and class dynamics as relations which underpin the development of Canada as a nation-state. It is important to note that these historical events are not presented as instances to support a particular theoretical proposition. Rather, I made use of a way of understanding the world which does not splinter the different historical events and moments into compartmentalized fields or areas of study.[8] In the latter approach, what upper class women did would be seen as "women's history," which has little to do with the organization of the labour market, and as the continuance of Anglo supremacy in nation building, which would be treated as "imperial history." The framework I put forward enables us to put together a picture of the formation of Canada as a nation-state with strong racist and sexist assumptions and policies—out of the seemingly separate pieces of history which are in fact pieces of the same jigsaw. It is thus that we come to see racism and sexism as the very foundation of Canadian nationhood.

Political Implications

On the basis of the above discussion I want to explore how we may work to eradicate sexism and racism from our praxis as feminists, as intellectuals, and as people of colour.

The first thing that needs to be said is that gender, race/ethnicity, and class are not fixed entities. They are socially constructed in and through productive and reproductive relations in which we all participate. Thus, what constitutes sexism, racism, as well as class oppression, changes over time as productive relations change. While racism today is seen in discriminatory practices directed mainly at coloured people (the Blacks, South Asians, Native people, for example), skin colour and overt physical differences were not always the criteria for determining racial differences. Historically, the Acadians were treated, by the Scots and the Irish, as people from a different race, and were discriminated and suppressed accordingly. Their experience of racial oppression is no less valid than that encountered by the Native people and today's ethnic and racial minorities. Within each racial and ethnic group, men and women, and people from different classes are subject to differential treatments. For example, while virtually no Chinese labourer or his family was allowed to enter Canada at the turn of the century through the imposition of the head tax, Chinese merchants and their families were permitted to immigrate during this period (Chan 1983).

Thus, it seems to me that it is not our project to determine whether gender, race/ethnicity class or the economic system is the primary source of our oppression. The task is for us to discover how sexism and other forms of gender, oppression (e.g., compulsory heterosexuality),[9] racism, and class oppression are constituted in different historical conjunctures so that the dominant groups maintain their hegemony over the means of production and reproduction. Meanwhile, it is important to see that the state in modern society is a central site of the struggles among different groups. Recognizing the way in which the state divides us at each historical moment would enable us to better decide how alliances could be forged across groups of people to struggle against racial, sexual and class oppression.

Secondly, from the above analysis, it becomes clear that racism and sexism are not merely attitudes held by some members of society. I am beginning to think that they are not even just structural—in the sense that they are institutionalized in the judicial system, the educational system, the workplace, etc.—which of course they are. More fundamentally, they are systemic: they have crystallized over time in the way we think and act regardless of our own gender, race and class position. Indeed, sexist, racist and class assumptions are embodied in the way we "normally" conduct ourselves and our business in everyday life.[10]

Thus, we cannot simply point our finger at, for example, the media or the school, and accuse them of gender and racial discrimination. While we begin from a recognition of the fundamental inequality between women and men, and between people from different racial and ethnic groups, at the everyday level we have to recognize that we are a part of these institutions. We must pay attention to the manner in which our own practices create, sustain and reinforce racism, sexism and class oppression. These practices include the mundane and unconscious ways in what and to whom we give credence, the space we take up in conversations with the result of silencing others, and the space we don't take up because we have learned to be submissive. We need to re-examine our history, as well as our own beliefs and actions, on a continuous basis, so that we become able to better understand and confront ways in which we oppress others and participate in our own oppression. While this in itself will not liberate us completely from own sexist, racist and class biases, it is a first step in working toward alternate forms of alliances and practices which will ultimately help us transform the society of which we are a part.

ENDNOTES

1. See, for example, the charge of racism by Native and Black women of Toronto's International Women's Day Committee (IWDC) in 1986, and the subsequent debates in socialist feminist publications such as *Cayenne* in 1986 and 1987.

2. See Karl Marx 1954 and 1969:475-495. For a critique of contemporary Marxists and a concise discussion of Marx's method, see Derek Sayer 1979.

3. Sandra Harding has called this "the standpoint approach" her book *The Science Question in Feminism* 1986. The major proponents of this approach, according to Harding, are Nancy Hartsock and Dorothy Smith. See Nancy C.M. Hartsock 1983, and Dorothy E. Smith 1987. While both Hartsock and Smith insist on the primacy of women's standpoint in social analysis, their theories differ in important ways. The way I make use of their work is to begin from the experiences of women of colour and to situate their experiences in the social organization of Canadian society. I make no claim to follow their theories exegetically. See Roxana Ng 1982:111-118.

4. For a critique, see Dorothy E. Smith 1987.

5. See Roxana Ng 1984, Endnotes 1 and 3 for a discussion on the exclusion of gender from ethnic studies.

6. See the works of Dorothy E. Smith, cited in this paper; lectures given by David Mole in the Dept. of Sociology, Ontario Institute for Studies in Education. 1979-80; and Derek Sayer 1979.

7. See Kari Dehli 1990, and Anna Davin 1978:9-65, for discussion on a similar phenomenon in Britain.

8. For a critique of sociology, see Dorothy E. Smith 1974:7-13; for a critique of political economy, see Dorothy E. Smith 1987.

9. This term is used by Adrienne Rich to describe the institution of heterosexuality which discourages and stifles intimate relationships among women. See Adrienne Rich 1983:139-168.

10. In examining racism embodied in feminist praxis, Himani Bannerji calls this form of racism "common sense racism". See Himani Bannerji 1987:10-12.

C h a p t e r   T w o

CANADIAN WOMEN'S MOVEMENTS

In the current context of neo-conservative politics, the women's movement in Canada has experienced a decline in influence. Because feminist organizations continue to push governments to ensure social equality through greater expenditures and new and more effective social programs, they have increasingly been cast as "special" interest groups—antithetical to the public good as defined by prudence and deficit reduction (Brodie 1995; Bakker 1995). But this has not always been the case. The readings in this section provide an overview of Canadian feminist organizing from a time in the 1970s and early 1980s when women's groups enjoyed influence and political legitimacy, to a current period characterized by marginality and new challenges. During the era of the second wave, feminist organizations have proliferated and as some of the readings acknowledge, dominant groups have become more internally diverse and inclusive.

In 1966, a number of Canadian women active in mainstream women's organizations[1] and an elected parliamentarian, Judy LaMarsh, were instrumental in calling for a Royal Commission on the Status of Women (RCSW). Upon learning of the government's resistance to this demand, Laura Sabia (later president of Canada's national women's organization, the National Action Committee on the Status of Women (NAC)) issued a public ultimatum threatening to "march two million women on Ottawa" (Prentice et al., 1988, 347). The Royal Commission was formally established in 1967 and delivered its final report in 1970. We have included the recommendations to provide you with a sense of the Report's breadth and also its omissions. The Commission focussed broadly on women and the economy, education, the family, taxation and child care, poverty, the participation of women in public life, immigration and citizenship, and criminal law and women offenders. When considered alongside comparable reports released in other western countries in the 1960s, the

RCSW can be viewed as quite radical, especially in its recognition of systemic sexism enforced by policy, and in the challenges it made to the public/private divide. In hindsight, however, there were also significant omissions, for example the failure to define violence against women as a central problem and the neglect of racism (see Williams, 1990 and Andrew and Rogers, eds., 1997).

The RCSW has been viewed as a formative event in the history of feminist organizing, both because of intense mobilization around its hearings and because of the organizing it produced. Canadian feminist organizing benefited from the federal government's decision to provide funding for women's groups, which was a key recommendation of the RCSW. In order to ensure that politicians acted upon the RCSW, the national umbrella group NAC was formed in 1972. Also important was the formation of a bureaucratic network to provide research and policy advice on women's issues (the establishment of agencies such as the Canadian Advisory Council on the Status of Women and the Women's Bureau of the Secretary of State). This internal bureaucratic network has now been effectively dismantled. While there have been some critiques of the Royal Commission (see Williams, 1990; Arscott, 1998; and Andrew and Rogers, eds., 1997), there can be no doubt that it significantly shaped the direction of the mainstream Canadian women's movement.

At the same time that some women's movement activists were focussing on the state and agitating for policy change, there was also an active grassroots feminist contingent. Radical and Marxist feminist grassroots organizing grew out of women's involvement in the student, peace and anti-war movements. One important founding document, "Sisters, Brothers, Lovers...Listen" (1967), challenges women's subordinate position within the New Left, as well as the Left's failure to recognize "women's liberation" as an important struggle. Emerging from the women's caucus of the student group Student Union for Peace Action, this manifesto argues that structures of production, reproduction, socialization, and sexuality intertwine to enforce women's oppression. Calling for an autonomous movement for Canadian women's liberation, while underscoring the necessity of radical structural changes in the economy, the family and sexuality, the authors set themselves apart from the state-focussed and equality-seeking mainstream organizations that grew from the RCSW.

One of the first scholarly accounts of the contemporary women's movement was *Feminist Organizing for Change* (1988). In this book, Adamson, Briskin and McPhail define the two predominant orientations of Canadian feminist organizing—"institutional" and "grassroots." "Institutional" women's groups were those that followed existing hierarchical conventions of leadership such as *Robert's Rules of Order* and focussed on making changes within existing institutions. Examples of such organizations would include the Liberal Party's Women's Caucus and the Young Women's Christian Association (YWCA). "Grassroots" encompassed those women's groups influenced by U.S. radical feminism and other social movements, who "reject[ed] ... notions of hierarchy and leadership, ... emphasize[d] ... personal experience, and ... believe[d] in the importance of process (234)." Grassroots groups highlighted by Adamson et al. include community-based anti-violence organizations, as well as groups like the Ontario Coalition for Abortion Clinics (OCAC), the Saskatoon Women's Liberation and the International Women's Day Committee. Adamson et al. define inclusion and participation as central concerns of grassroots feminist organizing. At the same time they note the difficulties groups have experienced dealing with differences and with power relations, especially those based on race. They advocate a socialist feminist strategy emphasizing multi-pronged social change, feminist engagement in coalition politics and the practical deployment of both institutionalized and grassroots forms of organizing.

Five years after the publication of *Feminist Organizing for Change*, Jill Vickers, Pauline Rankin and Christine Appelle examine the NAC in their book *Politics as if Women Mattered* (1993). Like Adamson et al., they argue that Canadian feminism has been shaped by both "reformist" and "radical" wings; but they seek to demonstrate how these two strands have been united, if tenuously, within NAC, which they describe as a "parliament" of women. This piece, "The Intellectual and Political Context for the Development of the NAC," is particularly useful in drawing attention to and defining the distinctive features of activism within the Canadian women's movement. The authors highlight: the radical liberal orientation of organized feminism; its state-centered vision of politics; and the systemic characteristics of its environment, specifically federalism and the existence of both a Quebecois nation and aboriginal nations within the federal state.

Vickers et al. chronicle the nature of feminist organizing in a period when NAC was considered a legitimate lobby group with entitlement to consultation in the policy making process, gender-designated funding, and special points of access within the federal bureaucracy. But since the mid-1980s much has changed. With the embrace of neo-conservatism and the erosion of governmental commitments to ensuring social equality, the women's movement has been placed on the defensive. In the national debacle on the 1992 Charlottetown constitutional agreement, NAC's active presence in the "No" Campaign earned it the label the "enemy of Canada." Increasingly, NAC and other feminist organizations have been constructed as "special interests" both by governmental actors and by the popular press. In this context, the representational claims of organized feminism have been undermined. Governmental cuts in funding for women's groups have affected the movement's ability to advocate for social equality.

Beginning in 1989, the federal government initiated a series of devastating cuts to women's groups. Accompanying these cuts has been a shift away from the provision of operating grants towards project grants (specific, time-limited grants that exclude funding for infrastructure) (Scott, Thurston and Crow, 1996). The implications of this kind of funding are that governments are increasingly able to dictate the women's movement's priorities and that organizations must devote increasing amounts of time to fundraising. Recently, NAC challenged project-driven funding and its own funding was cut. As we write, NAC, the most influential and significant organization of the second wave, faces a funding crisis that threatens its continued existence.

As legislators become more resistant to feminist demands, other forms of feminist strategy assume new importance. In 1981, at the height of its political influence, the Anglo-women's movement succeeded in achieving strongly worded guarantees of sexual equality rights in the new Canadian constitution. The Women's Legal Education and Action Fund (LEAF) was formed in 1985 to advance women's equality claims through the mechanism of Charter litigation. The piece included here written by LEAF defends the necessity of litigation as feminist strategy. Certainly there has been a significant debate within Canadian feminism about the use of law as a tool of progressive social change (Fudge, 1987). As LEAF itself acknowledges, rather than being used as an instrument to advance women's equality, the Charter has been increasingly deployed to challenge laws and policies benefiting women. LEAF achieved some early legal victories in the Supreme Court and has been somewhat successful in ensuring the legal embrace of a substantive, results-oriented conception of sexual equality. But there have also been some devastating defeats, especially when cases involve a conflict between the equality rights of sexual assault complainants and the legal rights of the accused (see Chapter Six, "Engendering Violence"). Nevertheless, the potential importance of Charter litigation as a defensive strategy is highlighted in a context where politicians seem intent on dismantling the past political gains of organized feminism.

As with many other feminist organizations, LEAF's early strategy was influenced by a conception of women's experience as homogenous and unified. As an organization, it was dominated by white, middle class lawyers (Gotell, 1995; Razack, 1992). But as this piece documents, LEAF's approach has recently shifted to encompass difference and to allow for an intersectional analysis of gender, race, ability and sexuality.

It is quite ironic that Canadian feminist organizations are being constructed as unrepresentative at the very moment when previously silenced groups of women have gained a greater voice and assumed leadership positions. In 1993, Sunera Thobani was the first woman of colour to be elected as NAC's president. This elicited a range of criticism both from within the organization (i.e. women of colour are taking over NAC) and from antifeminist politicians and political commentators (Rebick and Roach, 1996, 118). One Tory MP even suggested in the House of Commons, that Sunera Thobani was an illegal immigrant—"the incoming president of NAC…first is not a Canadian, and second does not have a work permit for this country…(should) the taxpayers of Canada be funding an organization with an illegal immigrant at its head?"[2]

The 1990s have indeed seen a new level of inclusionary politics within Canadian feminist organizations, but Vijay Agnew's article "Race, Class and Feminist Practice (1996)," and Becki Ross's article "Back to the Future: Concluding Notes (1995)" make it explicit that until very recently, practices of exclusion have been the norm. Their articles reveal the ways in which women of colour and lesbians were marginalized within the mainstream women's movement and have been organizing for social change autonomously. Agnew focuses on women from Asia, Africa and the Caribbean and argues persuasively that the race biases of the larger society have been reflected in multiple ways in Canadian feminist practice. As she suggests, if this has begun to change, it is largely because of the struggles waged by women of colour both within mainstream organizations like NAC and also within grassroots organizations like the International Women's Day Committee.

Becki Ross examines the history of the lesbian feminist group, Lesbian Organization of Toronto (LOOT). LOOT formed in 1980 in response to the heterosexism of the larger women's movement. In the grassroots tradition, LOOT collectively organized housing, work and politics. LOOT also identified lesbian visibility, pride, and the dismantling of the institutionalized heterosexuality as being fundamental to the fight for sexual equality. Ross illuminates the ways in which lesbians challenged and continue to challenge dominant heterosexist norms. Nevertheless, as she emphasizes, lesbian organizing in the 1990s has shifted away from the presumption of an instant and homogenous unity among lesbians and the exclusions and conformity that this generated. In the selection we have included from *The House that Jill Built*, Ross clearly establishes the contemporary diversity of the lesbian politics, as well as the ongoing barriers to living safe, public and legally protected lives.

There have been a range of tensions that continue to challenge the Canadian women's movement—how to organize, where to get funding, and what issues to prioritize. Should the women's movement continue to work in existing structures? What do "we" mean by inclusion? What kind of relationship do we want to have with governments? How do we make anti-racist, anti-heterosexist and class politics central to our movement? These questions are part of an ongoing conversation within Canadian feminism. Our conversations must continue in order to meet the many new challenges of feminist organizing in the twenty-first century. If it is true that feminist struggle faces an increasingly hostile political climate, it is also true that there have been impressive changes rendering movement organizations more representative and internally democratic.

ENDNOTES

1. In 1966, a 32 member Committee on the Equality for Women made up of groups such as the Women's Christian Temperance Union, Voices of Women and the National Council of Jewish Women supported a brief calling for a Royal Commission (Prentice et al, 1988, 346).

2. Hansard, House of Commons Debate Official Report, April 23, 1993, 183–84.

LIST OF RECOMMENDATIONS: REPORT ON THE ROYAL COMMISSION ON THE STATUS OF WOMEN IN CANADA

CHAPTER 2:

Women in the Canadian Economy

1. We recommend that the National Housing Loan Regulations be amended so that (a) for purposes of the gross debt service ratio, either husband or wife may be deemed to be the purchaser or owner and (b) up to 50 percent of time income of the spouse of the purchaser or owner, or of the spouse of the person deemed to be the purchaser or owner, may be included in computing the annual income. (paragraph 32)

2. We recommend that (a) both the Canada and the Quebec Pension Plans be amended so that the spouse who remains at home can participate in the Plan, and (b) the feasibility be explored of

    (i) crediting to the spouse remaining at home a portion of the contributions of the employed spouse and those contributions made by the employer on the employed spouse's behalf, and

    (ii) on an optional basis, permitting the spouse at home to contribute as a self-employed worker. (paragraph 103)

3. We recommend that the federal, provincial and territorial governments (a) make greater use of women's voluntary associations; and (b) increase their financial support to

    (i) women's voluntary associations engaged in projects of public interest, and

    (ii) voluntary associations working in fields of particular concern to women. (paragraph 155)

4. We recommend that the federal, provincial and territorial governments include in their selection standards for appointment to positions in their respective governments, the assessment of volunteer experience in evaluating the qualifications of applicants. (paragraph 161)

5. We recommend that a federal-provincial conference on labour legislation affecting women in Canada be called to prepare for Canada's ratification of the International Labour Organization Convention Concerning Equal Remuneration for Men and Women Workers for Work of Equal Value (Convention 100). (paragraph 218)

6. We recommend that the Yukon Territorial Council adopt legislation prohibiting different pay rates based on sex. (paragraph 221)

7. We recommend that the federal Female Employees Equal Pay Act be amended to apply to all employees of the Government of Canada. (paragraph 226)

8. We recommend that the federal Female Employees Equal Pay Act, the federal Fair Wages and Hours of Work Regulations and equal pay legislation of provinces and Territories require that (a) the concept of skill, effort and responsibility be used as objective factors in determining what is equal work, with the understanding that pay rates thus established will be subject to such factors as seniority provisions; (b) an employee who feels aggrieved as a result of an alleged violation of the relevant legislation, or a party acting on her behalf, be able to refer the grievance to the agency designated for that purpose by the government administering the legislation; (c) the onus of investigating violations of the legislation be placed in the hands of the agency administering the equal pay legislation which will be free to investigate, whether or not complaints have been laid; (d) to the extent possible, the anonymity of the complainant be maintained; (e) provision be made for authority to render a decision on whether or not the terms of the legislation have been violated, to specify action to be taken and to prosecute if the orders are not followed; (f) where someone has presented the aggrieved employee's case on her behalf and the aggrieved employee is unsatisfied with the decision, she have the opportunity to present her case herself to the person or persons rendering the decision who may change the decision; (g) the employee's employment status be in no way adversely affected by application of the law to her case; (h) where the law has been violated, the employee be compensated for any losses in pay, vacation and other fringe benefits; (i) unions and employee organizations, as well as employers and employer organizations, be subject to this law; (j) penalties be sufficiently heavy to be an effective deterrent; and (k) the legislation specify that it is applicable to part-time as well as to full-time workers. (paragraph 239)

9. We recommend that the minimum wage legislation of Prince Edward Island, Nova Scotia and Newfoundland be amended to require the same minimum wages for women and men. (paragraph 240)

10. We recommend that British Columbia adopt a Minimum Wage Act applicable to both sexes that will require the same minimum wages for women and men and will contain no sex differences in the occupations covered. (paragraph 241)

11. We recommend that the pay rates for nurses, dietitians, home economists, librarians and social workers employed by the federal government be set by compar-

ing these professions with other professions in terms of the value of the work and the skill and training involved. (paragraph 252)

12. We recommend that legislation on the Canada Pension Plan and the Quebec Pension Plan be amended so that the provisions applicable to the wife and children of a male contributor will also be applicable to the husband and children of a female contributor. (paragraph 259)

13. We recommend that the provinces and the territories amend their workmen's compensation legislation so that the provisions applicable to the wife of the person deceased will also be applicable to the husband of the person deceased. (paragraph 261)

14. We recommend that the Unemployment Insurance Act and Regulations be amended to provide a common definition for "dependents" of women and men contributors. (paragraph 268)

15. We recommend that the federal Unemployment Insurance Act be amended to apply to all employees working in an established employee-employer relationship. (paragraph 269)

16. We recommend the amendment of the federal Fair Employment Practices Act and the adoption of provincial and territorial maternity legislation to provide for (a) an employed woman's entitlement to 18 weeks maternity leave, (b) mandatory maternity leave for the six-week period following her confinement unless she produces a medical certificate that working will not injure her health, and (c) prohibition of dismissal of an employee on any grounds during the maternity leave to which she is entitled. (paragraph 284)

17. We recommend that the Unemployment Insurance Act be amended so that women contributors will be entitled to unemployment benefits for a period of 18 weeks or for the period to which their contributions entitle them, whichever is the lesser, (a) when they stop paid work temporarily for maternity reasons or (b) when during a period in which they are receiving unemployment benefits, they become unable to work for maternity reasons. (paragraph 288)

18. We recommend to the provinces and territories that protective labour legislation be applicable to both sexes. (paragraph 295)

19. We recommend the elimination of any discrimination on the basis of sex in terms and conditions of employment for air crew on air lines. (paragraph 298)

20. We recommend that the provinces and territories adopt legislation prohibiting the advertisement of a job opening in a manner that expressly limits it to applicants of a particular sex or marital status. (paragraph 301)

21. We recommend that sex-typing of occupations be avoided in the text and in the illustrations of all federal government publications. (paragraph 302)

22. We recommend to the Canada Department of Manpower and Immigration and to the universities that University Placement Offices refuse to make arrangements for firms to interview students in connection with positions for which the firms have specified sex preferences or sex requirements. (paragraph 305)

23. We recommend that all provincial and territorial legislation dealing with equality

of opportunity in employment specify that discrimination on the basis of sex and marital status be prohibited. (paragraph 331)

24. We recommend that (a) The Fair Employment Practices Act be amended to

    (i) include "sex" and "marital status" as prohibited grounds for discrimination, and

    (ii) apply to all employees of the Government of Canada; and

    (b) The Fair Wages and Hours of Work Regulations be amended to include "sex" and "marital status" as prohibited grounds for discrimination. (paragraph; 334)

25. We recommend that the provisions now included in section 22 (2) (b) of the Unemployment Insurance Act, amended to include sex and marital status as prohibited grounds for discrimination, be included in legislation applicable to Canada Manpower Centres. (paragraph 336)

26. We recommend that the federal government increase significantly the number of women on federal Boards, Commissions, Corporations, Councils, Advisory Committees and Task Forces. (paragraph 341)

27. We recommend that provincial, territorial and municipal governments increase significantly the number of women on their Boards, Commissions, Corporations, Councils, Advisory Committees and Task Forces. (paragraph 341)

28. We recommend that the federal government undertake a study of the feasibility of making greater use of part-time work in the Canadian economy. (paragraph 366)

29. We recommend that the differential treatment of Nursing Assistants and Nursing Orderlies in the federal Public Service be eliminated. (paragraph 377)

30. We recommend that the positions of secretaries in the federal Public Service be classified by one of the methods used for other classes in the federal Public Service. (paragraph 382)

31. We recommend that the federal Public Service Superannuation Act be amended so that (a) there will be no differences in the provisions on the basis of sex, and (b) the surviving spouse of a contributor will be paid the supplementary death benefits. (paragraph 386)

32. We recommend that the federal Removal Expenses Regulations be amended so that the expenses paid for the wife of an employee will also be paid for the husband of an employee. (paragraph 387)

33. We recommend that the federal Public Service Terms and Conditions of Employment Regulations be amended by (a) deleting section 50(2), and (b) substituting the provision that, during the six-weeks period preceding the expected date of an employee's confinement, a deputy head may direct the employee to proceed on maternity leave unless she produces a medical certificate that she is able to work. (paragraph 392)

34. We recommend that the federal government continue to pay the employer's contribution to the superannuation and Group Surgical-Medical Plans when an employee is on maternity leave. (paragraph 394)

35. We recommend that federal Public Service bindery positions at levels 1 and 2 be open to women and men on the same basis and that the job title "journeywoman" be eliminated. (paragraph 399)

36. We recommend that, until the sex-typing of occupations is eradicated, the federal Public Service Commission and federal government department (a) take special steps to increase the number of women appointed to occupations and professions not traditionally female, (b) review and, where necessary, alter their recruitment literature and recruiting programmes to ensure that it is abundantly clear that women are wanted in all occupations and professions, and (c) take special steps to obtain applications from qualified women when appointments for senior levels are being made from outside the service. (paragraph 402)

37. We recommend that the federal Public Service Commission and federal government departments have as an objective the elimination of the imbalance in the proportion of women and men in senior positions and (a) as much as is feasible, emphasize potential rather than experience as a basis for appointment or promotion; (b) ensure that vacancies are open to employees at a classification level low enough to permit consideration of qualified women; and (c) when a job opens, make sure that women candidates get full consideration including the evaluation of their experience in volunteer work and running a household if its relevant. (paragraph 422)

38. We recommend that the federal Public Service Commission and federal government departments (a) introduce programmes that will ensure the consideration of secretaries for administrative positions, and (b) open up intermediate and senior administrative positions to women in traditionally female professions. (paragraph 423)

39. We recommend that (a) a special effort be made to attract more women applicants for administrative training positions in the federal Public Service, and (b) federal government departments ensure that women administrative trainees are given the kind of training assignments that will prepare them for advancement to the senior levels. (paragraph 427)

40. We recommend that action be taken to increase greatly the enrolment of promising women in federal Public Service management courses, including the step of waiving salary floors and age ceilings where necessary in their case. (paragraph 428)

41. We recommend that, for the next 10 years, the number of women enrolled in each course in the Career Assignment Program of the federal Public Service be no less than 10 per cent of the total number of people enrolled in the course. (paragraph 436)

42. We recommend that (a) the federal Public Service Terms and Conditions of Employment Regulations be amended so that part-time employees will receive pay increases on the same basis as full-time employees, and (b) collective agreements for the federal Public Service contain this provision. (paragraph 442)

43. We recommend that federal Crown Corporation agencies (a) ensure that women scientists and technologists receive equal consideration with men for appointment, and (b) make a special effort to give graduate women employees a chance to take post-graduate degrees. (paragraph 455)

44. We recommend that federal Crown Corporations and agencies (a) develop transfer and promotion measures that will encourage women to move out of the traditionally female occupations into other occupations, and (b) emphasize in recruitment programmes that all occupations are open equally to women and men. (paragraph 458)

45. We recommend that each federal Crown Corporation and agency devise a long-term plan for the better use of womanpower within its organization. (paragraph 459)

46. We recommend that, where the size of staff warrants it, federal Crown Corporations and agencies appoint one or more qualified people whose primary duty for the next five to eight years will be to provide for the training and development of women in their organizations. (paragraph 460)

47. We recommend that federal Crown Corporations and agencies with rotational programmes between field and head offices ensure that women are considered for rotation on the same basis as men and are not judged in advance on their freedom to rotate. (paragraph 461)

48. We recommend that federal Crown Corporations and agencies (a) review their selection procedures to ensure that women are used in recruitment and selection programmes, and (b) have senior women officers on their personnel administration staffs. (paragraph 462)

49. We recommend that different provisions on the basis of sex be eliminated from superannuation and insurance plans for federal Crown Corporations and agencies. (paragraph 466)

50. We recommend that federal Crown Corporations and agencies (a) make clear to educational institutions, and to the public, that career opportunities within their organizations are open to women and that they are encouraging women to prepare themselves for such careers; and (b) require each private organization with which they do business to include in each contract, a clause that prohibits discrimination in employment on the basis of sex. (paragraph 467)

51. We recommend that sex-typing of the occupations of employees working in the Senate and House of Commons be discontinued. (paragraph 474)

52. We recommend that the Clerks of the Senate and the House of Commons devise a long-term plan for better use of womanpower and for opening senior positions to women as well as to men. (paragraph 475)

53. We recommend that the Royal Canadian Mounted Police Superannuation Act be amended so that its provisions will be the same for both female and male contributors. (paragraph 481)

54. We recommend that enlistment in the Royal Canadian Mounted Police be open to women. (paragraph 484)

55. We recommend that all trades in the Canadian Forces be open to women. (paragraph 488)

56. We recommend that the prohibition on the enlistment of married women in the Canadian Forces be eliminated. (paragraph 490)

57. We recommend that the length of the initial engagement for which personnel are required to enlist in the Canadian Forces be the same for women and men. (paragraph 494)

58. We recommend that release of a woman from the Canadian Forces because she has a child be prohibited. (paragraph 495)

59. We recommend that the Canadian Forces Superannuation Act be amended so that its provisions will be the same for male and female contributors. (paragraph 497)

60. We recommend that (a) the federal government issue a policy statement to the Ministers of all federal government departments, the heads of Crown Corporations and agencies, and the Speakers of the Senate and the House of Commons, expressing its intention to

    (i) ensure equality of opportunity in employment for women and the greater use of womanpower, and

    (ii) undertake short-term special measures where these are necessary to achieve its objectives; and

    (b) an information programme be undertaken so that management and supervisors at all levels in the Government of Canada be made aware of the government's policy regarding its employment of women. (paragraph 501)

61. We recommend that (a) a Women's Programme Secretariat be established in the Privy Council Office for promoting a programme for equality of opportunity for women in the federal Government Service and the greater use of their skills and abilities; (b) a Women's Programme Co-ordinator be appointed to each federal government department, Crown Corporation and agency, to the Royal Canadian Mounted Police, the Canadian Forces, and to the staff of the Senate and the House of Commons to promote within the organization the objectives of the Women's Programme and to maintain liaison with the Secretariat; (c) the federal government organizations referred to above be required to give periodic progress reports to the Women's Programme Secretariat of objectives undertaken; and (d) an annual report be tabled in Parliament on the progress being made in the federal Government Service toward the objectives of the Women's Programme. (paragraph 506)

62. We recommend that Chartered Banks (a) make it known that they intend to give women equality of opportunity; (b) eliminate the practice, where it exists, of requiring a longer attachment period for women than for men before promotion to management; (c) ensure that they have a record of women qualified for promotion to be considered as vacancies occur; (d) provide more opportunities for women to participate in both in-service and outside training programmes with the objective of their constituting at least 25 per cent of those trained by 1975; and (e) encourage their women employees to improve their knowledge and capabilities through management training courses and educational courses, such as those of the Institute of Canadian Bankers, in reasonable expectation that successful completion of these courses will lead to opportunities for promotion. (paragraph 513)

63. We recommend that department stores (a) ensure that women employees are considered for advancement on an equal basis with men; (b) investigate why, in areas where the staff is predominantly female, it is the practice to fill the senior positions with men; and (c) make a special effort to train more women employees for managerial positions. (paragraph 522)

64. We recommend that retail stores review their practices to ensure that exploitation of part-time workers does not exist. (paragraph 523)

65. We recommend that the Canada Department of Labour conduct a survey of the use of homeworkers, including handicraft workers, their wages and their other conditions of employment. (paragraph 533)

66. We recommend to the provinces and territories that household workers be cov-

ered by minimum wage laws, workmen's compensation and other labour legislation applicable to other paid workers. (paragraph 545)

67. We recommend that each provincial and territorial government establish a Household Workers Bureau which, with its network of local offices, would be responsible for (a) establishing and promoting employment standards for different categories of household workers; (b) maintaining a list of available workers according to their competence, training, experience, health and other relevant qualifications; (c) directing available household workers to families which require them; (d) maintaining a record of families which use or require the services of the Bureau, with indications of the conditions of work of each of them; (e) supplying these families with information relating to desirable conditions of work and social security benefits; (f) promoting training of household workers according to the needs of the market; (g) initiating, if necessary, training courses for household workers; (h) ensuring that household workers are not exploited; and (i) conducting studies and providing information on the current market situation of household workers. (paragraph 547)

68. We recommend that provinces and territories promote the establishment of agencies or co-operatives to (a) act as the employer of household workers to be assigned to suitable employment, and (b) collect for the services of the household workers, make income tax, social security, and other payroll deductions, and ensure that they have equitable pay, approved employment conditions and the protection provided by law. (paragraph 551)

CHAPTER 3:

Education

69. We recommend that the provinces and the territories adopt textbooks that portray women, as well as men, in diversified roles and occupations. (paragraph 53)

70. We recommend that women as well as men be admitted to the military colleges operated by the Department of National Defence. (paragraph 68)

71. We recommend that the federal government provide special funds for young women and men to acquire university education, such as is provided for young men who attend military college, leading to a degree in fields designated to be of special interest for aid to developing areas, the terms to include commitment to some specified national or international service. (paragraph 70)

72. We recommend that the federal government, the provinces and the territories set up committees to review all government publications concerned with the choice of occupations and careers in order to select and use only publications that encourage women to consider all occupations, including those which have been traditionally restricted to men. (paragraph 85)

73. We recommend that the provinces and territories (a) provide co-educational guid-

ance programmes in elementary and secondary schools, where they do not now exist and (b) direct the attention of guidance counsellors to the importance of encouraging both girls and boys to continue their education according to their individual aptitudes and to consider all occupational fields. (paragraph 87)

74. We recommend that, where they have not already done so, universities establish formal counselling services. (paragraph 88)

75. We recommend that (a) the federal government in co-operation with the provinces and territories set up a career information service in each local Canada Manpower Centre which would

    (i)   include personnel specially trained to give information to women on occupations, training requirements, financial help available, and labour market conditions and needs, and

    (ii) insist on the importance of a broad field of occupational choice for girls;

    and (b) subject to consultation and agreement with the educational authorities, this career information service be offered to all schools of the area. (paragraph 90)

76. We recommend that, where they have not already done so, the provinces and the territories set up courses in family life education, including sex education, which begin in kindergarten and continue through elementary and secondary schools, and which are taught to girls and boys in the same classroom. (paragraph 96)

77. We recommend that the provinces and territories (a) review their policies and practices to ensure that school programmes provide girls with equal opportunities with boys to participate in athletic and sports activities, and (b) establish policies and practices that will motivate and encourage girls to engage in athletic and sports activities. (paragraph 102)

78. We recommend that, pursuant to section 3 (d) of the federal Fitness and Amateur Sport Act, a research project be undertaken to (a) determine why fewer girls than boys participate in sports programmes at the school level and (b) recommend remedial action. (paragraph 103)

79. We recommend that the federal government, in co-operation with the provinces and territories, ensure that information on the federal Occupational Training for Adults Programme reaches women outside the labour force as well as those employed or actively seeking employment. (paragraph 126)

80. We recommend that the federal government, in co-operation with the provinces and territories, expand and widely advertise the part-time training programmes offered by the Department of Manpower and Immigration. (paragraph 127)

81. We recommend that section 3 (b) of the federal Adult Occupational Training Act be amended so that full-time household responsibility be equivalent to participation in the labour force in so far as eligibility for training allowances is concerned. (paragraph 130)

82. We recommend that the federal Department of Manpower and Immigration, in co-operation with provinces and territories, develop policies and practices that will result in (a) an increase in the number of women undertaking educational upgrading programmes and training for more highly skilled occupations, (b) the enrol-

ment of women in courses in line with their capacities without regard to sex-typing of occupations, (c) an increase in the number of women training for managerial and technical positions, and (d) the consideration by women of the whole spectrum of occupations before choosing training courses. (paragraph 134)

83. We recommend that the provinces and territories and all post-secondary educational institutions develop programmes to meet the special needs for continuing education of women with family responsibilities. (paragraph 143)

84. We recommend that the federal government, in co-operation with the provinces and territories, extend the present system of student loans to include part-time students. (paragraph 145)

85. We recommend that the federal government, in co-operation with the provinces, provide through the Occupational Training for Adults programme (a) training courses which will lead to a diploma for visiting homemakers for emergency assistance, the planning of which will be in conjunction with local welfare agencies, and (b) training courses leading to a diploma for household workers other than visiting homemakers. (paragraph 148)

86. We recommend that women be given the same opportunity as men to participate in any programmes at present or in the future, that are sponsored by government for the retraining and rehabilitation of rural people, such as those begun under the Agricultural and Rural Development Act (ARDA). (paragraph 169)

87. We recommend that the provinces and territories take appropriate action to study the current educational needs and interests of women in rural areas and, in consultation with local people, introduce more adequate programmes, ensuring that they are available to women. (paragraph 171)

88. We recommend that the Department of the Secretary of State, through its Citizenship Branch, in co-operation with the provinces and territories, (a) conduct surveys in all areas of Canada where immigrants are settling to ascertain the special educational needs of immigrant women, (b) suggest programmes by which these needs could be met, (c) make these needs and programmes known to voluntary workers in the community, and (d) assist volunteers in the implementation of these training programmes. (paragraph 176)

89. We recommend that the federal government, in co-operation with provinces and territories, review language training programmes in order to ensure that the needs of immigrant women are being met. (paragraph 177)

90. We recommend that the federal government, in co-operation with the Northwest Territories, make sure that the education programme in relation to housing is continued. (paragraph 189)

91. We recommend that the Northwest Territories amend its Housing Association by-laws so that both the lessee and the spouse of the lessee are members of the housing associations. (paragraph 190)

92. We recommend that the federal, provincial and territorial governments encourage Eskimo and Indian women to take training in adult education for work in the northern communities. (paragraph 191)

93. We recommend that the federal government, the provinces and the territories co-operate to (a) provide expanded, comprehensive courses for all public officials and employees and their spouses, working with Indians and Eskimos, to familiarize them with the cultures and traditions of the native people, including training in the native languages; (b) make available to Indian and Eskimo women education courses to provide at least functional literacy in either French or English; (c) encourage native women to participate in school planning and programming, and to serve on school advisory committees; (d) where it is not already being done, train native women as teachers and teachers' aides; (e) provide that teachers' colleges give special training courses in the instruction of English or French as a second language to Indians and Eskimos; (f) make sure that teachers' colleges provide courses in Indian and Eskimo culture, including training in the native languages for teachers planning to work with native People; and (g) make every effort to train Indians and Eskimos to provide the educational services in Indian and Eskimo communities now being performed by non-Indian and non-Eskimo public servants. (paragraph 193)

94. We recommend that universities establish or strengthen courses and research in Indian and Eskimo cultures. (paragraph 194)

95. We recommend to private industry that it provide training courses for employees working in the north, and their spouses, to familiarize them with the cultures and traditions of the native people, including training in the native languages. (paragraph 195)

96. We recommend that the federal government, in co-operation with the territories, include individual native women, as well as couples, in the programme under which Eskimos and Indians are brought south on learning trips. (paragraph 197)

97. We recommend that the federal government, in co-operation with the territories, ensure that management training programmes in the operation of co-operatives and small business enterprises be made available to native women as well as to men and be expanded to fit the growing needs of the northern communities. (paragraph 200)

98. We recommend that the provinces and territories, in co-operation with universities, arrange that educational television programmes, including credit as well as non-credit courses at elementary, secondary, general and technical college and university levels, be televised at hours, when both housewives and women in the labour force can take advantage of them. (paragraph 209)

99. We recommend that the governments and organizations which plan to use the Canadian satellite telecommunications system (a) consult knowledgeable women as to the types and quality of programmes and the hours of scheduling in order to meet the needs and convenience of women in Canada, and (b) include women professionals and specialists in all branches of programme production and broadcasting so that women will have equal opportunities with men in the development, operation and use of this new medium. (paragraph 212)

100. We recommend that committees, composed of citizens of the community, establish and direct Citizens' Information Centres for the purpose of providing free information on community resources, and that centres (a) maintain offices open to the public; (b) be responsible for the production and extensive distribution of booklets

listing community resources; (c) provide for free in-coming long-distance telephone calls from citizens who could not be expected to travel to the nearest centre; (d) provide information by correspondence on request; (e) make full use of radio, television, the newspapers and other mass media to ensure that citizens are well informed on the services provided; and (f) encourage mass media to provide, by means of articles, programme courses, news releases and other techniques, information on subjects that may give rise to problems for citizens. (paragraph 225)

101. We recommend that federal, provincial, territorial and municipal governments provide financial assistance to citizens' committees operating Citizens' Information Centres. (paragraph 226)

CHAPTER 4:

Women and the Family

102. We recommend that the federal government enact legislation establishing 18 years as the minimum age for marriage. (paragraph 39)

103. We recommend that the federal government change its passport application forms in order to indicate that a married woman may obtain her passport either in her maiden surname or in the surname of her husband. (paragraph 44)

104. We recommend that the federal government modify its policy so that a woman need not apply for a new passport after marriage unless she wishes to obtain it in her husband's surname. (paragraph 45)

105. We recommend that the provinces and territories amend their legislation so that a woman, on marriage, may retain her domicile or, subsequently, acquire a new domicile, independent of that of her husband. (paragraph 53)

106. We recommend that the Indian Act be amended to allow an Indian woman upon marriage to a non-Indian to (a) retain her Indian status and (b) transmit her Indian status to her children. (paragraph 59)

107. We recommend that those provinces and territories, which have not already done so, amend their law in order to recognize the concept of equal partnership in marriage so that the contribution of each spouse to the marriage partnership may be acknowledged and that, upon the dissolution of the marriage, each will have a right to an equal share in the assets accumulated during marriage otherwise than by gift or inheritance received by either spouse from outside sources. (paragraph 89)

108. We recommend that the provinces and territories, which have not already done so, amend their laws so that a wife who is financially able to do so may be held to support her husband and children in the same way that the husband may now be held to support his wife and children. (paragraph 98)

109. We recommend that the Criminal Code be amended so that the wife may be held to support her husband in the same way that the husband may now be held to support his wife. (paragraph 99)

110. We recommend that those provinces and territories which have established maximum amounts for maintenance orders remove such ceilings. (paragraph 107)

111. We recommend that the provinces and territories, which have not already done so, adopt legislation to set up Family Courts. (paragraph 111)

112. We recommend that the auxiliary services of Family Courts include an assessment branch dealing with the assessment and payment of alimony and maintenance. (paragraph 112)

113. We recommend that the Divorce Act be amended so that the three-year separation period provided in section 4 (1) (e) (i) be reduced to one year. (paragraph 135)

114. We recommend that the Divorce Act be amended so that the words "educational needs" be added to the list of exceptions where the maintenance of children over the age of 16 years may be ordered as a charge falling to the parents. (paragraph 142)

115. We recommend that fees for the care of children in day-care centres be fixed on a sliding scale based on the means of the parents. (paragraph 167)

116. We recommend that the provinces, where they do not already do so, pay not less than 80 per cent of the provincial-municipal contribution to day-care centres. (paragraph 170)

117. We recommend that the National Housing Act be amended to (a) permit the making of loans for the construction, purchase and renovation of buildings for day-care centres, and (b) permit the inclusion of space for day-care centres in housing developments, including university buildings, for which loans are made under the Act. (paragraph 173)

118. We recommend that the federal government immediately take steps to enter into agreement with the provinces leading to the adoption of a national Day-Care Act under which federal funds would be made available on a cost-sharing basis for the building and running of day-care centres meeting specified minimum standards, the federal government to (a) pay all the operating costs; (b) during an initial seven-year period, pay 70 per cent of capital costs; and (c) make similar arrangements for the Yukon and Northwest Territories. (paragraph 181)

119. We recommend that each province and territory establish a Child-Care Board to be responsible for the establishment and supervision of day-care centres and other child-care programmes, which will (a) plan a network of centres (as to location, type, etc.), (b) set and enforce standards and regulations, (c) provide information and consultants, (d) promote the establishment of new day-care services, and (e) approve plans for future day-care services. (paragraph 187)

120. We recommend that the Department of National Health and Welfare offer an extension of advisory services to the provinces and territories through the establishment of a unit for consultation on child-care services. (paragraph 188)

121. We recommend that birth control information be available to everyone. (paragraph 217)

122. We recommend that the Department of National Health and Welfare (a) prepare and offer birth control information free of charge to provincial and territorial authorities, associations, organizations and individuals and (b) give financial assistance

through National Health grants and National Welfare grants to train health and welfare workers in family planning techniques. (paragraph 218)

123. We recommend that provincial Departments of Health (a) organize family planning clinics in each public health unit to ensure that everyone has access to information, medical assistance, and birth control devices and drugs as needed, and (b) provide mobile clinics where they are needed particularly in remote areas. (paragraph 219)

124. We recommend that the criminal law be clarified so that sterilization performed by a qualified medical practitioner at the request of his patient shall not engage the criminal responsibility of the practitioner. (paragraph 223)

125. We recommend that the provinces and territories adopt legislation to authorize medical practitioners to perform non-therapeutic sterilization at the request of the patient free from any civil liabilities toward the patient or the spouse except liability for negligence. (paragraph 224)

126. We recommend that the Criminal Code be amended to permit abortion by a qualified medical practitioner on the sole request of any woman who has been pregnant for 12 weeks or less. (paragraph 242)

127. We recommend that the Criminal Code be amended to permit abortion by a qualified practitioner at the request of a woman pregnant for more than 12 weeks if the doctor is convinced that the continuation of the pregnancy would endanger the physical or mental health of the woman, or if there is a substantial risk that if the child were born, it would be greatly handicapped, either mentally or physically. (paragraph 243)

128. We recommend that the governments of the provinces, territories and municipalities make every effort to integrate the unmarried mother, who keeps her child, into the life of the community, by making sure that she (a) is not discriminated against in respect of employment and housing, (b) receives help with child care if necessary, and (c) has access to counselling to help her with emotional, social and economic problems. (paragraph 254)

129. We recommend that provinces and territories amend where necessary the regulations relating to provincial welfare programmes so as to prohibit the exertion of any influence on the unmarried mother to press for an order of affiliation. (paragraph 257)

CHAPTER 5:

Taxation and Child-care Allowances

130. We recommend that the federal Income Tax Act be amended in order that (a) the extra exemption allowed the taxpayer for the dependent spouse be reduced from the present $1,000 to $600 when the dependent spouse is under 60 years of age, and (b) the extra exemption allowed the taxpayer for a dependent spouse be the same as the individual personal exemption, when a dependent spouse is aged 60 and over. (paragraph 50)

131. We recommend that a federal annual taxable cash allowance in the order of $500 be provided for each child under 16 to be paid in monthly instalments to the mother as under the present Family Allowance system. (paragraph 51)

132. We recommend that the federal Income Tax Act be amended in order that husband and wife form a taxation unit and be permitted to aggregate their incomes, under a special tax rate schedule, in a joint return signed by both spouses with the option to file separately if they so desire. (paragraph 55)

133. We recommend that those provinces that have not already done so amend their respective Succession Duties Acts in order to abolish succession duties on assets passing from one spouse to the other. (paragraph 64)

CHAPTER 6:

Poverty

134. We recommend that the provinces and territories, in co-operation with municipalities and voluntary associations, provide a network of hostels for transient girls and women where counselling services on job opportunities and training facilities are made available. (paragraph 20)

135. We recommend that a guaranteed annual income be paid by the federal government to the heads of all one-parent families with dependent children. (paragraph 48)

136. We recommend that (a) the Guaranteed Income Supplement of the Old Age Security benefits be increased so that the annual income of the recipients is maintained above the poverty level, and (b) the Supplement be adjusted to the cost of living index. (paragraph 66)

137. We recommend that the federal government, the provinces, territories, municipalities and voluntary associations, in co-operation with native people, establish or expand friendship centres directed and staffed by people of Indian, Métis or Eskimo ancestry, to provide needed services. (paragraph 72)

CHAPTER 7:

Participation of Women in Public Life

138. We recommend that two qualified women from each province be summoned to the Senate as seats become vacant, and that women continue to be summoned until a more equitable membership is achieved. (paragraph 28)

139. We recommend that financial qualifications for eligibility for membership in the Senate be abolished. (paragraph 29)

140. We recommend that the federal government and the provinces name more women judges to all courts within their jurisdictions. (paragraph 33)

141. We recommend that the provinces which have not already done so, require women to be liable for jury duty on the same terms as men. (paragraph 37)

142. We recommend that women's associations within the political parties of Canada be amalgamated with the main bodies of these parties. (paragraph 55)

CHAPTER 8:

Immigration and Citizenship

143. We recommend that the Immigration Division of the federal Department of Manpower and Immigration review its policies and practices to ensure that the right of a wife to be an independent applicant for admission to Canada is always respected and that wives are made fully aware of this right. (paragraph 6)

144. We recommend that the federal Immigration Act and Regulations be amended by the elimination of the term "head of a family" wherever it appears in the legislation and by the substitution of the exact meaning which is intended in each case. (paragraph 7)

145. We recommend that the Canadian Citizenship Act be amended to provide for the automatic resumption of Canadian citizenship by women who lost it because they married aliens before January 1, 1947. (paragraph 16)

146. We recommend that the Canadian Citizenship Act be amended so that there is no difference between the residence requirements for the acquisition of Canadian citizenship by an alien husband and an alien wife of a Canadian citizen. (paragraph 18)

147. We recommend that sections 4 and 5 of the Canadian Citizenship Act be amended to provide that a child born outside Canada is a natural-born Canadian if either of his parents is a Canadian citizen. (paragraph 20)

148. We recommend that the Canadian Citizenship Act be amended so that either citizen-parent may apply for the naturalized citizenship of a minor child. (paragraph 22)

149. We recommend that section 11 (2) of the Canadian Citizenship Act be amended so that, in the case of joint adoption, the child may be granted Canadian citizenship if either of the adopting parents is a Canadian citizen. (paragraph 23)

CHAPTER 9:

Criminal Law and Women Offenders

150. We recommend that section 164(1)(c) of the Criminal Code be repealed. (paragraph 27)

151. We recommend that section 164(1)(a) of the Criminal Code be repealed. (paragraph 32)

152. We recommend that the words "of previously chaste character" be deleted from all the sections of the Criminal Code. (paragraph 38)

153. We recommend that the Criminal Code be amended to extend protection from sexual abuse to all young people, male and female, and protection to everyone from sexual exploitation either by false representation, use of force, threat, or the abuse of authority. (paragraph 42)

154. We recommend that subsection (3) of section 23 of the Criminal Code be amended to apply to both spouses. (paragraph 45)

155. We recommend that the provincial and territorial governments either provide or contract with suitable voluntary associations to provide homes for women on remand. (paragraph 49)

156. We recommend that the federal government, provinces, territories and municipalities, whenever possible, assign female instead of male police officers to deal with women taken into custody. (paragraph 51)

157. We recommend that the provinces and territories ensure that when the administrative policy of their corrections programme is being determined, the differences in the counselling and supervisory needs of women and men probationers be considered, staff requirements be based on these needs and caseloads be adjusted accordingly. (paragraph 55)

158. We recommend that the provinces and territories (a) develop a health and social welfare policy that would remove from the penal setting the handling of persons found apparently intoxicated and assign the responsibility for diagnosis and treatment to health and welfare administration; (b) ensure that there are treatment facilities for female alcoholics; and (c) in co-operation with health and welfare authorities establish treatment programmes, where they do not now exist, for female alcoholics being now detained in a penal setting for criminal offences. (paragraph 62)

159. We recommend that the federal Prisons and Reformatories Act be revised to eliminate all provisions that discriminate on the basis of sex or religion. (paragraph 66)

160. We recommend that the federal, provincial and territorial governments co-operate in order to provide flexible and imaginative programmes aimed at the rehabilitation of women offenders which would include (a) a system that provides appropriate living quarters, small "open" institutions where life follows a normal pattern rather than institutional living and is integrated as much as possible with the life of the neighbouring community; (b) programmes and services, such as education and vocational training, adapted to the needs of individual female offenders and taking full advantage of the resources of that district; and (c) personnel specially trained in dealing with female offenders. (paragraph 72)

161. We recommend that the federal Women's Prison at Kingston be closed. (paragraph 73)

162. We recommend that the National Parole Board make use whenever possible of members of band councils and government personnel, to provide parole supervision especially in rural and remote areas, for women of Indian and Eskimo ancestry. (paragraph 76)

163. We recommend that a network of halfway houses for women newly released from correctional institutions be set up in centres across Canada, supported by public and private funds and operated by voluntary groups and agencies, in accordance with approved government standards. (paragraph 79)

CHAPTER 10:

Plan for Action

164. We recommend that the federal government, the provinces, the territories and municipalities, each establish an implementation committee composed of a number of its senior administrators, to (a) plan for, coordinate and expedite the implementation of the recommendations made by the Royal Commission on the Status of Women to that jurisdiction; and (b) report from time to time to its government on the progress it is making. (paragraph 3)

165. We recommend that federal, provincial and territorial Human Rights Commissions be set up that would (a) be directly responsible to Parliament, provincial legislatures or territorial councils, (b) have power to investigate the administration of human rights legislation as well as the power to enforce the law by laying charges and prosecuting offenders, (c) include within the organization for a period of seven to 10 years a division dealing specifically with the protection of women's rights, and (d) suggest changes in human rights legislation and promote widespread respect for human rights. (paragraph 7)

166. We recommend that a federal Status of Women Council, directly responsible to Parliament, be established to (a) advise on matters pertaining to women and report annually to Parliament on the progress being made in improving the status of women in Canada, (b) undertake research on matters relevant to the status of women and suggest research topics that can be carried out by governments, private business, universities, and voluntary associations, (c) establish programmes to correct attitudes and prejudices adversely affecting the status of women, (d) propose legislation, policies and practices to improve the status of women, and (e) systematically consult with women's bureaux or similar provincial organizations, and with voluntary associations particularly concerned with the problems of women. (paragraph 17)

167. We recommend that, where it has not already been done, each province and territory establish a government bureau or similar agency concerned with the status of women which would have sufficient authority and funds to make its work effective. (paragraph 18)

SISTERS, BROTHERS, LOVERS... LISTEN...

Judy Bernstein, Peggy Morton,
Linda Seese, Myrna Wood

Fall 1967

The authors are movement women who were active at the time of writing this paper in the Student Union for Peace Action (SUPA), then Canada's leading New Left organization. The paper was written for a SUPA membership conference, and was part of the organizing of the first women's liberation group in Canada (in Toronto). This article was originally reprinted by New England Free Press.

This paper is intended to provoke thought and discussion. We hope that it will not be taken as vindictive but that certain directions may come from this discussion. Believing as Marx did that social progress can be measured by the social position of the female sex, we will attempt to describe the human condition in New Left terms as it exists today. We will also explore the position and role of women within this human condition. We will trace the history of the role of women in the New Left in Canada and show that this role is determined by the values of the dominant society. We will point out directions, methods for change and concrete suggestions for change both within and without the movement.

We trust that you will consider this paper with the seriousness with which it was written.

Human Condition

Embodied in all the things we stand for, are concerned with, and work for, as the New Left, is this concept we talk about as the *liberation* of human beings, a liberation that would enable us to develop the full potential that human kind may have. It is the concept behind our rhetoric on the black people of the U.S., the Vietnamese, the Canadian Indians, the developing Third World and the poor and middle classes.

Unlike lower forms of life, human beings are capable of becoming—becoming more than a living entity that is enslaved to the creation and maintenance of the species. The potential we human beings share is to develop our own creativity and make valid our humanism. We need not be caught up in the animalistic biological concept of physical survival of the fittest. Our level of survival and creativity is intricately bound up with the spiritual, social and economic level of society. Our level of survival and creativity is dependent upon our consciousness and the type of social relationships that allow the expansion of the consciousness.

We say that an acquisitive, frightened elite in society keeps all those who are dispossessed from growing in those areas which raise man to greater heights of creativeness, self-understanding, happiness than the more primitive past we come from. Liberation is to move freely through a lifetime's experience, learning from all, and regardless of one's supposed "place," expressing oneself in ways that have rarely been possible in our conformist society. We live in a time when this seems possible to us, within our reach; we have some knowledge, means of communication, aids like drugs for self-awareness and awareness of others, but are limited in our freedom to use them. Hence we develop underground methods of circumventing these restrictions put on us, whether cultural or revolutionary. However, since we hope for an extensive change in society, we constantly attempt to bring our way of living and thinking to the surface to start the change occurring.

However, so often it means that instead of understanding that concept we espouse, we use it mainly as rhetoric, as a shallow political explanation for our dissent. That is not to say that liberation should or could come before we can politically use the concept, but certainly among ourselves being and using should be simultaneous. We must learn by doing how people who have no power can liberate themselves.

The Human Condition as Reflected in the Position of Women

The direct, natural, necessary relation of human creatures is the relation of man to woman... The nature of this relation delimits to what point man himself is to be considered as a **generic being**. As mankind, the relation of man to woman is the most natural relation of human being to human being. By it is shown, therefore, to what point the **natural** behaviour of man has become **human**, or to what point the **human** being has become his **natural** being, to what point his human nature has become his **nature**.

Simone de Beauvoir has said in response to the above statement by Marx:

The case could not be better stated. It is for man to establish the reign of liberty in the midst of the world of the given. To gain the supreme victory, it is necessary for one thing. That by and through their natural differentiation men and women unequivocally affirm their brotherhood.

We believe they both state the case very well. We also see the human condition of this society as one of loneliness, alienation and fear. We all look for support against this. Men attempt to alleviate this fear by having someone—a woman—whom he can depend upon and dominate. He must see her as an inferior in order to strengthen his identity which is constantly threatened by an inhuman society. This leaves the woman with only one role with which to eliminate her similar fears. She must gain her identity through that domination. The woman begins to tie the man to her through his need for her. He is dependent on her playing the role of being his helpmate and being dependent on him for providing and protecting. The man's function is creation and procreation; the woman's is maintenance. This role chafes her. She realizes in her subconscious what Marcuse says: "Free election of masters does not abolish the masters or the slaves." The woman becomes possessive in retaliation for her forced role. She cannot allow him to be free because she is not free. Marcuse says, "In a society based on exploitation both the slave and the slaveholder are unfree...and this mutual dependence is...a vicious circle which encloses both the Master and the Servant." The human quality of love is destroyed. And we are the children of such relationships.

As Marian Ramelson writes: "Not only (will) men have to re-estimate women's place in the home and society, but women will have to re-estimate themselves, giving their work and potentialities a far higher value than they've been accustomed to do." Yes, the "woman problem" is a human "problem" but we women are beginning to understand the necessity of re-estimating ourselves. We are learning what Marcuse knew: "The range of choice open to the individual is not the decisive factor in determining the degree of human freedom, but what *can* be chosen and what *is* chosen by the individual."

Perhaps the position of women in the sexual act, most often lying underneath the man, illustrates the social and economic position of women in society. Women feel they are still on the bottom, in all respects. The notion of human liberation is in direct opposition to the notions of efficiency, profit, accumulation of possessions. The separation of man from woman contributes to the maintenance of such a society.

Historical Basis of the Position of Women

Juliet Mitchell, in an article on the position of women, "The Longest March," *New Left Review*, has set our four categories which she sees as operating dialectically to create and reinforce a subservient position for women in society: production, reproduction, sexuality and socialization. Her categories will be used to develop an outline on the historical basis of women's enslavement.

Production

Socialist writers have traditionally linked the origins and continuation of women's domination with the physical superiority of men and their consequent ability to perform work. This results in a division of tasks: men are creators and conquerors while women act as preservers and maintainers.

Historically, this is not true. While it is true that man's physical strength has given him a capacity for violence in war and conquest, and thus *political* control, the role of women in production has been a varied one. For example, in many agricultural societies, women have performed the bulk of work in the fields. In Britain during the period of early industrialization, women and children provided the bulk of the cheap labour force in the textile factories and the mines. In addition, women have, of course, performed socially necessary work, such as housework which falls outside the market economy. These examples show that coercion has and will be used to force women to engage in productive labour when the economic system demands it, or when men have decided that women will perform certain kinds of work.

In societies where women have not played a major role in the labour force, they are generally accorded the role of stabilizers of the social order. This occurs in the following way: Work is an alienating experience because men have no control over either the process or the products of their labour. An escape must be provided. The institution of the family has provided such an escape. Women have the job of maintaining a retreat from the alienating society. Without this release people in society might become alienated to the point of rebellion against the social order. In the same way that poor whites have been controlled by teaching them superiority to black people, men have been controlled by giving them a role superior to that of women.

It is obvious that the granting to women of equal rights to work and to be creative within the present society cannot be considered liberation, since work in a capitalist society is unfulfilling and alienating. The question of the role of women in production cannot be divorced from that of the necessity of a transition from capitalism to socialism, but the demand of rights in this area for women will be one step in breaking down the social order.

Reproduction

The problems of production and reproduction are closely linked. The inability, until recently, of women to control their own reproduction capacities has made it convenient to accord to women their present position. As long as women have no control over the number of children they wish to bear or when they wish to have them, they are easier to control, being more in need of protection and less useful as members of the labour force. "The pill" has the potential for making women free agents in this matter. The most optimistic thing about contraception is that once childbearing becomes one option among many, and women have some power to control their destinies, they may well be less ready to accept subservience as an inevitable part of their condition.

It is important to remember, however, that the questions of production and reproduction must be seen as social rather than strictly biological. Since the continuation of the race depends on reproduction, an economic system based on human needs rather than profit would see that women who are pregnant or who have young children should be provided for economically, especially if this removes them for a time from other productive labour. Capitalism, of course, makes no such social judgments.

Sexuality

The submissive role of women in the sexual act is inseparable from the values taught to people about how to treat one another and about the possibility or impossibility of a human relationship between men and women. Woman is the object; man is the subject. Women are screwed; men do the screwing. Men see sex as conquest; women see it as surrender. Such a value system in the most personal and potentially meaningful act of communication between men and women cannot but result in the inability of both the one who conquers and the one who surrenders to have genuine love and understanding between them.

The question of sexual liberation for both men and women is fundamental to both the liberation of women and to the development of human relationships between people, since the capacity for meaningful sexual experience is both an indication and an actualization of the capacity for love which this society stifles so successfully.

As "modern" women begin to recognize their own sexual potential and to demand sexual fulfilment, women begin to treat men as the object, so that we have two people, each treating the other as the object. This is natural, given that people are taught, in order to keep themselves alienated from one another, to treat other people, not as human beings but as the object of their wants and needs. The partial liberation that has taken place and is taking place for women in the sexual sphere does, however, hold out the possibility of more real human relationships between men and women. Both become equal and active participants: the potential for a mutual experience is greatly increased.

This kind of sexual liberation creates the possibility for people to unlearn those social roles which act to preserve an alienating society. Men can no longer act as conquerors, nor can women act as the dominated and conquered; this will in turn have its effect on the social roles that they must play.

Socialization of Children

Women are taught to be parasites—as Emma Goldman says—to live off men as dependent creatures. It is hardly surprising that since women are also the major socializers of children, children grow up not learning to be independent of others and able to make independent judgments about their own lives and the values of the society.

There is no particular biological reason, apart from early feeding, that women should act as the socializers of children. Indeed, the separate functions given to men and women in teaching children behaviour and in developing personality structure are in themselves evidence of the unintegrated personality structure that results from the roles of men and women in the society: the mother is the unconditional love symbol, the father that of authority. We see this also in the personality characteristics which men and women are taught—men are intellectual, strong, aggressive; women are passive, emotional, tender and so on. Such a division, biologically speaking, is of course so much nonsense.

The nuclear family, with the love symbol and the authority figure, also provides social stability in that it provides a structure in which frustration transference takes place. The man returns from work where he is unable to take out his frustrations in the appropriate place and transfers the hostility to wife and children. The mother allows this by accepting this as the male role: "Just wait until your father gets home and hears what you did—you're going to get it then." It also provides a way of socializing children that will teach them to obey authority by providing, in the early years, a complete authority system of adults which they must submit to.

In all of the areas mentioned above, biological necessity cannot explain the roles accorded to men and women. Biology is a useful excuse, since for the sake of efficiency many differentiations in social roles are made most easily in this way. However, maintenance of the social structure can also be seen as a primary cause for the division of roles between men and women that has taken place. Thus the liberation of women is a revolutionary demand in all aspects, for it demands the most complete restructuring of the social order. The realization of this would mean, in fact, human liberation.

Cultural Determination of the Role of Women

The role of woman as the centre of the family—childraiser, cook and housekeeper—and that of the man as the provider of the family has been assumed as natural. The nature of woman and of man has also been assumed. We contend that, in fact, culture could determine the exact opposite. There is no natural instinct for certain roles and personality traits.

Margaret Mead says this in her books *Sex and Temperament* and *Male and Female*. Let us review her findings. The Zuni, Arapesh, and Samoan tribes consist of men and women with the characteristics we attribute to women in our society. The women also actively enjoy sex while the men do not (Jung is turning over in his grave). The Mumdugumor tribe is the opposite—both men and women have the masculine characteristics of our society. The women, by the way, detest childbearing and childrearing (there goes the myth of maternal instinct). They are also the providers for the family. The Tchambuli and Zuni have their men raise the children. The former tribe finds men adorned with lovely ornaments, and long curls, while the women are unadorned and have shaved heads. The men spend their time with the children, doing the shopping and gossiping. The women work in the fields and forests to provide food and shelter for the family.

The other outstanding example of deviance from the norms of western society is the position of men and women in lower class Negro society in the U.S. Because of the old slave system, where the white women were allowed no freedom and black women were used by white men, black women have had a special role and a degree of freedom. There is an old Southern saying that the only free people in the South are white men and black women. A rueful addition by the white women in SNCC was, "So now we're fighting for the freedom of Negro men. When is it our turn?"

The lower class Negro *women* are the ones who can get the jobs. There are very few jobs for the men. Welfare reinforces this since women can receive welfare only when they prove they are not living with a man. Negro women are breadwinners. They are the rulers of the roost. They are assertive, active in politics within the confines of their caste society and the dominant force in their society. It is the women who are free to partake in affairs with men of other classes and colours. Men, if they remain in the family, are submissive, fearful and definitely the less favoured half of the relationship. They are also often forced to raise children.

The bulk of the membership and leadership of the Mississippi Freedom Democratic Party, the Mississippi Freedom Labor Union and the Poor People's Corporation (the only truly grass roots organizations in the South) were and are women. We mourn the loss of manhood of Negro men. It is easy to see that they have been deprived of their full humanity by the culture in which they live. Very few people mourn the loss of humanity of the exploited half of the human species—the women. Negro men are asserting their manhood in the ghettos of the U.S. Perhaps the women of the world will be asserting their womanhood soon.

Women in the New Left

We have mentioned the human condition and how we of the New Left deplore exploitation of all kinds. At the same time we realize that the revolution in this country will be a long hard pull. In order to keep the revolutionary movement alive it will be necessary that we attempt the most humane interaction. We must act as though the revolution had occurred by our relationships with one another.

We assert that SUPA people have the same hangups, frustrations and neuroses as the rest of society. One attempted solution to our lack of real ego identity was finding it within SUPA. We all know that this failed. We tried to identify with this group as if it were our family, our peer group and our society. We created father figures or allowed them to be created. While this proved harmful to all concerned, we hope that it was an experience from which we can learn. As a result of this kind of psychological seeking we never gained the principles of participatory democracy. A few people were allowed to lead. Many people were excluded from leadership. The largest excluded group was women. SUPA, in respect to women, totally accepted the mores of the dominant society.

Stokely Carmichael once said, "The only position for a woman in SNCC is prone." We cannot imagine any of the fine SUPA men uttering such a statement, but we can imagine many of them thinking it. In fact they put women in SUPA in two categories or roles—the workers and the wives.

One role for women is that of catering to the organization's men. These women maintain the stable, homey atmosphere which the radical man needs to survive. They raise the future radicals of Canada. They earn the money in the mundane jobs that our society pays people to do so the radical men can be political, creative and so forth. Of course, these relationships are ones of "freedom." But it is, in fact, a one-sided freedom and we all know which side is "free." This, we feel, is a situation not unlike that of the dominant society—"behind every successful man is a successful woman." While their real women are being women by earning money, cooking and housecleaning, their radical partners can be political and creative, write, think and ooze charisma.

But in order to do this, these men need followers and maintainers. Women in SUPA do this work. They are the typists, fundraisers and community organizers. The vast majority of community organizers were women and we must ask why. Community organizing was considered tedious. It required patience, sensitivity, understanding and more patience. It is a sad commentary that so few men felt they could do this kind of work.

Every so often one of these workers would try, through her efforts and work, to attain a position of leadership. As we all know too well, they were labelled "castrating females" and not "real women." In other words, they were no longer "good niggers." These women were forced out of the organization by various unconscious means, or accepted their subservient roles. The work of these women has been used to build a myth for SUPA but they must not try to gain recognition for this.

The myth of participatory democracy is just that, if one looks at the participation of women in SUPA. Old Leftists who agree totally with the aims and goals of SUPA are astounded that we permit the degree of male chauvinism that abounds in it. One sometimes gets the feeling that we are like a civil rights organization with a leadership of southern racists. This is disastrous for an organization. An organization that permits half its membership to be kept from using their talents and energies is in sad shape. Because of the attitude within the movement in the minds of both sexes, women are not free to think and act outside the limited role given to them in the broader society. We are allowed to speak but our thoughts are not given serious attention until expressed by a male. We are allowed sexual freedom but are still faced with a loss of respect on the part of many males if we take advantage of that freedom, or still expected to designate our "man" as our first priority. How many times have you heard a man express the sentiment that a woman in the movement is taking a particular position because that is what her "man" thinks?

As some of us women have become more aware of our intellectual and political powers we experience a loss of emotional identity in our personal lives. Men seem to find it difficult to relate to a person who combines both roles, i.e. "masculine intellectualism" and "feminine emotionalism." They insist we be one or the other.

If we refuse to be relegated to a womanly, wifely, emotional role and insist on being accepted as equally intelligent beings and capable of theoretical, strategic, and analytical work, most men will eventually accept us. But this acceptance will be on a tenuous basis while waiting for our first big slip. However, we find *then* that we are no longer "feminine" to them and must look for emotional involvements outside the left environment.

Some women react to this be reverting to the physically feminine and intellectually passive role. Hardly aware of it, they opt for the easier way to have their emotional and sexual needs fulfilled by men they respect at the expense of their chance for intellectual development.

It is our contention that until the male chauvinists of the movement understand the concept of liberation in relation to women, the most exploited members of *any* society, they will be voicing political lies.

Some movement women are ready for revolution. We have rejected many of the traditional leaders as irrelevant. We are thinking for ourselves. We are doing the necessary reading, writing, and conversing to find the analysis and theory for the task. We have the background of experience to do this. We have the frustration of being excluded to force us to do this. We are realizing that we have brains, that we can be political. It is the liberating feeling that black people have when they discover that being black is beautiful and therefore they are beautiful. It is a feeling of beauty and power. We are getting these kinds of feelings.

We are going to be the typers of letters and distributors of leaflets (hewers of wood and drawers of water) *no longer*. We are recognizing our own existential position and know the exploitations that affect us. At some time the men of the movement will have to understand our position. We are going to fight to change the atmosphere that forbids participation. We hope that those men who are excluded will join us in the fight.

FEMINIST ORGANIZATIONS AND FEMINIST PROCESS

Nancy Adamson, Linda Briskin,
Margaret McPhail

...The feminist critique of organizations did not emerge full-blown, but was pieced together over the early years of the women's movement through experimentation with alternatives. Although there is now an identifiable feminist model of organizational process, the process of experimentation and adjustment is ongoing. Fortunately, the grass-roots movement has largely resisted the pull to name one organizational structure as "correct." Instead, each organization takes the grass-roots feminist model (see below) and loosely applies it to its own analysis, goals, and strategies to create an organizational structure and process most useful to its members. Sheila Rowbotham has identified this as one of the strengths of the women's movement:

> As women encounter feminism they can make their own kinds of organising depending on their needs. It is this flexibility which it is extremely important to maintain. It means that for example groups of women artists or groups of women setting up a crèche or on the sub-committee of a trades council can decide for themselves what structure is most useful.[1]

The women's movement is not one organization, but the totality of a variety of organizations and individuals struggling to end the oppression of women. The distinction between movement and organization is an important one. An organization has structural form, organizational norms and goals, and a membership. It can be small or large, it can tend to homogeneity or heterogeneity, it can be focussed on personal or political goals or both. However it is constructed, an organization is identified by a structure, membership, politics, norms, and goals.

A movement, on the other hand, has an amorphous or fluid organizational quality; episodically, a more stable form might emerge. What holds a movement together is more ideological in nature than what is necessary to sustain an organization. So the women's movement, which really has no formal organization *per se*, is held together by a commitment to women's liberation. This is true even though what this liberation means to specific components of the women's movement may differ dramatically. Loosely, then, the ideology of women's liberation gives some coherence to the women's movement.

This chapter is about feminist organizational process. In it we are going to take the issue of feminist organization, and process out of the context of the women's movement. Although this approach separates organizations from their context, their tasks, and their strategies, it allows us to begin to examine in detail the specific organizational issues that have confronted the women's movement. While we are examining the structures themselves, it is important to remember that they exist only to facilitate the group's politics and strategies. In the women's movement we know how easy it is to be distracted from the goals by the structure.

Feminist Critiques and Models

Second-wave feminists quickly developed two different critiques of traditional organizational methods, which reflected the different origins of institutionalized and grass-roots feminisms. Each of these currents began with a critique and gradually developed a feminist model of organization and process. Organizational models included issues of leadership, membership, voting procedures, committee structure, and education of new members. Process models were designed to address the issues of power, democracy, and equality among group members. Though sometimes organization and process can be easily distinguished, often the two are closely interlinked.

Institutionalized feminism emerged from organizations such as the YWCA and the CFUW, which had traditional hierarchical organizational structures and traditional processes. Such forms include an elected executive (president, vice-president, secretary, treasurer), a committee structure, clear membership criteria (usually requiring a membership fee), and the use of *Robert's Rules of Order* to organize each meeting; decision-making is by majority vote. Because these were *women's* organizations, institutionalized feminists' experience of them was fairly positive: women were the leaders as well as the members, and women made the decisions as well as the coffee. This positive experience of traditional organizational norms helps to explain their continued use despite vociferous criticism by grass-roots feminists.

Grass-roots feminism had a very different origin from institutionalized feminism, and grass-roots feminists did not share a common experience of organizational forms. Many women who entered the grass-roots movement did so as individuals without experience in political organizations. Other grass-roots feminists came from other social movements, such as the student, native, civil-rights, anti-war, new-left, and counterculture movements of the sixties. While these movements were not associated with any particular organizational forms, the individuals who came from them into the women's liberation movement brought along a general, if often unarticulated, critique of traditional organizations. Their experiences in those groups ranged from positive—small groups and shared leadership—to negative—tightly structured organizations with élite leaderships.[2] In addition, some grass-roots feminists came from left organizations such as the Communist Party of Canada, the League for Socialist Action, and the Revolutionary Marxist Group. These women probably had the most experience with alternative organizational structures. Democratic centralism was the theoretical organizational model of left organizations, meaning, in theory, that all group members participated in making a decision (democracy) and then, once it was made, *all* members were responsible for carrying it out (centralism).[3] In practice,the democracy ranged from very traditional voting to other, more inclusive forms of decision-making.

In general, the experience of grass-roots feminists as *women* in the organizations of the 1960s social movements and left organizations was negative. Despite their critiques of the status quo, those organizations tended to be as hierarchical and male-dominated as traditional organizations. Women's experience was largely one of being members, not leaders, and of making coffee, not decisions—the reverse, as we have seen, of the experience of institutionalized feminists in their own women's organizations. For grass-roots feminists the struggle around organizational issues was in part a reaction against their experiences in other organizations.

Whatever the members' organizational experience—traditional, left, or none at all—the early years of the feminist movement were characterized by women critical of traditional organizing. For reasons discussed above, grass-roots feminists' suspicion of traditional organizational norms and leadership came out of our experience in organizations where we were denied any real access to positions of power. We rejected what we saw as the male, patriarchal, hierarchical, and élitist norms of traditional organizations as models. In the early years the question of organizational norms was high on our political agenda, and an enormous amount of time was spent developing alternatives that emerged slowly out of our feminist practice. In the mid-1960s there were *no* feminist organizations for women to join; we had to create each of the thousands of women's organizations that now exist in Canada and elsewhere. We did not like what existed, so we set out to build strong and effective alternatives.

What emerged from the feminist critique of traditional organizational forms and processes were two very different models, each suited to the politics and strategies of its originators. Institutionalized feminism retained many of the structures and processes of traditional organizations, but modified them to meet its own needs. Grass-roots feminism, on the other hand, initially rejected traditional organizational forms altogether and set out to build a new alternative. The result has come to be called "the feminist model" or "the feminist process."

1. The modified traditional feminist model

Institutionalized feminism, working largely within traditional organizations and having a strategy focused on changing "the system" from within, chose to modify traditional structures and processes to meet the needs of its members. Although these groups continued to use *Robert's Rules of Order*,[4] maintaining a hierarchical structure[5] with an elected executive and decision-making by majority vote, there was an emphasis on teaching members the rules of order and of ensuring that they were more aware of the executive's activities than in traditional organizations, and more involved. Sometimes, in groups such as NAC, the executive was gradually enlarged to include members-at-large representing regional concerns. In this case, the organization changed its structure to reflect its changing goals and strategies.

Feminists active in trade unions have attempted to work within the traditional hierarchical, male-dominated structure they found there. For many, the discovery that unions are as traditionally structured and as sexist as other institutions in our society has been discouraging;[6] these structures and attitudes often limit the possibilities for organizing women. Debbie Field has pointed out that the dilemma facing women's committees in trade unions is whether to try organizing autonomously, outside the trade-union structure, or within the structure in ways often determined by the (male) leadership.[7] Field concludes by linking the structure of women's committees to their effectiveness:

> In hindsight, and from the vantage point of no longer working at Stelco, I believe we made a mistake forming a women's committee so closely tied to the leadership. It would have been better to spend time, even a year or two, getting to know women in the plant before moving to structure a formal committee. This approach would have involved experimenting with new forms of organizing. ...

Unions could generally strengthen membership involvement if more informal methods of meeting and transmitting information were developed. Particularly when trying to mobilize women or new union members, it is important to develop creative tactics to make the union more accessible.[8]

While modified traditional forms work very effectively for some organizations, they are ineffective for others. In NAC the modified traditional structure works fairly well (although members do have criticisms)[9] because the member organizations have all agreed to the organization's goals. For trade-union women the modified traditional structures work less well, because these women are struggling with the contradictions of working in an overall organization that is male-dominated and sexist.

2. Organizing without organizations: the grass-roots feminist model

Grass-roots feminism, in contrast to institutionalized feminism, found traditional structures and processes inadequate and began to develop alternative structures and processes that have come to be called "the feminist alternative." Underlying it were three principles: a rejection of the notions of hierarchy and leadership, an emphasis on personal experience, and a belief in the importance of process. Grass-roots feminists totally rejected traditional structures and processes as fundamentally flawed and incapable of being modified to meet the needs of women. This rejection of hierarchy and leadership was a reaction to our perceived powerlessness in traditional organizations. One response was to refuse to consciously build any organization and to regard all aspects of organization—leadership, membership, structure, and decision-making—as innately oppressive to women and at odds with what the women's movement stood for. Initially feminists tried to find ways of organizing without organizations. In 1975, some five to six years after the first women's liberation organizations began in the U.S., Nancy Hartsock, an American feminist activist, wrote that "we have *only begun* to think about the way we should work in organizations with some structure, as opposed to the way we should work in small groups."[10]

As Hartsock suggests, the initial organizational structure in the grass-roots movement was the seemingly structureless small group. In Chapter 6 we discussed the importance of "the personal is political" to the grass-roots movement; this idea was very influential in how we thought about new organizational forms. It was imperative to recognize the importance of personal experience and to incorporate that into any organization. The organizational expression of this recognition was the small consciousness-raising group, which many feminists identified as basic to feminist organizing:

> The *practice* of small group consciousness raising, with its stress on examining and understanding experience and on connecting personal experience to the structures that define our lives, is the clearest expression of the method basic to feminism."[11]

The committee of the "Women Organize Alberta" conference in 1981 articulated this link between "examining and understanding experience" and "connecting previous experience to the structures in our lives":

> We feel that the act of continuously voicing our own realities and informing others of our developing understanding is an essential basis for women's organizing. ... Working from one's own interests is a personal political action in the context of an organizing process in that it potentially expresses the ways in which our realities are marked.[12]

The final principle guiding grass-roots feminist organizing was a belief in what is frequently referred to as the "collective process." Feminists from a range of backgrounds expressed the belief that it was the means, or the process, rather than the end that was central to feminism. In the late 1970s the Combahee River Collective, a small group of black American feminists, wrote:

> In the practice of our politics we do not believe that the end always justifies the means. Many reactionary and destructive acts have been done in the name of achieving "correct" political goals. As feminists we do not want to mess over people in the nature of politics. We believe in the collective process.[13]

Almost ten years later, in the mid-1980s, Gloria Steinem argued a similar place for the process in feminist practice: "The integrity of the process of change [is] part of the change itself. ... In other words, the end cannot fully justify the means. To a surprising extent, the end *is* the means."[14]

Grass-roots organizations had a particular means of operating. Typically, they were small groups of women organized collectively, with no office and no paid staff. The group met on a regular basis at a specific time, communicating with its members, and with interested women who were not members, through mailings, newsletters, and telephone networks. Membership was rarely formally defined; usually whoever came to a meeting was considered a member and could participate in all decision-making. Regular expenses, such as the cost of the meeting space and mailings, were paid for by donations from members and other interested women or organizations. The group as a whole made decisions for the organization, though sometimes a group would have a committee structure and delegate some decision-making to those committees. Groups frequently had both standing and *ad hoc* committees. The chairing of meetings was rotated among all members, agendas were prepared by the group as a whole, and minutes were sometimes kept and sometimes not. At meetings members sat in a circle.

Although the details of "feminist process" differed somewhat from group to group, its basic aspects—collective organization, no leadership, rotation of administrative tasks, agreement by consensus, and an emphasis on personal experience—were generally the same. These feminist assumptions emerged from, and are closely linked to, the two central aspects of feminist ideology: "the personal is political" and "sisterhood."

The importance of the feminist challenge to traditional structures and processes should not be underestimated. Both types of feminist organizations provided an opportunity to learn skills (for example, political organizing, lobbying, brief-writing, public speaking, administrative skills) that were frequently unavailable to women in traditional organizations. As a result women gained confidence in themselves, created alternative structures and processes, and built a powerful movement. Today, although traditional organizations are very slow to change, feminist organizational issues and questions are beginning to resonate there....

Decision-making and democracy. Out of grass-roots feminists' experience of being excluded from the power and decision-making structures within traditional organizations came a commitment to a model that included all members in decision-making. The decision-making model that seemed to best meet these criteria was consensus. Consensus allowed each woman to participate equally in decision-making; for the first time we had a say in the decisions that affected how our group functioned. Many of us learned to analyze and to strategize in those tedious but exciting meetings. The process not only allowed each woman a role in the decision-making, but meant that until each woman had agreed to the decision, the discussion continued; in other words, each decision had to be unanimous. Such decision-making was highly centralized—the entire group had to make every decision; delegation cannot exist with consensus decision-making. R. Seyd, a member of the Red Ladder Theatre collective in England in the mid-1970s, described such a group:

> Essentially, the group was structured so that every decision, however small, needed the unanimous agreement of every individual on it before it could be acted upon. Of course, in theory, this seems the perfect democratic approach. In practice it meant that those with the strongest personalities (the pushy ones) dominated the group. Through the course of an argument, those in a minority would eventually put up their hands and make the decision unanimous even when they did not agree with it, just so that the work could continue. ... When resentments built up to an intolerable level, explosions occurred, and often we would sit down for days in order to work out the problems. Because we believed there could be nothing wrong with the structure, since it was so democratic, this working-out led us into people's individual personalities and psychologies. The effect of this ultra-egalitarianism, this idealistic democracy, was in fact to individualise everything.[15]

The problem for the grass-roots women's movement was not with consensus *per se*, but rather with the way we analyzed the problems connected to it. Our fear of conflict stifled the potentially positive and creative ideas about how a group could function that might have been generated out of consensus decision-making.[16]

The grass-roots feminist belief that consensus was the "politically correct" form of feminist decision-making, together with a generalized fear of conflict, had several consequences. First, it meant that alternative models of decision-making, such as voting, committee structures, or delegation of decision-making, were rarely explored, although in practice we frequently used them—often with a sense of guilt. Second, it prevented feminists from developing a critique of consensus and thus validating the use of other forms. It also meant that women who disagreed with a general decision had to either "give in" to the group or "hold out" and stop any decision from being made—in other words, we pushed ourselves to homogeneity. For women who were new to the group, shy, or unsure of the group's politics and hence unsure of speaking, consensus decision-making reinforced the informal and unacknowledged leadership within the group. Although it appeared that all members made the decision, frequently the informal leadership was responsible. In such a situation the centralization of decision-making in the group as a whole is as problematic as the notion of consensus itself. The result was that we held ourselves hostage to our fear of conflict without understanding what was happening.

Conflict and disagreement are necessary and healthy signs that a group is functioning well. Conflict generates creativity, especially in the context of decision-making by consensus, and the resolution of conflicts can be energizing and empowering for the group. When groups create norms that discourage conflict, and when disagreement is seen as destructive to the group's unity, those members who have questions or who disagree with the generally accepted position silence themselves, usually by leaving. And the result is that, in trying to be democratic, the group comes to function in an undemocratic fashion.

The resolution of conflict in a healthy way has been difficult for many grass-roots feminist organizations, which have responded to conflict in one of two ways. Either the group would minimize the importance of dealing with conflict and maximize the importance of "getting on with it," because time was of the essence, our numbers small, and the tasks we were undertaking large, or it would focus entirely on conflict resolution and tend to turn the disagreements into personal ones. In 1978 Saskatoon Women's Liberation decided not to operate by consensus, and explained how their decision-making procedures avoided both these pitfalls: "We expect and welcome differences and debate. It can be one of our most constructive practices. We advocate majority decisions that will be acted upon (or at least not acted against) by every member of the group. Debate on the issue, though, may continue indefinitely."[17] This group also recognized the tendency to turn political differences into personality conflicts and cautioned against it. Like SWL, many grass-roots feminist organizations ceased to use a consensus model but retained the original feminist concern that every member's voice be heard.

The general approach of the grass-roots women's movement to democracy and decision-making can be seen as a form of participatory democracy. The thrust of participatory democracy is that everyone should participate in the group and that everyone is equally responsible for and to the group. Sheila Rowbotham has summed up the problems with participatory democracy:

> If you are not able to be present you can't participate. Whoever turns up next time can reverse the previous decisions. If very few people turn up they are lumbered with the responsibility. It is a very open situation and anyone with a gift for either emotional blackmail or a conviction of the need to intervene can do so without being checked by any accepted procedure. Participatory democracy only works if everyone accepts a certain give and take, a respect for one another's experience, a desire and need to remain connected. If these are not present it can be a traumatic process.[18]

2. Issues of form

The second set of issues facing feminist organizations includes type of organization, size, and homogeneity or heterogeneity. Like issues of feminist process, these choices are finally made in the context of a politic and strategy. We will now examine the general issues facing organizations in each of these areas.

Type of organization. The first question facing an organization is the range or scope of the issues it will address. It can choose to be an umbrella organization or coalition, a multi-issue, or a single-issue organization. This political and strategic decision has important organizational or structural components. All three types of organizations can be successful, as we will see below, but the organizational issues facing each are somewhat different. An umbrella organization, or coalition, is an organization of groups; it may or may not permit individual memberships.[19] Various groups agree on a basis of unity for the coalition, but each member group remains independent. One of the most effective examples in Canada is NAC, founded in 1972 and with a current membership of approximately 530 organizations, representing some three million women. The goal of such an organization must be either very specific or very general in order to hold together a range of groups that likely have more differences than similarities. Including groups with identified politics that cover the whole range of institutional and grass-roots feminisms, NAC has a general goal: to "unite women and women's groups from across the country in the struggle for equality." Such an approach allows the wide range of its member groups to work together within the context of that general goal and, at the annual general meeting of member groups, set specific policies by majority vote.

An example of an umbrella organization with a very specific goal is the Ontario Coalition for Abortion Clinics (OCAC), which focuses on the establishment and legalization of free-standing abortion clinics in the province. Like NAC, OCAC is a long-term organization with staff, membership fees, and so on. But many other coalitions are formed to work around a particular issue or to plan a particular event, and are seen as short-term from the start. In cities across Canada, for instance, coalitions are formed every year to plan celebrations for International Women's Day.

Umbrella organizations and coalitions have become an important form of feminist organization as the women's movement has come to comprise many organizations with clearly defined political analyses, strategies, and goals. The positive aspect of this way of organizing is that it focuses on what large numbers of organizations and individuals within the movement can agree on, and is thus able to validate the differences among groups while concentrating on their shared viewpoints. This type of organizing presents a powerful unified face to the world and is often effective in achieving change. The challenge is to present at the time the complexity and diversity of the women's movement.[20] As the critique of the movement by women of colour, lesbians, and disabled, francophone, native, and immigrant women shows, it has not often—some would say, rarely—been successful at balancing sisterhood and difference. As we suggested earlier, this is the current challenge facing the women's movement.

Multi-issue organizations are single groups that share a common political analysis and/or agree on a series of goals. These groups address a wide range of issues and are frequently members of coalitions. Examples include women's centres and groups that agree on a series of goals or services rather than a shared politic. For example, the Port Coquitlam Area Women's Centre states its objectives as follows:

> To be a women's drop-in, information-referral centre, serving women of all ages; to offer information and support through various programs; to offer volunteer opportunities for skill development, finding goals and breaking out of isolation; to provide a central place for women to meet; and to inform our elected representatives of the needs and concerns of the members.[21]

Another example of a multi-issue organization arising from a common political analysis is the International Women's Day Committee of Toronto, a socialist-feminist organization. The IWDC's goal is twofold: to work for "immediate concrete gains, as well as a much larger process of building alliances for a longer-term struggle for a transformed society."[22]

The strength of multi-issue organizations is that they address a range of issues from a shared political analysis and/or set of goals, and thus are able to link together the range of issues that feminism addresses and present them as a package. These organizations play an important role in linking single-issue concerns to feminism as a whole. Also, because these groups struggle to understand issues and action in the context of an overall political analysis, they have often been the initiators of important new practices. For example, in Toronto the IWDC played an important role in bringing many organizations into coalitions in the late

1970s. The group focused especially on making links with trade-union women, which in turn led them to recognize the different needs of immigrant women and, finally to recognize the importance of the issue of racism to the women's movement.

Single-issue organizations focus on *an* issue. Often these groups are made up of individuals with many different political analyses, but with agreement on the one issue and a strategy for change related to it. The single-issue group is now probably the most common type of feminist organization. The strength of these groups is that they bring a wide range of skills, experience, and numbers of members to focus on one issue. Thus the chance of "winning" is, obviously, greater than that of seeing a package of issues accepted, and single-issue groups therefore have clear successes and failures in a way that umbrella and multi-issue groups do not. And as Charlotte Bunch has said: "Women need to win.... Victories and programs, especially when linked to specific organizations, give us a clearer sense of what we can win and illustrate the plans, imagination, and changes that women will bring as they gain power."[23]

The struggle to legalize and implement midwifery in Ontario is an excellent example of a single-issue campaign led by several fairly small groups of midwives and consumers. Prior to 1986, the practice of midwifery in Ontario was in the twilight zone, neither legal or illegal. Concerned consumers and practising midwives came together to form the Midwifery Task Force and the Ontario Association of Midwives, both fairly small organizations. These groups decided on a specific focus: the legalization of midwifery as a self-regulating profession. Their struggle took place in the context of a Health Disciplines Legislation Review, without which their victory would have been much more difficult, if not impossible. This small group of activists learned the political skills of lobbying, brief-writing, and building a large base of support. In 1986 the Ontario government made midwifery legal and set up a Task Force on the Implementation of Midwifery in Ontario. Again, the midwifery community mobilized its support and has been very influential with the committee; in October 1987 the task force made recommendations that largely reflect its demands. Such "wins" are important not only because they improve the conditions of women's lives, but also because they give us a sense of our strength....

Heterogeneity/homogeneity. The issues of heterogeneity (the differences among feminists) and homogeneity (the similarities) have both arisen from our assumptions about the sisterhood of women. Grass-roots feminists are often torn between these two views of women. In the early years of this wave of the women's movement, we saw ourselves first as homogeneous—feminists, *the* women's movement, sisters; yet at the same time we experienced ourselves as heterogeneous—a wide variety of kinds of groups with differing political perspectives, objectives, and organizing methods; as lesbians and heterosexual women, as working-class and middle-class women, as white women and black women and women of colour. We are, of course, both things at once—the same and different. As we noted in Chapter 3, categories of difference are not neutral, but reflect complex relations of power. And for grass-roots feminists the understanding of difference is complex because it includes two different kinds of difference. One expression of difference is through the "politics of identity"; this includes the categories of race, class, ethnicity, and sexual orientation.[24] The other kind of difference is that of political strategies. Grass-roots feminists have had difficulty recognizing these two differences and often assumed that a political strategy flows directly from identity. Our problem has been not only a lack of understanding of our complex relationships, but also a failure to acknowledge ourselves as both homogeneous and heterogeneous. This failure is the structural expression of the feminist struggle to understand the complex relationship between sisterhood and difference.

Inside most feminist organizations that we have participated in, women have felt uncomfortable with heterogeneity, conflict, and change. The fact that these organizations too often played the role of personal networks meant that there was a drive to homogeneity, sameness, inside the organization. Groups often kept themselves small (and comfortable) by pushing out those who disagreed or who wanted to implement non-personal organizational norms. Desire for this kind of homogeneity was connected to creating a feeling of safety, which in turn was related to the role of the organization as a haven. Because differences are so threatening to a group where personal rather than political interactions dominate, it is difficult to acknowledge them openly. The more difficult this is, the less likely it is that the organization will be able to develop norms to deal with the differences.

The most recent example of this type of issue is the critique of the women's movement by women of colour. Black women, Native women, and other women of colour have argued for the centrality of their difference—race—to their feminist politics. The issues raised by women of colour are questions of power relations, and they remind us that organizational structures and processes, even feminist ones, are not neutral. Power relations are built into those structures and processes, and one of our tasks as feminists is to understand and expose them. Women of colour have criticized feminist structures and processes for allowing those power relations to exclude them:

> I've been working in women's organizations for years and I think there has been a serious attempt to try and have structures that are quite contrary to hierarchical, patriarchal structures. That is something we do not have in our history that we can build from. At the same time, there are things that are quite manipulative of immigrant women. On the one hand, you rotate chairs, minute taking, and so on, so that there will be some level of skill sharing between all members of the collective. There are clearing sessions where people can talk about how one person got to monopolize the chair. So there is some room to raise issues, but there are unspoken leaders . . . I feel that these women do manipulate the young, new, naive women in the group. You have to know how to talk like them, you have to be articulate, you have to know when to raise your voice.
>
> When I came over here, one of the things I didn't know was how meetings were conducted. I had never heard of *Robert's Rules* so I didn't know you had to speak through the chair. You couldn't come in and just say what you wanted to say. I was rendered completely neutralized, completely powerless by the structure of the meeting.[25]

For many of the reasons discussed above, women's organizations continue to have difficulty translating an anti-racist politic into concrete behavioural and structural changes. While this is a difficult process, it is a necessary one.

Socialist Feminism and Issues of Organization

As we discussed in Chapter 3, the socialist-feminist politic is based on a radical critique of the entire society, in particular of ideological practices, relations of power, and existing institutions. Our particular dilemma as socialist feminists is to combine diversity with unity, wide scope with focused action, and participation with direction. For socialist feminists, the feminist model of organization and process must be placed within this context as we try to avoid both marginalization and institutionalization.

Successful socialist feminism, as we noted in Chapter 5, depends on balancing a politic of mainstreaming and a politic of disengagement, and thus avoiding both marginalization and institutionalization. It is this unique pattern that helps to explain the difficulties of building socialist-feminist organizations, which must accommodate both the "inside" and the "outside" dimensions of the socialist-feminist task.[26] Socialist feminists face three dilemmas in building organizations, and they emerge directly out of our politic and practice.

In the first place, the concomitant pulls of disengagement and mainstreaming create a dilemma about what kinds of organizations are appropriate. Disengagement suggests the building of specifically socialist-feminist organizations. These might take the form of socialist-feminist political organizations, such as the International Women's Day Committee of Toronto or Bread and Roses of Vancouver, or a feminist trade union such as SORWUC.[27] Mainstreaming suggests entering into and participating in mainstream organizations from the standpoint of a socialist-feminist politic. This can take the form of organizing a women's caucus or committee inside a mainstream institution like a trade union. Inside such an organization (for example, the Toronto-based Action Day Care) socialist feminists, often unnamed as such, would fight for better day-care.

Although these choices are not necessarily mutually exclusive, it is difficult to sustain both strategies at once, as the above examples suggest. And when the decision is to disengage and build alternative organizations, the latter are often marginalized; SORWUC provides a clear and somewhat painful example of this process.[28] If the choice is to mainstream, co-optation and institutionalization often occur; the difficulty faced by trade-union women's committees in sustaining their challenge to the goals and practices of unions is one example.[29] Another is the difficulty Action Day Care faces in maintaining a radical position.

For socialist feminism the more difficult part of this dilemma is often that of marginalization. Many socialist feminists, among them Charlotte Bunch, argue that one way of building power is by creating alternative institutions "such as health clinics that give us more control over our bodies or women's media that control our communications with the public." However, Bunch recognizes the danger of such alternatives, and adds that, "alternative institutions should not be havens of retreat, but challenges that weaken male power over our lives."[30] Alison Jaggar argues that in that sentence Bunch sums up the difference between socialist-feminist ideas of building alternative institutions and the radical-feminist conception of a woman-culture, which would allow women to withdraw from the dominant culture.[31]

Second, the centrality of difference to the socialist-feminist politic and practice creates some contradictions around the building of socialist-feminist organizations. A politic of building sisterhood on the basis of difference is expressed organizationally through alliances and coalitions, rather than through large, homogeneous political organizations.

Inside such coalitions socialist feminists are torn between two political tasks: the need to build a broad-based, heterogeneous mass movement that can challenge dominant ideologies and practices (mainstream) and the need to win women to an alternative socialist-feminist vision (disengage). The first goal lends itself to the building of alliances constructed on a limited basis of unity, which would not offer much opportunity to highlight socialist feminism; the second suggests an explicit focus on building a socialist-feminist organization or current—that is, attempting to win women to a socialist-feminist perspective. The former functions in a politically heterogeneous environment; the latter aims for a degree of homogeneity and is, by definition, threatening to the coalition process.

Finally, the socialist-feminist belief in the necessity of a fundamental social transformation that challenges not only gender relations but also relations of class, race, and sexual orientation implies a commitment to the building or a mass heterogenous political movement. In principle this means forming alliances with organizations outside the women's movement, such as trade unions and progressive community groups that organize around peace, anti-racism, and environmental issues, and, if they exist, parliamentary and extra-parliamentary socialist and communist parties. In all these cases such a commitment also means organizing with men, which raises complex questions about the relation between the building of such alliances and autonomous feminist organizing.

The building of these kinds of alliances also constantly raises the strategic question of whether it is more appropriate to build socialist-feminist organizations or to enter into existing organizations and transform them. One of the dilemmas that arises here concerns the internal process of organizations. Feminists have developed an extensive critique of the process and practices of most social institutions (including the democratic centralism of far-left organizations), and have attempted to develop, although not always successfully, an alternative feminist process. The fact that feminist process is most easily developed and expressed in alternative organizations presents some difficulties for socialist feminists, who reject alternatives as an adequate political strategy and yet who simultaneously reject the practices of mainstream institutions.

As socialist feminists our particular strength in taking feminism out into the world is in the area of education. Socialist feminism unmasks how the system works; makes known the limitations of conventional political routes, thus empowering people with that information and perspective; and links one feminist issue to another to provide a complete picture of women's oppression. However, recruitment to socialist-feminist organizations is difficult because of anti-communism, the fear of change, and other factors discussed in Chapter 4. That difficulty might suggest that socialist-feminist organizations need to concentrate on the areas of education and outreach.

It is not so easy to juggle these various options, and in Canada, certainly, this has most often meant that building explicitly socialist-feminist organizations has not been a priority for many socialist feminists?[32] Moreover, it is important to point out that there is no consensus among socialist feminists that creating such organizations *per se* is the best strategy. And of course, at different historical and political conjunctures such organizations might be more or less viable. Notwithstanding, it is useful to situate the discussion of whether or not socialist feminists should focus their political energy on building such organizations inside the particular dilemmas that face such a project. In fact, it might be appropriate to suggest that part of the reason such organizations have so often failed, or that the project has been avoided, is precisely the contradictory nature of the task. Building socialist-feminist organizations is complex because we are pulled in different directions.

Conclusion

In building organizations, grass-roots feminists frequently got caught up in the organizational process itself, even when the organization in question was no longer effective. Organizational process can and does obscure the larger political goals that organizations set themselves, and also leads us to lose sight of the movement we are building. As we noted earlier, organizations are not a substitute for a movement, they are part of a movement; movement is a larger category, which gives meaning to individual organizations.

Organizational structures and processes do not exist for themselves. They have a purpose: to facilitate the political effectiveness of the organization. It is in the context of a particular group's political analysis and strategy that its structure and process must be evaluated. And though there has been a tendency in the grass-roots movement to regard "feminist process" as the correct way to structure every organization, the discussion above has demonstrated that different structures and processes are suited to different agendas. No one structure can meet the variety of political agendas found in the women's movement.

For socialist feminists, the strengths and weaknesses of feminist organizational models can best be understood in terms of the balance between disengagement on the one hand and mainstreaming on the other. Certainly the feminist model was a rejection of mainstream organizational theories and attempted to provide alternative structures using feminist process; as such it was a politic of disengagement. The danger of such a politic is that it can easily lead to marginalization and invisibility. And in fact, as we have seen, the practice of feminist process has been contradictory: while the theory operated as a politic of disengagement, the practice was often one of marginalization.

ENDNOTES

1.   Sheila Rowbotham, "The Women's Movement and Organising for Socialism," in Sheila Rowbotham, Lynne Segal, and Hilary Wainwright, *Beyond the Fragments* (London: Islington Community Press, 1979), 40-1.

2.   See Jo Freeman, "The Tyranny of Structurelessness" in Jane P. Jaquette, ed., *Women in Politics* (New York: John Wiley & Sons, 1974), 202-14 and Myrna Kostash, *Long Way from Home* (Toronto: Lorimer, 1980) for more detailed discussion.

3.   For a fuller discussion of democratic centralism, see Rowbotham et al., *Beyond the Fragments*.

4.   *Robert's Rules of Order* was first published in 1876 by U.S. Army general Henry M. Robert. Part I is subtitled "A Compendium of Parliamentary Law, Based Upon the Rules and Practise of Congress," and Part II is subtitled "Organization and Conduct of Business: A Simple Explanation of the Methods of Organizing and Conducting the Business of Societies, Conventions, and other Deliberative Assemblies." In North America these rules of order have come to be regarded as the standards for running a meeting and are very widely used. They are periodically revised and updated, and many organizations adapt them to their own needs.

5.   Hierarchical organizations have a structure that gives the most power to one or a few people and then gradually spreads different amounts of power to increasingly larger groups. There is a clear sense of power and authority *descending* from a few at the top down to those at the bottom.

6.   Linda Briskin. "Women and Unions in Canada: A Statistical Overview" in Linda Briskin and Lynda Yanz. eds., *Union Sisters* (Toronto: Women's Press, 1983); Julie White, *Women and Unions* (Ottawa: Canadian Advisory Council on the Status of Women, 1980).

7.   Debbie Field. "The Dilemma Facing Women's Committees," in Briskin and Yanz, *Union Sisters*, 293-306.

8.   Ibid., 300.

9. For example, see OCAC's proposal for structural change at the 1986 annual general meeting (CWMA/ACMF).

10. Nancy Hartsock, "Fundamental Feminism: Process and Perspective," *Quest* vol. 2, no. 2 (Fall 1975), 78 (emphasis added).

11. Josephine Donovan, *Feminist Theory* (New York: Frederick Ungar, 1985), 85.

12. Alice de Wolff, Judy Dragon, Julie Ann Le Gras, Trudy Richardson, Sandy Susut, Derwyn Whitehead, "Women Organize Alberta: Discussion Paper" (1981), 2 (CWMA/ACMF).

13. Donovan, *Feminist Theory*, 87.

14. Ibid.

15. C. Landry, D. Morley. R. Southwood, P. Wright, *What a Way to Run a Railroad: An Analysis of Radical Failure* (London: Comedia Publishing Group, 1985), 11-12.

16. For examples of forms of conflict resolution see Joan Holmes and Joan Riggs. "Feminist Organization Part II: Conflict and Change," *Breaking the Silence* vol. 3, no. 1 (Fall 1984), 16-22.

17. CWMA/ACME SWI papers. Constitutional Proposal, Jan. 1978. 4.

18. C. Landry, D. Morley. R. Southwood, P. Wright, *What a Way to Run a Railroad: An Analysis of Radical Failure* (London: Comedia Publishing Group, 1985), 11-12.

19. For a fuller discussion of this topic see Lorna Weir, "Tit for Tat: Coalition Politics," *Broadside* vol. 3, no. 4 (Feb. 1992), 10-11.

20. See Weir, "Tit for Tat," for the challenges of working with non-feminist groups in a coalition.

21. Bev Le François and Helga Martens Enns, *Story of a Woman's Centre* (Vancouver: Press Gang, 1979). 28-9.

22. Egan, 113.

23. Quoted in Allison Jaggar, *Feminist Politics and Human Nature* (Totowa, N.J.: Rowman and Allanheld, 1983). 335-6.

24. Linda Briskin, "Socialist Feminism: From the Standpoint of Practice" (paper given at the 3rd International Interdisciplinary Congress on Women, Dublin, Ireland, July 1987). 3-4.

25. Organizing Exclusion: Race, Class, Community and the White Women's Movement." *Fireweed: A Feminist Quarterly* no. 17 (Summer/Fall. 1983), 57, 59.

26. It is useful to note a distinction between organizing for change and building organizations to facilitate that process.

27. For a detailed discussion of the attempts of SORWUC (Service Office and Retail Workers Union of Canada) to organize the bank workers, see The Bank Book Collective, *An Account to Settle* (Vancouver: Press Gang, 1979).

28. Rosemary Warskett, in "Legitimate and Illegitimate Unionism: the Case of SORWUC and Bankworker Unionization" (unpublished paper prepared for the Political Economy Sessions of the Canadian Political Science Association, June 1987) documents the process of SORWUC's being constructed as an "illegitimate" union. In the language of this book, we might label this process marginalization.

29. For a discussion of the difficulties of building trade-union women's committees and the conditions under which such committees get coupled, see Field, "Dilemma Facing Women's Committees."

30. Quoted in Jaggar, *Feminist Politics*, 336.

31. Ibid., 336.

32. Some exceptions are Saskatoon Women's Liberation, the International Women's Day Committee of Toronto, and Bread and Roses of Vancouver.

THE INTELLECTUAL AND POLITICAL CONTEXT FOR THE DEVELOPMENT OF NAC

Jill Vickers, Pauline Rankin, Christine Appelle

Because the resurgence of feminism occurred in most Western industrialized countries at approximately the same time, studies of contemporary women's movements have tended to stress the things those movements have in common. By contrast, it is the purpose of this study to demonstrate the unique course that the English-Canadian women's movement took as it interacted with the federal state through its umbrella organization, NAC. This emphasis on differences rather than similarities is especially important for English-Canadian women, who have generally been so overshadowed by the U.S. movement that they lack a full sense of the unique achievements of their activism. Moreover, differences in each country's political opportunity structures, that is, its "institutions, alignments and ideology, have patterned the development, goals and values of feminist activists in each nation" (Gelb 1989:2). The structure of women's movements and the systemic characteristics of the country in which they operate also shape and constrain opportunities for effective action in each country....

An Overview of Women's Movements and the National Action Committee

In Western Europe and North America, the evidence is that women participate more in movements for change than men do, while men are vastly overrepresented in the offices of formal politics (Lovenduski 1986; McAdam 1988). It would be wrong, however, to assume that women *choose* one arena over the other. As Lovenduski (1986) argues, "It is because women are marginal to the political system and women's causes are seen as peripheral that it has been necessary for feminists to opt for social movement forms" (62). Traditional analysis stresses the spontaneity of movements, their limited capacity for organization, and their demise as the people, values, and demands they represent are integrated into the official political system. In subsequent chapters we will explore in detail some of the problems inherent in this characterization; here, we simply posit our hypothesis that women's movements represent values and demands that currently cannot be integrated fully into the official political systems of the liberal democracies. For this reason, we argue that, to be successful, women's movements must become institutionalized to ensure a continuity of activity over long periods of time.

Three distinct types of movements for change were evident in Canadian politics during the 1970s and 1980s: (1) equality-seeking movements, which include women's movements; (2) quality-of-life movement, wherein people seek change in such areas as peace and the environment directly, rather than under the auspices of a political party; and (3) reactionary movements, which arose in opposition to the first two types and were motivated by nostalgia for an idealized past. In each case, the movement existed because people shared a vision of change (or restoration) and because existing political parties could not accommodate the ideas, personnel, and energy involved. Women's movements have been at the centre of a new political dynamic in Canada that pertains to the search for equality. Their relative legitimacy and organizational stability has allowed them to play a key role in creating and sustaining coalitions with other equality seekers to achieve concrete ends that would improve the lives of otherwise marginalized people.

The attempt to understand women's movements in Canada is greatly complicated by their complexity. Already a highly decentralized state, Canada has spawned many movements at the provincial and territorial level. In the federal context, at least three distinct women's movements must currently be recognized: the movement we have chosen to term the "English-Canadian movement"; the francophone movement in Québec; and the movements of First Nations women. In ideological terms, one common approach has been to categorize feminism as liberal, leftist, or radical, largely ignoring organizational manifestations. Since it is our conviction that women's movements are shaped by the states to which they relate and by the political culture associated with those states, we have chosen to focus on the character of the movement in Canada as manifested in the political behaviour of its largest organization.

Understanding current women's movements is further complicated by the survival of feminist values articulated primarily in the language of responsibilities rather than in the language of rights (Vickers 1989). Such values survive in groups that were formed during the so-called first wave of women's mobilization, some of which are now a hundred years old. Groups such as the Federated Women's Institutes and the National Council of Women always involved women in Canadian politics even during periods of limited mobilization. These more traditional groups, revitalized by the Royal Commission on the Status of Women's energetic cross-country tour of the late 1960s, played a major role in shaping the current movement, endowing it not only with a capacity for organization, coalition building, and interaction with government, but also with a reformist stance, a preoccupation with service, and a weakness in theoretical development. To the extent that these groups participated in NAC—and many did—their values, rooted in an earlier era, coexisted with contemporary feminist values.

In the course of our research, we isolated some of the basic traits that characterized the English-Canadian women's movement as it related to the federal state between 1965 and 1985. Many of them reflect the mix of traditional and contemporary values and approaches that we have just described. For example, the movement was ideologically diverse, yet capable of maintaining coalitions. Far from rejecting involvement with the state, it relied heavily on government funding; nevertheless, it was both autonomous and multipartisan. Largely reformist in its goals, it displayed a high level of solidarity across class lines and generations. It focused on the federal government as best able to provide social support programs for women. Finally, its political culture is best described as radical liberalism. We shall now examine these characteristics in greater detail.

Many European observers distinguish between two "wings" in current women's movements: an older, *women's rights* wing and a younger, *women's liberation* wing (Lovenduski 1986). Jo Freeman, observing the U.S. movement, argued for a similar model. She saw the liberation groups as emphasizing their radicalism, fearing co-optation, seeing institutional structures as barriers, and rejecting accommodation with the state. The rights groups, by contrast, tended to think in terms of effectiveness and were interested in working within the existing political system (Freeman 1983). While these positions are also evident in the English-Canadian movement, they exist as tendencies present to some degree in most of the autonomous groups and institutions of the movement rather than as organizationally separate wings.

Ideologically, the English-Canadian movement is diverse, but it also displays a significant capacity to undertake collaborative action, maintain coalitions, and hold allegiances to several distinct political positions at the same time. The traditional political spectrum represented in the movement ranges from "red Tory," free enterprise, and libertarian feminism through liberal feminism to socialist, working class, and Marxist feminism. A second political spectrum was created initially around women's experiences of sexuality. In addition, there are integrative feminists, described by Angela Miles (1982:23) as women who "welcome the tremendous variety of participants, activities and thinking in the current movement and take relatively non-sectarian positions ... they tend to welcome diversity and debate as important contributions to growth and development." What motivates integrative feminists, in Miles's view, is "their sense of feminism as a potentially complete politics" that "unites them more closely with each other ... than with other feminists of like self-definition." (12) This strain of integrative feminism is one feature of the English-Canadian movement that enables it to build and maintain diverse coalitions and organizations that can encompass ideological difference. NAC, of course, is an organizational product of this aspect of the movement.

Politically, the movement is both autonomous—that is, independent of the state—and multipartisan, and both features have been a source of controversy. Sylvia Bashevkin (1985:4) identifies a tension between a desire for independence and an acceptance of partisanship in the political history of women in English Canada, and argues that this tension has limited women's political power. For example, many suffragists rejected political parties as corrupt and immoral devices fuelled by booze and male greed; more recently, many women working in small local groups have rejected the traditional structures of politics, including parties, in equally sweeping terms. As a result, fewer women than men seek to hold office in official politics. The desire to maintain an autonomous women's movement, however, has not involved a total rejection of the formal political arena. Even small groups who focus mainly on local projects have found occasion to join together in networks in order to influence government. Anne Collins (1985) has established that the first nationwide feminist network of small groups emerged as a direct result of the abortion issue and in response to the 1970 Abortion Caravan. Significantly, a number of networks comprising small grassroots groups, along with many individual groups, belonged to NAC during the period of study.

English-Canadian women who are active in official politics and political parties often rely on the autonomous women's movement as a source of ideas, analysis, and political leverage. The fact that there are feminists in all federal political parties and that each party has some sort of internal caucus or group devoted to feminist issues suggests a determination within the movement to reject an either/or choice. Angela Miles (1984) argues that women can and must insist on the right to participate fully in existing political institutions, while at the same time challenging their character and underlying principles. To follow this course, women have to operate on two fronts simultaneously: they must build autonomous, women-centred institutions in which to develop alternative ways of doing politics and they must be present, to whatever extent possible, within existing political institutions, to participate as women and thereby to challenge the logic of those structures. This dual focus need not be maintained by all individuals or groups; rather, the movement as a whole should operate on both fronts. Certainly, in the 1970s and 1980s the presence in NAC of individuals and groups with experience working in the official political system and from all the political parties reflected this dual focus and enhanced NAC's political skills.

The English-Canadian movement has been largely reformist in character: There have been no elements advocating the use of violence as there were, for example, in Italy (Lovenduski 1986), nor have the transformative goals in the programs of many of the more radical groups involved revolutionary change, whether violent or non-violent in conception (Adamson et al. 1988). During our period of study, these groups aimed at the transformation of society either through the creation of a counter-culture or through changes in individual consciousness. They did not aspire to some mirror-image system that would simply reverse roles, making women the power holders. They were, however, willing to use non-traditional tactics in their projects of transformation.

Although the English-Canadian movement has been largely reformist and transformative in character, it has also been progressive in many important ways. In particular, it displayed stronger solidarity across class lines and across generations than has either the U.S. or the British movement. Moreover, NAC's membership has included a number of unions, union caucuses, and other groups created by working-class feminists. NAC's second president, Grace Hartman, came from, and went on to lead, the Canadian Union of Public Employees (CUPE). Madeleine Parent, a beloved (or, depending on one's point of view, notorious) union leader from Québec, also played an important role in the organization. (Both these women were jailed for their union activities at one time or another.) The cross-generation continuity that has characterized the movement resulted, in part, from the involvement of first-wave groups in its alliances and coalitions. Perhaps more significant, however, was the presence of a transitional generation of women bridging the early and later periods of mobilization, women who passed their experiences on to the generation that came of age politically in the 1960s and 1970s. This transitional generation founded the Congress of Canadian Women in the 1950s and the Voice of Women in the 1960s. Many of its members remained active in NAC, and one, Kay Macpherson, became NAC's fourth chair.

Nevertheless, some participants of the movement have been very conscious of the limits of its progressive tendencies. For example, Lynn McDonald (1979:39), NAC's fifth president, wrote that "[while the movement] has not been inordinately concerned with the demands of middle class women ... neither has it gone so far as to challenge such basic institutions as private property." Margrit Eichler (1983), in her survey of NAC policy on the institution of the family and on the stay-at-home mother, argued that NAC followed a far less radical line in relation to the family than did feminists in Britain or the United States. This moderation on some key issues has often been seen as the inevitable dilution of positions that occurs when feminists of different theoretical stripes operate within a single organization. Other observers, however, have pointed to the moderating effects of certain characteristics unique to the English-Canadian movement, such as its ready acceptance of state funding, its service orientation, and its focus on the state as the primary instrument of change.

Historically, women's organizations in English Canada provided an alternative forum in which women could develop and debate public policy (Strong-Boag 1986). Many of the groups formed during the first wave of mobilization met annually with the federal cabinet, and several were designated to represent the government at the United Nations. Given this tradition, along with the strong intergenerational continuity that characterized the movement, it is not surprising that many of the women involved at the start of the wave of mobilization that began in the 1960s looked to the government as their initial policy focus.

The movement's tendency to see government as an instrument of change, combined with its propensity for creating coalitions, formed the basis on which institutions such as NAC could develop. A coalition of thirty-four traditional women's groups from both English and French Canada, formed in 1966, sought and obtained a Royal Commission on the Status of Women. With the establishment of the commission, many movement groups adopted a strategy that treated the commission's report as the focal point of their activity. The commission "received 468 briefs, more than 468 letters of opinion, and heard more than 890 witnesses during public hearings held in fourteen cities across the country" (Kome 1985:87).

While some have argued that the report, with its 167 recommendations, "became the blueprint for mainstream feminist activism during the 1970s" (Kome 1985:87-8), it was criticized by many of the new generation of feminists for failing to identify some of the basic elements of women's oppression. Its analysis of causes satisfied neither radical nor left-wing feminists. Although some representatives of the more radical groups presented briefs, the commission's overall approach was reformist, and it remained silent on certain key issues, such as violence against women and lesbian rights.

Some supporters of the commission's report praised it precisely because it did not offer a radical analysis. Nonetheless, Anthony Westell, writing in the *Toronto Star*, saw it as "A BOMBSHELL," "a political blockbuster," and "packed with more explosive potential than any device manufactured by terrorists." Westell concluded that, "as a call to revolution, hopefully a quiet one, it is more persuasive than any FLQ manifesto" (cited in Bird 1974:302). In Québec, although few observers found its recommendations radical, the report aroused ferment among women's associations just as it did in English Canada (Dumont et al. 1987). On balance, the judgment on the report was positive: "If we view the RCSW as an arm, or vehicle, of the women's movement, we must agree with feminist critics that it failed to adequately reflect feminist concerns and commitments. If, on the other hand, we view the RCSW as a step in the Canadian policy-making process, we cannot judge its composition deficient simply because it provided no representation for militant feminists" (Morris 1982:161).

With a focal document in place, both the English-Canadian and the Québec movements created yet another coalition, this time to establish a permanent structure to monitor the implementation of the Royal Commission's recommendations. The organization, created out of a process of interaction and conflict at the "Strategy for Change" conference in 1972, was NAC.

By 1972, groups associated with what was then called the women's liberation movement were sufficiently active in the large cities to be represented on the conference planning committee, and many were present at the founding conference itself. The new organization, however, relied heavily on Canadian women's past experiences in developing its political culture. Its umbrella structure was anchored by women from the National Ad Hoc Committee on the Status of Women, which included a coalition of groups experienced in federal politics. (As a result of their experience with "Cabinet Days," many of these women were familiar with the conventions governing polite interaction with politicians.) The newest elements in the movement were to be represented in NAC, but they were still a clear minority. We refer to them collectively as "grass-roots" groups—a myriad of small groups organized for specific purposes, from consciousness raising to undertaking local direct-action projects or initiating education in local workplaces. We distinguish them from the more traditionally organized groups that focused on interaction with governments. In time, these new groups developed an analysis of the oppression of women that was distinctly different from that of the royal commission, and they thereby came to represent a radical and leftist grass roots grafted on to NAC's founding coalition. Initially an organization of convenience, NAC became the arena in which such conflicting understandings of the condition of women could be debated and explored. As a result, it came to take on a unique role as a "parliament of women."

During this time, the various women's groups that existed in the United States remained ideologically and structurally separate (Ferguson 1984), despite the fact that they were reacting to many of the same social pressures and were exposed to a similar range of theoretical interpretations of women's subordination or oppression as were women in Canada (Macpherson and Sears 1976; Richardson 1983). What was it, then, about the environment in Canada that permitted enough cooperation across generational, ideological, and, at least initially, language lines to make possible the creation of an autonomous umbrella organization in which many could participate? Certainly, Canada's sparse population in relation to its vast land mass worked against the creation of ideologically distinct groups and services (Kostash 1980; McDonald 1979). But even in a large, densely populated metropolitan centre like Montreal, U.S. anthropologist Joan Richardson (1983:29) was surprised to find that there was no unbridgeable gulf in the 1970s between anglophone women's-rights organizations and radical-feminist groups. She argues (somewhat disapprovingly from her U.S. perspective) that "there is far too much borrowing from a variety of political sources and an absence of the terrific fear and antagonism which characterized U.S. feminist activity in the 1960s and 70s to allow for the construction of mutually exclusive categories." Historically, then, ideology has not been the central structural barrier in English-Canadian feminist organizing (although ideology does hold sway with some force within the francophone movement in Québec [Maroney 1988]). Furthermore, the fact that many of the movement's groups and activities were funded by some level of government may have resulted in their depoliticization, making cooperation easier. In 1986, more than seven hundred groups were receiving funding from the federal Secretary of State's Women's Program (Emergency Consultation of Women's Groups 1986). (At this time, there were at least two thousand groups that could be considered part of the women's movement [Burt 1986a].) Although it enabled many groups and services to develop to the stage of viability, the granting process reinforced the service components of projects and downplayed their political aspects. Richardson (1983:37) argued that "the general lack of initiative the groups demonstrated in devising stable and independent sources of funding also curtailed their social impact on the local environment and circumvented a valuable opportunity to incorporate more women in the movement."

The issue of funding and its effects was particularly critical for NAC during the period studied. NAC's members were groups, themselves already strapped for money. Government funding was a logical option and, in its fundraising efforts, NAC typically emphasized the government's obligation to support its representational costs. The organization's case was supported by the existing generous tax credit to federal political parties, which faced similar representational costs. Given the country's vast territory and sparse population, few pan-Canadian or even provincial/territorial groups could survive without government support. And government support remained another barrier to cooperation: it diminished competition among groups for funding from private sources. The federal government, moreover, encouraged cooperation in many ways.

Another characteristic of the English-Canadian women's movement was its strong service orientation. This was attributable, in part, to the availability of state funding for service projects, but it also reflected a strong tradition in Canadian women's political culture of women organizing locally to construct the services they, their families, and their communities needed (Andrew 1984; Vickers 1988a). In fact, the attitude towards the provision of service within the women's movement is one point of common perspective between feminists of the first and second waves of mobilization. Again, sparse population and vast territory meant that the provision of services had to be shared by people with quite different ideologies. Increasingly, the provision of services in small communities is even coming to require cooperation between feminists and anti-feminists (Angela Miles, personal communication to Jill Vickers, 1987)....

The English-Canadian women's movement has also been characterized by its centralized nature and its centrist orientation. Although the francophone movement in Québec considered the Québec state more progressive on equality issues and more open to feminist influence than the federal government, women in English Canada during the period studied considered the latter to be more progressive than most provincial/territorial governments. (The recent election of NDP governments in three provinces may cause this view to change.) In part, this centrist orientation reflected the symbiotic relationship that developed between the long-tenured Liberal government and a pan-Canadian women's movement that Liberals viewed as a positive force for unity with Québec. It also reflected the fact that the movement's focal document was the product of a federal royal commission and that the commission's recommendations applied primarily within the jurisdiction. Finally, the movement's centrism was attributable to the nature of Canadian federalism and the division of powers between the levels of government that put criminal justice (encompassing rape, pornography, prostitution, and abortion), constitutional matters, and most economic policies in the federal arena.

Adjusting to the environment of decentralization that has been encouraged by the Progressive Conservative government since its election in 1984 is possibly one of the greatest challenges facing NAC. Indeed, the free-trade debate and the constitutional talks reflected potential shifts in the power structure of Canadian politics that could leave a centrist women's movement targeting the wrong level of government. NAC's umbrella structure has been most effective in managing coalitions in relation to the centre of the federal system. By contrast, a chapter-based organization such as the National Organization of Women (NOW) in the United States, which mobilizes women at the local and state levels in ways an umbrella structure cannot, might be a better model in a decentralized federation. In addition, the English-Canadian movement is struggling to make common cause with many groups of newly mobilized women. These groups, which include women from racial minorities, lesbians, immigrants, prostitutes, battered women, and women with disabilities, see organizations such as NAC as mainstream and privileged, and meet their expressions of "concern" with demands for full access and equal treatment. The resulting politics of increased diversity within the English-Canadian women's movement has given governments a pretext for attempting to disrupt the cohesion and solidarity that the movement has managed to achieve.

Canadian Political Culture and Canadian Women's Movements

Canadian women's movements have always been somewhat overshadowed by their U.S. counterparts. The media invariably assume that the movements in the two countries are similar, if not identical, when in fact they are very different. As we had already noted, the English-Canadian movement has been skilled at coalition building and management, developing a multipartisan approach, a reliance on government funding, and a service orientation. All of these features are in distinct contrast to the U.S. pattern. Of course, U.S. women did not choose their options any more than Canadian women chose theirs. Rather, the political cultures of their respective societies and the political environments of their respective states have had an enormous influence on the shape of both countries' women's movements.

We understand political culture to encompass (1) norms and values about how to conduct politics; (2) understandings about the nature of politics; and (3) values about the proper limits of political action. Substantial political change, such as that sought by feminists, cannot be sustained without a basis in political culture, and consequently, every aspect of political culture can potentially be a contested zone from a women-centred perspective.

In this section, we argue that the English-Canadian movement's acceptance of radical liberalism as its operational code made possible the strong coalition-building behaviour that would begin to make women matter in federal politics. Radical liberalism, however, involved values that were somewhat familiar in Canada. NAC itself would have been impossible without this basis in Canadian political culture. By contrast, while the values about how to conduct politics that were developed by radical feminism in the United States reflected the character of U.S. politics, they were in conflict with many key aspects of Canadian political culture. In particular, the capacity of coalitions and umbrella organizations to operate effectively in the politics of the federal state would potentially have been threatened by this U.S. value system. An indigenous feminist political culture, however, was also developing, building on values from the earlier, local feminist traditions in Canada. Even among the women who worked within political parties, feminist values that had developed out of Canadian experience were taking root....

Women's Political Culture

In this section, we examine the values of political culture that were accepted by the member groups and activists of NAC. ...Given the importance of the revitalized traditional groups in NAC's original coalition, we will first explore the nature of women's political culture during the first seven decades of the movement's history. Once most Canadian women achieved the right to vote, what values did they hold about how to conduct politics? What did they think was political and what things did they think were properly left beyond the scope of politics?

In 1975, Thelma McCormack argued as follows:

> Women live in a different political culture from men, a culture based on differences in political socialization ... differences in political opportunity structures, and the way in which

the media of communication define each of them. Together, and reinforcing each other, these add up to a female design for political living that is dissimilar from that of the male. Long before a woman reaches voting age or is even told that politics is a "man's world," she can see that government is a male preserve. (25)

What McCormack brought home to observers was that, as a consequence of the over-whelmingly male nature of all of the state's institutions and of the dominant political system, women lived, quite literally, in a different political world than men. They conceived of politics essentially as a spectator sport. And, as McCormack also reminds us, men do more than dominate the *conduct* of politics; as journalists, political writers, and political scientists, they also dominate the *interpretation* of it. The inequality of the two political cultures means that men, "who are the 'haves,' are in a position to discredit the political behaviour and political insights of women without ever having to reflect on their own" (26).

Male political culture is lodged in formal political institutions, which perpetuate themselves and their values through the law and longevity. Many contemporary women, liberated by the realization that these institutions are neither natural nor inevitable, readily make a distinction between the "Big *P*" *Politics* of Parliament and elections and the "small *p*" *politics* of organizing to get things done in their communities (CRIAW 1987; Vickers 1988a). Linda Christiansen-Ruffman (1982) sees women's experience of local, volunteer activities as the source of their broader conception of what is political, and describes women's political culture as "rooted in the social organization of women's experience, which involves the nurturing of children and the organization of the family" (8). She defines political action as "all actions aimed at changing or maintaining the established order" (3).

In an empirical test of the existence of two political cultures, Sandra Burt (1986a:57) found that the men and women she interviewed displayed different values of political culture in three areas: (1) the meaning of politics; (2) the reasons for political participation, and (3) conceptions of the ideal citizen in a democracy. (Interestingly, she also found that, in addition to differences between women's and men's values, there were differences between the values of activists involved in traditional women's groups and those of women working at the grass-roots level for feminist goals, in either women's centres or rape crisis centres.)

Many of the value differences reflect women's clear understanding of the limited capacity of the institutions of the dominant political system to provide a context for meaningful participation by women engaged in ordinary women's lives. Many women do not consider the "right" to vote and hold office a basis for meaningful political participation, an attitude they have inherited from their mothers and grandmothers. Although women of the suffrage era may seem to have been fixated on the vote, we find that they did not, in fact, have a strong tradition of looking to formal politics for the resolution of their own problems. Instead, they had developed a strong tradition of informal ("small p") community politics, operating primarily in self-help groups (Vickers 1989; Strong-Boag 1986). The norm of self-help went along with a service-based conception of political life. Values of duty and responsibility motivated these women as much as, if not more than, abstract concepts of rights (Vickers 1989; Rooke and Schnell 1987)....

As we have suggested, then, women's movements in English Canada inherited a set of ideas about how to conduct politics to which we refer as "radical liberalism" (Richardson 1983; Vickers 1992).[1] In brief, this operational code embodied a commitment to the ordinary political process, a belief in the welfare state, a belief in the efficacy of state action in general to remedy injustices, a belief that change is possible, a belief that dialogue is useful and may help promote change, and a belief that service or helping others is a valid contribution to the process of change. The acceptance of this code gave the movement its ability to work and be effective in coalitions. It also limited the influence of ideas from the United States that rejected the ordinary political process and tended towards anti-statism. Certainly, the commitment of Canadian feminists to the welfare state put them strongly in conflict with this U.S. anti-statism.

Two major forces for the transmission of the values of radical liberalism were the Royal Commission on the Status of Women and the women's peace movement. Both contributed to a revitalization of women's organizations from 1950 to the late 1960s. But while many groups became more or less feminist in their purposes, they remained traditional in their views of politics and organization and adhered to a reformist, rather than radical, analysis of women's situation. Self-defined liberationists claimed the "grass-roots" label, believing that their movement "differs greatly from the middle-class women's rights groups which consist mostly of professional and church women" (Canadian Educational Women's Press 1972:9). Generally young, educated, and from white, middle-class backgrounds, these liberationists were ignorant or scornful of the movement's many decades of local activity (which was nothing if not "grass-roots").[2] Nonetheless, a sense of differentiation was developing, and the new "grass-roots feminism was already articulating a sense of itself as different from institutionalized feminism" (Adamson et al. 1988:53). (Adamson and colleagues define grass roots feminism as more community-based, emphasizing collective organizing, consciousness-raising, and reaching out to women "on the street" [12].)

In English Canada, these attempts at differentiation did not preclude cooperation between older and newer groups. Bonnie Kreps (1972:75) explained to the royal commission that "Radical feminism is called 'radical' because it is struggling to bring about really fundamental changes in our society." Her description of the indigenous women's liberation movement, however, reveals a position quite different from the determined exclusion of non-radical women in the United States. Describing women's liberation as "a generic term covering a large spectrum of positions," she divides it into the three familiar male-derived ideological "segments" (liberal, Marxist or socialist, and radical), adding that "all three have their own validity, all three are important. One belongs to one segment rather than another because of

TABLE 1.2   The operational code of "second-wave" women's movements in English Canada

Dominant strand: "radical liberalism"	Counter-strands
• A commitment to the ordinary political process	• A belief that "Power is not electoral"; support for community activism
• Pro-statism; a belief in the efficacy of state actions, especially of welfare-state programs	• Concerns for "the feminization of process" within feminist groups
• Pro-active; a belief that change is possible	• A belief that controversial/adversarial tactics are more effective as educative tools than the lobby/influence approach
• A belief that dialogue with those who differ may be useful	
• A belief that helping others, in terms of service, is a valid contribution to change	

Sources: Richardson 1983; Vickers 1986, 1988b, 1992

personal affinity with the aims being striven for" (74-5). This early example of the Canadian tradition of integrative feminism is no anomaly. In the United States, the very word *feminist* was rigorously reserved for the ideas of young, radical/revolutionary women. But in English Canada, quite radical women and groups were willing to work with quite traditional women and groups. Moreover, quite radical groups were also willing to accept (and received) state funding for their projects.

What, then, are the values of radical liberalism? First, it is characterized by a belief in dialogue and a willingness to engage in debate, not only for the purpose of eliminating differences, but also, in the case of differences that cannot be transcended, to understand them. Hamilton and Barrett (1986:1) put it this way: "Canadians talk to each other ... across barriers of theory, analysis and politics that in Britain, for example, would long since have created an angry truce of silent pluralism." They argue that Canadian feminists operate "from within a political culture built on the recognition rather than the denial of division and differences between people."(2) Finally, they conclude that, in Canada, the task of "apprehending diversity without becoming totally distracted by it" has been undertaken "with greater solidarity and less suspicion between activists and intellectuals, academics and reformers than have been the case in Britain or the U.S." (2)

While a willingness to engage in dialogue was central to the values inherited from first-wave feminists, the development of practices supportive of dialogue was also made necessary by the realities of Canadian political life. Chief among these realities was the need to achieve the involvement of some francophone women in organizations interacting with the federal government. Dialogue was maintained into the 1970s between anglophone and some francophone feminists through a process of élite accommodation, which was a familiar approach in Canadian politics. Laura Sabia revealed the somewhat opportunistic character of this tactic in her description of the delegation she led to Ottawa, on 19 November 1966 in search of a commitment by the government to establish a royal commission: "We chose women who gave us credibility, women of stature. We asked Thérése Casgrain to join us, and Réjane Colas, who was not a vocal person but she headed a lot of groups in Québec. The IODE was highly respected and a voice to be contended with in those days and we had Regina Tait, IODE President ... The leading women in Canada were doing our bidding" (interview with Chris Appelle, 10 January 1986).

The next fifteen years saw a rupturing of this tradition of cooperative interaction between anglophone and francophone feminists as feminism in Québec changed its perspective by embracing nationalism (Lamoureaux 1987), and English Canada failed to understand the nature of, and the reasons for, the new position. Nevertheless, a belief in the importance of interaction between English and French persisted in NAC, and other movement organizations, such as the Canadian Research Institute for the Advancement of Women (CRIAW), also adopted it as a goal. Certainly, claims by predominantly anglophone organizations such as NAC and CRIAW to represent Canadian women dictated at least lip-service to bilingualism.

As Hamilton and Barrett (1986:4) note, "A belief in undivided sisterhood was never very marketable in Canada," so the value placed on understanding and accommodating some, if not all, differences was considerable. Solidarity has been easier to maintain across class lines and between generations, however, than across the lines of linguistic, racial, and ethnic difference....

Also characteristic of radical liberalism is the belief that change is possible and that state action is an acceptable way of achieving change. The significant role that women played in creating Canada's welfare state may help to explain the greater sense of efficacy *vis-à-vis* the state among women of the English-Canadian movement than among women elsewhere. This belief, however, also reflects the pro-statism that, until recently, went largely unchallenged in Canadian society (Lipset 1990). Although neoliberal debates about welfare-state reform exists in Canada, relatively few feminists seriously question the view that "the state is turning out to be the main recourse of women" (Piven 1984:14; see also Andrew 1984). Most English-Canadian feminists still see the state as a potentially benign utility engaged in worthy redistributive efforts, provisions of services, and necessary regulatory tasks. Only in the area of abortion did the movement seek less government intervention, and even then, it was strictly in the sense of removing abortion from the criminal code, since feminists continued to demand that the state provide significant improvements in abortion services.

It is clear that the position of English-Canadian feminists is in stark contrast to the view that the state is unremittingly patriarchal and oppressive (MacKinnon 1989). Positions on this issue tend to be based on women's concrete experiences with the institutions of particular states in particular eras. In British Columbia, for example, where right-wing governments eliminated services that benefited women, as well as jobs occupied largely by women, the state was seen less as a benign utility and more as an oppressive force. (It is interesting to note that women active in service dealing with male violence against women also have a more critical appraisal of state institutions [Walker 1990]. This may be at least partially attributable to the fact that these women come into contact primarily with the judicial and police institutions of the state.)

Most English-Canadian feminists accept the premise that "helping others is a valid contribution which has intrinsic value" (Richardson 1983:28). Since most government funding has been tied to a service orientation, many groups have been forced to provide a service in order to gain funding. State funding has also resulted in the professionalization of feminist services, which has meant increased ranks of paid staff and growing bureaucracies— developments that may conflict with the more grass-roots approach that many feminists prefer.

What we have formulated as the operational code of radical liberalism is muted by a counter-force associated with certain local groups and unions. Even these elements, however, realize that "feminists who act only as critics of the system, and create too much distance from social institutions, run the risk of being unable to reach and activate people" (Adamson et al. 1988:179). Also present as a counter-current is the recurring debate concerning the proper orientation of umbrella groups such as NAC. Women espousing an ideology of egalitarianism, anti-hierarchy, and anti-leadership have repeatedly demanded a rethinking of the organization's purposes (Morris 1983). The overall picture, then, is of an operational code that generally supports involvement in the ordinary political process, tolerance of ideological diversity, encouragement of dialogue, and a commitment to service. Combined with these elements is a strong strain of dissent by more-radical elements that find themselves uneasily in harness, in NAC, with a coalition of more-conventional forces. Out of this political dynamic has come NAC's unique contribution to feminist politics.

Radical Influences on Feminist Political Culture

Radical feminism is an important, if little understood, influence in Canada. Throughout Quebec and the rest of Canada, "the radical-feminist message injected new energy into the liberal feminism which had existed ... for more than seventy years" (Dumont et al. 1987:364). It was at the level of general theory that radical feminism had its most important impact on women's movements both in Canada and throughout the liberal democracies. As we will demonstrate, however, these theoretical radical-feminist ideas, generated by French, Australian, Canadian, and U.S. writers, were different from the norms of political culture associated with the U.S. Women's Liberation Movement.

The major sources of radical-feminist theory were the writings of Simone de Beauvoir, of France (translated into English in 1952); Kate Millett, of the United States; Shulamith Firestone, of Canada; and Germaine Greer, of Australia. (The writings of the latter three were translated into French in the early 1970s.) These authors popularized ideas that were radical in two respects: They were based on the premise that sex oppression was fundamental and primary and that all other oppression sprang from it, and they held that all of society's institutions were permeated by and perpetuated male dominance. Although not all of these writers used the term, each demonstrated the existence of a political phenomenon called "patriarchy." In Canada, the influence of their ideas was threefold: (1) they helped to revitalize the existing traditions of liberal feminism and left feminism; (2) with their emphasis on personal and sexual relationships, they contributed to the widespread mobilization of young women; and (3) they motivated young women to join groups often established by U.S. émigré feminists. In the context of the feminist theory described above, the term radical referred to something quite new, because it focused on gender as the source of oppression....

The version of U.S. "radical" feminism that was first introduced into Canada (at a level other than general theory) is best represented by the ideas of Marlene Dixon, who moved to Montreal from the United States in 1969 to teach sociology at McGill University. Dixon felt she had come from a war zone, and her experience taught her that there was no place in an autonomous radical women's movement for liberals, traditional socialists, or women's-rights feminists. She saw no connection at all between her Women's Liberation Movement (WLM) and indigenous Canadian movements. Dixon understood the WLM as emerging out of the struggle against sexism in the organizations of the American New Left—specifically, Students for a Democratic Society (SDS) and the Student Non-Violent Co-ordinating Committee (SNCC) (Dixon 1971). The "terrific fear" of the police and other social forces mentioned by Joan Richardson (1983) as characteristic of U.S. feminism in the 1960s also contextualizes Dixon's views.

Dixon identifies three orientations in the early WLM in the United States, namely, those represented by the socialist groups, the consciousness-raising (C-R) groups, and the WITCH group, "with its wild and poetic imagery of kings, fairies, witches and power [that] involved a litany of oppression and rebellion" (1971:53). She notes that "at the [1965 Chicago] conference ... the basic division is usually referred to as 'consciousness-raising' vs. 'radical' or 'bourgeois' vs. 'revolutionary'" (56).

By 1969, Dixon was in Montreal acting as the prime mover in a group called WAM, the Women's Action Movement (Richardson 1983:14). The group promoted rapid polarization within the emerging WLM in anglophone Montreal. Indeed, the WLM soon splintered, leaving considerable disagreement as to which of the resulting two groups—the Young Socialists or the counter-culture women (as consciousness-raising women were now called)—was the "splinter group" (14-15).

By 1975, Marlene Dixon saw the conflict within the WLM as one between the "politicos" and the "so-called feminists" (1975:57). Announcing that she had become a Marxist-Leninist, she decried the joining of forces in the United States between the liberal feminists of the National Organization of Women (NOW) and "radical" feminists who espoused an ideology she described as "reactionary feminism" because of its explicit premise that "men are the enemy" (58-60). Calling reactionary feminism an "ideology of vengeance," she described how, "with the virtual expulsion of the left leadership," the "radical" feminists (previously described as C-R, counter-culture, bourgeois feminists) had assumed leadership over the portion of the U.S. movement that had not yet been co-opted into the reformist camp (NOW) (60). Finally, Dixon repudiated the methodology of consciousness raising, which she had taken in her missionary kitbag to Montreal, arguing that "the error ... was to substitute understanding psychological oppression for political education" (61). Seeing consciousness raising used as a tool for individualist self-realization (which is what made it attractive to white, middle-class, North American women who could not be "objectively oppressed," except by men), she rejected the program that radical feminists had constructed using it, especially the elements of "man-hating, Lesbian Vanguardism, reactionary separatism [and] virulent anti-communism" ... (61).

Few radical-feminist groups formed by U.S. émigrés in Canada followed the path of the U.S. movement, although the process of frequent splintering does seem to have been characteristic of groups that valued ideological homogeneity (Ricks et al. 1972). U.S. emigre Bonnie Kreps, cited earlier from her 1968 brief to the Royal Commission on the Status of Women, was a founder of the New Feminists (Koedt et al. 1973). While her brief shows a strong commitment to radical feminism as an ideology, with its focus on patriarchy and sexual oppression, it does not display hostility to other strains of feminism to the degree that Dixon's writings do.

None of these conflicts and divisions were inevitable results of adopting the ideas we attributed to radical feminism as an ideology earlier. Rather, they grew out of conflicts that were born within the U.S. New Left, in the context of U.S. politics. Because the United States was a vibrant imperial power and the U.S. feminists shared in that imperialism, the doctrine of a universal sisterhood was especially appealing to U.S. women. Many U.S. feminists, like Dixon, comfortably assumed that women in other countries were against the things they were against and for the things they were for. U.S. women reacted against the sexism of the male leadership of the New Left, who exploited women's sexuality and labour, denied them leadership roles, and denied their grievances status. Even after it emerged as an independent movement, however, the Women's Liberation Movement continued to share ideas about the politics of the state with the New Left, especially with the cultural radicals, who believed that "the struggle within the state and its institutions [was] hopeless and beside the point" Aronowitz 1984:22). Radical feminists saw themselves as striking out on a profoundly new course of analysing the condition of women from the perspective of a discourse of oppression and liberation. The sense of being oppressed by all of the large, impersonal institutions of U.S. society, as well as by men, shaped their efforts to define a sisterhood of those who were oppressed *because of their sex*. Ideas about the nature of oppression and liberations were in the air, and WLM women borrowed from them freely....

Women possessing a new world-view with no corresponding new world on the horizon and no map of how to get there could not easily go back to living compromised lives. They kept the faith by creating a fragment of a new world—a feminist community within a patriarchal society and an imperialist state. Feminist services, clinics, bookstores, literature, music, and scholarship all emerged as part of the process of "living our visions" in the here and now (Hawthurst and Morrow 1984). Simply living in a liberated way came to be seen as contributing to a feminist "revolution." This cultural version of radical feminism not only celebrated the social fragment that women created, but also involved a political quietism consistent with the ideas of the U.S. New Left. While it was perhaps an understandable option for women facing the enormous power of the U.S. imperial state, there was a lack of fit with the political culture of radical liberalism that prevailed in the English-Canadian women's movement.

The Women's Peace Movement and Feminism within the Canadian Left

Why were English-Canadian women influenced less by U.S. radical feminism's general ideas about politics than by its ideas about the proper functioning of feminists groups? We have argued that the intergenerational continuity of the English-Canadian movement allowed for the transmission of the political culture of radical liberalism to the new generation of feminists. We will now look at several ways in which that intergenerational communication about politics occurred. The first important arena of interaction between "old" and "new" feminists was the women's peace movement, especially in the context of the organization called the Voice of Women (VOW), founded in Toronto in 1960. The second was the caucuses of the democratic left, especially the Waffle, formed in 1969. We will also identify some of the features of the Canadian political system that may account for most feminists' commitment to radical liberalism and pro-statism.

The 1950s and early 1960s were active years for Canadian women, despite the success of societal and governmental pressures on women to return to their homes after the Second World War. In 1950, on International Women's Day, women's organizations, unions, ethnic groups, and peace groups joined together to form a new national women's alliance—the Congress of Canadian Women (CCW) (Macpherson 1975:40). The president was Rae Luckock, one of Ontario's first two women MPPs (the other was Agnes Macphail). The congress passed a Charter of Rights for Canadian Women, in which a commitment to feminism was clear: "We women of Canada assert that all human rights are women's rights." The charter's leftism was also evident in its claim to a "Right to livelihood, equal pay ... [and] seniority rights." Reproductive issues were conceptualized as the "Right to motherhood unhampered by lack of economic security, lack of hospital care and shelter, nurseries, hot meals" (Macpherson 1975:40). Finally, the centrepiece of the Charter was its claim to the "Right to peace." The CCW was founded in the same week that Canada's first equal-pay legislation was passed in Ontario. In 1954, a coalition of women's groups, including the YWCA, the NCWC, the Canadian Federation of University Women (CFUW), and the Canadian Federation of Business and Professional Women's Club (CFBPWC), lobbied successfully for the establishment of a Women's Bureau in the federal Department of Labour (Bannon 1975). This was to be the first of a long tradition of coalitions among women's groups to gain legal and structural changes of benefit for women.

As noted above, a major arena for the transmission of ideas about politics between generations was the Voice of Women. It appealed to women directly and was "dedicated to crusading against the possibility of nuclear war." VOW had a more respectable image that did earlier "ban the bomb" groups, because its leaders lent themselves to appellations such as "prominent" or "wife of the well-known ..." (Macpherson and Sears 1976:72). This aura of respectability won VOW early access to political decision-makers, but most VOW leaders were also genuinely respected for their feminist work. Thérése Casgrain, who led the fight for suffrage in Québec, for example, founded the Québec VOW and led a four-hundred-member delegation to Ottawa in 1961.

The VOW's activities interacted with those of the U.S. Women's Liberation Movement because of a shared focus on the war in Vietnam. But, as the VOW became increasingly nationalist and eager for "made-in-Canada" defence and foreign policies, it became critical of U.S. policy in areas that went beyond the conflict in Vietnam. Its members came increasingly to see Canadian economic, social, and political independence as the key to a Canadian role in achieving peace (Duckworth and Hope-Simpson 1981:172). None the less, many "Voicers" gave shelter and support to draft resisters and their partners, although the relationship was not always easy. Macpherson and Sears (1976:86) describe the 1971 conference in support of Indochinese women as especially difficult. Canadian women, swamped by the avalanche of "American imperialism of the left ... felt a new awareness of the need to establish their own national identity, while still acknowledging their bond with women everywhere."

The VOW was an organization within which several generations shared the values of their political culture. Certainly, NAC's determined multipartisan approach reflects a heedfulness of the warnings of older "voicers," that problems could result if members were allowed to use the VOW for partisan purposes. VOW members also taught the younger generation that "they could be agents of change in the world," and not just the causes of others, but also on their own behalf (Macpherson and Sears 1976:88). From 1961, the VOW was engaged in the campaign to legalize birth control, and in 1970, many "Voicers" lent support to the Abortion Caravan, which modelled itself on the old peace trains.

Both the English-Canadian and the Quebec movements, then, benefited from the existence of a bridging generation between first- and second-wave feminism. The democratic left also had the advantage of intergenerational continuity, provided through its socialist feminist tradition. Canada had a pattern of parties of the Left that was quite different from that in the United States. The institutionalized Left in Canada offered both a communist and non-communist option. In the CCF/NDP, moreover, the social gospel, Christian socialism, and rationalist Fabianism were at least as influential as Marxism. (Certainly, in English Canada, God is invoked as often by the Left as by the Right.) Many feminists were mobilized by the social-gospel tradition into left-wing causes, which thereby gained respectability in their communities. In particular, suffragist Nellie McClung's feminist version of the social gospel became a model for other women.

The evolution of socialist feminism within the non-communist Left, however, was hampered by the intense anti-communism of both the CCF and the NDP, which produced a deep suspicion of semi-autonomous groups or caucuses. In the late 1930s, the Toronto CCF Women's Joint Committee (WJC) was expelled from the party for forming common cause with communist women on certain issues (Manley 1980; Sangster 1989). Also in the 1930s, moreover, party traditionalists such as Winnipeg's Beatrice Brigden believed that "the CCF ... is firmly anchored to the most important social and economic institution, the home and the family" (Manley 1980:103). Nonetheless, even at that time, many women argued that socialism required a feminist analysis to be completed (Sangster 1989). In the 1960s, women in the NDP's Waffle caucus built on experience of that earlier generation of CCF socialist feminists.

On the surface, the Waffle's "Women's Lib" may have looked like a U.S. import. On closer examination, however, it becomes apparent that the Waffle's version of the New Left and its version of women's liberation are both quite different from their U.S. counterparts. The postwar renewal of the Left in Canada was represented primarily in the formation of the Waffle, but its adherents would reject the "New Left" label, seeing it as a manifestation of U.S. imperialism of the Left (Laxer 1960). Although the Waffle challenged the NDP's long-held premise that socialism could be attained exclusively through electoral and parliamentary activity, it in no sense rejected the ordinary political process or questioned the importance of state action. It offered community socialism as a supplement to, not a substitute for, the political process focused on the state. Community socialism involved three aspects: labour organizing, local neighbourhood organizing, and research on Canadian society.

Although the Waffle defined itself primarily around the issue of nationalism, it quickly spawned a women's caucus. A panel on the subject of women's liberation appeared on the agenda of the National Waffle Conference in 1970 (Public Archives of Canada [PAC] 1970b). Also, the resolutions booklet *For a Socialist Ontario in an Independent Socialist Canada*, prepared for the 1970 Ontario NDP Convention, included a ten-page section entitled "The Liberation of Women." It asserts the right of women to self-organization, arguing that "the oppression of women can only be overcome through women working together." And it adds that "the liberation of women must be a vital part of the struggle for socialism in Canada." (PAC 1970-2)....

Waffle women went through a process of reaction against the sexism of their male colleagues and, in the process, honed their consciousness as feminists. (Pat Smart, personal communication to Jill Vickers, May 1989). The Waffle as a group, however, responded positively to women's demands, providing an arena for the development of an analysis and policy proposals that integrated socialism and feminism in a new way. On the one hand, with their acceptance of the state, the party, and the ordinary political process, the Waffle women shared the operational code of radical liberalism; on the other hand, the values that underlay the community socialism they hoped to build echoed those held by their 1930s predecessors in the CCF, who also believed in extra-parliamentary action and local community decision making.

To summarize then, Canadian women of the 1960s were the beneficiaries of political cultures developed by women of earlier generations and transmitted through VOW or the CCF/NDP. This intergenerational cohesion would not only serve organizations such as NAC well, but would also prevent the political doctrine of anti-statism characteristic of U.S. radical feminism from making significant inroads in the English-Canadian women's movement.

NAC Political-Opportunity Structure: The Canadian Political System

The role of women in the formal politics of the Canadian state is equal to that of men only at the level of voting. The literature is replete with analyses identifying the barriers that limit both the "supply" and the "demand" for women activists within political elites (Brodie and Vickers 1982; Brodie 1985b; Bashevkin 1985; CRIAW 1987; Vickers and Brodie 1981; Burt 1986a). Certainly, the nature of the institutions of liberal democracy, such as political parties, is one such barrier. Democracy developed only as a "top dressing" in liberal states, which served competitive, individualist, market societies "through a system of freely competing though not democratic political parties" (Macpherson 1966). Indeed, a central feature of mainstream politics during the era of Liberal rule in Canada was élite accommodation. Despite rhetoric about "participatory democracy," women were excluded from the central process of political and economic policy making. Only within women's movement organizations were women "in charge" and only there were women-centred policies and processes the main order of business.

We have argued that women's movements are profoundly affected by the political culture in which they developed. In this section, we will illustrate that they are also shaped by the level of complexity of the ruling state and the nature of the prevailing regime during key periods of their development. NAC, in its dual role as a "parliament of women" and an interest group aggregating and representing the views of its member groups to the federal government, was particularly vulnerable to changes in both state institutions and the prevailing regime, especially to significant changes in the federal-provincial division of powers. In this section, we will explore some of the changing elements of Canada's federal political system, thereby providing the context for the actions and development of the English-Canadian movement, in general, and NAC, in particular....

The expansion of the welfare state by the federal government during the Liberal era (including, thereby, the provision of services important to women) cannot be understood as resulting primarily from the "ordinary" politics of élite accommodation. Lamarsh (1969:301) states: "Nothing was so hard to accomplish during all the time I was in cabinet as the appointment of a Royal Commission to inquire into the Status of Women."...

This precedent made it clear to women that the activist Liberal government would respond to massive public pressure from women under certain circumstances. It also taught them, however, that women's groups had to speak with one voice in order to achieve anything and that it helped to have a network of women within state institutions, and especially within the cabinet, working on the movement's projects.

The most important new element in postwar liberal-democratic politics was the rise of new and renewed movements for change. At the beginning of the Liberal era, they were of two distinct types: equality-seeking movements and quality-of-life movements, especially those concerned with the effects of a possible nuclear war. International human rights movements and the U.S. civil rights movement were the models that launched the equality-seeking dynamic. While women's movements had important links to the past and women enjoyed the basic civil and political rights won by first-wave activists, many felt that those rights had not made them "matter" in politics. Formal political equality had not resulted in any real political influence for women. Few policies or policy makers paid the slightest attention to women's needs or wants as women. Most women knew that, but they differed in their estimation of whether equality-seeking movements could get the official political system to respond and to change. In the United States, the tragic end of the Kennedy era and the shame of foreign entanglements in Vietnam and Cuba persuaded many women that the system was incapable of change. In English Canada, by contrast, most women remained more optimistic about the ability of governments to respond.

These new and revitalized movements for change threatened established political institutions, especially political parties. Federal Liberal governments, however, responded in an activist way. Government funding of the "voluntary sector" was expanded to include support that would enable citizen participation—even that of radical groups. To some observers this aspect of the Liberal government's activism is seen as an attempt to control and limit the effects of the new movements for change. Martin Loney (1977:457) for example, argues that such support served "to contain the debate within broad, but nonetheless definable parameters." During this period, something of a symbolic relationship developed between the organized portion of the women's movement, including NAC, and the federal state. The existence of a Liberal government with activist and centralist tendencies, one that was willing to fund movement groups and activities, encouraged the movement to "face the state." Findlay (1987:31) describes the government's approach as follows:

> Between 1966 and 1979, the Canadian state was engaged in organizing its formal response to women's demands for equality. Although some concrete legislative and policy initiatives were introduced in this period, the response of the state focused largely on integrating the representation of women's interests into the policy-making process. This was done both by establishing a network of programs and advisors to represent women's issues in the state bureaucracy, and by appointing a minister responsible for the status of women to represent women's interests at the executive level of the state.

The infrastructure developed during the era of Liberal rule included the Canadian Advisory Council on the Status of Women and Status of Women Canada. Such structures may well become permanent additions to the institutional equipment of the federal state, just as Women's Bureaus in Departments of Labour did several decades earlier....

What, then, were the major effects of the Liberal era with regard to women? Findlay (1987:31) observes that, during this period, "the state demonstrated a commitment to consult with the women of Canada, and in doing so not only validated the faith of liberal feminists in the strategy of reform by the state, but constructed a relationship with them that established liberal feminism as the public face of the women's movement." Sandra Burt (1986b) has argued that another key feature of this era was the state's deconstruction of feminism's systematic critique into a series of separate issues. The movement was largely accepting of the strategy of reform by the state and, to meet its commitment to provide services to women, found it necessary to develop its own expertise and policy proposals in areas that conformed to government-set agendas. This occurred in policy areas such as battering and child sexual abuse. Some of the early leaders of NAC were comfortable with the Liberal strategy of downplaying direct action (confrontation and demonstrations) in favour of lobbying government for specific policies and programs: it was an approach consistent with their values. Others, such as Lynn McDonald, believed it conflicted with NAC's responsibilities to its regional and community-based member groups and therefore tried to develop a more confrontational approach.

In the United States, the long-time existence of an entrenched Bill of Rights made equality seeking a familiar part of politics. By contrast, equality seeking was not a common feature of Canadian politics before the 1960s (Vickers 1986). During the Liberal era, however, many equality-seeking movements emerged that borrowed from the analysis and tactics of the women's movement, just as women had borrowed from the anti-slavery and civil-rights movements in the past. But this new dynamic in Canadian politics also included movements that adopted the language of collective, rather than individual, rights. The equality aspirations of Québec, for example, were being expressed increasingly in terms of a collective right to self-determination, and campaigns for individual rights in that province became entangled with campaigns for collective rights. The slogan of some members of the Québec feminist movement was "Pas de libération des femmes sans Québec libre, pas de Québec libre san libération des femmes" (Lamoureaux 1987:53). Third World struggles for national liberation also had influence on movements in Québec during the Liberal era. Two of the central challenges facing the Liberal government, then, were the rise of a radical movement to "decolonize" Québec and the rise of a democratic movement seeking to achieve Québec's separation from the rest of Canada.

Whether pursued in relation to individual or collective rights, equality seeking in Canadian politics was a contagious process. Racial minorities, gays and lesbians, immigrant groups, and people with disabilities all used civil-rights/equality-rights discourse and adopted tactics pioneered in part by women's movements. In addition, such groups found it possible to build coalitions, in which women were able to play a central role. The relative stability of women's movement organizations, achieved through the institutionalization of integrative structures such as NAC, allowed them to play a key role in the equality-seeking dynamic.

In the 1970s, an equality-seeking alliance was forged between some native women, including Mary Two Axe Early, and the member groups of the English-Canadian movement to oppose the elements of the Indian Act that discriminated against women. This alliance, whose aim was captured by the slogan "Indian Rights for Indian Women," believed in the primary of individual rights. Since that time, however, many aboriginal women have become increasingly sympathetic to the claims of First Nations to their collective rights to self-government. Divided from the "mainstream" white movements on the sorts of issues that also divide Western and Third World women, many aboriginal women are now seeking improved status exclusively within the First Nations. Non-status and Métis women, however, continue to struggle for individual rights and find support from many women's groups....

Until the late 1970s, there was little difference between the federal Liberals and Conservatives with regard to the propriety of state activism, especially in the realm of economics. As Janine Brodie (1985a:73) explains, "fundamental disagreements between the Liberal and Progressive Conservative parties over the question of state power and economic development have been relatively rare in our political history. The BNA Act provided for a strong federal government and, from the beginning, it was an active participant in Canada's economic development." In matters of social policy, there was somewhat more differentiation, with the Liberals supporting a more libertarian position on matters such as sex ("The state has no place in the bedrooms of the nation") and the Conservatives supporting a more libertarian position on issues such as gun control. But even in relation to social policy and the changes sought by equality seekers, there was no clear-cut polarization between the two parties.

In the late 1970s, a polarization did develop that has been described as follows: "The Progressive Conservatives became the party of free enterprise and decentralization while the Liberals became the party of state intervention in the economy and federal power" (Brodie 1985a:74; see also Laxer 1980)....

Some neoliberal forces in this debate believed that the welfare state had become overgrown and was in need of trimming by the new Conservative regime. They also tended to support a libertarian view of state intervention in "private" matters of social policy (such as abortion).[3] Neoconservative voices were present in this debate as well. Unlike the neoliberals, who favoured a reduction of the welfare state but not its elimination, neoconservatives advocated the virtual elimination of all and any regulation by the state, in order to "provide a level playing field" in the equal-opportunity "sweepstakes" (Vickers 1986).

Neoconservative groups, such as the National Citizens Coalition, were explicitly anti-feminist in their attacks on elements within the federal Conservative government that continued to support feminist issues and the funding of feminist organizations.

Neither the federal government nor the English-Canadian women's movement has chosen to pursue gender-gap politics, although polarization in some provinces has led to the emergence of electorally significant gender gaps. In the United States, where it was originated, the gender-gap approach involved an alliance between the Democratic party and major organizations of the women's movement based on the fact that U.S. women were more supportive than U.S. men of the state activism traditionally associated with the Democratic party. To further woo women voters, the Democratic party adopted affirmative action for party and convention offices and favoured policies supported by progressive women. In Canada, an alliance of this sort between women's groups and the second Mulroney administration was impossible, because both the government and the conservative feminists associated with it had come to view the actions of NAC as supportive of the NDP, although those actions reflected opposition to the government more than support for any other party.

Summary

In this section, we have argued that a strong equality-seeking dynamic was introduced into the federal political system in Canada during the 1960s. The ability of the English-Canadian women's movement to create conflict-managing institutions and to sustain coalitions despite difference made it a central player in this dynamic throughout the Liberal era. We have consequently rejected the vision of the Canadian state as a monolithic and unremittingly patriarchal oppressor (MacKinnon 1989), since this view is not sustainable in the light of the Canadian state's actual record of positive changes for women. Our analysis is based instead on a view of the state as a set of institutions that are often not fully consistent in their direction, partly because the government's ability to affect the behaviour of state institutions varies over time and partly because there is a competition within and among state institutions that complicates the implementation of a government's overall plans.

Furthermore, the limited ability of governments to deal with policy in anything other than short time frames can work to the advantage of the women's movement; indeed, it can potentially enhance the degree of influence that a movement with stable institutions engaged in long-term projects can attain. Sue Findlay (1987:48) maintains that "at times when the state is more vulnerable to women's demands, feminists can play a more active role in the development of state proposals to promote women's equality." Moreover, "taking advantage of the state's need for legitimation, they can establish feminist alternatives to the bureaucratic mode of operating that reinforces patterns of inequality, or advocate policies that challenge the ideology of capitalism and patriarchy." We would agree that, to be effective, strategies for making women matter in Canadian politics in the period under study required an understanding of when openings for the equality-seeking dynamic were imminent and of how they could be best utilized.

The development or successful strategies, however, also depended on the presence of networks of feminists within state institutions, as well as within legislatures. Some observers believe that if women are present in the institutions of the political system, they can change the agendas of those institutions (Freda Paltiel, cited in Burt 1986b). Findlay (1987:48) warns, however, that "the potential for successful challenges depends on the extent to which feminists inside the state have been able to maintain their relations with women's movement and to use their position to advocate reforms that will affect women's lives rather than reforms that have only symbolic value." Clearly, this could not be just a one-way street. Not only did women within political institutions have to be receptive to the women's movements, movement women also had to be open to women within the state and within political parties.

Finally, we maintain that it was essential for the contemporary movement to become institutionalized and for these channels of interaction to become as permanent as possible. This derives from our conviction that the struggle to gain equality for women is a multigenerational project that cannot succeed if it relies on the interpersonal relationships of a single generation. Reforms gained can never be taken for granted as permanent features. Nonetheless, "their value should not be underestimated as a response to the immediate needs of women and as a way of weakening the hegemony of the dominant groups that oppose women's equality" (Findlay 1987:48).

In the chapters that follow, we explore a number of structural reforms and policy changes achieved through NAC's interaction with the formal politics of the state over the period studied, arguing that the contribution of NAC to the achievement of the English-Canadian movement's goals reflects its successful institutionalization. In addition, we examine the political dynamic that led to the achievement of significant changes in Canada's Constitution, gained Canadian women their "ERA," and, more importantly, resulted in a recognition of the legitimacy of equality seeking by all disadvantaged groups in relation to the Constitution. In our view, the political engagement of the English-Canadian women's movement has contributed significantly to achieving major gains in women's struggle for real equality.

The remainder of our discussion is an assessment of the contribution of NAC to the movement's effectiveness. In particular, we consider the stresses on NAC as it undergoes institutionalization and strives to grapple with the task of providing representation for Canadian women from a wide political spectrum and from many newly mobilized groups. The issue of representation is critical to NAC's legitimacy, as it claims to represent women better than any existing political structure, including political parties. Finally, we discuss the pressures on NAC from various sources for decentralization and address the question of how NAC has adapted to politics since the end of the Liberal era. Our purpose, which is to present an account of politics "as if women mattered," will guide us in this project.

ENDNOTES

1. Many of these ideas were shared by both anglophones and francophones in the 1960s, when only the revitalized liberal feminism of the FFQ was present in Québec, but fewer are shared today (Micheline Dumont, personal communication to Jill Vickers, May 1989). Aboriginal women accepted the code to the same extent in the 1960s and early 1970s, but it was not shared in the 1980s by many First Nations women.

2. Intergenerational rebellion may well have been an important factor in shaping the attitudes of some young women to their political foremothers. Many considered their biological mothers to be "wimps" and knew little of their suffrage and post-suffrage grandmothers. One of the authors completed a BA in political science in the 1960s without ever hearing about the suffrage movement.

3. Recent Conservative ministers responsible for the status of women are excellent examples of neoliberal feminists. Highly supportive of free enterprise and of the federal state's use of its regulative powers to provide equality of opportunity for women. They have been less supportive of material programs (such as a national child-care program) that would in practice equalize opportunity.

RACE, CLASS, AND FEMINIST PRACTICE

Vijay Agnew

The absence of women from Asia, Africa, and the Caribbean from feminist activity in Canada is the result of the race biases of white feminists. But there has been no detailed account of how race-biased feminist theory articulates with exclusionary feminist practice. The values and norms embedded in the organizational structures and political processes of feminist struggles alienate and exclude some women. But feminist theory asserts that women's organizations can be brought together in coalition politics to represent the interests of all women equally.[1] Such an egalitarian view of social relations presumes that within a feminist context the biases, values, and hierarchies of the larger society do not operate or can be erased.

The exclusion of women from Asia, Africa, and the Caribbean from feminist practice has also been attributed to the differences in priorities of different groups of women. In the 1970s, the emphasis on issues of sexuality, reproduction, and abortion did not motivate women from Asia, Africa, and the Caribbean to join white, middle-class women in their struggles. As new immigrants, these women were far more concerned with racism in immigration policy and their lack of access to language-training programs (Agnew 1993b). A number of other issues, such as housing, employment, education, and social services, which cut across lines of race and class, had the potential of bringing women together. But there is little evidence that women from Asia, Africa, and the Caribbean participated in feminist struggles during the 1970s. For example, Nancy Adamson, Linda Briskin, and Margaret McPhail write:

> In 1973 a group of Spanish-speaking women in Toronto established the Centre for Spanish Speaking Peoples (CSSP). At the time these women and the CSSP were not seen as a part of the women's movement either by themselves or by feminists ... [W]omen's issues were still narrowly defined in a way that reflected the racial (white) and class (middle) assumptions of its founders. Individual feminists were supportive of such organizing efforts, but the women's movement as a whole did not regard such organizations as an integral part of its struggle.... Although more research needs to be done, it seems that the women of colour actively involved in feminist organizations were few. The reasons are complex: the origins of the women's movement, the definition of "women's issues," and racism. (1988, 60-1)

Common issues were not sufficient to bring white, middle-class women and working-class women and women from Asia, Africa, and the Caribbean together in feminist struggles.

The difficulty of incorporating the diversity of women's experiences and identities and yet retaining some focus on gender has created friction among feminists. Catharine MacKinnon argues that women's practice is based on the "notion of experience 'as a woman' and ... discrimination—based on sex" (1991, 14). But this was strongly disputed by women of colour:

> Writings by women of colour and Third World women acknowledge the existence of gender oppression, but they also maintain that gender oppression never occurs in a racially-neutral or culturally independent context ... Women's experiences which are not shared with white women have been the most difficult to admit into feminist discourse, usually because white feminists classify them as race-based rather than gender-based. We disagree with your notion of an empirical reality which would pervade all experiences "as a woman" in Third World and in white cultures ... [E]xamples of gender oppression often neglected by white feminists are: the industrial, domestic and supportive services women of colour provide for white women and men in the contexts of colonialism, imperialism, and slavery; the exploitation of women of colour which is gender specific but attributed to race; and the subordination of women as defined by Third World cultures, which differs from patriarchy in white culture. (Open Letters to Catharine MacKinnon 1991, 178-9)

A feminist practice involving women of different classes and races needs to identify its goals and objectives in terms that appeal to gender yet distinguish between the different forms of oppression of women.[2] In the 1980s, feminists tried to organize struggles at local levels and around specific issues. Alliances and coalitions among, a wide spectrum of organizations in support of each other's struggles would empower a large number of women. Not surprisingly, the process of "inclusion" has been difficult.[3] The diversity and range of feminist organizations create tension between feminists representing different organizations. Their coming together within umbrella organizations creates demands for representation and participation which challenge existing hierarchies and practices. The diversity of membership and issues makes it difficult for umbrella organizations to devise a strategy or political agenda that can satisfy all. Diversity is sometimes viewed as posing a threat to the survival of large umbrella organizations (Vickers 1988).

Conceptualizing the problem as one of integration or inclusion does not focus attention on the social and political contexts in which feminist theories and struggles are conceived and enacted. Race biases of the larger society are reflected in feminist practices—for example, in organizational structures, political processes, priority of issues, leadership, and unequal distribution of power. Consensual politics are difficult to achieve given the larger context, which distinguishes between women on the basis of race, country of origin, and class. The social context in which feminist practices are embedded creates barriers that exclude some women from them. This chapter explores the marginalization of women from Asia, Africa, and the Caribbean in feminist practice by examining the consciousness-raising activities of the 1970s and coalition politics of the 1980s....

Women's Organizations: Processes and Structure

In Ontario during the 1970s a number of new women's organizations emerged and existing women's organizations were revitalized. Health centres appeared, as well as rape crisis centres, abortion referral services, and transition houses for battered women (Black 1988, 84). Umbrella organizations like the National Action Committee on the Status of Women (NAC) were formed to bring these diverse groups together in support of women's struggles. Government departments and agencies responded to the revitalization of the women's movement by creating Status of Women offices or appointing advisers on women's issues (Findlay 1987, 31).

In the 1980s, women from Asia, Africa, and the Caribbean established a number of autonomous organizations that focused on issues of specific concern to themselves: racism, sexism, immigration policy, and access to social services (for example, Women Working with Immigrant Women, the National Organization of Immigrant and Visible-Minority Women, and the Congress of Black Women). At the same time, women from Asia, Africa, and the Caribbean formed umbrella organizations to give coherence, direction, and a higher profile to their issues with state agencies and feminist organizations dominated by white women.[4] Women Working with Immigrant Women was initiated by white social workers and immigrant and visible-minority women. However, the social workers slowly withdrew from its active functioning, which enabled immigrant women to manage their own organization (Women Working with Immigrant Women 1985-6).

State agencies supported women's organizations by allocating grants to them and encouraging the emergence of organizations for women from Asia, Africa, and the Caribbean, such as the Ontario Immigrant and Visible-Minority Women's Organization and the South Asian Women's Group (Ontario Women's Directorate 1987, 1). Support by government grants creates some tension in the politics of women's organizations. They must structure their organizations to conform to the requirements of the state, sometimes changing the character of the organization from a volunteer organization to an agency of the state (Ng 1988a). The dependence on state funds constrains the options available to women's organizations.[5] For example, it may restrain their espousal of militant politics or pressure them to become more inclusive of marginalized groups.

Feminist organizations have attempted to form alliances and coalitions with each other either in support of specific issues, such as abortion, or in support of broadly defined goals and objectives like the "women's movement" or "women's struggles." Criticism by women from Asia, Africa, and the Caribbean pressured organizations dominated by white women to address issues of women from Asia, Africa, and the Caribbean. Some organizations, like the National Action Committee and the International Women's Day Committee, after much dispute and acrimony, instituted changes to their structures to make them more representative of the different groups of women in their membership (Greaves 1991; Vickers 1991, Egan, Gardner, and Persad 1988). An analysis of some of these conflicts indicates the difficulties of forming coalitions across lines of race and class.

The critique of the exercise of power in a male-dominated society has motivated feminists to create structures and initiate processes that enable marginal groups to be heard along with the more privileged and the articulate. In ideal feminist organizational structures, there is no hierarchy: all tasks are rotated, and decisions are arrived at through consensus. They favour small groups, which allow for a "high degree of comfort and recognition of shared experiences," and they recognize "the absolute sovereignty of the individual as central to political decision making" and reject representative democracy in favour of direct or participatory democracy (Vickers 1991, 77). If these structures and practices are instituted in organizations dominated by white women, for example, in the NAC, rape and crisis shelters, and social service collectives, they can help working-class women and women from Asia, Africa, and the Caribbean come together with white, middle-class women. But despite theoretical commitment to non-hierarchical structures and the desire not to allocate privilege and power to individual women, in practice hierarchies and leaders emerge nonetheless (Ristock 1991, 41-55; Albrecht and Brewer 1990).[6]

Research indicates that small groups lead to greater homogeneity, conformity, and the development of an "us" and "them" attitude. Sheila Rowbotham notes: "Sisterhood can become a coercive consensus which makes it emotionally difficult for individual women to say what they feel rather than a source of strength ... Our lack of structure can make it difficult for women outside particular networks to join. It can lead to cliquishness and thus be undemocratic. The stress on personal experience makes it hard to communicate ideas" (quoted in Vickers 1991, 85). Members of small groups sometimes find diversity and difference threatening. A worker at a Canadian feminist collective notes: "We accommodate superficial differences but what that amounts to is real differences remaining hidden. The accommodation is just to allow women into the fold, to make them become one of 'us,'but differences in feminist analysis, skill and identity remain unacknowledged" (Ristock 1991, 48)....

Feminist processes and organizational structures assume that women have equal strengths, skills, and expertise. In reality, more privileged or articulate women manipulate the decision-making process to their advantage. Some women are able to manage the agenda of the organizations in subtle and indirect ways (Greaves 1991, 101-16; Ristock 1991). The coordinator of Women Working with Immigrant Women noted that her unfamiliarity with *Robert's Rules of Order* often placed her at a disadvantage with white women. White women familiar with these rules were able to marginalize the issues of women from Asia, Africa, and the Caribbean in the political agenda of these organizations (Interviews, 5 October 1989, 31 May 1989).

In theory, feminists abhor the exercise of privilege or expertise over groups and individuals. Feminists favour processes that distribute power among the participants. In practice, however, commitment to the theory has sometimes led to a refusal to discuss how power is exercised within these organizations. Power is exercised covertly. Power and leadership in feminist organizations shift from individuals to factions within the organization (Ristock 1991, 51-5). As "outsiders," women from Asia, Africa, and the Caribbean find it difficult to become part of "informal networks" or to join the different factions of white women. They may feel disempowered, suspecting that decisions have been made informally by different factions that excluded them. At other times, the issues of women from Asia, Africa, and the Caribbean may be "included" in order to consolidate power for a particular "faction." One black woman discussed her experience of alienation and marginalization at the Women's Press collective in Toronto: "The one black person or woman of colour is reduced to a minority voice and in the collective process that means one vote ... one voice. It is difficult for one voice to speak out as loudly as it should ... There is an undermining of self-confidence and you are constantly on the other side of the discussion facing nine or ten people who have an opposing point of view. It is always a minority situation ... I would like to see real involvement not just a token presence" (quoted in Kline 1989b, 59).

In theory, feminist political proposals are attempts to respond to the oppression of all women. However, since not all women are "victims" in identical ways, feminist practice must establish an agenda of priorities and allocate its limited resources to issues affecting women in different ways. Arriving at these decisions has been occasion for dispute. A basic conflict revolves around defining what is an appropriate feminist struggle. Is racism a feminist issue?

Even when common issues are identified, evolving an appropriate non-racist strategy may be difficult. For example, workshops on rape and wife battering may discuss how they affect some groups of women while the rest of the discussion purports to consider "all women" (Russo 1991, 288-96). A demonstration may indirectly reinforce racist stereotypes, such as when a group protesting rape marches through a black neighbourhood (Bhavnani and Coulson 1986, 84). Or an antiracist agenda may be adopted without initiating any structural change within an organization (Newsletter, International Women's Day Celebrations 1986). Such conflicts are about representation, accountability, responsibility, and equal sharing of power and authority.

Integrating people and their issues into organizations that are embedded in a racially stratified society has led to accusations of tokenism by women from Asia, Africa, and the Caribbean against white feminists and, in the caustic language of Trinh Minh-ha, to feelings of "being part of somebody's private zoo" (Minh-ha 1989, 82). Being outnumbered in an organization increases feelings of isolation, vulnerability, and powerlessness (Kline 1986b, 59). The issue of inclusion has exposed the racial, class, and ethnic composition of feminist organizations that purport to represent all women....

Consciousness-raising groups were informal, non-hierarchical, and egalitarian. The groups tried to create an environment that limited class privilege and encouraged participation by all women. Time was allocated equally, and everyone was allowed to finish statements without interruption. The groups attempted to avoid making comparisons or passing judgment, and they aimed to give everyone's experience equal validity. But some women, usually those who were middle class and well educated, were more articulate and could dominate discussions (Eisenstein 1983, 40).

Consciousness-raising groups could have provided a good opportunity for women from different classes and races to share their experiences. But the potential was never realized because the biases of class and race within the larger society influenced the dynamics of the group interactions. There is no indication that working-class women, women of colour, or black women participated in such groups. One reason for their absence was stated bluntly in 1970 in a position paper of the Leila Khalid Collective: "Women with little time, little education, with families and jobs, or women who have to fight hard to survive on welfare aren't interested in coming to weekly meetings to talk about sexuality and to read Engels." The absence of women from Asia, Africa, and the Caribbean from such groups is also explained by the influence of racism on their interaction and communication, their different understandings of the nature of their oppression and its sources, and their cultural and social alienation.

The focus of the consciousness-raising groups was gender, and gender oppression was the basis of solidarity and sisterhood. But this perspective was in itself exclusionary and alienating. Feminists within consciousness-raising groups regarded male supremacy as the most important form of domination, and all other forms of exploitation, such as racism, capitalism, and imperialism, were regarded as extensions of male supremacy (Roszak and Roszak 1969, 273).

The differences in interest and experience were alienating and exclusionary. Feminists of the late 1960s and 1970s were interested in cultural issues, particularly those related to sexuality, family, and socialization. The women shared intimate experiences with other women, such as incest, sexual molestation, rape, or abortion (Adamson, Briskin, and McPhail 1988, 44). Such experiences occurred among women from Asia, Africa, and the Caribbean too, but they did not provide a basis for solidarity between members of dominant and subordinate groups.

Cultural practices and mores also create social distance. For example, discussion of sexuality evokes acute embarrassment in South Asian women because their culture regards it as an intensely private and personal issue.[7] Further, members of a subordinate group who experience oppression on the basis of race are reluctant to discuss it, for this may only serve to confirm the pre-existing stereotypical images and attitudes of the dominant group. To articulate the existence of sexism within South Asian families would be to reinforce stereotypical notions of "traditional" societies and "oppressive" cultures. A feminist discussion would not necessarily help overcome deep-seated racist attitudes and assumptions, particularly when raising critical consciousness is perceived as referring to gender only.

Uma Narayan, a South Asian feminist, says:

> I often find myself torn between the desire to communicate with honesty the miseries and oppressions that I think my own culture confers on its women and the fear that this communication is going to reinforce, however unconsciously, western prejudices about the "superiority" of western culture. I have often felt compelled to interrupt my communication, say on the problems of the Indian system of arranged marriages, to remind my western friends that the experience of women under their system of "romantic love" seems no more enviable. (1990, 259)

Immigrants may also hesitate to criticize their new society, fearing they will provoke their audience to make comparisons with the "old country."

The status of women from Asia, Africa, and the Caribbean as immigrants and newcomers meant that they had different interests and experiences. The feminist movement did not address the specific conditions of their lives but focused its rhetoric and politics on the experience of white, middle-class women. For example, white feminists emphasized the oppression experienced by women within the family. They have been criticized by black feminists who argue that, in a racist and classist society, family is a source of emotional support and comfort for them (hooks 1984, 43-65; Parmar 1986). This is not to deny the existence of sexism within the family, but rather to say that women from Asia, Africa, and the Caribbean may be reluctant to identify with a movement perceived to be anti-family. The experience of discrimination by women from Asia, Africa, and the Caribbean increases their dependence on the family and ethnic community. Immigrant women who are confronted by attitudes and behaviours that are racist or classist are reluctant to identify with members of a dominant group on the basis of gender. As newcomers, they value the emotional shelter of the family and the sense of belonging in their ethnic group. They are likely to consider relations outside the family and community as stressful and alienating, while relations within the family and community affirm their dignity and identity as women.

Differences in class are also divisive and alienating.[8] Feminist theory sees all women as victims of discrimination, capitalist patriarchy, or biology. The experiential reality of women from Asia, Africa, and the Caribbean, however, is different from that of white, middle-class women. The labour market not only is segregated by gender but is ethnically stratified as well. Women from Asia, Africa, and the Caribbean may work either in job ghettos for immigrant women or in the lower strata of "female" jobs. Thus, women from Asia, Africa, and the Caribbean experience oppression not only by men but by women as well. The relations of subordination and domination are best exemplified in the nanny and mistress relationship. Thousands of women from the Caribbean and Asian countries have come to work as domestics in white households since the introduction of the Domestic Scheme in 1955 (Silvera 1983, 13; Daenzer 1991). In this situation it is rare for women from Asia, Africa, and the Caribbean to identify with white women as "victims" on the basis of gender. White, middle-class women may be oppressed by their gender, but they exercise great power and privilege when compared to women from Asia, Africa, and the Caribbean. Women can be both oppressors and oppressed. This is noted by bell hooks, a black feminist writer: "Women can and do participate in politics of domination, as perpetrators as well as victims—that we dominate, that we are dominated. If focus on patriarchal domination masks this reality or becomes the means by which women deflect attention from the real conditions and circumstances of our lives, then women cooperate in suppressing and promoting false consciousness, inhibiting our capacity to assume responsibility for transforming ourselves and society" (1988, 20). Women from Asia, Africa, and the Caribbean are more likely to share a common sense of victimization with men of their own class and race than with middle-class, white women.

Language can be a barrier to communication. The inability to speak English obviously keeps working-class women from Asia, Africa, and the Caribbean away from feminist meetings of white, middle-class women. Pauline Terrelonge has argued that accent and unfamiliarity with middle-class uses of language set up barriers between black and white women (1984). But knowledge of the language is not enough. Feminists have developed a complex jargon, with terms such as "herstory," "validation," and "knowings," which may be impenetrable for both working-class women and middle-class women from other cultures and societies. In addition, working-class and middle-class white women may share a colloquial language (e.g., the difference between being "at lunch" and being "out to lunch") and a store of familiar allusions (e.g., Harlequin romances and the Literary Guild), which are unfamiliar to immigrant women. And certain words have acquired negative connotations within a feminist setting which may disturb immigrant women (e.g., the use of the word "middle-class"). To women from Asia, Africa, and the Caribbean who have come to Canada in pursuit of a middle-class lifestyle, the disparagement of their goals by feminists is confusing and alienating.

A feminist practice that emphasized gender and ignored racism, colonialism, and imperialism could not gain much support from women who immigrated from Asia, Africa, and Latin America. The differences in experience and motivation for political activism have been a constant source of tension within feminist practice. This situation was outlined in the 1970 position paper of the Leila Khalid Collective, a group of white, college-going feminists:

> In practice and in our ongoing debate ... we treated women's oppression as special and related to other people's oppression only in a mechanical way. We thus reinforced the same abstract politics that had originally frustrated us ... [W]e see a women's liberation movement in North America attacking symbols (bras and beauty contests) and not the oppressor, concerned with individual liberation while black sisters are beaten and tortured, demanding freedom and equality from a decaying society where no one can be free and equal.

The feminist politics of middle-class women revealed "ignorance of the lives of other women and of factors beyond gender which determine women's lives" (Segal 1987, 61)....

A political analysis of mainstream feminist theory and practice of the 1970s enables us to understand that the absence of women from Asia, Africa, and the Caribbean from mainstream feminist practice results not from their culture and values but from their powerlessness, based on race and class. The issues, interests, and perspectives of white, middle-class women were those of women who could relate to each other. Within such a context, the perspectives of other women were either ignored or marginalized.

Coalition and Alliances in the 1980s

A political strategy of coalitions and alliances among different feminist organizations is widely supported by white feminists and women from Asia, Africa, and the Caribbean. In Canada, the recognition of the need to forge a unity amid diversity strikes a responsive chord. Canada's official policy of multiculturalism is based on a need to recognize the contributions of the many different cultural groups that form part of the Canadian mosaic.

The debates within feminism resonate with questions about the role of "other Canadians" in Canadian society and about the political necessity of integrating "other Canadians" to achieve a unified society based on a diversity of cultures. Critics argue that multiculturalism emphasizes the cultural differences between groups rather than their differences of power and privilege. They see multicultural policy as a strategy meant only to reduce conflict between different ethnic groups who desire a greater share of resources, power, and privilege. Multiculturalism offers compensation to the powerless by "accepting" them but not by giving them power or privilege. In other words, multiculturalism does not challenge the nation's political and social structures; it perpetuates them (Peter 1981). A similar complaint may be directed against feminist theory and practice. Recognizing the different experiential realities of oppression in women's lives does not challenge the differences that give power to some women and withhold it from others, and it may reinforce them.

The difficulties of forming alliances and coalitions across lines of race and class can be explored by examining the struggle of women from Asia, Africa, and the Caribbean to gain representation for themselves and their issues in a large national feminist organization such as the National Action Committee on the Status of Women (NAC) and in the socialist-feminist coalition of the International Women's Day Celebrations (IWDC), which is also referred to as the March 8th Coalition.

NAC is a large umbrella organization which originated in 1972 with a mandate to monitor the implementation of the recommendations of the Royal Commission on the Status of Women (National Action Committee 1986, 2). By 1988 its membership had expanded to 570 groups, representing a wide spectrum of organizations from across Canada (Greaves 1991, 102). Autonomous organizations of women from Asia, Africa, and the Caribbean and their umbrella organizations are members of NAC. But until very recently NAC was essentially a white, anglophone network to which "others" sought entrance (Vickers 1988, 59). The diversity of its membership led to demands that NAC change its structure and enable different groups of women to participate. An editorial in IWDC's newsletter of 1986 notes: "NAC must look to itself and question why different groupings of women have been inhibited from joining. Perhaps the present structure, political approach to issues [and] method of work discourage the building of a more representative participatory movement. We must be open to change." At the same time, newer members demanded that NAC's executive members be made more accountable to the general membership.

NAC is regarded as the "formal women's movement in Canada, the official women's opposition, and the public voice and symbol of feminism in Canada." It has the responsibility to simultaneously "lead and mirror the Canadian women's movement" (Greaves

1991, 103-4). An organizational review conducted in 1988 recommended that NAC open itself to "more diversity and ground itself more thoroughly in the grass-roots women's movement." It recommended that NAC ensure that its structure and internal processes include those whom it purports to represent. But Jill Vickers questions whether NAC "can incorporate in its processes black feminism, ethnic feminism, disabled women's feminism, lesbian feminism, etc.... It may well be that there is a limit to the number and diversity of groups which can operate under the umbrella structures like NAC" (1991, 91).

NAC's primary role has been to manage conflict within the women's movement, which would encourage coalitions between different women's organizations. The relations between small, local organizations and large, "mainstream" organizations can be cooperative. Large organizations, like the NAC, provide some coherence and political direction to feminist politics at the national level. They need the support of organizations of women from Asia, Africa, and the Caribbean to dispel the impression that the Canadian women's movement is primarily a white, middle-class movement. NAC has to demonstrate that it represents all Canadian women regardless of race, ethnicity, and class. It needs to prove its representative character to state agencies whose material support is necessary for the organization to survive. These pragmatic issues of survival have pressured NAC to graft issues of race and class onto existing agendas. Women who were previously excluded can now be included.

Cooperation and participation between women's organizations are mutually beneficial. The presence of small organizations of women from Asia, Africa, and the Caribbean within NAC enables these small groups to introduce issues that are of special interest to themselves and which may otherwise be neglected by NAC. Small organizations often need the resources and organizational expertise of large organizations for lobbying politicians and state agencies. Their issues receive wider publicity at a national level through the media attention attracted by large organizations.[9] But occasionally disputes erupt, particularly over representation, priorities, and leadership.

NAC has introduced some structural changes in an attempt to become more representative and more responsive to the demands of women from Asia, Africa, and the Caribbean. Its lack of well-defined structures disadvantages those groups who are not part of the informal networks among white women. For example, NAC policy and resolutions of the annual general meetings are developed within committees. NAC executive members chair committees in particular areas, and executive members are lobbied before or after election for promises to promote a policy committee. Since resolutions are developed within committees, this activity constitutes an informal priority-setting exercise for NAC agenda (Greaves 1991, 106-8). The absence of a committee from a particular area or of a committee serving a particular constituency results in the marginalization of other members and their issues.

NAC committees do not function under a particular plan or structure, and there are no definite guidelines that determine the process of acquiring a budget. The lack of structure gives particular significance to the skill of the chair of a particular committee, her networks within the organization, and the lobbying of committee members. A NAC executive member notes: "executive members would compete, posture, bargain and trade at the first executive meeting of the year to establish as much money as possible for their favourite committee. Inexperienced executive members, were often less successful at this, not realizing that cooperation and openness were likely to render them 'losers' in the budget allocation process" (Greaves 1991, 106).

In 1984, as a result of lobbying by women from Asia, Africa, and the Caribbean, an Immigrant and Visible-Minority Women's Committee was added to NAC's other committees. Until this committee was created, the issues of women from Asia, Africa, and the Caribbean were virtually unrepresented. A South Asian feminist who was active in the process of initiating the committee notes. "Before that [1984], NAC put forward two resolutions relevant to the immigrant women's network—five years apart, in a seven-year period. Just two proposals." The new committee's "purpose was not to ghettoize our issues, but it was to get our issues on the floor, get them integrated, and then disband the committee at the proper time" (Interview, 14 August 1989). During the 1991 meeting, the Immigrant and Visible-Minority Women's Committee refused to discuss racism in a separate forum, demanding instead that it be integrated into the themes of the constitution and reproductive technologies that the meeting was highlighting (statement circulated by the Immigrant and Visible-Minority Women's Committee, Annual General Meeting, 1991).

Women from Asia, Africa, and the Caribbean have formed the Women of Colour Caucus within NAC to develop strategies for making their issues an integral part of NAC's agenda. But achieving this goal could be difficult. Since NAC is a national organization, different groups are brought together primarily during its annual meetings. Women from Asia, Africa, and the Caribbean coming to the annual meeting as delegates may represent organizations that focus on women from Asia, Africa, and the Caribbean, or on women's shelters, health cooperatives, or support services. But there is no continuity of delegates from one year to the next. Only those members of the executive or regional representatives of NAC can have some impact on NAC's policies (Women of Colour Caucus, Annual General Meeting, 1991.). A change in NAC's structures to make them more inclusive and representative of different groups of women thus takes on added significance.

Under strong pressure from activist women from Asia, Africa, and the Caribbean, NAC instituted an affirmative action policy for its executive. During the 1991 annual general meeting, a Filipina and a South Asian woman stood for election for an executive position. There were already three women from Asia, Africa, and the Caribbean on the executive. However, an amendment from the Women of Colour Caucus asked that four additional members-at-large be designated as affirmative action positions for aboriginal women, women of colour, immigrant women of colour, and women with disability (Women of Colour Caucus, Amendment to Resolution #7, Section 2c, Annual General Meeting, 1991). And they asked that one vice-president be a woman of colour or an aboriginal woman. The implementation of these "affirmative actions" was resisted by the Lesbian Women's Caucus, whose members believed that their issues were marginalized within NAC as well (statement issued by the Lesbian Caucus, Annual General Meeting, 1991).

During the 1991 annual general meeting, anglophone, francophone, immigrant, and lesbian women were consistently represented at all plenary sessions.[10] But despite its symbolic significance, this representation does not by itself indicate that power is being equally shared among these different constituencies. Which group of women exercises power and authority within the organization remains a difficult and contentious issue.

NAC's mandate to represent the women's movement in Canada means that it must find a balance among the different issues and priorities of women. These issues and priorities have different impacts upon women and these differences must be reconciled as well. But it may be difficult for NAC to satisfy the many groups that it represents.

NAC is responding to the pressure and changing its structures and processes to accommodate new constituencies. Although the changes may be small and achieved with difficulty, they indicate that the relations between white feminists and feminists from Asia, Africa, and the Caribbean are being addressed. A black feminist active within NAC notes: "It takes a lot of fighting on our part and a lot of challenging to get NAC to listen to what we are saying. From 1986 we have had to push and challenge and insist and get angry and yell and call people racist, but at least when people come out they don't only see white faces on the stage, which is also very important" (Interview, 14 August 1991).

International Women's Day Celebrations, 1986–91

Racism divides women from Asia, Africa, and the Caribbean and white feminists both within the feminist movement and in society at large. Women from Asia, Africa, and the Caribbean have argued that white feminist practices ignore or marginalize racism or replicate the racist practices of the larger society within feminist struggles. Although white, middle-class feminists of the 1980s have recognized the different oppressions experienced by women from Asia, Africa, and the Caribbean, developing an antiracist agenda and an antiracist movement can be difficult. It gives rise to several issues: how to introduce an antiracist perspective into the organizational agenda; how to initiate antiracist action; and who is to exercise authority and leadership in the struggle (Bunch 1990; Anzaldúa 1990). The white feminists' assumption of leadership in forming policy and implementing projects for "their" movement is interpreted by women from Asia, Africa, and the Caribbean as racist. This situation makes alliances across lines of class and race difficult.

The struggle by women from Asia, Africa, and the Caribbean to integrate the issues of gender, race, and class oppression into white feminist practices has been contentious and divisive. But some feminists argue that the differences among women do not have to be a source of misunderstanding and separation but can be used to devise more inclusive feminist theories and practices. Audre Lorde notes: "We have been raised to view any difference other than sex as a reason for destruction, and for black women and white women to face each other's angers without denial or immobility or silence or guilt is in itself a heretical and generative idea. It implies peers meeting upon a common basis to examine difference, and to alter those distortions which history has created around our difference. For it is those distortions which separate us" (quoted in Russo 1991, 309). In practice, however, the coming together of individuals or groups in a common understanding has not been easy. Differences of perspective and power continue to divide women....

Problems in feminist practice raise the issue of how, and on what basis, do individuals overcome gender, race, and class biases and participate in "common" struggles? Feminist theory has not sufficiently explored how differences in experience can be overcome to create a common understanding. These differences pose the threat of relativism, which "implies that a person could have knowledge of only the sorts of things she had experienced personally and that she would be totally unable to communicate any of the contents of her knowledge to someone who did not have the same sorts of experiences" (Narayan 1990, 264). Can white feminists understand the oppressions of another group? Or does understanding come only from lived experience of oppressions?

Feminists argue that experience of oppression gives one insights into a particular oppression that is not shared by others. Even those sympathetic to the oppressions of a particular group may be unaware of the various nuances of how that oppression is experienced. Uma

Narayan notes: "The view that we can understand much about the perspective of those whose oppression we do not share allows us the space to criticize dominant groups for their blindness to the facts of oppression. The view that such an understanding, despite great effort and interest, is likely to be incomplete or limited, provides us with the ground for denying total parity to members of a dominant groups in their ability to understand our situation" (1990, 265).

Newly empowered groups may be wary of forming alliances with members of the dominant group. They have experienced white domination and the suppression of the experience, culture, individuality, and dignity of the colonized. Women from Asia, Africa, and the Caribbean, conscious of the biases of feminist theory and practice in the 1970s, may question the motives behind white feminists' interest in their struggles. They fear that white women who are sympathetic to their cause may use that as a pretext to speak on their behalf, thereby suppressing their "voice" once again. The alliance of women from Asia, Africa, and the Caribbean and white feminists is motivated by a common commitment to struggle against a male-dominated society. But women from Asia, Africa, and the Caribbean experience race, class, and gender oppression simultaneously, and this experience puts them at odds with white feminists and makes a working relationship between them problematic.

The exercise of privilege and domination in feminist practice has expressed itself in different ways over a period of time. The biases of feminist theory of the 1970s meant that feminist practices were ethnocentric. In the 1980s the emphasis on the different identities of women in feminist theory made feminists more sensitive to the different experiences and issues of women from Asia, Africa, and the Caribbean. Feminist practices are embedded in institutional structures that assign power and privilege unequally on the basis of gender, race, and class. Problems arise when white feminists act on assumptions that their experiences categorize as "normal," "natural," or merely "routine". Their activities are experienced by the subordinate group as oppressive. Inequalities based on race and class are articulated within feminist practices through the constant struggle and tension between women representing diverse identities and perspectives.

The process of challenging white feminist practices has empowered women from Asia, Africa, and the Caribbean. Hilary Lips identifies the ability to doubt, question, and resist the status quo as a power that subjugated groups can exercise. "The challenge, coming as it does from a new confidence in one's own meanings and metaphors, may be more transformative and ultimately disturbing to the established system than would any change coming from within the hierarchical framework" (1991, 9). Women from Asia, Africa, and the Caribbean have had some success in challenging the status quo of race relations in small and in large diversified feminist organizations. They have successfully exercised the "power to" name their oppressions and to define the conditions of their participation in feminist struggles dominated by white women. However, the liberating and energizing power of discovering their own strength and the collective capacity to act are balanced by the power relations in feminist organizations.

ENDNOTES

1. For example, see the articles in Albrecht and Brewer 1990 and in Wine and Ristock 1991.

2. For another example of the difficulty of developing a theory and practice that retains the signif-

icance of gender while acknowledging the diversity of women's experiences, see Ramazanoglu 1989.

3. Gloria Anzaldúa discusses some of the tensions in forming alliances among women across lines of race: "Despite changes in awareness since the early eighties, racism in the form of 'your commitment has to be to feminism, forget about your race and its struggle with us not them' is still the biggest deterrent to coalition work between white-women and women-of-color" (1990, 221-2). For a discussion of the power relations involved in the experience of women from Asia, Africa, and the Caribbean in feminist theory and practice, see Spelman 1988.

4. This is discussed in detail in Chapter 7 of *Resisting Discrimination.*

5. State funding of community groups is discussed extensively in Chapter 8 of *Resisting Discrimination.*

6. For a Canadian example of the power struggle and tension among white feminists and feminists from Asia, Africa, and the Caribbean, see Dewar 1993, 32-47.

7. I refer here to traditional norms and values. South Asian women who have lived in the West or are identified as "Westernized" in South Asia may not feel so inhibited in discussing women's sexuality.

8. In this discussion I focus primarily on the differences that class creates between white women and women from Asia, Africa, and the Caribbean. But there are also class divisions among women from Asia, Africa, and the Caribbean which make it difficult for them to form alliances among themselves. Work with community organizations brings working-class and middle-class women together to struggle against racism and sexism. This is explored in chapters 7, 8, and 9 of *Resisting Discrimination.*

9. For example, in 1991 the rally of the NAC to Parliament Hill in Ottawa and attempts to meet with various ministers were broadcast on CBC's national evening news and were the subject of a CBC documentary.

   The NAC championed the cause of some refugee women in 1993 and brought it to the attention of national media. Two articles appeared in the *Globe and Mail* on 5 March 1993: "'Siege' of immigration offices threatened" (Andre Picard) and "Fourteen face violence if deported, committee says."

10. Delegates representing women from English Canada, French Canada, women from Asia, Africa, and the Caribbean, and lesbian women were present at all plenary sessions, meetings with the minister in charge of women's affairs, press conferences, and entertainment.

BACK TO THE FUTURE: CONCLUDING NOTES

Becki Ross

During the 1970s in Toronto and other Canadian cities, following the American lead, autonomous lesbian-feminist organizing signalled the first of many fractures within the largely heterosexual-dominated women's movement. Eager to differentiate themselves from straight women, sexist gay men, and non-political gay women, "new lesbians" invented lesbian-feminist discourse, subject positions, and identities through avenues of life/style, sexuality, culture, and politics. In the 1980s, women of colour and immigrant women, Jewish women, disabled women, and working-class women charged feminism, and lesbian feminism, with its white, Christian, able-bodied, middle-class character.[1] Splinter groups increasingly committed to a particular brand of identity politics proliferated. The 1980s also yielded the subdivision of activist lesbians into specialized groupings: lesbians of colour, Jewish lesbians, working-class lesbians, leather dykes, lesbians against s/m, older lesbians, lesbian youth, disabled lesbians, and so on (see below).

In 1995, lesbian culture and politics have undergone an extraordinary redefinition through shifts in emphasis and group membership since the heyday of LOOT and similar lesbian-feminist projects. Today, among increasingly savvy lesbian and bisexual activists, the commitment to learning how differences of age, race, ethnicity, and class complexly intermix with sexual identity is serving to unsettle the normative "whiteness," unexamined class assumptions, ageism, and ableism that hobbled lesbian feminism in the 1970s. Though the drive to congregate and organize has far from disappeared, idyllic notions of "Lesbian Nation" have all but been abandoned.

Concentrated in large urban centres, support groups include Lesbians of Colour (Toronto); Vancouver Island Support Group (Victoria); Gays and Lesbians Aging (GALA, Toronto); Lesbian Youth Peer Support (LYPS, Toronto); Lesbian Youth Group (Vancouver); Black Socialist Dykes (Toronto); Gays and Lesbians at the University of Manitoba (Winnipeg); Fredericton Lesbians and Gays; Nice Jewish Girls (Toronto); Truro Lesbian Support Group; Asian Lesbians of Toronto (ALOT); Atish, for "lesbigays" of South Asian Heritage (Vancouver); Two-Spirited Peoples of the First Nations (Toronto); the lesbian caucus of the Disabled Women's Network (DAWN); and Outrageous, Wiser Lesbians (OWLS, Toronto).[2] There is a range of social services: counselling services, coming-out groups, funding foundations, and community halls and centres, such as the Vancouver Gay and Lesbian Centre and the Lesbian and Gay Community Centre in Montreal. Legal issues are the focus of organizations Equality for Gays and Lesbians Everywhere (EGALE), in Ottawa; the Coalition for Lesbian and Gay Rights in Ontario (CLGRO); Action Network for Gay and Lesbian Rights (Montreal), Canadian Committee against Customs Censorship (CCaCC); Censorstop; and lesbian and gay caucuses in unions like the Canadian Union of Educational Workers (CUEW), Bell Canada, and the Canadian Union of Public Employees (CUPE). Socially, needs are met by lesbian/gay bars and assorted "Dyke Nites" at straight clubs; Lesbian and Gay Pride Day committees; church groups; choirs; recreation clubs; potluck dinner clubs; and lesbian softball, soccer, golf, swimming, bowling, water polo, and curling leagues. Bisexual women have also begun to build their own networks and enunciate their own political program.[3]

In the domain of representation, identified by editors of *Radical America* as the central site of queer political contests in the nineties, there are Quota, *a lesbian magazine* (Toronto), *Khush: a Newsletter of South Asian Lesbians and Gays* (Toronto), *X-tra!* (Vancouver, Toronto, Ottawa), *Sami Yoni, for Lesbians of South Asian Descent* (Toronto), *Angles* (Vancouver), *Labrys* (Ottawa), *CLUE! magazine* (Calgary), *Perceptions* (Regina), *Gayzette* (Halifax), and *Lezzie Smut* (Vancouver). Canadian lesbian anthologies have been published by the Women's Press, Sister Vision Press, Ragweed/Gynergy, and Queer Press, and there are lesbian/gay radio shows on community and campus stations. Lesbian/gay/queer issues have been published by *Border/Lines*, *Fireweed*, and *Fuse* magazines. Culturally, lesbians are making significant contributions to the fields of theatre, music, visual and performance art, film/video, and photography.

From my vantage point as a white, middle-class academic/activist, I devour cartoons by Noreen Stevens; prose by Dionne Brand, Jane Rule, Makeda Silvera, and Beth Follett; computer porn by Shonagh Arielman; poetry by Brenda Brooks, Leleti Tamu, Daphne Marlatt, Betsy Warland, Carolyn Gammon, Tamai Kobayashi, and Mona Oikawa; and music by Faith Nolan, Seven Cent Posse, Sugar and Spice, k.d. lang, lngrid Stitt, and Women With Horns. The films/videos of Midi Onodera, Candy Paulker, Michelle Mohabeer, Shanni Mootoo, Marusia Bociurkiw, Rose Gutierrez, and Gita Saxena (Gitanjali) and the art of Stephanie Martin, Grace Channer, Karen Augustine, Anna Camilleri, River Sui, and Racy Sexy examine intersections of racial identity, racism, and sexuality, and offer a stinging antidote to the sanitized and commodified white-lesbian "flavour of the month" peddled by *Newsweek*, *Vanity Fair*, and *New York* magazines.

Academic ventures, though much less robust in Canada than in the United States, include the Toronto Centre for Lesbian and Gay Studies and their newsletter, *Centre/Fold*; a smattering of credit and non-credit courses in colleges and universities; and assorted campus-based lesbian and gay groups, conferences, and seminars.[4] Lesbians have been involved in many forms of AIDS activism, including direct-action groups like AIDS Action Now! and support groups for persons living with AIDS.[5] Moreover, lesbians continue to make up the leadership of sex workers' rights organizations such as the Canadian Organization for the Rights of Prostitutes (CORP), Maggie's—the Prostitutes' Safe Sex Project, and Sex Workers Alliance of Toronto (SWAT). Indeed, in a departure from the 1970s, there are greater numbers of lesbians who have chosen to work alongside pro-feminist gay men across a wide spectrum of community-based activities.

In contrast to LOOT, today there are no groups that attempt to be all things to all lesbians. Instead, the diffuse, partitioned character of lesbian-feminist organizing predominates. Almost all former members of LOOT are currently involved in politically oriented undertakings as lesbians and feminists yet not in organizations that identify explicitly as lesbian feminist.…

It is unclear to me whether communities of bar lesbians, closeted, suburban gay women, and lesbian feminists are closer together today than they were twenty years ago. The majority of lesbians (and gay men) continue to live double lives, hiding their sexuality in fear of damaging consequences. It's possible that greater numbers will come out in the 1990s, buoyed up by a splendid twenty-five-year legacy of activism and the tenacity of lesbian and lesbian/gay/queer institutions intent on realizing greater visibility, dignity, and equality in the future. Whether closeted or partially closeted lesbians then place their lesbian identity in a public, political context as a site of personal/political agitation for change remains an open question.

Since the 1970s, the presumption of an instant unity among lesbians qua lesbians has been proven both false and intolerant to differences. Given the limitations of LOOT and early lesbian-feminist praxis more generally, the increasing recognition of diversity and the naming of difference/s as a site of organizing would seem to mark a positive step. But as Cherrie Moraga warns, "Failure to move out from there will only isolate us in our own oppression—will only insulate rather than radicalize us."[6] And bell hooks adds that "the ability to see and describe one's own reality is a significant step in the long process of self-recovery; but it is only a beginning."[7]…

Within the past several years, in Toronto, Montreal, Vancouver and several smaller cities, networks of mixed-gender, multi-sexual, and multiracial coalitions have emerged in the wake of successive political crises: the police shootings of black youths in the late 1980s; the Chantal Daigle and Barbara Dodd abortion cases (1989); the Montreal Massacre (1989); police violence directed against lesbians and gay men in Montréal (1990); the invasion of First Nation territories at Kanasatake (1990); the Gulf War (1991); the police raid on the gay men's leather bar, Katacombes, in Montréal (1993); the trumped-up targeting of Somali Canadians as welfare defrauders (1993-94); the rise of anti-Semitism and anti-immigration sentiment and practices; and the recent escalation of gay/lesbian bashing in most urban centres. Throughout, lesbian, gay. and bisexual activists have struggled to forge tenuous, fragile bonds with other progressive constituencies. Reminiscent of joint organizing in the 1970s, participation in alliance building is still fraught with miscommunication, suspicion, and the fear of co-optation. Though concerted efforts have been made to promote and realize inclusivity, problems of sexism, racism, homophobia, and unexamined class privilege persist.[8]…

On the one hand, small victories have been secured. On the other, most Western capitalist cultures are besieged by the ascendancy of moral and economic conservatism and the erosion of political gains, the rootedness of heterosexism deepened by the AIDS/HIV crisis, and the sluggishness of social-change movements. In Canada, two lesbians recently lost custody of their children in part because they were lesbians and deemed "unfit" care-givers and role models by a judge in Renfrew County.[9] On sex- and gender-related issues, the state has re-tooled obscenity legislation: the Supreme Court *Butler* decision (1992) has been used by Ontario judges to confiscate lesbian and gay sexually explicit images/texts from Canadian bookstores, and Memorandum D-9-1-1 continues to dictate the U.S./Canada border seizures of lesbian/gay print and visual materials en route to lesbian/gay, women's, and left bookstores.[10] Passed hurriedly in the summer of 1993, the "youth pornography" bill, Bill C-128 (Section 163.1 of the Criminal Code), has increased controls on sex-trade workers and criminalized young gay-male hustlers. A last-minute electoral ploy intended to advance the federal Tory government's tough anticrime agenda, the law provides for up to five years in prison for simple possession and up to ten years for production, distribution, importation, or sale of sexually explicit images of anyone under eighteen (or anyone who *appears to be* under eighteen).[11]

The federal House of Commons has yet to include sexual-orientation protection in the Charter of Rights and Freedoms, though courts ruled in the *Haig and Birch* decision (1992) that sexual orientation is an "analogous ground" and must be "read into" both the Charter and the Canadian Human Rights Act. The Human Rights Commission alone is currently faced with over eight cases concerning discrimination, harassment, and employment benefits launched by lesbians and gay men in Canada. When the Canadian Union of Public Employees (CUPE) passed a resolution to amend its pension plan so its gay and lesbian workers could name their partner as beneficiary, the Minister of Revenue denied the union eligibility for tax benefits that other employers receive for contributions to employee pension plans under the Income Tax Act.

On a positive note, over the past twenty-five years, a significant handful of victories have been secured. In 1991, the "Douglas" decision made at the Supreme Court level determined that homosexuality is no longer grounds for discrimination in the Canadian Armed Forces.[12] A number of corporate employers have decided to extend spousal benefits to their lesbian and gay employees. ... In June 1994, the Quebec Human Rights Commission recommended that provincial legislation be amended to extend to lesbian and gay couples the same rights and benefits enjoyed by heterosexual couples, except the right to adopt children.[13]

In December 1990, the Ontario New Democratic Party (NDP) extended job benefits— including health, dental, and leave time—to same-sex couples in the civil service. In 1992, Michael Leshner won a four-year legal battle requiring the Ontario government to extend survivor pension benefits to its lesbian and gay employees. Though the body of judicial and quasi-judicial rulings recognizing the rights of lesbians and gays is growing, the process is expensive and time-consuming and deals ineffectively with discrimination on a case-by-case basis.

In 1993, the ruling Ontario NDP government introduced the omnibus Bill 167—the Equality Rights Statute Law Amendment Act—intended to rewrite over fifty laws to provide equal rights for same-sex couples. Among the laws to be revised are the Family Law Act, Landlord and Tenant Act, Insurance Act, Cemeteries Act, and Land Transfer Tax Act.[14] The sweeping bill championed by Attorney General Marion Boyd was designed to legalize lesbian/gay adoption, spousal pension benefits upon death of the partner, and tax benefits for lesbian and gay couples.[15] In May 1994, it passed first reading by a narrow margin of 57-52 votes; the debate in and outside the legislature whipped up considerable moral anxiety about the stability of "the family.[16] Indeed, an Ontario provincial by-election in the Victoria-Haliburton riding was won in April 1994 by Chris Hodgson, a Progressive Conservative candidate who campaigned exclusively against the provincial NDP's promise to extend legal rights to same-sex couples. Hodgson's campaign literature argued that "new spending schemes" (that is, same-sex spousal benefits) will "increase the cost of doing business in Ontario and drive jobs away."[17]

In May 1994, the Roman Catholic Archbishop of Toronto, Aloysius Ambrozic, addressed more than one million Catholic parishioners. In a letter mailed to two hundred parishes in the greater Toronto area, he proclaimed: "Any attempt to promote a homosexual lifestyle as the equivalent of legal marriage must be vigorously opposed. It is a matter of considerable urgency, and to that end we are asking you to write to your local member of provincial parliament to protest the proposed legislation."[18] Dignity, a group for gay and lesbian Catholics with country-wide chapters, vociferously condemned the archbishop's decree, as did a number of progressive Catholic, Jewish, United Church, and Anglican leaders. Meanwhile, in Alberta in 1994, backed by the support of several influential church groups, provincial Tory Premier Ralph Klein appealed a court decision that would extend human-rights protection to lesbians and gay men.[19] At the same time, gays, lesbians, and supporters have mobilized bodies and resources to combat the damage of active, repressive forces.

On 9 June 1994, the second reading of Bill 167 in the Ontario Legislature was defeated by a margin of 68-59 after a charged, emotional debate. Twelve members of the majority NDP government voted against the bill. While thousands of lesbians, gays, bisexuals, and supporters protested the defeat at a downtown demonstration later that evening, fundamentalist leaders such as Ken Campbell hailed the quashing of the bill as a victory for the "majority of the province."[20] Over the course of several months of heated skirmishes, these fiercely competing positions approached the character of an informal national referendum on homosexuality, sexual liberation, and the family with all the properties of a full-scale moral panic reminiscent of Anita Bryant's "Save Our Children" crusade and the police incursion on *The Body Politic* magazine in 1977.

Notwithstanding the fiery backlash, it is clear that law reform in and of itself is a limited avenue for change—a reality that lesbian feminists had predicted in the late 1970s. Sociologist Didi Khayatt has documented how lesbian teachers in Ontario continue to perform elaborate "passing" strategies to hide their lesbian identities in spite of legal protection for sexual orientation via antidiscrimination legislation.[21] Legal scholar Didi Herman warns against the liberal thrust underlying the civil-rights reforms sought by organizations of lesbians and gay men in the Canadian context.[22] Writer Carol Allen is concerned about who will be excluded by legislation change. She cautions: "We must stop making legal arguments which, if successful, will only help other professional, white, middle-class, able-bodied lesbians and gays whose family form looks very much like the traditional heterosexual ideal."[23] Moreover, the law provides an inadequate measure of protection for vulnerable constituencies such as lesbian and gay teachers, child-care workers, nurses, anti social workers. As such, legal reform in isolation from massive educational offensives will not necessarily dismantle homophobic and heterosexist attitudes and practices....

In the 1990s, perhaps more than ever, contests over what "lesbian" means rage on. Exhibiting "authentic" behavioural, ideological and style codes (however much authenticity itself is debated) is still esteemed among many politicized lesbian feminists as one method of revealing one's inner self, securing high moral rank, and locking up political credibility. Today the drive to determine identity-based codes—the ongoing preoccupation with *being a "real" lesbian*—seems to betray an even greater urgency and intensity. And yet there seems to be remarkably less consensus among the players: a potentially liberating dilemma given the challenges posed to the silences constructed by white, middle-class lesbian-feminist discourse, icons, and narratives, yet one that may also immobilize. *Village Voice* columnist Alisa Solomon warns that "a lesbian can wag her finger as righteously as any patriarchal puritan, defining what's acceptable according to what must not be ingested, worn and especially desired.[24] And reporting on the National Lesbian Conference in Atlanta in 1991, Donna Minkowitz reported: "The main business emerged: an inquisition into the sins of conference goers, from working for Uncle Sam to preferring thin women as sex partners ... Attendees were so obsessed with setting up a *cordon sanitaire* that no one organized to do anything concrete to change the real world."[25] In 1995, most urban lesbian activists in Canada and the United Status have demonstrated little enthusiasm for the prospect of bridging balkanized constituencies.

At the same time, attempts within lesbian-feminist communities to supplant old prescriptions with liberal-individualist codes for fashionable, politically sophisticated "queerdom" in the 1990s threaten to mandate new notions of who's in and who's out. Such a focus harkens back to the inward-looking nature of preceding Lesbian Nations rather than forward to the promise of mobilizing against actual state and social discrimination. Exclusionary parameters police populations and operate to compartmentalize constituencies as acceptable or unacceptable. I argue that no movement for gender and sexual liberation can afford the evacuation of a male-to-female lesbian transsexual, a leather dyke into s/m fantasy, a lesbian (or any woman) who is HIV+, a softball playing and factory-working gay woman, a rural lesbian who has never heard of Susie Sexpert, or a lesbian of colour who refuses to splice her self into identity-pieces with lesbian on top.[26]

Certainly, there is no obvious or guaranteed correlation between "otherness" and community-based militancy. However, in the lesbian-feminist 1970s, formal and informal strictures worked to deny the benefits of belongingness to those least acquiescent to conformity. Positioned on the outside (though insiders did not always feel inside) were those lesbians, whether or not they identified as feminists, who came to terms with their lesbian selves primarily in lesbian/gay bars, hostels, prisons, baseball and hockey leagues, recreation clubs, house parties, and workplaces. I am not suggesting that these sites were void of codes and rules; I suspect that they were governed by a sophisticated infrastructure of norms and meanings intrinsic to every subculture. What remains worth interrogating, however slippery and contradictory, is the power wielded within social formations to make manifest certain possibilities and to preclude the attainment of others.

The knowledge and meanings of polymorphously diverse lesbian experience have been silenced, distorted, denied, and/or omitted from the historical record. During the period of 1977-80, members of the Lesbian Organization of Toronto identified lesbian visibility, lesbian-feminist pride, and the dismantling of heterosexual hegemony as fundamental to the collective fight for sexual and social freedom for all women. LOOT-goers set out to operationalize what it means to *be* a full-time lesbian feminist in all facets of their lives— "the unified epistemological and volitional agent," to quote Shane Phelan.[27] Coming out— perceived as the first necessary and prideful step towards liberation—was not just a linguistic act; it was a physical and psychic dramatization of one's essential lesbianness. Members of LOOT insisted on the radical specificity of lesbian feminism through what Judith Butler might call the self-disclosing, repetitive acts of gender and sexual insubordination.[28] Reinvesting the feminist dictum "the personal is political" with bold, fresh lesbian faith served as an intense flash point for a newly forming feminist constituency.

Several former LOOT members claim that the genesis of all social/recreational, support, political, and legal action by and for lesbians in Toronto in the 1990s can be traced directly back to the concretization of lesbian-feminist visions internal to the Lesbian Organization of Toronto. Without question, young activists today owe a debt to LOOT's fecund seedbed of ideas, energy, and hutzpah. The richness of contemporary lesbian/gay/queer organizing attests to the profound impact of LOOT's existence in spite of the difficulties of transfering grass-roots political and cultural acumen from generation to generation. At the same time, LOOT's legacy is not an unproblematic one. The varied successes and limitations of the

LOOT experiment at once inspire and haunt contemporary efforts to contest debilitating discourses and practices of heterosexism, as well as sexism, racism, and class inequality. Figuring out how to accomplish liberatory politics and gains without reproducing past mistakes will preoccupy grass-roots activists for decades to come.

Amid the current profusion of multi/queer/culture and identities, tensions persist between organizing autonomously and building coalitions across diverse constituencies. The often painful, exasperating, and yet indispensable work of grass-roots activism is most cogently articulated by African American Bernice Johnson Reagon in "Coalition Politics," a speech delivered at the West Coast Women's Music Festival in 1981.[29] Almost fifteen years later, to me it appears easier at times to abandon the commitment to devoted, militant struggle than to persevere in spite of disillusionment. Yet, in urban and rural milieux, lesbian/gay/queer and queer-positive resources are multiplying, not shrinking—a testament to the fortitude and imagination of those faced with adversity, hostility, and feelings of non-existence. Indeed, the proliferating tentacles of anti-heterosexist resistance emerge by necessity to challenge the diffuse, micro-techniques of power that socially organize heterosexuality as the only allegedly "normal," "natural," and "universal" human sexual expression. While post-structuralist theorists illuminate the instability and performativity of identity categories to the point of deconstructing queerness altogether, many lesbians/gays/queers stubbornly promulgate their perverse identifications. And they are joined by increasing numbers of organized cross-dressers, transvestites, transsexuals, and transgenderists: a phenomenon that suggests the multiplication rather than the dissolution of identities.[30] And yet, as Judith Butler heeds, though "outness" demands affirmation, the term may present an impossible conflict between racial, ethnic, or religious affiliation and sexual politics. In other words, we need to ask, For whom is outness an available and affordable option?[31] We need to recall that the vast majority of lesbians (and gay men) are not out, lead double lives, and struggle to be whole human beings.

Many lesbian stories need to be told, retold, and remembered. *The House That Jill Built* offers one book of stories that aims to stem the corrosive tide of amnesia. In the end, I am still uncertain as to what the determinate content of a lesbian-feminist politics might be. While some lesbian commentators argue for the assimilationist right to "family" monopolized by heterosexuals, others hope that future queers will embrace their role as "recruiters" of those foundering in the alien worlds of families. Some endorse the power of pink consumerism to change mainstream attitudes; others agitate for the efflorescence of a radical movement, or movements, not a market. Some are concerned to highlight the vulnerability of women (and lesbians) to sexual victimization, while others insist on the urgent need to assert sexual optimism and jouissance.

ENDNOTES

1. Much has been written on diversity from a lesbian standpoint since the late 1970s. For a sampling, see Joan Gibbs and Sara Bennett, eds., *Top Ranking: A Collection of Articles on Racism and Classicism in the Lesbian Community* (Brooklyn, NY: February Third Press 1980); Gloria Anzaldua and Cherrie Moraga, eds., *This Bridge Called My Back: Writings by Radical Women of Colour* (New York: Kitchen Table Press 1981); Evelyn Torton Beck, *Nice Jewish Girls: A Lesbian Anthology* (Watertown, Mass.: Persephone Press 1982); Hortense Spillers, "Interstices: A Small Drama of Words," in Carole Vance, ed., *Pleasure and Danger: Female Sexuality Today* (Boston and London: Routledge and Kegan Paul 1984), 73-100; Audre Lorde, *Sister Outsider:*

Essays and Speeches (New York: The Crossing Press 1984), and *A Burst of Light* (Ithaca, NY: Firebrand Books 1988); Juanita Ramos, ed., *Companeras: LaCina Lesbians* (New York: Latina Lesbian History Project 1987); Jackie Goldsby, "What It Means to Be Colored Me," *Out/Look*, Summer 1990: 8-17, and "Queen for 307 Days: Looking B(l)ack at Vanessa Williams and the Sex Wars," in Arlene Stein, ed., *Sisters, Sexperts and Queers: Beyond the Lesbian Nation* (New York: Penguin Books 1993), 110-28; Ekua Omosupe, "Black/Lesbian/Bulldagger," *differences: A Journal of Feminist Cultural Studies* 3, 2 (1991): 101-11; Kate Rushin, "Clearing a Space for Us: A Tribute to Audre Lorde," *Radical America* 24, 4 (1993): 85-8; Margaret Randall, "To Change Our Own Reality and the World: A Conversation with Lesbians in Nicaragua," *Signs*, Summer 1993: 907-24; Karin Aguilar-San Juan, "Landmarks in Literature by Asian American Lesbians," Ibid., 936-43; Jewelle Gomez, "Speculative Fiction and Black Lesbians," Ibid., 950-5; Barbara Smith and Jewelle Gomez, "Taking the Home out of Homophobia: Black Lesbians Look in Their Own Backyard," *Out/Look* 8 (Spring 1990): 32-7; and Alicia Gaspar de Alba, "Tortillerismo: Work by Chicana Lesbians," *Signs*, Summer 1993: 956-63. For an introduction to new, Canadian-based voices, see the work of Black, Native, and Asian lesbians living in Canada: Leleti Tamu, "Casselberry Harvest," *Fireweed*, Spring 1989: 47; Donna Barker, "S & M Is an Adventure," *Fireweed* 28 (Spring 1989): 115-21; Li Yuen, "International Lesbian Sex Week Poster," *Angles*, September 1987: 15-16; Tamai Kobayashi, "Untitled," *Fireweed* 30 (Spring 1990): 52-3; Milagros Parades, "Christmas Eve Imaginings," *Fireweed*, Spring 1989: 79; Makeda Silvera, ed., *Piece of My Heart: A Lesbian of Colour Anthology* (Toronto: Sister Vision Press 1992); Karen Augustine, "Bizarre Women, Exotic Bodies and Outrageous Sex," *Border/Lines,* Winter 1994. On lesbians and disability, see the recent NFB film *Towards Intimacy*, and the 1993 pamphlet "Women with Disabilities Talk About Sexuality," produced by the Disabled Women's Network (DAWN) of Toronto; Joanne Doucette, "Redefining Difference: Disabled Lesbians Resist," in Sharon Stone, ed., *Lesbians in Canada* (Toronto: Between the Lines 1990), 61-72. On aging see Jeanette Auger, "Lesbians and Aging: Triple Trouble or Tremendous Thrill," in Stone, ed., *Lesbians in Canada*, 25-34. On class in the 1950s, see Line Chamberland, "Projet de communication: Sur la culture lesbienne, les armies 1950s Montréal" (trans. as "Social Class and Integration in the Lesbian SubCulture"), in Sandra Kirby, Dayna Daniels, Kate McKenna, and Michelle Pujol, eds, *Women Changing Academe* (Winnipeg: Sororal Publishing 1991). 75-88. And from her research on sexualities in Egypt, Didi Khayatt has written "A Subject in Limbo: Redefining the Categories," paper presented at Queer Sites conference, Toronto, May 1993.

2. On issues specific to small-town lesbian/gay life, see Eleanor Brown, "Lives Are Changing in Small Towns: Lesbians and Gay Men Across Ontario Are Risking Much to Come out in Support of Family Rights," *X-tra!* 252 (24 June 1994): 18.

3. Bisexuality is taken up by CKLN radio, "Bi and Out: Discussing the Les/Bi Divide on Queer Radio," *Fireweed*, Summer 1992: 62-7; Carol Queen, "Strangers at Home: Bisexuals in the Queer Movement," *Out/Look*, Spring 1992: 23-33; and Lorraine Hutchins and Lani Kaahumanu, *Bi Any Other Name: Bisexual People Speak Out* (Boston: Alyson Publications 1990).

4. The Toronto Centre for Lesbian and Gay Studies sponsors an annual "Lesbian and Gay Academic Forum," the University of British Columbia planned a lesbian/gay speakers' series for the fall of 1993, and lesbian/gay/queer conferences have been held at Concordia/Université du Québec à Montréal (1992), New College, University of Toronto (1993), and York University (1994).

5. On the topic of lesbians, AIDS, and HIV, see Mary Louise Adams, "All That Rubber, All That Talk," in Inez Rieder and Patricia Ruppelt, eds, *AIDS: The Women* (San Francisco: Cleis Press 1988), 130-3; Mona Oikawa, "Safer Sex in Santa Cruz," *Fireweed: Asian Canadian Women* 30

(Spring 1990): 31-4; Diane Richardson, *Women and the AIDS Crisis* (London: Pandora 1987); Pat Califia, *Macho Sluts* (Boston: Alyson Publications 1989); The ACT UP/NY Women and AIDS Book Group, eds., *Women, AIDS and Activism* (Toronto: Between the Lines 1990); Sue O'Sullivan's interview with Cindy Patton, "Mapping: Lesbians, AIDS and Sexuality," *Feminist Review*, Spring 1990: 120-33; Jackie Winnow, "Lesbians Working on AIDS: Assessing the Impact of Health Care for Women," *Out/Look*, Summer 1989: 10-18; and Ruth L. Schwartz, "New Alliances, Strange Bedfellows: Lesbians, Gay Men and AIDS," in Stein, ed., *Sisters, Sexperts and Queers*, 230-44. For a cogent analysis of African American women and AIDS, see Evelynn Hammonds, "Missing Persons: African American Women, AIDS and the History of Disease," *Radical America* 24, 2 (1992): 7-23.

6.   Cherrie Moraga, "La Güera," in Moraga and Anzaldua, eds., *This Bridge Called My Back*, 29.

7.   bell hooks, *From Margin to the Centre* (Boston: South End Books 1984), 24.

8.   On the problem of theorizing and implementing a class-conscious lesbian and gay politics, see Dorothy Allison, "A Question of Class," in Stein, ed., *Sisters, Sexperts and Queers*, 133-55; and Steven Maynard, "When Queer Is Not Enough," *Fuse*, Fall 1991: 14-18. And see Alexander Chee, "Queer Nationalism," Steve Cosson, "Queer Voices," and Maria Maggenti, "Women as Queer Nationals" *Out/Look*, Winter 1991: 12-23. On homophobia in racial communities, see bell hooks, "Reflections on Homophobia and Black Communities," *Out/Look*, Summer 1988: 22-5; and Smith and Gomez, "Taking the Home out of Homophobia," 32-7.

9.   Gay Doherty, "The Trauma of Our Justice System," *Quota*, September 1993: 1, 4.

10. The categories of public and private have been, and continue to be, integral to the state regulation and administration of sex. Most recently announced sex legislation includes Bill C-49, which criminalizes "communication for the purposes of prostitution," and Bill C-61, which criminalizes "corrupting morals" (Section 159), "keeping a common bawdy house" (Section 193), and "procuring and living on the avails of prostitution" (Section 195). Bill C-128 provides for up to ten years' imprisonment for the production, distribution, and importation or sale of "child pornography": the sexually explicit representation of anyone under 18, or anyone who appears to be under 18. For criticism of the federal "Kiddie Porn" bill, see Brenda Cossman, "How the State Created a Bunch of Paedophiles," *X-tra!* 236 (12 November 1993): 17.

11. For analysis of the debate that swirled around the passage of the new youth-pornography law, see Heather Cameron, "Who's Really Being Targeted? Kiddie Porn Will Allow Police a 'Foot in the Door,'" *X-tra!* 226 (25 June 1993): 15. Also see Brenda Cossman, "How the State Created a Bunch of Paedophiles," 17. Cossman argues that the North American Man-Boy Love Association (NAMBLA) was used and demonized to justify the new youth-pornography law. "The message conveyed was that all gay men are paedophiles ... [which] is a central element in the hate campaign being waged by the religious right and its efforts to depict gay men and lesbians as the new evil enemy. The debates around Bill 128 gave reasoned legitimacy to this homophobic rhetoric." And see Eleanor Brown, "Hustler Speaks Out on Obscenity Charge," *X-Tra!*, 13 May 1994: 11.

12. Eleanor Brown, "Canadian Forces Surrender: Court Decision Opens Gates for Lesbian and Gay Soldiers," *X-Tra!* 209 (30 October 1992.): 15.

13. Richard Mackie, "Quebec Urged to Follow Ontario on Gay Benefits," *Globe and Mail*, 2 June 1994: AS.

14. In "Who Gets to Be Family," Carol Allen makes the valuable point that poor lesbians on social assistance might suffer economically when the definition of spouse changes in the Family Benefits Act. It is possible, Allen argues, that one woman might then be considered financially depen-

dent on her (female) spouse, which would make the couple vulnerable to cut-backs in family benefits in Linda Carty, ed., *And Still We Rise: Feminist Political Mobilizing in Contemporary Canada* Toronto: Women's Press 1993, 105. For a compelling argument in favour of same-sex spousal benefits from the standpoint of a lesbian mother, see Katherine Arnup, "We Are Family: Lesbian Mothers in Canada," *Resources for Feminist Research* 20, 3 & 4 (Fall 1991): 101-7. Also see Coalition of Lesbian and Gay Rights of Ontario, *Happy Families: The Recognition of Same-Sex Spousal Relationships*, 1993.

15. Two days before the second reading of Bill 167, Attorney General Marion Boyd elected to remove a provision that would have given same-sex couples the right to apply for child adoption. She also agreed not to change the current legal definition of spouse or of marital status. Lesbian and gay activists expressed outrage and disappointment that the amendments weakened the initial bill and capitulated to the right wing. See Craig McInnes, "Boyd Backs Off on Gay Spouses," *Globe and Mail*, 9 June 1994: Al, Al0.

16. Craig McInnes, "To Homosexual Parents, A Family Is a Family," *Globe and Mail*, 2 June 1994: Al, A4. In 1993, an Unemployment Insurance Commission appeals board ruled that two women are spouses. The ruling argued that one of the women had "just cause" to quit her job (to relocate to be with her lover) and should receive unemployment benefits. The UI Commission is appealing the decision to a federal-court judge. See Eleanor Brown, "These Two Women Are Spouses," *X-tra!*, 7 January 1994: 1.

17. Chris Hodgson Campaign, "Same-Sex Benefits," *Lindsay Post*, 11 March 1994.

18. Julie Smith, "Archbishop Assails Same-Sex Benefits," *Globe and Mail*, 30 May 1994: AS.

19. Scott Feschuk, "Alberta Tories in a Bind over Gay-Rights Decision," *Globe and Mail*, 14 April 1994.

20. Craig McInnes, Martin Mittelstaedt, and James Rusk, "Ontario Bill on Gay Rights Defeated," *Globe and Mail*, 10 June 1994: Al, Al0.

21. Didi Khayatt, "Legalized Invisibility: The Effect of Bill 7 on Lesbian Teachers," *Women's Studies International Forum* 13, 3 (1990): 185-93.

22. For an informative, well-argued consideration of the limitations of civil-rights strategies pursued by lesbian and gay activists, see Didi Herman, *Rights of Passage: Struggles for Lesbian and Gay Legal Equality* (Toronto, University of Toronto Press 1994).

23. Allen, "Who Gets to Be Family," in Carty, ed., *And Still We Rise*, 103.

24. Alisa Solomon, "Dykotomies: Scents and Sensibility," in Stein, ed., *Sisters, Sexperts and Queers*, 215. In the same collection, see Lisa Kahaleole Chang Hall, "Bitches in Solitude: Identity Politics and Lesbian Community," 218-29.

25. Donna Minkowitz, "The Well of Correctness," *Village Voice*, 21 May 1991: 39.

26. Susie Bright (a.k.a. Susie Sexpert), *Susie Sexpert's Lesbian Sex World* (San Francisco: Cleis Press 1990), and *Susie Bright's Sexual Reality: A Virtual Sex World Reader* (San Francisco: Cleis Press 1992).

27. Shane Phelan, *Identity Politics: Lesbian Feminism and the Limits of Community* (Philadelphia: Temple University Press 1989), 138.

28. Judith Butler, "Imitation and Gender Insubordination," in Diana Fuss, ed., *Inside Out: Lesbian Theories, Gay Theories* (London and New York: Routledge 1991), 13-31.

29. Bernice Johnson Reagon, "Coalition Politics: Turning the Century," in Barbara Smith, ed., *Home Girls: A Black Feminist Anthology* (New York: Kitchen Table Press 1983), 356-69.

30. On transsexuality, see Chris Martin, "World's Greatest Cocksucker: Transsexual Interviews," *Fierio, International* 22 (San Diego: San Diego University Press 1992), 101-22.

31. Judith Butler poses this question in her essay "Critically Queer," *GLQ: A Journal of Lesbian and Gay Studies* 1, 1 (1993): 18.

INTRODUCTION: EQUALITY AND THE CHARTER: TEN YEARS OF FEMINIST ADVOCACY BEFORE THE SUPREME COURT

Women's Legal Education and Action Fund

15. (1) Every individual is equal before and under the law and has the right to equal protection and equal benefit of the law without discrimination, and in particular, without discrimination based on race, national or ethnic origin, colour, religion, sex, age, or mental or physical disability.

(2) Subsection (I) does not preclude any law, program or activity that has as its object the amelioration of conditions of disadvantaged individuals or groups. Including those that are disadvantaged because of race, national or ethnic origin, colour, religion, sex, age, or mental or physical disability.

28. Notwithstanding anything in this Charter, the rights and freedoms referred to in it are guaranteed equally to male and female persons.[1]

The story of the Women's Legal Education and Action Fund (LEAF) is a story about women undertaking law reform and legal analysis in a very particular way. Using traditional legal tools, they continually assert women's rights to be recognized as "human beings equally deserving of concern, respect and consideration."[2] This book presents a portion of these women's work, with a minimum of embellishment. It is 10 years since LEAF launched its first case. Certainly it is time for an overview but in the arena in which LEAF operates—litigation of Charter issues before Canada's highest court—10 years is a brief interlude. It is not yet possible to judge LEAF's effect on equality jurisprudence in this country in a definitive way. However, it is possible to present what LEAF has done.

LEAF, occasionally in coalition with other organizations, has submitted 23 facta (the briefs used in legal appeals) to the Supreme Court of Canada. They are found on the following pages. There are cases in lower courts in which LEAF's work was significant,[3] but this book is limited to the Supreme Court of Canada because, arguably, that is where our greater influence has been. This limitation also provides thematic consistency, for the facta possess a continuity of language and argument that is occasioned by the legal forum for which they were written.

This book will be of interest to feminist activists, legal practitioners and historians, students of equality theory and advocacy, and people who have followed and supported LEAF's work. The facta represents a sizeable portion of LEAF's legal history. They are impressive for both their technical and creative quality. They also provide a means of assess whether LEAF has been able to sustain its feminist roots while transforming its beliefs into legal action.

A History of LEAF

On April 17, 1985, section 15 of the Canadian Charter of Rights and Freedoms became law. On the same day, the creation of LEAF was formally announced. The link was intentional, for the women[4] who founded LEAF were among the many who affected Canadian constitutional history by ensuring that their views were considered during the constitutional negotiations on the equality sections of the Charter: sections 15 and 28. Their success convinced these women that they had a continuing role to play to ensure that the promise of section 15 was converted into tangible gains.

The LEAF founders' conviction sprang from their understanding that the development of true equality in Canadian society could not be achieved through constitutional amendment alone. To continue and expand upon the influence gained at the constitutional table, many of these women concluded that they needed to participate in the ensuing law reform and constitutional litigation. The task of conceiving and implementing a strategy for this participation was facilitated by the three-year delay between the Charter's proclamation in 1982 and section 15's enactment in 1985. However, as Sherene Razack notes in her book *Canadian Feminism and the Law* the idea of a legal action fund was percolating among the core LEAF group as early as 1981.[5]

A number of conferences and consultations were organized. A group known as the Charter of Rights Educational Fund (CREF) organized the Study Days on January 15 and February 19, 1983. The study days attracted more than 170 participants from Canada and the United States who pondered issues ranging from the systemic nature of sex discrimination to the exact meaning of section 28 of the Charter. CREF also struck a committee to undertake an audit of federal and Ontario legislation in violation of section 15. The enormous document was released in January 1985.[6] Similar audits, mostly spearheaded by women, took place across the country.[7] These initiatives, impressive in themselves, were all the more so when arrayed against the relative inaction of the federal and provincial governments in undertaking similar surveys, when this was the very purpose for which section 15 was delayed three years.

The Canadian Advisory Council on the Status of Women funded a research study to identify the type of agency that would enable women to both develop expertise on equality rights and influence the application and interpretation of those rights. Entitled *Women and*

Legal Action, the study was released on October 1984. After examining landmark legal cases for Canadian women, existing advocacy organizations in Canada and the American experience with litigation funds, the study concluded that "... a legal action fund to concentrate on issues of sex-based discrimination is an essential component of an effective strategy to promote the interests of women in the Canadian legal system."[8]

The result of these various initiatives was a rich resource for LEAF in coming years: a starting point for LEAF's equality analysis and a focus to its litigation.[9]

Litigation is an expensive business. Between August 1984 and April 1985, LEAF's founders principally applied themselves to the daunting task of generating sufficient capital to establish the operations of an organization devoted to legal activity. They were successful, in no small part, because among them were some of the most prominent feminist lawyers, activists, and fund-raisers in the country. In fact, the creation of LEAF in such a short period of time is a clear illustration of privilege transformed into progressive social activity.

Today, LEAF is a non-profit organization governed by a national board of directors. Branches and chapters exist across Canada. Board and committee members are volunteers. There is a national office in Toronto with paid staff as well as an office in Vancouver run by West Coast LEAF, a legally separate organization.

LEAF's mandate is two-fold: to participate in litigation that promotes equality for women and to educate the public about this litigation and its relationship to women's equality. Litigation is overseen by a committee of the board called the National Legal Committee. The Legal Committee is composed of women who possess extensive litigation experience and/or a sophisticated understanding of equality issues.

The mandate of the Legal Committee is to select and manage LEAF's litigation. This responsibility entails working toward the development of a comprehensive theory of substantive equality for all women, developing fundamental principles of legal analysis, establishing case and project selection criteria, and setting priority issue areas.

Cases come to LEAF's attention in a variety of ways: through regular examination of case law digests; through an informal network of lawyers, academics, and women's organizations; and through the approximately 1,000 inquiries LEAF receives from the public each year.

Once a case is identified, it is, assessed according to certain criteria. These criteria have changed during the past 10 years. In April 1985, the women who founded LEAF agreed upon the following criteria:

1. The case would be an equality rights case.

2. It would arise under the Charter, or equivalent provisions of other provincial legislation.

3. It would be a test case: it would involve breaking new ground, challenging a discriminatory law or advancing the interpretation of equality rights guarantees, and would have the potential to improve women's rights significantly.

4. It would present strong enough facts so that there would be little chance of its being decided on grounds that did not require an equality analysis.

5. Ideally, it would result in significant gains for women, or gains for a significant number of women.

6. It would be of special interest to LEAF if it raised issues of multiple discrimination, or discrimination on grounds other than and in addition to sex.

These criteria were developed at a time when LEAF's staff and board envisioned their work as proactive: identifying discriminatory law and practices and initiating court actions to eliminate them. As will be discussed in the next section, this vision was severely tested by the plethora of cases in which LEAF had to respond to challenges raised by others. The criteria were also closely tailored to sponsoring individual cases—a practice that proved to be prohibitively expensive. They did not necessarily address the issues that arise in interventions, the activity that has come to dominate LEAF's legal work.

Over the years, the guidelines have been further developed to reflect LEAF's current work and priorities. They currently read as follows:

1. The case must promote substantive equality for women; ideally, a case will result in significant gains for women, or gains for a significant number of women.

2. Preference will be given to cases arising under the Charter. A case arising under provincial human rights legislation may be taken if it otherwise meets the criteria.

3. The case must involve breaking new ground and/or establishing a legal precedent that affects the collective interests of women. (Note that the words "test case" have been removed because interventions are not generally recognized as test-case litigation.)

4. The case must enable the Court to decide the equality issue, or, in the alternative, it must otherwise advance the equality jurisprudence.

5. Regardless of the merits of the case, it must also lend itself to fashioning a remedy capable of concretely advancing women's equality rights.

6. Cases that allow for follow-up with respect to education, monitoring, and implementation of a successful decision will be given preference.

7. The Legal Committee will give priority to cases that will address issues of multiple discrimination and diversify LEAF's caseload.

Before being adopted, cases are summarized to the Legal Committee in a case proposal. Aside from detailing the precise nature of the equality issues, case proposals address other questions unique to LEAF's litigation philosophy including: avenues for addressing the inequality besides litigation; coalition and consultation possibilities; and the case's potential impact on women who experience diverse forms of discrimination.

Litigating Equality for Women: Underlying Principles

LEAF acknowledges that inequality is a continuing state for many different groups in society. However, LEAF's particular mandate is to address the inequalities experienced by women. With this in mind, three main principles animate LEAF's equality theory:

1. Women as a group, compared with men as a group, experience widespread and pervasive discrimination.

2. Women who are oppressed on the basis of, for example, their race, class, sexual orientation, religion or disability, experience inequality different in degree and/or kind, in various contexts.

3. Law can be an effective tool for egalitarian social change.

In accordance with the first principle, LEAF recognizes that women suffer sex-based discrimination in specific and concrete areas of their lives, such as: physical safety, access to fulfilling and fairly paid work, family and childcare responsibilities, reproductive choice, and economic security; in addition, LEAF recognizes that these concrete forms of discrimination represent persistent attacks on women's dignity, autonomy, credibility, power, and membership in community.[10]

Once the systemic inequality of women is understood as a pervasive social and legal condition. LEAF argues that litigating equality for women under section 15 of the Charter must proceed in a particular way. From the inception of its Supreme Court of Canada litigation, beginning with the *Andrews* case, LEAF advocated a purposive approach to section 15.

LEAF argues that the purpose of section 15 is to redress injustices and enhance the position of those groups who have been and remain subject to systemic discrimination. With respect to women, section 15 must be used to reject laws and practices that reinforce and shape their disempowerment. Conversely, section 15 supports laws and practices that promote women's equal enjoyment of legal, political, economic, and social benefits that historically have been reserved for men as a group.

The purposive approach to equality is articulated in LEAF's work in a variety of ways. LEAF firmly rejects any approach to equality which contains or promotes what is called the "similarly situated test." This approach, also known as the Aristotelian or formal equality approach, posits that equality is achieved by treating like persons alike, and unlike person unalike. As a test of rational consistency, it accords well with what are known as process claims. Process claims relate to the law's administration; they do not and cannot address how law is made, to whom it applies, its impact on oppressed groups, or its contribution to systemic inequality.

What the similarly situated test cannot answer are the following questions: How are persons or groups found to be alike? How are they found to be unalike? Who determines the categories for comparison? What are the underlying criteria that form the basis for the comparison? As the Ontario Court of Appeal held in an early Charter case, these unanswered questions represent the fatal defect of the similarly situated test:

> It is not always clear whether persons are or are not similarly situated, and whether, even if they are not, this is relevant to a section 15 inquiry.... It is usually possible to find differences between classes of persons, and, on the basis of these differences, conclude that person are not similarly situated. However, what are perceived to be "differences" between classes of persons could be the result of stereotypes based on existing inequalities which the equality provisions of the Charter are designed to eliminate, not perpetuate.[11]

In other words, the similarly situated test carries with it the risk of importing into an equality analysis the values of an unequal society. For example, differences that arise through socially imposed disadvantage may become the criteria for unequal treatment that maintains and even promotes that disadvantage. When the subjects compared are men and women, the problem becomes particularly acute because biological and gender differences (both real and perceived) may be classed as differences that justify disadvantageous treatment of women; the historical refusal to recognize women's particular needs during and after pregnancy and childbirth is one example.

LEAF has also developed arguments to build upon the recognition in human rights law that discrimination often assumes indirect and unintentional forms. Very few laws deliver blatantly unequal treatment of women. Instead, much discrimination occurs indirectly and is attributable to systemic biases that are difficult to identify and more difficult still to eliminate. Many laws can be shown to have developed in accordance with standards for entitlement or recognition of social needs that appear neutral but are actually based upon male experience.[12]

Laws can be deficient both in what they do and what they fail to do. For example, until recently, sexual harassment was not recognized as an actionable harm in the human rights or criminal law context. This is understandable only if one adopts the view that men's exploitation of women's sexuality is not only *not* harmful, it is natural. Even after sexual harassment was deemed unacceptable conduct, there continued to be resistance to recognize it as an important obstacle to women's equality because the term appears gender-neutral and could in theory, refer to harassment of men by women. In reality, sexual harassment is something that is almost exclusively done to women by men. Moreover, the sexual exploitation of any person is intrinsically linked with a socially ascribed status that is uniquely female. Looked at in this broader way, sexual harassment can be seen for what it is, and indeed what the Supreme Court has recognized as such: sex-based discrimination.[13]

The second principle by which LEAF operates is that different women experience inequality differently. Although LEAF's mandate states that the organization seeks to promote equality for all women in Canada, LEAF recognizes that inequality is experienced in many ways and on many levels. Women experience disadvantage not only because of their sex but because of other characteristics such as race, national or ethnic origin, sexual orientation, or disability. Where multiple discrimination is experienced by the same person or groups of persons, the resulting inequality may call for a very different analysis.

LEAF has been criticized for failing to address women's inequality in all its complexity and diversity. This criticism is not without foundation. Because LEAF's founding board and staff were white, middle class professional women, there was legitimate skepticism of LEAF's ability to respond to and incorporate the interests and experiences of diverse women. Furthermore, the nature of the litigation process, and in particular the intervention process, is such that schedules and time constraints are often non-negotiable and extremely limiting. This makes it difficult to engage in the kind of extensive consultation with women and women's organizations which is essential if the final product is to reflect women's diverse realities in a respectful and meaningful way. In responding to court deadlines, LEAF has, on occasion, taken shortcuts that were insufficiently attentive to the impact of LEAF's positions on more marginalized women. Furthermore, it must be acknowledged that the goal of a comprehensive equality theory that accommodates women's differences is an elusive one. The issues raised are uniquely difficult, as is translating them into legal theory and argument.

It bears pointing out that LEAF's internal struggle to become more responsive to the needs of all women mirrors the struggle in the greater feminist community.[14] Feminist legal theorists have been confronted with the stark reality that, in choosing to examine women's experience without reference to their particular and unique realities, they render those women with the bleakest realities invisible.[15] To its credit, LEAF has not shied away from this daunting challenge, and has organized a three-fold response: organizational, theoretical, and experiential.

Organizationally, LEAF adopted a Diversification Policy in 1990,[16] which it applies in many ways: actively pursuing a broad representation of women throughout the organization; recognizing the importance of inclusiveness and accountability in its administration and governance processes; and selecting and litigating cases that will involve and affect the greatest possible number and range of women. The development and adoption of the policy has been a long-term commitment. Perhaps the policy's most important accomplishment to date is that it has forced LEAF to confront the barriers to diversity posed by LEAF's commitment to litigation, an activity that relies upon skills and qualifications obtainable only through privileged processes.

On a theoretical level, LEAF's staff and National Legal Committee attempt to incorporate into their legal work the conflicting insights that often accompany the recognition of women's difference. All case proposals must address the potential impact of a case on different groups of women. More specifically, LEAF demands that serious and sustained thought be given to the question: how will a particular case, and the equality strategy LEAF adopts, impact on the most disadvantaged women in society?

Finally, to broaden its knowledge and understanding of different women's lives, LEAF has relied to an ever-increasing degree upon the insight and expertise of other women's organizations. In particular, LEAF has approached these organizations for assistance in forming the analysis around particular cases. That is why, more recently, LEAF has intervened not in its own name but as one member of a coalition.

The move to coalition work has had several implications. It has highlighted the difficulty of putting a theory of inclusiveness into practice. It is difficult to condense complex legal and social issues into a 20-page factum, even when only one organizational viewpoint—LEAF's—must be reflected. It is more difficult when many organizations are involved whose viewpoints are diverse and often conflicting.

Coalition work has further acknowledged the expertise of women who are not formally trained in the study of law but who have clear insight into how the law works to oppress women. Organizationally and through its membership, LEAF has the aura that comes from being a player in the legal arena. This imparts to LEAF, and the women behind it, a particular kind of privilege, which in part explains LEAF's continued access to the legal process. However, feminist litigation requires blending the power of the legal process with the rich detail and nuances of women's reality. It is crucial for the litigation process to take note of the varied ways in which the law actually operates in women's lives, which are not immediately apparent to those who make the arguments in court.

Finally, by including more and different women in the discussion and activity surrounding a case, LEAF has fundamentally changed its litigation processes. In this work to increase its experience base and expertise, LEAF perhaps comes closest to employing the consciousness-raising that many scholars have identifed as critical to a feminist method.[17]

LEAF's third principle is a committment to the law's utility as a tool for egalitarian social change. LEAF believes that women need to participate in Charter litigation based on principles of substantive equality—that is, principles dcsigned to make changes in the material conditions of women's lives. This belief has been stringently tested over the past 10 years. LEAF has had to reassess its expectations as well as its strategies. Significantly, however, LEAF has never abandoned this founding belief.

LEAF's first annual report, *LEAF Litigation: Year One*, stated: "The primary focus of LEAF is to do proactive work. The ability to control the litigation agenda, to decide the timing and the substance of the challenges, is one very significant reason why women find LEAF empowering."[18] Adopting the stratgegy of advocacy groups such as the National Association for the Advancement of Coloured People, LEAF's founders hoped the organization could occupy the field of women's equality litigation, become recognized as an expert, and, by selecting appropriate cases, ensure that small but important progressive steps were made.[19]

This proactive vision was severely tested by early equality cases that often involved male litigants who sought to undermine benefits achieved by feminist law reform. For example, men challenged the criminalization of sexual assaults, previously viewed as consensual, between older men and underage girls. Men also lost no time challenging evidentiary rules designed to ensure fair, non-sexist treatment of complainants during sexual assault trials. On other fronts, men challenged laws such as those providing economic assistance to single mothers, which were enacted to address the severe hardship of the most impoverished women.

In these and other cases, LEAF participated simply to ensure that existing positive schemes for women were not dismantled. This participation was different from what LEAF originally envisioned. Instead of initiating a challenge on behalf of a woman or women adversely affected by existing laws, LEAF's role was as an intervenor—a third party permitted to make arguments in order to assist the court in its deliberations.

These developments had several implications for LEAF's litigation strategy. First, because an intervenor must always obtain leave of the court to participate, LEAF had to expend resources to ensure its right to intervene, both in particular cases and through policy work on the need for public interest intervention. Second, as intervenor, LEAF had to deal with the case as framed by the parties. Third, LEAF had to act within very short timelines and be in a state of continual readiness. Fourth, in its role as an intervenor, LEAF could not easily maintain contact with individual women litigants and the complexities of their lives.

Because of those and other difficulties that are not limited to LEAF, many feminists strongly oppose Charter litigation as a means to effect progressive social change. The critique of Charter litigation includes the following perceived problems: it is undemocratic because it judicializes what are in fact political issues,[20] it drains women's resources, especially financial, that are better deployed in more overtly radical activities,[21] it is the domain of privileged men in which women are at a profound disadvantage,[22] and it is illusory because it fosters the belief that real change is possible, when in fact existing social and political structures remain intact and may even be strengthened.[23]

These are powerful charges of which women engaged in law reform and litigation must take note. LEAF does not have simple answers to these concerns. However, LEAF's experience over the past 10 years has allowed it to develop strategies to deal with these limitations.

Certainly the judiciary is an unrepresentative segment of society. However, elected institutions are no more representative and in recent years have been positively hostile to women's concerns and indeed equality issues in general. That members of the bench are not accountable in the same sense as elected representatives is not entirely negative since their independence is accompanied by the freedom to accept politically unpopular arguments. Similarly, their lengthy and uninterrupted tenures provide groups such as LEAF the opportunity to create and implement strategies that recognize that equality-seeking is a long-term endeavour.

With respect to allocating women's resources, there is no doubt that litigation is tremendously expensive. But it is wrong to assume that the women who support LEAF's work have abandoned other methods of effecting social change. Litigation is simply one strategy among many. At some point, however, it is a strategy that must be considered because inevitably legal schemes will be vulnerable to Charter attack. In the words of one commentator, "[the] women's movement cannot abjure the Charter. The Charter will not abjure us."[24] Challenges to progressive legislation cannot go unanswered. The early section 15 cases present a striking display of the clash between two possible methods of Charter interpretation: a civil libertarian model focused on individual rights and freedoms, and a systemic model that continually presses for the recognition and amelioration of existing group-based inequalities. LEAF, indeed women in general, cannot afford to shun this battle.

As well, the law *itself* often operates as a clear and direct impediment to women' equality. For example, women's legal status has been impaired or even denied through disciminatory provisions such as those found in the immigration and Indian acts. Their exercise of reproductive autonomy has been criminalized. The systemic legal barriers that adversely affect women's daily lives require, at some point, the pursuit of legal remedies to remove them.

Certainly, women are at a preliminary disadvantage when they litigate under the current conditions of male power and privilege, which are paramount in the legal arena. However, within LEAF itself, litigation has come to encompass processes quite alien to its conventional meaning. LEAF's continued success, and the success of other organizations, in obtaining leave to intervene in a variety of cases is evidence that the parameters within which such cases are defined can be influenced and even changed. LEAF's interventions in private civil actions[25] have illustrated that equality issues arise in cases traditionally considered too narrow and individualistic to warrant the application of public law principles. LEAF's interventions in criminal cases, perhaps the archetype of the individual rights model of Charter interpretation, sends a clear message that the criminal law involves more than the rights of an accused person measured against the state's interest in law and order; it involves women's rights to equal protection of the criminal law and equal security of the person, in both civil and criminal law cases; LEAF's intervention arguments set precedents merely by the fact that the Court allowed them to be made.[26]

Finally, there is the argument that the Charter is illusory and dangerous because it precludes real systemic change. What constitutes real systemic change is a matter of debate and an issue on which women can legitimately differ. Some scholars point to feminist equality challenges as a bright light in an otherwise gloomy 10 years of Charter litigation.[27] Certainly, there are cases presented in this book that represent significant symbolic and material gains for women.

Criticisms of the Charter's efficacy as a tool for egalitarian social change must be badanced against the realization that the Charter is a fact of our legal and social universe. Although most women did not specifically ask for a constitutionally entrenched bill of rights, the women who founded and continue to support LEAF responded to the Charter's advent by demanding that it harm women as little as possible and live up to its rhetorical claims. These women welcomed the challenges posed by the Charter, and their work over the past 10 years highlights the Charter's potential not only to vouchsafe women's equality, but to advance it.

ENDNOTES

1.   Canadian Charter of Rights and Freedoms. Part I of the Constitution Act, 1982, being Schedule B of the Canada Act 1982 (UK), 1982, c. 11.

2. *Andrews v. Law Society of British Columbia*, per McIntyre J. 171.

3. See Appendix H of *Equality and the Charter*.

4. Some men were also involved in founding LEAF, and today many men are among LEAF's supporters.

5. Sherene Razack, *Canadian Feminism and the Law* (Toronto: Second Story Press, 1991), 36.

6. Charter of Rights Education Fund, *Report on the Statute Audit Project: A Preliminary Analysis of Selected Federal and Ontario Laws Based on the Sex Equality Provisions of the Canadian Charter of Rights and Freedoms* (Toronto: 1985).

7. See, for example, Charter of Rights Coalition (BC), *Women's Equality and the Charter of Rights and Freedoms: Preliminary Review of Selected British Columbia Legislation*.

8. M. Elizabeth Atcheson, Mary Eberts, and Beth Symes, *Women and Legal Action* (1984: Canadian Advisory Council on the Status of Women), 163.

9. Charter of Rights Education Fund, *Study Day Papers* (Toronto, 1985).

10. *Andrews v. Law Society of British Columbia*, LEAF Factum, paragraph 57.

11. *Century 21 Ramos Realty Inc. v. The Queen* (1987), 5B OR(2d) 737, 756-57.

12. Helena Orton, "Litigation for Equality—LEAF's Approach to Section 15 of the Charter," March 1989, 5, in Karen Busby et al., eds., *Equality Issues in Family Law*.

13. *Janzen and Govereau v. Platy Enterprises Ltd. et al.* (1989) 1 SCR 1251.

14. See, for example, Marlee Kline, "Race, Racism and Feminist Legal Theory" (1989), 12 *Harvard Women's Law Journal* 115.

15. Martha Minow, "Feminist Reason: Getting It and Losing It" (1988), 38 *Journal of Legal Education* 47, 56.

16. Copy available from the National Office on request.

17. See, for example, Richard F. Devlin, "Normos and Thanatos (Part B): Feminism as Jurisgenerative Transformation or Resistance Through Partial Incorporation?" (1990), *Dalhousie Law Journal* 123, 171.

18. Mary Eberts and Gwen Brodsky, *LEAF Litigation: Year One*, March 31, 1986, 8.

19. Razack, supra, 52.

20. Michael Mandel, *The Charter of Rights and Legalization of Politics in Canada* (Toronto: Wall and Thompson, 1989), Chapter 2.

21. Judy Fudge, "The Effects of Entrenching a Bill of Rights upon Political Discourse: Feminist Demands and Sexual Violence in Canada" (1989), 17 *International Journal of Sociology and the Law* 445, 457.

22. Elizabeth Shilton, "Charter Litigation and the Policy of Government: A Public Interest Perspective" (1992), 30:3 *Osgoode Hall* LJ 653, 654.

23. Allan Hutchinson, "Waiting for Coraf (or the Beautification of the Charter)" (1991), 41 *University of Toronto* LJ 332.

24. Shilton, supra, 655.

25. *Norberg v. Wynrib*, (1992) 2 SCR 226; K.M. v. H.M., (1992) 3 SCR 6; and *Moge v. Moge*, (1992) 3 SCR 813.

26. Sharon Lavoie, "Advocating Values: Public Interest Intervention in Charter Litigations" (1992-93), 2 *National Journal of Constitutional Law* 26.

27. Richard Sigurdson, "The Left-Legal Critique of the Charter: A Critical Assessment" (1993), 13 *Windsor Yearbook of Access to Justice* 117, 130-34.

THE GENDERED DIVISION OF LABOUR AND THE FAMILY

In the mid-sixties, many U.S., British and Canadian feminist scholars and activists were debating the origins of women's oppression. As outlined in the introduction to "Canadian Feminist Theories," some consulted existing theoretical frameworks to understand women's oppression, while others totally dismissed them. Those who worked with existing theoretical frameworks, particularly Marxism, exposed the faulty logic and androcentric assumptions that precluded an understanding of women's oppression. In 1969, Margaret Benston's pivotal piece "The Political Economy of Women's Liberation" provided one of the early insights that changed the way in which we would come to understand productive and unproductive labour. Benston was writing in a context where there was, and still remains, a deeply rooted belief that women's labour in the home was natural, that it was simply a labour of love. In such a context, drawing attention to the invisible, essential and unpaid character of domestic labour provided an important window of analysis into women's oppression in the home, and helped to explain the low wages women receive in the paid labour force. Benston made explicit the ways in which women's unpaid labour is critical to capitalism. Deploying a Marxist analysis, she emphasized women's work in the home as a distinct form of production—the production of use values for direct consumption. Subsequently, many Canadian feminist scholars and activists have attended to the important relationships between unpaid domestic labour and the economy. In fact, though somewhat overstated, Meg Luxton and Heather Jon Maroney contend that Marxist feminist analyses of women's work in the home is the "only instance where Canadian contributions have been internationally recognized"(1987, p.18).

A decade after Benston's article was published, Bonnie Fox brought together many influential Canadian Marxist feminist scholars in the edited collection *Hidden in the*

Household (1980). In keeping with a materialist method, Fox argues that we need to shift the analysis of women's oppression from an experiential to a structural level. In particular, the household as site of women's oppression needs to be examined more fully, from a historical perspective and in relation to capitalist production. She calls for "a theoretical analysis of women's domestic labour… (which) must clarify the *particular nature* of domestic labour and thus women's oppression *under capitalism*" (italics in the original, 11). As well, although not included in this collection, Meg Luxton's *More than a Labour of Love* (1980) (and her subsequent work on socialist feminism and feminist political economy) carefully documents and theorizes the ways in which reproductive and productive labour are entwined. *More than a Labour of Love* undertakes an empirical study of women's work in the home, from childcare, through to housework, cooking, and caring for husbands. Luxton argues that until the gendering of domestic labour ends, sexual equality is impossible.

The changing relationship of domestic labour and the sexual division of paid labour are brought to the fore in this reader by Pat Armstrong's "Restructuring Public and Private: Women's Paid and Unpaid Work" (1997). Armstrong has written extensively on the gendering of paid and unpaid work (see 1993, with Hugh Armstrong) as well as more recent articles on the health care system and women's work in health care occupations (1996). In the article we include here, Armstrong persuasively demonstrates how women's work continues to be shaped by shifting meanings in the public and private spheres. She describes a dramatic shift in the equation of public with masculine that occurred in postwar Canada as increasing numbers of women entered the paid work force. In addition, after much feminist political struggle, policies were implemented to enhance women's economic opportunities and ease their private responsibilities (for example, paid maternity and parental leave, tax deductions for childcare, and anti-discrimination laws).

Despite these decisive changes in the gendered composition of the workforce and in public policy, Armstrong illustrates how the sexual division of labour remains almost intact in the heterosexual family and in the workforce. Moreover, in the current context of neo-conservatism, characterized by government cutbacks and increased privatization, inequalities have intensified. As Armstrong argues, neo-conservative policy rests on a discourse of re-privatization, in which the family is reconstituted as the building block of society. The embrace of neo-conservatism has meant an erosion of policies aimed at addressing the burden of the double day, just as it has brought about a redesignation of previously "public" responsibilities as "private" duties to be born by women.

The privatized framing of caring work is nowhere more apparent that in the realm of childcare. Clearly, as more and more women engage in paid labour there is a need for good quality, affordable childcare. As the RCSW recognized 30 years ago, the implementation of a national and accessible childcare program is an essential prerequisite for sexual equality (1970). Sixteen years later, the federally appointed Task Force on Childcare (1986) conducted extensive public consultations and recommended a fully funded childcare system. Since that time, the promise of a national childcare strategy has reappeared in electoral platforms only to be dropped from the political agenda. Assumptions about the inherently private nature of "motherwork" have framed federal and provincial government responses to the childcare crisis in the last decades of the twentieth century.

The failure to establish a national childcare program has been accompanied by measures such as enhanced tax deductions, increased (yet very inadequate) amounts of funding for the creation of new child care spaces, and continued subsidization of costs for low income women. Underpinning this piecemeal strategy and reinforced with the embrace of neo-conservatism, is a construction of childcare "as a series of private arrangements to be negotiated by individuals"(Teghtsoonian, 1997, 122). This has left most women relying on unstable and un-regulated forms of childcare. Moreover, reflecting the overall devaluation of women's work, childcare remains a very poorly paid job in which workers earn half of the average Canadian wage (ibid., 123-128). The only exception to this piecemeal strategy is Quebec's recent establishment of a publicly-funded "$5 a day" daycare programme. Its implementation has yet to be systematically studied, but it has been suggested that childcare workers (largely women) continue to subsidize this public programme through low wages.

The interrelation between women's paid work and their ongoing responsibilities for caring work and domestic labour has been a central terrain of inquiry for a generation of important Canadian socialist feminist scholars. They have carefully dissected these relationships, drawn out their consequences for women's oppression and succeeded in highlighting the distinctions between the ideology of familialism, material relations within families, and historically changing family forms. As Mackie contends, feminist scholarship has shown us how the structure of families and family roles are not biologically determined but are instead socially constructed and influenced by state policy, the nature of the economy and many other institutions. This scholarship has also challenged the idealization of the traditional nuclear family model (a family form that is statistically in decline) and is attending to the diversity of family forms. Finally, the dominant notion of "the family as a haven in a heartless world" has been effectively deconstructed through feminists analyses of intimate violence (see Chapter Six), power relationships within families, and inequalities in domestic labour.

Despite the critical importance of such writings on work and family within Canadian feminist theory, socialist feminist scholarship has been insufficiently attentive to the ways that race, heterosexuality, able-bodiedness and age shape women's paid and unpaid labour. Moreover, much of the socialist feminist scholarship that did attempt to integrate these concerns often did so through the strategy of addition. Hamilton has argued in *Gendering the Vertical Mosaic* that "(i)n additive models of race, gender, and class ... white women are viewed solely in terms of their gender, while women of colour are 'doubly' or 'triply' oppressed by the cumulative effects of race and gender, or race, class, and gender. Such additive models are resistant to acknowledging the relational nature of each social division, the fact that each is positioned and gains in meaning in relation to the other" (1996, p. 179).

The interrelationship of heterosexism, racism and gender are taken up in this chapter in a series of readings seeking to complicate and deepen a feminist analysis of families. As these readings demonstrate, while feminist theory has drawn attention to the family as a site of oppression and challenged the equation of women and the family, for many Canadian women, families are not prisons, but instead represent precarious achievements. In Das Gupta's critically important article, "Families of Native Peoples, Immigrants, and Peoples of Colour (1995)," she demonstrates how racism and state policies in the area of immigration and native affairs have historically impacted upon the families of indigenous people, immigrants and people of colour. This article demonstrates how the right to family formation has very often been denied to many groups of Canadian women on the basis of race. While not dismissing the insight that families can be oppressive for women of colour, Das Gupta critiques the tendency among many white feminists to reduce the family to oppression. Family forms are not uniform, nor are women's experiences of family life. Das Gupta argues for the embrace of a complex, historical understanding of family forms that would demonstrate how some kinds of families are sanctioned while others are discouraged. She also calls for an appreciation of families as both sites of gender oppression, as well as places of resistance to, and havens from, racism.

Kline's article "Complicating the Ideology of Motherhood (1993)" on the devaluation of native motherhood, echoes the critique framed by Das Gupta. As both authors contend, the Canadian state's historical project of assimilating and colonizing native peoples has had the impact of threatening native families. Native womens' role as mothers has been eroded through such assimilationist policies as: Indian Act provisions removing status from Indian women who married non-Indians; the residential schools policy by which native children were taken away from their families to be educated in Western ways; and the "sixties scoop" during which thousands of native children were seized by child welfare agencies and adopted by white families (see "Our Story," in Chapter Six). As Kline points out, the dominant ideology of motherhood is class and race specific. She investigates contemporary child welfare law and shows how the dominant ideology of motherhood is legally reproduced, constructing native women as "bad" mothers and leaving them vulnerable to losing their children.

The manner in which law and public policy work to privilege the heterosexual nuclear family, while devaluing lesbian motherhood, is taken up by Arnup in her article "Living on the Margins: Lesbian Families and the Law (1997)." While custody law is changing and no longer explicitly discriminates against lesbian women, those who live openly and politically still risk losing their children. As the legal cases discussed in this article reveal, homophobic assumptions continue to frame judicial interpretations of the best interests of the child. In most provinces non-biological partners are not able to legally adopt their children and thus cannot gain legal recognition of their parental rights. While there have been some important legal decisions recognizing "same-sex" partners, heterosexual marriage and common-law relationships remain privileged in many ways.

In the current context, the traditional nuclear family is being reasserted. In our home province, Alberta, "gay marriage" has assumed the status of a moral panic within the governing Conservative caucus. Danielle Crittendon's recent and nationally debated book *What Our Mothers Didn't Tell Us: How Happiness Eludes the Modern Woman* advises women to delay careers, marry early and stay at home with their children (Crosbie, 1999). In this chapter, we have presented the careful and diverse Canadian feminist literature on the gendered division of labour and the complexities of families. We believe this provides an essential basis for informed engagement with such positions.

THE POLITICAL ECONOMY OF WOMEN'S LIBERATION

Margaret Benston

The position of women rests, as everything in our complex society, on an economic base.

Eleanor Marx and Edward Aveling

The "woman question" is generally ignored in analyses of the class structure of society. This is so because, on the one hand, classes are generally defined by their relation to the means of production and, on the other hand, women are not supposed to have any unique relation to the means of production. The category seems instead to cut across all classes; one speaks of working-class women, middle-class women, etc. The status of women is clearly inferior to that of men,[1] but analysis of this condition usually falls into discussing socialization, psychology, interpersonal relations, or the role of marriage as a social institution.[2] Are these, however, the primary factors? In arguing that the roots of the secondary status of women are in fact economic, it can be shown that women as a group do indeed have a definite relation to the means of production and that this is different from that of men. The personal and psychological factors then follow from this special relation to production, and a change in the latter will be a necessary (but not sufficient) condition for changing the former.[3] If this special relation of women to production is accepted, the analysis of the situation of women fits naturally into a class analysis of society.

The starting point for discussion of classes in a capitalist society is the distinction between those who own the means of production and those who sell their labor power for a wage. As Ernest Mandel says:

> The proletarian condition is, in a nutshell, the lack of access to the means of production or means of subsistence which, in a society of generalized commodity production, forces the proletarian to sell his labor power. In exchange for this labor power he receives a wage which then enables him to acquire the means of consumption necessary for satisfying his own needs and those of his family.
>
> This is the structural definition of wage career, the proletarian. From it necessarily flows a certain relationship to his work, to the products of his work, and to his overall situation in society, which can be summarized by the catchword alienation. But there does

not follow from this structural definition any necessary conclusions as to the level of his consumption . . . the extent of his needs, or the degree to which he can satisfy them.[4]

We lack a corresponding structural definition of women. What is needed first is not a complete examination of the symptoms of the secondary status of women, but instead a statement of the material conditions in capitalist (and other) societies which define the group "women." Upon these conditions are built the specific superstructures which we know....

In sheer quantity, household labor, including child care, constitutes a huge amount of socially necessary production. Nevertheless, in a society based on commodity production, it is not usually considered "real work" since it is outside of trade and the market place. It is pre-capitalist in a very real sense. This assignment of household work as the function of a special category "women" means that this group does stand in a different relation to production than the group "men." We will tentatively define women, then, as that group of people who are responsible for the production of simple use-values in those activities associated with the home and family.

Since men carry no responsibility for such production, the difference between the two groups lies here. Notice that women are not excluded from commodity production. Their participation in wage labor occurs but, as a group, they have no structural responsibility in this arm and such participation is ordinarily regarded as transient. Men, on the other hand, are responsible for commodity production; they are not, in principle, given any role in household labor. For example, when they do participate in household production, it is regarded as more than simply exceptional; it is demoralizing, emasculating, even harmful to health. (A story on the front page of the *Vancouver Sun* in January 1969 reported that men in Britain were having their health endangered because they had to do too much housework!)

The material basis for the inferior status of women is to be found in just this definition of women. In a society in which money determines value, women are a group who work outside the money economy. Their work is not worth money, is therefore valueless, is therefore not even real work. And women themselves, who do this valueless work, can hardly be expected to be worth as much as men, who work for money. In structural terms, the closest thing to the condition of women is the condition of others who are or were also outside of commodity production, i.e., serfs and peasants.

In her recent paper on women, Juliet Mitchell introduces the subject as follows: "In advanced industrial society, women's work is only marginal to the total economy. Yet it is through work that man changes natural conditions and thereby produces society. Until there is a revolution in production, the labor situation will prescribe women's situation within the world of men."[5] The statement of the marginality of women's work is an unanalyzed recognition that the work women do is *different* from the work that men do. Such work is not marginal, however; it is just not wage labor and so is not counted. She even says later in the same article, "Domestic labor, even today, is enormous if quantified in terms of productive labor." She gives some figures to illustrate: In Sweden, 2,340 million hours a year are spent by women in housework compared with 1,290 million hours spent by women in industry. And the Chase Manhattan Bank estimates a woman's overall work week at 99.6 hours.

However, Mitchell gives little emphasis to the basic economic factors (in fact she condemns most Marxists for being "overly economist") and moves on hastily to superstructural factors, because she notices that "the advent of industrialization has not so far freed women." What she fails to see is that no society has thus far industrialized housework. Engels points out that the "first premise for the emancipation of women is the reintroduction of the entire female sex into public industry. And this has become possible not only as a result of modern large-scale industry, which not only permits the participation of women in production in large numbers, but actually calls for it and, moreover, strives to convert private domestic work also into a public industry."[6] And later in the same passage: "Here we see already that the emancipation of women and their equality with men are impossible and must remain so as long as women are excluded from socially productive work and restricted to housework, which is private." What Mitchell has not taken into account is that the problem is not simply one of getting women into *existing* industrial production but the more complex one of converting private production of household work into public production.

For most North Americans, domestic work as "public production" brings immediate images of Brave New World or of a vast institution—a cross between a home for orphans and an army barracks—where we would all be forced to live. For this reason, it is probably just as well to outline here, schematically and simplistically, the nature of industrialization.

A pre-industrial production unit is one in which production is small-scale and reduplicated; i.e., there are a great number of little units, each complete and just like all the others. Ordinarily such production units are in some way kin-based and they are multi-purpose, fulfilling religious, recreational, educational, and sexual functions along with the economic function. In such a situation, desirable attributes of an individual, those which give prestige, are judged by more than purely economic criteria: for example, among approved character traits are proper behavior to kin or readiness to fulfill obligations.

Such production is originally not for exchange. But if exchange of commodities becomes important enough, then increased efficiency of production becomes necessary. Such efficiency is provided by the transition to industrialized production which involves the elimination of the kin-based production unit. A large-scale, non-reduplicative production unit is substituted which has only one function, the economic one, and where prestige or status is attained by economic skills. Production is rationalized, made vastly more efficient, and becomes more and more public—part of an integrated social network. An enormous expansion of man's productive potential takes place. Under capitalism such social productive forces are utilized almost exclusively for private profit. These can be thought of as *capitalized* forms of production.

If we apply the above to housework and child rearing, it is evident that each family, each household, constitutes an individual production unit, a pre-industrial entity, in the same way that peasant farmers or cottage weavers constitute pre-industrial production units. The main features are clear, with the reduplicative, kin-based, private nature of the work being the most important. (It is interesting to notice the other features: the multi-purpose functions of the family, the fact that desirable attributes for women do not center on economic prowess, etc.) The rationalization of production effected by a transition to large-scale production has not taken place in this area.

Industrialization is, in itself, a great force for human good; exploitation and dehumanization go with capitalism and not necessarily with industrialization. To advocate the conversion of private domestic labor into a public industry under capitalism is quite a different thing from advocating such conversion in a socialist society. In the latter case the forces of production would operate for human welfare, not private profit, and the result should be liberation, not dehumanization. In this case we can speak of *socialized* forms of production.

These definitions are not meant to be technical but rather to differentiate between two important aspects of industrialization. Thus the fear of the barracks-like result of introducing housekeeping into the public economy is most realistic under capitalism. With socialized production and the removal of the profit motive and its attendant alienated labor, there is no reason why, *in an industrialized society*, industrialization of housework should not result in better production, i.e., better food, more comfortable surroundings, more intelligent and loving child-care, etc., than in the present nuclear family.

The argument is often advanced that, under neocapitalism, the work in the home has been much reduced. Even if this is true, it is not structurally relevant. Except for the very rich, who can hire someone to do it, there is for most women an irreducible minimum of necessary labor involved in caring for home, husband, and children. For a married woman without children this irreducible minimum of work probably takes fifteen to twenty hours a week; for a woman with small children the minimum is probably seventy or eighty hours a week.[7] (There is some resistance to regarding child-rearing as a job. That labor is involved, i.e., the production of use-value, can be clearly seen when exchange-value is also involved—when the work is done by baby sitters, nurses, child-care centers, or teachers. An economist has already pointed out the paradox that if a man marries his housekeeper, he reduces the national income, since the money he gives her is no longer counted as wages.) The reduction of housework to the minimums given is also expensive; for low-income families more labor is required. In any case, household work remains structurally the same—a matter of private production.

One function of the family, the one taught to us in school and the one which is popularly accepted, is the satisfaction of emotional needs: the needs for closeness, community, and warm secure relationships. This society provides few other ways of satisfying such needs; for example, work relationships or friendships are not expected to be nearly as important as a man-woman-with-children relationship. Even other ties of kinship are increasingly secondary. This function of the family is important in stabilizing it so that it can fulfill the second, purely economic, function discussed above. The wage-earner, the husband-father, whose earnings support himself, also "pays for" the labor done by the mother-wife and supports the children. The wages of a man buy the labor of two people. The crucial importance of this second function of the family can be seen when the family unit breaks down in divorce. The continuation of the economic function is the major concern where children are involved; the man must continue to pay for the labor of the woman. His wage is very often insufficient to enable him to support a second family. In this case his emotional needs are sacrificed to the necessity to support his ex-wife and children. That is, when there is a conflict the economic function of the family very often takes precedence over the emotional one. And this in a society which teaches that the major function of the family is the satisfaction of emotional needs.[8]

As an economic unit, the nuclear family is a valuable stabilizing force in capitalist society. Since the production which is done in the home is paid for by the husband-father's earnings, his ability to withhold his labor from the market is much reduced. Even his flexibility in changing jobs is limited. The woman, denied an active place in the market, has little control over the conditions that govern her life. Her economic dependence is reflected in emotional dependence, passivity, and other "typical" female personality traits. She is conservative, fearful, supportive of the status quo.

Furthermore, the structure of this family is such that it is an ideal consumption unit. But this fact, which is widely noted in Women's Liberation literature, should not be taken to mean that this is its primary function. If the above analysis is correct, the family should be seen primarily as a production unit for housework and child-rearing. Everyone in capitalist society is a consumer; the structure of the family simply means that it is particularly well suited to encourage consumption. Women in particular *are* good consumers; this follows naturally from their responsibility for matters in the home. Also, the inferior status of women, their general lack of a strong sense of worth and identity, make them more exploitable than men and hence better consumers.

The history of women in the industrialized sector of the economy has depended simply on the labor needs of that sector. Women function as a massive reserve army of labor. When labor is scarce (early industrialization, the two world wars, etc.) then women form an important part of the labor force. When there is less demand for labor (as now under neocapitalism) women become a surplus labor force—but one for which their husbands and not society are economically responsible. The "cult of the home" makes its reappearance during times of labor surplus and is used to channel women out of the market economy. This is relatively easy since the pervading ideology ensures that no one, man or woman, takes women's participation in the labor force very seriously. Women's real work, we are taught, is in the home; this holds whether or not they are married, single, or the heads of households.

At all times household work is the responsibility of women. When they are working outside the home they must somehow manage to get both outside job and housework done (or they supervise a substitute for the housework). Women, particularly married women with children, who work outside the home simply do two jobs; their participation in the labor force is only allowed if they continue to fulfill their first responsibility in the home. This is particularly evident in countries like Russia and those in Eastern Europe where expanded opportunities for women in the labor force have not brought about a corresponding expansion in their liberty. Equal access to jobs outside the home, while one of the preconditions for women's liberation, will not in itself be sufficient to give equality for women; as long as work in the home remains a matter of private production and is the responsibility of women, they will simply carry a double work-load.

A second prerequisite for women's liberation which follows from the above analysis is the conversion of the work now done in the home as private production into work to be done in the public economy.[9] To be more specific. this means that child-rearing should no longer be the responsibility solely of the parents. Society must begin to take responsibility for children; the economic dependence of women and children on the husband-father must be ended. The other work that goes on in the home must also be changed—communal eating places and laundries for example. When such work is moved into the public sector, then the material basis for discrimination against women will be gone.

These are only preconditions. The idea of the inferior status of women is deeply rooted in the society and will take a great deal of effort to eradicate. But once the *structures* which produce and support that idea are changed then, and only then, can we hope to make progress. It is possible, for example, that a change to communal eating places would simply mean that women are moved from a home kitchen to a communal one. This *would* be an advance, to be sure, particularly in a socialist society where work would not have the inherently exploitative nature it does now. Once women are freed from private production in the home, it will probably be very difficult to maintain for any long period of time a rigid definition of jobs by sex. This illustrates the interrelation between the two preconditions given above: true equality in job opportunity is probably impossible without freedom from housework, and the industrialization of housework is unlikely unless women are leaving the home for jobs.

The changes in production necessary to get women out of the home might seem to be, in theory, possible under capitalism. One of the sources of women's liberation movements may be the fact that alternative capitalized forms of home production now exist. Day care is available, even if inadequate and perhaps expensive; convenience foods, home delivery of meals, and take-out meals are widespread; laundries and cleaners offer bulk rate. However, cost usually prohibits a complete dependence on such facilities, and they are not available everywhere, even in North America. These should probably then be regarded as embryonic forms rather than completed structures. However, they clearly stand as alternatives to the present system of getting such work done. Particularly in North America, where the growth of "service industries" is important in maintaining the growth of the economy, the contradictions between these alternatives and the need to keep women in the home will grow.

The need to keep women in the home arises from two major aspects of the present system. First, the amount of unpaid labor performed by women is very large and very profitable to those who own the means of production. To pay women for their work, even at minimum wage scales, would imply a massive redistribution of wealth. At present, the support of a family is a hidden tax on the wage earner—his wage buys the labor power of two people. And second, there is the problem of whether the economy can expand enough to put all women to work as a part of the normally employed labor force. The war economy has been adequate to draw women partially into the economy but not adequate to establish a need for all or most of them. If it is argued that the jobs created by the industrialization of housework will create this need, then one can counter by pointing to (1) the strong economic forces operating for the status quo and against capitalization discussed above, and (2) the fact that the present service industries, which somewhat counter these forces, have not been able to keep up with the growth of the labor force as presently constituted. The present trends in the service industries simply create "underemployment" in the home; they do not create new jobs for women. So long as this situation exists, women remain a very convenient and elastic part of the industrial reserve army. Their incorporation into the labor force on terms of equality—which would create pressure for capitalization of housework—is possible only with an economic expansion so far achieved by neocapitalism only under conditions of full-scale war mobilization.

In addition, such structural changes imply the complete breakdown of the present nuclear family. The stabilizing consuming functions of the family, plus the ability of the cult of the home to keep women out of the labor market, serve neocapitalism too well to be easily dispensed with. And, on a less fundamental level, even if these necessary changes in the nature of household production were achieved under capitalism it would have the unpleasant consequence of including *all* human relations in the cash nexus. The atomization and isolation of people in Western society is already sufficiently advanced to make it doubtful if such complete psychic isolation could be tolerated. It is likely in fact that one of the major negative emotional responses to women's liberation movements may be exactly such a fear. If this is the case, then possible alternatives—cooperatives, the kibbutz, etc.—can be cited to show that psychic needs for community and warmth can in fact be better satisfied if other structures are substituted for the nuclear family.

At best the change to capitalization of housework would only give women the same limited freedom given most men in capitalist society. This does not mean, however, that women should wait to demand freedom from discrimination. There is a material basis for women's status; we are not merely discriminated against, we are exploited. At present, our unpaid labor in the home is necessary if the entire system is to function. Pressure created by women who challenge their role will reduce the effectiveness of this exploitation. In addition, such challenges will impede the functioning of the family and may make the channeling of women out of the labor force less effective. All of these will hopefully make quicker the transition to a society in which the necessary structural changes in production can actually be made. That such a transition will require a revolution I have no doubt; our task is to make sure that revolutionary changes in the society do in fact end women's oppression.

ENDNOTES

1. Marlene Dixon, "Secondary Social Status of Women." (Available from U.S. Voice of Women's Liberation Movement, 1940 Bissell, Chicago, Illinois 60614.)

2. The biological argument is, of course, the first one used, but it is not usually taken seriously by socialist writers. Margaret Mead's *Sex and Temperament* is an early statement of the importance of culture instead of biology.

3. This applies to the group or category as a whole. Women as individuals can and do free themselves from their socialization to a great degree (and they can even come to terms with the economic situation in favorable cases), but the majority of women have no chance to do so.

4. Ernest Mandel, "Workers Under Neocapitalism," paper delivered at Simon Fraser University. (Available through the Department of Political Science, Sociology and Anthropology, Simon Fraser University, Burnaby, B.C., Canada.)

5. Juliet Mitchell, "Women: The Longest Revolution," *New Left Review*, December 1966.

6. Friedrich Engels, *Origin of the Family, Private Property and the State* (Moscow: Progress Publishers, 1968). Chapter IX, p. 158. The anthropological evidence known to Engels indicated primitive woman's dominance over man. Modern anthropology disputes this dominance but provides evidence for a more nearly equal position of women in the matrilineal societies used by Engels as examples. The arguments in this work of Engels do not require the former dominance of women but merely their former equality, and so the conclusions remain unchanged.

7. Such figures can easily be estimated. For example, a married woman without children is expected each week to cook and wash up (10 hours), clean house (4 hours), do laundry (1 hour), and shop for food (l hour). The figures are *minimum* times required each week for such work. The total, 16 hours, is probably unrealistically low; even so, it is close to half of a regular work week. A mother with young children must spend at least six or seven days a week working close to 12 hours.

8. For evidence of such teaching, see any high school text on the family.

9. This is stated clearly by early Marxist writers besides Engels. Relevant quotes from Engels have been given in the text.

INTRODUCTION FROM *HIDDEN IN THE HOUSEHOLD:* WOMEN'S DOMESTIC LABOUR UNDER CAPITALISM

Bonnie Fox

The writers came together in the fall of 1977 to write a book that would carry forward the discussion of domestic labour that began with such promise in the late 1960s. In so doing, we hoped to help develop the Marxist theory of women's oppression that is an essential tool in the struggle for women's liberation.

The importance of the roles of mother, wife and "housewife" in defining women's social identity today is clear. And while being a housewife does not always involve being a mother or even a wife, having children and being married both entail a host of household chores and responsibilities. Indeed, domestic labour-broadly defined and including child care is most women's primary responsibility and it is also often exclusively *their* responsibility. In fact, being adult and female means involvement in domestic labour for all except perhaps bourgeois women. Moreover, domestic labour is basic to society: it involves the reproduction of daily life itself. Therefore, in order to understand women's position in the family and in society, we must look to the organization of their daily work in the home.

If the material conditions of women's household work are central to the determination of women's social position, then an understanding of them is key in formulating a strategy for women's liberation. The struggle must begin from an understanding of the structural features of the household that are most oppressive to women, the origins and sustaining foundations of these household features, the ways in which the household is changing and the obstacles to significant social change.

An understanding of the material situations of working-class and middle-class women requires sifting through the details of their daily lives: the emptiness of the early morning home with its unmade beds, dirty dishes and universal chaos; the energy drain caused by growing kids with boundless energy and unceasing demands; the escapist relief offered by the soap operas; the psychological onslaught waged by the ad men and the idiocy of the directions on their products. For some, it also means the conflicting demands of a double workload—in the home and at a waged job. In the early days of the women's movement, much attention was focussed on women's experiences of these conditions of their daily lives. The personal perceptions articulated in countless consciousness raising sessions contributed to a collective understanding of the oppressive features of women's common experience. However, questions about the sources and sustaining structures of women's oppression cannot be answered through immediate experience alone.

Because appearances are especially deceptive in capitalist society, we need a rigorous analytic approach to questions about women's condition. For example, the true source of the value of commodities (namely labour), is mystified under capitalism so that commodities' useful characteristics and their exchange appear to give them value. Similarly, the real relations between the part of the production and reproduction of society that occurs in the household and that productive sphere known as the economy are hidden and mystified.

Marx successfully penetrated the surface of the appearances of capitalist commodity production, revealing its basic structure and historic tendencies. He focussed his attention on production because he assumed it to be the ultimate basis of social organization and ideology. In writing about this materialist conception of history, Engels argued that:

> the determining factor ... is, in the final instance, the production and reproduction of daily life. This, again, is of a twofold character: on the one side, the production of the means of existence, of food, clothing and shelter and the tools necessary for that production; on the other side, the production of human beings themselves, the propagation of the species. The social organization under which the people of a particular historical epoch and a particular country live is determined by both kinds of production. . .[1]

This statement suggests that without an understanding of the organization of the household we will not fully understand the organization of society. It also points out that women's domestic role involves a type of production. Only the implication that the conceptual separation of the production of the means of existence and of human beings is paralleled by a physical separation of their production between the economy and the household—makes the statement less than definitive. For part of the means of daily existence are produced through domestic labour and labour power is partly produced by workers outside the household. Furthermore, this conceptual vagueness preceded the subsequent omission by both Marx and Engels of any analysis of the production that occurs in the household, as it develops under capitalism.

Nevertheless, Marx's method of historical materialism makes clear the importance of domestic labour as the other half of the production and reproduction of daily life and a necessary counterpart to the capitalist production of subsistence goods. And a systematic use of Marx's methods can disclose the key features of that labour process. In order to analyze capitalist production, Marx abstracted from its details and thus isolated its determinant elements; he then slowly reintroduced the detailed specifics of capitalist development. This sort of theoretical abstraction reveals dynamic tendencies in society that are mystified by appearances. Therefore, such theory is not only essential, it is also a powerful tool in the struggle for change.

So, a theoretical analysis of women's domestic labour is called for. This analysis must clarify the *particular nature* of domestic labour and thus women's oppression *under capitalism*. Those attempts at an analysis of women's oppression that begin with the assumption of women's universal subordination are inherently limited. In ignoring the marked historical and cross-cultural variations in women's position, these analyses abandon the search for causally related material and social factors before it has really begun. Yet, a clear understanding of the factors influencing women's social position must account for variations in that position and the relation of these variations to other aspects of the society.

Under capitalism, most women and men are oppressed by a social order that separates them from the means necessary to produce their own subsistence, from the products of their labour and from each other in their daily work lives. Additionally, however, women are oppressed in special ways when the dominant mode of production is capitalist. Not only is the sexual division of labour highly elaborated, it entails the relegation of women's chief productive role to the household, which is separated from the sphere of socialized (or cooperatively organized) labour, where capitalism's dominant form of production occurs.

In stark contrast with capitalist production, in which the direct producer is clearly compelled by necessity to sell his or her capacity for work, domestic labour presents itself as a labour of love. Instead of being mediated by a market sale between two formally contracting parties, domestic labour accompanies a personal commitment to family members. While work for the capitalist is physically and temporally separated from the rest of daily life, household labour is interwoven with "personal life" and totally enmeshed in the worker's most intimate personal relationships. Consequently, while the wage worker is caught up in a clearly delimited process of production for sale, the household worker is perpetually striving to meet personal needs.

That household work is a privatized labour has consequences for the workers' class consciousness and implications for their ability to organize for collective action. Furthermore, the fact that no wage is paid to the worker affects her or his social status and power within the household. It is not surprising that labour occurring in the home, creating no clear product, drawing no obvious payment and performed in a society where wage work dominates, appears to be non-work and confers on the worker little social recognition.

Nevertheless, domestic labour, as one of the major ways that the means of daily living are produced, is of primary importance: it not only produces the next generation, it also produces and continually reproduces the working capacity of the wage earner(s). In an economy based on the historic dispossession of people from their means of production, the majority of adults is left with only one saleable possession, the capacity of work. Because that same historic process of dispossession entailed the commoditization of the means of subsistence, the household depends for its survival on the continual sale of this labour power. In selling labour power to capital, the worker submits himself or herself to a routine that drains his or her energies and returns only a pay cheque. Physical nourishment, recreation and relaxation, emotional development, intellectual stimulation, the cultivation of personal relationships—in short, most of what human living and growth comprise—must occur outside of work. "Personal life" must be found in the time left over from wage work. Yet, personal life depends upon successfully earning a wage; and not only the wage worker's personal life but also his or her family's continued existence depends upon that wage. Nevertheless, the worker could not return to work without the material and emotional rejuvenation he or she experiences at home, at the end of each day. Should he or she fail to recover, at home, from the daily wear and tear of work, his or her work capacity and even his or her life expectancy will shrink.

Much of household work involves meeting the needs of the wage earner, in obvious ways (e.g., feeding him or her, clothing him or her) and in ways that are more subtle (e.g., providing a rewarding home environment and family life). Of course, much of this contribution towards the reproduction of labour power by the domestic labourer involves spending the wage for commodities that require her or his labour before they are ready for consumption. So, she or he unites the labour of those wage labourers who produce consumer commodities with her or his own in order that the wage worker might continually return to work and that the family might survive.

From the perspective of capital, wage labour is the source of profits. Consequently, the production and reproduction of labour power must be of concern to capital. It is, then, somewhat paradoxical that the domestic work process has fallen progressively behind the capitalist production process with respect to productivity. The work continues to be carried out by the individual working alone, a situation that precludes elaboration of a division of labour and consequent increases in productivity. Actually, the long-term trend has been towards a shifting of the burden from the shoulders of several household members to the shoulders of one. Its continued privatization largely explains why domestic labour continues to be time consuming despite its increased mechanization over the last several decades.

While the consequences of privatization are fairly clear, the basis of the peculiar coexistence of the capitalist economy and the private household is not well understood. Whether the private household is only one of many formations possible with capitalist development, or whether it is a structurally necessary component of an economy dominated by capitalist production is unclear. Similarly, the nature of the continued relationship between the daily work that occurs in the domestic sphere and capitalist commodity production remains at issue. The answers to these questions are crucial: they will indicate the extent to which changes in the position of women are possible under capitalism.

Subsumed under this broad question are more specific and immediate questions. The fact that married women are increasingly involved in wage work raises the question of how capital activates the reserve labour pool latent in the household. The trend towards a double work day for most women also raises the question of whether the relationship between the household and capitalist production is changing. Similarly, the increased assumption by capitalist production and the state of more and more of the tasks involved in the reproduction of labour power, a trend related to the influx of married women into the labour force, may have a significance as yet unexplored. Is the socialization of domestic labour in fact possible under capitalism?

Equally crucial is the issue of the relationship between patriarchy and capitalism. The way in which class relations shape the relations between the sexes demands the attention of all struggling for women's liberation. The question is not only whether the demise of the capitalist organization of production is a precondition for women's liberation, but also what specific changes must be made subsequent to that transformation before women will be truly free.

These are the key questions addressed by the articles in this book. They are not addressed here for the first time, however. The women's movement of the late 1960s and early 1970s generated an array of serious, if often crude, discussions of the sources and specific shape of women's oppression under capitalism. The writing that focussed specifically on domestic labour set the context within which we all work now....

ENDNOTE

1. Frederick Engels, *The Origin of the Family, Private Property and the State* (New York: International Publishers, 1942), 71-72.

RESTRUCTURING PUBLIC AND PRIVATE: WOMEN'S PAID AND UNPAID WORK

Pat Armstrong

The terms "public" and "private" have at least two meanings, both of which have significant implications for women and their work. At times, we use "public" to refer to those services, supports, and regulations established by governments. The term "private," in this case, refers to what is not done by governments. Although this kind of "private" can include both for-profit and not-for-profit organizations, as well as households, we are usually thinking of divisions within the formal economy when we talk of the private and the public sectors. At other times, we use "public" to refer to the world outside the private household, to what is done in the public sphere. These two meanings of "public" and "private" often overlap, as do both kinds of private and public spheres....

In the period following the Second World War, governments at the municipal, provincial, and national levels in Canada were faced with considerable pressure from unions, women's organizations, community groups, and returning veterans to provide services and supports that would allow individuals and families to meet the heavy disabilities of serious illness, prolonged unemployment, accident and premature death (Marsh 1975). Keynesien economic theory taught that another depression could only be avoided through state support of individual purchasing power....

...Although some of these services and supports had been provided previously by the private sector, by charitable organizations, and by families, it was clear that this kind of support was insufficient. The depression had certainly demonstrated that unemployment was not primarily the fault of the individual. Many people did not have families, and many families did not have the necessary resources to purchase or otherwise provide the kinds of supports required to face severe illness, unemployment, or a lengthy old age. Many charitable organizations did not have these resources either. Those that did often restricted their services to particular groups such as those with religious affiliations or those from certain cultural backgrounds, or set conditions, such as financial need or age, that excluded a wide range of individuals. Private services were expensive and also usually set conditions that excluded a large numbers of people, particulary the many women who did not have income from paid work or other sources (see, e.g., Yalnizyan 1994)....

The economic boom that was both a product of and contributor to what has come to be called the welfare state also helped women's groups to demand more regulation of relationships in the private and public spheres (Armstrong 1996; Armstrong and Armstrong 1998). The private and the public in both senses of the terms were restructured.

But as the economic boom began to fade in the late 1960s attacks on the welfare state became more vociferous.... Financial institutions within and outside the country used the debt that they had helped create to demand that states downsize and deregulate (Martin 1993). There were increasing calls for a reduction in the public sector and for deregulation of the private sector. High unemployment levels weakened the claims of those defending extensive state intervention and meant employers faced weaker unions. In response, governments have been dismantling the welfare state, transferring much of the work to the private sector in the formal economy and to the private sphere. At the same time, they have been deregulating in ways that let private decisions of individuals govern the conditions of work and of relations in both the private and public spheres.

This chapter examines the consequences of restructuring for the conditions and relations of women's work, as well as for the construction of the public and private in the two senses of those terms. The current restructuring is once more altering women's lives, and cannot be understood without an analysis of what has gone before. This, then, is the purpose of this chapter....

The Public as Formal Economy

Education

The postwar period saw a dramatic growth in the number of women remaining in school beyond the elementary level. Between 1951 and 1991 the proportion of women 15 to 24 years of age who were students more than doubled from 21 per cent to 52 per cent (Armstrong and Armstrong 1994). In the 1950s three times more men than women received bachelor or first professional degrees, six times more men than women graduated with master's degrees, and women accounted for only 6 per cent of those granted doctorates (Statistics Canada 1990, 47). By 1991 women accounted for the majority of those enrolled in bachelor and first professional degree courses, almost half of those in master's programs, and just over a third of those doing doctoral work (Statistics Canada 1994a, 6).

This change was the result of the large growth in public, post-secondary educational institutions, the increase in government economic support for students, and changes in admissions policies as well as in attitudes. Many of the new public colleges did not change tuition fees, and tuition fees in universities were kept relatively low. The state covered the overwhelming majority of the costs. Moreover, most students were eligible for the federally funded Canada Student Loans and many were also eligible for bursaries. These developments reflected the government's belief that investment in human capital was necessary for economic growth. They also reflected demands from students based on studies demonstrating that the high costs meant access to education was based mainly on sex and class (see, e.g., Porter, Porter, and Blishen 1973). Few of the studies used to justify these changes considered race or disability; however, we now know that these groups had even more difficulty getting advanced education (Henry et al. 1995; Satzewich 1992)....

Paid Work

The postwar period has witnessed an enormous expansion not only in post-secondary education but also in women's participation in the paid workforce. In 1951 less than one in four women over age 15 was counted as part of the labour force. By 1991 this was the case for 60 per cent of women over 15 years of age (Armstrong and Armstrong 1994). The increase was primarily accounted for by the movement of married women into paid work. The most dramatic increase has been among mothers with children under age 16 at home. In 1993 more than two-thirds of such mothers were in the labour force, and this was the case even for women who had children under 6 years of age, if they lived in two-parent families. However, by contrast to the improving situation of married women, only 46 per cent of lone-parent women with young children were in the labour force (Statistics Canada 1994a). A number of factors contributed to the increased number of women in the paid labour force.

Economic Need

The most important factor in the rising female participation rates was economic. In the case of single women, the need for earned income seems obvious and continuous. Few would challenge the notion that older single women, at least, need the earned income. Although some may argue that many younger single women can turn to their parents for economic support, the high proportion of young women who are both in school and in the labour force suggests that most need to at least supplement parental support (Armstrong 1995).

Economic need also seems an obvious reason for the labour force participation of separated and divorced women. Their numbers have increased over the past two decades, partly as a result of government regulation. Pressure, especially from women's groups, helped to create legislation that made it easier to divorce or separate, and gave women more access to the assets of the marriage (Mossman 1994). But these legal changes seldom left separated or divorced women free of economic need. Governments, and support enforcement agencies, have not been very effective in ensuring that men followed the rules, and only a minority of men make support payments after a marriage ends....

Separated and divorced women certainly need money, but many have difficulty finding decent employment. If there are children from the marriage, they are most likely to be left in the custody of their mothers (Statistics Canada 1995b). The high cost, scarcity, and low quality of day care services make it difficult for these women to take full-time paid work, although some are able to take advantage of government-subsidized day care. These subsidies may help to explain why a higher proportion of lone-parent families use day care services regularly, compared with two-parent families (Lindsay 1992)....

Government assistance at the federal, provincial, and municipal levels has allowed many of these women to survive, especially while their children are young. "On average, transfer payments made up 30% of the income of these families, compared with 13% for lone-parent families headed by men and just 7% for two-parent families with children" (Lindsay 1992, 37).... In short, government intervention permitted some women to leave their marriages with some assets and provided some support, but it left one in two single mothers living below the poverty line, many of them ill-equipped for the labour force (National Council of Welfare 1990).

Elderly women are also often in need of income, given that few have pensions from paid employment and many are widowed or married to men with no or low pensions. This pattern will not change significantly in the future because the number of men covered by employer-sponsored pension plans is declining, and the number of women covered by such plans is significantly below that of men (Frenken and Master 1992). The labour force participation of elderly women has not grown, however, in part because most have little labour market experience, and many have low levels of formal education....

The economic need of married women is less obvious and more often challenged. However, study after study in the late 1960s and early 1970s demonstrated that there was a clear connection between husband's income and wife's labour force participation....

Since the 1960s there has been a growing income disparity among heterosexual families. The value of the male wage relative to prices started to decline then and has decreased more rapidly in recent years. Two things countered this growing inequality: increasing female labour force participation and government transfer payments (Armstrong and Armstrong 1994, Chapter 6; Morissette, Myles, and Picot 1993). ...Clearly economic need was a major factor in married women's growing labour force participation, even though governments contributed significantly to household income.

The rise in female labour force participation over the past thirty years, then, partly reflected the fact that the growing number of single women staying in school needed at least part-time income to support their studies. It also reflected the economic need of the increasing number of women who were separated and divorced. As well, as male wages failed to keep up with household economic requirements, it reflected married women's growing need for income. But to some extent this economic need was alleviated by government transfer payments and services in kind.

Demand

While women's economic need was increasing, so was the demand for their labour. Whether we look at industrial growth or occupational growth, the same picture emerges. Jobs grew where women have traditionally worked and where women are perceived to be most likely to have the skills considered necessary.

In 1951, 45 percent of all employed men worked in mining, logging, agriculture, fishing, construction, and transportation. By 1991, however, jobs in these industries accounted for only 20 per cent of all employment and for less than 30 per cent of male work (Statistics Canada 1993). Many men have found highly paid, unionized jobs in these industries. Indeed, to a large extent it was just such jobs that made it possible for many men to be the sole economic support for a family. But these jobs are disappearing. Meanwhile, jobs have been growing in the service industries, and a majority of these new jobs went to women. In 1951 more than two-thirds of employed women worked in the service sector. By 1991 this was the case for just over 80 per cent of them (Armstrong and Armstrong 1994)....

Not surprisingly, the same kind of picture emerges if we look at occupations instead of industries. Growth was rapid in traditionally female jobs. Women were, and continue to be, highly concentrated in clerical, sales, and service work. While 55 per cent of women employed in 1993 worked in such jobs, this was the case for just over a quarter of the men (Statistics Canada 1994a).

These broad industrial and occupational divisions hide even greater segregation. Women are not only segregated into certain industries and occupations, they are also segregated into female-dominated jobs. Of the 200 jobs selected in the 1991 Census summary, 35 are at least 70 percent female and 81 are at least 70 percent male. More than two-thirds of the women, 68 per cent of them, are employed in these 35 female-dominated jobs (Armstrong 1993)....

The gendered segregation is not limited to the kinds of work women do, however. It is also found in terms of wages. The salaries in the female-dominated jobs range from $13,037 to $37,694, while those for male-dominated occupations go from $16,135 to $111,261....

The wage segregation is particularly evident if we look at the ten lowest and ten highest paid occupations. Women accounted for only 20 percent of those in the ten highest paid occupations, but made up over 70 percent of those in the ten lowest paid occupations. While nearly 5 percent of employed males were in the ten highest paid occupations, this was the case for just under 2 percent of the employed women. Meanwhile, nearly 6 percent of women worked in the ten lowest paid jobs, while just over 1 percent of the employed men were in such jobs (Armstrong and Armstrong 1994). Clearly the demand in low wage jobs grew.

There is yet another kind of segregation in the labour force that also helps to explain the rising demand for female labour. Since 1975, the number of part-time jobs has more than doubled (Pold 1994).... More than a quarter of employed women held part-time jobs, but only a third of these women said they did not want full-time work (Statistics Canada 1994b)....

Overall, while women's labour force participation has grown dramatically, the segregation of the labour force has remained remarkably stable throughout the postwar period. This pattern suggests that there was a growing demand for workers in traditionally female areas and in low-paid and part-time work. Much of the work was in the public sector, and more of the work was homework....

...While women employed full-time, full-year averaged only 60 per cent of the equivalent male wage in the early 1970s, they were earning 72 per cent of the male wage in the early 1990s (Statistics Canada 1994a). Because so many women are employed part-time, the overall wage gap is much larger. If all earners are taken into account, women were paid only 64 per cent of what men were paid in 1992, but this still represented an improvement over 47 per cent in 1971 (Ibid.).

Of course, average wages hide inequalities among women. Unionized women did significantly better than those without a union. For example, in 1988 unionized professional women earned $101 more per week than did those without a union, and clerical workers with a union earned $108 more than non-unionized clerical workers (Statistics Canada 1992). Although there was little difference between immigrant and non-immigrant women in terms of wages, visible minority women were paid less than other women. "In 1990 the average employment income for visible minority women was $24,700, about $1,400 less than other women who earned an average of $26,000" (Statistics Canada 1995b, 23, 138). Aboriginal women averaged over $2,000 less than non-Aboriginal women (Ibid., 152). However, women's wages in general are low, with nearly 60 percent of women earners paid less than $20,000 a year in 1993 (Statistics Canada 1995c). At the same time as so many women were at the bottom of the earnings categories, there was a small decrease in the number of women in the top income bracket. Moreover, the inequalities among women remain much smaller than those among men.

Unions clearly played a significant role in raising women's average wage, particularly in the public sector where more than half the women union members worked. Women's groups' successful demand for legislation requiring first equal pay for equal work and then equal pay for work of equal value was also important (Fudge and McDermott 1991). The prohibition of discrimination in determining benefits also helped improve women's economic position. Less obvious was the raising of the minimum wage and the requirement that this minimum be the same for women and men. Women are almost twice as likely as men to work at minimum wage, the only pay protection many women get. "Close to a quarter of a million adult women worked for the minimum wage or less sometime in 1986" (Akyeampong 1989, 10). However, even minimum wage did not protect many women from poverty. "Women accounted for 61% of adult low-paid workers who collected welfare" (Ibid., 16).

Similarly, minimum employment standards legislation was particularly important for women, because for many the legislation is the only protection they have from employers who resist providing vacations or safe conditions of work. Those who are excluded from the legislation are especially vulnerable (Ocran 1997). Indeed, that the state specifically excludes some women from such protection indicates its contradictory role in relation to women. In the case of domestic workers, for example, the state has not only limited the application of minimum standards. It has also restricted their access to other employment if they come from other countries, as many do (Carty 1994).

In addition to pay and minimum standards legislation, the state introduced other measures that helped women obtain and keep employment. Human rights and employment equity legislation are obvious examples. Sexual harassment became recognized as sex discrimination, and employers were prohibited from discriminating on the basis of marital status and from laying off or dismissing pregnant women (Majury 1991). Indeed, the state went even farther, requiring that women be granted maternity leave and that unemployment insurance be paid to pregnant women who met particular employments requirements (see Iyer 1997).…

Unquestionably, inequalities and barriers remain. For example, although immigrant women are only slightly underrepresented in professional and managerial work compared with other women, they are still disproportionately slotted into manufacturing work (Statistics Canada 1995b, 122). Visible minority women with university degrees are more likely than other women with university degrees to do clerical work and to be in sales, service, and manual jobs (Ibid., 137). Aboriginal women are the least likely of all women to have professional or managerial jobs, and women with disabilities face higher rates of unemployment than other women. Moreover, some programs are administered in ways that perpetuate inequalities. But most women have been better off with state intervention and union support, even though they have not shared equally in the gains.

The Private as Household

The dramatic changes in education and in labour force participation in the postwar period were not accompanied by similarly dramatic changes in the household. Domestic work has remained primarily "women's work," whether or not they also work in the labour force. Research in the early 1970s (Clark and Harvey 1976) and in the early 1990s (Ornstein and Haddad 1991) demonstrated that the work of cleaning, cooking, shopping, and child care is primarily women's work.…

Although women receive little support in their domestic chores from either their spouses or the state, they do receive some help in child care. A recent national survey found that 57 percent of Canadian children "under the age of 13 participate in at least one non-parental child care arrangement in a given week" (Goelman et al. 1993, 13). The federal, provincial, and municipal governments have not moved very far or very fast into the provision of day care (Teghtsoonian this volume), but they have provided some support in the form of subsidies to low-income mothers, in the form of capital subsidies to non-profit centres, and in the form of regulations for care. Some after-school and lunch programs, along with expanded public recreational facilities and publicly supported weekend events have also helped women with their parenting work....

The state became much more active during the 1960s and 1970s in terms of services for the elderly and the disabled....

The state also intervened to offer some protection to women in the home. In response to pressure from women's groups and to pressure from those women working within government on women's issues, the state supported research on household relations. This research, along with that done by women's groups, accompanied by continued demands for intervention, resulted in the state making criminal laws more sensitive to wife battering and making wife rape illegal (Koshan 1997; Walker 1990). The state helped support women who left abusive relations through counselling services and group homes. Many women gained greater control over their own bodies, as both birth control and abortion became legal (Kleiber and Light 1978; McLaren 1992). But disabled women remained significantly disadvantaged in all respects, from protection from abuse to access to financial or emotional support and their right to decide about care (Statistics Canada 1995b). Although much of this state initiative has been criticized for its structure, content, and implementation (Koshan 1997), it did nevertheless help many women. State regulations on housing and household products also helped make the home safer, although many significant hazards remain (Rosenberg 1990).

Laws were also changed to ensure not only that women had a right to a division of the marital property on divorce, but also to some of the pensions earned by their spouse. Not all women were successful in acquiring the benefits that the law appeared to offer (Mossman 1995, 1994), even when they were helped by state-supported legal aid programs. Women whose first language was not English or French experienced particular problems in gaining access to such programs. Moreover, these family law rights were not, in general, extended to gay and lesbian couples (Boyd 1994).

Thus, the state has made the private sphere of family relations somewhat more of a public concern. This development is in many ways consistent with the old feminist slogan claiming that the personal is political. In some cases, such as social welfare and child welfare, this approach has meant that the state invaded the privacy of the home and served to perpetuate unequal relations (Mosoff 1997). State intervention also has often meant more protection for women and less unpaid work for women.

Redefining the Public/Private Divide

In the postwar period, then, the state expanded enormously in terms of services....

At the same time, the state increasingly regulated the for-profit and not-for-profit sectors. A range of legislation and regulations helped protect women from various hazards and types of exploitation. Some of this intervention required that women be treated like men, while other measures recognized women's unequal position in the market and their different roles in reproduction. Although not all women were protected by such state initiatives as labour codes, and although much of the legislation remained unenforced, poorly enforced, or inappropriately interpreted, many women did benefit from minimum protections. Moreover, women working within the legal system often helped overcome such problems in the legislation or used it to push for additional reform.…

Restructuring Public and Private Today

From the 1950s to the 1980s the public sphere grew enormously, both in terms of the state expanding what it did and how it intervened in the market and in terms of what the state did in relation to the home. Recently, however, this kind of intervention has come under attack, primarily in the name of reducing the public debt and of making government more efficient. Yet it has also been defended with reference to feminist critiques of past practices. Indeed, feminist criticisms of many state initiatives are being used increasingly to justify cutbacks done in the name of reform. For example, sending women home hours after childbirth is explained in terms of feminist concerns over medicalization of birth.…

It is not only jobs that are being eliminated in the public service. It is also the monitoring of what the civil service does for women. The agencies that were at least nominally established to protect women's interests within the state and to support research on women's issues have been cancelled or reorganized. For example, the Canadian Advisory Council on the Status of Women was dismantled in 1995. Financial support provided by government to non-governmental agencies is under attack and is increasingly defined as support for special interests. Such interests must be privately funded in the new state.

At the same time governments at all levels are significantly reducing funding for education, health, and welfare. These cutbacks have an impact on women as both providers and users, given that they are the majority of both. In terms of employment, jobs are being eliminated rapidly in these areas, and work is increasingly being contracted out to private sector firms that pay women less and offer less job protection (Armstrong and Armstrong 1996). New work organization techniques transferred from the private sector are transforming many of the public sector jobs that remain (Armstrong et al. 1994). In the name of improving quality, public sector employers are appealing to women's desire to provide high quality services, to participate in decision-making, and to work in teams as a way of reengineering work. But too often these processes end up de-skilling the job. At the same time these private sector techniques frequently pit women against each other, undermining their traditional ways of working together. With government cutbacks, private sector for-profit firms are moving in to fill the demand for services. These employers tend to be non-union. Moreover, they are more likely than public sector employers to rely on part-time and short-term work, to vary their hours in ways that make it difficult for women to arrange child care, and to pay low wages and benefits. Because women form the majority of this labour force, the impact will be greatest on them.

In terms of service reduction, women will be particularly disadvantaged. For example, the proposed hike in post-secondary education tuition fees will return us to the time when parents and students had to cover a significant part of the costs. In those times, parents forced to choose which children to support chose sons over daughters, and declining incomes mean that more parents will again be forced to choose (Porter, Porter, and Blishen 1973). Moreover, the proposed payback scheme based on earnings will mean that women will be paying back their student loans for much longer, given that they earn less than men....

The state is not only withdrawing from the provision of services, however. It is also withdrawing from the regulation of the non-profit and for-profit sectors.... Certainly this is the case in Ontario, with the election of the Harris Conservative government in 1995 made it clear that employment equity legislation as we know it is gone and that there will be no money for pay equity. Cutbacks will mean that those last hired will be first fired, and, without protection; the women who did benefit from employment equity legislation are likely to suffer disproportionately. Labour legislation that made it easier for some women to organize into unions is also slated for removal, as are many aspects of health and safety protection. Highway safety patrols, for example, have been eliminated, leaving women on the road to fend for themselves.

These changes in the public arena have a significant impact on women in the household and the community. Services not provided by women paid and trained for the work are being rapidly transferred to women in the home or to voluntary agencies. Some new techniques and technologies are eliminating or reducing the labour required in some areas, making it possible to significantly alter services. So, for example, day surgery has become possible as a result of new surgical techniques and new ways of relieving pain. However, much labour is still required and this necessary labour is skilled labour. Indeed, precisely because the labour is related to new techniques, most of it has never been done at home (Armstrong 1994; Glazer 1991). Yet a great deal of this work is being sent home, where it is expected that it will be done by women without pay. However, most women now have labour force jobs, few have the necessary skills, and many do not have the desire to do the work. Particularly disadvantaged are poor women who cannot hire assistance, single women who do not have partners to help, and women without relatives in Canada who can support them in this work.

Some of the work transfer has no relation to new techniques. In Ontario and Alberta, for example, kindergarten and day care are being cut. In both cases governments indicate, both explicitly and implicitly, that this work should be done by mothers or female relatives rather than by the state. Such a position not only deprives women of services, it also directly challenges their right to employment and defines them as the people responsible for child care....

Changes in social assistance will also have a significant impact on women, given that they form the majority of recipients. In Ontario, for example, the payments for welfare have been significantly reduced and the rules for eligibility altered to make it much more difficult for anyone, even the disabled, to claim benefits. Aboriginal women in particular will suffer because a high proportion of them have been eligible for assistance in the past (Statistics Canada 1995b, 151-3). Similarly, proposed federal changes in unemployment insurance regulations would make payments based on household income. This change would not only transform the program from an insurance scheme based on right to a welfare program based on need; it would also disproportionately affect women. Under the current scheme each worker is treated as an individual who has rights based on contribution and job search. Under the proposed scheme women would be assessed as spouses dependent on the men who usually earn more, or at least enough, to make the women ineligible.

As is the case in the public arena, the state is also deregulating the household. Services for battered women have been dramatically reduced, along with other kinds of support like counselling. Legal aid to support women's claims is very much under threat, making it difficult for women to find protection under the rules that remain. Environmental regulations that help reduce hazards in the home and on the street are being altered to reduce their impact. And the federal government has virtually refused to regulate the new reproductive technologies that may endanger many women's lives.

The restructuring currently under way thus means both more unpaid work and less protection for women, in terms of social support, unionization, or regulation. It also means more responsibility and less power. As more work is transferred to community and home, more state surveillance enters the household. But this surveillance, in such forms as new regulations for welfare and for home care services, means that what has been private becomes public, without the kinds of protection such a shift usually provides. Home care workers, for example, enter the home at their convenience, following rules made by others about what can be done for whom. The new intervention in the household is more about policing women than about making private troubles public issues....

Conclusion

...[T]he postwar expansion of the public both in the sense of what the public sector took over from or regulated in the market, and in the sense of what the state did in and for the household, did have two distinct advantages for women. First, the state did help many women and did help reduce inequality in many instances. Second, the state is much more open to democratic influence than is the case within the private sector or when women have to fight battles within their individual households.

As many feminists have pointed out, the state has never been a neutral arbitor or primarily a defender of women. But the state can, and does, set rules or provide services that can protect the weakest. Private firms and individual households offer much more arbitrary and unreliable protections, especially for the weakest. As the public shrinks in the sense of regulating and servicing, the private prevails. The impact will be greatest on women. Women's labour force participation has already declined and their unemployment rate grown as a result of the shift from the public to the private sphere (Statistics Canada 1995a). The problems that will be increasingly hidden in the household will take longer to become evident in the data. Meanwhile, the shifts in public and private will be played out in women's lives.

COMPLICATING THE IDEOLOGY OF MOTHERHOOD: CHILD WELFARE LAW AND FIRST NATION WOMEN

Marlee Kline

Introduction

The damage wrought by child welfare systems on First Nation people and communities is well known and documented.[1] A number of studies have suggested this damage is explained in part by the way child welfare law is implicated in and informed by racist processes.[2] I have argued, for example, that the ideological form[3] and substance[4] of child welfare law established a discursive framework that naturalizes the removal of First Nation children from their extended families, communities, and Nations. Racism is central to the relationship between law and ideology in this context. Racism does not, however, exist in a vacuum. Rather, it operates in complex interaction with gender and class and other social relations. This is particulary important for class and other social relations. This is particularly important for understanding child welfare law, in which the spotlight of judicial scrutiny is on First Nation women often living in poverty. While consideration of the intersection of race, gender and class informs the analyses of particular cases in earlier work on the application of child welfare law to First Nations,[5] there has not yet been an attempt to construct a theoretical framework for understanding this intersection more generally. My aim here is to develop such a framework.[6]

I want to argue that a key to understanding the effects of child welfare law on First Nations lies in the way courts assess the mothering capabilities of First Nation women. Most problematic is the tendency of courts to construct First Nation women as "bad mothers," and thus apparently justify removing their children and placing them in state care. Importantly, the construction of First Nation women as "bad mothers" is mediated by the dominant ideology of motherhood.[7] Understanding the race, gender, and class specificity of this ideology therefore provides some insight into the complex relations of oppression and power that inform the material and discursive dimensions of child welfare law.[8] First Nation women are particulary vulnerable to being constructed by courts as "bad mothers" because, as a consequence of colonialist oppression and different cultural norms, they do not always meet the dominant cultural and middle class expectations that constitute the ideology of motherhood....

I.   *The Dominant Ideology of Motherhood*

By the dominant ideology of motherhood, I mean the constellation of ideas and images in western capitalist societies that constitute the dominant ideals of motherhood against which women's lives are judged. The expectations established by these ideals limit and shape the choices women make in their lives, and construct the dominant criteria of "good" and "bad" mothering. They exist within a framework of dominant ideologies of womanhood, which, in turn, intersect with dominant ideologies of family.

There are several core expectations that constitute the dominant ideology of motherhood. First, motherhood is understood as "the natural, desired and ultimate goal of all 'normal' women;"[9] in other words, a woman must be a mother before she will be considered "a mature, balanced, fulfilled adult."[10] This dictate of compulsory motherhood applies not only to pregnancy and birth, but also to the matrix of behaviours deemed to constitute "good" mothering,[11] namely:

> A "good" mother is always available to her children, she spends time with them, guides, supports, encourages and corrects as well as loving and caring for them physically. She is also responsible for the cleanliness of their home environment.
>   A "good" mother is unselfish, she puts her children's needs before her own.[12]

A further expectation is that "[t]he individual mother should have total responsibility for her own children at all times."[13] I will refer to this expectation as the primary care requirement. Finally, a mother is expected to operate within the context of the ideologically dominant family form, one that is "heterosexual and nuclear in form, patriarchal in content,"[14] and based on "assumptions of privatized female dependence and domesticity."[15] The latter assumptions have limited women's ability to participate in the workforce on equal terms with men, and contributed to the devaluation of women's paid work, child care, and domestic labour.[16] Perhaps to counter the lack of status and financial rewards accorded to motherhood, the role of "mother" has been idealized as "important, worthwhile and intrinsically rewarding."[17]

The dominant ideology of motherhood is an historically and culturally specific phenomenon, consolidated in the late nineteenth century; in Canada and other Western capitalist nations.[18] It has undergone a number of shifts from that time, some of which correspond to changes in the political economy of capitalism. Since the 1960s and 1970s, for example, with rising numbers of women in the workforce, the ideology has increasingly countenanced some forms of "working mother," rather than dictating full-time stay-at-home motherhood.[19] As well, in the last ten years or so, fathers have come to be constructed as also having a vital role to play in raising children, additional to, though different than, the role of mothers.[20] Though changes such as these have had effects on the ideology of motherhood, they have not weakened its considerable power in disciplining women. Mothers who deviate from the ideals of motherhood are constructed as "bad mothers," thereby justifying their social and legal regulation, including regulation by child welfare law.

Importantly, however, it is not just mothers *as anomalous individuals* who are judged harshly against the ideals of motherhood.[21] Motherhood has been constructed ideologically as compulsory only for those women considered "fit," and women have often been judged "unfit" on the basis of their social location. This has been the case (at various times during the last century and in different places) for disabled women, black women, First Nation women, immigrant women, Jewish women, lesbian women, sole-support women, poor women, unmarried women, young women, and others.[22] For these women, procreation has often been devalued and discouraged.[23] The ideology of motherhood, therefore, speaks not only to gender roles and behaviour, but it also constructs some locations within social relations of race, class, sexuality, ability, and so on as more appropriate for motherhood than others. Thus, motherhood is better conceptualized as a privilege, than as a right,[24] a privilege that can be withheld, both ideologically and in more material ways, from women who are not members of the dominant groups in society or who are otherwise considered "unfit."

Within this framework, so-called "unfit" women who want to have children are often confronted with serious barriers and difficulties. Single heterosexual women, lesbian women and/or disabled women, for example, are "expected to forgo mothering in the 'interest of the child,'"[25] and lesbians in particular find it difficult to gain access to safe alternative insemination processes.[26] Moreover, though there is variation along lines of race and class,[27] young women who become pregnant and who choose to carry their fetuses to term are often pressured, both externally and through the internalization of motherhood ideology, to give up their babies for adoption.[28] When women considered "unfit" do have and raise children, it is difficult, if not impossible, for them to meet the societal image of the "good mother."[29]

Historical analyses of motherhood discourses provide insight into the development of the race, class, and gender specificity of contemporary meanings of motherhood.[30] Dorothy Roberts, for example, has examined the ideological devaluation of black motherhood, and the corresponding valuation of white motherhood, during the period of slavery in the United States.[31] Dawn Currie argues that contemporary meaning of motherhood have some roots in late nineteenth and early twentieth-century North American eugenics-derived birth control discourses which expressed concerns about controlling both the growth of potentially unruly populations and the racial quality of future generations.[32] In contemporary discourses of motherhood, however, the origins and operation of motherhood ideology within social relations of oppression, including overlapping ones of race, gender, and class, are submerged. Instead, the expectations of "good" mothering are presented as natural, necessary and universal. The "bad mother," by corollary, is constructed as the "photographic negative" of the "good mother,"[33] again with the operation of racism and other such factors rendered invisible. Moreover, the realities of poverty, racism, heterosexism, and violence that often define the lives of mothers who do not conform to the ideology are effectively erased. As Marie Ashe writes:

> Consideration of the material conditions or women's lives is made irrelevant through construction of the "bad mother" as a pure and essentialistic figure. She is defined as a woman whose acts or omissions constitutes "bad mothering" whatever her class or race or household relationships.[34]

Thus, the construct of "bad mother," though historically embedded in oppressive social relations, is presented as universal and thus innocent of its origins and effects.[35] This dynamic then helps to naturalize and legitimate intersecting oppressive relations of race, gender, and class in particular contexts, such as that of child welfare law.

II. The Ideology of Motherhood, Child Welfare Law and First Nation Women

The imposition of child welfare law on First Nations in Canada vividly illustrates the intersection of multiple axes of power within the ideology of motherhood. Understanding this dynamic, I want to suggest, helps explain why the child welfare system has had such destructive effects on First Nations, and most directly, on First Nation women and children. Before illustrating this point by analyzing recent child welfare cases, I would like to make some preliminary observations....

At both the initial stage of child welfare proceedings, when it is determined whether a child is in need of protection, and at the dispositional stage, when support services and/or alternative care placements are ordered, courts draw on ideological conceptions of motherhood which form part of the common sense knowledge of judges.[36] This happens in two interconnected ways.[37] First, judges focus on and blame *individual* First Nation mothers for the difficulties they face without recognizing the roots of those difficulties in the history and current structures of colonialism and racial oppression. Second, the dominant ideology of motherhood operates to impose dominant cultural values and practices in relation to child-raising on First Nations, and correspondingly devalue First Nations values and practices in this context. These two tendencies operate in conjunction with each other with other processes, to shape the final results arrived at by courts....

Individuation, Obfuscation, and Mother-Blaming

An important feature or the ideology of motherhood is the way it individuates mothers and the practice of mothering. This can be understood as related to the primacy of the individual in liberal ideology more generally. The individualistic focus of the dominant ideology of motherhood, and the related expectation that individual mothers will take full responsibility for their children, means that when there is a problem with a child, the individual mother's mothering practices are subjected to critical scrutiny.[38] The implication is that mothers are to blame for child neglect....

Though, as a general feature of the ideology of motherhood, mother-blaming does not appear culturally or racially specific on its face, I want to argue that its application to First Nation women must be understood in these terms. Most directly, mother-blaming obscures the wider context of racism, poverty, ill-health, and violence within which many First Nation women who appear in the cases are struggling to survive. More fundamentally, it obscures the roots of these conditions in historical and continuing practices of colonialism and racial oppression, including land dispossession, destruction of the traditional economies of First Nations, and the transgenerational effects of residential schools, and the child welfare system itself.

The focus on individual "bad mothers" as the source of difficulties in First Nations child welfare cases effectively blames First Nation women for the effects of social ills that are largely the consequence of this history and present. Vivid illustrations of this individualized mother-blaming focus can be found in child protection cases involving First Nation women who are dependent on drugs or alcohol, or involved in a relationship with a violent man. In such cases, judges often refer to the alcohol and drug dependencies of First Nation women as their "personal lifestyle" problems, implying they deserve what comes (the removal of their children) if they do not rehabilitate themselves within a "reasonable" time.[39]

In *Director of Child Welfare of Manitoba v. B.*,[40] for example, the Court referred to substantial alcohol abuse by the mother as an aspect of her "lifestyle,"[41] stating that it included personal traits and problems that severely limit her parenting abilities.[42]

Even more disturbing is the tendency, to characterize the subjection of First Nation women to violence by male partners as simply a "personal problem" or a problem of "lifestyle." In *Child and Family Services of Western Manitoba v. J.H.B.*,[43] a First Nation mother was characterized as beset by a "chaotic lifestyle"[44] resulting from an abusive relationship and alcoholism. The Court concluded that her children were "entitled to be free of the detrimental consequences which flow from care being provided by someone whose life is resumed and subsumed by *personal problems*" [emphasis added].[45]... Altogether, the characterization of battering and alcohol and drug dependency as personal problems reinforces the placing of blame for child neglect on the deficiencies of individual mothers, and obscures the roots of the difficulties First Nation mothers face in more systemic oppressive relations including historical and continuing colonialist and racist practices.

This dynamic is also at work in the way the ideological expectation that mothers be unselfish and self-sacrificing is applied to First Nation women. Women are labelled "selfish" and "immature" when they are found not to meet this expectation, and there are several ways this specifically affects First Nation women. For example, the presumption underlying the expectation that it is possible to separate the needs of mothers from those of their children is particularly onerous for many First Nation women who, because of poverty and other difficulties struggle to survive on a day-to-day basis. In *Re J.H. and N.H.*,[46] for example, a battered First Nation woman without employment or appropriate housing, who often required assistance from social welfare authorities to provide her children with basic necessities, was characterized by the Yukon Territorial Court as, at bottom, "preoccupied with her own needs."[47]...

Illustrations of mother-blaming can also be found in cases that draw upon ideological constructions of the physical home environment "proper" for raising children. Women whose living situations do not meet these standards are judged as inadequate mothers. A mother is presumed *not* to be a "good mother" if, for example, she moves from place to place, or if the place where she lives is not clean and tidy....

...This poses particular difficulties for First Nation women in child protection cases. Once again, the specificity of the application of the "proper" home requirement to First Nation women takes a "mother-blaming" form. The difficult life circumstances of many First Nation women, which are largely the consequence of historically rooted structures of colonialism and racial oppression, are regarded by judges as indicators of, and risk factors for, inadequate mothering. This is particularly apparent in cases which manifest ideological expectations that a home be an established if not permanent one, and that it be "clean and tidy."

With respect to permanency, First Nation women are sometimes characterized by judges as not meeting the ideological requirement of having a "proper" home environment on the ground they live "nomadic" or "transient lives."[48] In *L. (P.)*,[49] for example, a First Nation woman, whose three children had been apprehended from her, lived first with the father of her children, then off and on with her sister in Manitoba, and then with "another boyfriend."[50] The judge was concerned that even when the two parents were together they had no fixed home.[51] He considered the woman's situation to be "more than a 'nomadic life.'" It indicates instability, insecurity, a lack of permanency—all of which are not positive factors for any family, and are more devastating for a young child."[52] The lack of an established home, in other words, was for the Court *ipso facto* a risk factor....

In *New Brunswick (Minister of Health and Community Services) L.M. and F.G.*,[53] all parental rights and responsibilities in relation to three First Nation children were transferred from a mother (and disinterested father) to the New Brunswick Minister of Health and Community Services. This was done, in part, because the mother "ha[d] been moving from one place to another and [was] simply not in a position to receive custody of her children."[54]...

Like the "permanent home" requirement, dominant middle-class ideals of cleanliness and tidiness are central to ideological constructions of good motherhood, and have particularly oppressive effects for many First Nation women confronted by child welfare law. A particularly vivid example can be found in *L.O. and S. O. v. Superintendent of Child Welfare*.[55] A nineteen-month-old Inuit girl suffering from serious skin rashes was apprehended from the Inuit couple who had taken her in when she had been abandoned as a baby because, according to the Court, their house "was just not tidy enough for such a tender-skinned little girl."[56]...

...[T]here is an unfortunate implication that standards of hygiene in First Nation communities are the result of cultural differences, rather than a material consequence of poverty, overcrowded and substandard housing, and so on, which are in turn related to histories of colonialism and racial oppression.[57]

A final example of mother-blaming and the individualist focus on the ideology of motherhood can be found in the expectation that mothers assume primary care of their children, regardless of their circumstances. A mother must be self-reliant and care for her children with minimal or no assistance.[58] Again, the individualistic focus of this requirement ignores and obscures the colonialist roots of the problems faced by many First Nation women. Poverty is often responsible for the difficulties mothers, and in particular lone mothers, have in providing primary care to their children,[59] and this has specific implications for First Nation mothers who disproportionately live in poverty[60] largely as a result of colonialist practices and policies. These facts are obscured, however, by the focus on primary care. In *Re J.H. and N.H.*,[61] for example, because a 32 year old First Nation mother in the Yukon was unable to "provide *primary care* for herself and her children [emphasis added],"[62] the children were committed permanently to the care of the Director of Family and Children's Services. The many times she had approached child welfare authorities or relied on relatives for caregiving assistance in crisis situations were taken by the Court to indicate "little improvement on *her* part in dealing with *her* problems *on her own*" [emphasis added].[63] Yet, part of what created her need for assistance in the first place was her lack of suitable housing, and her inability to supply her children with basic necessities because of her poverty....

ENDNOTES

1. See: H.B. Hawthorn, ed. *A Survey of the Contemporary Indian of Canada: A Report on Economic, Political, Educational Needs and Policies* (Ottawa: Indian Affairs Branch. 1966); H.P. Hepworth, *Foster Care and Adoption in Canada* (Ottawa: Canadian Council on Social Development, 1980); P. Johnston, *Native Children and the Child Welfare System* (Ottawa: Canadian Council on Social Development 1983); P. Hudson and B. McKenzie. "Child Welfare and Native People: The Extension of Colonialism" (1983) 49 *Soc. Worker* 63; Review Committee on Indian and Métis Adoptions and Placements, *No Quiet Place: Final Report to the Honourable Muriel Smith, Minister of Community Services* (Winnipeg: Manitoba Community Services, 1985) (Chair: Kimelman A.C.J.): Indian Association of Alberta, *Child Welfare Needs: Assessment and Recommendations* (Calgary: Indian Association of Alberta. 1987) [hereinafter Child Welfare

Needs]; Canada, Child and Family Services Task Force, *Indian Child and Family Services in Canada: Final Report* (Ottawa: Indian and Northern Affairs, 1987) [hereinafter Final Report]; W. Warry, *Ontario's First People: Native Children* (Toronto: The Research Policy Nexus, (1989); A. Armitage, "Family and Child Welfare in First Nations Communities" in B. Wharf, ed., *Rethinking Child Welfare in Canada* (Toronto: McClelland and Stewart, 1993).

2. See: E. Carasco, "Canadian Native Children: Have Child Welfare Laws Broken the Circle?" (1986) 5 *Can. J. Fam. L.* 111; P. Monture, "A Vicious Circle: Child Welfare Law and the First Nations" (1989) 3 *C.J.W.L.* 1; M. Kline "Child Welfare Law, 'Best Interests of the Child' Ideology and First Nations" (1992) 30 *Osgoode Hall L. J.* 375 [hereafter "Best Interests of the Child Ideology"]; M. Kline, "The Colour of Law: Ideological Representations of First Nations in Legal Discourse" [forthcoming, Social & Legal Studies] [hereinafter "The Colour of Law"].

3. Kline, "'Best Interest of the Child' Ideology," Ibid.

4. Kline, "The Colour of Law," supra note 2.

5. See Monture, supra note 2, and Kline, "'Best Interests of the Child' Ideology," supra note 2.

6. Sexual orientation and ability are also implicated in the application of child welfare law to First Nations, but because the available cases do not consider these dimensions, this paper will focus only on intersecting relations of race, gender, and class.

7. The ideological conception I rely on comes out of a socialist feminist tradition; see S.A.M. Gavigan, "Paradise Lost, Paradox Revisited: The Implications of Familial Ideology for Feminist, Lesbian and Gay Engagement to Law" (1993) 31 *Osgoode Hall L.J.* (forthcoming). It is materialist in the sense that I recognize the beliefs, images, explanations, and evaluations that constitute ideology as constructed historically in conjunction with and in relation to, material and cultural conditions and power relations, which are then represented as natural, inevitable, and necessary — as simply part of "common sense" — in the current social order. See also Kline, "The Colour of Law," supra note 2.

8. In complicating how we understand the ideology of motherhood, I am building on some of the groundbreaking work in this area by feminists working in law, such as that of Susan Boyd, who has examined gender-specific aspects of the ideology, and their impact on women with paid work seeking custody of their children. See Boyd, "Child Custody, Ideologies, and Employment" (1989) 3 *C.J.W.L* 11] [hereinafter "Ideologies and Employment"]; From Gender Specificity to Gender Neutrality: Ideologies in Canadian Child Custody Law" in C. Smart and S. Sevenhullsen, eds., *Child Custody and the Politics of Gender* (London: Routledge, 1989) 126 [hereinafter "From Gender Specificity to Gender Neutrality?"]; "Investigating Gender Bias in Canadian Child Custody Law: Reflections on Questions and Methods: in J. Benckman and D. Chunn, eds., *Investigating Gender Bias: Law, Courts, and the Legal Profession* (Toronto: Thompson Educational Publishing, 1993) 169 [hereinafter "Investigating Gender Bias"]. See also Katherine Arnup, who has focused on heterosexist aspects of the ideology and their impact on lesbians seeking custody of their children in "Mothers Just Like Others: Lesbians, Divorce, and Child Custody in Canada" (1989) 3 *C.J.W.L.* 18. More recently, the interaction of race and class relations with gender relations within the ideology of motherhood has begun to be explored both historically and in its present manifestations in different contexts by, for example, Susan Boyd and Dawn Currie in Canada, and Dorothy Roberts and Martha Fineman in the United States. See: S.B. Boyd, "Some Postmodernist Challenges to Feminist Analyses of Law, Family and State: Ideology and Discourse in Child Custody Law" (1991) 10 *Can. J. of Fam. L.* 79 [hereinafter "Postmodern Challenges"]; D. Currie, "Class, Race and Gender: Re-Thinking the 'Motherhood Question' in Feminism" (Paper presented at the Fifth International Interdisciplinary Congress of Women, San Jose, Costa Rica, February 1993); D.E. Roberts, "Racism and Patriarchy in the Meaning of

Motherhood" (Paper presented at the Workshop of Motherhood, Feminism and Legal Theory Project, Columbia University School of Law, December 4-5, 1992); M.A. Fineman, "Images of Mothers in Poverty Discourse" (1991) *Duke L.J.* 274. See also Leonore Davidoff, ed., *Special Issue on Motherhood, Race and the State in the Twentieth Century* (1992) 4(2) *Gender and History*.

9. M. Stanworth, "Reproductive Technologies and the Deconstruction of Motherhood" in M. Stanworth, ed., *Reproduction Technologies: Gender, Motherhood and Medicine* (Minneapolis: University of Minnesota Press, 1987), 14.

10. B. Wearing. *The Ideology of Motherhood: A Study of Sydney Suburban Mothers* (Sydney: George Allen & Unwin, 1984), 72.

11. Carol Smart, "The Woman of Legal Discourse" (1992) *Social & Legal Studies* 29, 38.

12. Wearing, supra note 11, 72.

13. Ibid.

14. Gavigan, supra note 7.

15. Ibid., citing D. Chunn, "Rehabilitating Deviant Families Through Family Courts: The Birth of 'Socialized' Justice in Ontario, 1920-1940" (1988) 16 Int. J. *Sociology L.* 137. See also: J. Lewis, "Dealing With Dependency: State Practices and Social Realities, 1870-1945" in J. Lewis, ed., *Women's Welfare, Women's Rights* (London: Croom Helm, 1983); J. Acker, "Class, Gender and the Relations of Distribution" (1988) 13 *Signs* 473.

16. See, e.g.: M. Mollay. "Citizenship, Property and Bodies: Discourse on Gender and the Inter-War Labour Government in New Zealand" (1992) 4 *Gender and History* 293.

17. Wearing, supra note 10, 72.

18. See: C. Backhouse, "Shifting Patterns in Nineteenth-Century Canadian Custody Law" in David H. Flaherty, ed., *Essays in the History of Canadian Law* (Toronto: The Osgoode Society, 1981); V. Strong-Boag, *The New Day Recalled: Lives of Girls and Women in English Canada, 1919-1939* (Toronto: Copp Clark Pitman, 1988); Boyd, "From Gender Specificity to Gender Neutrality," supra note 8.

19. Boyd. Ibid.

20. See: M.A. Fineman, "The Neutered Mother" (1992) 46 *University of Miami Law Rev.* 653; C. Smart, "The Legal and Moral Ordering of Child Custody" (1991) 18 *J. of Law and Society* 485. Despite this change, fathers still escape the child care responsibility expectations accorded to mothers, as well as the stigma attached to failure to meet these expectations. See K. Swift, "Contradictions in Child Welfare: Neglect and Responsibility" in C. Baines, P. Evans, and S. Neysmith, eds., *Women's Caring: Feminist Perspectives on Social Welfare* (Toronto: McClelland & Stewart, 1991).

21. Roberts, supra note 8, 17.

22. See: A. Asch and M. Fine, "Introduction: Beyond Pedestals" in A. Asch and M. Fine, eds., *Women with Disabilities: Psychology, Culture and Politics* (Philadelphia: Temple University Press, 1988); Karen A. Blackford, "The Baby Crib and Other Moral Regulators of Mothers with Disabilities" in H. Stewart, B. Percival, and E.R. Epperly, eds., *The More We Get Together...* (Charlottetown: gynergy books, 1992); G. Bock, "Racism and Sexism in Nazi Germany: Motherhood, Compulsory Sterilization, and the State" in R. Bridenthal, A. Grossman, and M. Kaplan, eds., *When Biology Became Destiny: Women in Weimar and Nazi Germany* (New York: Monthly Review Press, 1984); P. H, Collins, *Black Feminist Thought: Knowledge, Consciousness,*

and the Politics of Empowerment (Boston: Unwin Hyman, 1990); Roberts, Ibid.; Currie, supra note 8; R. Solinger, "Race and 'Value:' Black and White Illegitimate Babies in the U.S.A., 1943-1965" (1992) 4 *Gender and History* 343; L. Gordon, "Family Violence, Feminism, and Social Control" (1986) 12 *Feminist Studies* 453 at 466-7. These categories set out as examples are not necessarily distinct; but may cross-cut one another.

23. Roberts, supra note 8, 17.

24. Molloy, supra note 16, 301.

25. Stanworth, supra note 9, 15. See also Asch and Fine, supra note 22.

26. See: M.A. Coffey, "Of Father Born: A Lesbian Feminist Critique of the Ontario Law Reform Commission Recommendations on Artificial Insemination" (1986) 1 *C.J.W.L.* 434; D. Cooper and D. Herman, "Getting The Family Right: Legislating Heterosexuality in Britain, 1986-1991" (1991) 10 *Can. J. Fam. L.* 41; K. Harrison, "Fresh or Frozen: Lesbian Mothers, Sperm Donors, and the Concept of the Limited Father" (Paper presented at the Workshop on Motherhood, Feminism and Legal Theory Project Workshop, Columbia University School of Law, December 4-5, 1992); R. Wigod, "Lesbian Couple Who Want Child Denied Sperm" *The Vancouver Sun* (22 July 1993) A 1.

27. Solinger, supra note 22.

28. This emphasis on adoption has shifted over time and place to apply to some groups of women and not others, depending on factors such as the "value" of particular children on the adoption "market." Solinger, supra note 22, argues that the increased encouragement of young, unmarried white women to give up their children for adoption in the 1950s in the United States was a reflection in part of the "value" of white babies on this "market." She contrasts this encouragement to the experience of young black women who were then, and continue now, to be expected to keep their babies. See also P. Williams. *The Alchemy of Race and Rights* (Cambridge, Massachusettes: Harvard University Press. 1991), 227. Such analysis of the "market value" of babies might help to explain the ideological context which facilitated the great increase in adoption and fostering of First Nation children by non-First Nation families which occurred in the 1960s in Canada and the United States. Other factors which have contributed to this shift include the imperative of the white middle-class family as the best context within which to raise children, constructed through familial ideology [see infra notes 130-141, and accompanying text), and a decrease in taboo against cross-cultural adoption (as reflected e.g., by the comment of Wilson J. in *Racine v. Woods.* [1984] 1 *C.N.L.R.* 161 (S.C.C.) at 171—"I believe that inter-racial adoption, like inter-racial marriage, is now an accepted phenomenon in our pluralist society").

29. This is not to say, however, that white middle-class women find it easy to meet the ideals of motherhood or necessarily experience motherhood as fulfilling and rewarding. As Adrienne Rich (1976) observed in her classic work *Of Women Born: Motherhood as Experience and Institution* (New York: W.W. Norton, 1976), there are certainly "cracks" in the "sacred calling" of motherhood, and a great disjuncture between these ideals of motherhood and the experiences of many mothers, who feel "endlessly burdened, anxious and blamed." Set J.F, O'Barr, D. Pope, and M. Wyer, "Introduction" in J.F. O'Barr, et al. eds., *Ties That Bind: Essays on Mothering and Patriarchy* (Chicago: University of Chicago Press, 1990) 1 at 14. But such negative experiences do not negate the ideology of motherhood. As Gavigan, supra note 7, has argued in regard to familial ideology more generally, it simply "illuminate[s]…what some feminists identify as the oppressive implications of the generality of the idealization and romanticization of the [ideology]." For reasons inherent in the ideology, however, it is more difficult for women who are poor or working class and/or First Nation and and/or black and/or lesbian, and so on, to meet the dominant expectations of motherhood. See: S. Boyd, "Postmodernist Challenges," supra note 8; Gavigan,

Ibid. This complicates and provides insight into the further link drawn by some between the failure of women to conform to ideal patterns of mothering, and violence, poverty, and social disarray. See: Fineman, supra note 8; Roberts, supra note 8: M. Young, "Reproductive Technologies and the Law: Norplant and the Bad Mother" (forthcoming, *Marriage and Family Review*).

30. H. Land, "Introduction: (1992) 4 *Gender and History* 283.

31. Supra note 8. See also Collins, supra note 22, and E. Fox-Genovese, *Within the Plantation Household: Black and White Women of the Old South* (Chapel Hill: University of North Carolina Press, 1988).

32. Supra note 8. See also A.Y. Davis, *Women, Race and Class* (New York: Vintage Books, 1981) at 213-15; L. Gordon, "Why Nineteenth-Century Feminists Did Not Support 'Birth Control' and Twentieth-Century Feminists Do: Feminism, Reproduction, and the Family" in B. Thorne and M. Yalom, eds., *Rethinking the Family: Some Feminist Questions* (Boston: Northeastern University Press, 1992); A. McLaren, *Our Own Master Race: Eugenics in Canada, 1885-1945* (Toronto: McClelland & Stewart, 1990).

33. J. Swigart, *The Myth of the Bad Mother: The Emotional Realities of Mothering* (New Yolk: Doubleday, 1991), 8.

34. Marie Ashe, "'Bad Mothers' and 'Good Lawyers:' Reflections on Representation and Relationship" (Paper presented at the Workshop on Motherhood, Feminism and Legal Theory Project Workshop, Columbia University School of Law, December 4-5, 1992), 8.

35. This point is analogous to Peter Fitzpatrick's general discussion of how law's claim of innocence obfuscates its role in reproducing and reinforcing racism. See Fitzpatrick, "Racism and the Innocence of Law" (1987) 14 *J. Law & Sociology* 119.

36. See Boyd, "Ideologies and Employment," supra note 8. Interestingly, ideological conceptions of motherhood play out even at the dispositional stage where the judicial mandate is to do whatever is in the "best interests of the child." See Kline, "Best Interests or the Child" Ideology, supra note 2, 389 n. 57.

37. I have separated these two tendencies, not to imply that they are distinct processes, but for analytical clarity.

38. A.I. Griffith, Alison I., and D.E. Smith, "Constructing Cultural Knowledge: Mothering as Discourse" in J.S. Gaskell and A.T. McLaren, eds., *Women and Education: A Canadian Perspective* (Calgary: Detselig Enterprises Limited, 1987), 97.

39. Implicit in this construction is the notion that the rewards of mothering should be enough to motivate a woman to overcome an alcohol or drug dependency. See Swift, supra note 20, 258-9.

40. (1979), [1981] 4 *C.N.L.R.* 62 (Man. Prov. Ct Fam. Div.).

41. Ibid., 64.

42. Ibid.

43. (1990), 67 *Man. R.* (2d) 161 (Man. Q.B.).

44. Ibid., 161.

45. Ibid., 164.

46. Supra note 40.

47. Ibid., 287.

48. Mobility is a useful indicator of socio-economic conditions, as well as the availability of goods and services and employment and educational opportunities. See N.H. Lithwick, M. Schiff, and E. Vernon, *An Overview of Registered Indian Conditions in Canada* (Ottawa: Indian and Northern Affairs, 1986) at 46. This 1986 study (based on 1981 data) found that the mobility rates or off-reserve Indians, and in particular, Indian women off-reserve, were higher than those of the general reference population. As well, more off-reserve Indians surveyed had moved residence and locale in the preceding five year than on-reserve Indians. A more recent study in Vancouver found that: 11.5% of the First Nation people surveyed had lived in only one residence in the preceding five years; 23.9% had lived in two different residences: 38% had lived in three to five different residences; and the rest had lived in six to twenty-five different residences. With respect to movement between locales, the same study found that over one-third (37.7%) had lived in only one locale in the preceding five years, another third had lived in two locales, 14.7% had lived in three different locales, and the rest had lived in 4 to 15 different locales. See Rowe & Associates, *The Vancouver Urban Indian Needs Assessment Study* (Vancouver: Ministry of Labour and Consumer Services, 1989). See also V. Satzewich and T. Wotherspoon, *First Nations: Race, Class and Gender Relations* (Scarborough, Ontario: Nelson Canada, 1993), 97-8.

49. Kenora—*Patricia Child and Family Services V.L. (P.)* [1987] O.J. No. 1858 (Q.L.).

50. Ibid., 3.

51. Ibid., 5.

52. Ibid., 5-6.

53. (1989), 93 *N.B.R.* (2d) (Q.B. Fam. Div.)

54. Ibid., 265.

55. (1984) *N.W.T.R.* 295 (Nwt. S.C.) [hereinafter L.O. and S.O.]

56. Ibid., 298.

57. See Monture, supra note 2, 14.

58. Swift, supra note 20, 257.

59. See: e.g., National Council of Welfare, *Women and Poverty Revisited* (Ottawa: National Council of Welfare, 1990). The correlation between poverty, and involvement with child welfare authorities is also well documented. See: National Council of Welfare, *Poor Kids* (Ottawa: National Council of Welfare, 1975) at 276; J. Campbell, *An Analysis of Variables in Child Protection Apprehensions and Judicial Dispositions in British Columbia Child Welfare Practice* (M.S.W. Thesis, University of British Columbia British Columbia); *Making Changes: A Place to Start—Report of the Community Panel, Family and Children's Services, Legislation Review in British Columbia* (Victoria: Minister of Social Services, October 1992) at 9-20 [hereinafter Making Changes]; Callahan, supra note 39, 182-191.

60. See: Department of Indian and Northern Development, *Basic Departmental Data, 1990* (Ottawa: Ministry of Indian and Northern Development, 1990) at 55-7; Satzewich and Wotherspoon, supra note 48, 101; Kline. "'Best Interests of the Child' Ideology," supra note 2, 378, n. 8.

61. Re. *J.H. and N.H. (1988),* 3 Y.R. 282 (Yuk. Terr. Ct.), 100.

62. Ibid., 287.

63. Ibid., 288.

LIVING IN
THE MARGINS:
LESBIAN FAMILIES
AND THE LAW

Katherine Arnup

Like all women, lesbian mothers are profoundly affected by the political and legal climate within which they live and raise their children. In many jurisdictions, lesbianism is still considered a "crime against nature" and a revelation of lesbianism can lead to criminal charges and imprisonment. As the American poet and essayist Minnie Bruce Pratt reminds us, "How I Love is Outside the Law."[1] While the sexual activities in which lesbians engage are no longer criminalized in Canada, provided they take place within the privacy of their own homes, nonetheless lesbians' relationships with each other and with their non-biological children remain largely outside the law. Furthermore, in a number of American states, even "private acts" between same-sex partners remain criminalized.[2] The recent flurry of anti-gay initiatives in the United States coupled with the huge opposition to the inclusion of any further sexual orientation protection in Canada indicate that the battles we have fought for the past twenty-five years are far from over....

An examination of the history of lesbian mothers efforts to secure custody of their children conceived within heterosexual relationships reveals that, in this respect at least, lesbians are still, if not outside, then barely on the margins of the law. Prior to the 1970s, few lesbian mothers contested custody in court. Fearing the implications of open court battles and recognizing that they were almost assured of defeat at the hands of a decidedly homophobic legal system, many women "voluntarily" relinquished custody, in exchange for "liberal" access to their children. On occasion lesbian mothers were able to make private arrangements with former husbands, often lying about their sexual identity in order to retain custody of the children. Such arrangements are still common today, although the numbers are impossible to determine, given the necessarily private nature of the agreements.

During the 1970s and and 80s, with the support of the gay and lesbian movements and of feminist lawyers and friends, lesbians began to contest and, in a limited number of cases, win the custody of their children conceived within heterosexual marriages. In contrast to many American jurisdictions, in which lesbianism per se has been deemed a bar to custody,[3] judges in Canada have adopted what might appear to be a more "reasonable" approach. Examining closely aspects of each applicant's lifestyle, the judge has sought to determine what effect, if any, the mother's lesbianism will have on the well-being of the child.[4]...

Case v. Case was the first Canadian case to deal specifically with the issue of lesbian custody. In July 1974, Mr. Justice MacPherson of the Saskatchewan Queen's Bench granted custody of the two children to their father. In considering the significance of their mother's lesbianism the judge noted that "it seems to me that homosexuality on the part of a parent is a factor to be considered along with all the other evidence in the case. It should not be considered a bar in itself to a parent's right to custody." [5] That statement is contradicted by the judge's discussion of the mother's "lifestyle." Describing the father as a "stable and secure and responsible person," the judge added that, "I hesitate to put adjectives on the personality of the mother but the evidence shows, I think, that her way of life is irregular." In considering her role as vice-president of the local gay club, he added, "I greatly fear that if these children are raised by the mother they will be too much in contact with people of abnormal tastes and proclivities." [6] Thus, while Mrs. Case's lesbianism was not in itself a bar to custody, her "lifestyle" was.

K. v. K., a 1975 Alberta custody dispute, provides an interesting contrast. Comparing the two cases, the judge stated:

> The situation before this court is, in my view, different. Mrs. K. is not a missionary about to convert heterosexuals to her present way of life. She does not regard herself as gay in the sense that heterosexuals are "morose." Mrs. K. is a good mother and a warm, loving, concerned parent. [7]

The judge stated further that "Mrs. K's homosexuality is no more of a bar to her obtaining custody than is the fact of Mr. K's drug use." Having had the opportunity to examine both Mrs. K. and her lover, the judge concluded that "their relationship will be discrete and will not be flaunted to the children or to the community at large." Mrs. K. was awarded custody of her child.

Discretion on the part of the homosexual parent has continued to be cited as a justification for awarding custody to that parent. In a 1991 Saskatchewan case, the judge awarded custody of two children to their aunt, a woman who had been involved in a lesbian relationship for twelve years. In discussing the relationship between the two women the judge noted:

> I found these two women to be rather straightforward. Their relationship does not meet with the approval of all members of society in general. They were neither apologetic nor aggressive about their relationship. They are very discreet. They make no effort to recruit others to their way of living. They make no special effort to associate with others who pursue that lifestyle. In short, D. and H. mind their own business and go their own way in a discreet and dignified way. [8]

A 1980 Canadian case followed the pattern set by *Case v. Case*. Gayle Bezaire had originally been granted custody of her two children, but as a result of "changed circumstances" the original order was reversed, giving custody to the father. The second custody order was upheld on appeal. The details of this case, as in many custody battles, are complex. It is apparent that the mother violated a number of provisions of the original order. At least one of these, however, represented a "catch-22" situation. In his original order, the judge had ordered the mother to live alone. He explained: "I am attempting to improve the situation, and this includes any open, declared, and avowed lesbian, or homosexual relationship." In this order, Judge MacMahon sought to inhibit the lesbian "life-style" of Mrs. Bezaire while declaring that her lesbianism was not in itself a bar to custody.[9]

Imposing conditions like these is a common practice in cases involving a lesbian or gay parent. The practice is based on the assumption that a parent's homosexuality may negatively affect the child, but that those effects can be overcome if the parent meets certain conditions, such as not co-habiting with a lover, not sharing a bedroom with a lover, and not show-ing affection of any kind in front of the child. Paula Brantner has recently commented on the unfairness of these conditions: "Heterosexual parents are not routinely asked to forgo sex-ual relationships with other adults to obtain custody of their children—lesbian and gay par-ents are." The impact of these conditions on the lives of lesbian and gay parents is severe. Brantner notes: "Gay parents are forced to make impossible and intolerable decisions. Parents who fail to comply with the court's restrictions my lose their children. If they do com-ply, they may lose their partners or the ability to be openly gay and to maintain contact with other gay persons, which takes its own psychological toll." [10]

The contradiction between the liberal acceptance of homosexuality and the setting of con-ditions is evident in dozens of cases involving lesbian and gay parents. As early as 1974, an Australian judge noted that "[T]he days are gone when courts will disqualify a woman from the role of parent merely because she has engaged or is engaging in some form of extra-mar-ital sex, be it heterosexual or homosexual." Despite this statement, Judge Bright ordered the mother not to sleep in her lover's bedroom overnight or to let her lover sleep in her bed-room overnight. As well, the children were required to visit a psychiatrist at least once a year. [11]...

These cases illustrate the distinction which judges have drawn between what they deter-mine to be "good" and "bad" lesbian mothers. "Good" lesbian mothers, women who live quiet, discreet lives, who promise that they will raise their children to be heterosexual, who appear to the outside world to be heterosexual single parents, have in recent years increasingly succeeded in winning custody of their children. "Bad" lesbian mothers, women who are open about their sexual orientation, who attend gay and lesbian demonstrations and other pub-lic events, and who view their lesbianism positively or as one aspect of an entire challenge to society, are almost certain to lose custody of their children to their ex-husbands....

With the passage of family law reform legislation in Canada in the 1980s, criteria for determining custody were amended and, as a result, parental behaviour *in and of itself* could no longer be considered a bar to custody. In Ontario, for example, the *Children's Law Reform Act* specifies that the "best interests of the child" shall be the determining factor. The legislation directs the judge to consider "all the needs and circumstances of the child," including the relationship between the child and those persons claiming custody, the pref-erences of the child, the current living situation of the child, the plans put forward for the child, the "permanence and stability of the family unit with which it is proposed that the child will live," and the blood or adoptive links between the child and the applicant. [12] The sec-tion explicitly states that "the past conduct of a person is not relevant to a determination of an application—unless the conduct is relevant to the ability of the person to act as a parent of a child."[13]

While the revised legislation might appear to improve a lesbian mother's chances for suc-cess, there are a number of ways these provisions can be interpreted by a homophobic judge to rule against her application for custody. First, a judge may refuse to recognize a "homo-sexual" family as a permanent and stable family unit. Homosexuals, after all, are not permitted to marry and therefore do not meet this standard heterosexual measure of "stability." The "closeted" nature of many gay and lesbian relationships, and the absence of any census cat-egory to "capture" same-sex partnerships, also render it virtually impossible to offer sta-tistical evidence of the longevity of same-sex relationships. Given these obstacles, a lesbian mother might find herself unable to demonstrate the "permanence and stability" of her "family unit."

A "lesbian life-style" may also be used to find that a lesbian mother is unlikely to provide a "suitable" home for her child. As *Case v. Case* demonstrates, judges have deemed activities like attending lesbian rallies and dances, exposing the child to other lesbians and gay men, and discussing lesbian issues openly in the home negative factors in considering the application of lesbian mothers for custody of their children. Thus, despite the apparently fair-minded language of family law reform, judges can and do find ways within the law to deny lesbian mothers custody of their children.

This reality presents a lesbian mother seeking court-ordered custody with a number of difficult choices. If she presents herself in court as an "avowed lesbian," if she admits to coming out at work or at school, she stands less chance of winning custody of her children, especially if she meets a determined challenge from her ex-husband. Within this legal context, most lesbians "choose" to act as "straight" as possible to win custody of their children. Such strategies tell us far less about the belief systems of lesbian mothers than about the attitudes and prejudices of the courts. As Julia Brophy has noted: "A custody dispute is not the forum in which to mount a feminist critique of the family." [14]...

A recent custody case in Richmond, Virginia, serves as a startling reminder of the fact that the issue of child custody for lesbian mothers is far from resolved. In September 1993, Henrico Country Juvenile and Domestic Relations Court Judge Buford M. Parsons Jr. awarded custody of Tyler Bottoms to his maternal grandmother, removing the two-year-old child from the care of his biological mother and her lesbian partner. The judge's ruling was based on solely on the fact the mother is a lesbian. Parsons relied on *Roe v. Roe*, a 1985 Virginia Supreme Court case that found homosexual parents to be unfit parents with no custodial rights to their children.[15] In that case, the court found that living with a lesbian or gay parent placed "an intolerable burden" on a child. While Sharon was successful in her initial appeal of the decision, Tyler remains with his grandmother, pending yet another appeal. [16]

While initially most lesbian mothers who came to public attention were women who had conceived and given birth to children within heterosexual partnerships or marriages; in the past fifteen years, increasing numbers of lesbians have chosen to conceive and bear children, either on their own, or within a lesbian relationship. Since the late 1970s, an undermined number of lesbians have requested artificial insemination services at infertility clinics and sperm banks across North America. Many of these requests were denied once the applicant's sexual orientation was revealed. In some instances women were informed that the clinic had decided not to inseminate *any* single women, claiming that they feared single mothers would launch child support suits against the medical facility should the insemination be successful.[17]

To date, no legal decisions have been issued concerning infertility clinics which discriminate against single women or lesbians. In the only documented American case, a woman launched a legal action against Wayne State University when its medical centre rejected her application for artificial insemination. Fearing the repercussions of a protracted legal battle, the clinic abandoned its restrictive policy, granting her application before the case could be heard by the courts.[18] In Canada, a similar complaint was upheld by the British Columbia Council of Human Rights in August 1995. The complaint, alleging discrimination on the basis of sexual orientation and family status, was filed by Sandra Benson and Tracy Potter against Dr. Gerald Korn for his refusal to provide artificial insemination services to them solely on the grounds that they are lesbians. The B.C. Council of Human Rights awarded Benson and Potter $2,500 as compensation for emotional injury and $896.44 for expenses. [19] Although applicable only in British Columbia, the decision represents an important precedent in the struggle for the provision of donor insemination services for lesbians.

Perhaps anticipating requests for donor insemination from single heterosexual women and lesbians, legislative initiatives in a number of jurisdictions in the United States have restricted access to insemination services to married women. [20] No Canadian legislation yet exists, although recommendations to this effect have been made by a number of commissions.[21] Most recently, the Royal Commission on New Reproductive Technologies supported the right to assist insemination for single women, and explicitly for lesbians. The report recommends that "[c]riteria for determining access to assisted insemination services should not discriminate on the basis of social factors such as sexual orientation, marital status, or economic status.[22] This recommendation took many feminists by surprise, particularly since it contravened a public opinion poll which indicated that a majority of Canadians surveyed (seventy-one percent) opposed lesbians' access to reproductive technologies. [23]

In light of access barriers to clinical services, it is not surprising that many (if not most) lesbians prefer to make private insemination arrangements. Here, however, legal measures designed to medicalize the practice of alternative insemination present yet another roadblock. In recent years, a number of jurisdictions in the United States and elsewhere have passed legislation declaring artificial insemination to be a practice of medicine, thereby legally restricting its use to licensed practitioners. The Ontario Law Reform Commission in 1985 recommended the passage of similar legislation. [24] Should such a measure be implemented, it would force women engaging in private insemination arrangements to remain "clandestine" about their activities in order to avoid legal sanctions. Surprisingly, perhaps, the Royal Commission report condones the practice of private insemination, recommending that "[s]perm should be provided to individual women for self-insemination without discrimination on the basis of factors such as sexual orientation, marital status, or economic status."[25] To date, however, that recommendation has not been enacted.

Another legal issue faced by lesbians is the legal status of the sperm donor. While artificial insemination was initially treated by the courts as the legal equivalent to adultery against the woman's husband, gradually the courts have moved to a position that recognized the child as the legitimate offspring of the recipient's husband, provided he had consented to the insemination procedure. Most legislation now specifies that the parental rights and obligations of the donor are replaced by the paternal rights of the husband.

The issues are considerably more complex in the case of a lesbian or unmarried heterosexual women and a known donor. In such instances, women who arrange a private insemination—most of whom are lesbians—face the risk of paternity claims by sperm donors. To date, no Canadian cases have been reported, but in six of the seven reported American cases, sperm donors seeking paternity rights have had their claims upheld by the courts. The decisions have ranged from placing the sperm donor's name on the child's birth certificate to granting access rights. [26] Such decisions have been made even in cases where the insemination was performed by a licensed practitioner, thereby ignoring relevant legislation which extinguished the rights and obligations of donors. In one 1989 case, the Oregon Appeal Court concluded that, despite the statute, the donor had shown himself interested in performing the duties of a father and was therefore entitled to paternity rights similar to those of an unwed father. [27] In a similar Colorado case, the Colorado Supreme Court ruled in favour of the donor, crediting the donor's claims of having bought toys, clothing, and books for the child, as well as establishing a trust fund in the child's name, as evidence of his desire to parent. [28]...

In the final American decision, the Oregon Court of Appeal upheld a lower court decision which denied the sperm donor any paternal rights. In that case, the donor had signed an agreement waiving his paternal rights. When a dispute arose over visitation, the parties entered into mediation. After several sessions, they reaffirmed and re-signed their original agreement. [29] It was on that basis that the appeal court upheld the original decision.

While all of the cases to date have involved only the issues of access and a declaration of paternity, the implications extend far beyond those claims. A declaration of paternity can accord any or all of the following: sole or joint physical or legal custody, visitation, decision-making in such areas as education, religion, and health care, custody in the event of the mother's death, denial of permission to change residence or to adopt, obligation to provide child support, and inclusion of the donor's name as father on the child's birth certificate. [30] As the National Center for Lesbian Rights in the United States has noted: "In our system of law there are only two options. Either the donor is merely a donor, with no parental rights or relationship with the child whatsoever, or he is a father, with all of his parental rights intact. There are no gray areas in the law here, and, when in doubt, the courts tend to grant donors full parental rights in cases involving single mothers."[31]

In marked contrast to sperm donors, the legal status of non-biological lesbian mothers has for the most part been denied by the courts in both the United States and Canada. [32] While these women have helped to care for and financially support the children of lesbian families, courts have repeatedly *refused* to grant their claims for visitation rights upon dissolution of the lesbian relationship or custody rights upon the death of the biological mother. In the only reported Canadian case dealing with this issue, the judge rejected a lesbian mother's application for support for herself and her children born during the course of her relationship with her former lesbian partner. The court sided with the non-biological mother who maintained that she had no legal obligation to support either the biological mother or the children. [33]

As more lesbian couples choose to become parents, courts will increasingly be faced with the issue of the rights and responsibilities of non-biological lesbian mothers. Many areas of childrens' (and parents') lives are affected, including medical authorization, visitation, support, and custody upon dissolution of the parental relationship, and guardianship in the event of the death of the biological mother. To date, in an effort to secure legal rights for the non-biological parent, lesbian parents have sought a variety of legal mechanisms including second-parent adoption and joint custody. Second parent adoption, the option used by step-parents in heterosexual relationships when they create a new parenting arrangement following the dissolution of the original marriage, allows the "new" parent to assume rights and responsibilities without requiring the original parent of that sex to forfeit his or her parenting status. Such an option has not been widely available to lesbian and gay parents. [34]

In May 1995, lesbian mothers in the province of Ontario won an important legal victory, when Judge Nevins granted second-parent adoptions to four lesbian couples. [35] In a far-reaching decision, Judge Nevins rejected all of the standard arguments used to deny parental rights to homosexuals, concluding that:

> When one reflects on the seemly limitless parade of neglected, abandoned and abused children who appear before our courts in protection cases daily, all of whom have been in the care of heterosexual parents in a "traditional" family structure, the suggestion that it might not ever be in the best interests of these children to be raised by loving, caring and committed parents, who might happen to be lesbian or gay, is nothing short of ludicrous. [36]

Ontario thus joins the growing list of jurisdictions in which second parent adoptions can be granted to lesbian and gay couples. [37] In most jurisdictions in the United States, and throughout Canada, only one parent of each sex can have legal rights to a child. Thus, the birth mother must relinquish her rights to enable the non-biological mother to adopt the child.…

The effort to secure second-parent adoption or joint custody may also pose a danger for lesbian families. As Nancy Polikoff has noted: "The stress of entering the legal system and potentially submitting the family to evaluation according to standards rooted in homophobia and heterosexism is as much a deterrent as the uncertainty of asserting untested legal theories." [38] Lesbian families pursuing such options must weigh carefully the financial and emotional costs of state intervention against the benefits of the legal recognition of their family constellation, should their application be successful.

In the absence of effective, risk-free legal mechanisms, the following documents can be drawn up in an attempt to insure that the non-biological mother's parental rights are recognized by the courts: co-parenting agreement, statement of guardianship in a will, and a medical authorization form. While none of these mechanisms is a guarantee, they serve at least, to indicate the intention and wishes of both parents. [39]…

The legal position of lesbian mothers has improved considerably since the first custody cases began to appear before the courts in Canada, the United States and elsewhere, some twenty years ago. Lesbian mothers and their children are gaining acceptance in schools, daycare centres, and communities across North America. Lesbians are contesting homophobic laws and practices in the areas of adoption, foster parenting, and child custody. No longer is it a judicial certainty that a lesbian mother will lose custody of her children. Despite these gains, lesbian mothers still risk losing their children and many are fighting these battles every day. In the realm of family law, there is no one strategy, no right way to proceed. Lesbians facing these issues should seek legal counsel, since laws vary tremendously from province to province, state to state and country to country. [40] Equally importantly, they need the support and help of other lesbian parents who understand the anguish that these struggles bring.

ENDNOTES

1. Minnie Bruce Pratt, "Poetry in Time of War," in *Rebellion: Essays 1980–1991*, (Ithaca: Firebrand Books, 1991), 228.

2. In *Bowers v. Hardwick*, the U.S. Supreme Court upheld the constitutionality of a Georgia statue which criminalized homosexual acts. That 1986 decision represented a major setback for efforts to improve the custodial position of lesbian and gay parents cannot be fit parents. See *Bowers v. Hardwick*, 106 S.Ct. 2841 (1986).

3. For a discussion of the *per se* approach, see Robert A. Beargie, "Custody Determinations Involving the Homosexual Parent," *Family Law Quarterly*, 22, 1 (Spring 1988), 71–86.

4. For a discussion of these cases, see Wendy Cross, "Judging the Best Interests of the Child: Child Custody and the Homosexual Parent" *Canadian Journal of Women and the Law*, 1 (1986), 505-31; Katherine Arnup, "Mothers Just Like Others: Lesbians, Divorce, and Child Custody in Canada," *Canadian Journal of Women and the Law*, 3 (1989), 18-32.

5. Not all cases which appear before the courts are reported in legal journals. It is a common occurrence in cases in which homosexuality or lesbianism is a factor to seal the records, ostensibly to protect the privacy of the individuals involved. This practice presents a problem for both lawyers

and researchers in the field of lesbian custody. Those cases which are reported become accessible to judges and lawyers for their use in future cases, and thereby assume an importance beyond their individual significance.

6. *Case v Case,* (1974), 18 *R.F.L.* 128 (Sask. Queen's Bench).

7. Ibid.

8. *K. v. K.*, (1975), 23 *R.F.L.* 63 (Alta. Prov. Ct.), 64.

9. D.M. v. M.D., 94 *Sask. R.* 315, [1991] S.J. No. 672.

10. Paula A. Brantner, "When Mommy or Daddy is Gay: Developing Constitutional Stands for Custody Decisions," *Hastings Women's Law Journal*, 3, 1 (Winter 1991), 105, 107.

11. *Campbell v. Campbell*, (1974), 9 SASR, 25 at 28, cited in Margaret Bateman, "Lesbians, Gays and Child Custody: An Australian Legal History," *Australian Gay and Lesbian Law Journal* 1(1992), 49.

12. *Bezaire v. Bezaire*, (1980), 20 *R.F.L.* (2d)365(Ont.C.A.).

13. *Children's Law Reform Act*, R.S.O. 1980, c.68, section 24.

14. Julia Brophy, "New Families, Judicial Decision-Making and Children's Welfare," *Canadian Journal of Women and the Law*, 5 (1992) 496.

15. *Roe v. Roe*, 228 Va.722,324 S.E.2d 691 (1985). The Virginia Supreme Court found that living conditions would "impose an intolerable burden upon her [the child] by reason of the social condemnation attached to them." The court noted as well that "the father's unfitness is manifested by his willingness to impose this burden upon [his daughter] in exchange for her own gratification."

16. For an initial report on the case, see Nancy Wartik, "Virginia is no Place for Lesbian Mothers," *Ms.* (November/December 1993), 89. The appeals court decision overturning Judge Parsons' original order was unanimous. Judge Sam W. Coleman III wrote that "a child's natural and legal right to the care and support of a parent and the parents' right to the custody and companionship of the child should only be disrupted if there are compelling reasons to do so." (AP wire service, June 21, 1994).

17. For a discussion of such arguments see Katherine Arnup, "Finding Fathers: Artificial Insemination, Lesbians and the Law," *Canadian Journal of Women and the Law*,7,1 (1994), 97-115.

18. *Smedes v.Wayne State University*, No. 80-725-83, (E.D. Mich., filed July 15, 1980). The case was widely reported in the American press.

19. In the Matter of the *Human Rights Act* S.B.C. 1984, c.22 (as amended) and in the matter of a complaint before the British Columbia Council of Human Rights between Tracy Potter and Sandra Benson versus Gerald W. Korn and/or Korn Management Ltd.

20. On this issue, Robert H. Blank notes "the question of allowing single or lesbian women access to AID has been approached explicitly in few jurisdictions and rejected in virtually all." Blank, *Regulating Reproduction*, (New York: Columbia University Press, 1990), 151.

21. See, for example, Saskatchewan, Law Reform Commission of Saskatchewan, *Proposals for a Human Artificial Insemination Act*, (March 1987).

22. Recommendation 99 (9). *Proceed With Care: Final Report of the Royal Commission on New Reproductive Technologies*, 485.

23. The report noted: "Although most Canadians surveyed did not support lesbians having access to

DI, to provide a service in a discriminatory way by denying access, without evidence that a resultant child would be harmed, is contrary to the Charter and also contravenes our ethics of care." *Proceed With Care*, 456

24. Ontario, Ministry of the Attorney General, Ontario Law Reform Commission, *Report on Artificial Reproduction and Related Matters*, (1985).

25. Recommendation 94 (f), *Proceed With Care*, 480.

26. See Sperm Donor wins Fight With Lesbians" *Toronto Star* (26 July 1991), F1. For a discussion of these cases, see Katherine Arnup, Finding Fathers…" (see above). See also Arnup and Susan Boyd, "Familial Disputes? Sperm Donors, Lesbian Mothers, and Legal Parenthood" in *Legal Inversions*, Didi Herman and Carly Stychin (eds.), (Temple University Press, 1995).

27. In *Kevin N. McIntyre v. Linden Crouch*, while the insemination was not performed by a licensed practitioner, the court determined that the relevant Oregon legislation did apply. That legislation specified that, when as insemniation is performed by a licensed practitioner, the donor has "no right, obligation or interest with respect to a child born as a result of artificial insemination" and the child has "no right, obligation or interest" with respect to the donor. ORS 109.239 section 5, 1, and 2. *MacIntyre v. Crouch*, 780 P.2d 239 (Or.App.1989). Despite that finding, the court ruled that, if the donor could demonstrate that an agreement had existed between himself and the mother regarding his parental involvement with the child, then his constitutional rights would have been violated. They directed him to a lower court to make arguments on this issue.

28. Interest of R.C., (1989, Colo)775 P2d 27.

29. *Leckie v. Voorhies*, Case NO. 60-92-06326 (Ore. Circuit Court, April 5, 1993) (unreported); and *Leckie v. Voorhies*, No. A797857, May 25, 1994, 128 Ore. App. 289.

30. For a discussion of the implications of donor rights, see National Centre for Lesbian Rights, "Lesbians Choosing Motherhood: Legal Implications of Donor Insemination and Co-parenting", reprinted in William B. Rubenstein, ed., *Lesbians, Gay Men, and the Law*, (New York: New Press, 1993), 543.

31. Ibid., 546.

32. For an in-depth discussion of the parental rights of non-biological mothers, see Nancy D. Polikoff, "This Child Does Have Two Mothers: Redefining Parenthood to Meet the Needs of Children in Lesbian-Mother and Other Nontraditional Families," *Georgetown Law Journal*, 78 (1990-91), 459-575.

33, *Anderson v. Luoma*, (1986), 50 *R.F.L.* (2d) 127 (B.C.S.C.) The biological mother did succeed in winning a property settlement.

34. According to a 1996 newsletter of the Gay and Lesbian Parents Coalition International (GLPCD), the following jurisdictions have granted at least one second-parent adoption: Alaska, California, Colorado, District of Columbia, Illinois, Indiana, Iowa, Massachusetts, Michigan, Minnesota, Nevada, New Jersey, New York, Ohio, Oregon, Pennsylvania, Rhode Island, Texas, Vermont and Washington, England also recently granted a second-parent adoption. GLPCI Network, Winter/Spring 1996, 14.

35. *Re. K.* (1995) 23 O.R. (3d) 679 (Ont. Ct. Prov. Div.)

36. Ibid., 708

37. *Re. K.* has since been followed by a decision at the Ontario Court General Division and by numerous unreported cases. *Re. C.E.G.* (No.1) [1995] O.J. No. 4072 and Re. C.E.G. (No. 2) [1995]

O.J. No. 4073 (Ont. Ct. Gen. Div.).

38. Polikoff, "This Child Does Have Two Mothers," 526.

39. For a discussion of these efforts, see Karen Spallina: "Lesbians Choosing Parenthood," *Guild Practitioner*, 50, 1 (Winter 1993), 21-4.

40. For assistance in finding a knowledgeable and supportive lawyer, contact your local lesbian/gay rights organization. If no such organization exists, try a women's centre or other support centre. It is extremely important to find a lesbian positive lawyer. For other organizations, see the resource section in this volume.

FAMILIES OF NATIVE PEOPLES, IMMIGRANTS, AND PEOPLE OF COLOUR

Tania Das Gupta

This chapter presents an antiracist perspective on the "family" in Canada that departs from traditional discussion. It is often assumed that the "family" is of a standard form, and thus variations are neither acknowledged nor discussed. Authors implicitly assume that the "family" unit is male-dominated, white, middle-class, nuclear, and heterosexual. This image does not allow for variations of class, ethnicity, or sexuality. Such a stereotype is reinforced by ideological institutions and processes in society, most conspicuously the mass media.

Therefore, traditional discussion of the "family" falls into an essentialist trap, reinforcing a functionalist notion of the "complementary" roles played by men and women. Conflicts and oppressions are not acknowledged—and if they were would be defined away as "deviance" (Parsons and Bales, 1955). Variations of "family" forms among people of colour, for example extended families, single-parent families, and multiple-parent families, would also be seen as deviant and in need of being resocialized to conform to the dominant form.

This chapter will look at variations in families among Native peoples and people of colour in Canada and then analyze how these variations, in most instances, have been socially organized according to the imperatives of a capitalist society and its associated interventionist state (Panitch, 1977). State policies in the area of immigration and racism have historically had a fundamental effect on families and on communities of colour. We will see that people of colour have frequently been denied the right to have the "family" form of their choice and that this denial has been historically motivated by racism, an ideology that has been fully capitalized on by the Canadian state. Also, we will see that the demand for "a family" has been one of the major organizing principles of communities of colour in Canada.

I use quotation marks around "family" to indicate that the word has sexist and racist connotations. Carol Yawney, an anthropologist, commented that we could use other words to refer to a household, such as *clan* or *band*. As a compromise, I will use the plural *families* to indicate that there are many different forms of households operating in different communities.

CRITICAL REVIEW AND THEORETICAL FRAMEWORK

The most powerful critique of traditional theories and reports on the "family" came from feminist writers, activists, and theoreticians (Beauvoir, 1952; Greer, 1970; Steinem, 1983) who pointed out that the roles played by women within their families were far from ideal and in fact reinforced a second-class role for women marked by oppression, boredom, and non-recognition. By ignoring the problems in families, particularly those arising from relationships between men and women, we were delivering not a complete picture of the institution but rather a partial picture, one that represents a patriarchal vantage point. By not looking at the experiences of women in families, we were perpetuating the invisibility of women's work as well as our silence in academic discourse. Feminist contribution to sociological theory has been, therefore, a focus on women's experience and making gender a framework for analysis (Smith, 1977)....

Cross-cultural variations in families have been pointed out by feminists such as Nett (1988: 83) and socialist feminist anthropologists such as Reiter (1975); however, variations have been linked to different stages of economic development in societies. In other words, communities of colour have been studied anthropologically by white women but frequently in the context of looking at pre-capitalist societies.... Since the 1980s, there has been a growing literature documenting, from women's standpoints, the experiences of immigrant women and women of colour in families and communities in Canada (Brand 1991; Brant 1988; Das Gupta 1986; *Fireweed* 1983; Iacovetta 1987; Latham and Pazdro 1984; *Polyphony* 1986). Much of this has been written by Native women, women of colour, and immigrant women....

Such a perspective has boiled down to the following assertions about the "family":

1.   The "family" form has not always been nuclear and heterosexual (Das Gupta, 1993; Latham and Pazdro, 1984).

2.   Women and men of colour and immigrants have not always had the right to live in a "family" context in Canada, a right that white Canadians take for granted (Thornhill, 1991; Brand, 1991). Therefore, roles played by men and women of colour have not been the stereotyped ones that white feminists often take for granted as a point of departure.

3.   When they have been allowed to live in it, the "family" form has generally been oppressive to women of colour. But it has also been a support and refuge in an otherwise hostile environment.

4.   Immigrant women and women of colour have to go beyond gender to understand their situations in the world. This means that we have to take into account race and class oppressions as well as privileges (*Fireweed*, 1983; Vorst et al., 1991) and thus make alliances with the working class, and with men of colour on these grounds.

5.   Forms of resistance that have emanated from these varied realities and experiences have historically not been recognized as "feminist" because they don't adhere to a traditional mould. The mould itself needs to be re-examined because of its exclusionary parameters.

The demand for a "family" historically became an antiracist, feminist, and working-class agenda, given oppressive state policies. The state has maintained a capitalist mode of production as well as reproduced racist, sexist, and classist structures through its various policies, including immigration policies and such laws as the Indian Act. Through such policies, the state has regulated the "family" form of Native peoples, immigrants, and people of colour. It has rationalized doing so with various hegemonic ideologies, such as racism and gender. Hence, the "family" has become a terrain of struggle not just for men and women but also for communities of colour and immigrant communities vis-à-vis the state....

NATIVE PEOPLES

Genocide of the Culture, Genocide of the Family

It is erroneous to talk about Native families for two reasons. First, Native peoples are composed of a number of distinct nations with different histories, cultures, economic bases, languages, and dialects. So it is important to be specific when making sociological assertions. Second, the devastation of Native families has been only one part of the Canadian government's genocidal policies....

When Europeans landed on this continent, they encountered well-developed, highly organized, and stable formations of Native societies, including family formations. Families varied in lineage and locality, but they were extended, and women and men related to each other with reciprocity and sharing (Bourgeault, 1991; Brant, 1988)....

However, these arrangements were a hindrance to the European project of colonization and capitalism. In order to subjugate and disempower Natives, the mercantile colonizers embarked on a campaign to penetrate, exploit, and distort Native families, and finally to destroy them altogether....

In the absence of white European women, white officials took "wives," often by force, initially from the Native community and later from the racially preferred Métis community (Bourgeault, 1991: 104; CANSP, 1978: 34). These women were used to transport goods, prepare furs, make shoes, knit, stitch, and "keep house" for white men. Native men became the hunters and trappers for the companies and also acted as middlemen in the fur trade. Women's labour was thus diverted from their own communities toward the maintenance of individual men and the colonial trading companies. Native men sometimes resorted to "several wives" in order to accomplish their middlemen roles....

As capitalism predominated and immigration from all over the world took hold, the labour of Native peoples, including the Métis, was not as crucial as it had been in the early years of capitalist development. Nor was Native peoples' labour as malleable as that of immigrants, since Natives retained the option of not assimilating into the predominant capitalist system. So the European colonialists, with the help of the church, adopted a strategy of biological and cultural assimilation of Native peoples. At the centre of this approach lay an effort to destroy Native family formations, including the destruction of Native children. Two institutions that have played very key roles in this process are the schools and the child welfare agencies....

Frideres (1987) describes the policy of assimilation pursued through education. Religious-based education before 1850 was followed by missionary-led residential schools and then the standardization (read assimilation) of Native with non-Native education in the 1960s.

Perhaps the residential schools provide the most dramatic examples of what education did to Native children and to families. York (1989: 22) presents vivid documentation of the horror of missionary teachers and government officials threatening bodily harm or arrest to force Native parents to send their young children to residential schools. Residential schools were hostels where children were separated from their families, prevented from speaking their own languages and practising their own traditions, and made to practise a semi-militaristic lifestyle, including wearing uniforms and having their hair shaved off. They were brainwashed to believe in the "goodness" of the Bible and the "barbarism" of Native religions. All this happened with the aid of severe corporal punishment and, frequently, sexual abuse of these children. Generations of depression, alcoholism, suicide, and family breakdown are the legacy of such traumatic experiences and are described as the "residential school syndrome" by Native peoples themselves (York, 1989: 37).

The abuse at such schools seems to be only one stop in a whole litany of abuse, including sexual abuse, that Native children experience at the hands of non-Native men in powerful positions. In some Native communities, up to 94 percent of the residents were sexually abused as children (York, 1989: 30). Most children attending residential school started young and many stayed for years without holidays and without any contacts with their parents and their communities. Separating children from their families was one of the chief ways the institution could break all cultural links with Native education, culture, and language.

In the absence of good parental role models and the total absence of Native role models, residential schools produced generations of Native adults with minimal parenting skills, coupled with symptoms of residential school syndrome. This frequently produced abuse within Native families (Locust, 1990). Diana Nason, a past program supervisor at Native Child and Family Services of Toronto, confirmed the persistence of this vicious cycle (interview with author, 1992)....

Just as the residential school system was being phased out in the 1960s, the child welfare system stepped into view in the form of Children's Aid Services, which removed Native children from their parents on the pretext that the parents were "inconsistent" or "abusive." This was a dominant phenomenon in most Native communities on- and off-reserve.

In 1979, a national report on adoption and welfare found that 20 percent of children in foster care were Native, while only 6 percent of the Canadian population was Native (Hudson and McKenzie, 1981: 63). In Manitoba, 60 percent of children in foster care were Native, while the overall Native population in the province was 12 percent. In the 1970s, 80 percent of Native children in Kenora, Ontario, were in "care" (NCFS, 1991). This trend continued into the early 1980s (York, 1989: 206). Most children were placed in non-Native homes, including homes outside Canada.

How did this come about in cultures where "kids are considered as sacred gifts" and where "nobody owned the children, except the community" (Diana Nason, interview with author, 1992)? Hudson and McKenzie (1981) have answered this question by analyzing the non-Native child welfare system as an agent of colonization of Native peoples. They have argued that this colonial relationship has three characteristics, namely the lack of decision-making power in the Native community, the devaluation of Native parenting and child welfare practices, and the nature of interaction between Native and non-Native societies that reproduces the subordination of the former and the domination of the latter....

Native peoples are unique in Canada as being the only communities that have been defined by the government in a piece of legislation, namely the Indian Act, which was passed in 1876 (Midnight Sun, 1988: 78). The descendants of those who did not sign treaties or become registered are not defined as "Indian." Until 1960, a Native person had to renounce "Indian" status in order to vote, go to university, buy liquor, or live off-reserve. Before

1985, Native women who married non-Native men lost their status as "Indians" (as did their children) unless they subsequently married Native men. This meant that they could not reside on-reserve and they lost all inheritance rights. Moreover, they and their children could not go back to their families on-reserve in case of being widowed, separated, or divorced (CASNP, 1978: 4). This policy was challenged by Jeanette Corbiére-Lavell in 1973. Although she did not win her case, the campaign united large numbers of Native women and started a movement to reform the Indian Act.

The social workers and child welfare workers are mainly middle-class non-Natives who undoubtedly bring their own biases in defining "abuse" and "dysfunctional families" (York, 1989; Johnston, 1983). Carol Locust (1990) discusses several examples of classifying traditional child-rearing practices as "abusive." The practice common to extended families of a child living with her or his grandparents, aunts, or uncles has often been interpreted as abuse. Diana Nason (interview with author, 1992) related a situation in which a Native couple used to leave their child with her/his grandparents over weekends while they indulged in drinking. These parents were defined as "inconsistent parents" and thus their child was removed from them.

Children in Native cultures are treated as fully developed human beings deserving of full respect. Children are therefore not "forced" or "disciplined" into anything, a characteristic mentioned also by John (interview with author, 1992). Older Native children have been known to take on significant household responsibilities, particularly around child care. These roles have sometimes been interpreted as "contributing to delinquency."

Similarly, Native parents who encourage their children to participate in traditional ceremonies, which may require them to be absent from school, have been blamed for not providing an environment for educational success.

A "blaming the victim" mentality has always existed, as far as the Native community is concerned. Disproportionately high rates of post-neonatal deaths and a variety of illnesses are often used to justify classifying Native parents as "unfit," without explaining that these health problems occur predominantly as a result of poverty and discrimination.

In the face of such systematic genocidal policies, many in the Native communities have resorted to self-destructive behaviours such as alcoholism, sniffing gasoline, and suicide to escape the pain of daily survival (York, 1989; Midnight Sun, 1988: 78). This in turn has reinforced the predominant racist stereotypes that non-Native societies hold about Native peoples.

Resistance to Genocide

After generations of colonial domination and the resulting politics of divide and rule, Native peoples have achieved a sense of unity for a common goal—self-government....

Self-government in the area of social services and child welfare is also a growing movement, with organizations such as Anishnawbe Health Toronto (which provides culturally sensitive health care to Native peoples in Toronto), and Native Child and Family Services of Toronto (NCFS), which tackles child welfare in the off-reserve population in Toronto. Even though it is not yet mandated to take children into protective custody, NCFS has launched several innovative programs, based on Native values, to intervene in situations of child abuse in Native families. For instance, they can remove a Native child to a "Native support home" in the same city. They have also started a "customary care program" (NCFS,

1991), which is an adaptation of the principle of the extended-family form so important in Native cultures. If parents are in need of child-care support, they have the right to name an extended family member or trusted friend as an alternative care giver. In the absence of such options, NCFS can match parents with other Native families who have volunteered to extend such help. By means of these programs, NCFS is trying to use Native values and traditions in promoting child welfare. An important departure here from the non-Native system is the maintenance of ties between children and their natural parents, keeping Native families together as well as caring for children in their Native communities.

IMMIGRANTS AND PEOPLE OF COLOUR

The Construction of "Single" and "Temporary" Status

Chinese Families

In the absence of appropriate and adequate European immigration in the late 1800s, and because of the near genocide of Native peoples, about 15 000 Chinese men were admitted into Canada to work on the railways, despite protests from B.C. politicians and people at large. However, once the railway was completed in 1885, the Chinese Immigration Act was passed to restrict the entrance of the Chinese by imposing a $50 head tax, which rose to $500 per head by 1903.

The wives of Chinese labourers usually stayed behind in China, not always because they wanted to but because they or their husbands could not afford the head taxes. Valerie Mah, a Toronto teacher and historian, called the Toronto Chinese community between 1878 and 1924 the "bachelor" society because of the absence of women (Dunphy, 1987). The head tax was a way of systemically excluding a group of people because of race, ethnicity, and sex.

The women who did come numbered under 100 in 1885, and either were the wives of merchants or were prostitutes (Van Dieren, 1984). The tiny middle class of traders and merchants in the Chinese community was given an option of bringing their wives free of charge before 1900; after 1900, all women were charged a head tax. Given capitalism's constant search for investment, Canada has always encouraged entrepreneurial immigrants. The wives of immigrant businessmen became important as comanagers and unpaid workers, thus saving on labour expenses and also maintaining a passive labour pool.

The sexuality of people of colour is always a problem for a racist society. Single male Chinese workers posed a threat of miscegenation to white Canadians. Importing female Chinese prostitutes seemed to be the solution to this "problem." However, the presence of prostitutes raised fears of a rise in the population of Chinese immigrants as well as the seduction of white boys (Van Dieren, 1984).

South Asian Families

As in the case of Chinese immigrants, immigrants from the Indian subcontinent, referred to as South Asians, were prevented from coming to Canada by systemic barriers. By an immigration stipulation of 1908, South Asians could land in Canada only by continuous journey. Yet the Canadian Pacific Railway, which operated the only continuous steamship passage on that route, was forbidden to sell any tickets. Moreover, under the Immigration Act of 1910, each Asian immigrant had to possess $200 to enter Canada. These two rules effectively prevented the entry of South Asians.

South Asian women were banned from Canada, although, in 1910, the wives of two professional men entered (Doman, 1984). Immigration of South Asian women of all classes was decried by society at large, including white women's groups, for fear of encouraging the settlement of South Asians in Canada.

It was not until 1919 that South Asian women could enter Canada, and then only as wives. Repeated pressure from British colonial officials at the Imperial War Conferences, between 1917 and 1919, had the ban removed. Yet few women and children immigrated because they were formally required to be registered as legitimate "wives and children" in India, and few procedures facilitated marriage registrations there until 1924. Between 1921 and 1923, only eleven women and nine children entered (Doman, 1984: 102). Older children could not immigrate to reunite with their parents, a rule that disregarded the fact that, unlike Canadian children, older children often lived with their parents up to the time of their marriage....

Japanese Families

Before 1908, evidence suggests that the Japanese in Canada were mainly a community of single males and that some may have sought solace with prostitutes (Adachi, 1976; Kobayashi, 1978). Most lived with other men in company shacks, bunkhouses, and boardrooms near their workplaces, just like their Chinese and South Asian counterparts.

In 1907, self-regulation of immigration from Japan was negotiated in the form of a gentlemen's agreement, according to which the Japanese government voluntarily restricted the number of emigrants to Canada. Canada resorted to this approach to maintain diplomatic relations with Japan, an ally of Britain at the time. The agreement covered the immigration of domestic and agricultural workers; wives, children, and parents were allowed to arrive freely until 1928. The agreement came on the heels of a race riot in British Columbia aimed at Chinese and Japanese immigrants.

Adachi describes the period after 1908 as the "family building phase" (1976: 87), when single men sought wives in several ways. Some visited Japan for arranged marriages; others sent for "picture brides" from a catalogue (Kobayashi, 1978, 4)....

Japanese women, like many women in other communities, were expected to be completely devoted to their husbands, children, and the home, although they laboured on farms as well as fulfilling their domestic obligations. Their labour played a crucial role in the success of Japanese farms, particularly in berry and small fruit production (Adachi, 1976: 149). Perhaps the reason the Canadian government was open to the formation of families among the Japanese, but not among the South Asian and Chinese communities, was that unpaid family labour is an asset in small farming, as it allows the farmer to greatly minimize labour costs. Interestingly, this concern exists today in the administration of the seasonal farm workers' program, in which family members are encouraged to migrate to Canada under contract. Most of these contract workers are Caribbean blacks and Mexicans (Singh Bolaria and Li, 1988). This contrasts sharply to the conditions under which domestic workers come into Canada. The latter have historically been encouraged to work in Canada as "single" women, away from their family members, including their young children. In their case, family members are seen as potential burdens on Canadian social services.

After 1928, however, in an effort to further limit the number of Japanese immigrants, women and children were included in the annual quota. This was a period of heightened racism against Asians in general and the Japanese in particular. There was intense paranoia among white Canadians about being outnumbered and economically dominated by Japanese Canadians. By 1931, the number of picture brides coming into Canada had declined significantly.

Anti-Japanese feelings reached a zenith in the war years with the bombing of Pearl Harbor. In the name of national security, mass evacuations of Japanese were begun in January 1942; all males between 18 and 45 had to be removed from the west coast by April 1942. This resulted in the dismantling of families and the disruption of children's schooling. Most of the men were removed to work in road camps in other parts of Canada. Women and children were, initially, forced to reside in hastily converted public buildings, lacking complete privacy, before being moved to camps in the B.C. interior, first to tents and then to shacks.

On June 24, 1942, the Canadian Security Commission decided to reunite married men in detention camps with their families, by transporting wives and children to the camps for the winter. As a result, the camps became extremely crowded and ill equipped, and the movements of residents were closely monitored by security officials. Unmarried men in the camps were prevented from marrying lest they should try to stay with their wives. Even though the commission was supposed to provide the basic necessities of life, evacuees had to buy their own food with incomes between 22 and 40 cents an hour (Adachi, 1976: 259). The old and the infirm lived on provincial relief based on the number of family members. Japanese children were excluded from provincial schools, so that camp residents themselves had to build their own schools with their own finances and staff them with hastily trained Japanese teachers.

Familial authority and socialization processes were transformed in the semi-communal camp life (Maykovich, 1980: 68). The authority that Issei (first generation) parents had over their children was weakened, which then weakened parents' abilities to transfer their indigenous language and culture.

The disruption of families continued in the postwar years, when all Japanese Canadians were encouraged to go back to Japan or to work on sugar beet farms, extremely back-breaking work. Many young, single members of the *Nisei* (the second generation) chose to move to Ontario and other eastern provinces, away from their parents....

Black Caribbean Families

If we look at the history of white European immigrant women, we find a pattern of large numbers coming to Canada as poor, single, young domestic workers (Barber, 1986; Conway, 1992; Lindstrom-Best, 1986). White women had a choice of settling in Canada or returning to their home countries. Between 1900 and 1930, about 170000 British women came under this category. In 1929, 1 288 out of 1 618 Finnish women arrived as domestics. Immigration policies differed for domestics who were women of colour. If they came as temporary or contract domestic workers, they could not alter this status in Canada. If they did not fulfil their contractual agreements, they were forced to go back to their home countries.

Women of colour who have been brought to Canada as contracted domestic workers have been predominantly black Caribbean and Filipina women. These women have been, and still are, admitted for limited contractual periods. They remain in Canada only in the job and with the employer with whom the contract exists. The periods during which these women could, in fact, use the domestic scheme[1] to immigrate to Canada have been brief, so that few women have been able to take advantage of it. As a result of political lobbying by community organizations since 1981, domestic workers have been able to apply for immigration after two years of contracted work.

However, systemic barriers remain, since applicants have to fulfil certain conditions such as maintaining stable employment, demonstrating financial management skills, and demonstrating their involvement in the community. Just as in the case of Asian male immigrants in the early part of the twentieth century, it has been a policy of the government not to encourage the possibility of developing families among women of colour who came as domestic workers. Thus, their status as "single" and as "temporary" is deliberately organized by immigration policies.

Even when Chinese and Japanese women worked as domestic workers, they were restricted to working for Asian families. A law that restricted Chinese families from employing white domestic workers stood until 1929 (Dunphy, 1987). This could only reflect racism and the fear of miscegenation. The decision to admit certain groups of women as domestic workers while excluding others was perhaps guided not only by racial and ethno-centric concerns. It is noticeable that the groups admitted under the domestic schemes have been, by and large, English-speaking and Christian and more akin to Western, Anglo-Canadian culture. One can only suggest that these concerns were paramount, since many of these women would work as babysitters and nannies and would therefore have a strong socializing influence on white children. Moreover, the role of black women as care givers is a holdover from the history of slavery, of racism and sexism.

The first Caribbean domestic scheme admitted 100 women from Guadeloupe in 1910 and 1911 (Calliste, 1991). However, the scheme was ended because of information that these women were allegedly not completely "unattached," that is, that they had children. Many of these women were later deported on alleged grounds of being "public charges." The real reason was of course that unemployment among white female domestic workers had gone up and women from the Caribbean were seen as competition. Also, part of the reason lay in the assumption that single mothers would become public dependants.

Black Caribbean female nondomestics and men who wanted to immigrate to Canada were systemically excluded by immigration regulations that admitted only farmers, farm labourers, domestics, wives, and minor children of residents in Canada, and British subjects from English-speaking countries (Calliste, 1991: 142). Besides, the Immigration Act of 1952 officially excluded "people on the basis of nationality, citizenship, ethnic origin...and their probable inability to become readily assimilated" (Calliste, 1991: 143).

The "singleness" of black domestic workers from the Caribbean was maintained in the second domestic scheme (1955-67), when only unmarried women without children and not in common-law relationships were admitted into Canada as immigrants on a quota basis. Proposed changes to the immigration regulations in the early 1960s may have been what eventually prompted many of these women to apply to sponsor their close relatives, fiancés, and children. Not only was this very disappointing to immigration officials (Calliste, 1991: 151), but they could not reconcile the fact that women breadwinners were sponsoring men as fiancés, a departure from traditional gender roles.

However, as other writers have pointed out, historically, black women have often been heads of households (Brand, 1988 and 1991; Turritin, 1983; Yawney, 1983)—out-migration of male members to urban centres in the hope of increased income turned a significant proportion of families in Montserrat into female-headed ones (Turritin, 1983; 313). Brand (1988: 122) has argued that the depressed economic condition of black men generally has prevented them from participating in child and family maintenance. Therefore, black women have, out of necessity, been economically independent in supporting themselves and their children. Even though they earn some of the lowest incomes in Canada, their labour-force participation is one of the highest.

The determination of immigration officials to maintain the singleness of black Caribbean women was dramatized in the case of the seven Jamaican mothers who applied to sponsor their children, previously unreported, in 1976. They were ordered to be deported for failing to report their children on their applications to come to Canada (Leah and Morgan, 1979). After an intensive struggle that involved community and labour groups, the seven women won their cases and were allowed to stay in Canada....

When black Caribbean workers applied to sponsor their fiancés and children in the early 1960s, the government responded by bringing in middle-class black Caribbean men who were university students, which in effect continued the lack of family reunification for these women (Calliste, 1991). An unequal sex ratio existed in the black Caribbean community until very recently.

Today, domestic workers come into Canada on temporary work permits, an arrangement begun in 1973. For two years, these workers remain as "unfree," after which they can apply for permanent residence. But, as mentioned before, this transition is marked by many barriers (Silvera, 1983: 18). In 1992, the Ministry of Employment and Immigration announced changes in the Foreign Domestic Movement program such that applicants now must have Grade 12 education and health-care training (Primera, 1992: 12). According to Intercede, a Canadian domestic worker rights organization, these criteria will effectively exclude women from the Philippines, India, and the Caribbean, where such training is unavailable or inaccessible to working-class women.

Immigrant Domestic Workers and White Families

One of the issues that has rarely been discussed is the contribution of domestic workers in reproducing white Canadian-born families in Canada. By definition, they "mother" white Canadian-born children by cooking, cleaning, washing, dusting, and even fulfilling sexual services under coercion (Silvera, 1983: 61). While their own families, including those with very young children, are forced by immigration laws and employment conditions to remain far away from their mothers, these women nurture, feed, dress, and nurse their employers' children. They enable mainly upper-class and middle-class white women to escape their traditional gender roles to develop lucrative careers or to enjoy leisure time. By the same token, the government can save on crucial day-care services, which are urgently needed by working women with preschool children. In this process, domestic workers are prevented from ever establishing their own families and communities. There is almost an assumption that "they" don't "need" these families since they are assumed to be racially and socially incapable of nurturing and properly socializing their own children. This attitude has sometimes also been directed toward white non-English-speaking European domestic workers, such as Finnish domestics (Lindstrom-Best, 1986: 20), although black domestic workers have been subjected to it most frequently.…

Characteristics of Families Among "Temporary" Working-Class Canadians

Even though the Canadian government deliberately and systemically prevented the formation of families of colour before the 1950s, women, men, and children have organized themselves into households in order to create a sense of stability, of "family," and of community. These formations have often provided solace from the otherwise hostile environment permeated with racism and ethnocentrism.

Turritin (1979: 321) writes that the "sibling household" among black women from Montserrat was the predominant social arrangement in the postwar period; a woman and her siblings lived together. Friendship networks were also very significant in choice of residence. Silvera (1983:31) writes about black Caribbean women referring to close friends as "church sisters." Unfortunately, even this was disrupted by government efforts to disperse domestics across the country (Calliste, 1991: 153). Women also created social clubs, centres, and recreational programs to facilitate social networks and support, friendship, and, later, self-advocacy organizations (Calliste, 1991: 152; Das Gupta, 1986: 17; Silvera, 1983: 125).

Brand (1988) speaks of the extended family in the black community, which is based on matrilineage and strong female support across generations, going beyond rules of paternity and "blood" relationships. Yawney (1983) discusses how lower-class family life in the Caribbean is marked by matrifocality, where women are heads of households and responsible for supporting their children. Extended relatives, neighbours, and friends take part in looking after children. In this network, elderly grandmothers, unemployed members, family friends, and unattached individuals, particularly women, become key players in providing support to one another, particularly in child-rearing responsibilities.

Even in times of slavery, black people struggled to create families on their own terms. Research reveals that naming black children after their fathers and blood relatives was a way of maintaining family relations (Dill, 1992: 221). Preserving of African traditions in kinship ties was also significant. Constructing slave quarters using African building technologies and design reveals cultural resistance to racist oppression in blacks' efforts to maintain family ties and privacy.

Chinese and South Asian men from the "bachelor" period continued their long-distance family lives by visits and sending money. Dill refers to this as the "split household family" (1992: 225). In Canada, Chinese men formed kinship associations based on surname, dialect, or territory (Johnson, 1983: 364). These were also social support associations and facilitated the maintenance of links with their wives and children, and also enabled them to deal with the prejudices of the larger society.…

Among South Asian men, village and kin relations were used to establish "family"-like formations. During the long voyage to Canada, in restricted and crowded conditions, the men lived communally, cooking and eating together and supporting each other. This pattern continued once they were in Canada. Four to twelve men would live together in a household, creating an extended "family"-like structure based on the Indian norm (Buchignani and Indra, 1985: 33). They pooled their money for their necessities of life and shared household duties. It was apparently common for an unemployed member to do the cooking. In this set-up, the sick and the unemployed were well looked after. Living collectively also allowed these men to save money, despite the low wages that they earned....

In these early years, the banning of wives and children, which prevented them from reuniting with their families, provoked the most intense anger and fuelled political organizing among British Columbia's South Asian community. The men realized that without women, children, and families, their community would remain temporary, unstable, and stripped of social and political rights in Canada.

Evidence suggests that families among Japanese Canadians, once they started developing, were nuclear. Kobayashi (1978) writes that this resulted in the Nisei, the second generation, missing out on contacts with their grandparents, who traditionally would have played a significant role in the socialization of children. She questions the implications of that for these children and for future generations.

Family Building Among Postwar Immigrants of Colour

Even though the government made an effort to encourage family reunification in the postwar era, many barriers were erected. Some of these were institutionalized and systemic, while others were a legacy of past and family and racist government policies. These barriers continue up to today, even though one of the cornerstones of the current immigration policy, as phrased in the Immigration Act of 1976, is "to facilitate the reunion in Canada of Canadian citizens and permanent residents with their close relatives from abroad" (Toronto Coalition for a Just Refugee and Immigration Policy, 1987).

When reunification took place, communities had to deal with the estrangement of couples (Dill, 1992) and with the fact that children born later than usual meant greater differences in age and in values between parents and children (Johnson, 1983).

Similar problems have been mentioned with regard to black Caribbean women who sponsored their children to Canada in later years and who experienced tension in these relationships because they had been separated and had to deal with feelings of hurt, rejection, and indifference (Christiansen, et al., n.d.: 76). These children faced new lives, separated from their siblings and care givers, and had to develop, almost overnight, new relationships with their natural mothers, from whom they may have been separated for years. Some of these mothers may have married here, had other children, and established a "family" with which these newly arrived children had no familiarity.

With the repeal of the Chinese Immigration Act, Chinese immigration was restricted to wives and unmarried children under 18; this was later expanded to include sponsored relatives. However, these groups could not apply to come into Canada as independent immigrants until 1962 (Li and Singh Bolaria, 1983: 93).

Unlike other landed immigrants, South Asians could not freely sponsor parents, grandparents, fiancés, or unmarried children (Das Gupta, 1986: 68). South Asian immigration was also restricted by yearly quotas. For instance, the quota for India was 150 in 1951 and 300 in 1957 (Buchignani and Indra, 1985). These were men by all accounts, since it was assumed that these immigrants could later sponsor their wives and unmarried children under 21.

Social Construction of Gender, Race and Class in Postwar Families of Colour

To facilitate family reunification, a category of immigrants was labelled as the "family class"; these would be given priority simply because they had "very close relatives" in Canada. Critics have pointed out that, in practice, the arbitrary definition of "family" and delays in the processing of these applications often keep families separated for long periods (Toronto Coalition for a Just Refugee and Immigration Policy, 1987). For instance, "family" does not include brothers and sisters over 21, nor sons and daughters over 21. Fathers are not recognized as parents. A natural father has to legally adopt his child before he can sponsor her or him. An adoption process has to happen before the child's thirteenth year and can be fairly complicated. It has been said that overseas immigration officials tend to reject these applications. Similarly, de facto parents, such as aunts or grandparents who may have brought children up in the absence of natural parents, are not recognized. Like natural fathers, they also have to legally adopt the children before sponsoring them over to Canada.

The formal definition of who would be considered "family" members illustrates the cultural and racial bias of the state. According to government definitions, several members of an extended family are not seen as "close" family members. Moreover, children, who are young adults, are assumed to be financially independent, living separately from their parents, and are thus not part of their parents' "family unit." There are also assumptions about neolocality, which may not have relevance for matrilocal or patrilocal communities.

Even though family class immigrants are said (according to immigration regulations) to be of first priority, in practice they are less of a priority than entrepreneurial immigrants ("Processing of Family Class Applications," Cross Cultural Communication Centre, Toronto). In some countries, such as ones in the Caribbean, family class applications fall in priority after student and work authorizations. Besides, the process of family reunification is often lengthy because of lack of resources in overseas immigration offices as well as bureaucratic obstacles. Normal processing time for family class applications from the United States and Britain is between 71 and 116 days; those from India take 203 to 413 days, those from Guyana take 518 days, those from Trinidad and Tobago take 462 days, and those from Zaire take 637 days (Cross Cultural Communication Centre).

The reasons for these delays in countries consisting mostly of people of colour are the lack of personnel and other resources to process the volume of applications. This practice of systemic discrimination allows "neutral" structures and practices to have an adverse effect on one group of people. For instance, there are five immigration offices in the United Kingdom, ten in the United States, four in France, and two in Germany, while there is only one in India, serving eight other jurisdictions; of six in Africa one serves 23 other jurisdictions and two are in South Africa....

Historically, it is noticeable that when women have been allowed to enter Canada, they have been able to do so as wives and as dependants (Pope, n.d.; Estable and Meyer, 1989). Their dependent status is maintained by various institutional processes upon their arrival in Canada. The point system of immigration perpetuates systemic barriers for women and people of colour who want to immigrate as independent candidates since it emphasizes such things as education, skills, training, employability in "open occupations," and knowledge of English and/or French. Most women from the working classes and from racial minority groups would never qualify to immigrate on the basis of such criteria as they lack access to the required training. Thus, when women have come to Canada on their own, they have done so as "unfree" labour, as slaves, domestic workers, or seasonal farm labourers. Mostly, these have been black, Filipina, and Mexican women. Despite the recent demand for domestic workers, this occupation has not been added to the list of "open occupations" and thus does not earn any immigration points (Estable and Meyer, 1989: 39).

As soon as anyone is defined as family class, it is assumed that they are not good enough to work outside the home (hence the lack of insistence on earning points) and that their primary responsibility is with child care and housework. Another family class assumption is that women are not destined for the labour force. This in effect reproduces traditional gender ideology, even though the majority of immigrant women participate in the paid labour force (in the most ill-paid and insecure sectors) at a greater rate than Canadian-born women.

However, women's dependence on men is reinforced by a variety of institutional processes. Government-subsidized English/French as a Second Language (ESL/FSL) Courses are not made accessible to those who have been sponsored. "Breadwinners" (read men) are given first priority. This policy affects women adversely, since 43 percent of women immigrants in 1986 did not know either official language (Estable and Meyer, 1989: 20). This situation is exacerbated for older women.

Moreover, women are not eligible for most subsidized social services unless they can prove that their sponsorship has broken down (Ng and Das Gupta, 1981; Pope, n.d.).... For job-training courses, a minimum level of English or French is necessary. So once again women are denied access if their spoken English is poor. In the absence of recognition of prior professional experience and qualifications, women are streamed into dead-end entry-level jobs (Estable and Meyer, 1989: 23).

The dependence of immigrant women is dramatically perpetuated when they are in abusive relationships. Recently, as a result of pressure from immigrant women's advocacy groups, abused women who have been allowed to remain in Canada have become eligible for subsidized social services.

Conclusion

The community histories presented here illustrate the politicization of the family vis-à-vis the Canadian state and dominant interest groups. Historical writings reveal that women, men, and children of colour have not always had the right to live in a "family" situation on their own terms. The descriptions of the conditions under which working-class Chinese, South Asian, and Japanese men and women in the early twentieth century and, later on, black Caribbean women lived and worked illustrate that they existed as "single" people in the Canadian context. Official immigration policy, as well as informal practices, ensured this pattern. Families were, and continue to be, disrupted and actively prevented from forming, thus preventing the reproduction of the group and its community. Family disruption also ensures the temporariness of their residence in Canada. Moreover, it ensures the predominant whiteness of the population overall.

The birth of the Métis was a result of coercive miscegenation practised by male colonists with Native women. Simultaneously, those women's indigenous family forms, which had been extended and egalitarian, disintegrated. Later on, the extended families and close relationships between Native parents and their children were broken down for the express purpose of terminating Native cultures, languages, religions, education, and economies. This was accomplished initially by missionary-led residential schools and later by non-Native child welfare agencies, both of which operated on the philosophy of superiority of white Christian culture and the natural inferiority of Native peoples.

At the same time, the Indian Act defined out many members of the Native communities, particularly women married to non-Natives and their children, as nonstatus, which, among other indignities, denied them the right to live on reserves with their families. The experience of blacks who came from the United States as slaves, Loyalists, and fugitives can be seen in the context of slavery in the Americas. Families of enslaved black people were completely controlled by white slave masters. Decisions regarding marriages, sexual relations, pregnancies, and cohabitation were made by white men. Like various Native nations, blacks during slavery were also subjected to forced miscegenation, a form of violence toward women and a way to reproduce the slave population. In the absence of adequate research, I have speculated that this history must have had profound effects on their later migration to Canada and the establishment of their families here.

The Native nations, as well as immigrants of colour who were held captive as single and temporary workers, provided a pool of cheapened labour to fuel the development of colonial mercantile capitalism and, later, industrial capitalism. Native peoples provided labour for the fur trade, and blacks and immigrants of colour were instrumental in land clearing, farming, lumbering, and the like. Later, all these communities were employed in factory, service, clerical, and domestic work.

The absence of immigrant families meant that the quantitative cost of reproduction was lower, since their families were not present in Canada. The spouses and family members of these immigrants, who lived outside Canada, subsidized them with their unpaid labour at home. This enabled Canadian employers to keep wages at a super-exploitative level and thus to reap high profits. However, qualitatively and psychologically, the absence of families meant increasing costs for these immigrant workers in the form of loneliness, alienation, and depression. For Native peoples, these effects reached an extreme level with high incidences of self-destructive behaviour. The destruction of Native communities hardly presented itself as a problem to Canadian employers, since labour was plentiful through immigration. In fact, the presence of Native peoples and their rights as the original peoples of this land were seen by many as an impediment to the capitalist employment of land and natural resources.

Family members were generally allowed in for certain groups, such as Chinese merchants and the Japanese. Perhaps in these cases the value of families for stability and for reproduction was recognized by the government. The contribution of women and children as unpaid labourers in small businesses and on family farms (for which the Issei were gaining a reputation before their internment) was recognized also.

Legitimization functions of the state were accomplished by the genocide of Native families and the obstruction of family formation among immigrants. By pursuing such policies, governments were catering to a racist public while maintaining the "cheapness" of people of colour and of Native peoples.

This removed any basis of power for them and was the formula for maintaining their vulnerability. That vulnerability was rationalized on overt and covert racism, thus fanning white racism hegemonic in Canada at the time. By pursuing such policies, governments were catering to a racist public while maintaining the "cheapness" of people of colour and of Native peoples.

When family reunification was declared an official policy in the post-war period, traditional gender roles with their associated ideologies were reproduced through various institutional processes. Even if we are to accept these gender relations, family reunification has remained an uphill battle for many immigrants. Despite this history, Native peoples and people of colour have formed families in order to establish permanence, mutual support, and solidarity with each other. Same-sex, communal, and quasi-extended families have been formed as a bulwark against genocide and racism. These alternative families create a sense of support and solace from the harsh realities of life. The struggles for family reunification and for civil rights have been two of the most important organizing principles for immigrants and people of colour. For Native peoples, self-government in every aspect of their lives has been the fundamental demand for the restoration of their families and nations.

ENDNOTE

1.   "Domestic Schemes" refers to special programs that the Canadian government has had to allow specified types and numbers of domestic workers to enter Canada.

SEXUALITY

The feminist analysis of sexuality joins together with reproduction in several important ways. Perhaps most obvious are the reproductive consequences of heterosexual intercourse. Until the early twentieth century, women's sexuality and sexual expression was firmly equated with reproduction; this ideological linkage was challenged with the sex reform and birth control movement beginning in the early twentieth century. The challenge to dominant sexual norms intensified in the 1960s in the midst of what has been called the sexual revolution. In this period, "sexual repression" was refuted by the fledgling gay and lesbian movement and by the New Left, with an emphasis on sexual pleasure and freedom and a critique of marriage and monogamy. But a specifically feminist interrogation of sexuality did not emerge until the beginning of second wave feminism. With the rallying cry "the personal is political" feminists of many different perspectives challenged both the connections between reproduction and women's sexuality and the power relations embedded in both. In making sexuality a political issue, feminists conceptualized sexuality as changeable, and thereby undermined the dominant view that sexual desires and practices are fixed by nature. Moreover, the slogan "the personal is political" expressed a new awareness that experiences of sexual coercion or being valued only for their sexuality were common for most women and were evidence of a pervasive system of male sexual power.

Like the feminist literature on new reproductive technologies (see next chapter), Canadian feminist contributions to sexuality studies are diverse. Feminists speak in many and sometimes oppositional voices. Indeed as Stevi Jackson and Sue Scott comment, "...sexuality has been a contested terrain amongst feminists since the nineteenth century. No sooner had it been identified as a major area of concern by the modern movement, than significant disagreements began to emerge" (1996, 1). Writings on sexuality represent a burgeoning field in Canadian

Women's Studies. Although constrained by space, we have tried to reproduce material that is reflective of the diversity of Canadian feminist thinking in this area since the 1970s. If there is one unifying theme in this set of readings, it is the construction of a challenge to the representation of and compulsory nature of heterosexuality. Together with gay scholarship and queer theory,[1] feminist theory has been a central voice in gaining recognition of the socially constructed character of sexuality. Wresting sexuality away from its framing as natural and biological has been a formidable challenge; but it has opened the way for an interrogation of dominant sexual norms. Several of the readings in this section, most explicitly Valverde and Overall, draw upon Adrienne Rich's groundbreaking theorization of heterosexuality as an institution. Rich analyzes heterosexuality as a means of ensuring the male right of physical, economic and emotional access to women and suggests that heterosexuality is institutionalized—that is, constructed ideologically and through physical coercion (1986).

The coercion inherent in dominant heterosexuality has been identified most clearly by feminists working on gender violence (see "Engendering Violence" chapter). It emerges here in the powerful antipornography feminist polemic written by Cole, entitled "Pornography" (1992). Cole was a key player in what some have termed the feminist "porn wars" that emerged in Canada in the 1980s. By the 1980s, feminists had successfully wrested pornography as an issue away from previously dominant moral conservative/civil libertarian voices. Before feminist interventions, the central question in the pornography debate was whether sex should be depicted, not how it should be depicted. Cole defines pornography not in the non-gendered terms of sexual explicitness, but in explicitly gendered terms as the eroticization of women's subordination for men's sexual pleasure. She goes on to outline a number a mechanisms by which pornography harms women. Following American anti-pornography feminist Catharine MacKinnon, she contends that law, (specifically in the form of a civil rights regime that would allow those harmed by pornography to sue), needs to be harnessed against pornography.

Anti-pornography arguments are often presented as the feminist orthodoxy. Burstyn's intervention in the Canadian feminist debate on pornography represents an opposing and feminist position. In "Political Precedents and Moral Crusades" (1985) Burstyn challenges the definition of pornography as harm and contends that it is not pornography that causes women's oppression. Instead we must be cognizant of the manner in which pornography draws its meanings from wider cultural narratives through which masculinity and male sexuality are constructed. Informed by socialist feminism, Burstyn contends that we cannot rely on law to reweave the delicate fabric of social life. Censorship, she argues, is likely to be used against feminist efforts to redefine and reinscribe women's sexuality and against gay and lesbian sexual expression. Burstyn's writings were prescient. In 1992, in the *Butler* decision, the Supreme Court shifted the legal definition of obscenity to embrace anti-pornography feminist contentions that pornography is harmful towards women. As Cossman, Bell, Gotell and Ross outline in their book, *Bad Attitudes on Trial* (1997), the first obscenity prosecutions post-Butler targeted gay and lesbian pornography. The moral basis of obscenity law seems resistant to feminist redefinition.

Shifting away from the question of representation, many of the readings in this section elaborate upon the feminist contention that heterosexuality is a social and political construct that works to preclude the recognition of sexual diversity and of women's sexual identity and expression. Valverde's critical book *Sex, Power and Pleasure* (1987) remains to this date the most successful publication of the Toronto Women's Press. In the chapter included here, "Lesbianism: A Country That Has No Language," she outlines a social constructionist perspective on lesbianism, refuting the view of lesbianism as essence (existing always and unchanged throughout history). She contends that lesbianism as a specifically sexual identity came into being with turn of the century sexology. This is not to argue that "lesbian" practices and desire did not exist before. Instead, it was only with turn of the century sexology that it became possible to say "I am a lesbian." Before this, this identity category did not exist. As Valverde argues, lesbian cultural and political movements have, over the course of the twentieth century, mobilized on the basis of this identity, challenging its construction as deviant and pathological. Despite this mobilization, lesbianism remains silenced within a culture that continues to define heterosexuality as natural and paradigmatic. Valverde contends that the struggle against compulsory heterosexuality is a struggle for all women, not only lesbians. Crucial to this struggle is cultural work that contributes to lesbian visibility.

Rule's essay, written in the 1970s, represents an early example of this kind of cultural work. Rule is an acclaimed novelist whose fictional writing on lesbian lives, including her groundbreaking lesbian romance *Desert of the Heart* (1964), have consistently represented a positive lesbian sexuality. In the essay included here, she describes growing up in a context where the only available images of lesbians were negative. She contemplates the effects of homophobia and in particular, the effects of internalized homophobia on lesbian relationships, arguing that women's failure to treat each other as "peers" constrains the possibilities of "loving equality."

Lee Maracle's more recent essay "Isn't Love a Given" (1996) seeks to value lesbian sexuality from the perspective of heterosexuality. In this way, she takes up Valverde's call for common feminist front against compulsory heterosexuality. Like Rule, Maracle is an important Canadian novelist; her fictional and theoretical work have been important contributions to a developing native feminist literature (see Maracle 1999). Here Maracle situates the negation of native women's sexuality in racism, in colonization, and in the resulting destruction of native cultures and communities. In this context, she argues, sex becomes little more than physical release. Native women are constructed as less than fully human, as mere vessels for male gratification. As she writes, "in our society it is loving women that is prohibited," so naturally "we are going to hate women who love women" (24,26). The struggle against compulsory heterosexuality is crucial in order to reclaim the "sacred right of women to love and be loved."

Maracle's powerful essay drawing out the links between valuing lesbianism and a redefinition of heterosexuality refutes the claim made by some lesbian and radical feminists that heterosexuality is incompatible with feminism. The relationship between heterosexuality and feminism is taken up explicitly in Overall's (1990) influential article. While defining heterosexuality as an institution that is enforced and arguing that heterosexual privilege must be acknowledged, she contends that choosing lesbianism means the corollary possibility of choosing heterosexuality. In drawing a distinction between heterosexual practice and the institution of heterosexuality, she suggests that to pose heterosexuality as a choice undermines the compulsory nature of heterosexuality.

MacDonald's piece "Critical Identities" (1998), moves beyond the binary of heterosexual/lesbian to engage with debates about transgender, a diverse category of sexual expression and identity that occupies the spaces inbetween. MacDonald contests the dismissal of transgendered peoples by some lesbian feminists. She illustrates the rigid and exclusionary conception of identity that underlies the claim that transgender is but a patriarchal plot.

Similarly, she challenges the manner in which queer theory/postmodernism appropriates transgender as an expression of diversity that breaks down foundational binaries of man/woman and hetero/homo. Both positions, she argues, operate to deny the validity of trans-gendered people's experience. MacDonald suggests that feminism can benefit from an engagement with transgender theory—a theory that sheds productive insights on the meanings of man and women/straight and gay. In particular, she suggests that feminism must re-theorize its conception of identity in light of the questions raised by transgender theory. This article is a complex piece that demonstrates the proliferation of new sexuality literature within Canadian feminism and the challenging directions that are now being pursued as feminists seek to problematize gender in multiple ways.

Bell's article on female ejaculation, "Feminist Ejaculations" (1991), returns us to the question of sex, biology and social construction. Bell is a political theorist, a sex teacher and a performance artist whose work underlines the necessity of a politics of desire within feminism. Deploying a postmodern perspective, Bell demonstrates how restrictive definitions of women's sexuality within medicine and sexuality have literally been written on and into women's bodies. Sexological literature has obscured women's capacity to ejaculate. Bell contends that women must reclaim ejaculation as a potent bodily experience. But the article does far more than tell women that they need to learn more about their "G spots." Bell promotes female ejaculation in a literal sense; but she also uses ejaculation as a metaphor of female sexual power and agency. Contesting the dominant equation of female passive provides a means for Bell to articulate a feminist politics of pleasure. At the end of the millennium, when so much talk of sex centres on "danger," the recognition of power and desire must play a central role in feminist sexuality theory and politics.

ENDNOTE

1. The appropriation of postmodernism by gay and lesbian scholars has led to the development of queer theory. Rather than setting up categories such as "lesbian" as the basis of political identities, queer theory has sought to destabilize the boundaries between woman and man and straight and gay. Queer theorists contend that sexual identities are not fixed, given or the property of individuals. Instead, sexual identities are fluid and shifting; they are to be adopted or discarded, played with and subverted, strategically deployed in different contexts. As MacDonald describes in her contribution in this section, the aim of queer theory is to demonstrate that gender and sexuality are not given realities but are instead the products of discourse, maintained by their endless performance and repetition.

PORNOGRAPHY

Susan G. Cole

...Two basic principles underlie the analysis of pornography in this book. The first is that women matter, and an analysis of pornography that does not take women into account is badly skewed. Second, pornography is not just a picture, a two-dimensional artifact or an idea. It is a practice[1] consisting of specific activities performed by real people. The notion that pornography is a practice helps do away with the issues of taste, interpretation and offended sensibilities that muddy the debate on pornography, and it gets at the crucial issue of who is doing what to whom. Defining pornography as a practice and not as a picture transforms the way pornography is discussed. Instead of asking "does pornography cause violence?," we discover that women are abused to make the materials that (male) consumers use in ways that are abusive to women. Abuse is not *caused* by pornography, it is part of what pornography *is*. Through this perspective the linear argument of cause and effect gives way to the description of a cycle of abuse in which pornography reinvents itself.

To get a sense of how this perspective challenges pre-existing notions of what pornography is, consider these two examples:

> You are watching a movie. On the screen, a woman is lying down on what looks like a bed, though it could be a table. A movie director filming all of this walks to the table and cuts off two of her fingers with a pair of garden shears. He then saws off her arm. Then he carves her open from the sternum to the belly and eviscerates her. The camera crew is shown becoming sexually aroused. The movie ends with the killer holding up the woman's guts triumphantly as he howls his pleasure.
>
> You are watching a movie. On the screen a woman is lying on a table. A doctor in uniform approaches. She takes his penis in her mouth and sucks on it, apparently greedily. He joins her on the table. She is smiling. She always smiles. He comes. So does she, in cataclysmic tandem....

Much of the time, the violence is real in pornography. So are the women who have been bought and sold to appear in the pornography. Why then do the pictures not move observers to notice that something terrible is happening to the women shown? Perhaps the myopia has something to do with a widely shared fascination with movie magic. Moviemakers, after all, serve up fantasies and illusions, and pornography, which in 25 years has gone from 30-second black-and-white loops to full-length features with costumes and plot lines (a term used loosely here), appears to be just another movie. But the truth is a liar: when a woman is tied up so that the ropes cut her flesh, the ropes are as tight as they appear; if a woman is beaten, there is no assurance that she is being tapped lightly and not slugged. Besides, once she is tied up, a woman has lost all immediate control of what will happen next in the production....

The pervasiveness of pornography tends to make women invisible as human beings, visible only as things or objects. The women in the pictures are not considered human enough to worry about. An example of this syndrome was the response given by a Canada Customs official in the wake of women's protests against the distribution of the December 1984 edition of *Penthouse*. In that edition, a photographic feature showed women tightly bound and hanging motionless from trees and poles or splayed on rocks. The spread looked like a revelation of the necrophiliac pornographic mind, and a sign that dead women were sexually appealing. When asked to comment on how these materials escaped the scrutiny of otherwise over-vigilant border guards, a Customs representative hemmed and hawed and finally allowed that "the violence was implied."[2]...

Feminism has always taken women's real experience as the basis for theory, and a perspective on pornography should not be any different. It is important to dispense with appearances and to reject any assumptions about what women are and what is real for us. Behind the facade of marital bliss, there could be wife assault. Similarly, behind the appearance of consent and pleasure in pornography, there could be rape and violation. To find out if there is, rigorous questions have to be asked, questions that probe women's actual experience and the way the products of pornography are used. *Pornography is a practice of sexual subordination. Its producers present sexual subordination for their own sexual pleasure, and its consumers get sexual pleasure from the presentation of sexual subordination.*

To understand pornography as a practice, it's necessary to dispense with the idea that pornography is a thing, a two-dimensional artifact, and consider it more a series of activities. Compare it to the practice of photography in which a photographer carries out a number of functions. S/he sets up the subject, focusses the lens, takes the picture, develops it and then sells it or exhibits it. Or compare it to the practice of advertising. The advertiser does market research, designs the ad, produces it, secures the ad space and displays it. The advertiser who practices advertising produces an advertisement. The photographer practicing photography produces a photograph. The pornographer practicing pornography produces...what? Resurrecting the word pornograph[3] makes the scheme consistent. The elements of presentation and sexual subordination are already contained in the word "pornography." Pornography comes from the Greek words *graphos*, meaning depiction, and *pornos*, the lowest of female sexual slaves. *Graphos* suggests that the activity of presentation is a crucial part of the process. Up until recently, depiction would have meant drawings or words or stage productions, in contemporary usage it can refer to the taking of pictures, or recording on video or audio tape as well. *Pornos* reminds us that the word was never used for playful or loving couplings but for the of the most degraded female slaves....

...[T]he fact is that rarely will a person encounter sexually explicit materials featuring adults that are not records of sexual subordination. The abuses experienced by women in these products range from the pain of assault and torture acted out in violent pornography; to prior sexual assaults that distort women's perceptions of themselves and their choices and drive them into the pornography business where they get paid for what has previously been stolen from them—their bodies; to the coercion of poverty that limits women's job opportunities and makes the pornography business seem lucrative; to the subtler conditioning that teaches women that being a sex object—even in *Playboy*—is what every woman should dream of. Still, many people have a hard time looking at pornography and seeing victimization. Perhaps the best way to grasp the pain of these women is to put yourself into the picture and imagine how it would feel....

Defined as the presentation of sexual subordination for sexual pleasure, pornography is not presented here as a neutral term. Thus it differs from the term "sexually explicit materials," which is often used to define pornography and which makes it possible for pornography to go either way: it could be positive, it could be negative. Defining pornography as a practice of subordination embodies the harm, the negative, in the very definition. Subordination means that someone is being made less than someone else. It contains connotations of inequality and oppression. Where there is a presentation of sexual subordination for sexual pleasure, there is pornography. Where there is no sexual subordination in a presentation, there is no pornography. This means that some materials heretofore identified as pornography, by law or by moralists, would not be covered by the definition. For example, public displays of sexuality are not necessarily pornography. Neither are home-made videos of sexual activity. Crucially, with this definition, the only way to be "pro-pornography" is to take a stand in favour of sexual subordination....

Sexual subordination occurs in a number of different ways. One example of sexual subordination occurs when explicitly violent pornographs present women being hurt—killed, tortured or beaten. When I refer to violence in pornography in this instance, I am not referring to mainstream pin-ups caressed by leather (although as we shall see, these too have subordinating qualities), but to explicitly violent scenarios like those in *Water Power*, or home-made bondage films in which the violence is not staged. In these scenarios, objectification is obviously taking place. Objectification is the process through which the person on the bottom of the hierarchy is dehumanized, made less human than the person on the top of the hierarchy, who in turn becomes the standard for what human is. In violent pornography, objectification takes place so effectively that many people can look at these pictures and not see anyone getting hurt.

Sexual subordination also occurs anytime a woman is forced into a sexual act for its presentation. This is Linda Marchiano's experience and the experience of many women who have been forced to perform sexually for a camera. For example, in one Ontario shelter, a woman confided to a counsellor that her husband had tied her to the bed, forced her into sexual acts with the family dog and then took her picture. When this kind of subordination takes place, it is often very difficult to identify from the picture itself, since often the women are depicted as getting pleasure from the sexual abuse even in explicitly sexually subordinating scenes.

One of the favourite fictions of pornography is that women play an acquiescent role in their own degradation. Pornographers espouse this egregious lie when they depict women enjoying rape. In clinical circles where the effects of these scenes on viewer attitudes have been studied, researchers call these scenes rape myths.[4] The promulgation of the rape myth is an important pornographic strategy, for it provides the means for disguising whatever force may have been used in the making of the pornographs. What looks like rape suddenly becomes sex when the victim moans with delight. We are already reluctant to see violation in the pictures that show explicit violence, and the sight of a woman apparently getting pleasure from torture skews our perceptions even more. We see a woman raped, but wait, she's enjoying it. Maybe it isn't rape at all. We don't see what is going on off camera, who else is there, or how she got there in the first place.

Even as technological advance has defined contemporary culture, many movie lovers become unsettled when they see a film and then see footage of how the film was made. We don't want to see the lighting crew, the heavy equipment, the painted set, the truck, the stunt men, the make-up crew and the director telling the actors exactly how to read the lines against the blazing sunset. We want the fantasy intact. We agree to suspend disbelief when pornography replaces the blazing sunset on the screen. Movie myths obscure the coercion that goes into the making of pornographs. So it is not surprising that while watching pornographs of women being brutalized, some people forget that there is real pain there.

The myths of pornography have become more credible than the voice of real women. Faced with a film in which she performs fellatio with apparent eagerness, people do not believe Linda Marchiano when she says it was an act, that she didn't like it, that she was forced to do it. Marchiano's performance was real, and not simulated. She did "deep throat" Harry Reems, her co-performer, just as women really do get hurt in violent pornography. This is why I do not use words like "simulated" when referring to the action in specific pornographs. There is, after all, no such thing as a simulated vagina. I do not think there is any such thing, for that matter, as simulated sex. Just because there is no penetration does not mean that the women in the pictures are not real. Similarly, I avoid other words that have been associated with the discourse on pornography, like "images" and "representation". These are words that have an important meaning in art criticism, but they tend to distance us from what is happening to the women in pornographic pictures. Instead of the word image, use "document." Thus, pornographs are not images of sex, they are documents of sexual events. And pornography is a presentation of sexual subordination. It does not represent anyone or anything.

A woman has been sexually subordinated when pictures of her are used or sold without her consent. This can happen when a woman discovers that her husband has sent in photographs of her as part of the reader participation feature in pornographic magazines, it happened to former Miss America Vanessa Williams and to pop star Madonna, who early in their careers had both posed in the nude for photographers. *Penthouse* publisher Bob Guccione was able to let legal loopholes and rubber-stamp releases pass as consent and then published pictures of these women when they became public figures. He made immense profits without financially compensating the two women. In *Screw* Al Goldstein presented a drawing of Gloria Steinem's face on a body that had an explicit rendering of genitalia. These public displays of major figures are meant to be humiliating, and the damage can and has been devastating.[5]

When a woman in a pornograph is owned by a pornographer, when she is his possession, then she is being sexually subordinated. This applies to the Hugh Hefner syndrome in which bunnies, many of whom have had sex with Hefner, are paraded on the page as a graphic depiction of the pornographer's virility. It also applies to husbands who take pictures of their wives in the bedroom to show proof of ownership. And it applies to women who sell themselves so that pornography can be made. In fact, the industry's ability to churn out commercially available pornography depends on the traffic in real women.

When people look at women in pornography, they often do not see victims subordinated in the practice. They see pornography's collaborators: Why do these women do it?, they ask. If they stopped, wouldn't the industry collapse immediately? These questions are part of a syndrome called blaming the victim. Victim-blamers who look at pornography wonder why the women are there rather than why there is such an enormous market for sexually abusive entertainment. The fact is that the women in pornography are usually women trapped in systems of prostitution. Either they lack the skills to do anything else or, as we will see in the last chapter, selling their bodies has become a logical extension of other sexual abuses in their lives....

The pornographic universe also remains intact in the pornography lesbians and gay men produce for their own communities. The women and men who "perform" are in pornography because they are poor, have been recruited into pornography in the course of a sexual assault, or, having fallen into the victimization syndrome, are being revictimized. Not only are the experiences of these pornography "stars" like those of the women victimized in straight pornography sold to men, but the ideologies embedded in gay materials also usually mimic the messages in heterosexual pornography. The ideology of dominance and submission is deeply entrenched in the overtly sadomasochistic material in lesbian magazines like *On Our Backs*. The fact that the ideology of dominance and submission can transcend heterosexuality speaks to the power of gender stereotypes, in gay male pornographic scenarios of dominance and submission, the person doing the fucking is often called "he," while the fuckee is called "she." This is the way gay pornography, even though it is same-sex material, still manages to gender sexuality. The sexes are the same but the roles remain different—masculine and feminine, powerful and powerless.

In the pornographic universe, racism is very sexually appealing. When pornographers use black women, they place them in scenarios of slavery that fuse male dominance with racial superiority. In her chains, the black pornographic female looks as if she enjoys being enslaved in both the racial and sexual senses. The pornography of Asian women is often a pornography of torture and ultra-passivity, perpetuating white western stereotypes of Asian women as passive and subservient. Some people have suggested that any stereotype of race constitutes the pornography of race, but they miss the fundamental point that the sexual component cannot be removed from a definition of pornography. Racism per se is not pornographic. Rather, pornography eroticizes racism. And one of this society's most successful strategies for instituting values is to eroticize them....

Pornographers like to describe themselves as the bearers of dissident ideas. But women are not ideas, and pimping women to readers is not an expression of political dissent. The numbers speak most eloquently. The notion that pornographers are struggling against a repressive status quo is difficult to take seriously in the face of industry profits greater than those of the conventional film and record industries combined....

Men use pornography primarily because it feels good. What feels good is male domination and female submission. What feels good is watching women in conditions of subordination. What feels good is the apparently unlimited and protected access men have to female sexuality in the form of commercially available pornographs. What feels good is the existence of a population of women for them. Many consumers, and even non-consumers, believe that this population of women materializes naturally to service men's sexual needs. Some women, they think, are "like that." The fact that these women appear in postures of humiliation and abuse in pornography only proves the point, and becomes a self-fulfilling prophecy for men who look at the pictures and decide that the women in them must be less than human or they would not do these things. The unobstructed access to female sexuality, coupled with definition of female sexuality as "less than" that of men, reinforces male power and turns women into a group that cannot be perceived as equal....

Many women are not in situations where they can choose whether to participate with men in the sex promoted by the magazines. Women who have escaped to shelters for assaulted women have described how their spouses, inspired by pornography, have forced them to participate in sex they did not want.[6] When Diana Russell asked a random sample of women, "Have you ever been upset by someone trying to get you to do what they'd seen in pornographic movies or books?" 10 per cent of her respondents said yes.[7] We do not know how many of her sample were forced into sexual acts that they could not know were connected to pornographic materials....

Russell's study provided some of the first evidence that the sexual subordination in the practice of pornography goes on not only during the process of production but during the process of consumption. And the evidence is growing. Many women report being forced to buy videos and watch them. They describe being bullied by partners who wonder why they don't look and act like the women in the pictures.[8] Now that the video boom has brought such a huge volume of new pornographs into the home, where most of the violence against women takes place, these conditions of force are worsening....

...[I]f we believe what women say about their own lives—admittedly a radical research methodology—the case for the connection between pornographs and violent acts is strong enough. Saying so does not make the assailants less responsible for what they do. Identifying the dynamic of pornography, however, does place some responsibility on pornographers for promoting this kind of assault. Pornographers do not trade in fantasy. They trade in the sexual subordination they hope will sustain their customers' erections. What, we should ask, is supposed to happen to these erections? If we take what women say seriously, it is obvious that men do not confine their sexual activity in pornography to masturbation.

Feminists have found that violence against women is systematic and that pornographers have turned that violence into an erotic spectacle. It is painful to have to face the fact that terrible things are done to women to create this spectacle, and that the documents of this abuse, the pornographs themselves, are displayed and sold publicly with the assumption that not much will be done about the abuses shown; it has a devastating effect on women's sense of personal security, for all of this reinforces the suspicion (and the experience) that if these things were to happen to women outside of the practice of pornography, not a great deal would be done about it either. When a woman confronts the products of pornography she feels as if she is being targeted for abuse. In this way pornography acts as a form of public terrorism for women....

What it does to sex itself is another distressing matter. Laboratory studies have tested the attitudes of men who have looked at repeated scenarios of the rape myth and compared them with the attitudes of men who had not been exposed. Men exposed to the rape myth believe that women enjoyed rape and sex that was forced on them in significantly greater numbers than those who were not so exposed.[9] Pornography, it seems, has the effect of convincing consumers that women invite sexual advances, that sexual harassment is not harassment and that rape is only good sex preceded by women's sexiest protest: please don't....

At the same time as pornography merges rape with sex, it has the effect of changing women's status to something less than human. Men exposed to violent pornography tend to trivialize the violence in the films.[10] Crucially, this callousness towards women's injuries has been shown to cross over into real life. In one study, male subjects were asked to participate in a (mock) rape trial after viewing violent pornography. They failed to see the seriousness of a woman's real rape, and they gave a significantly shorter sentence to the rapist than did men who had not seen the films.[11] Similar studies using the so-called non-violent "just sex" materials have produced similar results. It seems that when men see women engaged in sex, whether forced or apparently consensual, they think women are inferior and care about them less....

For years feminists have insisted that pornography lies about women, and lies about men too. Women are not this way, feminists insist. Men do not really do these things. But when sexual abuse is so prevalent that women are paralyzed with fear, unable to get on with their everyday lives, worried that looking a man in the eye will be confused with giving him the eye; when it is so easy to eroticize conflict between women and men; when the operative language of sexuality is that men take and women surrender; when assaulted women complain that they have trouble distinguishing between their spouses' controlling behaviour and love; when incest survivors report that they cannot trust their own orgasm; when it becomes clear that pornography is not a fantasy but a practice of sexual subordination; and that this subordination is made sexy so that it will be reproduced, then the reality has to be faced. Pornography is an effective agent of social control, and the lies of pornography are becoming the truth about life....

In our political culture, it is the pornographer who builds his empire of propaganda and forced sex while women protest in the face of liberal platitudes. There is a pathetic irony in the fact that the three words that have been used most effectively to subvert women's activism against pornography have been "freedom of speech." And one of the most effective agents in negating women's voice has been the pornographer, who reduces women to objects so that their credibility is undermined. Women are increasingly frustrated with the deep entrenchment of liberal values that assume that just by saying everyone has equal rights, those rights will automatically materialize. The romanticization of free speech and other individual freedoms will never subvert male dominance and will instead continue to buttress existing power structures. Women have to ask: why should we let the pornographer speak when he does so much to keep us silent?

As the forces of repression meet those of expression, one wonders why oppression is left out. While observers, whether male or female, choose up sides in the pornography question, other anti-pornography feminists and I redefine the terms of the debate. The right thinks pornography is a moral issue of good and evil, I see it as a political problem of power and powerlessness.[12] The civil libertarian defends pornography as an idea or speech, I am fighting it as a practice of sexual subordination. The moralist says pornography unbridles male sexuality, I say it directs it. The civil libertarian wants to protect freedom, including the pornographer's. I yearn for the day when women will have freedoms to defend.

Ultimately, by questioning pornography's relationship to women, the feminist arguments wind up cutting through the tension between the two traditional sides of the dichotomy. The right-winger warns that the pornographer poses a danger to ordered society, the civil libertarian defends the pornographer's right do so, while I insist that the pornographer is the champion of a very ordered status quo. And while the decency contingent fears the pornographer, the liberator, and the civil libertarian defends the pornographer, speaker and dissident, I know the pornographer is a pimp.

ENDNOTES

1. This idea was first promoted by Andrea Dworkin in *Pornography: Men Possessing Women* (New York: Perogee, 1981), and by Catharine A. MacKinnon in "Francis Biddie's Sister;" in *Feminism Unmodified: Discourses on Life and Law* (Cambridge: Harvard University Press, 1987). The two have recently coauthored *Pornography and Civil Rights: A New Day for Women's Equality* (Minneapolis: Organizing Against Pornography, 1988).

2. "Five Officials Who Scan Porn Rule What Enters Country;" *Toronto Star*, 20 November 1984. "The difficulty with the Penthouse editorial is that the violence is implied, not explicit;" according to Customs official Tom Greig. See also *Regina v. Metro News Limited*, unreported (Ont. D.C.) per Sheard J., in which the materials were deemed obscene. The decision was unusual in that it identified the materials as obscene even though there was not, legally speaking, any sexual explicitness. This kind of so-called feminist decision in obscenity cases is discussed in depth in Chapter II.

3. According to the *Oxford Dictionary*, a "pornograph" is defined as an "obscene writing or pictorial illustration." I am resurrecting the word, not the definition.

4. This term was coined by researchers James Check and Neil Malamuth, whose groundbreaking studies will be discussed later, and by Wendy Stock, who applied their research strategy to women.

5. Vanessa Williams described how after publication of the photos she "had hit rock bottom," in *People*, 6 August 1984, 81. Gloria Steinem described the experience of being humiliated by *Screw* in *Outrageous Acts and Everyday Rebellions* (New York: Holt Reinhart and Winston, 1983), 23.

6. This unpublished study was undertaken by myself with the assistance of the Ontario Women's Directorate. Women staying at shelters in Ontario were surveyed and asked five questions: Does your partner use pornography and if so, what kind? Does he ask, expect or force you to buy it? Does he ask, expect or force you to use it? Does he ask expect or force you to replicate the activities in the pictures? How does this make you feel?

7. Diana E.H. Russell, *Sexual Exploitation: Rape, Child Sexual Abuse, and Workplace Harassment*, (Beverly Hills: Sage, 1984).

8. In the shelter study (see note 6 above), of the 105 women surveyed, 24 per cent of the women whose spouses used pornography were forced to buy the materials, representing 13 per cent of the entire sample. 25 per cent of the women whose spouses used pornography were forced to look at it. Further, a full 48 per cent of the women whose spouses used pornography, representing 25 per cent of the entire sample, reported having to replicate the activities in the pictures against their will. All of the women described these experiences as dehumanizing in some way.

9. Malamuth and Check, "Penile tumescence and perceptual response to rape as a function of victim's perceived reactions," *Journal of Applied Social Psychology* vol. 10 no. 6: 528-554. The questionnaire administered to subjects contained questions of a true/false nature, like "A woman who hitchhikes deserves to be raped," or "A woman who dresses scantily is asking for it." See also Malamuth et al., "Testing Hypotheses Regarding Rape, Exposures to Sexual Violence, Sex Difference and the Normality of Rapists," *Journal of Research in Personality*, vol. 14 (1980): 121-137; and Malamuth and Check, "The Effects of Mass Media Exposure on Acceptance of Violence Against Women: A Field Experiment," *Journal of Research in Personality*, vol. 15 (1981): 436-446.

    It's interesting to track the results of similar studies performed on women. See Wendy Stock, "The Effects of Pornography on Women" invited testimony for the Attorney General's Commission on Pornography, third hearing, September 11 and 12, 1985, Houston, Texas. Stock discovered that exposure to rape myths increased women's sexual arousal to rape and increased their rape fantasies. It did *not*, however, convince them that women liked force in sex.

10. This research and the work that preceded it is described in Ed Donnerstein, "Pornography: Its Effect on Violence Against Women," in *Pornography and Sexual Aggression*, 115-138. See also Daniel Linz, "Sexual Violence in Mass Media: Effects on Male Viewers and Implications for Society," University of Wisconsin, unpublished (1985).

     While the study results have been very useful, it is fascinating to note what male researchers do to find harm in pornography. They show violent pornography to male subjects, wiring up their brains, their hearts or their penises to see what effect the materials have on them, when the violence done to the women in pornography is right in front of their eyes on the screen.

11. In Donnerstein's study (see note 10 above), he took his subjects to participate in a mock rape trial held at the university law school. The subjects heard testimony from a woman who had been raped and were asked to assess her evidence and pass sentence on the perpetrator. The subjects trivialized the woman's injuries significantly more than a control group which had not seen the films, and passed a significantly lighter sentence than the control group. The results indicate that prolonged viewing of violent pornography has effects that cross over into real life situations. I think that the studies also show that as long as violent pornography is a mass media staple, we will have a hard time getting people to take sexual assault seriously.

     As Wendy Stock did with the Malamuth/Check research program. Carol Krafka applied the Donnerstein/Linz strategy to women. She discovered that like the male subject group, her female subjects grew less upset with the violence the more they saw, and that they rated the materials less violent the more they saw. But these women did not trivialize a rape victim's injuries at the mock trial. C.L. Krafka, "Sexually Explicit, Sexually Violent and Violent Media: the Effects of Multiple Naturalistic Exposure and Debriefing on Female Viewers." University of Wisconsin. unpublished (1985). In both Stock's and Krafka's studies on women, the materials did affect the women adversely, but it did not change their *attitudes* about sexual assault. Perhaps this is because many of them know what it feels like to be victimized.

12. MacKinnon's work, cutting through the traditional dichotomies of right and left, immoral and moral, makes her one of the most important feminist thinkers. "Obscenity is a moral idea; pornography is a political practice;" she writes in her article "Not a Moral Issue" in *Feminism Unmodified*. There she makes the distinction between feminist politics and right-wing moralism. See also Lorenne Clark's excellent article "Liberalism and Pornography" in D. Copp, and Wendell, eds., *Pornography and Censorship* (New York: Prometheus, 1983). Clark writes, "Why then has the demand for privacy centred so exclusively on preserving the traditional domain of male privilege? And why do the staunchest defenders of that view fail to see that in invoking these principles within a domain characterized by fundamental inequality they are in fact reinforcing that inequality and sanctioning its worst abuses?"

BEYOND DESPAIR: POSITIVE STRATEGIES

Varda Burstyn

…Ideas about women's liberation and sexual equality struggle for—and within—our hearts and minds, battling notions about sexuality, reproduction and sex roles that date from Victorian times. These social splits haunt us: we live with polarization in society, and confusion, uncertainty and fear uneasily coexist with our pleasures, hopes and satisfactions.

Most disturbing is the way violence seems to permeate our culture. If we are women, however, there is an extra measure of fear, even of panic. For interwoven into women's experience of social violence is a fear unique to women: that generic form of terror, "violence against women." Because aggression against women often takes a sexual form, and because of the stigma attached to women whose sexuality, is expressed outside the conventions of marriage, deep anxiety about danger colors all women's hopes for sexual pleasure.

This kind of violence is rooted in the virgin/whore, good woman/bad woman dichotomy of patriarchal cultures, where control of women's sexuality is a core mechanism in their overall subordination. It is not new nor peculiar to our times. Still, antipornography feminists claim that we are seeing a qualitative escalation, virtually an epidemic, of violence and sexual hatred. We simply do not have statistics to allow us to compare what is taking place today with what existed 15, let alone 30 or 60 years ago. When we survey the social landscape, we must be sure to register the fundamental gains women have made. But though we cannot be sure of the rates of violence against women, it is possible that some types are increasing.…

But if we are to construct loving, responsible relations between people of all ages and sexes, we must ground our legal and social actions in the best of what people are living today, not the worst. For though the sexual morality of the previous period is breaking down, along with the patriarchal family, and though there are casualties from this disintegration, it is also true that seeds of a new, responsible, life-positive morality, are growing, and it is these we must nurture and cultivate. The sexism inherent in so much pornography requires not the repressive response of censorship. Rather, we must make our own explorations of sexuality, known throughout society. The exploitive values so obvious in pornography should not be obscured by censorship, but *challenged* by noncommercial, pluralistic and life-affirming work that reflects the variety of sexual lifeways that exist in our society, and that will, given half a chance, create new kinds of family-friendship groups.

Resolving the issues of sexuality is absolutely crucial to the continued existence and the extensions of the gains we have begun to make. Feminists are correct when they insist that sexuality is "central" in gender politics. But a censorious focus on pornography does not adequately address sexuality. This is why this volume, though entitled *Women Against Censorship*, argues that in addition to rejecting censorship as such, we must also avoid strategies that emphasize legal reform and social control, for these give the state instead of communities of people the power to determine what can be expressed. It puts primary emphasis on the legal system and the punitive, criminal arms of the system at that, and little or no emphasis on changing the real conditions of women's and men's lives. It encourages, even if inadvertently, top-down models of state intervention into sexual life instead of fostering the more creative, organic changes that are slowly emerging—changes based on a commitment to gender equality and freedom of sexual orientation.

The final portion of this chapter is dedicated to constructive alternatives to both censorship and pornography, to giving concrete content to a strategy based in responsible pluralism in sexual life. This approach recognizes the variety of sexual arrangements that now exist in our urban, multicultural society and seeks to use this pluralism as a way of teaching mutual respect, emotional and procreative responsibility, and solidarity between the sexes in place of bitter antagonism.

Our approach has to reflect the morality we want to build, which we struggle for in our daily lives and we try to convey to our children, because it embodies our vision of the future....

The Legal Front

All prior censorship of all media must be stopped. No exceptions to this fundamental democratic right can be tolerated, for if we censor the voices of our opponents and enemies, they will surely find ways to censor us.

All sections dealing with "obscenity" in the Criminal Code should be dropped; no sections substituting legislation on "pornography" should be added. To be judged, all sexual material must be interpreted; all interpretation is subjective; all interpretation must pass through a judicial system geared to the stabilization of the social order currently organized along lines of economic hierarchy and masculine power and privilege.

All powers at present conferred upon customs and postal officials to decide what may or may not enter the country should be rescinded.

All laws that enshrine a double standard that treats homosexual material or practice as more harmful than heterosexual material or practice must be removed from the books.

Human rights legislation should not be used to prosecute sexual material. No matter how offensive and grotesque some material is, the problem is not the sex per se, but the violence and hatred depicted in it....

We must be aware that laws, even when enacted under feminist pressure, are never enforced in a social vacuum: whether they are used for or against feminism depends much more on how strong the women's movement is than on the original initiative behind the laws....

If women find themselves coerced into sexual activity for pornographic production, they should lay assault and rape charges against those responsible. If they are paid less than promised for their work, they can sue for breach of contract. If their pictures are published without their consent, they can sue for harassment, slander, libel and damages, or new legislation can be devised to deal specifically with this problem. Similarly, if women are coerced by their husbands or lovers into sexual acts inspired by pornography, they should lay assault and rape charges. But to suggest, as Andrew Dworkin and Catharine

MacKinnon do in the U.S., and Susan Cole does in Canada, that the makers of the pornography in question be sued because the pornography itself is responsible for the assault is dangerous....

Alternatives to Pornography

We must target sexist and heterosexist values in pornography and in sex education. But this is not enough to change the way sexuality is represented in society, because the identification of sexism can't be achieved in the abstract. We must work to effect change in the very forms of culture that organize and transmit information about sexuality. We have to reclaim our right to a sexual culture, shaped by us, for us. There are many ways to accelerate the process.

At present "sex education" is included in the curricula of most primary and secondary schools; is part of, in a more extended and sophisticated way, certain courses at the university level; and in some urban centres is offered by groups such as Planned Parenthood. The curricula are shaped, in the main, by sexologists and social workers, who represent a skilled but still narrow and specialized approach to sexual questions. Opponents of sex education have argued that though we have more programs for the discussion of sex, we have not seen a reduction of such "sexual problems" as teenage pregnancy and sexually transmitted disease. Supporters of sex education are concerned about these, but their concern extends to other issues as well. Notably, many feminists are worried that due to the hypersexualization of our culture, girls are losing the de facto right to approach sexual experience on the basis of their own needs and personal timing. If 20 years ago it was difficult for a girl to say yes, today it is harder for her to say no.

In terms of sex education for children and youth in the school system, there are a number of big problems. Children often feel uncomfortable discussing sexuality with teachers, who are also authority figures and whom students fear, rightly or wrongly, may use information against them. They often do not feel comfortable talking about sex in the arbitrary grouping of a class, preferring the safety of a chosen peer group. The official programs deal not with the real-life experience of kids, but with a predetermined and not always relevant set of facts and opinions. Finally, confining sex education to schools mistakenly assumes that the only people who need to discuss and learn about sex and sexuality are students. As a beginning, the following changes in sex education would constitute worthwhile and necessary improvements....

We must find the means and ways to substitute a true plurality of images and meanings for the false "average" or stereotyped meanings created by the mass media.

As it now stands, most commercial material is produced with corporate financing, whether through direct sponsorship (television, many films) or indirect sponsorship (some films, magazines). If noncommercial work is to succeed, it must be able to reach as broad an audience as the commercial media and be of comparable quality. To attain this goal requires a number of things.

Through government action we must put some limits on commercial access to and monopoly over the public arena. As it now stands, women, sexual, racial and ethnic minorities, lacking funds and networks of power, are disenfranchised. Ways must be found to untangle the imperatives of profit from the politics of information without substituting state control for that of commerce, thus giving voice to the true plurality of our society. As a starting measure, taxes on the commercial media—which have, it is generally acknowledged, a licence to print money—should be used to help finance noncommercial undertakings.

At present, there is very little material that is produced for television by organizations such as Planned Parenthood, and feminist, gay, even forward-looking church groups, because they do not, as a rule, have the necessary economic resources, although the talent is not lacking. Furthermore, in the case of feminist and gay work especially, were such material to be produced much of it would be censored under present laws, which, as feminist Susan Cole has observed, make it possible to depict a woman sucking a gun but outlaw images of fellatio.

Therefore government arts bodies at all levels—municipal, provincial, federal—should be involved in financing material by cultural producers who speak for those without the resources to create work on a mass scale. In the area of sexuality, this means subsidizing feminist and gay cultural workers and their projects in particular.

With respect to magazines, at present *Playboy* and *Cosmopolitan* are available on virtually every newsstand in North America, but it is impossible to obtain copies of, say, *Fuse* or *Broadside* or *The Body Politic* (have you even heard of these alternative arts, feminist and gay publications?) except in a few bookstores in major urban centres. Government action must be undertaken to enable noncommercial publications to be distributed on a much wider basis....

But while we must fight for governments to develop an enlightened cultural policy, we must not wait for them to act or rely on their funding or intervention. We must become actively involved in making and promoting the use of progressive work on sexuality within our own communities and social and political movements.

All cultural organizations and enterprises need to be brought under mandatory affirmative action legislation. If women are able to make work that expresses their concerns as women without fear of reprisals and other negative consequences, particularly if they do not have to account to corporate sponsors, they will produce material that will illuminate sexuality for all. The National Action Committee on the Status of Women has recommended that women have a television station of their own. This is precisely what we need....

The Sex Industry

...But for the most part, women's working conditions in the sex industry are far from good, and in many cases, quite dreadful. And indeed, although it is impossible to say with accuracy what proportion of adult sex-workers perform under conditions of real coercion and brutality, for a significant number of women their "choice" of sex work is a choice only in the most literal of senses. They "choose" to work under terrible conditions, without control over environment, clientele or the nature of the spectacle, because they have no other option but to starve. Others turn to sex work because they see this course as less damaging to their health and well-being than factory work, cleaning or waitressing, which are often unsafe and frequently involve constant sexual harassment.

A feminist-oriented approach to the sex industry must ensure that women are no longer victimized by police and social politics; that greater criminalization of neighborhoods and risk to women as workers is discouraged; that the audience for sexist pornography and the market for alienated sex is reduced. This kind of approach means that we must address the needs of sex-workers both by improving the quality of their present working lives and by seeking to create real alternatives to alienating sex work. On both planes, repressive measures are harmful and counterproductive. Censorship only worsens the position of sex-workers vis-à-vis those who control the industry—pornography producers, sex emporium entrepreneurs, and pimps, corporate or individual—by criminalizing sex work and its products and putting the women who work in this field at greater risk in relation to police and the courts....

There is a debate as to whether we should legalize prostitution and regulate pornographic production and other sex work. The answers are complex. On the one hand, legalization would mean that sex-workers would be registered with the state, and therefore theoretically their working conditions, wages and other rights would be monitored. On the other hand, certain kinds of sex work—especially classically defined prostitution—would thereby be institutionalized in ways that tend to give government and corporate entities more control over the women workers in the industry, rather than increasing their autonomy in relation to clients and employers. Instead, along with the Canadian National Action Committee and the U.S. National Organization for Women, we must demand the decriminalization of prostitution. The present laws (in Canada, laws against soliciting and the keeping of a "bawdy house"; in the U.S. against prostitution per se) put prostitutes at constant risk, and create an entire group of women who are socially ostracized and saddled with criminal records, which make finding alternative employment extremely difficult. We must demand the annulment of criminal records for sex work, and find ways to deal with prostitution on a local level without victimizing women. While this is not a simple matter, if communities work in conjunction with prostitutes, and if prostitutes are allowed to operate independently and without harassment, a solution can be found. In the case of sex emporiums, strip joints and similar spots, laws regulating working conditions, minimum wages and unionization should apply, since only such regulation can prevent the worst sort of exploitation.

In terms of the longer-term fate of prostitution, again the issues are complex. Many feminists, though they argue against the victimization of prostitutes, nevertheless believe that sex work is more problematic than other kinds of work. In part, this evaluation stems from a sense that there is something especially alienating in intimate physical contact with strangers, particularly under conditions of poverty and stigmatization. Many sex-workers report such feelings about their work, saying that over time it affects how they feel about themselves and about men. If we believe that sexual encounters are best in conditions of free affectional choice— a position that I hold both emotionally and intellectually—then we must work toward the creation of meaningful alternatives to alienated sex work. This means that in keeping with a more general commitment to full and meaningful employment, we must demand educational and economic support for women who want to leave this work so that they can live dignified lives without economic hardship while preparing for new ways of earning a living....

Reproductive and Erotic Rights for Women and Sexual Minorities

Sexual mores and norms are not naturally predetermined but socially created. They take the raw material of sex—two sexes, a drive to find pleasure from the body and a desire to procreate—and organize it into socially ordered practices. In our society, the dominant sexual norms—those reflected in law, education, church life and the mass media—reflect men's systematic dominance in social and political life. Although there are great differences among the major cultural institutions and their views of sex (differences, for example between the old-fashioned patriarchalism of orthodox Catholicism and the slick new "masculinism" of *Penthouse*), they all reinforce men's power over women and sexual arrangements compatible with that power. From a feminist point of view, then, sexual morality must be a political issue as well. The kinds of norms we want to develop must reflect our goals of equality and self-determination.

For women, the sine qua non of sexual rights has been embodied in the slogan "Control of our bodies, control of our lives." Part of the antifeminist backlash we have been experiencing is a reaction against women's move to take control of their own bodies and lives. The key planks in a program of reproductive and erotic rights are:

(a) Safe, reliable contraception, universally available to women of all ages; increased awareness of contraception in community programs; and improved methods developed through subsidized research and government manufacture, if necessary. For example, the technology now exists to produce a condom that would be so sensitive that neither partner would feel deprived of the sensation of contact. Condom and drug companies are refusing to manufacture this condom because if would undercut existing contraceptive devices and destroy the almost criminally lucrative oral contraceptive market. The pill has many dangerous side effects, and is increasingly implicated in diseases of the endocrine and immune systems. The new "supercondom" would be completely safe and have no side effects.

(b) A woman's right to choose abortion, and to have that choice supported by safe, easily accessible medical services. Women must be able to have the procedure done in their communities and, when necessary, by staff who speak their native language. Professional, supportive counselling both before and after, should women need help to get through this often painful and distressing operation is also critical, as is the right to have the procedure covered by medical insurance.

(c) The right to choose or to refuse sterilization. All over North America, as well as in the Third World, women of racial and national minorities find themselves sterilized without their consent after childbirth or abortion. This must stop. At the same time, many white, middle-class women who want sterilization are refused because their doctors believe that they should reproduce or go on reproducing.

(d) An end to compulsory heterosexuality: we know that sex between people of the same gender is the choice of a significant minority of the population. We also know from the study of other cultures that same-sex practices have often been a central part of mainstream sexuality. From these facts we can deduce that our own sexuality is very much shaped by the taboos placed on same-sex practice, taboos that work in the context of masculinism to reinforce gender hierarchy. If these taboos were lifted, sexual encounters would likely occur between people of the same sex much more often than they do now.

The present prohibitions on homosexual practice give rise to deep prejudices, which in turn lead to fear and mistrust. People with homosexual preferences are seen as "perverted" and "deviant," hence dangerous and contaminating, while those with heterosexual preferences are considered "normal" and "healthy." These prejudices set ordinary people against one another, and divert attention from the crimes of institutionalized, compulsory heterosexuality: incest, molestation and rape, and a generalized, though rarely acknowledged, atmosphere of coercion that subtly forces women to serve men sexually and to subordinate their own needs to men. So pervasive are these values that, like the air we breathe, for the most part we do not even notice them. But they are a major part of what keeps our sexual lives in line with gender hierarchy.

Because homosexual practice—as part of or as the exclusive component of an individual's sex life—is so stigmatized, we need to take some affirmative action on this front. Sex education programs must include gay-positive content to break down the stigmatization of same-sex choices, and the way homosexual people are isolated from mainstream life. Similar measures are necessary in other spheres. Given the deep biases against homosexuality, and the way that they tend to colour media productions on gays and lesbians, this material needs to be developed under the leadership of gay and lesbian people, who can speak for themselves....

Feminists who oppose censorship—a strategy that takes little time or reflection to expound—do not have another slogan, another quick solution, another panacea to offer in its place. We do have a comprehensive list of tasks we must carry out to bring sexism and violence to an end. Working on any one of these is more helpful—immediately, not in the distant future—than supporting censorship of any kind today, for these tasks get at the structural basis of sexism and violence, and thus ensure that we will have a future.

Whenever major change takes place in society, whenever people who are underprivileged challenge the structures of inequality that have kept them down, political polarization takes place. Women are challenging sexism, and the system of masculine dominance is responding in powerful ways. Its responses are interwoven with the defences of a crisis-ridden economic system based on so great a need for profits that it jeopardizes the health, well-being and even basic existence of millions of people—indeed, of the planet as we know it. Many people are afraid and confused; it is easy to lose hope, easy to fall into the politics of fear and despair; tempting to grasp at straws if, in the current troubled seas, they see the lines that may pull us to safety. But this illusion is dangerous; it disorients us and drains the strength we need for the tasks ahead.

There is no effective—no *realistic*—substitute for basic change, no alternative to social transformation. In times of crisis, such as our own, social movements need to firmly and publicly state their overall solutions to the problems in society. Now more than ever it is madness to abandon the program for human dignity that feminism has embodied since its second wave began in the 60s. Now more than ever the women's movement must hold to the vision of a good life for all, translate it into solid, practical policy and fight to implement that policy, at all levels of society. Now more than ever we must insist that public funds that finance police, jails, the armed forces and weapons manufacture be redirected to cooperation and life, not domination and death.

Women—and men who support feminism—are too important a political force to be ignored if we fight together for this vision. Remaining steadfast now will yield positive results when, inevitably, it becomes clear that the right-wing program was able to solve nothing, that the Mulroney and Reagan governments have only worsened the lot of most people. If at that point we are ready; if we have done the groundwork, fought in our communities, confronted, educated, negotiated; if we have not abandoned the arts and the media to sexists and exploiters; if we have worked hard to build profeminist political parties willing to bring about social change, then we will be in a position to offer alternative social leadership to the antiwoman, antihuman politics of the patriarchal right and the masculinist multinationals whose need for profits stands in direct contradiction to our needs for security, self-determination and community.

We will not then have to spend precious time and resources disentangling ourselves from the snares in which we have become caught. We will not have been gagged or silenced or frightened into retreat. We will not have to start over, rebuilding our forces, reeducating ourselves and our supporters. If we remain steadfast now, when that moment comes we will be able to build the power that will take us from incremental to giant steps along the road to freedom for women and sexual joy for all.

HOMOPHOBIA AND
ROMANTIC LOVE

Jane Rule

"Do you mean there are lesbians here, in this room?" a young woman asked, horrified. For her the experience of women meeting together once a week, sometimes as many as fifty of them, to break up into small groups and discuss the problems shared by women, had been literally liberating from the sexual pressure she always felt when men were around. That she might have to be on her sexual guard again, this time with women, depressed her badly. A man, reviewing Kate Millett's *Sita* in the *New York Times*, confessed to a depression (the sincerity of which I doubt) because even in a lesbian relationship one woman dominated the other emotionally and, more blatantly, sexually. If lesbian sexuality poses all the same problems, while being "a problem" in itself, it is automatically worse. The onus is on the lesbian to prove to heterosexual women and men that her experience is essentially better, if it is to be accepted at all. There is a lot of attractive arrogance, particularly among younger lesbians setting out to do just that, and they have my candid applause for every point they win in the debate. Having grown up in the lesbian silence of the 30s and 40s, having had no sense of community through the 50s, having broken the silence for myself in the early 60s with a gentle and romantic novel, I have developed no skills for that debate, but Adrienne Rich's invitation to enter into a conversation about homophobia with women, not necessarily in political/feminist terms, but to discover "what's really going on here," calls to my own endless wondering at experience.

If I had been the same age as the young woman who was threatened by the idea of lesbians in the same room, I would perhaps have been angry with her, though when I was her age and a friend of mine expressed the same kind of horror ("What would you do if you ever met a lesbian? I think I'd throw up or faint or die.") I said not a word; and later, in my brooding, neither anger nor any doubt about my silence ever crossed my mind. I felt simply horribly and inevitably alone. Twenty-five years later, I wanted to be instructive, and I think I was gentle and reassuring enough to encourage that young woman to be courteous if not open-minded about experience. I suspect my own sexuality, because of my age and my position as a university teacher, was unreal to her, as I am sure the sexuality of her male teachers even older than I was not. I could not, in good faith, have told her that no lesbian would ever find her attractive and make sexual advances. Most in my generation are timid and circumspect enough to be generally harmless, but lesbians her own age might certainly not only desire her but feel some political zeal in converting her, challenge and bully with as much ego investment as any young male for conquest. Nor, of course, could I have assured any young lesbian that one of her adventuresome heterosexual sisters might not take advantage of her feelings for the experience of it. The young call it "doing numbers" on each other.

I *am* sincerely depressed by how often lesbian relationships are accurate caricatures of heterosexual relationships, though it doesn't surprise me. It's important for Kate Millett to chart accurately what has happened to her, whether anyone is depressed by it or not. It is clear that Kate's obsession with Sita depends on Sita's indifference at this stage in the relationship. The moment Sita relents, offers Kate the sexual security and attention she craves, Kate feels claustrophobic and longs to be free. Over and over again I was reminded of Willa Cather's statement: "Human relationships are the tragic necessity of human life; that they can never be wholly satisfactory, that every ego is half the time greedily seeking them, and half the time pulling away from them."

True. For my much younger self. I was sexually so hungry, humanly so isolated, psychically so traumatized by social judgment that I required of myself a purity of motive so self-sacrificing, a vision of love so redeeming that to be a lover was an annihilation of all the healthy instincts of self-preservation I had. I am still not free of all the phobic reactions that sweet, strong, young self had to resort to in order to stay singularly alive. And though we say over and over again that the young now are not traumatized as we were, I do not really believe that the sexual revolution of the women's movement has reached most nervous systems yet. I was interrupted in the middle of this paragraph by a phone call from a younger friend who said, "My lover, ever since a political fight about tenure at her university eighteen months ago, has vomited every time we have made love, which has been no more than once every two months, and now she's moved into the guest room and says I should make love to anyone else I want." There's the homophobia in ourselves, Adrienne, whether we've known from age eight or only discovered after years of marriage and childbearing that we love each other. No wonder the homophobia in heterosexual men and women is so outrageous to us. Before we confront it in them, never mind that's where we got it, we must understand it in ourselves.

As honestly as I can recall, before I knew any psychological or moral definitions, I turned to women for love because I knew how I wanted to be loved, and I knew only women knew that. From my mother certainly. I had a cherishing father when he was around, but he was rarely around, and so he loved ideas he had made of his children. My mother loved us through our vomiting, broken bones, sulks; listened to our jokes, theories about the world, egomanias, and sorrows. (My father, this day, loves as I think a woman can, but it has taken him seventy-odd years to come to it, and he's rarely gifted.) I did not think then about being loved, though I needed to be. I thought about being loving.

I was not good at it, "half the time greedily seeking...half the time pulling away..." I could not get clear of the separation of roles, beloved or lover. Like Kate and Sita, I seesawed between senses of power and dependence. Power required too much responsibility. Dependence was too humiliating. In each is the failure to be peers, failure that is so appalling in the heterosexual model, never mind that some men and women together figure out how to be free of it.

Do we begin by disliking ourselves as women because women are unequally loved? Do we carry that dislike into our love of other women and therefore struggle under a burden: knowing we are worse, we must, therefore, be better? Are we the unclean bitches who must transform ourselves into goddesses? To try to be too good to be true is spiritually so expensive that our failures not only nauseate but destroy numbers of us. I wrote some years ago, "I'd like to try being simply good enough."

It was my lovers who suffered nauseous guilt, not I. They returned to husbands, the church, celibate scholarship. I, instead, found I could not walk down a city street, stand before an audience, eat in front of anyone. I slept, drank, masturbated through days to avoid writing and believed my will to defy those escapes and get back to work would finally kill me. It is not simply a story of the terrible 50s. I hear it all around me now in the "liberated" 70s.

I understand why Bertha Harris wants to insist that lesbians, the only true lesbians, are monsters. She is trying to take our homophobia into her arms and transform herself/us into lovers "bad enough to be true," incestuous, self-centered, addicted, mad. Begin to love there.

I lack the romantic flair, live in too small a community (by choice), have been too long in a central relationship (twenty-three years, by choice). I need more ordinary solutions. Or hopes.

One of my heterosexual friends told me that her lover had said she wasn't a good "wife" to him. She asked him for his definition of a wife. When he had finished telling her, she said, "You're not talking about a wife; you're talking about the mother of a child under six." I am always nervous about the suggestion that, as lesbians, we should mother each other, though I understand that the image comes from our first source of love. Our mothers are also the first source of rejecting power against whom we screamed our dependent rage. As adults, if we cry out for that mother love, the dependent rage inevitably follows, and what is even more disconcerting is that, given total attention and sympathy, we are soon restless to be free, for we aren't any longer children. A young man asked me, in a seminar on Willa Cather, "Don't you think only people of the same sex can have a real marriage, not only of the flesh but of the imagination?" "I don't know," I answered, "but what a dreadful thought!" "One flesh" has always struck me as spurious, since each is importantly defined by a sack of skin, and children are not metaphors of union but individuals often made up of gene banks hard to recognize as in any way similar to either parent. "One imagination" is an even more terrifying invasion of the autonomous mind and spirit.

The Greeks treated romantic passion like any other illness, expressed sympathy and a hope for early recovery. Yet we put the state of being in love as the highest good. When I encounter people "entirely in love," I wonder why we couldn't just as well celebrate any delirious fever, say pneumonia, as a state infinitely to be desired. Surely we would be kinder to ourselves and our friends to hope for a cure than to encourage a lifelong ailment, fortunately very rare.

I am not being cynical. The love which Kate Millett describes in Sita is finally degrading to both people, patterned as it is on the relationship between a mother and a dependent child. Kate's instinct to get out, to get back to her own work, is her cure. Both the pain of her own dependence and Sita's return to men as lovers strengthen the homophobia in each of them. There can be no lasting delight and nourishment between people when one is always afraid the other will return to "Daddy" with his superior sexual power, the other sure to be suffocated by a possessive child who refuses to grow up and leave home.

I don't think there is any way to root out our homophobia until we also deal with the infantile in romantic love as the weed that it is, choking out the young and real sisterhood that begins to flower among us. We have got to be peers, respecting each other's strengths without dependent envy, sympathetic with each other's weaknesses without cherishing or encouraging them, interdependent by choice, not by terrified necessity.

I love the eroticism among women who like their own bodies, the hard discussion between those who require their own minds, the joy among strong spirits. The young woman who was terrified to be in a room with lesbians learned her fear from men who tried to dominate her. The man depressed at the old pattern of sexual politics, even between two women, was first disillusioned about relationships in heterosexual terms. Each is projecting onto lesbians the basic failure of romantic love between the sexes. If we try to be better at that, we will over and over feel worse.

Sex is not so much an identity as a language which we have for so long forbidden to speak that most of us learn only the crudest of its vocabulary and grammar. If we are to get past the pattern of dominance and submission, of possessive greed, we must outgrow love as fever, as "the tragic necessity of human life," and speak in tongues that set us free to be loving equals.

LESBIANISM: A COUNTRY THAT HAS NO LANGUAGE

Mariana Valverde

...Lesbianism is not a disease. It is not even a natural physiological or psychological condition. It is a complex social fact. Sex between women may have taken place for thousands of years, but the formation of a distinct lesbian identity—perceived as inherent, persisting even in the absence of sexual activity—is a relatively recent event. We cannot understand the position of lesbians in today's society without knowing some of the history of when and how this distinct sexual identity was formed.

A Bit of History

Historian Lillian Faderman has pointed out in her ground-breaking book *Surpassing the Love of Men: Romantic Friendships and Love Between Women*[1] that both sex and love between women were part of European and American culture from the sixteenth to the nineteenth centuries, while strictly speaking there were no lesbians until the turn of the twentieth century....

...The "romantic friendship" of the late eighteenth and nineteenth centuries was an accepted feature of a social life that did not assume the women involved were in any way deviant or anti-heterosexual. Historian Carroll Smith-Rosenberg was the first to uncover a whole tradition of such long-lasting bonds of love between American women in the nineteenth century. She discovered many cases of women friends who would even displace the husband from the marital bed when visiting one another.[2] Sometimes the women did not marry and lived together as a couple, an arrangement known as a "Boston marriage." This was more common in the late nineteenth century, and only in urban settings since pioneer women tended to marry.

Faderman suggests that these passionate and sensual relationships that involved all the earmarks of passionate love, as we can see in surviving letters and other documents, were not usually based on genital sexual contact. The women might have slept in the same bed, hugged and kissed each other, and experienced all the signs of falling in love, but they probably did not think of their kisses or their racing pulses as indicators of a specifically genital desire. After all, in this era women were supposed to have only emotional desires, and there is evidence to show that most if not all women internalized this idea. For most, "sex" probably meant less than satisfying contact with overbearing husbands, or simply reproduction.

When "in love" with another woman, they would not associate those feelings with either reproduction or with "base" desires....

It was only after the 1880s that love between women began to be regarded with suspicion and investigated for signs of perversion. Havelock Ellis in Britain, Richard von Krafft-Ebing in Germany, and other doctors and scientists began to take an interest in classifying human sexual behaviour according to "types." They established criteria for distinguishing the various types, especially the normal and the abnormal. Some of these types were the fetishist, the sado-masochist and the necrophiliac. But foremost among the abnormal sexual types was the "invert" or homosexual....

For women, the impact of the new sexology was mixed. On the one hand, women who felt sexual urges toward other women could now put a name to their feelings, and argue, as did Radclyffe Hall's heroine, that they could not help being what they were, and hence need not be ashamed. But on the other hand, the new homosexual identity was not on par with heterosexuality. To be a lesbian was to be abnormal, and as the heroine of *The Well of Loneliness* also said, to be something other than a real woman. By adopting the sexologists' categories one might achieve inner peace knowing that one's feelings and experiences had a name and were shared by other women. However, one could never be at peace with the world since lesbianism was so stigmatized that even speaking about it was not allowed....

Making Heterosexuality Compulsory

With women increasingly defined and evaluated according to their heterosexual market value, and with marriage viewed neither as an economic partnership nor a parenting project but as a glorious romance, the stage was set for the social institution that had come to be known as "compulsory heterosexuality."[3] This institution is not located in any downtown skyscraper or in any government department, but it is so pervasive in today's society that it resembles the proverbial water of which fish are unaware.

Sexism creates femininity and masculinity as we know them, since our gendered egos are constituted by psycho-social conditioning. Compulsory heterosexuality refers to the ideology and social practice that pushes properly gendered women and men into couples and makes them believe this is a free choice. It must be emphasized that compulsory heterosexuality need not rely on extreme bigotry against homosexuality in order to achieve its goal of instituting the heterosexual couple as the *sine qua non* of personal success and social stability.

Heterosexism is not only present when someone actively discriminates against or harasses a gay person. It is also present in many places where gay people are not involved, for example in bridal industry ads that portray diamonds and white wedding dresses, and indirectly traditional marriage, as universally desirable. In this sense, heterosexism oppresses not only homosexuals but anyone who is either celibate or is in a casual sexual relationship. It is even oppressive to coupled heterosexuals who enjoy its privileges, since the whole weight of a social institution is imposed upon their individual shoulders. Bridal industry ads are offensive to married women who are happy in their marriage but do not derive their identity from it. Women who want to take a job in a different city and feel guilty about commuting between job and husband are also oppressed by heterosexism. The relationship is supposed to be more important to them than to the husband, who would not be expected to have to make those choices.

Although heterosexism oppresses gay men and all men who do not fit "the norm," it weighs particularly heavily on women. Women suffer more pressure to "find a man" than men do to find a wife. Women are the ones who are constantly being told—by the advertising industry, movies and novels, and by family and friends—that they have to work at improving their appearance and their cuisine in order to get a man, or if they have one, to keep him. Men gain extra social status from having a woman at their beck and call, and can be stigmatized as "queers" if they fail to produce a woman for the appropriate social occasions. However men do not need female validation for their very identity. They change neither their name nor their social class upon marriage. A garbageman married to a schoolteacher is still a garbageman; a university-educated woman who marries a farmer becomes "the farmer's wife." We see then that because women are denied an autonomous identity, the consequences of being in or out of a heterosexual couple are greater for them....

...[W]e are surrounded by heterosexist ideology; we enter heterosexual relationships accompanied by a whole series of expectations and ideals about what "it" is supposed to be like. Whether our fantasy entails being swept off our feet by a tall millionaire, or whether we sigh after a non-sexist man in a crumpled shirt, we all have expectations and hopes and we are all more or less affected by the stories of "great loves" we have read about or seen in movies. From Romeo and Juliet to the soaps there is a constant stream of ideology about what heterosexuality is like or should be like.

By contrast, the almost complete dearth of images of lesbianism in our culture means that when a woman begins to feel attracted to other women she has no preconceived notion of what "it" is supposed to look or feel like. The few lesbian enclaves in large cities have created some ideal conceptions of what love between women is or could be about. But these ideals are not part of the general culture, and to seek them out one has to visit feminist or gay bookstores, listen to hard-to-get lesbian songs, or attend the few and not widely publicized events the community organizes. Even for those lesbians living in large cities where lesbian communities do exist, one has to make a real effort to go out and find the like-minded women and the culture that speaks to us. The culture of heterosexism, of course, washes over us constantly.

When I began to fall in love with a woman, I was completely unacquainted with any depictions of lesbianism. The descriptions and ideals produced by lesbian feminism had never come to my attention, and I did not become aware of them until I was already deep into the most intense love relationship of my life. I thus did not expect or hope or fantasize: I simply explored with great wonder everything that happened in those early months of our love, all the feelings and thoughts that seemed to be arising out of the blue in my previously "normal" heart....

Lesbians, the State, and Society

Most people think we live in enlightened times, and that outright persecution of lesbians and other unpopular minorities is confined to outposts of bigotry. Most people are unaware that divorced women are routinely deprived of custody of their children if ex-husbands bring evidence of lesbianism into the courtroom. Few people know that as late as the seventies there were cases in Canada of women being committed to psychiatric hospitals and subjected to heavy drugs and electroshock because their parents or husbands convinced doctors that lesbianism was a sign of madness. And today, many young lesbians are forced out of their homes by irate fathers.

It is important to understand that lesbians are not only subjected to occasional perse-cutions but also to the everyday grind of societal oppression. Constant tension and stress is felt even by those lesbians living in relatively privileged settings. Every day we have to decide how we will appear before the world. Should I, in a coffee-break conversation with coworkers, speak about "my lover" the way other women talk about their boyfriends? Will I hide all the tell-tale lesbian books and posters in my home because an aunt is visiting?…

However lesbians choose to respond to specific situations—and there is not a lesbian alive who can possibly be "out of the closet" in all circumstances—they are not free to simply live their lives without making an "issue" of their lesbianism. If they try to avoid the stress of going public they will succeed only in internalizing the conflict, and making themselves unhappy by the constant self-censorship which alone can keep the closet door shut. On the other hand, if one tells one's family and friends about one's sexual choices, one is not then exempt from future dilemmas. Many lesbians struggle for years with the difficult question of telling one's parents, only to discover that after the "big talk" silence once more descends upon them.…

Social prejudice and heterosexist attitudes are certainly one big obstacle preventing lesbians from living freely. However, the mechanisms of the state (laws, courts, police, school systems) are not at all neutral with respect to lesbians. For instance, in Canada it is illegal to engage in gay sex until one is twenty-one years old, while the heterosexual of consent is fourteen or sixteen depending on the province.…

The police and the bureaucracy are not the only agencies of the state that exercise their power in such a way as to reinforce lesbian oppression. Lesbians are also often deprived of custody of their children by the courts. Furthermore, lesbian couples are not allowed to adopt children under the rules of Children's Aid, and a lesbian who wants to be artificially inseminated will find it virtually impossible to find a sympathetic doctor who will help her. Fortunately new networks have developed to allow lesbians who want to have children to get in touch with volunteer gay men, but these networks are almost underground.…

But legal changes must go hand in hand with changes in the public perception of homo-sexuality. Just as one of the first tasks of the post-1968 women's movement was to challenge the media stereotypes of women and to project new, positive images of women's strength and capabilities, so one of the key tasks of lesbian communities is to present an alternative image of who we are.…

The Women's Movement: Lesbianism Is An Issue for All Feminists

If we look at lesbianism as a social category identifying women who are permanently inde-pendent from men and look to each other for love, sex, and day-to-day support, then it is clearly in the interest of all feminists to defend lesbianism as a positive choice. Conversely, when lesbians are sneered at for being "too ugly to get a man" or for "aping men," hetero-sexual feminism is also being attacked. All women are kept down and prevented from freely choosing if and how they will relate to men or conform to male standards of femininity. Thus, defending lesbian rights and supporting lesbian culture is not something that heterosexual feminists ought to do as a matter of charity; rather defending lesbianism is an integral part of the struggle for women's independence. Attacks on lesbians are implicitly attacks on all women who deviate from the traditional pattern. If heterosexual feminists expect to increase the social space for women, they have to defend the right of all women to choose lesbianism if they so desire.

Unfortunately, not all feminists see the issue this way, because not all have grappled with internalized homophobia and heterosexism. Many heterosexual feminists are uneasy about lesbians speaking publicly for the women's movement, because they fear people will get "the wrong impression" and dismiss all feminists as man-hating lesbians. Instead of challenging this prejudice, many heterosexual feminists run away from it and give in to it. In the early seventies, the American National Organization for Women (NOW) carried out a witch-hunt against lesbians precisely because it did not want to "create the wrong impression" and ruin its public image. The irony of this purge was that the divisions and hard feelings it caused were probably far worse for the organization's morale and cohesion than anything male attacks on lesbian feminism might have caused. Today, mainstream women's organizations would probably not undertake the same kind of divisive marginalization of lesbians. But nevertheless, lesbians are often perceived within the mainstream women's movements as "uncomfortably sexual," as Lorna Weir has put it.[4]

Heterosexual feminists tend to have a certain split between their private erotic life with men and their political activities with women. But for lesbian feminists "the personal is political" in a much more direct way. Often, political coworkers are also lovers (or ex-lovers, or the ex-lovers of one's present lover!). There is an unmistakable erotic energy that sometimes surfaces not just in social gatherings but even in meetings or more formal settings. Grassroots feminist organizations often accept this, but more "respectable" organizations frown on any manifestations of lesbian erotic energy or even on women who talk about lesbian sexuality....

...The politics of the women's movement are often set by articulate, well-educated women who are usually middle-class, white, and heterosexual (publicly at least). Their point of view is presented as being that of women in general. By contrast, lesbians, women of colour and other "minority" women are seen as representing only women like themselves and not women in general. Lesbian issues are constructed as "particularistic," "special-interest" issues. Women who are known to be lesbians are treated, by the media and even by many feminists, as unable to speak about anything *but* lesbian issues, as though lesbians did not need equal pay and indeed pensions as much as anyone else. This is heterosexism at work. To be heterosexual is regarded as average, normal, and non-problematic. But to be anything else is instantly problematic and relegates one to the status of "minority." And if no vocal members of that minority group are present to voice their views, then their concerns will be routinely forgotten. A feminist movement that claims to speak for all women must make sure that it does in fact include the concerns and views of all sectors, without falling into the trap of dividing women into "normal" or "average" on the one hand, and "fringe" groups on the other.

Seen from this perspective, it becomes clear that lesbianism is an issue for all feminists, just as child care and child rearing is an issue for all feminists regardless of whether or not they are mothers. For example, almost all feminist organizations have a clear position on women's right to abortion, and many lesbians have worked long and hard to defend this right even though they do not personally need abortion facilities. This is because it has become clear that what is at stake is not just abortion itself, but the larger right of all women to make their choices around childbearing and sexuality free from state and church coercion. Similarly then, when lesbians fight to gain access to the media or other public spaces, what is really at stake is the right of *all* women to define their own sexual identity and have access to cultural resources in order to create positive images of their eroticism and their lifestyle. All women who long for a woman-centred sexuality will find it in their best interests to take an active interest in the development of lesbian culture. To fight for lesbian rights and against heterosexism is to fight against male-defined feminine roles, and for autonomy. Active support for lesbian cultural and political initiatives is hence an integral part of being a feminist.

When heterosexual feminists fail to support lesbian initiatives, it is not only through incorrect political ideas. It is also because certain emotional reactions and gut feelings prevent them from thinking clearly. Lesbians by their very presence often make heterosexual women uncomfortable and anxious. These anxieties have to be examined one by one and dealt with in a calm manner, always remembering they are not individual failings. Rather they are the inevitable result of having grown up with homophobia and having had homophobia repeatedly used to undermine the women's movement. Sometimes lesbians do not remember this and turn on individual heterosexual feminists with such cheap shots as "You shouldn't sleep with men, they are the enemy." This is designed only to produce guilt and divisiveness, and to overcompensate for lesbian invisibility by turning the tables on heterosexual feminists and telling them they cannot be real feminists. These oversimplifications are explosions of anger and have no place in political discussions. Feminism asserts the right of all women to make their erotic choices, and this includes choosing men exclusively. Feminism also rejects the hierarchy of sexual practices, and so does not seek to substitute a lesbian priority for heterosexism. The goal of feminism in the area of sexuality is to establish true sexual pluralism, where no one choice is presented as "the norm."

However, having once or twice been faced by dogmatic lesbian chauvinism, sometimes heterosexual feminists retreat and refuse to ask any critical questions about their own views and practices. Being attracted to men is definitely neither unfeminist nor oppressive to lesbians, but since it necessarily fits into the institution of heterosexuality certain questions are helpful. Here are examples of what seem to me to be possible critical questions for heterosexual feminists:

- Do I, even though I am heterosexual, have a "lesbian streak"?
- If so, am I panicked about releasing that energy, and wish lesbians would go away so that I don't have to deal with it?
- Or do I have absolutely no attraction to other women, and think any woman who does must be bizarre?
- Am I afraid a lesbian will try to seduce me?
- Am I secretly hoping a lesbian will seduce me?
- Do I have stereotyped views about lesbian role-playing in relationships? If so, where do those views come from? From actual experience, from the media, from one or two novels or movies?
- Do I assume that all women I meet are heterosexual? Do I think I don't know any lesbians just because none of my friends have explicitly told me they are lesbians?

- If my daughter, sister, or mother came out as a lesbian, would I be embarrassed? If so (and this is only to be expected), do I have any way to develop a more positive attitude and get over my initial anxiety?

- Do I think that having lesbians in the women's movement is a public embarrassment? If so (and this is only to be expected), do I and my heterosexual friends have ways to deal with this? Do we fear guilt by association?

- Can I talk to a lesbian about my fears and concerns? Can I talk to anybody about all these questions?

All these questions are legitimate. Everyone has to struggle with them at some point or another, and this takes time. Heterosexism is so deeply ingrained in us that it takes a concerted effort to overcome it. Being lesbian-positive is not easy, and does not come automatically on joining a women's group, or for that matter on becoming a lesbian.

This means that dialogue is crucial, not just between lesbians and heterosexual women, but among heterosexual women as well. During this dialogue one will probably be faced with questions that have never been asked before, such as "Why am I heterosexual anyway?" Or for lesbians, "Do I secretly think feminists who are not lesbians are second-class feminists?"

The first precondition of dialogue is mutual respect. But the second condition is an awareness that not all sexual choices are created equal. Lesbians are oppressed because of their sexual preference, while heterosexual women acquire certain privileges from society as a result of their sexual preference. Thus, even if we find a lot of common ground and discover that sexual relationships tend to have the same problems, we should not end our investigation with a bland "It's really all the same anyway." Lesbian oppression is not experienced by heterosexual women, and they need to educate themselves about it by talking with lesbians, by reading, and by any other available means.

Once we have mutual respect as well as an awareness of both lesbian oppression and heterosexual privilege, we can move on to discuss our personal concerns and our views about how the women's movement can best fight against heterosexism, which oppresses all independent women, and against the specific oppression of lesbians. This discussion is already taking place in small groups, but it needs to take place more publicly and on a larger scale.

The final goal is a strong women's movement which represents the interests of women of all sexual orientations, and which vocally defends the right of lesbians not only to have private relationships but also to build a visible and public lesbian culture. This culture will of course be of more direct benefit to lesbians. But all women can gain inspiration from seeing the tremendous possibilities that are released when we begin to think about woman-centred eroticism, about woman-oriented culture, about woman-positive politics.

ENDNOTES

1. Lillian Faderman, *Surpassing the Love of Men: Romantic Friendships and Love Between Women* (New York: Morrow, 1981).

2. Caroll Smith-Rosenberg, "The Female World of Love and Ritual: Relations Between Women in 19th Century America," *Signs*, vol. 1 no. 1, (1975), 1-29.

3. Adrienne Rich, "Compulsory Heterosexuality and Lesbian Existence," *Signs*, vol. 5 no. 4, (Summer 1980).

4. Lorna Weir and Leo Casey, "Subverting Power in Sexuality," *Socialist Review*, No. 75-76, 152.

HETEROSEXUALITY AND FEMINIST THEORY

Christine Overall

Heterosexuality, which I define as a romantic and sexual orientation toward persons not of one's own sex, is apparently a very general, though not entirely universal, characteristic of the human condition. In fact, it is so ubiquitous a part of human interactions and relations as to be almost invisible, and so natural-seeming as to appear unquestionable. Indeed, the 1970 edition of *The Shorter Oxford English Dictionary* defines "heterosexual" as "pertaining to or characterized by the normal relation of the sexes."[1]...

This is, then, the first of what I shall refer to as the paradoxes of heterosexuality: As an expected, supposedly normal characteristic of adult and even pre-adult life, it is so pervasive that it melts into our individual lives; its invisibility as a social condition makes it seem to be just a matter of what is personal, private, and inevitable. Heterosexuality is simultaneously the only "real" form of sexuality, and yet (for that very reason) very difficult to perceive. Heterosexuality is transparent, in the way that a piece of plastic wrap is transparent. Yet, like plastic wrap, it has the ability to hold things in place, to keep things down, and to provide a barrier to prevent other things from coming in contact with that which it seems to be protecting....

The Institution of Heterosexuality

...By the institution of heterosexuality, or what I shall call for short the heterosexual institution, what I mean is the systematized set of social standards, customs, and expected practices which both regulate and restrict romantic and sexual relationships between persons of different sexes in late twentieth-century western culture....

In referring to heterosexuality as an institution, I am rejecting an essentialist or reified view of sexual orientations. Human sexuality is culturally constructed, that is, it is "a social," not [only] a biological phenomenon.[2] There is no reason to suppose that sexual activity and expression are more immune to the effects of enculturation than are other apparently "natural" human activities such as caring for children, or eating. Of course, the fact that sexuality is culturally constructed does not entirely preclude the possibility that some form of sexual expression is innate or "natural," or that we have "biological inclinations" toward some form of sexual activity. But it does imply both that the evidence for such a natural sexuality will be virtually impossible to detect, and that the stronger hypothesis is that there is no such natural sexuality. One cannot even refer to primordial feelings or irresistible passions as natural, since enculturation processes, including the heterosexual institution, help to define what feelings we do and do not, or ought and ought not to have....

...[F]or, whatever our inherent proclivities may or may not be, there is undeniably tremendous social pressure toward heterosexuality. This pressure is a part of the heterosexual institution. Indeed, I wonder why, if heterosexuality is innate, there are so many social voices telling us, ad nauseum, that that is what we should be. These voices include the ideology that surrounds heterosexual romance, dating, and marriage; the mythology of falling in (and out of) heterosexual love, of flings, crushes, affairs, passions, and helpless attractions; the cultural apparatus that purports to assist women to be heterosexually attractive, to be coy, alluring, "sexy," and flirtatious, in order to "find true love" or to "catch a man," and then to maintain his interest once he's caught; the psychotherapies and medical treatments, together with literature ranging from self-help manuals to scholarly treatises, that claim to prescribe the nature and forms of and adjustment to healthy female heterosexuality and the cures or panaceas for its disfunctions; the cultural images, in popular music, paintings, dance crazes, novels, stories, advice columns, films, videos, plays, and advertising, that interpret human sexuality and love exclusively in terms of two by two heterosexual pairing; and the predominant instruments of western social life—the bars, dances, parties, clubs— that recognize only the heterosexual couple. Why is there so much insistence, via these intensive socialization mechanisms, that all women be heterosexual and *learn* to be heterosexual, if that is what we are all naturally inclined to be anyway? So the presence of that strong social insistence upon heterosexuality is, to my mind, one very large piece of evidence that heterosexuality is not innate. But, whether it is or it is not, it is the heterosexual institution that is the subject of discussion in this paper....

The Politics of Heterosexuality

...My question about the object of the heterosexual institution is akin to questions about the object of other institutions such as the state, the family, the educational system, or religion. And one way of starting to answer such questions is by looking to see what individuals or groups of individuals benefit from the institution, what the benefits are, how those benefits are created and distributed, and at whose cost the benefits are acquired.

For the past two decades, radical feminists have offered disturbing answers to these questions. They have argued, first, that the heterosexual institution primarily benefits men, not women; and that it affords men easy sexual gratification and material possession of women, as well as reproduction of themselves and their offspring. Second, these benefits are created and distributed through what Adrienne Rich and others have described as the compulsory nature of heterosexuality: female heterosexual desire and activity must be enforced and coerced, through a myriad of social practices in the family, in culture, in religion, education, and law.[3] This process has been described as the deliberate recruitment of women into active participation in heterosexuality.[4] Mariana Valverde states:

> [G]iven the enormous social weight of heterosexism, one cannot accurately describe heterosexuality as merely a personal preference, as though there were not countless social forces pushing one to be heterosexual. People do not generally choose heterosexuality out of a number of equally valid, equally respected lifestyles. . . . As long as certain choices are punished while others are presented as natural, as the norm, it is naive to describe the com-

plicated process of the construction of conformity and/or deviance by reference to a consumer-type notion of personal preference.[5]

Third, whatever its rewards may be (and they are more than amply celebrated in romantic fiction, films, songs, and everyday mythology) the costs for women of providing the benefits of female heterosexuality for men are of two types: First, violence, degradation, and exploitation of women's bodies and women's sexuality, through such practices as prostitution, rape and other forms of sexual assault, woman battering, pornography, and incest; and second, the deliberately cultivated separation of women from their allies, each other. The operation of the heterosexual institution is a very successful demonstration of the political maxim that to keep a subject group down, it is important to keep its members divided, to prevent them from developing loyalties to each other, and to direct their trust and commitment to members of the oppressor group. In short, the heterosexual institution is the strongest arm and most powerful manifestation of patriarchy; and therefore one of its most important objects is the oppression of women.

As an agent of patriarchal oppression, the heterosexual institution generates a second paradox in heterosexuality: the conjunction of heterosexual privilege and heterosexism. On the one hand, the heterosexual institution grants a certain privilege to heterosexual women that is not possessed by non-heterosexual women. A heterosexual woman is validated for having (or at least wanting) men in her life: the presence of a boyfriend or husband—or even the search for a male partner—confirms that the woman is a "real woman"; that (some) men (sometimes) find her attractive; that, whatever else she might be or feel or think, she is not (so the assumption goes) a "manhater" and therefore beyond the moral pale (even though woman hating is considered a fairly normal part of human civilization). A woman's heterosexuality, visibly demonstrated, shields her from the vicious attacks reserved for non-heterosexual women.

At the same time, heterosexual privilege is coupled with heterosexism, that is, discrimination on grounds of non-heterosexual orientation. Hence, heterosexual privilege has its price: strict conformity to the standards and requirements of heterosexual behaviour and appearance. On the one hand, deviations, even apparent ones, are usually noticed and punished, through verbal and even physical violence, ostracism, and the threatened loss of employment, reputation, peace and safety, home, children, or financial security. In many instances to be a feminist (regardless of one's sexual activities) is to invite heterosexist vituperation; many people, including some feminists as well as non-feminists, are inclined to regard the word "lesbian" as a dangerous term whose application to oneself undermines one's credibility and acceptability. Yet on the other hand, successful conformity to heterosexual standards of behaviour and appearance may also be painful, and necessitate contortions, self-abasement, and continual self observation in order to regulate one's feelings, speech and behaviour to fit the image of the heterosexual woman. Hence, not only are there tremendous costs for the person who is non-heterosexual, but also the heterosexual woman is in a classic double-bind situation: to avoid the damages of non-conformity, she must incur the damages of conformity....

Heterosexuality and Choice

In one of my favourite cartoons, a young woman asks her tough and savvy feminist mother, "Ma, can I be a feminist and still like men?" "Sure," replies the mother, "Just like you can be a vegetarian and like fried chicken." When l recounted this joke in an introduction to feminism course, my young female students were disturbed rather than amused. And this is not surprising. To some, the mother's reply may seem to be a reductio ad absurdum of combining feminism and heterosexuality. A good vegetarian, one might think, just does not like fried chicken; or she certainly *ought* not to like it. And if, in a moment of weakness, she does consume fried chicken, then she is either not a good, moral, consistent vegetarian, or, worse still, she is not a vegetarian at all. So also with the feminist. While many of my students hoped that it would be both logically and empirically possible to be a feminist and still like men, or even lo love them, they also saw considerable tension in being both heterosexual and feminist. Some feminists who love men have expressed both doubt and guilt about the legitimacy of their lives, and some non-heterosexual feminists have encouraged those feelings....

Is, then, a "feminist heterosexuality" possible?[6] To answer that question, it is necessary first to consider the nature of choice. If, as some feminists have argued, heterosexuality in women is coerced, it would seem that no woman chooses to be heterosexual. When there are not several recognized and legitimate options, when there are so many pressures to be heterosexual, and when failure to conform is so heavily punished, it is difficult to regard heterosexuality as the genuine expression of a preference. In fact, as one (heterosexual) woman remarked to me, given the damning indictment of heterosexuality which has been presented by some feminists, it might seem that any woman would be heterosexual only if it were *not* a choice.

But this is not all that can be said about the possibility of choosing heterosexuality. For, first, a single-minded focus on the coercive aspects of the heterosexual institution absolves heterosexual women of any responsibility for their sexual practice in a way that seems inappropriate, at least in the case of feminist women, who have had some opportunities to reflect upon the role of heterosexuality in patriarchal oppression. The idea that all heterosexual women (unlike non-heterosexual women) just can't help themselves and are somehow doomed to love and be attracted to men gives too much weight to the view of women as victims, and too little credit to the idea that women can act and make decisions on their own behalf. Moreover, it implicitly imputes to all heterosexual women a sort of false consciousness. Most such women will not see themselves as victims of coercion. Although they may not think of heterosexual practice as a choice they have made, they also do not necessarily feel like helpless victims of the heterosexual institution. But if no woman can choose to be heterosexual, then all heterosexual women either fail to correctly understand their own sexuality, or they can correctly understand their sexuality only by seeing themselves as helpless victims.

On the contrary, I would argue, it is a mistake to summarily dismiss *all* heterosexual women's experience as a failure to understand their own sexuality. Indeed, it is possible that some such women may

> have actively chosen, rather than fallen into, a life of heterosexual marriage and children...and that in their heterosexual relationships, they have control over their own sexuality and share equally in the enjoyment of and participation in their sexual relationships.[7]

I am not saying here only that some heterosexual women may lead exceptional lives in the sense that their relationship with their man (or men) is experienced as egalitarian and uncoercive; I am saying that there is an important sense in which a woman can genuinely and even sanely choose to be heterosexual, although the conditions and opportunities for that choice may be fairly rare. Beyond the claim that heterosexuality is innate (which seems to be an insuf-ficiently grounded essentialist claim) and the claim that heterosexuality is coerced (which seems true in regard to the heterosexual institution as a whole) there is a third possibility: that heterosexuality is or can be chosen, even—or especially—by feminists.

If it is possible to choose *not* to be heterosexual—and most radical feminists have argued that it is—then it is possible to actively choose to be heterosexual. To some degree, each of us is able to make ourselves into the kinds of sexual beings we are, through a process of interpretation and reinterpretation of our past and present experiences and of our feel-ings and emotions, and through active interaction with other persons, not just passive recep-tivity to their influence. By choosing one's heterosexuality I mean not merely acquiescing in it, or benefiting from heterosexual privilege, but actively taking responsibility for being heterosexual. Admittedly, most apparently heterosexual women never make, and never have an opportunity to make, such an active conscious choice. In what cases, then, might it be correct to say that a woman has genuinely chosen her heterosexuality? The following remark by Charlotte Bunch provides a crucial insight into the paradoxical answer to that question:

> Basically, heterosexuality means men first. That's what it's all about. It assumes that every woman is heterosexual; that every woman is defined by and is the property of men. Her body, her services, her children belong to men. If you don't accept that definition, you're a queer—no matter who you sleep with....[8]

For a heterosexual woman, to start to understand the institution of heterosexuality and the ideology of heterosexism is already to start to leave standard heterosexuality behind. For part of what is customarily meant by the ascription of heterosexuality is its unconscious "perfectly natural" character. Persons who are non-heterosexual never have the luxury of accepting their sexuality in this way....

...Marilyn Frye has pointed out that in discussions of sexual prejudice and discrimination one may often hear a statement such as "I don't think of myself as heterosexual"—pre-sumably said by a person who engages in heterosexual activity.[9] Heterosexuals ordinarily extend to others the somewhat dubious privilege of assuming that everyone is like them; since to be sexual is to be *hetero*sexual, "[t]he question often must be *made* to arise, blatantly and explicitly, before the heterosexual person will consider the thought that one is lesbian or homosexual."[10] On the other hand, such persons often perceive non-heterosexuals as being unnecessarily preoccupied with their sexuality, unable to stop talking about it and "flaunting" it to the world. But, Frye suggests:

> Heterosexual critics of queers' "role-playing" ought to look at themselves in the mirror on their way out for a night on the town to see who's in drag. The answer is, everybody is. Perhaps the main difference between heterosexuals and queers is that when queers go forth in drag, they know they are engaged in theater—they are playing and they know they are play-ing, heterosexuals usually are taking it all perfectly seriously, thinking they are in the real world, thinking they are the real world.[11]

The person whose sexual practice is heterosexual and who honestly and innocently states that she does not think of herself as heterosexual shows herself most clearly to be heterosexual in the standard sense. Paradoxically, then, for a woman to firmly and unam-biguously affirm her heterosexuality may already begin to leave it behind, that is, to cease to be heterosexual in the unthinking unconscious way she once was: she ceases to participate wholeheartedly in the heterosexual institution, and begins the process of disaffiliation from it.[12] When that sort of reflection takes place, I believe, the woman is beginning genuinely to choose her heterosexuality; and she is choosing heterosexual practice without a concomitant endorsement of the heterosexual institution.

Of course, for such a woman, heterosexuality is still something which is enforced, in Rich's sense; that is, persistent cultural pressures strive to ensure her conformity, and deviance from heterosexuality is penalized, often severely. No amount of awareness of the heterosexual institution can, by itself, change the compulsory nature of heterosexuality, and disaffiliation by one woman will not rock the institution.

Nevertheless, that awareness can make a difference, for the previously unawarely heterosexual woman, in the dimensions of her own sexuality: she can begin the process of shaping her own sexuality, by making decisions and choices based upon an understanding of the power and the limits of the heterosexual institution. For she can explore her own personal history and determine how and when her sense of the erotic became separated from women and connected to men.[13] In so doing, she can no longer regard her heterosexual orientation as something over which she has no power or control, as something which just dominates her sexual feelings and practices. Instead, she can distinguish between sexual passion and attraction, on the one hand, and dependence, need, fear, and insecurity on the other. She can become aware of her feelings about women's and men's bodies, and discover whether and/or to what degree she has internalized a socially validated revulsion toward the female body. She can genuinely ask herself whether sexual activity with men is something she wants, or merely something in which she engages. (For, of course, we cannot assume that all women whose sexual practice is heterosexual also enjoy their sexual activities.)

If the answer is no, it is not something she wants, she then has the prospect of choosing to be non-heterosexual. On the other hand, if the answer is yes, she can, in a way, begin to come out as a heterosexual: Not in the heterosexist fashion by which almost all heterosexuals, male and female, ordinarily mark their heterosexuality, but rather in terms of an informed and self-aware feminist evaluation of her life as a heterosexual,[14] renouncing as far as possible the privilege accorded by heterosexuality,[15] and recognizing both the different varieties of oppression non-heterosexuals undergo and also the affinities she shares with non-heterosexual women. She can support non-heterosexual women, validate their relationships, and refuse any longer to be complicitous in the erasures they often undergo. She thereby chooses to be heterosexual as a matter of sexual practice, but not as a matter of the exclusive heterosexist alignment or orientation of her life.

Nevertheless, although it may now seem that heterosexuality can be genuinely chosen by women, for some feminists the question may still remain whether it *ought* to be chosen, whether it is ever a good choice, a choice a feminist could responsibly make. Although some heterosexual feminists pride themselves on their "exceptional" heterosexual relationships, relationships which are, apparently, non-oppressive and egalitarian, still, whatever the particular relationship is like, it nonetheless remains *possible* for the man to take advantage of his potential power. All that stands in the way of his using that power is his own good will, while he is not similarly dependent on the woman's good will. And he still benefits, however indirectly, from male hegemony, and "even the advantages that he is in a position to refuse are waiting for him if he changes his mind."[16]

> [C]hanging our expectations will [not] by itself change the unequal power relationship. It does not, for instance, change the expectations and behaviour of the man. Neither does it remove the institutional power vested in the male in heterosexual relationships.[17]

Moreover, the woman in such a relationship is still giving her energies very largely to a man, consorting intimately with a member of an oppressor group, and hence, indirectly withholding her energies from a woman. For any woman, heterosexual orientation seems to mean putting men, or at least a man, first. And even while rejecting the heterosexual institution, such a woman also still benefits from heterosexual privilege. Thus, no matter how idyllic her relationship, it seems to fail of its very nature to challenge the status quo, and to reinforce the apparent exclusive loyalty of a woman to her man. Together, the two persons in the relationship still appear to participate in and contribute to the perpetuation of an institution which is oppressive of women, particularly of non-heterosexual women and unattached women of any orientation, as well as of heterosexual women in abusive relationships.[18] And of course having an exceptional relationship does not in any way spare a woman from the worst excesses of the heterosexual institution as they may be visited upon her by men other than her immediate sexual partner(s).

The foregoing observations appear to call into question the *legitimacy* of a woman's deliberately deciding to be heterosexual, and I have only very tentative responses to them. The first involves taking seriously the distinction between the institution of heterosexuality on the one hand, and on the other hand, specific heterosexual relations and the persons who become involved in them. This is the same sort of distinction made by Adrienne Rich in her discussion of motherhood. Rich has urged us to recognize that while motherhood itself is an oppressive institution, mothering particular children may be a delightful, worthwhile, valuable human activity.[19] Similarly, while heterosexuality is an oppressive institution, not all heterosexual relationships are valueless as a result. Glimpsing this possibility might also encourage feminists to make a distinction between what could be called the *institution* of manhood on the one hand and individual men on the other....

...[T]his answer, by itself, has of course all the weaknesses of any "individual solution" to problems of oppression. For it depends upon a commitment of the man in the relationship not to avail himself of the power of his position. And so, it must be said, for a woman to actively choose to be heterosexual is an act of faith-faith first of all in the fundamental humanity of the men whom she chooses to love. By actively choosing to be heterosexual, a feminist woman is rejecting the view that male sexuality is inevitably and innately violent and exploitive, and that men are hopelessly fated to engage only in aggressive and oppressive relationships. Although members of the two sexes acquire very different roles, men just as much as women learn to participate in the heterosexual institution. And it is a lesson which men can reject. The heterosexual institution is a social artifact that can be changed, and men themselves may be the allies of women in changing it.

ENDNOTES

1. *Shorter Oxford English Dictionary*, Addenda (1970), my emphasis.

2. Carole S. Vance and Ann Barr Snitow, "Toward a Conversation About Sex in Feminism: A Modest Proposal," *Signs* 10 (1984) 127.

3. Adrienne Rich, "Compulsory Heterosexuality and Lesbian Existence," in Catharine R. Stimpson

and Ethel Spector Person, eds., *Women: Sex and Sexuality* (Chicago: University of Chicago Press 1980) 62-91.

4. Beatrix Campbell, "A Feminist Sexual Politics: Now You See It, Now You Don't," in The Feminist Review, ed., *Sexuality: A Reader* (London: Virago Press 1987) 23.

5. Valverde, 114.

6. The question is taken from the title of Angela Hamblin's article, "Is a Feminist Heterosexuality Possible?," in Sue Cartledge and Joanna Ryan, eds., *Sex and Love: New Thoughts on Old Contradictions* (London: The Women's Press 1983) 105-23.

7. Ann Ferguson, "Patriarchy, Sexual Identity, and the Sexual Revolution," in Nannerl O. Keohane, Michelle Z. Rosaldo, and Barbara C. Geipi, eds., *Feminist Theory: A Critique of Ideology* (Chicago: University of Chicago Press 1982) 159.

8. Charlotte Bunch, "Not For Lesbians Only," in Charlotte Bunch et al., eds., *Building Feminist Theory: Essays From Quest* (New York: Longman 1981) 69.

9. Marilyn Frye, "Lesbian Feminism and the Gay Rights Movement: Another View of Male Supremacy, Another Separatism," in *The Politics of Reality*, 147. Michael Ramberg has pointed out to me that to say "I don't think of myself as heterosexual" could also mean "I am not only heterosexual" or "I will not always be heterosexual."

10. Marilyn Frye, "On Being White: Toward A Feminist Understanding of Race and Race Supremacy," in *The Politics of Reality*, 116, her emphasis.

11. Marilyn Frye, "Sexism," in *The Politics of Reality*, 29, her emphasis.

12. Frye, "On Being White," 127.

13. Marilyn Frye, "A Lesbian Perspective on Women's Studies," in Margaret Cruikshank, ed., *Lesbian Studies: Present and Future* (Old Westbury, NY: The Feminist Press 1982) 197.

14. See Katherine Arnup, "Lesbian Feminist Theory," *Resources For Feminist Research/ Documentation sur la recherche feministe* 12 (March 1983) 55.

15. Amy Gottlieb, "Mothers, Sisters, Lovers, Listen," in Maureen Fitzgerald, Connie Guberman, and Margie Wolfe, eds., *Still Ain't Satisfied! Canadian Feminism Today* (Toronto: Women's Press 1982) 238-9.

16. Sara Ann Ketchum and Christine Pierce, "Separatism and Sexual Relationships," in Sharon Bishop and Marjorie Weinzweig, eds., *Philosophy and Women* (Belmont, CA: Wadsworth 1979) 167, 168.

17. Hamblin, 117.

18. See Leeds Revolutionary Feminist Group, "Political Lesbianism: The Case Against Heterosexuality," in *Love Your Enemy? The Debate Between Heterosexual Feminism and Political Lesbianism* (London: Onlywomen Press 1981) 5-10.

19. Adrienne Rich, *Of Woman Born: Motherhood as Experience and Institution* (New York: Bantam Books 1976).

ISN'T LOVE A GIVEN?

Lee Maracle

I am appalled by the fact that I have been asked on numerous occasions to state my position on the question of women and lesbianism. What really appalls me is that the person thinks that I ought to take a position on the sacred right of women to love and be loved. Isn't love a given?

But if I am appalled at being asked, I am doubly appalled and shamed by the fact that the question needs to be answered. We have not come a long way, baby. The prohibition of women's right to choose is all-encompassing in North America. It is the most deep-seated bias in the history of class society. Racism is recent; patriarchy is old.

Colonization for Native women signifies the absence of beauty, the negation of our sexuality. We are the females of the species: "Native," undesirable, non-sensuous beings that never go away. Our wombs bear fruit but are not sweet. For us intercourse is not marked by white, middle-class, patriarchal dominant-submissive tenderness. It is more a physical release from the pressure and pain of colonialism—mutual rape. Sex becomes one more of the horrors of enslavement, driving us to celibacy. The greater the intellectual paralysis, the more sex is required and the more celibacy is desired.

Does this seem incongruous? Yes, but so are paralysis and movement.

Our life is lived out schizophrenically. Our community desires emancipation. The greater the desire, the more surely do we leap like lemmings into the abyss of alcoholism, violence and suicide. We cannot see our enemy, but we know we must have one. We are standing at the precipice of national destruction.

Women kid themselves that traditionally we were this way or that way. In the name of tradition we consent to all kinds of oppressive behaviour from our men. How often have we stood in a circle, the only female Native, and our contributions to the goings-on are not acknowledged?—as though we were invisible. We are the majority of the membership of almost every Native organization at the lowest level, the least heard and never the leaders. It is not for want of our ability to articulate our goals or lead folks, either. We have been erased from the blackboard of our own lives.

What pains me is that I never saw this before. How often do we read in the newspaper about the death or murder of a Native man, and in the same paper about the victimization of a female Native, as though we were a species of sub-human animal life? A female horse, a female Native, but everyone else gets to be called a man or a woman. (I will qualify this by saying that I do not recall the death of a black woman ever being reported. Gawd, Cj, let's hope it is because no black woman ever died on skid row. But we know different, don't we?)

I have been to hundreds of meetings where the male members demand written submissions from female members while giving themselves the benefit of collective discussion and team development prior to any attempt to write it up, thus helping male speakers to sharpen their ideas. Worse, I have watched the chairperson sit and listen to an endless exchange between two male colleagues while a patient woman holds her hand in the air, waiting to be recognized.

It doesn't stop there. This anti-woman attitude by Native males seems to be reserved for Native women. The really big crime is that our men-folk rise when a white woman walks into the room. Native men go to great lengths to recognize her, and of course, where there is controversy, her word is very often the respected one.

We must and will have women leaders among us. Native women are going to raise the roof and decry the dirty house which patriarchy and racism have built on our backs. But first we must see ourselves as women: powerful, sensuous beings in need of compassion and tenderness.

Please bear with me while I try to unravel the tangled roots this bias against love and choice. We must try to look at why women reject women's rights to choose, and understand why women treat the love between women as some sort of leprous disease that is contagious. I cannot write for women who love women; so far, the only lovers in my life have been men. I can address the feelings of homophobia which preclude our ability to accept lesbians among us.

Homosexuality has been named abnormal. If love were a matter of mathematics, averages and so forth, then that would be a fitting way to look at it, since the majority of us are heterosexual. However, love is a thing of the spirit. It finds its major expression through the heart and body. Since contemporary society is based largely on the economics of class and power, norms and mathematics usually prevail. The nature of love, its spiritual, emotional and physical origins are never considered in the white, male point of view.

When men talk about love between people of the same sex as abnormal, they are not referring to love at all, but to sex. Since we are speaking about love, we will have to ignore the male viewpoint. When women refer to women who love women as unnatural, what they really mean—and this is pathetic—is that it is almost unheard of, and, they agree, it is not allowed. Men loving women is almost unheard of: does its scarceness make it abnormal, unnatural? Any love women can garner for themselves will appear unnatural if women are generally unloved.

Nowhere in the white, male conception or history has love been a motive for getting things done. That is unnatural. They can't see love as the force which could be used to move mountains, change history or judge the actions of people. Love/spirit is seen as a womanly thing and thus is scorned. Women love their sons but men influence, direct and control them. Women love their husbands; men provide for women in exchange for a stable home and conjugal rights and that ever-nurturing womanly love. Men scorn love. We are expected not only to accept this scorn in place of love, but to bear untold suffering at the hands of men. That there is violence in North American homes is taken for granted: "Everyone knocks the wife around once in a while." And does anyone want to admit that very often after a beating on a drunken Friday, a woman is expected to open up to further scorn by moaning and groaning happy sounds while the man who beat her helps himself to her body?

Have you ever heard a man honestly admit that a woman's fear, her surrendering as a result of having been intimidated, excites and arouses him? Rape, ladies and gentlemen, is commonplace in the home. In the home, it is not a crime. What is worse, in our desperate fear of being unloved, a good many women pleas for mercy and accept responsibility for the beating and beg forgiveness for imaginary transgressions. Could this be where men get the idea that women "like it, ask for it" when the subject of rape is discussed?

To be quite frank, my friends, if that is how we feel about ourselves, then it is quite likely that we are going to be vitriolic about women who are not victimized in the same way. A woman who has found love apart from men is seen as a traitor, just as a woman who has found the love of a gentle man is seen undeserving. He, of course, must be a wimp—pussy-whipped. In our society it is loving women that is prohibited.

Sexuality is promoted as the end-all and be-all of womanhood, yet perversely it is often a form of voluntary rape: self-deprecation and the transformation of women into vessels of biological release for men. Our bodies become vessels for male gratification, not the means by which we experience our own sexual wonderment. Any other sexuality is considered abnormal and to be derided. White women spend a lifetime striving for the beauty of large breasts, a small waist, clear skin and that practiced look of submissive stupidity that indicates they will quietly acquiesce to brutal sex.

A woman close to myself and my lover left her husband not too long ago. He beat her on a regular basis for some fifteen years. Between beatings, she told us that he would get on top of her and without ever looking at her, relieve himself of sexual tension. Over the years, she was never sure if, every time he had sex, she had volunteered herself for rape. That is the kind of story I have heard over and over again just too frequently. It is the kind of sex that is going on in too many homes of the nation.

How many women on Saturday night face beer-breathed husbands in the darkness of their rooms, saying, "Please, no," to men who carry on without their consent? They don't scream because they would awaken their own children. Marriages end over a woman's right to say no in her own bedroom. The law says she must allow her husband conjugal rights. This amounts to reducing women's bodies to soft knots in deformed trees.

Divorce alone gives a woman the right to deny her husband rutting privileges on his terms. We certainly cannot go beating our husbands as they do us. We are not usually their physical equals. Before the shame of colonization caught up to us and our men-folk started behaving like lesser white men (the more brutish type), Native men used to respond to flirting from women. Some still do. We used to believe that men responded to women, naturally. We also believed that choice was sacred, and that women were sexually passionate beings. We had better get back to some of the traditions that kept us human.

Nearly every woman in North America, particularly if she is a woman of colour, knows that vacant look of a man who is "getting his rocks off," that phrase unspoken in polite company. Men say it to each other more often than anyone cares to face. The very thing we never bring up in mixed company is that basically men take great pride in referring to sex in just that way: "getting your rocks off," "changing your oil," etc. For those of you who think that feminism or women's liberation has brought about a change in this attitude, just go to a leftist social event and bring up the subject of fucking. There is no way to clear a room more quickly than to ask a man if he "got his rocks off much in high school." He will squirm and deny that he ever put it quite that way. If he merely squirms, like as not he was one of the boys who listened to other boys talking like that on the high school football field and laughed. If he squirms and turns red, he is lying.

Homophobes are quick to vilify love between women because the idea of women loving each other is diametrically opposed to volunteering yourself up for rape. The danger of women who love women, in the decrepit minds of patriarchal males, is that men may be challenged to love women too. No more "getting your rocks off." No more venting your frustrations on your wife. If you've got a problem you'll have to solve it.

What else is there? Some man will have to answer that question. I am not about to help you to be more human; I have enough trouble doing that for myself. It is hard enough to reach inside myself and find my own humanity without carrying your load too.

I didn't always feel that way, as my friend Cj commented:

> *The Servant*
>
> Lee, you make me hysterical
>
>> yes, you do
>>
>> this white man wants to be served
>
> and you trot out your daisy apron
>
> and serve him
>
> in his own language!

Listen to the tone of the women who curse "Damn dyke!" It is filled with resentment and laced with a very mysterious kind of awe. You just know that "Who does she think she is?" follows closely on the heels of that first epithet. If we accept brutal sex as the best we can get, the norm, then naturally we are going to hate women who love women and don't have to put up with the violence that degrades most women in North America. Hate is itself perverse and so of course we get even by referring to dykes and faggots as diseased or mind-sick individuals.

Even the feminist movement has a hard time with love. I have heard it said that lesbianism is "women identifying with women." I admit I am at a loss for words that would embrace the very intimate love between two people who happen to be women. I am at a loss as to how to describe it as anything other than love between Sue and Carol, or whoever they happen to be. But calling it "women identifying with women" feels like a misnomer. Sex, love, intimacy are not about identification, they are bigger, deeper and broader than that. I am at a greater loss to describe the phenomenon here in North America where lesbianism has become a liberating force, as though it were an alternative to love. Having the freedom of love, be loved, determine the nature of the physical expression of that love, the power to name it, govern it, is liberating, whether the person you enjoy this freedom with is the same sex as you or different from you. It is just as powerful to enjoy the freedom to love with a man as it is with a woman. What is lacking for all women is the absolute right to be cherished and the absolute freedom to govern our love's expression.

All of our conversations about women who have women lovers are couched in terminology which escapes my comprehension: homosexuality, heterosexuality, lesbianism, homophobia… I have a very simple and straightforward philosophy, learned from my grandmother: "in the end, granddaughter, our body is the only house we will ever truly own. It is the one thing we truly own… What is more, in the end, command of it will only amount to the sacred right of choice."

From my grandmother's words I understand that there is human sexuality, a biological need for sex, and there is love. (All those who are easily embarrassed can put the book down.) Sex is sex. Sex and love are not the same thing and they are not equal. Sex is the one thing that we can enjoy completely on our own. (I suspect that good many women do just that.) Few other animals have the wherewithal to gratify themselves sexually quite like we do. We do not need a partner or lover to have sex. When you up-grade sex to the level of love, you erase love completely.

When someone says she is a lesbian she is saying that her sexual preference is toward women. She is not saying that she does not like or love men. I have heard from women that so-and-so was bitter about her marriage so she went gay. It sounds so dangerously logical and absurd at the same time. It's as though "gay" were some place women go as opposed to, say, "shopping," and that there are only two attitudes women can have toward men, bitter and not bitter. Those who are bitter go gay and those who are not go shopping. The danger of the logic is that rather than respecting women as beings, it consigns them to going toward men or away from the men. It accepts that men and our attitudes toward them determine our sexual being. We get all tangled up in the web of our own misunderstanding and then ascribe that colossal ignorance to someone else.

Sex can sometimes go hand-in-hand with love. If it does, so much the better. But it is not necessary to be in love to enjoy sex. When I first said that in public, an indignant, uncoupled woman said, "Well, sex and love have to go together." I responded brutally: "Yes, I am going to fuck my mother, my father, my sister, my daughters and all my friends." She didn't mean that.

What she thought is that women cannot have sex without love. Nonsense. I once went to a bar, looked around the room, saw a nice smile with a reasonable male body attached to it, walked over to the table and sat down. After a beer I grabbed hold of the gentleman's arm and let him know that any more of that stuff might impair his performance. To which he responded, "Are you interested in my performance?" I had hold of his hand already so I just nodded. "Why are we still here then?"

We left. The sex was not bad. There was no love, no illusions whatsoever, just the two of us rutting and being gratified.

Sex is good but love is precious. It is our passion and compassion. Love defines our humanity. Focussed, love binds two people together in a relationship that can be lifelong. If we truly loved ourselves as women, the question of who we choose to engage with sexually would be irrelevant. Let us stop elevating rutting to the position of defining our humanity. Despite the pressure of sexually oriented billboards and TV ads, let us stop placing fucking on a plane alongside moral principles which confine women to being sexual vehicles rather than sexual beings.

The result of telling young women that they cannot have sex until they are married and in love is that the shame of desiring sexual gratification will mis-define their lives from pubescence onward. My daughters know, as all girls do, that if they want sex no one can stop them from getting it. It is one of the most available commodities on the market, if you don't mind my cynicism. It is mis-defining their lives around sex that is degrading, and it usually comes from mothers at the behest of fathers. Some mothers, in the interest of equality, try to convince their sons that they should also abstain from sex until marriage.

Pardon my heresy. I taught my children not to confuse love with sex, just as my mother taught me. I wanted them to learn about love from birth on. Surely we do not expect our babies to begin enjoying sex at birth. Is it love then that we seek to deny them? I am convinced that equating sex with love is what is behind all the perversity of child sexual abuse. Some people have taken the bullshit seriously.

The last little note I want to make on sex and sons is a curious one. We are dichotomous in the rearing of our sons and daughters. In order that our sons not grow up to be faggots, we teach them to be macho and to hate girls, loathe all that is gentle, loving and tender. We teach them to pursue sex with girls, who have been taught that sex without love is evil and immoral. We are ashamed when our daughters are discovered to be sexually active, but proud of our sons' sexual proclivity. "He is a real lady-killer." Listen to that: a killer, and we say it with pride.

Love is both a social and personal phenomenon. The dictates of individualism in North America put social love somewhere in the ashcans of the mind. I love men, but I choose one lifelong partner. I love women but sexually I prefer men, so the women I love will be enjoyed at the spiritual level and not the physical. Or the converse, I love men but prefer women sexually, therefore it is men who will be enjoyed on the spiritual level. Sound simple?

Love presumes the right to choose. That means it is no one's business but my own what goes on in my bedroom. Neither my children, my friends, my neighbours nor the world at large has the right to choose my partner. In fact, we don't practise that: our friends and families are notorious for pressuring us into choosing a "suitable" mate. Women influence their children to choose a partner that is compatible with them as mothers. Men extort from their sons the right to direct their choice of a life-long partner. And yet we make loud noises about our freedom of choice compared to people in places like Africa and India, where arranged marriage is still a reality. In practice, there is little choice in partner selection, right here.

The right to choice is as false in this society as the right to be free. Feminists are fond of analyzing the practices of societies in Africa and pointing out the horrible roles of women in such places. Pointing fingers at the oppression of women elsewhere changes not a damn thing for women here.

Before we force women who love women to parade their intimate affection for all to examine, we should talk about rape—the kind that goes on in the home between partners. Before we ask women to justify themselves, we had better talk about why we hate each other. And before we bestow the right on society to judge women who love women, we had better demand that society rectify itself.

The next time a woman asks me what my position on lesbianism is, I am going to ask her what her position is on her husband "getting his rocks off." If she gives me a straight answer, I am going to tell her that I am absolutely opposed to rape and that forcing a woman to accept my definition of who she may love amounts to rape.

To be raped is to be sexually violated. For society to force someone, through shame and ostracism, to comply with love and sex that it defines, is nothing but organized rape. That is what homophobia is all about. Organized rape.

FEMINIST

EJACULATIONS

Shannon Bell

This text is about the ejaculating female body. How did it cum to be that male ejaculation has never been questioned, debated, analyzed; just accepted as a given feature of the male body and male sexuality? An odd question. Yet it is no more odd than what has actually happened to female ejaculation throughout history. There are two questions that have not been raised about female ejaculation, from its discussion by the early Greeks to the most recent. The first is how can women have control over ejaculation; the second, and more recent question, is: why have feminist voices failed to speak about and embrace female ejaculation?...

The expulsion of female fluids during sexual excitement was thought by a number of Greek and Roman doctors and philosophers to be a normal and pleasurable part of female sexuality, the debate evolving around whether female fluids were or were not progenitive. Aristotle argued against the general belief that female seed was produced by women; Hippocrates and Galen were the most well-known of those ancients who argued that women emit seed. Hippocrates (460-377 B.C.) advocated a "two semen" theory of generation based on the belief that both male and female fluids contributed to conception.[1]

In *The Generation of Animals*, Aristotle (384-322 B.C.) argued against the two semen theory of generation and connected female fluid with pleasure:

> Some think that the female contributes semen in coition because the pleasure she experiences is sometimes similar to that of the male, and also is attended by a liquid discharge. But this discharge is not seminal ... the amount of this discharge when it occurs, is sometimes on a different scale from the emission of semen and far exceeds it.[2]

Galen, supporting the theory of female seed, made a distinction between female fluid that was procreative and female fluid that was pleasurable. He identified the source of pleasurable fluid as the female prostate:

> ... the fluid in her prostate ... contributes nothing to the generation of offspring ... it is poured outside when it has done its service ... This liquid not only stimulates ... the sexual act but also is able to give pleasure and moisten the passageway as it escapes. It manifestly flows from women as they experience the greatest pleasure in coitus ...[3]

Western scholars and doctors throughout the Middle Ages remained faithful to

Hippocrates' and Galen's notion of female sperm, which came to them through Arab medicine. In fact, the theory of the female seed survived long after the Middle Ages.[4]...

Female ejaculation also came to be considered a figment of the male imagination. References to female ejaculation can be found in *The Pearl*, a two volume Victorian journal (reprinted in 1968), which contains short stories, poems, ballads, and letters. These and other references in late nineteenth-century and early twentieth-century erotic literature have subsequently come to be marked figments of the male imagination. Steven Marcus, for example, states in *The Other Victorians: A Study of Sexuality and Pornography in Mid-Nineteenth Century England* (1966) that in pornographic writings:

> [T]here is first the ubiquitous projection of the male sexual fantasy onto the female response—the female response being imagined as identical with the male ... and there is the usual accompanying fantasy that they ejaculate during orgasm.[5]...

Despite the descriptions of female ejaculation in medical, anthropological, philosophical, and popular literature from time to time throughout Western history, female ejaculation has been practically ignored until the late 1970s and 1980s.

De-eroticizing Female Pleasure: Female Ejaculation and Sexual Science

The clearest and most complete description of the physiological process and anatomical structure of female ejaculation was published in *The International Journal of Sexology* (1950) by Grafenberg, a German obstetrician and gynecologist. In his "own experience of numerous women," Grafenberg observed that:

> An erotic zone always could be demonstrated on the anterior wall of the vagina along the course of the urethra ... Analogous to the male urethra, the female urethra also seems to be surrounded by erectile tissues ... In the course of sexual stimulation, the female urethra begins to enlarge and can be felt easily. It swells out greatly at the end of orgasm ... Occasionally the production of fluids is ... profuse ... If there is the opportunity to observe ... one can see that large quantities of a clear transparent fluid are expelled out of the urethra in gushes ...[6]

Despite Grafenberg's clear description, female ejaculation was ignored and/or denied by the dominant scientific discourses defining female sexuality from 1950-1978. Kinsey, Pomeroy, and Martin (1953), writing three years after Grafenberg, mention female ejaculation only to deny its existence.[7] Masters and Johnson (1966) note that "female ejaculation is an erroneous but widespread concept."[8] As recently as 1982, Masters, Johnson, and Kolondy continue to refer to female ejaculation as "an erroneous belief"[9] and suggest that the fluid could be the result of "urinary stress incontinence."[10]

Grafenberg's analysis remained in obscurity until Sevely and Bennett reintroduced it into sexological discourse in their review of the literature on female ejaculation, "Concerning Female Ejaculation and the Female Prostate" (1978) published in *The Journal of Sex Research*. Their review originated the contemporary debate among sex researchers, gynecologists, urologists, and sex therapists regarding the existence of female ejaculate and its source. This debate has focused on three areas of concern: efforts to prove that women do or do not ejaculate; analysis of the chemical composition of ejaculate to determine whether or not it is urine; and, the potential of ejaculation for constructing a new theory of sexuality....

Male sexologists still have an investment, perhaps an investment in holding onto asexually privileged position where sexual activities revolve around their "spending" or "withholding" of ejaculate, in questioning whether women can ejaculate. Female ejaculation is, for some, a matter of belief, rather than a physiological response. Alzate, who conducted a clinical study of 27 women, disregarded what he termed a subject's "emphatic" affirmation that she often ejaculated and discounted his recorded observation of her doing so, to claim that "the ignorance and/or confusion still prevalent among women about the anatomy and physiology of their sexual organs may make them mistake either vaginal lubrication or stress urinary incontinence for an 'ejaculation.'"[11] There is a recurrent tendency for researchers to disregard, reinterpret, and overwrite women's subjective descriptions of ejaculation. Sex researchers Davidson, Darling, and Conway-Welch, in the most extensive social survey of a female population regarding their experience of ejaculation (1289 women responded), state that anecdotal data suggests that the physiological sensations associated with the expulsion of fluid are very similar to those physiological sensations associated with voiding of urine.[12] I was presenting a paper in a session on "Female Ejaculation" at the World Congress of Sexology in December 1989 in Caracas, Venezuela. I discussed representations of female ejaculation and showed slides of the ejaculating female body; a Spanish medical team showed vaginal photographs of the glands and ducts surrounding a woman's urethral. An older hegemonic male member of the audience, publicly contended that "we have just seen pictures of this fluid shooting out of the female body and slides of its location but he would believe women ejaculated if one pathologist declared that they did."…

Female ejaculation was legitimated and popularized for the first time in *The G Spot and Other Recent Discoveries About Female Sexuality* (1982). A large portion of the chapter "Female Ejaculation" is composed of self-reports from, and case vignettes of, female ejaculators. Some of the women had been diagnosed by their companions and by the medical profession as suffering from urinary incontinence. Other women depicted the act of ejaculation as an experience of pleasure and a regular part of their sexuality. The authors of *The G-Spot* suggest that because "female ejaculate can only serve one purpose: pleasure"[13] and that women have historically been absented from the realm of pleasure, the knowledge of ejaculation has not been accepted and socially appropriated by professionals or the public.

Josephine Sevely, *Eve's Secrets: A New Theory of Female Sexuality* (1987), has provided the most comprehensive study of female ejaculation. Her theory not only sexualizes the urethra but also emphasizes the simultaneous involvement of the clitoris, urethra, and vagina, which function as a single integrated sexual organ. The implications of Sevely's theory are threefold. First, a woman's sexual organ ceases to be fragmented into clitoris and vagina: it is an integrated whole composed of clitoris, urethra, and vagina. Second, this integrated whole is a multiplicity "full of things," all alive with sensation. The [w]hole is an active w[hole]; no more clitoral activity versus vaginal passivity. Third, the "anatomical difference" between male and female genitals upon which phallocentric culture and society is premised is challenged by an alternative construction of anatomical symmetry. Both male and female bodies have prostate gland structures and both have the potential to ejaculate fluids during sexual stimulation. The female body, free from the limiting economy of the male psyche-libido, reveals physiological difference within anatomical symmetry. The female body can ejaculate fluid from thirty-one ducts; with stimulation can ejaculate repeatedly; can ejaculate more fluid than the male body; and, can enjoy a plurality of genital pleasure sites: the clitoris, urethra, vagina, the vaginal entrance, the roof of the vagina, the bottom of the vagina, and the cervix.

Feminism and Ejaculation

The ejaculating female body has not acquired much of a feminist voice nor has it been appropriated by feminist discourse. What is the reason for this lacuna in feminist scholarship and for the silencing of the ejaculating female subject? It has to do with the fact that the questions posed, and the basic assumptions about female sexuality, are overwhelmingly premised on the difference between female and male bodies: "the most visible difference between men and women, and the only one we know for sure to be permanent ... is ... the difference in body."[14] The most important primary differences have been that women have the ability to give birth and men ejaculate. Women's reproductive ability has been emphasized as a central metaphor in feminist critiques of patriarchal texts and has been theorized into a "philosophy of birth" and an economy of (re)production. Feminists, in their efforts to revalorize the female body usually devalued in phallocentric discourse, have privileged some form of the mother-body as the source of écriture féminine: writing that evokes women's power as women's bodily experience. Mary O'Brien, for example, in *The Politics of Reproduction* (1981), provides a feminist model for interpreting masculinist political philosophy. O'Brien begins her project by posing the question: "Where does feminist theory start?" She replies: "Within the process of human reproduction. Of that process, sexuality is but a part."[15] O'Brien names her reappropriation and theorization of the mother-body as a "philosophy of birth." Luce Irigaray writes that "historically the properties of fluids have been abandoned to the feminine."[16] The fluids, reappropriated in feminine sexual discourse and theorized by French feminist philosophers such as Luce Irigaray and Julia Kristeva, have been the fluids of the mother-body: fluids of the womb, birth fluids, menstrual blood, milk: fluids that flow. Ejaculate—fluid that shoots, fluid that sprays—has been given over to the male body. To accept female ejaculate and female ejaculation one has to accept the sameness of male and female bodies.

Contemporary feminism, however, has rejected sameness as being defined from the perspective of the male body, as conformity with the masculine model. To avoid identification with a male phenomenon, women have suggested that the term "ejaculation" should not be used. I argue that the term should be kept while using the distinctive characteristics of female ejaculate to redefine and rewrite the meaning of the term: female ejaculate is not "spent"; with stimulation one can ejaculate repeatedly; and, a woman in control of ejaculation may ejaculate enormous quantities.

The second factor in feminists' failure to embrace ejaculation as a powerful body experience is their understandable concern regarding possible male control over female ejaculation in the context of a masculinist and heterosexual script in which ejaculation is presented as something men do to women's bodies. The Boston Women's Health Collective, editors of *Our Bodies, Our Selves* (1984), warn women that the G-Spot and female ejaculation could be "used to re-instate so-called 'vaginal' orgasms as superior" and could "becom[e] a new source of pressure" to perform.[17] Ehrenreich, Hess and Jacobs, in *Re-making Love. The Feminization of Sex* (1986) misconstrue the emphasis in *The G-Spot* on the urethra as a return to Freud's primacy of the mature vaginal orgasm. Ehrenreich et al, argues that Chapter Four of the *G-Spot*, "The Importance of Healthy Pelvic Muscles," which links strong pubococcygeus muscles (PC muscles) with ejaculation and G-Spot orgasms and provides case vignettes of women who discuss the merits of strengthening their PC muscles, encourages women to strengthen "the muscles that hold the penis in place."[18] In my experience these muscles do not in fact hold the penis in place; rather, they push it out and spray the ejaculate. The penis (if one is around) may then re-enter until the glands and ducts surrounding the urethra become so enlarged in size through stimulation that they expel the penis and spray again. Ehrenreich et al, also claim that "the acrobatics necessary to achieve the 'new' orgasm privilege male-dominant sexual positions."[19] This criticism is odd since Ladas et al. provide case vignettes of ejaculation in many different positions: woman on top, rear entry, man on top, partner using his/her hand, and woman using her own hand. They provide case histories from lesbians and note that "preliminary reports indicate that there may be a higher incidence of female ejaculation in the lesbian population than there is among heterosexual women."[20]

Female ejaculation is about power over one's own body. For many women who do experience ejaculation, however, it is a passive experience—something that happens, not a capacity and process they control. If feminists are going to appropriate and reclaim the female body, it is very important that women provide feminist scripts of the ejaculating body in *control* of ejaculation....

ENDNOTES

1. Hippocrates, *De geniture*, eds. and trans. W.C. Lyons and J.N. Hattock, (Cambridge: Pembrooke Press, 1978), chap. 6 (74-78).

2. Aristotle, *De Generation Animalium*, trans. Arthur Platt, in *The Complete Works of Aristotle*, eds. J.A. Smith and W.D. Ross, (Oxford: The Claredon Press, 1912), II 728a.

3. Cited in Josephine Sevely, *Eve's Secrets: A New Theory of Female Sexuality*, (New York: Random House, 1987), 51.

4. Danielle Jacquart and Claude Thomasset, *Sexuality and Medicine in the Middle Ages*, trans. Matthew Adamson, (Great Britain: Polity Press, 1988), 66-74.

5. Steven Marcus, *The Other Victorians: A Study of Sexuality and Pornography in Mid-Nineteenth Century England*, (New York: Basic Books, 1966), 194.

6. Cited in Sevely, 85-6.

7. Alfred J. Kinsey, Wardell B. Pomeroy, and Clyde E. Martin, *Sexual Behavior in the Human Female*, (Philadelphia: W.B. Saunders Co., 1953), 634-5.

8. William H. Masters and Virginia E. Johnson, *Human Sexual Response*, (Boston: Little Brown, 1966), 135.

9. William R. Masters, Virginia E. Johnson, and R.C. Kolodny, *Masters and Johnson on Sex and Human Loving*, (Boston: Little, Brown, 1982), 69.

10. Ibid., 70.

11. Heli Alzate, "Vaginal Eroticism: A Replication Study," *Archives of Sexual Behavior* 14 (1985): 530-33 and Heli Alzate and Zwi Hoch, "The 'G-Spot' and 'Female Ejaculation': A Current Appraisal," *Journal of Sex and Marital Therapy* 12 (1986), 217.

12. J.K. Davidson, Sr., C.A. Darling, and C. Conway-Welch, "The Role of the Grafenberg Spot and Female Ejaculation in the Female Orgasmic Response: An Empirical Analysis," *The Journal of Sex and Marital Therapy* 15 (1989), 120.

13. Ladas et al, 79.

14. Elaine Showalter, "Feminist Criticism in the Wilderness," *The New Feminist Criticism: Essays*

on Women, Literature and Theory, ed. Elaine Showalter, (New York: Pantheon Books, 1985), 252.

15. Mary O'Brien, *The Politics of Reproduction*, (London: Routledge Kegan Paul, 1981).

16. Luce Irigaray, *This Sex Which is Not One*, (New York: Cornell Press, 1985), 116.

17. The Boston Women's Health Collective, *Our Bodies, Our Selves*, (New York: Simon & Schuster, Inc., 1984), 171.

18. Barbara Ehrenreich, Elizabeth Hess, and Gloria Jacobs, *Re-Making Love. The Feminization of Sex*, (New York: Anchor Press, 1986), 158.

19. Ibid., 184.

20. Ladas et al, 84.

CRITICAL IDENTITIES: RETHINKING FEMINISM THROUGH TRANSGENDER POLITICS

Eleanor MacDonald

Introduction

Feminist theorists have responded to the emerging political movement of transgendered people and the corresponding theorization of transgendered identities in a variety of ways, all of them disquieting.[1] By turns, feminists have denounced transgendered people as dangerous to feminism, depoliticized the experiences of transgendered people, or celebrated the transgendered identity as emblematic of the subversive character of feminist postmodern theory. None of these positions is adequate for the real challenges that transgendered people offer to the categories of both identity-based and postmodern feminist theorizing.

All too frequently feminism's relationship to transgender politics has been expressed as one of direct hostility and exclusion. The classic (and until quite recently, nearly the exclusive) feminist statement on the issue of transsexualism was Janice Raymond's book, *Transsexual Empire: The Making of the She-Male*. Raymond's dramatic opposition of feminism to transgendered people and politics is made clear throughout; it is perhaps most evident when she likens the transsexual woman to a rapist:

> All transsexuals rape women's bodies by reducing the real female form to an artifact, appropriating this body for themselves. However, the transsexually constructed lesbian-feminist violates women's sexuality and spirit, as well. Rape, although it is usually done by force, can also be accomplished by deception. (1979, 104)

This reasoning has regularly been used to justify the exclusion of transgendered women, from women-only services, events, gatherings.[2] And, while transgendered women are portrayed as utilizing a Trojan Horse style of infiltration and violation of the "safe space" of the women's community, transgendered men are, in turn, often treated as dupes of the patriarchy and as traitors to their sex, as women who might have been "sisters in the struggle," but who instead joined the ranks of (presumably always anti-feminist) men. Raymond, in fact, treats transgendered men not as choosing their transition, but as having it inflicted upon them as patriarchy's way of destroying women who challenge femininity....

While Raymond's position seems extreme in its gender determinism, it reflects a deep ambivalence in the relationship of feminism to the question of gender. We find simultaneously the contradictory positions that gender is an inherently patriarchal structure that women can, indeed must, defeat to transcend, and that gendered femininity is itself an expression of feminism. This latter position is expressed in terms of, for example, the belief in an inherent strength, spirituality, sexuality, and/or creativity that women can draw upon. Gender is viewed as mutable and socially constructed while, in the same breath, it is contradictorily presented as determined immutably by one's assigned sex at birth and upbringing. No thought is given to the unique perspectives that transgendered people might have to contribute to the understanding of gender experience, gender relations or of women's oppression.

Perhaps the more common, but less vocal attitude of most feminists has been to sidestep transgender issues as inherently apolitical. The assumption has been, by feminists and by society more generally, that transsexualism is a medical or psychiatric problem, and therefore the private concern of rare individuals. Again, with this attitude, transgender experience is effectively eliminated from political concern; the gender concerns raised by transgendered individuals are not incorporated into feminist theories of gender at all.[3]

More recently, postmodern feminist theory has begun to embrace transgender as an expression of diversity and difference, and as playing a strategic role in breaking down the binary dualisms of Western metaphysical thought. The new pluralist celebration of diversity is certainly vastly preferable to the hostility or dismissiveness expressed in other models of feminism. Nevertheless, it may run the same risks as liberal tolerance of difference, which in the end does little to recognize the specificity of particular subject positions. In its promotion of transgender identity as a transcendence of identity, postmodern theory assimilates transgender to its own intellectual project through presenting transgendered experience as chimera, play, performance or strategy. It does so at the expense of investigating the actual lives, political demands, or feelings expressed by transgendered people of having an identity that is often experienced as "authentic" or "integral" and that is considered to be neither "chosen" originally nor "performed" strategically....

It is my argument that transgender politics and transgendered people's experiences must be taken seriously by both more traditional gender identity-based feminism and contemporary postmodern feminism. In addressing transgender politics' challenge to the boundaries of gender identity, traditional feminist approaches need to critique their own exclusionary practices, and challenge their own understanding of gender and sexuality. In the direct and visceral terms in which transgendered people experience the boundaries and instability of identity that are celebrated in the postmodern feminist theoretical approach, the latter must take seriously the demand for a more programmatic agenda for postmodern feminist thought.

In what follows, my arguments are based on the insights that may be gained from examining transgender as an "identity." It is my hope that out of examining the distinctive contributions of transgender identity to identity politics, new grounds may be found for alliances among varied social movements. These grounds would be based not in identity as much as in understanding and in a recognition of the power of exclusion.

Transgender Identity Politics

The growth of new social movements, organized around the salient experiences of oppression of different identity groups, has engendered a corresponding intellectual study of identities, of how we come to acquire an identity, of what an identity means, and of how identities become socially recognized, defined, and politicized. Each identity-based social movement has made unique contributions to these debates.

The transgender political movement has only recently gained public recognition. Alongside this newfound political status, new ways of conceptualizing and defining what transgender means are also emerging. And, as with other identity-based movements, transgender politics is providing singular challenges to how we think about identities and their politicization. In what follows, I argue that what transgender identity specifically problematizes is identity itself. Transgender identity is about identity experienced as problematic; the experience of being transgender problematizes the relationship of the self to the body, and the self to others. In doing so, it also problematizes issues of identity boundaries, stability and coherence.

I also intend that, as with the study of other identity groups, the insights that can be gained from an exploration of transgender identity do not apply only to transgendered people, but can be extended to other identities as well.

Identity as Problem

The term "transgender" has only very recently come into popular and political use, and its definition is critical to the politics that it engenders. The term, as I use it, includes all those people whose internally felt sense of core gender identity does not correspond to their assigned sex at birth or in which they were raised. This includes people who identify with the gender other than that assigned at birth as well as those who do not identify with any gender at all. It includes those who present themselves in their originally assigned sex, as well as those who present themselves in the sex which coheres with their actual identity (and therefore may include non- and pre- and post-operative transsexual people) and those who move back and forth between self-presentation as women and as men. I also includes those whose gender presentation is ambiguous in ways which don't permit them to present as either gendered male or female. In this usage, the term does not include those who are both physically and emotionally comfortable in their assigned sex and gender, even while they are challenging the social meanings that have been traditionally assigned to that sex and gender. What is radical, then, to the definition of "transgender" is its origin in problem, a disjunction between one's feelings of who one is or is not, and how one is (or has once been) perceived, recognized, and understood by others.

Gender and sex are both complex terms, whose complexity is not acknowledged in their daily usage. Sex includes, at a minimum, chromosomal sex, gonadal sex, hormonal sex, internal reproductive organs, external genitals, assigned sex, and gender role (Natal 1996, 14). Much scientific evidence not only points to the non-congruence of all these variables in all cases, but also to their non-binary nature. Despite this, it is customary to presume the presence of two and only two fully congruent and "opposite" sexes, male and female. Moreover, external genitalia remain the primary factor in attributing sex (O'Donovan, cited in Natal, 14; Kessler in Nelson and Robinson 1995, 13).

Gender, in turn, is expected to cohere unproblematically with sex. But gender too involves a rich complex of variables, including: gender assignment (which generally takes place at birth, after which it is considered immutable); roles (specific social activities which are assigned masculine and feminine status); identity (one's internally felt or experienced sense of being either male or female); status (social rank which is accorded to males or females or those performing masculine or feminine roles); relations (socially appropriate behaviours evinced by males or females in relation to other males and females); attribution (perception by others of one's sex that takes place in all social interaction); behaviour (use of the gestures, mannerisms, language, clothing, comportment considered appropriate to one's biological sex); and biology (genetic or sexual-physical predeterminants of any of the above).

What transgender identity is about is identity as the incoherence of these elements, as the felt incoherence of self and body; it is identity as non-identity of the self, according to one of the principle means by which the coherence of the self is supposed to be unconsciously achieved. For some transgendered people, the experience of a non-coherence of body and self is a permanent condition; for others, this coherence is achieved a conscious, very often medicalized process.

Much of what is unique about transgender identity, as an identity, is this reference to the identity as, in itself, problematic, as based in the profound sense of gender "dysphoria," of a disruption between one's sense of one's own gender and one's body. It is therefore simultaneously a problem of the relationship of self to self (mind/body) and self to others (the individual to culture, society, etc.) Transgender politics points to the refusal of this problem to be exclusively resolved either at the individual level or at the societal level.

The individual solutions (self-denial, passing, surgical sex re-assignment) are, to many, unacceptable. As Kate Bornstein remarks, regarding the advice given to post-operative transsexuals to "invent" a new childhood, and a new past for oneself, and to destroy evidence of one's previous sex: "transsexuality is the only condition for which the therapy is to lie" (1994, 62). Non-recognition, or discontinuity between one's felt self and the perception of others merely continues in a new guise. These solutions also ignore the voices of those who feel that their gender cannot be recognized within the binary categories of male and female, and who wish to create a space for recognition of themselves as transgender, third sex, two-spirited, intersex, epicene, or androgyne.[4]

While individual solutions seem inadequate in their repetition of the denial, incoherence, or intransigence of the transgender condition, solutions at the societal level are frankly insensitive to the specific needs of transgendered people, and not infrequently utopian in their goals. The desire to move to a point where "gender doesn't matter," either through the abolition of gender (one of the goals of many versions of feminist politics), or through the proliferation of gender in performance and play (the postmodern feminist take on the problem) has wide appeal and credibility (including within the transgendered community), but too often is used as an excuse either to criticize or deny the experiences of transgendered people.

In light of this, I must remark upon how the pronouncement that "gender shouldn't matter" is used by many feminists to portray transgendered people as inherently gender conformists, and consequently anti-feminist in their politics. First, it is necessary to acknowledge that the use (both playful and serious) of stereotypes and gender conformity may be a very real pleasure for those who have long desired recognition in their gender. And, aside from the strong likelihood that some transgendered people will feel relief and pleasure in a new gender role, this unfair criticism serves to stereotype transgendered people and denies the existence of those—and they are many—who also challenge those stereotypes. As well, it should be emphasized that stereotypically gendered behaviour and attitudes are often a prerequisite for being taken seriously as transgendered, especially by the medical community, on whom transgendered people are entirely reliant for receiving hormones or surgery. And, further to all of this, an appropriate rejoinder to the critic might be, simply, that one way of being gender-nonconformist is to refuse to accept the mandatory congruence of sex and gender.

Further to this, there has been insufficient recognition among feminists who do not experience a core sense of gender-incongruity, of their own participation in maintaining a rigid binary sex/gender system. With the goal of ending women's oppression, feminists have themselves often maintained gender systems, albeit "alternative" ones, designed to stand in direct opposition to those of the dominant society. These are manifest throughout feminist writing and organizing. One sees them in the continued assignment of femininity and masculinity to specific behaviours, in the differential treatment of women and men, in the celebration of specific aspects of femininity (often, and justifiably, to redress the common social repudiation of these human qualities and characteristics by mainstream society). Similarly, the gay and lesbian communities, while clearly challenging the heterosexual norms that are corollary to the sex/gender system, and while often creating welcoming space for androgynous people, for passing men and women, and for a range of gender expression, have nonetheless not questioned deeply what it means to be attracted to a particular "sex." Far too often, transgendered people are criticized for changing or desiring to change their sex, for not having "transcended" the link of body to gender expressed as "sex," by others who readily and comfortably desire a "sex," an embodied gender. From both the feminist and the gay and lesbian communities, the critique of traditional gender systems has stayed at the level of criticizing the attribution of specific gender behaviours to specific sexes, and not moved beyond this to consider the implications of having a gender at the level of personal identity. It needs to be said that few among the non-transgendered have pondered for long the luxury of living in a body that feels at ease and consonant with the self.

The criticism that transgendered people have too great an investment in gender finds a strong opponent in the now postmodern celebration of transgender as transcending gender. But this postmodern reading of transgender, too, unfortunately effaces much of the transgender experience. When Kate Bornstein (1994), a transgender performance artist, comments in distinctly postmodern tones on the fluidity she has found in her expression of identity, she writes:

> I love the idea of being without an identity, it gives me a lot of room to play around; but it makes me dizzy, having nowhere to hang my hat. When I get too tired of not having an identity, I take one on: it doesn't really matter what identity I take on, as long as it's recognizable. I can be a writer, a lover, a confidante, a femme, a top, or a woman. I retreat into definition as a way of demarcating my space, a way of saying "Step back, I'm getting crowded here." (39)

Yet what is significant about Bornstein's list of chosen identities is its limitations, as much as its freedom. Despite what she says, it does indeed matter to her what identity she takes on; it matters that it be "recognizable."…

Bornstein is among the most postmodern-influenced of current transgender activists. This is evident in her discussion of the fluidity of identity, the problem of categorization. And yet even in this celebration of difference and non-identity, Bornstein's work reflects something which the postmodern advocation of the proliferation of all identities and all categories cannot explain—the sense of authenticity of a particular identity or closed set of identities. Bornstein is representative of, as Califia argues, the more recent political transgender activists who have been influenced by feminism, postmodernism, and sexual liberation politics. So it is striking the degree to which even while arguing for postmodern post-identity, she continues to adhere to the "truth" of certain experiences and identities.

Much of what is published about transgender identity takes autobiographical form, and throughout these autobiographies, the authors deal with the problem of how to describe to others the need for an integrated and authentic sense of self and the relief that comes through attaining this in sex reassignment. To take only one example, Max Wolf Valerio explains:

> I think most people don't understand how transsexuals feel about our original biological selves. Everyone experiences this discontinuity between identity and body slightly differently, but there's a commonality. For me, it wasn't so much that I hated my body or hated being a woman. First of all, even as I say that I was a woman, that feels as though somehow, it really wasn't true. At some point, I realized that my deepest, most abiding sense of myself was male. When I saw that there was an alternative, that the hormones really work, I knew that I would rather live my life as a man. As a man, a more integrated sense of myself began to emerge. (Feinberg 1996, 142)

Perhaps, in responding to the postmodern challenge to the fixity or stability of identity, what we discover is that there is a range of identities within which one can "manoeuvre" but the transgender experience suggests that there are limitations, too, on one's sense of who one is, outside of which one feels oneself harmed, mis-recognized, mis-taken. To extend this challenge beyond transgender is to suggest to other identity politics movements that it is still necessary to discover the problematic aspect of an identity that is too readily overlooked in the claiming of, for example, lesbian, gay or bisexual pride, or of feminist consciousness.

Identity As Contested

Transgendered people's experience of gender identity as inherently problematic is compounded by the experience of it as both contested and contestable. One's gender is, of course, not one's own decision. Typically assigned at birth, it is, happily, one supposes, experienced by most people as unproblematic. When issues arise over it, they usually regard the content socially accorded to gender (of socially appropriate femininity or masculinity, for example, and these in turn are often further specified within class or race dynamics), not the assignment of gender itself. Feminists, for example, and rightly, struggle over changing the meaning of what it is to be a woman, expanding the boundaries of possibilities to allow for greater freedom in women's (and men's) lives. Transgender politics, on the other hand, is often about how the categories of, and the boundary between, male and female, or masculine and feminine, are set at all.

There are at least two sites in which the contestation over transgender identity takes place. The more obvious is, of course, the entire social sphere of the transgendered person's life. Virtually no social spaces exist in which the existence of transgendered people is recognized and accepted. The lesbian, gay and bisexual movement protests the presumption of heterosexuality; the transgender movement protests the even more common presumption of sex/gender identity congruity. For transgendered people, to "come out" as transgendered means frequently to have one's gender identity disputed, contested, disbelieved, or fully denied. Having to prove to others that you really are who you say you are is a task which might appear surreal if it weren't also, for many transgendered people, quotidian.

Transgendered people are faced with a limited range of options for living with an identity that is both felt within as problematic and continuously contested by the society without. Many choose medical intervention and surgical sex reassignment. But doing so requires confronting another site in which one's transgender identity is contested, in which further "proof" is required. Transgender identity is eligible for medical intervention in accordance with its status as a psychiatric condition, currently listed as "gender dysphoria" for which the diagnosis is based on a fixed set of diagnostic criteria. Transgendered people seeking sex reassignment must prove to a committee of medical authorities that they indeed meet these criteria. More than one author has noted the conservative effect of these measures—individuals seeking medical assistance are usually both aware of, and fully prepared to conform to whatever criteria they understand will provide them with the medical diagnosis needed for sex-reassignment surgery and hormone treatment to be offered. Thus, the diagnostic tools are repeatedly confirmed in this process.

Aside from the considerable social stigma of claiming an identity which is also considered a psychiatric disorder, the medicalization of transgendered people also may be experienced as disempowering; one's own identity can be disputed or overturned by a panel of medical personnel. *The Standards of Care: The Hormonal and Surgical Sex Reassignment of Gender Dysphoria Persons*[5] also leaves little room for individual variations or preferences of transgendered people in determining the course of any medical assistance they may seek. A rigid binary gender system remains the basis for evaluating and reassigning sex.

Despite all the difficulties presented in the medical treatment of transgendered people, there is very real concern and debate in the transgendered community that the demedicalization of "gender dysphoria" would put an end to all insurance coverage of drugs or surgery, effectively putting surgical options out of reach for all but the most wealthy. Ironically, the very site of contestation of an identity also serves societally, in many respects, as its validation and support.

Identity As Liminal

Postmodern theory has introduced the concept of "liminality" as critical to our understanding of identities. What is liminal is on the threshold, the edge, or the border, the "no-man's" land that exists in places between borders, where no rules hold, where contests over authority sometimes take place. The concept of the liminal is valuable for critical thinking, for asking questions about what establishes the boundary limits of the categories we use, and for considering how these categories can be destabilized, or how these boundaries are transgressed. At times, however, postmodern theorists risk romanticizing this concept of liminality.

Transgender identity is useful in giving flesh to this postmodern conceptualization of "liminality" in identity. Because transgender identity is experienced as exclusion from or harm by the existing categories of "gender," it provokes the question of how those categories are established. How are they maintained? How are the boundaries of what is normal "policed?" How can they be transgressed? Transgendered people often experience, and frequently painfully so, living on these borders, and the costs of transgressing them.

To the degree that the categories themselves, and the social investment in maintaining them, are politicized, transgender politics raise questions of how one disrupts and destabilizes existing category boundaries. In doing so, transgender politics directly challenge the stabilization of category boundaries that has become part of the quest of many other identity-based movements (i.e. who qualifies as gay or lesbian, who can be a feminist, who is a woman, etc.)

The category of "transgender" also rapidly proliferates in interesting ways suggesting that there may be unique aspects to the creation of any sort of solidarity within the transgendered movement. Consider the range of MTF, FTM, non-op, pre-op, post-op, third sex, androgyne, epicene, two-spirited, and intersexed identities. When one considers as well that transgendered people frequently go through transitions which move them from one of these categories into another, one gets a sense too of the fluidity of identifications that transgendered people may experience. Transgendered people may also experience leaving the identity of "transgendered" behind, as they, through surgery or hormones, come to experience a sense of mind/body and societal/self congruity more typical of the non-transgendered. Add to this that all of the categories are, of course, made infinitely more complex by the necessary intersection of all transgendered identities with the full range of class, race, sexual orientation, cultural and other identities (and that all of these have an effect on how gender, and with it, transgender, will be experienced).

Conclusions

...Transgender politics is not (and, I would argue, cannot be) based on identities that are experienced as solid, permanent, exclusionary, whole. Rather it is in the nature of the identity itself to be problematic, contested, transgressive, and liminal....

To a very large degree, these aspects of transgender identity have appeared to align it most closely with postmodern theory in its celebration of fluidity, dispersal, liminality, and so forth. But I argue that what characterizes transgender identity can also serve to indicate some of the limitations of the postmodern theoretical approach. Too often postmodern approaches validate difference at a linguistic level without considering the lived experience of difference. Outside of concrete proposals for social change, such an approach seriously risks minimizing the experience of really living on borderlines, of the incoherence that often accompanies shifts in identity, of the difficulty in establishing a self that can withstand its contestation, and thus risk taking an attitude of indifference or complacency toward these experiences. To postmodern theory, transgender argues, then, for the reality of difference, and the need to investigate the social structures which enforce sex/gender identity congruity and stability at every level.

To identity-based feminist theory, on the other hand, transgender politics argues for a destabilization of the categories of woman and man, of lesbian, gay and bisexuals. Instead, I argue that what transgendered identity politics generates is new motivation to move beyond identity as the basis of social movement politics and into new exploration of the ethical bases of alliances and formation of communities. As well, and critically, it demands an exploration of the structural and systemic production of "contested" and "liminal" sites within every political community, including feminism, and the responsibility for breaking down the exclusionary and limiting effects that these boundaries have on us all.

ENDNOTES

1. The term "transgender" was first brought into use by Virginia Prince in her book, *The Transvestite and his Wife*. While the term has the narrower definition (intended by Prince) of non-operative transsexual, I have chosen, following current usage in the transgendered community, to use it in its broader sense which is meant to include "transgendered men" and "transgendered women" so that gender attribution refers to the identity claimed by the person concerned, regardless of their sex assignment at birth or status as pre- or post-operative transsexual. This is at odds with medical convention which generally continues to refer to people according to their birth-sex up until, and even after sex-reassignment.

2. One of the more notable instances of this has been the Michigan Women's Festival's institutions of a "womyn-born-womyn only" policy created to exclude transgendered women from the site. See Califia, 277-279. Another instance was the threatened boycott of Olivia Records, a feminist recording label, in the wake of the publication of Raymond's book, in which Raymond criticized Olivia for having Sandy Stone, a transgendered woman, as a member of their collective. After several months of receiving hate mail, death threats and threats of assault, and fearing the financial collapse of the business, Stone was asked to leave the collective. See Califia, pp. 106-7 and Sandy Stone, "The Empire Strikes Back: A Posttranssexual Manifesto," in Julia Epstein and Kristina Straub, eds., *Body Guards: The Cultural Politics of Gender Ambiguity*, (New York and London: Routledge), 280-304.

3. The exception to this might be, again, where the transsexual experience is then appropriated to the feminist demand to change the attributions of specific gender characteristics to a particular sex. This approach assumes that gender attributes or roles always equal gender identity. Transsexuals who undergo sex change are thereby understood as lost to the feminist project. Margrit Eichler, for example, argues that "transsexuals are people who suffer so deeply from the sex structure that they are willing to endure terrible pain and loneliness in order to reduce their suffering. This group of people—potentially—be the most potent group of people pressing for changes in the sex structure, because their aversion to 'sex appropriate' roles is apparently insurmountable. By declaring them, by surgical fiat, as members of the other sex, this change potential is diverted and becomes as conservative as it could have been revolutionary." (Eichler, "Sex Change Operations: The Last Bulwark of the Double Standard" in E.D. Nelson and B.W. Robinson (eds.) *Gender in the 1990's*, 36).

4. "Third sex" refers to people who define themselves as neither male nor female, but instead as belonging to another gender group. There are historical instances of societies which have a third gender group, such as the *hijra* in India. For this and other examples, see Ramet, 1996 and Feinberg, 1996. "Two-spirited" is a term used by some native North American cultures to refer to people understood to have both male and female qualities. Some transgendered people have adopted this self-definition. "Intersex" refers to those whose sex at birth is not readily defined as either male or female, usually because the baby had full or partial genitals of both sexes. Typically, these children receive surgery and/or hormonal treatment to conform to either male or female anatomy. "Androgyne" refers to someone whose sex is not readily apparent, often someone who combines both male and female gender characteristics, or who avoids gender presentation altogether. "Epicene" is the least familiar of these terms, but gaining popularity. It is both adjective and noun, and means "partaking of the characteristics of both sexes; common to both sexes; worn or inhabited by both sexes."

5. *The Standard of Care: The Hormonal and Surgical Sex Reassignment of Gender Dysphoric Persons* were developed by the founding committee of the Harry Benjamin International Gender Dysphoria Association in 1979 (Walker et al., 1979). Pat Califia offers some insightful commentary on the historical shaping of medical conventions in the "treatment" of transgendered people in *Sex Changes* (Califia 1996, Ch. 2 especially).

REPRODUCTION

In 1971, Eleanor Wright Pelrine wrote one of the first books analyzing the effects of the criminalization of abortion in Canada. She began the task of documenting the work of Dr. Henry Morgentaler who was performing abortions in Montreal and being prosecuted for his actions. According to section 251 of the Criminal Code (1969):

> 251. (1) Every one who with the intent to procure the miscarriage of a female person, whether or not she is pregnant, uses any means for the purpose of carrying out his intention is guilty of an indictable offence and is liable to imprisonment for two years.
>
> (2) Every female person, who, being pregnant, with the intent to procure her own miscarriage uses any means or permits any means to be used for the purpose of her intention is guilty of an indictable offence and is liable to imprisonment for two years.

Women could attain abortions with the approval of a Therapeutic Abortion Committee (TAC) consisting of "not less than three members each of whom is a qualified medical practitioner, appointed by the board of that hospital for the purposes of considering and determining questions relating to terminations of pregnancy within that hospital" and:

> ...if, before the use of those means, the therapeutic abortion committee for that accredited or approved hospital, by a majority of the members of the committee at which the case of such female person has been reviewed,
>
> (c) has by certificate in writing stated that in its opinion the continuation of the pregnancy of such female person would or would likely to endanger her health,...

It was not until 1988 that abortion was decriminalized in a Supreme Court case launched by Morgentaler. As Brodie, Jenson and Gavigan discuss in their brief overview entitled "The Politics of Abortion (1992)," while abortion was decriminalized in this decision, the decision continued to privilege the regulation and care of abortion by the medical profession and the Court strongly insisted that this matter should be decided in the legislative assembly and not in the Courts. Only one Supreme Court judge, Justice Bertha Wilson, contextualized abortion in relation to women's circumstances and their bodies. In her decision, she stated:

> The decision [to terminate a pregnancy] is one that will have profound psychological, economic and social consequences for the pregnant woman. The circumstances giving rise to it can be complex and varied and there may be, and usually are, powerful considerations militating in opposite directions. It is a decision that deeply reflects the way the woman thinks about herself and her relationship to others and to society at large. It is not just a medical decision; it is a profound social and ethical one as well. Her response to it will be the response of the whole person. (1988, p. 171)

Despite decriminalization, abortions are still difficult to obtain in most rural areas and the "right-to-life" movement has increased its surveillance of doctors who perform abortions and the use of violence to deter service providers has also increased. This has had the overall effect of decreasing the availability of abortion. More recently, the discourse on abortion has created an adversarial role between women and fetuses. The fetus has garnered the status of a person. Conceptualizing and advocating personhood for fetuses has meant that they enjoy more privileges than most women (Daniels 1993).

While the Canadian women's movement has struggled over the freedom not to reproduce, more recent feminist scholarship has revealed the racist, heterosexist, ableist, and classist assumptions in the pro-choice movement. Feminist scholars such as Petchesky (1990) have shifted the terms of the debate from reproductive choice to reproductive freedom. The freedom to reproduce includes access to pre- and post-natal care, and artificial insemination and more recently, access to safe and publicly funded reproductive technologies. This freedom to reproduce is critical to addressing the intersection of race, gender, sexuality and class. For example, this shift highlights the reproductive struggles of First Nations women, women with disabilities who have been sterilized, and single mothers and lesbian parents who have had their children forcibly removed (Das Gupta 1995 in this collection, Arnup 1997 in this collection, Monture 1998).

Reproduction has been used to divide women. White middle- and upper-class women are encouraged to reproduce and are rewarded for having children, while others are discouraged. This issue is highlighted in the *G.(D.F.)* case, discussed in Dawson's contribution to the reader, "First Person Familiar: Judicial Intervention in Pregnancy" (1998). In this highly controversial case, a pregnant drug-addicted native woman was detained in a drug treatment program in order to "protect" her fetus. This extreme case parallels recent trends in the U.S. where poor, black women have disproportionately been targeted for court-ordered prenatal interventions. Although the Canadian Supreme Court overturned the original order in *G.(D.F.)* and argued that the law does not recognize the unborn child as a fetus possessing rights, the majority decision failed to grapple with the racial dimensions of this case. Moreover, as Dawson contends, the case illustrates the conceptual limitations of a legal framework based upon separation that is incapable of grappling with the experience of pregnant embodiment.

While some Canadian women struggle for the conditions to raise healthy children through living wages and accessible and affordable childcare, other women are struggling to reproduce their "own" children. The debate about new reproductive technologies[1] is a problematic one for Canadian feminist scholars. On the one hand, some reproductive technologies can assist women with carrying a pregnancy to term and birthing a live child. The availability of reproductive technologies thus increases reproductive choices and allows some women an opportunity to achieve this experience. On the other hand, the availability of reproductive technologies has also exerted new pressures on women to do everything they possibly can to reproduce, despite the experimental nature of many processes (Burstyn 1992, 1993). Some feminist scholars have even gone so far as to suggest that reproductive technology, dominated by male-defined priorities and medicalized discourses, is but a "male counter-attack" by the "technodocs"(Corea, 1985; Diamond, 1990).

The articles in this reader suggest the need for a rethinking of the debate on new reproductive technologies. In "The Social Construction of Reproductive Technology" Menzies (1993) argues that technology is socially constructed and "involves how we go about the business of life" (p. 18). With this broad definition of "technology," Menzies locates reproductive technology in social, cultural, political and economic structures. For Menzies, technology is a tool, a method and a process. Through a range of examples she illustrates the ways in which we have come to value some technologies over others. She wants us to "re-focus...on women as technological practitioners" (20) and work from a "woman-defined" approach to technology. Menzies advocates a "woman-centred critical analysis of the new reproductive technologies" (21). This position allows us to ask some new and different sets of questions about reproductive technologies.

While Menzies provides us with ways to rethink technologies from the point of view of women's experiences, Thelma McCormack (1988) puts forward suggestions for how to ensure public policies that provide men and women with agency in "Public Policies and Reproductive Technologies." McCormack outlines the various philosophical and theoretical positions of the Catholic Church, social critics, and feminists that shaped the debate on new reproductive technologies in the early eighties and how these positions have relied on sociobiology and technological determinism. By exposing these assumptions, she demonstrates how these positions are faulty and suggests that public policy on reproductive technologies must encompass a view of reproduction as a continuum to include "both the problems of fertility and infertility" (370) and must also emphasize a "developmental and holistic model of the mind/body, the moral accountability of institutions, and a more collective model of child-caring" (370).

The "politics of reproduction" continue to shape Canadian feminist scholarship and activism. The more than 20 year struggle to decriminalize abortion has not translated into publicly funded, safe and accessible abortion; policy recommendations of the Royal Commission on New Reproductive Technologies have not been implemented. Legislative and policy initiatives are not enough to ensure Canadian women's reproductive freedom. These issues still need to be at the forefront of the women's movement in order for Canadian women to attain bodily integrity.

ENDNOTES

1. The Royal Commission on New Reproductive Technologies in their final report, *Proceed with*

Care (1993) defined new reproductive technologies in the following manner:

1) the prevalence, risk factors, and prevention of infertility;

2) assisted human conception;

3) prenatal diagnostics and genetics; and "the use of fertility drugs, assisted insemination using a partner or donor sperm, in vitro fertilization, sterilization reversal, and newer developments such as gamete intrafallopian transfer" (GIFT); and

4) research involving human zygotes, embryos and fetal tissues (Volume I, 6–7).

THE POLITICS OF ABORTION IN CANADA

Janine Brodie, Shelley Gavigan, Jane Jenson

…In the history of abortion shifts in the meanings assigned to reproduction have resulted in complex interrelationships among discourses, political mobilization, and public policy. Historians remind us that women have always exercised choice, terminating their pregnancies as a means of fertility control.[1] Nevertheless, the meanings and legal prohibitions associated with this choice have varied significantly across time and cultures. Canadian practice, for example, has been strongly influenced by Christian tradition and by British law, both common law and statute.

The early legal history of abortion was inextricably bound up with theological doctrine. This is most clearly illustrated by the centuries-long entrenchment in English criminal law of the concept of quickening, a concept directly derived from an ecclesiastical concern to determine the first moment of vitality of the foetus. While the early Christian church stressed the sanctity of life from its very beginning, this "moment" was not conception. Life was thought to commence only when the unborn infant first moved in the womb, that is, when it quickened. It was thought as well that only at quickening was the foetus infused with a soul. Abortion was thus initially regarded as an ecclesiastical offence, and, later, as a minor common-law offence if performed after quickening. In the early years of the nineteenth century, the significance of quickening as a momentous event in pregnancy was attacked by religious, medical, and legal authorities alike, not the least because the threshold determination of whether quickening had occurred was triggered by the word of the pregnant woman herself, and confirmed (or not) by a jury of matrons.[2]

The secular state's entry into the regulation of abortion has been relatively recent. In Britain, Lord Ellenborough's Act (1803) was an early example of such regulation. All abortions performed after quickening became punishable by death, while those performed before quickening were criminalized for the first time. Quickening as a significant distinction in abortion law was eliminated by an Act of 1837 which also dropped the death penalty for the offence. In 1861 the British House of Commons adopted the *Offences Against the Persons Act* which consolidated the offence as a felony punishable by three years imprisonment and for the first time explicitly extended criminal liability to a pregnant woman who attempted to obtain or self-induce an abortion. Abortion in Britain was governed by this Act until 1967. Nevertheless, in 1939 a British case opened space for the limited provision of legal abortions.[3] In the celebrated *Bourne* case, a jury acquitted a doctor who testified that he had performed an abortion on a fifteen-year-old who had been brutally gang-raped by three soldiers, because he had formed the opinion that the procedure was medically necessary to preserve the mental health of the young woman. Thereafter, medical practitioners who performed abortions, having formed a good faith opinion that the miscarriage was medically necessary, were reasonably secure that they would not be prosecuted. If prosecuted, they were of the view that an acquittal would surely follow. While the trial judge who charged the jury in *Bourne* did not make express reference to the defence of necessity, the case was taken to have rendered this defence available in abortion prosecutions.

Canada's legislative regime largely followed the British path. By the early 1840s, some of the colonies had legislation which imitated Lord Ellenborough's Act. The *Offences Against the Persons Act* was incorporated into Canada's Criminal Code enacted in 1892. It made abortion an indictable offence and those convicted were liable to imprisonment for life. It also made women who attempted to abort themselves liable to up to seven years imprisonment.... This general legal prohibition remained virtually unaltered until 1969.[4]

Canadian women, however, continued to resort to abortion as a means, albeit illegal and often dangerous, of fertility control. The practice was usually carried out in secrecy either by women themselves or with the aid of an illegal abortionist. Historical evidence suggests that abortion services were also offered overtly, but in a disguised form. Newspapers at the turn of the century and later, for example, openly advertised services and products for women designed to make their periods *"regular"*.[5] This extra-legal abortion regime, however, was not without its costs: many Canadian women died and many more became infertile as the result of desperate last resorts to gain control over their reproductive capacities.

Canada finally moved to change the regulation of abortion in the late 1960s. The new law, Section 251 of the Criminal Code, maintained a general ban on abortions, but allowed a "therapeutic exception" for a doctor who received certification from a Therapeutic Abortion Committee (TAC) in an accredited hospital that the continuation of the pregnancy "would or would be likely to" endanger the life or health of the pregnant woman.... In effect, this reform of the law replaced judicial control after the fact for medical control before the fact.[6]

...[T]he 1969 reform was framed and achieved within a discourse of medicalization. Reproductive decisions—especially those related to contraception and abortion—were designated as medical ones; the moral or political content was downplayed. As a result doctors were assigned control over women's reproductive decisions. This change had been motivated by the concerns of some doctors who had been performing abortions but who were becoming increasingly concerned about their criminal liability in the face of mounting demand. The principal motivation for the new legislation was to clarify the doctors' legal liabilities and define the state's interest in regulating the procedure. During these years, the voices of women as collective actors with different interests in the abortion issue were largely marginalized and muffled. To the extent that women figured in the debate, they were seen as objects—the victims of "the backstreet abortionist"—and in need of protective legislation. As Jenson points out, this medicalized definition made abortion reform possible, but it was soon challenged by the emergence of new actors with new definitions of their interests and the issue. Feminists immediately began to make claims for women's control over reproduction. By the mid-1970s, pro-choice groups began to challenge the prevailing medical definition, using instead a language of rights. By the 1980s the politics of abortion encompassed forces advancing either the rights of women or the rights of the foetus.

The struggle over competing definitions of abortion was propelled with full force into the political arena by the Supreme Court's judgement in the 1988 *Morgentaler* case. Pro-choice groups celebrated the decision because the court appeared to embrace and legitimize key themes of their rights-based discourse. The majority ruled that the Criminal Code's provisions infringed upon a woman's right to security of the person and that the requirement of approval by a TAC was inconsistent with the principles of fundamental justice. Nevertheless, as Shelley Gavigan observes in the last chapter of this book, the *Morgentaler* decision, like many other apparent victories, was contradictory, fragile, and incomplete. The Court continued to insist that abortion was a medical matter, and that the growing struggle between pro-choice and pro-life forces about these respective rights of women and the foetus had to be settled through political rather than legal mechanisms.

...Janine Brodie traces the politics of abortion after the *Morgentaler* decision until the Senate's defeat of Bill C-43 in January 1991. The chapter examines the failed attempts of the federal government to depoliticize the abortion issue and then to locate a compromise position on this deeply divisive issue. After the Morgentaler decision both pro-choice and pro-life groups attempted to seize the opportunity to displace once and for all the medicalized language of abortion and replace it with their respective discourses around rights. At stake was the content of the new state regulatory regime. The ensuing struggle reflected the dual nature of politics. It took the form of conventional politics—lobbying, mobilizing, and demonstrating. At another level, however, it was a struggle over vocabulary and meaning because the content of any new policy was premised upon particular understandings of the objects of regulation—in this case women's fertility and access to self-determination. While both the pro-choice and pro-life arguments centred on the issue of abortion per se, each promoted very different understandings of women, their place in society, and their rights. Unlike the 1969 parliamentary moment, when the collective interests of women were obscured within the discourse of medicalization, this time their interests were pitted against a relatively new actor in the politics of abortion—the foetus.

The foetus, much like the body of the pregnant woman, is a technical term which pro-life discourse has very powerfully imbued with social meaning. According to medical parlance, an embryo becomes a foetus when it completes its basic organ development, approximately eight weeks after fertilization.[7] At this stage, it is roughly an inch in length and can only be categorized as "human" by reference to its genetic structure. The development of the foetus is a biological process, but the point at which we elect to represent the foetus as a human and assign human qualities to it is very much an issue of interpretation and social construction.[8]

Historically, western societies have not defined the foetus as a person and certainly not a person with rights which take precedence over those of the living. To the extent that it was valued, it was valued as a father's property.[9] As Shelley Gavigan explains,...the discursive construction of the foetus as a person is a relatively recent innovation in Canadian legal practice and a critical victory for pro-life forces. Although the courts have not, as yet, granted constitutional protection to the foetus, they have moved in ways to "protect" the foetus from the threat supposedly posed by pregnant women. Again, the real targets of this pro-life campaign are women who wish to retain their status as autonomous individuals.

...[T]he law, like legislative politics, constitutes a site for struggles over meanings—meanings which feminists have attempted to influence but do not control. The power of law is to reflect and reinforce particular meaning systems over others. Feminists have sought to focus judicial treatment of abortion on the matter of women's rights, but their reliance on rights-based claims also has given rise to counterclaims about the rights of the foetus and of fathers. Nevertheless, Canadian courts' continued adherence to a medicalized definition of abortion may paradoxically protect Canadian women from many of the setbacks suffered by women in countries such as the United States, where abortion has been subsumed under the constitutional protection of individual privacy....

ENDNOTES

1.   Petchesky, *Abortion and Woman's Choice* (New York: Longman, 1984); Linda Gordon, *Woman's Body, Woman's Rights: A Social History of Birth Control in America* (Middlesex: Penguin Books, 1977); Angus McLaren and Arlene Tigar McLaren, *The Bedroom and the State: the Changing Practices and Politics of Conception and Abortion in Canada* (Toronto: McClelland and Stewart, 1986); Barbara Brookes, *Abortion in England 1900-1967* (London: Croom Helm, 1988); Shelley A.M. Gavigan, "On 'bringing on the menses': The Criminal Liability of Women and the Therapeutic Exception in Canadian Abortion Law," *Canadian Journal of Women and the Law* 2 (1986), 279.

2.   See Shelley Gavigan, "The Criminal Prohibition As It Related to Human Reproduction: The Genesis of the Statutory Prohibition of Abortion," *Journal of Legal History* 4 (1984), 20-43.

3.   Ibid.

4.   Gavigan, "On 'bringing on the menses'".

5.   McLaren and McLaren, *The Bedroom and the State*: Chapter 2.

6.   Mollie Dunsmuir, *Abortion: Constitutional and Legal Developments* (Ottawa: Library of Parliament, 1989), 7.

7.   Law Reform Commission of Canada, *Crimes Against the Foetus* (Working Papers 58) (Ottawa: Supply & Services, 1989), 7.

8.   See Rosalind Pollack Petchesky, "Foetal Images: The Power of Visual Culture in the Politics of Reproduction," in *Reproductive Technologies: Gender, Motherhood, and Medicine*, Michelle Stanworth, ed. (Minneapolis: University of Minnesota Press, 1987).

9.   Petchesky, *Abortion and Woman's Choice*: 263.

PUBLIC POLICIES AND REPRODUCTIVE TECHNOLOGY: A FEMINIST CRITIQUE

Thelma McCormack

Reproductive technology covers a wide range of medical strategies for increasing the effectiveness of contraception, overcoming infertility and reducing the risk of genetically transmitted deformities....

In recent years, the demand for these services has increased many times over. ...One explanation for the demand is an increase in infertility (WHO, 1975); another...is the precipitous drop in the number of babies available for adoption. Improved contraceptive information and practice, the desire of teenage mothers (married or unmarried) to keep their babies, as well as the legalization of abortion account for the shortage.[1] Since none of these trends is likely to be reversed, the long-term expectation is that more couples will turn to the new technologies....

Philosophically, the most difficult and intractable questions are about research in embryology, but the bitterest and most divisive debates are over the applications and communication of existing knowledge....Artificial insemination by donors (AID) and surrogate parenting have become the most problematic legally and contentious socially—not because they involve non-coital procreation, although the unconscious responses to that extraordinary fact cannot be discounted, but because they involve third parties and, in some instances, a payment of money to the outside person....

...Because the impact of reproductive practices and policies is immediately and most directly on women, it is from their perspective that these policies will be evaluated, while recognizing that reproductive policies are part of a larger, more comprehensive set of population policies. ...In this context the term feminist perspective refers to an analysis which discloses how patriarchal values about the subordinate status of women, about the nature of motherhood, infertility and the family are both implicit and explicit in our thinking about reproduction....

Subtexts: Sociobiology and Technological Determinism

The uses of reproductive technology pose a number of minor and several major questions. But like any complex set of questions the answers elude us, in part, because of deeper and unresolved subtexts. Fears, for example, that the new reproductive technology will lead to a form of eugenics, a neo-Nazi effort to improve the species and create a Master race are prompted by the formation of sperm banks whose donors are Nobel prize winners. One physician who carried out artificial insemination procedures insisted that the women have high IQs (Gordon, 1987). No matter how often these theories of intelligence are discredited, they recur regularly by some Gresham's law. What keeps them alive is the more fundamental schism in modern thinking over nature and nurture; that is, over whether our inherited genetic scripts are immutable, insulated against environmental influence, and ultimately determine our attitudes and social behaviour, or whether they are developmental, and sensitive to environmental factors that can produce wide variations and mutations....

The second debate is over technology, the extent to which we can predict determinate outcomes, and the importance of technology in altering our values and social practices (Rothschild, 1983). Much of the literature on reproductive technology is based on speculations about the impact of the technology, from the "redundant male" (Cherfas and Gribbin, 1984) as a result of test-tube parthenogenesis to the partial extinction of women who are destined to become scarce as a result of sex determination (Guttentag and Secord, 1983).[2]...

Meanwhile the debates about reproductive technology are conducted against the noise of sociobiology versus technological determinism, and the challenge offered to each by a political perspective, in this instance, feminist that measures progress by the degree to which women achieve control over their own fertility. In the foreground is a more immediate struggle shaping up between 1) the Catholic church, 2) social critics (chiefly legal scholars and concerned scientists) and 3) feminists....

1   The Catholic Church

In 1987 the Vatican released a text stating the Church's opposition to any form of procreation outside of the "natural" form of sexual intercourse between lawful husband and wife (Instruction, 1987). It acknowledged the problems of sterility and infertility and approved medical treatment wherever possible, but artificial methods of procreation such as in vitro fertilization or artificial insemination or surrogate parenting were all and equally unacceptable. Bearing children and the act of conjugal love must be one.

Governments have an obligation to control the activities of scientists who, for purposes of scientific inquiry, experiment with human embryos.[3] The state is asked to reaffirm the sanctity of life by making these activities illegal and restraining the professionals who regard themselves as the group best qualified to establish regulatory guidelines.

2   Social Critics

But the modern secular state with is heavy investment in scientific research may not wish to curtail or even control what it may see as the leading edge of biology, preferring, instead, to let the scientists themselves draw up their own agendas and ethical codes....

However, the co-operative relationship between the state and the scientific community is neither permanent nor static; it is continually renegotiated, and it is in this process that critical opinion becomes part of the debate. In general, social critics—mainly legal scholars, social scientists, and concerned scientists who fall between the technical professionals at one extreme, and the dogmatic religious groups at the other—have discussed (a) economic inequities (Ince, 1984), (b) the allocation of resources and (c) both the legal and social issues involved in surrogate contracts.

Economic inequities arise out of the organization of medical services. In vitro fertilization is often described as a technology for the rich, while surrogate parenting has been assumed to be the upper middle classes exploiting low income groups.... Inflammatory phrases like "babies for sale" are commonplace....

But to some extent these class-gender disparities depend on health insurance. In the U.S. in vitro fertilization may be four or five times the cost of the same procedure in Australia or in Britain where it is carried out under the National Health Service. ...In France and Sweden where sperm donation is treated like blood donation, the sperm donors receive no monetary compensation....

One may also question the wisdom of funding clinics to improve fertility when zero population growth might be more socially responsible (Newton, 1983). Funds could be better allocated to therapies and other techniques, including environmental controls, to preventing infertility and finding a cure for it (Zimmerman, 1982). Our alarm about overpopulation, however, is not always matched by the people in developing countries who...fear underpopulation...(Newman, 1972). Cross-cultural studies suggest widespread anxiety about infertility and harassment of women who are barren (Ford, 1964).

On the matter of surrogate contracts, critics do not reject the idea of a contract as intrinsically offensive, nor do they look upon the payment of money to a surrogate mother as a purchase price (Black, 1981; Mady, 1981; Benditt, 1983; Mawdsley, 1983; Hollinger, 1985; Katz, 1986). A father cannot buy his own child, Benditt writes (Benditt, 1983)....

3   *Feminist Criticism*

The feminist agenda has traditionally emphasized reproductive safety and reproductive choice. From Margaret Sanger's campaign for family planning to the current focus on abortion rights there is a straight, unbroken line. "Biology is not destiny," "Our bodies our own," "Every child a wanted child" are the shorthand expressions of protest against the over-medicalization of pregnancy and childbirth, the passive dependency on the medical professions, and the loss of self-determination.

Reproductive freedom which is measured by choice and control is a crucial part of a larger program to achieve structural equality and cultural liberation. The denial or frustration of these objectives is as much in science as in law, economics or politics. Medical science, in particular, has been damned with faint praise in feminist discourse where it is frequently described as part of a system of social control which both extends and legitimates the patriarchal status quo (Wikler, 1986). Feminists and feminist theory are, then, less preoccupied with medical ethics and the wayward practitioners who deviate from professional standards, than with the larger political script....

Each of these groups—the Catholic church, the critics and the feminists—provide a definition of the public interest. But we are not totally without laws, legal precedents and policies which can be adapted. The right to have children can be extended to cover noncoital conception. There are also adoption and custody laws. In addition, some equate the payment of a fee to surrogate mothers with black market adoption, which is illegal in most jurisdictions....

No one, however, is satisfied with these expedients, least of all lawyers and judges who want legislation. ...The truth is that both of these ideas—noncoital reproduction and surrogate parenting—raise complex issues about the family and parenting for which we have incomplete knowledge and inadequate frameworks, frameworks which are themselves changing (Black, 1981; Mady, 1981; Hall, 1985; Stumpf, 1986; Eichler, forthcoming). What are the options?

The choice of options is circumscribed by the liberal state; specifically, the importance of protecting individual privacy, allowing the professions to regulate themselves through licensing and peer-group review, and giving clients or consumers the opportunity to nego-tiate with the suppliers through a market mechanism. In addition, there is a built-in political disinclination to enact legislation which is difficult to enforce because it is contrary to pub-lic opinion or inconsistent with the political culture. Finally, there [is]…the Charter of Rights and Freedoms.

Reproductive rights have typically been treated as privacy rights; to beget or not to beget is an individual not a state matter; the right to have children is set out in Article 16 in the United Nations *Declaration of Human Rights*. Hence, it is unlikely that Canada or any country will prohibit all forms of noncoital procreation; policies will more likely be selec-tive and a compromise between no regulations, at one extreme, and the Criminal Code, at the other.…

The Family, the Donor Father and the Surrogate Mother

Whatever policy Canadians adopt—laissez-faire, professional self-regulation, government regulation or some combination—it must inevitably impinge on our concepts of the family and motherhood. Is motherhood biological or social? On what basis do we make judge-ments about the competence of mothers? Does the family require two parents? What role does the third party, the donor have?

Our cultural legacy is a dual image of mothers, negative and positive. The first includes the stereotype of the pregnant teenager who was either too ignorant or too careless to pro-tect herself.…

At the other end of the spectrum are women in stable, married relationships, middle-class women who have a firm grasp of their domestic role and female identity, but may be unable to conceive. Such women are "childworthy" (Snowden and Mitchell, 1981) and deserve our understanding and the opportunity to use scarce resources. Yet, before they can avail them-selves of in vitro fertilization or some other form of artificial pregnancy they must be checked since not all "child worthies" are suitable applicants. In a study of Ontario physicians who carry out the IVF procedures, a third indicated they would not treat unmarried couples; they were unanimous in insisting on the consent of husbands even though it is the woman who is subjected to the tests and bears the physical and emotional risk (Ontario Law Reform Commission, 1985).

The (nuclear) family bias is often equated with "the best interests of the child". The full realization of the child's freedom can only be achieved, according to Ribes (1978), in an environment with two parents. For "a mother to block that relation, restrict it to herself, is the equivalent of mutilating her child" (Ribes, 1978:132).…

Given the ideal of a two-parent nuclear family, does conception which requires a third party undermine family structure? Lygre (1979) claims that the surrogacy pattern cheats the family history of pregnancy. Black (1981), on the other hand, suggests that it strength-ens the family by making it possible for childless couples to have a family, and, in any case, family history is made by parenting not pregnancies.

Are children who are conceived through artificial insemination by donor or through a surrogate parent legitimate? ...In most countries, the legal status of the child has been resolved by the courts which have held that the husband of the biological mother is deemed to be the father in law; the donor has neither financial responsibilities nor social rights. In effect, then, the courts have held and the philosophers have concurred that fatherhood is social, not biological.

Almost all writers, ethicists, lawyers, and medical persons recommend that male sperm donors be protected by anonymity, even though this may expose the child, at some future date, to risk in terms of health, and even though the child may wish to trace his or her roots as many adopted children do. Any disclosure, these writers claim, would discourage donors and disrupt the husband-wife relationship through sexual jealousy. No empirical evidence is offered to support this crude notion of male rivalry. However, and this is more important conceptually, donor anonymity reduces the person to being a "stud". Donors many not wish to know which children they father, yet wish to be known as a person altruistic enough the help others; they may find it degrading to be denied any status except as sperm donor (Poyen et al., 1980). Women who act as surrogates are unable to conceal their role; and, they, too may wish to have their non-pecuniary motives acknowledged. A woman who volunteers to be a surrogate mother may be expressing her personhood in the way she prefers and understands, and may resent the depiction of herself as a "breeder," a woman so desperate for money she is willing to "rent her womb," or as someone who is exploited by brokers acting on behalf of the affluent (Parker, 1983). In short, by insisting on the model of the two-person nuclear family, the third party becomes a nonperson.

Sperm donors are required to satisfy both medical and social criteria. The social criterion means being able to match the physical characteristics of the couple with those of a potential donor so as to insure an appearance of racial and ethnic continuity. "Experience with adopted children has shown," Snowden and Mitchell write, "that a physical likeness to the adoptive parents helps the child to identify with the parents and the parents with the child." They imply that interracial marriages and interracial adoptions place an unnecessary strain on family relationships. But studies of interracial families do not support this, and, in any case, the risk is for the couple themselves to assume if they wish....

The distinction between a pregnant woman and a mother has been a part of liberal social science which has attempted to make parenting more accountable and would give an adoptive mother the same status as a "natural" mother. Yet, the surrogacy question has reopened the issue. Should priority be given to the gestating mother or to the potential adoptive mother? Marxists assert that since the contract mother is the producer she has the right to the product; it is her baby more than it is the natural father's and certainly more than his wife's; psychoanalysts claim there is a special bonding between fetus and mother that must be respected in the interests of the child....

In summary, the literature tends to be biased in terms of the nuclear family. There is no awareness that in Canada, as elsewhere in the Western world, new forms of family life have been evolving as couples marry, divorce, remarry, and the children of these marriages have several sets of parents. As a result of custody arrangements, children may live in more than one parental household with other sets of siblings. Because of the rigid notion of the two-parent nuclear family, the literature demeans the third parties who are involved in either surrogate relationships or artificial insemination by donor by limiting them to a biological function. Finally, in defining "the best interest of the child," there is a tendency to define fatherhood as social (the husband of the natural mother) and motherhood as biological.

Although feminist literature is more critical of the nuclear family, it has not always been consistent on some of the issues involved (Wikler, 1986). There is no one feminist approach to reproduction technologies. Rushing and Onorato (1987, 26) summarize the differences:

> For liberal feminists, these technologies should be regulated to promote equal access and to protect women from their indiscriminate or unnecessary use. Radical feminists worry about the fact that these technologies are developed and implemented in an environment which is male-dominated, even woman-hating. For radicals, these technologies can only be liberating if women control them. Socialist feminists argue that the new reproductive technologies will further oppress women as long as they are used in the context of capitalist patriarchy....

General Principles: Structural, Ethical and Biological

A new and more positive paradigm would start from the assumption that reproductive policies must include both the problems of fertility and infertility, contraception and abortion as well as artificial insemination and in vitro fertilization. Logically, they belong together....

The second set of assumptions is based on ethical systems which emphasize a developmental and holistic model of the mind/body, the moral accountability of institutions, and a more collective model of child-caring that would include divorced parents, grandparents, step-parents and others who might reside in the household and want to be part-time parents. (Sherwin, 1984-85; Sherwin, n.d.) None of this should deprive women or be used as an excuse to deprive women who are infertile of their right to have children. If "biology is not destiny" for the fertile, it is also not destiny for the infertile.

Fertility and infertility would be conceptualized as natural stages in the life cycle, and considering the life span, people can expect that during the major parts of their lives they are in phases of infertility or sub-fertility. And since men also change with respect to sperm production, the bonds of affection men and women develop for each other expressed in sexual intimacy are imperfectly related to their stages of fertility. It follows that noncoital reproduction is an option which is not limited to a group who have been defined by the medical profession as impaired. It is available to all regardless of their health, sexual orientation or marital status.

Based on these broad principles, a set of feminist guidelines for a public policy on reproductive technology can be indicated.

1. The Demedicalization of Infertility

Reproductive services are social services first, medical services second. They can be carried out in a variety of non-hospital settings. Ideally, they would be available through a women's health centre with its typical emphasis on prevention and maintaining health rather than on pathology. It is important, too, not to exaggerate the medical risk to the fetus or woman when a pregnancy has been achieved.

2. Eligibility and the Nuclear Family

The nuclear family is no longer the statistical norm in Canadian society, nor is it always the most desirable form for either adults or children. But our social policies tend to treat the alternative models as "crisis management" rather than as part of a pluralistic approach to family systems which includes parents who may be living apart, step-parents, and grand-parents. Parenting may be spread over many persons. The result is a different family ethic closer to the older extended family. Hence, any policies about eligibility should not be contingent on the nuclear family.

3. From Gatekeeper to Facilitators

Our current practices with respect to noncoital reproduction create two classes of women: those who do not need permission to bear and those who must meet some sort of social criterion (Ontario Law Reform Commission, 1985). The latter give up a substantial part of their privacy and their right to control and manage their reproductive processes. They do this in the hope of fulfilling a desire to have children and they do not expect the same freedom as women who conceive easily and without complications. Nevertheless, there is an obligation to protect privacy and reaffirm choice. Redefining the role of gatekeepers to facilitators, and removing any non-medical restrictions would go a long way toward restoring women's self-confidence and self-esteem damaged by the stigma of childlessness.

4. A Donor is a Socially Constructed Social Role, not a Biological One

Following this guideline, a surrogate mother would be defined as a donor or a male donor would be designated as a surrogate father, but the distinction between them as donors would be reduced. As outsiders who are expected to disappear after they have carried out their biological function, they have equivalent roles. Although there is a big difference between ejaculation and a pregnancy of nine months, it is degrading to either to be obliged to deny their social identity. But if we take the further step and define the donor's contribution as a gift, neither a commodity nor a service, it must be like a gift, with no strings attached. That is easier said than done; some set of contractual rights must be clarified.

5. Genetics and Information on Gender

A sex-selection technology is or soon will be refined and readily available, while abortions based on sex already occur. In view of our previous discussion of the moral challenge to raise children of either sex, no encouragement should be given to the uses of this technology while recognizing that there is no way of enforcing a prohibition (Warren, 1985). However, women have an absolute and unconditional right to the information where there is a history of hemophilia or some similar sex-related disorder.

These constitute minimal tentative guidelines for developing public policies on reproductive technology which would be consistent with feminist standards. Some issues have not been dealt with. For example, we are eventually going to have to face the question of racism in the identification of sperm donors by "race." Can the state condone what some may see as segregated sperm banks? How is this to be balanced against the views of visible minorities, ethnic and religious groups who object in principle to this "melting-pot" approach?

In summary, the new reproductive technologies may only serve a small minority but the interest and strong feelings they arouse suggest that they serve as a text for the projection of our fears about the misuses of science and technology. We are no longer confident that science is liberating, and women in particular have been critical of its methods and direction. The new reproductive technology is not anti-woman but modern social history is more problematic....

ENDNOTES

1. The possibility that babies available for adoption in Third World countries may be either kidnapped or bought by agents has been a growing cause of concern among couples who were encouraged to seek children whom they were led to believe were orphaned, abandoned or freely given up by their parents. Hence couples who might have adopted these children are deterred.

2. "In a nutshell, when women are scarce and men are readily available a protective morality develops that favors monogamy for women, limits their interactions with men, and shapes female roles in traditional domestic directions" (Guttentag and Secord, 1983:231).

3. Since the 1970s in the U.S. there has been a ban on federal support for fetal research.

THE SOCIAL CONSTRUCTION OF REPRODUCTIVE TECHNOLOGIES AND OF CHOICE

Heather Menzies

…What I offer here is a reflection on the social construction of reproductive technologies and of women's choices around them. It's a reflection drawn from women's experience and use of these and other technologies—i.e. women's actual and historical technological practice. It's also an attempt to break the dichotomy which positions us either outside the technology with no opportunity to control it, or totally within its control, little more than its helpless victims.

Conventional wisdom—associated with dictionary definitions, educational curricula and media coverage of technology—reinforces women's sense of being either outside technology or on the passive receiving end of it. We are schooled to think of technology as industrial tools, machines and systems: factory production systems primarily, but also military systems and energy systems. In other words, big stuff, capital-intensive stuff, designed by engineers.[1] However, this is a restricted definition of technology, associated with capitalist, industrial, patriarchal society, which admittedly has a near-monopoly on thinking and doing around the world. However, if we dare think for ourselves and be broadly inclusive, technology can be better defined as plain, everyday know-how (Macdonald, 1987) and as practice (Franklin, 1990). At its simplest, technology involves how we go about the business of life. Not so much as individuals in isolation from each other, but as groups and communities.…

Technology varies from society to society and even among groups within society and in different settings—such as women in the home or native people living on the land. The key is the social relations and organization, and the values inspiring them. Because what emerges as the customary way of doing things and how this is formalized as customs and systems depends on the prevailing world view, including what is seen as valuable and important to the people of that society or group.…

The corporate, competitive, controlling perspective is the dominant way of seeing things in our society. It has been called the "dominator model" (Eisler, 1988) and is represented both as patriarchy and in capitalism, where the ability to amass money (through the production and marketing of goods and services) is the medium of control. There is a dominant technological practice associated with this world view. My friend Ursula Franklin calls it "the production model" (Franklin, 1990). It's a top-down systems approach, through which everything from the identification of problems and needs to the articulation of solutions—

in the form of commodified goods and services—and the production and delivery of those solutions, through instructions, prescriptions, protocols and practices, is controlled through designated ranks of people. Although the production model is best known in factories and offices, it has spread into health care and other social services as well. Sometimes described as the "medical model," it helps explain why one response to problems such as infertility and breast cancer is favoured over others—namely, individualized, commodified treatments versus collective, social and environmental measures for healing and prevention. However, this production-model practice will only become the exclusive practice if other ways of seeing things, from which other conceptions of technology can emerge, are completely eclipsed from the public imagination. Hence the importance of women re-membering[2] ourselves within our rich legacy of technology use and personal practice and using it to define our own approach to technology in reproduction.

Re-focusing on women as technological practitioners will give us a place to stand on the new reproductive technologies beyond the narrow dichotomy of being for or against the mainstream production-model idea of fit. Standing inside a woman-defined approach to technological practice will help us resist the production-model approach to women's reproductive health and replace it with a model of our own. For instance, the goal of assisting and protecting women's capacity to have healthy babies with a minimum of intervention and related dependency might emerge from a woman-centred analysis of women's reproductive health needs, and a related definition of technology as social practice and know-how. This in turn would give us a positive framework in which to critique others' stated goals....

Such a goal would also allow us to focus on preventing over time, but without exchanging the immediate, and hopefully only short-term, needs of women with blocked fallopian tubes who could benefit from *in vitro* fertilization (IVF). The larger framework would help us to support these women in their efforts to use IVF on their own terms: refusing the all-or-nothing choice which many doctors try to impose—that is, consent to total intervention including a complete drug "work-up"—and instead choosing, as at least one woman I interviewed did, to do IVF without the hormonal drugs.... With adequate support for the women-patients, the IVF experiment could be an opportunity for women to assert their power as users and practitioners of technology and to resist the production model's efforts to reduce women to objects and victims of a male and corporate-controlled technology.

Exploring this option for women would help us to open up the choices for infertile and, in the case of artificial insemination, lesbian and single women who want to bear a child. We could widen the choice from the current one of either using artificial insemination (AI) and IVF on the production-model terms provided, or not using them at all. The first option, using the technology on the terms dictated by the doctors, leaves women vulnerable to being hurt and abused. The second choice, namely repudiating the technological option altogether, leaves those women who want to bear a child, but who can't do it without technological assistance, with no hope and little support in a painful personal situation. Furthermore, both choices leave control over these and other medical technologies largely with the people who control them at present (Benston, 1993), and leave unexamined the assumption that women can never negotiate effective control themselves....

Technology As Tool and System

Popular wisdom tells us that technology is a tool, a neutral means to an end. It only takes on a bias when it is applied and used in certain ways by whoever uses it. Hence, a rolling pin or hammer can be productively used to make pastry or build a house, but they can also be used as weapons. However, the choices around what technology is developed, what form it takes and how it is marketed and represented are not neutral. These are highly political choices.

Birth control technology was sold to women as a tool. Epitomized by the pill, birth control was seen as the key to women's sexual liberation. The pill's packaging reinforced this: a self-contained circular dispenser with a clear plastic cover, it invited women to see the pill as something which did all the thinking for them, and contained its action neatly within the circumference of women's reproductive organs. All we needed to do was to take the little pill every morning. Like the IUD, the pill did its work silently. Out of sight, out of mind. Nearly 20 years later, a 1985 federal report on oral contraceptives warned that women on the pill face two to four times the risk of developing deep venous thrombosis (blood clots, which are linked to strokes) and pulmonary embolism (Rauhala, 1987).

Analyzed in the context of women's historical oppression in a patriarchal society, the pill can be seen as part of the same pattern which caused the IUD and, earlier, the diaphragm, to be developed as contraceptives. These "tools" emerged from a sexist choice that the innermost part of a woman's body (rather than a man's body) should necessarily be the site of contraceptive intervention, and that women should bear the cost and any risks associated with their use....

The pill also emerged from a male-oriented understanding of sexual relations between men and women: namely that women's "liberation" meant that women were available to men without risk of paternity, and that intercourse was the essence of sex....

There are important lessons here which we can apply to our thinking about *in vitro* fertilization, genetic screening and other new reproductive technologies which are being presented to women as tools of liberation and choice. For instance, is *in vitro* fertilization, which represents a major and risky intervention into women's bodies and hormonal systems, justifiable as a way to circumvent low male sperm count when sperm banks can match donor sperm according to hair and eye colour, height and weight? Is genetic parenthood, on both sides, essential or equally important, to having and rearing a child?...

In terms of the particular technology chosen for development, we could ask, if genetic screening is a neutral research tool, what priorities have pushed this technology to the forefront of reproductive health care so fast, and during a time of health-budget restraints and cutbacks? Whose goals do these technologies serve—parents who are prepared to love a baby unconditionally, or corporations and the state who want resilient workers and healthy taxpayers? And once it is in place so that this is what is being "offered" to women, is our choice and consent truly of our own making, or assumed like our compliance in "liberated" sex?...

In fact, choices are being made. They're being made by global pharmaceutical, medical-equipment and other institutions who then market (or offer) these choices to the general public as if the consumers or users were the ones making the choice.

What happened to the Women's Health Trial for breast cancer prevention in the U.S. is an excellent case in point. Initiated in 1983 when it was approved by the National Cancer Institute, it was a large-scale long-term study to test the hypothesis that a low-fat diet could help prevent breast cancer. First, some faulty research discrediting the link between diet fat and cancer was used to postpone this study. Then, the institute jumped on the bandwagon of "chemo-prevention" by sponsoring a $70 million study which involves giving healthy women regular doses of the drug tamoxifen, which is used to treat malignancies

(Rennie, 1993). A similar production-model pharmacological fix, which was publicized in a keynote address at a major 1992 cancer conference (interestingly, cosponsored by the Harvard School of Public Health and the General Motors Cancer Research Foundation), involves treating women with a patented hormone-replacement therapy costing $350 a month (Rennie, 1993).

What's happening vis-à-vis women and breast cancer gives us some important questions to raise about women and infertility. For example, where are the measures for preventing infertility by criminalizing toxic work environments, eradicating sexually transmitted disease and ensuring safe contraceptive technologies? Why has there been virtually no action toward a universal childcare system in Canada, which would allow people to combine child rearing and career development and could mitigate infertility caused by age; yet 13 hospital-based IVF and related programs have been set up across the country at a time of hospital and health-budget cutbacks (Stephens and McLean, 1993).

A woman-centred goal of ensuring and protecting women's capacity to have healthy babies with a minimnm of intervention and dependency would compel us to challenge the lack of prevention as biased against women's reproductive health, and to insist that prevention be considered a top priority. At the same time, it would compel us to support those women who are incurably infertile and want to experiment with IVF. One of the ways we can support these women is by helping them critique the IVF and other technologies as given.

The key question for us to ask in such a critique is how the technologies of IVF, or AI, are organized: in an open, democratic way so that every person using the technology is able to control how, and how much, she uses it? Or is it a closed system, with little or no leeway for personal discretion and innovation by individual users?...

...This model, the "medical model" in health care, recognizes autonomy only on the part of doctors, not the women-patients. Like the "production model" in the working world (Franklin 1990) monopolized by management under the legal title of "managerial prerogative," the medical model emphasizes control from the top down, and expertise and competence in the hands of doctors and technicians, not the women. Furthermore, this mode constantly reproduces itself—in the way most doctors are trained, most hospitals are run, and in the way individual pieces of technology are designed, manufactured and set up for daily use....

Patients are admitted only if they fit certain criteria, established and policed by the physicians running the clinic, which generally excludes lesbian couples and single women. Once the women are selected, their control over the techniques and technologies associated with AI, IVF and other treatments is limitcd to giving or withholding consent, based on limited information supplied by doctors in language which is often extremely difficult to understand (Stephens and McLean, 1993). The doctors assume (appropriate) the same "managerial prerogative" in their capacity as health-care professionals as management does in the workplace. Intrauterine insemination and AI are often accompanied by superovulation drugs (Stephens and McLean, 1993); yet unless the woman is infertile with all identifiable hormonal problem, there seems little reason to subject her to the risks, and costs, associated with fertility drugs.

On the other hand, there is the precedent of a Winnipeg AI program which sends out sperm by bus, packed in dry ice, to rural couples, who insert the sperm themselves (Stephens and McLean, 1993). While in some provinces insemination has been officially designated as a "delegated medical act" to be performed only by licensed professionals, in Manitoba technological users are still free to be technological practitioners, using techniques perfected by women over years of using tampons. So the system isn't necessarily closed.

The story of midwifery's comeback over the last 20 years offers us one of the best precedents for seeing how the production model approach to women's reproductive health can be overturned, and alternative technologies, such as techniques in assisting natural childbirth organized around women's physical and cultural priorities can be put in place even in mainstream hospitals....

In the area of abortion, I have written elsewhere (Menzies, 1991) that if women could negotiate the use of abortion technology according to their own needs and priorities, they might organize the procedure so as to mitigate the pain and anguish many women suffer around this experience. Thus, a woman-defined abortion service might begin by acknowledging this pain, and provide some support in dealing with it as part of the abortion service. In addition to the technical-medical act, there might be a grieving ritual and opportunity for counselling and support from friends, peers and professionals.

The trouble is, there is little public discussion of these precedents. Or rather, they are part of another discourse on technology, one that is centred in women's actual experience, women's technological practice, not on technology divorced from the social context and on the officially designated experts. Meanwhile, the dominant or official discourse on abortion, as with other technologies, has been organized to virtually mirror the biases of the production model in the choice and organization of technology. It's organized as a debate for or against a given choice and organization of technology. Furthermore, it's a debate governed by designated experts, speaking the de-contextualized language of objective evidence and facts.

Technology As Discourse

...It's useful to think of discourse as a type of technological system—a cultural system of knowledge production rather than the more familiar material system producing and marketing things. We can ask, therefore, whether the discussion is open and democratic, with every participant contributing equally to its direction and outcome, or whether it's closed through pre-determined terms of reference governed and administered by some authority figure such as the chairperson of the Royal Commission on the New Reproductive Technologies?

Women's experience with the discourse on abortion since the 1960s is instructive, First, it wasn't a discourse created by women, but by men associated with medicine, law and the church....

Trying to represent women within the discourse, feminists were forced to adjust themselves to its overall structure: a debate for or against women's access to abortion as currently given—that is, as a procedure completely controlled by doctors acting as managers of the technology. The structure of the debate precluded discussing another way of organizing the technology, with women able to negotiate their use of it according to their personal needs and priorities. Furthermore, the language of the debate, the disembodied language of women's rights ("versus" so-called fetal rights) precluded talking about women's direct experience of abortion out of which a sense of women's actual needs could emerge. In addition to the abstract language, the polarized nature of the discourse styled as a debate kept women from testifying to the anguished choice which abortion represented to many women, lest they give ground to the other side in the debate. The silencing of this anguish not only aggravated many women's suffering. It also left women unsupported and alone in the hands of doctors who sometimes prolonged their pain and suffering in the way they treated them (Menzies, 1991 and Bowes, 1990)....

...[T]he lesson is not to concentrate too much on trying to reform the official discourse. Perhaps the lesson is to ground ourselves in our own discourse. One that is consciously open and democratic, and centred in women's actual experience.

The Personal Is Political

For me, the positive and revolutionary part of the phrase "the personal is political" focuses on personal, lived experience, and how its evidence and example can change our society. It was by focusing on women's unpaid work in the home, and taking it seriously as work (not leisure and/or consumption), that Maggie Benston and other feminists made the breakthrough in thinking about women's liberation and women's work: that women's liberation would not be accomplished simply by women going out in the paid labour force and taking on the double burden of paid as well as unpaid work. It also requires that women's work in the home, the family and community be validated as productive labour (Benston, 1969).

With a similar focus on women's actual experience, feminist historians such as Jennifer Brown and Sylvia Van Kirk have revised conventional historical accounts—for instance, of the timetrade period—by including women's conception of events, such as food preservation and translating from one language to another, and by including the women who did these things as bona fide historical agents. In science, feminists such as Margaret Alic have revised conventional understandings of what constitutes science by taking seriously the science women have done over the centuries, on their own terms. Building on and overlapping this, others such as Ursula Franklin and Maggie Benston have opened the frame of reference to welcome a broader range of inquiry and activity, including a lot of the citizen science and grassroots science which women continue to do in the community and in the peace, environmental and other activist movements.

...[I]t was by focussing on women's actual experience, as telephone operators and office workers, that I could break out of the mould of the official discourse on technology in the workplace, with its limited options of being for or against a particular choice and organization of technology (Menzies, 1989). It was by taking these women seriously as technological practitioners that I could begin to see another option: that of organizing the technology their way—which tended to be in ways that enlarged and extended public service and didn't just automate what services were presently provided. Similarly, it was by focusing on women's actual experience with abortion that I was able to see how the feminist discussion on abortion could and even must move beyond the limits set by the official discourse: namely, women's access to safe abortions. Women don't just need access to the technology. We need to be able to control it. And there's no reason why we can't—given the precedents I mentioned earlier.

The feminist discourse on the new reproductive technologies is just beginning. This book demystifies the technology and offers a preliminary analysis of it. The next step is to stimulate an open, democratic discussion about women's reproductive health, out of which a sense of the appropriate choice, place and organization of various technologies will hopefully emerge. If the personal is political, then an open, inclusive discussion in which every woman's experience is recognized as valid and true, will yield an open, inclusive approach to the goal of empowering women to have healthy babies and healthy sex lives with the minimum of intervention and related dependency....

ENDNOTES

1. The word engineer derives from the latin word *genre*, which means to sire; the male role in procreation.

2. Re-member means to put together again, to rejoin pieces of things, and bodies, which have broken apart. The word is used here to deliberately evoke a bodily and organic sense of women remembering.

FIRST PERSON FAMILIAR: JUDICIAL INTERVENTION IN PREGNANCY, AGAIN: G. (D.F.)

T. Brettel Dawson

At the end of October 1997, the judges of the Supreme Court of Canada released their decisions in *Winnipeg Child and Family Services (Northwest Area) v. G. (D.F.)*[1] This case attracted nationwide attention (and a raft of interveners)[2] after a Manitoba judge, on a motion by a provincial agency providing child protection services, ordered in early August 1996, that Ms. G.—a young, Aboriginal woman pregnant with her fourth child—be detained at a health sciences centre and undergo substance abuse treatment until childbirth on the basis that her active addiction to glue sniffing was placing her fetus at substantial risk of developmental harm.[3] This order was stayed two days later[4] and was subsequently set aside on appeal to the Manitoba Court of Appeal.[5] Ms. G. voluntarily remained at the medical centre until discharged in mid-August, stopped sniffing glue, and gave birth to an apparently healthy child in December 1996. The agency's appeal to the Supreme Court of Canada to restore the legal basis for the original order (in particular, drawing on tort law and the *parens patriae* or wardship jurisdiction of the court) was dismissed by a majority of seven judges to two.

The events of August were not the only actions in 1996 that brought the status of the relationship between a pregnant woman and her fetus in Canada to the attention of the law. In May, a pregnant woman, Brenda Drummond inserted a pellet rifle into her vagina and fired a pellet, which lodged in the brain of her fetus. Two days later she gave birth; when her infant's condition deteriorated, surgeons discovered and surgically removed the pellet in order to preserve his life. Drummond was charged with attempted murder. The charge was quashed as disclosing no offence known in law, in so far as one cannot be convicted of attempting to do something (kill a fetus) that, had one been successful, would not have been an offence (a child must be born alive and then die to support a charge of homicide based on actions against a fetus).[6] Again, in December, a New Brunswick judge held in *Dobson v. Dobson* that a child could sue his mother for (insurance) damages for injuries suffered while he was a fetus on account of his mother's negligent driving, which had resulted in an automobile accident.[7]

Together, these decisions affirm a number of well-established and familiar legal propositions,[8] which include: Canadian law does not recognize a fetus as a legal person possessing rights;[9] the line of demarcation for a fetus to become a legal person—the so-called "born alive" rule—"is the requirement that it be born completely extruded from its mother's body and be born alive;"[10] remedies for negligent behaviour cannot be pursued until a cause of action is brought by a legal person;[11] once a child is born, alive and viable, the law may recognize that its existence began before birth for certain limited purposes,[12] by means of a legal fiction;[13] the courts do not have a wardship jurisdiction over unborn children;[14] orders for detention or forced medical treatment of pregnant women are impermissible;[15] the pregnant woman and her unborn child are one—prior to birth, the fetus does not exist as a person and in law is part of its mother;[16] and that regarding an unborn child and its mother as separate legal or juristic persons in a mutually separable and antagonistic relationship would be a radically new conception in law.[17]

One clear message to police, physicians, child protection agencies, and judges of first instance is that during the period of pregnancy the fetus is outside their jurisdiction.[18] This message is resolutely positive—in fact—for all who are concerned with protecting and enhancing the sphere of women's reproductive autonomy. However—in law—the decision raises some issues of fundamental concern. One feature of the decision is that it carries the weight of unusual dissent in this area by two Supreme Court judges.[19] Another dimension is that the decisions engage so little with the challenges of feminist theory, Aboriginal voices, and medical complexity. Finally, the limitations of the conceptual framework adopted by the majority and minority judges—that of legal personality—are made starkly clear. It is with these issues that I engage in this comment.

Legal personhood has been a basic building block and reference point in common law and, together with the concept of legal individualism, is of central ideological importance in the common law. Roger Cotterrell has noted that "the concept of the legal person or legal subject defines who or what the law will recognize as a being capable of having rights and duties."[20] According to the jurist, G. Paton, in his text on jurisprudence; "[L]egal personality … refers to the particular device by which the law creates or recognizes units to which it ascribes certain powers and capacities … Just as the concept 'one' in arithmetic is essential to the logical system developed … so a legal system must be provided with a basic unit before full legal relationships can be devised which will serve the primary purpose of organizing social facts. The legal person is the unit or entity adopted."[21] Cotterrell draws our attention to the ideological significance of this "logical system":

> [The concept] allows legal doctrine to spin intricate webs of interpretation of social relations, since the law defines persons in ways that empower or disable, distinguish and classify individuals for its special regulatory purposes. For example, children, slaves, mentally disordered individuals, prisoners or married women may be partially or wholly, invisible to the law in particular societies and eras; not recognized as persons at all, or treated as possessing only limited legal capacities to contract, to own property, or to bring legal actions. In this way, throughout history, law has not merely defined social relations, but defined the nature of the beings involved in them.[22]

Of course, legal persons need not be human beings or animate beings who are able to articulate their own interests directly. Corporations are legal persons and so-too are religious idols, which can be endowed with juristic identity.[23] There is nothing inherent in the fetus itself that disqualifies it from being ascribed legal personality; nothing that is except for the clear and irreconcilable conflict with the twin concept of legal individualism/individuation: although it is a distinct biological entity, the fetus has no separate existence from the pregnant woman, it is literally within the human being and legal personality of the pregnant woman, and has no capacity for severable rights or interests. Within the framework of legal personality and the rights-embued individual that flows from it, the fetal/maternal social and legal relation, then, is a conundrum for the law.

This observation is not new. The problem was explicitly addressed to the Supreme Court of Canada several years ago by the Women's Legal Education and Action Fund (LEAF) in its factum as intervener in the 1991 case of *R. v. Sullivan*,[24] in which two midwives were charged with criminal negligence as a result of the death of a fetus during childbirth. LEAF unsuccessfully argued that the harm to the fetus should be regarded as harm to the mother. The judges held that the fetus had not become a human being and that independent harm had not been caused to the birthing mother. In its factum, LEAF stated:

> Traditionally legal method proceeds by analogy and distinction, making it tempting to compare the relationship between a pregnant women and her fetus to relations already mapped by law. However, there are no adequate analogies to pregnancy and childbirth and attempts to find them distort reality. Had women not been excluded from participation in the legal system, the unique relationship between the woman and her fetus and the experience of pregnancy in the life of women—hardly new facts—might have engendered their own fundamental legal concepts and doctrine, as elaborate as [doctrines dealing with commercial partnerships for example].[25]

Nevertheless, this conundrum has been side-stepped in recent cases, with the judges choosing to base their decisions on relationships already mapped by law and building their reasoning around legal personhood/individualism.

In one sense, this approach has been inevitable in so far as the tools for an alternative approach or another option in law have not been clearly articulated. There is, too, a concern that deviating from the established reasoning might place at risk the hard-won position in Canadian law that permits women the choice to continue or terminate their pregnancies.[26] Finally, there is the issue of the fundamental and apparently intractable policy concerns that are raised in this area. In her majority judgement in *G. (D.F.)*, Justice Beverley McLachlin identified a "host of [seemingly unanswerable] policy considerations" that "may be raised against the imposition of tort liability on a pregnant woman for lifestyle choices that may affect her unborn child."[27] These considerations included a need to avoid creating maternal/fetal conflict over decision-making power;[28] the absence of "bright lines" to distinguish tortious from non-tortious behaviours: difficulty determining what will cause "grave and irreparable harm to a fetus";[29] the observable factor that the women most likely to "fall afoul" of a new duty would be "minority women, illiterate women, and women of limited education;"[30] and the reality that the proscribed behaviours "may be the products of circumstance and illness rather than free choice capable of effective deterrence by the legal sanction of tort."[31] McLachlin J. concluded that the potential increase in outside levels of scrutiny of the conduct of pregnant women would be highly problematic,[32] particularly, given the paucity of evidence that a duty of care to the fetus, such as that proposed by the appellant, would reduce the incidence of substance-abused children or would produce healthier mothers.[33]

In *G. (D.F.)*, however, Justice McLachlin's solution—which could not have been more explicitly stated—was to refer the matter to the legislature and remove consideration of the policy questions and expansion in the area from the common law. She referred over fifteen times in the course of her relatively brief reasons to the fact that these issues were of such gravity and significance that they should be left to the legislature. However, the core of the issue, in my view, is not *who* should make the change but *what* the change should be: a shift of conceptual frameworks is required when considering the social relationship of pregnancy.

In *G. (D.F.)*, the judges clearly disagreed as to what their roles should be when confronted with the limits of existing law. McLachlin J. appeared, somewhat inchoately, to recognize that the concept of legal personhood could take the matter only so far; she chose to hold the existing line. Mr. Justice Major in dissent was not so circumspect. In his view, the line of demarcation of legal persons has been wrongly drawn and should be shifted in order to locate a fetus being carried to term within its range.

McLachlin J. began her decision with the comment:

> Ascribing personhood to a foetus in law is a fundamentally normative task. It results in the recognition of rights and duties—a matter which falls outside the concerns of scientific classification. In short, this court's task is a legal one. Decisions based upon broad social, political, moral and economic choices are more appropriately left to the legislature.[34]

Conceptual change and normative limitations, however, were not of significant concern to Major J., and he was quite straightforward that he considered his decision to be a challenge to the status quo. However, his was not a progressive activism. The dangerous inversion in his approach was apparent in his rejection of McLachlin J.'s (admittedly timid) reference to the Court's task in *G. (D.F.)* as being solely a "legal one."

In McLachlin J.'s reference, there is the sound of a distant echo that Major J. appears to have heard. In the well-known "Person's Case,"[35] the judges of the Supreme Court of Canada rejected the argument that women were within the meaning of the term "persons," in the context of their eligibility for appointment to the Senate in section 24 of the *British North America Act, 1867*. They too had been at pains to point out that they were deciding only a legal question. Their decision, of course, was subsequently swept away by the Judicial Committee of the Privy Council. In sounding the echo, Major J. was quite explicit:

> Precedent that states that a fetus is not a "person" should not be followed without an inquiry into the purpose of such a rule. In the well-known case of *Edwards v. Attorney General for Canada*, the Privy Council overruled precedent and a unanimous Supreme Court of Canada ... and held that women were "persons" with respect to s. 24 of the *B.N.A. Act, 1867*. Rigidly applying precedents of questionable applicability without inquiry will lead the law to recommit the errors of the past.[36]

However, seeking to cast off precedent in the area of women's reproductive autonomy without engaging with the complex theoretical and conceptual issues it raises is no remedy to error. Indeed, I consider that Major J. went on to propose a regime that would not only be an "error in the present" but would almost certainly guarantee recommission of errors in the past.[37]

The foundation of Major J.'s decision was that the "born alive" rule should be set aside as an "outdated" and "indefensible" evidentiary presumption given the advances in medical knowledge and technology that "show us that a foetus is alive and has been or will be injured by the conduct of another."[38] In this reasoning, Major J. drew on the assessments of improving medical knowledge and technological advances, which appear to tell us (or to tell male judges) more about the fetus. He posited that these assessments provide a basis to extend the pur/view of law in relation to the fetus. Clearly, he felt he could more clearly "see" the fetus and thus could more confidently expand the reach of law towards it. Yet, his challenge to the "born alive" rule was based on a static and ascribed view of the rule's rationale that was exclusively medical and dated from a time at which it was not medically possible to determine the status of the fetus and the impact upon it of human conduct. This is not the only available rationale. As LEAF pointed out in its factum, another rationale is that only upon birth does "the live infant become individuated and capable of entering into the types of social relationships with others which are the proper province of law."[39] LEAF further argued that the "acceptance of birth as the defining moment of legal personhood is the only position which is consistent with, let alone protective of, women's equality rights."[40] A biological focus is radically incomplete given that procreation is socially gendered and its terms are a matter of social (economic, legal, and technological) construction. Surely a Supreme Court judge should not fall so easily into the thrall of biological determinism in such a fundamentally policy-based area.

However, based on his rationale and with faith in the science of medical technology as a guide, Major J. set his path. He commented at the outset of his decision that, "to the extent that a change in the law is required, the much admired flexibility of the common law has proven adaptable enough over centuries to meet exigent circumstances as they arise."[41] Not surprisingly, by the end of his decision, a fetus had become a person "for purposes of the *parens patriae* jurisdiction," who was in a "particularly vulnerable position" in that "absent outside assistance," it had "no means of escape from toxins ingested by its mother."[42] Ms. G., and all addicted pregnant women in her situation, had been constructed by Major J. as "reckless" mothers,[43] "who had chosen to continue their substance abuse,"[44] had unreasonably rejected culturally appropriate and benevolent care,[45] and, in so doing, had caused "devastating harm and a life of suffering" which could have "so easily [been] prevented,"[46] to "a child [they] had decided to bring into the world."[47] A woman's choice was thereby limited to aborting her fetus or to undertaking "some responsibility for its well-being,"[48] which was enforceable by the courts although involving a "fairly modest" imposition on the mother[49] and a "relatively modest" intrusion on her liberty interests[50] that "must bend when faced with" such a situation.[51] To Major J., "Where the harm is so great and the temporary remedy so slight, the law is compelled to act."[52] What was exercising Major J. was that he did "not believe our system, whether legislative or judicial, has become so paralysed that it will ignore a situation where the imposition required in order to prevent terrible harm is so slight ... outdated medical assumptions should not provide any license to permit the damage to continue."[53] He could not accept the prospect of the law, "standing idly by end watching the birth of a permanently and seriously handicapped child who has no future other than as a permanent ward of the state."[54] In this world view, the normal conservative response to feared fetal harms, in which the pregnant women "disappears" in favour of consideration of the fetus,[55] is inverted by Major J. to one in which the fetus "disappears." Instead, it becomes a "person" that is seen by the benevolent gaze of the law while, at the same lime, the law imposes surveillance on the very present woman who is disciplined for everyone's good, including her own.

In his willingness to expand the law, Major J. was directly invoking the common law role of judges to define the nature of beings and to profoundly alter their social relations. In doing so, he drew on a particular factual, medical, and cultural context in conjunction with the legal context that was posited. In his story, which drew heavily upon the factum of the appellant child protection agency, Ms. G. had consistently refused all earlier offers of treatment and had refused to attend the treatment program offered by the appellant agency during her fourth pregnancy at which time a place had been immediately available. Moreover, he accepted the evidence of an expert witness as establishing that although the first sixteen weeks after conception are the most critical development period for the central nervous system, "any reduction of toxic exposure during pregnancy would reduce the central nervous system damage."[56] Reduced to terms of such stark intransigence (notwithstanding contrary voices in the Manitoba Court of Appeal), the temptation for action through legal intervention in the face of a legal conundrum was clearly overwhelming for Justice Major. While he crafted an apparently restrictive regime in which action would be limited to extreme cases, a procedurally fair process, and the least intrusive remedy, he clearly considered that the *G. (D.F.)* case would fall within such a regime.

If Major J.'s opinion is a good example of how the law sees and who it sees, it is also a good exemplar of the constructed nature of this legal approach and, hence, of the possibility of constructing alternative response. To deconstruct for a moment, the Women's Health Rights Coalition pointed out in its factum that the factual basis laid out in the lower courts in *G. (D.F.)* was incomplete. There was no trial and what evidence there was, was introduced during litigation that proceeded "at breakneck speed and was handled on an emergency basis." There was little or no opportunity for cross-examination or contrary evidence to be introduced because of the nature of the proceedings.[57] Similarly, the Canadian Civil Liberties Association made the obvious point in its factum that "it is inevitable that most if not all applications for foetal protection will be brought under urgent conditions. Emergency conditions prevailed in virtually every one of the American cases referred to ... the courts have recognized the inherent difficulty of doing justice in this situation."[58]

Significantly, the Women's Health Rights Coalition provided information in their factum that established that a far more nuanced and complex situation existed than was depicted by Major J. It appears that Ms. G. did seek treatment for her glue sniffing on several occasions. Moreover, in early June 1996, she had applied voluntarily to enter an addiction treatment centre in Winnipeg only to be told that there was a waiting list of several months but to "keep in touch." After the appellant agency became involved in mid-July, Ms. G. again expressed her willingness to obtain treatment. When the agency worker tried to take Ms. G. to the treatment centre she was intoxicated; she said she would get treatment, but "not right now." Instead of returning to repeat the invitation when Ms. G. was sober, the agency sought judicial intervention.[59] The coalition also suggested with compelling references that the expert medical evidence relied upon by Major J. is in fact far more ambivalent and equivocal and suggests only that there was some evidence of fetal harm from solvent exposure, that benefits to discontinuance, although expected, are not fully known in that the data are incomplete, and that the existence of a fetal solvent syndrome had not been established.[60] This case, then, was far from the starkly framed scenario presented by Major J.

An additional dimension of Major J.'s decision was the cultural context that was accepted by him as forming part of the factual basis of his decision. He appeared to accept that "mental and physical disabilities in children as a result of substance abuse by their mothers while pregnant" is "a 'crisis situation' in many Aboriginal communities."[61] He noted that one of the two Aboriginal interveners[62] intervened, in part, to urge upon this Court the creation of a legal remedy to use in their fight against fetal alcohol syndrome/fetal alcohol effects (FAS/FAE). These interveners submitted that such a remedy would be consistent with the aboriginal world view, and that the common law should be expanded to help alleviate what is particularly an aboriginal problem."[63]

A clear difference in approach is apparent in the arguments made in *G. (D.F.)* by the two interveners most representative of Aboriginal communities. On the one hand, Southeast Child and Family Services emphasized as "clear and overwhelming" the evidence of a link between substance abuse by pregnant women and FAS/FAE. They suggested that Aboriginal leaders had advocated "strategies to intervene and prevent FAS/E"[64] and argued that "[t]he traditional Aboriginal perspectives regarding world view, pro-natal care and the place of children in Aboriginal cultures support the conclusion that an expectant mother had a responsibility, not only to her child *in utero*, but also to the community to take appropriate care of herself and the child."[65] Moreover, they argued that in early Aboriginal societies, "[p]renatal care often involved restrictions and rules concerning diet and activity"[66] and, while non-intervention was part of the belief system, it had "not been necessary" because "each member accepted" her responsibility.[67] Pending a return to traditional values and teachings about pregnancy and birthing, this intervener seemed willing to have the court step in: "Courts should encourage and support community based support which in turn will encourage traditional values and teachings."[68]

A significantly different stance was taken by the other Aboriginal intervener—the Women's Health Rights Coalition. The coalition addressed the responses of Aboriginal communities to fetal health issues, arguing strongly that "resort to involuntary confinement and treatment *has not been endorsed* by Aboriginal peoples" and there has been "no call for judicial intervention issuing forth from inside or outside Aboriginal communities" [emphasis in original].[69] Instead, rather than recommendations for coercion through court orders, innovative community health and voluntary treatment strategies are being formulated and implemented as holistic and helping approaches.[70] The coalition urged the Court to listen carefully and sensitively to the concerns, frameworks, and options put forward by Aboriginal communities and to avoid recommitting the egregious errors of past, "well-intentioned" interventions. In its factum, LEAF also clearly made the point that "for Aboriginal women in particular, the use of coercive powers against them is viewed as the next phase in government control over their mothering."[71] The debate between these groups clearly draws attention to the non-unitary nature of the views about Aboriginal world view, culture, and tradition. It should surely caution (non-Aboriginal) judges from the expedient assimilation of one view over another in support of decisions framed around European legal concepts.

This analysis leaves us, however, with the nub of the problem: the current options and approaches in law seem unsatisfactory—fetal rights advocates are touching a nerve in calling attention to the fetus, and feminist legal theorists have little in place as an alternative response beyond reassertion of the non-personhood of a fetus. In its factum in support of intervention, the Attorney-General of Manitoba used a rather breathtaking example to advocate for a switch from fetal non-personhood to fetal personhood:

> It is submitted that in extreme eases, the need for intervention would be obvious to all. For example, if a woman in the last week of pregnancy held a gun to her stomach and threatened to shoot, one would be hard pressed to suggest that there should be no power to intervene to protect the child, even though the mother has the right to take her own life.[72]

Of course, something similar was the scenario in *Drummond*. In that case, however, the response to a charge of attempted murder by the mother of her fetus was that such an offence was not known in law. Nothing visible to the law had happened. Pressing the point, in the *Sullivan* case, in which the alleged negligence of two midwives led to the death of a full-term fetus in the birth canal, the legal response was that "no-one" had died.[73] This result is undeniably where the law takes us and leaves us within the current legal personhood analysis and its options. Fetal rights advocates are not the only ones ill at ease; this situation can also be troubling for those, like myself, who support non-intervention into women's reproductive sphere.[74]

Some of the argumentation and reasoning in *G. (D.F.)* was directed towards seeking appropriate legal responses to the scenarios that were presented. One option, of course, was to place the relationship of the pregnant woman and fetus outside of legal regulation by constructing legal exclusions premised on the pre-eminent equality and life, liberty, and security interests of pregnant women. Such an approach was favoured by McLachlin J. who affirmed the need to protect the very sphere held so lightly by her colleague Major J. In her view, "the order at issue in this trial can only be upheld by a radical extension of civil remedies into the most sacred sphere of personal liberty—the right of every person to live and move in freedom."[75] In its factum, LEAF also stressed that there is no period in any woman's life when she is outside the protection that the *Canadian Charter of Rights and Freedoms* guarantees.[76] They argued that the right to refuse medical treatment "even during pregnancy, exists for all forms of treatment," and thus, state-sanctioned interference with women's physical being and their authority to make prenatal caretaking decisions must necessarily be prohibited.[77]

A second option suggested in *G. (D.F.)* is to recognize positive state obligations to provide the appropriate conditions for ideal pregnancies. What is most interesting in *G. (D.F.)*, of course, is that Ms. G., once treatment became available, to her, remained voluntarily until her approved medical discharge in mid-August. It is tempting to recast this case to be one involving judicial intervention into inadequate and inconsistent social and health services. In this light, Ms. G. could be seen as having mobilized law as a means to finally be able to obtain treatment![78] The Women's Health Rights Coalition argued that, rather than changing or "expanding" the common law (which they argued would be wrong in principle and would send the wrong message to governments),[79] responsible public policy is required to attack the underlying social causes of addiction and provide innovative treatment interventions. With refreshing bluntness, they submitted that governments in Canada are avoiding their obligation to ensure social health and well-being and are failing to move quickly in establishing new, women-specific addiction treatment programs. The problem is especially acute for Aboriginal communities. The coalition continued, stating that if governments are going to ignore their social responsibilities, the Court should not try to solve the ensuing crisis by creating dubious new legal tools.[80]

A third option explored in argument was implementation of an "ethic of care" or a non-intervention, drawing on insights from alternative world views or frameworks.[81] This idea was most clearly articulated by the Women's Health Rights Coalition, which argued that "the health interests of mothers and children must be understood as inherently linked rather than opposed."[82] They posited that a woman has a moral duty to nourish and care for her fetus but stressed that this should not be cast as a coercible legal duty.[83] The coalition discussed an "ethic of non-interference" as being an important and widely accepted cultural value in Aboriginal culture, promoting positive interpersonal behaviour by discouraging coercion of any kind, be it physical, verbal, or psychological and stemming from a "high degree of respect for every individual's independence."[84] While accepting that "this is a case which cries out for 'something to be done,'" they posed a question rather than an answer: "precisely what should be done?"

The message I take from *G. (D.F.)* is that it is important—indeed pressing—to work to develop new responses, which are audible within law, to reproductive issues. To start, such responses need to accept that the fetus exists as a living being and proceed from the premise of a complex and ongoing relationship between fetus and woman that does not pit them in opposition but equally avoids creating a unitary entity based on the woman alone.[85] It must also respect the particular experience, needs, and capacities of women in relation to their fetuses and uphold their own bodily/relational integrity.[86] It is, therefore, timely to seek ways to move beyond the paradigm of personhood, individuation, and rights-based analysis in the area of women's reproduction. This situation is inherently relational; to disconnect woman and fetus is to create, rather than to solve, problems. An ethic of care, interconnection, and responsibility provide the basis for beginning to imagine new legal frameworks. We will undoubtedly have continuing opportunities to work towards a new approach to this area. In the meantime, the decision in *G. (D.F.)* protects pregnant Canadian women while this work, itself, gestates.

ENDNOTES

1. [1997] S.C.J. No. 96 (Q.L.) [Thereinafter *G. (D.F.)*].

2. The interveners at the Supreme Court of Canada were: the Attorney General of Manitoba: the government of Yukon; the Evangelical Fellowship of Canada, and the Christian Medical and Dental Society; the Catholic Group for Health, Justice and Life; the Alliance for Life; the Association des Centres jeunesse du Quebec; the Southeast Child and Family Services; the Canadian Abortion Rights Action League; the Women's Legal Education and Action Fund (LEAF); and a coalition (the Women's Health Rights Coalition) comprised of the Women's Health Clinic, the Métis Women of Manitoba, the Native Women's Transition Centre, and the Manitoba Association of Rights and Liberties.

3. (1996). 111 Man. R. (2d) 919 (Q.B.) *per* Shulman, J.

4. *Per* Helper J., Manitoba Court of Appeal, 8 August 1996.

5. (1996) 113 Man. R. (2d) 3 (Man. C.A.).

6. *R. v. Drummond*, [1996] O.J. No. 4597 (Ont. Prov. Div.), *per* Hansen, P.C.J. interpreting *Criminal Code*. R.S.C, 1985, c. C-46. s. 223, [hereinafter *Drummond*].

7. [1997] N.B.J. No. 17 (Q,B.) (Q.L.). *per* Miller J, [hereinafter *Dobson* (Q.B.)]: upheld (1997), 148 D.L.R. (4th) 332 (N.B.C.A,) [hereinafter *Dobson* (N..B.C.A.)]; leave to appeal to S.C.C. granted: [1997] S.C.C.A. No. 406 (Q.L.).

8. Many of these propositions became familiar in a preceding line of cases at the Supreme Court of Canada: *Borowski v. Attorney General for Canada*, [1989] 1 S.C.R. 342; *R. v. Morgentaler*. [1988] 1 S.C.R. 30; *Daigle v. Tremblay*, [1989] 2 S.C.R. 530 (abortion rights); *R. v. Sullivan*, [1991] 1 S.C.R. 489 (criminal negligence) [hereinafter *Sullivan* (S.C.C.)]. That the appellant's position represented a radical departure from these principles was noted in the factum of the Women's Legal Education and Action Fund, in *G. (D.F.)*, *supra* note 1 at para. 7 [hereinafter LEAF Factum].

9. *G. (D.F.), supra* note 1 at paras. 15-16.

10. *R. v. Sullivan* (1988). 43 C.C.C. (3d) 65 at 78 (B.C.C.A.) [hereinafter *Sullivan* (B.C.C.A.)]; affd. *Sullivan* (S.C.C.), *supra* note 8. As cited in *Drummond, supra* note 6 at para. 38.

11. *G. (D.F.), supra* note 1 at para. 23; *Dobson* (Q.B.), *supra* note 7 at para. 8.

12. *G. (D.F.), ibid.* at para. 14; *Dobson* [Q.B.). *ibid.* at para. 4, citing *Montreal Tramways v. Leveille*, [1933] S.C.R. 456 [hereinafter *Montreal Tramways*].

13. "For these reason, I am of the opinion that the fiction of the civil law must be held to be general application. The child will, therefore, be deemed to have been born at the time of the accident to the mother." *Montreal Tramways, Ibid.* at 465. At first instance in *Dobson* (Q.B.), Miller J. expressed some difficulty "in understanding the rationale" of such a fiction but resolved the matter by concluding that "the fiction recognized [in the case] must mean that two persons—the mother and the foetus—have the same enforceable rights." *Dobson* (QB.) *supra* note 7 at para. 6. Miller J. ultimately settled on the idea that "although a foetus is not recognized in law as a 'person,' certain rights do accrue and can be asserted upon being born alive." *Ibid.* at para. 28. Similarly, the majority in the Supreme Court in G. (D.F.) considered that "any rights or interest the fetus may have remain inchoate and incomplete until the child's birth." *G. (D.F.) supra* note 1 at para. 15. See Mark S. Scott, "Note: Quickening in the Common Law: The Legal Precedent Roe Attempted and Failed to Use" (1996) 1 *Michigan Law and Policy Review 199*.

14. *G. (D.F.), supra* note 1 at para. 51,

15. *Ibid.* at para. 59; See also *Re Baby R* (1988), 15 R.P.L (3d) 225 (B.C.S.C).

16. *G. (D.F.). supra* note 1 at para. 55; *Dobson* (N.B.C.A,), *supra* note 7 at para. 3; *Drummond, supra* note 6 at para. 41. citing *Sullivan* (B.C.C A.), *supra* note 10 at 80.

17. *G. (D.F.), supra* note 1 at para. 29.

18. This situation is also consistent with the majority recommendation against judicial interventions during gestation and childbirth made by the Royal Commission on New Reproductive Technologies in its final report, *Proceed with Care*, vol. 2 (Canada: Minister of Government Services, 1993) at 949 [hereinafter *Proceed with Care*].

19. Earlier decisions in the area of abortion, injunctions with respect to abortion, and so on have tended to be unanimous decisions by the judges of the Supreme Court of Canada.

20. Roger Cotterrell, *The Sociology of Law*, 2nd ed. (London: Butterworths, 1992) at 123-4.

21. G. Paten. *Textbook of Jurisprudence*, 4th ed. (London: Oxford University Press, 1972) at 392. See also F.H. Lawson, "The Creative Use of Legal Concepts" (1957) 32 *New York University Law Review* 913–16.

22. Cotterrell, *supra* note 20 at 123-4.

23. P.J. Duff. "The Personality of an Idol" (1923) 3 Cambridge Law Journal 42 Note also *Bumper Development Corporation v. Commissioner of Police for the Metropolis*, [1991] 4 All E.R. 638, in which the English Court of Appeal accepted that an "Indian Hindu temple [was] recognized as a legal person in Indian law, [and was] entitled to sue, through its representative, in an English court for the recovery of stolen property."

24. *Sullivan* (S.C.C.), *supra* note 8.

25. Factum of the Women's Legal Education and Action Fund in *Sullivan* (S.C.C.), *ibid.* at para. 29. See the factum as published in Women's Legal Education and Action Fund, *Equality and the Charter: Ten Years of Feminist Advocacy before the Supreme Court of Canada* (Toronto: Edmond Montgomery Publications, 1996) at 16.

26. It is noteworthy that all judges and interveners accepted that this case was not about abortion rights, but rather, about a woman's situation after she has exercised her decision to carry a fetus to term.

27. *G. (D.F.), supra* note 1 at pare. 36.

28. *Ibid.* at para. 37.

29. *Ibid.* at para. 39.

30. *Ibid.* at para. 40.

31. *Ibid.* at para. 41.

32. *Ibid.* at para. 42.

33. *Ibid.* at paras. 43-4.

34. *Ibid.* at para. 12.

35. *Edwards v. Attorney General for Canada*, [1930] A.C. 124, a reference case concerning whether women were to be included in the term "persons" in the context of the interpretation of section 24 of the *British North America Act, 1867*, which outlined eligibility for appointment to the Senate.

36. *G. (D.F.), supra* note 1 at para. 118, *per* Major J.

37. See comments, *infra* note 711.

38. Major J. cited Clarke Forsythe, "Homicide of the Unborn Child: The Born Alive Rule and Other Legal Anachronisms" (1957) 21 *Valpariso University Law Review* 563. See also Mary Lynn Kime, "Note: *Hughes v. State*: The 'Born Alive' Rule Dies a Timely Death" (1995) 30 *Tulsa Law Journal* 539; Charles Kester, "Is There a Person in That Body?: An Argument for the Priority of Persons and the Need for a New Legal Paradigm" (1994) 82 *Georgetown Law Journal* 1643; and Stephanie Ritrivi McCavitt, "The 'Born Alive' Rule: A Proposed Change to the New York Law Based on Modern Medical Technology" (1991) 36 *New York Law School Law Review* 609.

39. Supra note 8 at para. 23.

40. *Ibid.* at para. 24.

41. *G. (D.F.), supra* note 1 at para. 61.

42. *Ibid.* at para. 103.

43. *Ibid,* at para. 95.

44. *Ibid.* at para. 62.

45. *Ibid.* at para. 81.

46. *Ibid.* at para. 93. In this view, Major J.'s oversimplification of the situation before him is breath-taking. In its Factum at para. 81, LEAF pointed out that the attempt to use legal coercion to respond to these very complex situations "is to privatize fault and punish women. Pregnant women will be held personally responsible for systemic problems." LEAF Factum, *supra* note 8.

47. *Ibid.* at para. 95.

48. *Ibid.* at para. 116.

49. *Ibid.* at para. 132.

50. *Ibid.* at para. 133. In its factum, LEAF pointed out that the position of Child and Family Services "grossly underestimates women's constitutional rights." LEAF Factum, in *ibid.* at para. 21. Major J. appears to have taken women's constitutional rights similarly lightly. He failed to notice that this "relatively modest" intrusion was sex-specific (and pregnancy-specific) and thus raised additional constitutional equality interests. In the words of LEAF in its factum: "Court orders mandating the conduct of women during pregnancy ... create a sex-specific burden which reinforces limiting cultural stereotypes and further entrenches existing inequalities." LEAF Factum, ibid. at para. 34. See also *Brooks v. Canada Safeway*, [1989] 1 S.C.R. 1219.

51. *Ibid.* at para. 93.

52. *Ibid.* at para. 138.

53. *G. (D.F.), supra* note 1 at para. 138.

54. *Ibid.* at para. 53.

55. See my comments in T. Brettel Dawson, "A Feminist Response to 'Unborn Child Abuse': Contemplating Legal Solution" (1991) 9 *Canadian Journal of Family Law* 157 at 169. See also Christine Overall, "'Pluck the Ferns from Its Womb': A Critique of Current Attitudes to the Embryo/Fetus" (1986) 24 *University of Western Ontario Law Review* 1.

56. *G. (D.F.). supra* note 1 at para. 83.

57. Factum of the Women's Health Rights Coalition, in *G. (D.F.), ibid.* at paras. 8-10 [WHRC Factum].

58. Factum of the Canadian Civil Liberties Association, in *G. (D.F.). ibid.* at para. 45.

59. WHRC Factum, in *supra* note 57, at paras. 13-16.

60. *G. (D.P.), supra* note 1, at para. 17.

61. *Ibid.* at para. 88.

62. Southeast Child and Family Services.

63. *Ibid.*

64. Factum of Southeast Child and Family Services and West Region Child and Family Services, in *G. (D.F.), supra* note 1 at para. 16-17.

65. *Ibid.* at para. 22.

66. *Ibid.* at para. 31.

67. *Ibid.* at para. 36.

68. *Ibid.* at para. 47.

69. WHRC Factum, *supra* note 57 at para. 46.

70. *Ibid.*

71. LEAF Factum, *supra* note 8 at para. 14. The earlier phases identified by LEAF included residential schooling and child welfare removals ("the Sixties Scoop"). See also, *Report of the Aboriginal Justice Inquiry of Manitoba* (Winnipeg: Province of Manitoba, 1991) at 520; Anne McGillivray. "Therapies of Freedom: The Colonization of Aboriginal Childhood," in Anna McGillivray, ed. *Governing Childhood* (Aldershot: Dartmouth Press, 1996). LEAF analyzed the process of social and legal categorization that a case such as this one invites: "[I]ndividuals [can be] assigned to a group and then special categories of socially constructed difference are invoked in an attempt to explain prejudicial treatment and justify force ... If pregnant women have been historically and socially devalued, an aboriginal woman who is solvent addicted and poor has been marginalized to the point where some people redefine coercion and force as help and care." LEAF Factum, *supra* note 8 at para 50. The Women's Health Rights Coalition in their factum reported a comment made by a participant during a sharing circle of women who had been involved in some form of substance addiction: "Why would you go and see your doctor when you know they will end up taking your baby away?" WHRC Factum, *supra* note 57 at para. 33.

72. Factum of the Attorney General of Manitoba, in *G. (D.F.)* at para. 16.

73. *Sullivan* (S.C.C.). *supra* note 8. Even in *Dobson* the policy limitations of the person-based framework were starkly shown. As things currently stand, after a child is born and becomes a legal person there is nothing to distinguish actions by a third party from actions by the mother during pregnancy as the basis for legal action, precisely because the basis for the legal rule does not recognize women's reproductive autonomy or bodily integrity nor does it accept a collectively-based relation. In *Dobson* (Q.B), Miller J. reasoned that "if an action can be sustained by a child against a parent, and if an action can be sustained against a stranger for injuries suffered by a child before birth, then it seems to me a reasonable progression to allow an action by a child against his mother for prenatal injuries caused by her negligence," *Dobson* (Q.B.), *supra* note 7 at para. 26. The New Brunswick Court of Appeal upheld on appeal and added that the action arose based on a pregnant mother's general duty to drive carefully—a duty which "even the mother at the wheel owes to her fetus." (Citing John Fleming, *Law of Torts*, 8th ed. (Sydney: Law Book Company, 1992) at 168.) When the *Dobson* case reaches the Supreme Court of Canada on appeal, a range of policy arguments can be anticipated including a focus on the bodily integrity of the woman. One argument is likely to be that "suits taken by children against third parties for damage caused *in utero* reinforce a woman's bodily integrity by providing additional deterrent to negligent intrusions on her body and should not be used as precedent for obligations which would detract from that integrity and infringe her equality." See LEAF Factum, *supra* note 8 at para. 31, in the specific context of arguing against a creation in tort of a maternal duty of care towards her fetus. Another policy argument focuses on the distinct and unique aspect or maternal/fetal relationship: "[A] pregnant woman and her fetus share physical interdependency that a third-party and the fetus do not. The nature of the relationship between the pregnant woman and her fetus makes problematic tort liability against the

mother for prenatal injuries," American Medical Association, Board of Trustees Report, "Legal Interventions during Pregnancy: Court-Ordered Medical Treatments and Legal Penalties for Potentially Harmful Behaviour by Pregnant Women" (1990) 264 (20) *Journal of the American Medical Association* 2663 at 2664; as cited in WHRC Factum, *supra* note 57 at para. 25.

74. It might also be noted that reproduction is not the only area that raises such concerns for law. Complex, ongoing economic relationships raise similar dissonance with the individuated paradigm of obligation. See further T. Brettel Dawson, "Estoppel and Obligation: The Modern Role of Estoppel by Convention" (1989) 9 *Legal Studies* 16.

75. G. (D.F.). supra note 1 at para. 46.

76. *Canadian Charter of Rights and Freedoms*, Part I of the *Constitution Act, 1982*, as enacted by the *Canada Act 1982* (U.K.). 1992.

77. LEAF Factum, *supra* note 8 at paras. 30, 33, and 43.

78. In flipping the situation in this way, I do not mean to negate the very real disempowerment felt by, and imposed upon, Ms. G. by the state actions in her situation. Interestingly, in its factum, LEAF points out that Child and Family Services "should not be able to argue that coercion against individual women is now necessary because the government of Manitoba has failed in its duty to provide adequate services," LEAF Factum, *ibid.* at para. 67. See also Martha Jackman, "Constitutional Contact with the Disparities of the World: Poverty as a Prohibited Ground of Discrimination under the Canadian Charter and Human Rights Law" (1994) 2 *Review of Constitutional Studies* 76.

79. LEAF Factum, *supra* note 8 at para. 35

80. *Ibid.* at para. 39.

81. *See Proceed with Care, supra* note 18 at 962:

In line with the ethic of care, we believe that the best approach is to seek ways to ensure that the needs of both the woman and fetus are met—in other words, to prevent a situation developing in which child welfare, medical, or other authorities might consider judicial intervention appropriate or necessary. The ethic of care offers a means of avoiding the conflicts inherent in judicial intervention by promoting two fundamental values: respect for the rights and autonomy of the pregnant woman and concern for the health and well-being of the fetus. The best way to accomplish this is not by compelling pregnant women to behave in certain ways, but by providing a supportive and caring environment in which they can make informed decisions and choose among realistic options before and during pregnancy.

82. WHRC Factum, *supra* note 57 at para. 21.

83. *Ibid.* at para. 74.

84 *Ibid.* at para. 49.

85. Recall Sir William Blackstone's words in his eighteenth-century *Commentaries*:

[B]y marriage, the husband and wife are one person in law: that is, the very being or legal existence of the woman is suspended during the marriage, or at least is incorporated and consolidated into that of her husband; under whose wing, protection, and cover, she performs everything.

Sir William Blackstone, *Commentaries on the Laws of England*, Vol. I (Chicago: University of Chicago Press, 1979), 442.

86. See also Elaine Hughes, "Fishwives and Other Tales: Ecofeminism and Environmental Law" (1995) 8 *Canadian Journal of Women and the Law* 502, in which an alternative relations paradigm for environmental law is suggested.

ENGENDERING VIOLENCE

...we witnessed with horror the spiraling momentum of woman-hating explode, in the early evening of December sixth, with the massacre of fourteen women at the University of Montréal. The historical context of our individual and collective experiences as intellectual women enabled me to see that what the media had labelled as the "idiosyncratic" madness of this young man actually reflected infinitely multiplying images of male power transformed into violence—a polished surface facing the mirror of masculine privilege. (Lewis, 1993, 151-152)

The Montréal Massacre functioned as a clarion call to action on the problem of violence against women. From the societal denials that had impeded responses for much of the 1970s and 1980s, the 1990s emerged as a time of reckoning with the pervasive and systemic nature of gender violence. But even this sad and dramatic event would not have been sufficient to prompt recognition had it not been for the decades of feminist activism and intellectual work preceding it.

For more than 30 years, Canadian feminists have theorized, documented, pressured governments, and constructed independent responses to violence against women. Against the dominant understanding of sexual violence as a series of uncommon events perpetuated by deviant criminals, feminist analysts have illuminated its widespread incidence and structural nature. Canadian feminists have insisted that we recognize how the threat of violence is a constant companion for all women and has operated to restrict their freedom, mobility, and aspirations. Three of the readings in this chapter are important parts of this effort in societal consciousness-raising.

The first Canadian book on rape, Clark and Lewis's *Rape: The Price of Coercive Sexuality* (1977) represented a devastating indictment of the criminal justice system. This study established that law had not only failed to deal fairly with women's complaints of rape, it also embedded and perpetuated a set of rape myths. In examining police handling of rape complaints in the early 1970s, Clark and Lewis demonstrated how the classification "unfounded" seemed to depend on perceptions of the victim's character. Flipping on its head the dominant understanding of law as the answer to the problem of rape, the study claimed that legal practices actually encouraged the assault of particular groups of women (through the dichotomous characterization "good" women and "bad" women).

The politicization of "wife battering," like rape, emerged from feminist grassroots activism. But attention to violence in intimate relationships lagged behind the definition of rape as a social problem. The RCSW (see Canadian Women's Movements chapter) was completely silent about wife battering. It was feminist front-line activism that led to the establishment of the first transition houses in the early 1970s. In 1981, when a parliamentary committee released a report documenting the prevalence of wife battering, many members of parliament responded with nervous laughter. Clouded by patriarchal constructions of the family as "haven," the naming of intimate violence posed a serious challenge to the dominant, romanticized idea of the traditional nuclear family.

The intent of Linda MacLeod's *Wife Battering: The Vicious Circle* (1981) was to question the many myths about intimate violence with glimpses of "reality," provided first through the use of stories about woman abuse in outwardly happy middle class families, then through empirical study. We live in a society where quantification implies legitimacy and "Truth." Consequently, breaking the silence surrounding men's violence necessarily involved statistical documentation. Early feminist investigations underline the paucity of empirical analyses and indeed it was not until 1993 that the first national Statistics Canada study on violence against women was released (Statistics Canada 1993). MacLeod's study estimated that one in ten women married or living common law, regardless of class or race, experienced intimate violence. Her analysis pointed towards structural factors, rather than poverty, individual pathology or "faulty" family interaction as the foundations of intimate violence.

If the existence of intimate violence threatened strongly held beliefs about the nuclear family, breaking the silence on child sexual abuse was even more disruptive. But it was not empirical research that first unsettled the climate of denial surrounding sexual abuse of children. Instead, it was women's life writing. Standing out among the Canadian texts released in the 1970s and 1980s is Elly Danica's (1988) unsettling *Don't: A Woman's Word*. Critically acclaimed, *Don't* has been described as, "…the beginning of a survivor's lexicon. The birth into language of her own savage abuse …the imperative assertion of [Danica's] own agency, 'don't'" (Williamson, 1990, 140). As a child and an adult, Danica had tried to tell her story again and again and in each telling, her claims were denied. Her project speaks in a different way than the social scientific discourses deployed by Clark and Lewis and MacLeod. Danica opens a space in language which her story can find meaning and finally, be heard. Her "speaking against the injunction to silence," provides a feminist experiential standpoint for knowing sexual abuse.

Together, significant texts such as these played a crucial role in releasing the problem of violence against women from its denied past. But this was only the first step in attempting to undo the problem of violence against women. In their effort to challenge the conditions that sustain gendered violence, feminists have employed three inter-related strategies. First, since the emergence of early interventions that sought to name violence as a systemic problem, the Canadian feminist literature on this subject has ballooned into a now impressive collection of texts that theorizes, documents and seeks to address this continued problem in all of its dimensions. The feminist texts described above sang almost solo; the cry that "this is the first study, book or narrative" is one that can no longer be made.

The second strategy used was direct grassroots action, informed by the radical feminist recognition of the necessity of autonomous organizations, devoted to the empowerment of women experiencing violence. The creation of what is now a national network of over 60 rape crisis centres and approximately 400 transition houses has been instrumental in providing services for survivors and in raising awareness. At the end of the millennium, these important services face proliferating crises, including declining governmental support and a growing societal backlash. Capturing the thrust of this backlash, a national newspaper feature report on rape crisis centres and battered women's shelters emphasizes a pervasive climate of mismanagement and internal conflict. In this article, feminist anti-violence organizations are represented as mere indoctrinators of their clients and most definitely undeserving of continued funding (LaFramboise, 1998).

Perhaps because it is more consistent with the dominant construction of gender violence as "crime," the final feminist strategy—criminal law reform—has had greater success. Since the 1970s, there have been important initiatives tightening legal definitions and creating practices to improve the treatment of those who have experienced violence. But many analysts now contend that law reform as strategy needs to be carefully evaluated.

The text by Jennifer Scott and Sheila McIntyre outlines the impact of more than two decades of feminist efforts to rewrite Criminal Code provisions on rape/sexual assault. While informed by feminist academic study, this analysis is excerpted from a submission made to a parliamentary committee by the national feminist litigation organization, the Women's Legal Education and Action Fund (LEAF). It is, therefore, feminist lobbying in action.

This submission highlights the central feminist insight that sexual violation must be analyzed as both function and effect of social inequalities. Systemic inequality makes all women vulnerable to sexual violence—but other forms of social power "particularize" this vulnerability. In underscoring how race, class, age, and disability increase the vulnerability of many women and simultaneously diminish their credibility in law, this piece demonstrates an important evolution in feminist thinking. For much of the 1970s and 1980s, violence against women was seen exclusively as an outgrowth of male domination. For example, feminist analyses most often failed to explore the racialized character of the violation experienced by aboriginal women, emphasizing instead the common vulnerability of "all women." It was not until the 1980s and 1990s that feminist anti-violence analysis and activism began to be influenced by a politics of difference. This shift resulted out of struggles waged by women of color, women with disabilities, aboriginal women and others, who challenged the silences of gender essentialist constructions of violence (Levan 1996, 331).

Scott and McIntyre outline several important changes to Criminal Code provisions on sexual assault—the most fundamental being the 1992 "no means no" amendments that explicitly define "consent" as voluntary agreement. Despite strongly worded legislation that is the envy of feminist law reformers in other countries, the incidence of sexual assault remains shockingly high (39%) and at the same time the least reported of any violent crime (6%) (Statistics Canada, 1993). Courts have struck down provisions aimed at improving the treatment of women complainants as infringements of the legal rights of accused persons.

In this way, progressive sexual assault law reforms have been undermined. In addition, rape myths continue to ground legal interpretation. For example, in *R. v. Ewanchuk*, a 1998 Alberta Court of Appeal decision recently overturned by Supreme Court, McClung J. contended that even though a young woman had repeatedly said "No, stop" to the escalating sexual advances of a potential employer in a job interview, her behaviour and what she wore could have led to an assumption of "implied consent."

By the end of the millennium, the problem of violence against women has entered into the mainstream. In this context, feminist anti-violence work faces different challenges. A critical challenge lies in maintaining the legitimacy of feminist representational claims. As government actors increasingly embrace the problem of gender violence as their own, there is a danger that feminist voices will be pushed to the margins. The federally appointed Canadian Panel on Violence Against Women illustrates this potential danger. When this national inquiry was announced in 1991, feminist activists insisted that some of its members be appointed by the organized women's movement. What was at stake was the very legitimacy of feminist knowledge. The government's resistance to movement appointees produced a rift between the Panel and organized feminism, exacerbated by the glaring under-representation of women of colour, immigrant women, and women with disabilities.

The *Final Report* of the panel, released in 1993, was written without the input of major feminist groups who had made the difficult decision to boycott. But this report nonetheless signaled a profound turning point in how "violence against women" was constructed as a policy problem. The report's rhetoric and recommendations reflected feminist perspectives on "violence against women." Gotell's, "A Critical Look at State Discourse on Violence Against Women," calls attention to the manner in which the Panel appropriates feminist analysis and discourse and represents women as "victims." Feminist anti-violence work has strategically deployed the claim that "women are victims of male violence," often at the same time stressing the strength of women's resistance and the necessity of empowerment. Gotell argues that for many reasons, feminists must be wary of constructing women as powerless victims, even for strategic reasons. Representing women as silent victims feeds all too easily into a justification of state protectionism and also allows for feminist knowledge and representation to be discounted. When the state claims to speak on behalf of women victims, feminist voices can be silenced. In the current context, then, a time of broken silence and a proliferation of government gestures, the real challenge for feminist activism will be to continue to speak for women and to maintain the claim of expertise gained through research and grassroots work.

Recognizing the complexity of gender violence and the manner in which it is rooted within overlapping power structures, affecting us all in different ways, is a formidable task. We need to continue to speak about violence and to listen to women telling their stories and experiences in new ways. The final reading in this chapter points us in the direction of this more complex future. In the 1980s, native feminists castigated white middle class feminists for appropriating their voices and experiences. By the early 1990s, aboriginal women organized to ensure that their specific experiences and history could begin to be told, heard, and dealt with on their own terms.

In the reading "Our Story," the pervasiveness of violence against native women is set within the context of racism and colonization that has eroded native communities. The thrust of this text, produced by the Aboriginal Women's Circle of the Canadian Panel on Violence Against Women, is to argue for the development of community-based approaches linked with the political empowerment of aboriginal women. This conclusion, while calling attention to the specificity of violence against native women, is one that should frame the future direction of anti-violence activism—ending gender violence requires women's empowerment.

DON'T:

A WOMAN'S WORD
Elly Danica

1.1　DON'T. I only know this word. This is the only word I have ever learned. Don't. I can not write with only this word. A woman's vocabulary: Don't.

1.2　Don't tell. Don't think. Don't, what ever else you do, don't feel. If you feel, the pain will be there again. Don't.

1.3　But the pain is there anyway. It exists even when I don't. See? I warned you. You can't afford to feel. Pain will reach out of your belly and grab you by the throat. Choking. His hands around my throat. It is only pain. Old friend. I thought it was him. Again. Only pain. I can stand the pain. I can drown it in words or wine or smoke. Something can be done. If it was him again, that would be different.

1.4　Feeling. Exploring. Pain like a mountain. I climb. More pain. The mountain never ends, it grows in me daily, my belly expanding to hold it. Nothing is born of this pain. Nothing I want to hold up to the light. Monster. Monstrous. Me. Mary, Mary, quite monstrous in my belly Mary Shelley. I know what you mean. I live here too. But only just survived the ritual incisions thrice carved on my pale belly.

1.5　I know death too. Death looks like the man my mother married. His pants down. Kids don't remember. I was a four-year-old adult. I remember. I was never a kid. I don't remember being a kid. I remember nothing useful. I remember yearning for innocence. Yearning for not knowing. Four. Nine. Eleven. Twelve. Thirteen. Fourteen. Fifteen. Fifteen began the time of yearning for memory. A different memory. I don't want to remember this. This never happened. The world is dark. There is no memory. Only his hands around my throat. Blocking. Memory gone. Speech gone. Feeling gone. No I. Nothing left.

1.6　She washes dishes. She's good at washing dishes. What else do we need her for? Why should I feed her? She's useless. I'll get a dishwasher, you plug them in, they don't talk back. She doesn't talk. Talk when I tell you. Smile god-dammit. Smile or I'll fix your face so it will do what I want.

1.7　Wanting. He always wants. I don't want. Who asked you? He wants. He gets. He knows how. Hands. Beating. Choking. Screaming? Who is that screaming? That's not me screaming. I no longer know how to scream. Except inside. Co-operate or I'll kill you. Do this or I'll hurt you. I already hurt. Inside. He can't see inside. Almost victory. There is something he can't touch. Inside. Very far away. Just a little light. Inside. Almost smile. Don't. He wants. He always wants.

1.8 Don't tell. Your mother. She doesn't understand. Our secret. Every time you tell I'll hurt you worse. Remember that. This is so you'll remember to keep your mouth shut. This is so you'll do as your told. This is because you're ugly. This is so you'll learn you are a woman. I know how to hurt you so there are no bruises. I'm not stupid. Stupid is female. Stupid cow. Stupid slut. Do what I tell you. Open your mouth. Put it in. If you bite again I'll kill you. Simple. Open your mouth. I'm already dead. What does it matter? Who will help me? My mother will not meet my eyes. My mother walks away. My mother knows. She knows. She always knows.

1.9 Children don't remember. Anyway. What does it matter? Who will believe the kid? I know what I'm doing. There are no visible bruises. Nobody will ever know. I'll kill you if you tell.

1.10 I know. Twenty-five years since the last secret. Thirty-six years since the first secret. I know. I don't know how to tell. Fear is the taste of my own blood in my mouth. Hands again. Always hands. Always hurting. Jaw. Neck. Throat. Arms. Belly. Genitals. Thighs. Always hurting.

1.11 Soul. A tiny light. If he doesn't know about it I can keep it. My secret. My soul. A self. A star. Millions of light years away. I search. I don't tell. He thinks I don't remember. He is puzzled by hate. After all he did for me. After all he gave me. I only hate. I do not murder. I have my star search. I believe in soul. He believes in hell. His own invention. He will reap what he sows.

1.12 Justice. How can I believe? He is free. I carry chains. He killed all that was beautiful in me. He is free. He has comfort. My mother. I don't know my mother. I don't know comfort. All I know is pain. Not just hands. Not just penis. Pain is like a stone growing in my belly. The mountain. I push it before me. It will never be born. Monstrous. Hate. I wear a girdle of hate. Days deformed. Life. This is not life. This is hell. The hell of the hands, choking. The hell of the penis, pushing. No. The hell of the four-year-old adult. Who doesn't remember. Who never forgets. Hate.

1.13 Hate as a promise. Never forget. Don't remember. Just never forget. Hate. Chains of hate. At least you won't forget to hate. The chains help you to remember. Bound to him. Bound to remember sooner or later. Later. I am forty. Now memory grows like a tree he planted. I hate the tree. I hate everything. When I was eleven he said he would teach me what it meant to be a woman. Again. He forgot the other times. Maybe I was a kid then. He doesn't have to remember. I can never forget.

1.14 I am not grateful. I am never grateful. Hands again. He'll teach me to be grateful. I am still not grateful. Thank it. Get down on your knees and thank it for making you a woman. That? Laughter. I'll kill you. Hands. Where is the light? Why is it so dark? Hands. My throat hurts. I can't kiss it. You can't make me. He knows how to use his hands. My throat doesn't exist. I don't exist. You can't make me. He is tired of hurting me. Go away, he says, I'll teach this lesson again. Tomorrow.

1.15 Another day. Always another day. Why doesn't he die of his evil? Only I will die of his evil. Ugliness. Something rotten. He sees it in my face. He laughs. Look in the mirror, stupid. Boils. On my face. Why is the evil of the fathers only visited on the daughters? Why do I have boils? Why not him? He wants to carve the boils from my face. He wanted to be a doctor. They wouldn't let him. He hates 'they'. He hates me. He will fix my face. I hide. He fixed my leg once. Dug in with a pocket knife. Made a hole in the muscle. Why should he care?

1.16 Kid's got no guts. Kid's got no brains. Just a stupid cunt. I said spread them. Now! Why? Because I said so. Because that's all you're good for. Do what you're told. Aren't you ever going to learn to do what you're told? Why do you make me hurt you? Do you think I like to hurt you? Smile I said. See what I mean? You never do a goddamn thing I ask. You never do anything right. No guts. No brains. Stupid.

1.17 He says I'm stupid? What he wants is stupid. Why don't you get somebody else for your stupid games? I like you. Daddy's girl. Wanna be daddy's girl? No. Just think that. Don't say no. Say nothing. I said don't you want to be daddy's girl? I expect a yes. Say yes. Say thank you daddy. That's what he wants. Don't say it. Don't say anything. Don't be part of his evil. If you don't say yes it's only a venial sin. You have to say yes. He wants a yes. He'll get a yes. He'll use his hands to get a yes. He'll rip the hair from your head. He'll get a yes. Now it is your sin. Now it is your fault.

1.18 Memory. Process. Year of the Rabbit. Running from memory. Can't run from him. No place to run. Nobody believes he hits me. How can I make them believe the rest? Where would I go? He said he'd find me and kill me, even if I run. No hope. Only hate. Hate as a live and growing thing. Hate keeps me alive. For tomorrow: a day when somebody believes me. Dawn. Someday. All I live is night. How can you live only night? Easy. Twenty-five years of darkness. Not easy. Hate as a companion. Nobody believes me at eighteen. Twenty. Twenty-three. At twenty-five I am declared a fuck-up. Useless. Again. I vow to leave town with my hate. I vow to look for sunshine. I see a shrink. Another shrink. Another. Finally a woman. Compassion. Now hate has sewn my lips down, stitched them to my teeth. I can no longer speak. Twenty-seven. Twenty-nine. Paralysis of the will. Fuck-up. Useless. Always useless. To everybody. Even to myself. Useless.

1.19 I lose hope. Nobody believes me. Thirty. It's now or never. I learn to live with never. Never again. I don't remember. I don't want to remember. Memory pursues me. Memory uses a pen to pursue me. Memory runs out the ends of my fingers and makes marks on paper. I don't have to read this. This is useless. What does this mean? Indulgence. Sin. No right to write of how I feel. Bitter. Indulgence. Bitter, but hold on. Don't let it go. Don't let the tears come. Indulgence. A sin. The sin of the women to live only in their pain. The sin of the women never to see the universal. Stuck in the mundane. You'll never be spiritually evolved. Stuck. Making marks on paper. I never stop. I scream in frustration. I live alone. Now I can scream. And again. And again. I don't remember. Don't make me remember. You never forget. Hate has a purpose. Hate serves memory's purpose. The marks on paper weigh fifty pounds. I can't carry this weight anymore.

1.20 Nightmare. I'm awake. How can this be a dream? I wish it was a dream. I could forget if it was a dream. Please tell me this was a dream. Tell me I'm wrong. Tell me I can't remember it. Tell me it was too long ago. Tell me kids get it wrong. Tell me I don't have to remember.

1.21 Forty. The Year of the Hare. The year of light in darkness. Rebirth. Memory as talisman. The dawn of hope. Somebody believes me. I can't keep the secret anymore.

The secret is killing me. Hands around my throat. Forty. Nightmares. Gray skies. March hare. Madness. I need rage. I only know how to rage at myself.

1.22   Descent again. Follow the March hare. The Goddess Inanna on a meathook in hell. Dead meat. Spread your legs, dog meat. Dead dog meat.

1.23   There is still hate. There is more. Always more. I find one shard implanted under my skin. I rejoice. I remove it with care. I try not to leave scars. I don't use a pocket knife. I try to heal the wound. Why no relief? There are two? I will remove the second then. Still no relief. There are more? Still more?

1.24   The woman made of potshards. Pieces. Not herself. Never herself. Who is herself? Only broken pieces. Each one removed grows a new piece in its place. The wounds fester. There is no healing. The bleeding cannot be staunched. There is no healing. Fear again. The pieces cannot be removed. Can't cut out your soul. What soul? Remember the star search? No. Only the pieces. Only the pain.

1.25   Inanna had insurance. If I'm gone too long, come for me. Who will be my insurance? Who will bribe the guardians of darkness and bring me back to the light? Who could find all the pieces? How can this be done? How can this not be done? Faith in the process. Descend. Enter. Memory.

THE PROBLEM
OF RAPE

Lorenne Clark and Debra Lewis

The fear of rape affects all women. It inhibits their actions and limits their freedom, influencing the way they dress, the hours they keep, and the routes they walk. The fear is well founded, because no woman is immune from rape.

But in the public mind there are two quite different attitudes to rape, the rape victim, and the rape offender. At times we condemn rape as a monstrous, criminal act; at others, we slough it off as a mildly dirty joke, treating it as nothing more serious than a minor skirmish in the inevitable "battle of the sexes".

As the archetypal, antisocial crime, rape is kept alive in the public conscience by sensational newspaper accounts of grisly sex-murders, presented as titillating warnings to young women about the dangers of hitch-hiking or other "unladylike" conduct. This reinforces what every woman has been taught from childhood—rape is the worst thing that can happen to a woman. Within this perspective, rape calls forth our greatest moral outrage and our greatest cry for vengeance. But co-existing with these attitudes are others, in which rape is dismissed with a knowing wink as a natural consequence of the sexual game in which man pursues and woman is pursued. What is called "rape," then, is thought to be only an unsophisticated seduction; at most, it is a minor breach of our social standards.

This contradiction in public attitudes is reflected in society's inconsistent treatment of rapists and rape victims. At the level of codified law and public pronouncements, we repudiate rape as a serious offence. Our laws against rape imply that the accepted moral standard of sexual relations is one of mutual consent, where neither party uses any kind of physical coercion or threat. But at the level of actual practice, women have found little real protection in the judicial system. Few cases come to court, fewer rapists are convicted, and the victim, rather than the rapist, is put on trial. Our courts do not fulfill the promise of the law, and rape remains a serious threat to women.

Among the many questions to be answered, the most basic ones are "Why are some rape victims taken seriously while others are not?" and "Why are some rapists punished while the overwhelming majority are not?" It is clear that we lack an analysis which can explain both the myths and the realities of rape. And it is also clear that, without a deeper understanding of what rape is and why it occurs, we can never eliminate the problems surrounding it, much less eliminate rape itself....

For all practical purposes, the popular reaction to the problem of rape began with an article by Susan Griffin in *Ramparts Magazine* in 1971.[1] This article, entitled "Rape: The All-American Crime," was a powerful attack on some basic assumptions which seemed to dominate official attitudes towards rape and rape victims. Her tone was strident, and her first concern was to set before the reading public the feelings and reactions of women. Nowhere in the rape literature was there any record of how women, the victims of rape, felt about the offence, either in terms of their own personal experience of rape, or in terms of the judgments made about them by others. While many people in the academic community were aware of the risks run by a rape victim in reporting the offence, no one had thought it significant to document, or even explore, the truth of the feminists' allegation that the trial of a rape offender was also—perhaps primarily—the trial of a rape victim. This view of the rape victim as the victim not only of a criminal act but of the judicial process as well, continues to dominate much recent writing on the subject.

During the early 1970s, rape relief or crisis centres sprang up across North America with the dual purpose of providing support to rape victims, and pressuring governmental and other public agencies for changes which would lessen the impact on the victim of reporting the offence. Independent groups and persons—"independent" in the sense that they had no connections with official institutions or with the academic, social scientific community—began to carry out detailed studies; they examined both the methods used by the police, the courts, and the medical profession in dealing with rape victims, and attitudes which members of these institutions brought with them to their tasks. These investigators had an admitted and partial objective: they wished to document the more general thesis that rape was just another form of women's oppression in a sexist society which assumed the natural inequality of the sexes, and the natural domination and superiority of the male.

They called attention to the fact that rape was not treated as a serious offence, despite the heavy maximum sentences allowed by law, and to the common belief that most women who were raped simply got what they were asking for or deserved. They substantiated their claims by pointing to alarming increases in rape's rate of occurrence, despite rape victims' continuing reluctance to report the offence, low ratios of "founded" to "unfounded" cases at the level of police classification, the special rules of evidence used to discredit rape victims in court, low conviction rates, and sentences far, far below the maximums. If a belief in the moral gravity of the offence existed in the public consciousness, it did not filter down to the only levels upon which it could be acted. As these writers concluded, with justification, the divergence between alleged values about rape and the actual practices surrounding it constituted but another, glaring instance of the hypocrisy of a male supremacist society. While the laws against rape were supposed to represent real respect for the sanctity and purity of womanhood, their implementation reflected the true value placed upon women in our society.

Another fact which feminist writers hammered home again and again was the virtual conspiracy of silence surrounding the whole question of rape. As a very grave and outrageous act, it is assumed to be an unusual occurrence, and this assumption is thought to justify the fact that rape isn't much talked about. In fact, rape happens a great deal, and is happening with greater frequency everywhere. But like incest and wife-beating, it was for a very long time one of those embarrassing facets of the human condition that one simply did not mention. This silence no doubt reflects the common belief that rape doesn't happen very often, but it also reflects the opinion that even if rape does occur, it should not, and therefore it shouldn't be made public. As far as the victim is concerned, the prevailing attitude is that rape is shameful and degrading to her, and the less said about it the better. Advertising the fact that one has been raped is an open invitation to social disaster....

The net effect of this conspiracy of silence is to discourage many rape victims from reporting the offence. Silence perpetuates the misconception that rape does not happen very often (who wants to look like the rare case of disaster?); it reinforces the view of rape as a shameful and degrading experience (who wants to reveal herself as having suffered a woman's worst fate?); and it reflects the belief that "nice girls don't get raped" (who wants to advertise that she's been raped, given the automatic implication that she wasn't then, and certainly isn't now, a "nice girl"?). To the extent that our society's silence rests on a presumption that rape is a natural fact, and that there can, hence, be no point in prosecuting rape offenders beyond a simple desire for revenge, the women who report rape appear to be tilting at windmills for no better purpose than revenging an affront to their outraged dignity; if rape is seen as a natural (though regrettable) event, a source of shame to its victim, and a crime of low incidence which mainly affects women who in some sense invited it, what woman in her right mind would want to avail herself of the slim chance of justice afforded by the judicial process, particularly when her motivation is likely to be perceived purely as a desire for vengeance?

The conclusion which the feminist writers reached was that social attitudes and the legal and judicial processes all conspire to keep women from having effective exercise of their political and human rights. Despite the fact that laws against rape exist on the books, ostensibly for women's protection, there are effective social and legal constraints which prevent women from utilizing their legal rights. The law is the illusory pot of gold at the end of an illusory rainbow, according women neither the protection of their rights nor the guarantee of redress for their injuries. Women are afraid, and are made afraid, to seek the protection and redress of the law. Their best strategy is to remain silent, and when one considers that it is the rapist who has most to benefit from this silence, it is hard to escape the conclusion that social attitudes, and their articulation in the legal process, operate to protect not the victim but the rapist. As things stand, it is *being* raped that is punished, and it is being raped that is the crime.

It has been argued that rape is simply the ultimate weapon which men use to exercise power over women and to exhibit that alleged natural domination which is their assumed birthright.[2] Many feminists contend that rape is as much an expression of the need to illustrate that power, as it is an expression of the desire for sexual gratification, and that the exercise of that power is condoned and encouraged by existing attitudes and practices. If the laws against rape provided the model of consensual sexuality which some assume they do, serving as much as an ideal to be striven for, as all articulation of the basic standards to be maintained, and if these laws were enforced with that goal in mind, then the inequality of power between the sexes upon which male supremacy rests would disappear. But those in control of our society do not want that imbalance of power to disappear; therefore, they have a vested interest in undermining the extent to which the laws against rape could constitute such an ideal. In order to preserve and enhance male supremacy, rape must be both possible and probable; it must remind women who has power over them and keep them solidly in their places. Thus, it is hardly surprising that the practices surrounding rape are what they are; to preserve the sexual *status quo*, it is not accidental, but *necessary*, that they remain so.

One of the most important contributions which feminists made was to force people to see rape in a larger social, economic and political perspective. The social scientists who tried to deal "objectively" with the problem of rape never seemed aware that rape takes place within a social setting, and that it cannot be treated or analyzed apart from the larger framework of social attitudes and practices in which it is embedded. This led them to make many assumptions which were clearly false, and a good many more which were highly questionable. Most importantly, the social scientists never really asked why rape occurs, and what social attitudes and beliefs support it. They brought their own biases with them into their research but conducted their research, and drew their conclusions, as if those biases did not exist. Whatever claims may have been made about the "objectivity" of the social sciences, even a cursory study of the rape literature reveals much to contradict it.

One of our basic contentions is that rape is a *social*, not a natural fact. It is produced by a certain kind of society and not by an eternal, immutable human nature. The attempt to treat rape as a natural fact, as an inevitable consequence of a fixed human nature, is simply a way to avoid doing anything important about it. But if rape is a social fact, it can be eliminated through social change.

Some people may believe that certain social arrangements are necessitated by some fixed aspects of human nature, and they may or may not believe that rape can be eliminated, depending on what aspects of human nature they take to be constant, and what social arrangements they take to be not merely conventional, but necessary because of it. If rape is really believed to be a problem, however, experience surely dictates that we at least try to rearrange society and to change the natures adapted to suit the present one, in an attempt to eliminate not merely the adverse consequences of the problem, but the cause and the problem itself. It is our deeply-held conviction that the causes of rape lie within the present social system, a system which is, among other things, fundamentally sexist. Rape is one of the products of a sexist society; it is the price we must pay for a society based on coercive sexuality.

ENDNOTES

1. Susan Griffin, "Rape: The All-American Crime," 26-35.

2. Susan Brownmiller, *Against Our Will*.

WIFE BATTERING CAN HAPPEN IN YOUR FAMILY

Linda MacLeod

KAREN W.[1]

Karen was just 14 when she met Richard. He came with his family to one of her parents' summer barbeques. He was 19, a journeyman electrician, working in the construction business, as did both their fathers. Karen's father liked him immediately. It wasn't every young man nowadays who would stick through an apprenticeship with the long hours and low pay. He himself had apprenticed as a bricklayer, and now he owned his own construction firm. Rich looked like a young man who could do the same thing.

Rich came often to the house after that, becoming a part of the family activities. It was easy enough to set another place at the table with Karen and her five brothers and sisters.

By the time she was fifteen, Karen and Rich were "going steady". Most of their social life was with Karen's sisters and brothers, and it was generally a happy time. Occasionally, when there were other boys from Karen's school included, Rich would become moody and silent. He said they were immature, and he made her promise she wouldn't pay any attention to them. He talked about getting married as soon as Karen was old enough. Plans became more specific; they were to be married soon after Karen's 17th birthday.

It was a huge wedding. Karen looked beautiful, her parents were pleased. Rich was hardworking, he was Catholic. They weren't particularly concerned that she hadn't finished high school; she would be getting married anyway, and certainly materially she would never want for anything.

They began their married life in the three-bedroom house that Karen's parents had given them for a wedding present. Within three months she was pregnant. It was soon after this, after a party at her sister's, that they arrived home and no sooner had the door closed than Rich suddenly viciously punched her in the face. She reeled back in horror and surprise. He accused her of flirting with her brother-in-law—suggested she had probably been carrying on an affair with him. She denied this and he hit her again. She locked herself in the bathroom until she heard him go to bed. She spent the night on the living room chesterfield. She told no one. The beatings continued. At the same time, she and Rich continued to take part in all the activities of her large, warm family. Her first baby, a girl, was born, and 14 months later, a boy. There were baptism parties; the family went to mass together; in summer they went to the lake for family picnics. Karen, ashamed, told her parents nothing of the beatings. When the bruises couldn't be hidden by sunglasses or high-necked sweaters, both she and her husband would lie about them.

When finally he threatened to kill her or her baby daughter, she tried to tell her parents. They wouldn't believe her. Such things didn't happen. She was exaggerating. She should just go on being as good a wife and mother as she could, and everything would be alright. One day she heard a staff member from a transition house for women who have been battered being interviewed on the radio. Four days later Rich beat her up again. The next day, after he had gone to work, she packed up the children and went to the house. She had been married five years. She had bruises on her face, neck and abdomen. Finally her parents were forced to face the fact that something terrible had been happening. They were very supportive of her decision to get a separation agreement. Her husband was ordered by the courts to keep the peace. Karen's father persuaded him to leave the house, and had the locks changed.

Karen stayed at the transition house for three weeks while she went through the court process. During that time she met with a counsellor from the community college, and discussed, with growing excitement, the possibilities for further education. Before she left the transition house she had enrolled for the coming term in an upgrading program to complete her high school. Day care would be provided by the college, and her parents would support her until she was self-sufficient.

Two weeks after she had returned to her home, Rich broke in, locked the two children in the bedroom, beat Karen, and finally shot her. He then went into the basement and hanged himself. That was how Karen's father found them all when he dropped by two days later for a casual visit.

SUSAN A.

Susan had been a pretty, quiet, studious English major. After graduation she took a job writing advertisements for a department store. She met Gary, an outgoing extroverted sales representative for an appliance company. He was full of energy, a lot of fun; he knew where all the exciting places were, and he seemed to have hundreds of friends. He loved a party; maybe he drank a bit too much, but he always had a good time. She was 22 when they got married. She gladly quit her job right away, because Gary wanted her to be a full-time wife. Their first child was born within a year. The violence started almost at the beginning. She had tried to overlook it, had forgiven him, because she knew his job put him under a lot of pressure, and he would have a few drinks to relax. He would never hit her, she was sure, if he wasn't drinking. A second child was born. Finally the situation was too much; she tried to leave, as she was to try several times over the next few years. Each time he would persuade her to give him another chance, he would promise to reform. Two more children were born. Gary was promoted to sales manager: the pay was higher but Gary, who was not comfortable in a managerial job, was under even more strain. Occasionally Gary would have to stay home because of his drinking, but he was a good salesman and a good provider. They looked like the perfect family in their split-level suburban home with its outdoor swimming pool. When the youngest child was in nursery school Susan got a clerical job and prepared the way to leave eventually. The beatings continued. Finally, on one occasion the oldest child, Lori, tried to intervene, and Gary beat her up too. Susan took the children and left. She found herself an apartment, bought a second-hand car. Lori looked after the younger children after school until her mother got home.

She had not told Gary where she was, but he found out easily enough by simply phoning the company where she worked. He came one day while she was still at work and persuaded the youngest child, Kenny, to let him in. When Susan returned home he beat her, and Lori as well. Susan called the police and laid an assault charge, but she realized she was no longer safe in the apartment. She and the children moved into a transition house until she could earn enough money to pay the first and last month's rent on another apartment.

Staff at the transition house noted that the youngest child was terrified if men came to the door. Gary was put on a peace bond—ordered by the court not to hit his wife again, Susan proceeded to get a separation agreement and interim custody of the children. However, as she drove into the parking lot at work one morning, Gary was waiting for her. He smashed the windshield in with a crowbar and attacked her. One eye was severely gouged, the other also injured, and she sustained a concussion. The terrified security guard called the police.

For three weeks there was some doubt as to whether or not Susan would lose an eye. Finally she recovered.

Gary was charged with attempted murder. When he finally came to court four months and several adjournments later, he was found guilty of assault causing bodily harm, and given a one-year suspended sentence. He has therefore spent a total of one day in jail for this crime—the day he was arrested.

Susan, her prettiness marred by a badly scarred left eye, continues to live on her own with her four children, supporting them on $904 per month. She is determined to make it without any help from anyone.

Wife Battering Must Come Out of the Closet

Wife battering is a fact of life in families across Canada. Women are kicked, punched, beaten, burned, threatened, knifed and shot, not by strangers who break into their houses or who accost them on dark streets, but by husbands and lovers they've spent many years with—years with good times as well as bad.

In every neighbourhood there are women who are battered by their husbands or live-in lovers. Wife battering crosses geographic and income lines. It is as common in rural households as in urban. It spans all ages, races and nationalities. In some families it is an isolated or occasional occurrence, but in others it is a daily routine.

Wife battering is, of course, not the only kind of family violence. We are all horrified at stories we read of child abuse and incest, and more recently cases of husband beating and "granny bashing" have come to public attention. While we have no conclusive statistics on "granny bashing," the number of families which include three generations are relatively rare. Child abuse is receiving widespread public attention and reporting of known child abuse cases by some citizens outside the family has become legally mandatory. Husband battering also does exist, but its existence relative to wife battering must be put in perspective. A number of studies on family violence have reported on this phenomenon and have concluded that:

> The few women who resorted to counterviolence did so as an act of desperation associated with failure of other options.[2]

While men are killed by their wives as well as women by their husbands:

> *long-term* physical abuse between spouses is almost always perpetrated by the man.[3]

and

> If one uses injuries as a criterion, then wife-beating would far outdistance husband beating.[4]

In other words, wife battering and husband battering are very different phenomena. The few women who inflict serious harm on their husbands usually do so for self-preservation, after enduring prolonged violence against themselves or their children.

Wife battering has not received the public attention it deserves. Too often it is explained away as atypical or as an individual aberration, and its seriousness is lightened by making it the subject of jokes. But wife battering is too serious to be laughed away and too common to be explained away as an "illness" or a "personal problem." Wife battering is much more than an individual dilemma or an occasional outburst. It is a way of life which touches us all indirectly or directly because it is perpetuated by our beliefs, traditions and institutions.

What Is Wife Battering?

To clarify how wife battering will be used throughout this report, an operational definition will be offered which enumerates what wife battering is not as well as what it is.

Wife battering is *not* just the result of an isolated argument that has got out of hand. According to a British study of wife abuse, more than three-quarters of the women surveyed reported that physical assaults were usually *not* preceded by verbal arguments.[5] Neither is wife beating to be confused with sado-masochistic behaviour on the part of two consenting adults. It is not playful, fun, or sexually stimulating for the woman.[6]

Wife battering is *not* confined to legally married couples. It applies equally to couples in common-law marriages and to couples living together. It does *not* occur only in heterosexual couples—it can also refer to battering of the partner who adopts the "wife" role in a homosexual or lesbian relationship. The terms "wife," "husband" and "marriage" will, however, be used throughout largely for convenience and also as a reminder that the battering we are discussing cannot be separated from the family context, or from the "husband" and "wife" roles which *can* be just as strong inside or outside a legal marriage.

> Wife battering *is* violence, physical and/or psychological, expressed by a husband or a male or lesbian live-in lover toward his wife or his/her live-in lover, to which the "wife" does not consent, and which is directly or indirectly condoned by the traditions, laws and attitudes prevalent in the society in which it occurs.

The violence women who are battered experience, is therefore a combination of three types of violence: physical violence, psychological violence directly initiated by their husbands in the form of constant denigration, taunts, purposeful inconsistencies or threats, and the psychological violence these women experience when they try to get help outside the family to stop the battering and find that help is too often just not there.

Women who are battered and look for help, learn very quickly that violence is an integral part, not just of certain family interactions, but of our whole society and that violence in the family is indirectly supported by practices and policies which condone some violence by husbands against wives.

From the first hand reports of women who have been battered, an experiential definition emerges which brings the three sides of wife battering to life. Being battered is feeling confused, feeling dead inside, feeling worthless, having no friends—not even one that you can call when you're feeling really low. It's not knowing when he'll turn on the kids—

always feeling jumpy, never knowing when it will start again, its being afraid all the time—not just of him but of everything—not really trusting anyone or anything. It's feeling guilty and in some indefinable way responsible, even though you're the one who's being beaten.

How This Study Was Done

Most of the facts for this report were gathered from groups and agencies taking an active role in the intervention/prevention of wife battering. Transition houses across Canada—houses where battered women and their children can stay temporarily for protection and support—and some hostels which accept battered wives—73 in all[7]—were contacted and given in-depth telephone interviews on the process of wife battering. Barriers to effective help experienced by women who have been battered and obstacles that transition house workers encounter in providing effective support for these women were discussed. Transition house workers were also asked to send any statistics they had collected on the women who stayed at their houses, as well as any detailed reports or pamphlets they had prepared. Forty-seven houses did send statistics: the others, usually recently opened, did not yet have an organized data collection system, because they had been open too short a time, or didn't have enough staff to include data collection in their duties.

In addition, provincial police departments were contacted, as were some local police departments (in randomly selected centres in each province), provincial family court offices, offices of attorneys-general, provincial social service offices, selected children's aid society offices and a few larger hospitals across Canada in an attempt to gather further statistical information on the subject.

Unfortunately this search proved virtually fruitless. Although all police departments were very cooperative, we found that they have figures on assaults but do not separate assault cases by sex of the victim or offender, or by the relation between them. None of the other services contacted collected statistics on wife battering in any systematic way.

The Focus of This Report

This report will emphasize the frustrations, dilemmas and barriers women experience when they make others aware that they have been battered. It will expose the incidence and characteristics of wife battering. It will examine common myths about wife battering as well as the legal, medical and counselling procedures which help perpetuate these myths. It will look at an image of the family, developed centuries ago, but still perpetuated by our laws and traditions, which places the family outside the law and reinforces the right of men to beat their wives. It will look less at the individual characteristics of "battered wives" and "battering husbands" but focus more on the social system which perpetuates and accepts wife battering throughout our society. Finally this report will look towards directions for change—change which will protect women from being battered, change which will revise procedures that leave women who have been battered with nowhere to turn, change that will enable people to live in families without violence.

ENDNOTES

1. For the sake of the women and their families, some of the details in these case histories have been changed.

2. Hilberman, Elaine, & Munson, Kit. *60 Battered Women*, 4. Prepared for American Psychological Association Meetings, Toronto, Ontario, May 5, 1977.

3. Hamlin, Diane. *The Nature and Extent of Spouse Assault*. Center for Women Policy Studies. Clearinghouse Director, Washington, D.C., October 1978, 1.

4. Strauss, Murray. *Behind Closed Doors: Violence in the American Family*. Doubleday, N.Y. (to be released in 1980). Reported in the Calgary Herald, October 2, 1979.

5. Support Services for Assaulted Women, *Wife Assault in Canada—A Fact Sheet*, Toronto, Ontario.

6. Carol Victor found in her survey of 80 battering cases that no wives who were battered desired sexual relations with their husbands, after being beaten, although 18 husbands who committed the attacks did. Reported in Davidson, Terry, *Conjugal Crime*, 65-66.

7. Not all houses contacted were in operation at the time of this survey. Two had closed during 1979, but the former workers were contacted to discover why they had closed, to make use of their insights about wife battering and to include their 1978 statistics in our estimates.

SUBMISSIONS TO THE COMMITTEE ON JUSTICE AND LEGAL AFFAIRS REVIEW OF BILL C-46

Sheila McIntyre and Jennifer Scott

Inequality in Sexual Assault Law

For centuries, the substantive doctrine defining sexual offences and the unique evidentiary and procedural practices governing the prosecution of such offences have reflected and perpetuated the social, economic, political and legal inequality of all women, particularly those women distinctively disadvantaged by one or more of their race, class, disability, aboriginal ancestry, sexual orientation or occupational or immigration status. Until the first comprehensive overhaul of rape law in Canada in 1983, all laws relating to sexual assault were developed, promulgated and administered by men, a group responsible for 99% of all sexual offences. These laws were framed without regard for the experience and perspective of women and children—i.e. the primary targets of male sexual aggression—in what remains a pervasively sexually unequal culture. By default, they reflected and normalized the unequal rights, roles and sexual standards assigned by men to women.

Under such sexually inegalitarian conditions, both the common law and the Criminal Code permitted, and even mandated, discriminatory legal treatment of sexual assault complainants.[1] Until 1983, husbands were legally entitled to rape their wives. Until 1983 most of the rules governing rape were overt exceptions to general rules of evidence. Rules requiring evidence of "recent complaint" and corroboration of complainants' testimony; rules governing the admissibility and probative value of the complainant's reputation for chastity; and rules admitting evidence of the complainant's sexual history as an indicator of her propensity to lie or propensity to consent indiscriminately to sexual activity are the most infamous examples. In the eyes of the male lawmakers, this gender-specific crime required a departure from the Rule of Law. Equality before and under the law was suspended in the case of a crime disproportionately committed by adult men against women and children. On their face, the laws were sexually discriminatory.

Each of these discriminatory rules derived from a single foundational myth that has entrenched the unequal treatment of sexual assault complainants in law for at least 400 years. This myth is that women and child victims of male sexual violence are uniquely prone to lie about rape and fabricate false allegations against innocent men. Though demonstrably ungrounded in fact and explicitly misogynist, this myth has proved both intractable and subject to endless mutations. One of its earliest and most often cited expression was articulated by Lord Matthew Hale in 1678: "Rape is an allegation easily to be made and hard to prove, and harder to be defended by the party accused, tho' never so innocent."[2] Rape accusations, in fact, have never been easily made. Rape remains one of the most under-reported serious crimes. According to Statistics Canada's National Violence Against Women Survey in 1993, only six percent of all sexual attacks and unwanted sexual touching are reported to the police.[3] Of that minority of sexual offences reported, a disproportionately high percentage are still deemed "unfounded" by police. If prosecuted and tried, sexual offences have always been harder to prove than defend against, not least because of the unique rules framed to indulge the unfounded fear of lying complainants.[4]

The foundational myth that women and children have a propensity to lie, and lie often, about sexual violence has spawned a host of subsidiary myths purporting to account for the imagined female propensity to lie about sexual violence: women lie to protect their sexual reputations or to appease disapproving parents; women lie out of some peculiarly female vindictiveness or malice or mischief or fickleness; women and children are prone to rape fantasies or sexual delusions; women and children yearn to be sexually overpowered but bring false charges rather than admit their desires. It has also spawned overtly discriminatory applications distinguishing between that minority of complainants male lawmakers are inclined to believe and the majority deemed in law and society unworthy either of belief or, even if believed, of law's protection.

Police and prosecutorial filtering practices, evidentiary rules and jury instructions codified this differential treatment of those women a sexually discriminatory culture labelled "good girls" and "bad girls". "Good girls," though, are believable because they do not readily consent to sex with anyone other than their husbands; and "bad girls"—i.e. those with any pre- or extra-marital sexual history—are deemed prone to consent to any and all men so cannot be believed when they report a rape and, in any case, are natural born liars. Hence the alleged relevance of past sexual history evidence. "Good girls" may not consent to extra-marital sex, so say "No" meaning "Yes". Hence, law must exculpate through the "mistake of fact" defence those rapists who self-servingly mistake a clear no for consent. "Good girls" cannot be raped against their will, can only be overpowered by deviant strangers, are never violated by the "good" men they know and, when defiled, send up an immediate hue and cry to tell the world of their violation. Hence, the old definition of rape requiring non-consent plus force; the exemption until 1983 of marital rape from criminal redress; and the recent complaint rule. "Bad girls" ask for it or deserve it; or falsely allege rape following consensual sex to extort profit from hapless men; or have no legitimate claim to law's protection either because they have no virtue capable of being recognized as injured or they have insufficient worth to merit any man's incarceration. Hence the admissibility until 1983 of evidence of "general" sexual reputation and the continuing unjust treatment of prostitutes, hitch-hikers, women who were drinking with the accused prior to their rape, as unworthy of law's protection.

Because pernicious stereotypes based on race, disability, class and sexual orientation have constructed Aboriginal, black, Asian, poor, mentally disabled and lesbian women as promiscuous, "over-sexed" or sexually indiscriminate, such women have historically not only been disproportionately vulnerable to sexual exploitation and abuse, but disproportionately treated as beneath law's protection. The rules which presume unchaste women more likely to consent to sex and less worthy of belief, *per se* discredited the allegations of such presumptively unchaste women. As Madame Justice L'Heureux Dube observed in 1991 in her dissenting opinion in *Seaboyer*, the result has been that:

> The woman who comes to the attention of the authorities has her victimization measured against the current rape mythologies, i.e. who she should be in order to be recognized as having been, in the eyes of law, raped; who her attacker must be in order to be recognized, in the eyes of the law, as a potential rapist; and how injured she must be in order to be believed. If her victimization does not fit the myths, it is unlikely that an arrest will be made or a conviction obtained.[5]

Sexual Violence as a Practice of Inequality

Research on sexual violence reveals that two factors operate in a rapist's selection of victims: vulnerability and availability.[6] The more disadvantaged, dependent or relatively powerless an individual, the more she or he is vulnerable to sexual exploitation and violence, particularly by individuals she or he knows, especially where they occupy positions of power, authority or trust in relation to their victims. These inequalities which correlate with sexual victimization also insulate many abusers from exposure and legal sanction. Contrary to rape mythology, only a minority of sexual assaults are committed by strangers. The non-strangers who sexually exploit their positions of social, economic and institutional power also exploit the differential credibility accorded those of high and low social status. They presume that their dependents or professional subordinates or those socially defined as their racial or sexual inferiors are unlikely to report them not only for fear of direct reprisals[7] but for fear of being disbelieved should they actually report an abuser of higher social standing. A legal system which indulges the actual or mythic belief in the uncreditworthiness of individual members of the disadvantaged or dependent constituencies most targeted for sexual violence overtly violates the purpose of s. 15 of the *Charter*: the protection and promotion "of a society in which all are secure in the knowledge they are recognized at law as human beings equally deserving of concern respect and consideration"[8]

The Supreme Court has acknowledged that sexual assault is a gendered crime wherein 99% of offenders are male and 90% of victims are female and that its gendered dimensions constitute a "denial of any concept of equality for women".[9] Men are not biologically fated to rape women and children. They are socialized to equate sexual initiative, prowess and aggressiveness with masculinity. In our sexually unequal culture, many men are socially, occupationally or economically situated to exercise control and power over women and children, and to equate that superiority with masculinity as well. Sexual aggression is used by men in a sexually unequal society "to underscore women's difference from, and by implication, inferiority with respect to the dominant male group" and "to remind women of their inferior ascribed status."[10] Rape and the fear of rape, in effect, function as a mechanism of social control over women, enabling men to assert dominance over women and maintain the existing system of gender stratification. Where laws ostensibly prohibiting a male crime against women actually deter the majority of women from reporting such crime, subject that minority who do report to invasive and intimidating discreditation tactics common to no other criminal context and facilitate acquittals on the basis of discriminatory logic, they are directly implicated in perpetuating the socio-legal cycle by which actual or threatened male violence keeps all women in their socially devalued and disempowered place.

Although systemic sexual inequality makes all women vulnerable to male sexual violence and to unequal legal treatment following such violence, other inequalities compound and particularize such sexual and legal vulnerability. Young people are at particular risk from men they know. In the case of male child victims, age and dependency produce vulnerability; in the case of girls, dependency, age and gender exacerbate abuse. Where racial or economic inequalities play an influence in subjecting racial minority, Aboriginal or poor youth to the control or authority of, e.g., adult male foster parents, probation officers, group home staff or child welfare authorities, societal discrimination further heightens their vulnerability to sexual violence. At least one in eleven children under the age of seven is sexually assaulted by someone in a position of parental authority; 99% of their assailants are males; 71.8% of those sexually assaulted for the first time as children are female; 68% of all sexual assaults happen to women between ages 16 and 25.[11]

Boys, girls and women with disabilities are at least 150% as vulnerable to sexual predation as their non-disabled peers, disproportionately by family, paid or institutional caregivers on whom they are dependent.[12] Stereotypes about people with disabilities—e.g. that physically disabled women should be grateful for any sexual attention or that mentally disabled women are naturally promiscuous—not only provoke some assailants or help them rationalize their abusiveness, but ground discriminatory beliefs in police, prosecutors and juries that disabled complainants are more likely to have consented to sexual attention and their claims that sex was unwanted are less worthy of belief.[13]

First Nations women and children are particularly vulnerable to male sexual violence.[14] The breakdown of family ties and communal values intentionally achieved through the residential school system and the high incidence of physical and sexual violence normalized within residential schools has been directly linked to sexual violence within aboriginal communities.[15] Aboriginal women are also highly vulnerable to sexual violence perpetrated by white men steeped in degrading and dehumanizing stereotypes of "Indians" in general and "squaws" in particular.[16] Racist stereotyping has also been shown to infiltrate criminal proceedings involving aboriginal complainants. The high incidence of abuse experienced by aboriginal women has been cited as reason to discount the injury they experience when assaulted; stereotypes about "drunken Indians" have operated to blame aboriginal complainants for their victimization, whether or not they had been drinking at all prior to their rape.[17] Research has also established links among the high rates of sexual violence against black women, racist stereotypes of black women as promiscuous and low prosecution and conviction rates for those who sexually prey on black women.[18]

The historic and present inequalities which augment the vulnerability of racial minority and/or disabled women and children to sexual violence also diminish their perceived credibility. Evidentiary rules premised on the propensity of all sexual assault victims to lie, will disproportionately insulate from prosecution or exculpate men who trade on their victims' inequality. In the result, those most vulnerable to sexual violence by reason of their social inequality will receive the least equal treatment before and under criminal law and the least benefit and protection of criminal law.

Legislation to Curb Inequality in Operation of Sexual Assault Law

On three separate occasions in the last twenty years, Parliament has sought to reduce the operation and unjust results of rules based on discriminatory myths and logic in sexual offence proceedings. On each occasion, defence counsel have successfully persuaded courts to disregard Parliament's intent or to "discover" new rationales for reinstating formally abrogated rules.[19] In the last five years, the Supreme Court of Canada has formally discredited a few of the most transparently groundless of these discriminatory myths and inferences. It has pronounced against the myths that: lack of chastity equates with a propensity to lie and to consent to sex; a virtuous woman cannot be raped against her will and/or that lack of overt resistance equates with consent; honest women will report their rapes immediately and that women who delay before reporting are less worthy of belief; and that the testimony of child victims of sexual abuse is inherently unreliable.[20] Regrettably, the Court has also issued reasons contradicting these holdings by invoking mythic stereotypes as hypothetical risks criminal law must guard against. The spiteful complainant and the extortionate prostitute appear in *Seaboyer*; the teenage girl who lies to salvage her reputation and avoid parental censure in *Osolin*. The Court has also recognized new myths without a scintilla of evidence to warrant such judicial notice: it has apparently credited the pseudo-scientific invention known as "false memory syndrome"[21] by crediting its inventors' defamatory and paranoid spectre of evil or man-hating (feminist) therapists calculatedly implanting false memories in susceptible clients.[22] As noted by Professor Busby, the discriminatory belief that malicious or dishonest feminist therapists manipulate their clients into "remembering" assaults which never occurred was "plucked out of the air" in *O'Connor*:

> there were no allegations to this effect in the case and no evidence was presented to support this notion. Given the [Supreme] Court's oft-stated reluctance, even refusal, to consider issues absent a factual base, the mere fact [they considered] this belief is ... troubling.[23]

Until Bill C-46, no statutory law reform or judicial decision has sought to challenge at its root the foundational myth underlying the historic and continuing unequal treatment of those targeted by virtue of their social, economic and political inequality for male sexual violence. This long overdue legislative corrective can be expected to face fierce resistance. LEAF urges the Committee to be vigilant to distinguish legitimate concerns from alarms reliant on rape mythology.

Bill C-49: Reforming Sexual Assault Law to Conform to All Charter Guarantees

Parliament's last intervention to correct against the operation of legal bias in sexual assault law occurred in 1992 after the Supreme Court of Canada's decision in *Seaboyer*. The *Seaboyer* case challenged two evidentiary provisions contained in the 1983 package of reforms introduced by Parliament to reduce discrimination in sexual offence doctrine. Section 276 had prohibited the admissibility of evidence of a complainant's sexual history with persons other than the accused save in three narrowly defined circumstances. Section 277 banned resort to evidence of a complainant's "general sexual reputation". The Court unanimously upheld s. 277, but a majority struck down s. 276 on the ground that its exemptions risked impairing an accused's right to a fair trial in those rare, but hypothetically imaginable, cases where the type of evidence exempted might raise a reasonable doubt as to the accused's guilt. The majority opinion authored by McLachlin, J. held that judges must have discretion in such rare cases to admit arguably relevant evidence of a complainant's sexual history with persons other than the accused. It issued guidelines for judges indicating purposes for which such evidence may not be used, and calling on judges to instruct juries about the permissible use to which sexual history evidence may be put once admitted.

Despite granting leave to intervene to a coalition of women's organizations defending the constitutionality of s. 276 on anti-discrimination principles, the majority decision virtually ignored s. 15 of the *Charter* as well as the substantial evidence demonstrating the irrelevance, discriminatory underpinnings and discriminatory effects of sexual history evidence. Section 15 was not even mentioned under the sub-heading. "Relevant Legislation," where McLachlin J. reproduced the text of the constitutional and Criminal Code provisions she deemed applicable to the case. Section 15 is referred to only once in the majority judgment as an "interest" subsumed within s. 7, not as a full-fledged and free-standing constitutional right. Despite compelling empirical, legal historical and scholarly evidence to the contrary and without offering any evidence, the majority decision simply asserted that the "twin myths" that unchaste women are more likely to consent to sex and more likely to lie about rape "are now discredited" within the legal system. The majority disregarded recent examples of judicial sexism in reported cases, and simply declared such manifest bias a thing of the past.[24]

The release of the *Seaboyer* decision provoked an immediate and sustained public outcry. Within a month the federal, provincial and territorial ministers of justice began to discuss immediate corrective reforms. Although many members of the public called on Parliament to exercise its power under s. 33 of the *Charter* to override the decision, such extraordinary action was not necessary, precisely because seven of nine Supreme Court justices had ignored s. 15 in their decision. Their constitutional omission created the constitutional opening to enact new legislation consistent with all, not just some, *Charter* guarantees.

Before introducing new legislation, the then Minister of Justice, Kim Campbell, took two steps unprecedented in Canadian legal history. First, in seeking input from legal practitioners and legal scholars, she consulted experts in all, not just some, *Charter* guarantees to ensure that equality law was fully incorporated into the proposed amendments. More, she consulted with those non-lawyers most expert on the operation of inequality in the enforcement of sexual assault law: women from across the country who are veteran staffers of rape crisis centres and women's shelters. Instead of simply trusting the opinions of legal professionals knowledgeable about the law on the books, she recognized that to refashion sexual assault laws consistent with the *Charter*'s equality guarantees she had to credit the knowledge of those most familiar with every dimension on which sexual assault laws in practice operate unequally in an unequal world. Instead of building from criminal law and constitutional precedents constructed from women's exclusion and then trying to tuck women in, this reform process began from the fact of women's inequalities as reflected in and reinforced by criminal law and reconstructed law to deliver what the Charter promises: equality before and under criminal law, equal protection and benefit of criminal law and the equal security of women and children from physical, emotional and sexual violation according to s. 7. Bill C-49 became the first sexual assault law in Canadian history substantively responsive to the equality guarantees of the *Charter*, not least because it was shaped from start to finish by meaningful, direct consultations with those whom the proposed law was designed to benefit, protect and secure and whom prior laws have systematically failed.

For the first time in Canadian legal history, Bill C-49 defined the meaning of "sexual consent" in criminal law. This positive definition of consent as "voluntary agreement," to the sexual activity which is subject to criminal charges, was designed to focus rape trials off rape myths and irrelevant inquiries which distort the fact-finding process and on to the only relevant factual question in a sexual offence trial: did this complainant actively and freely agree to sex with this accused on this occasion? Here, consent is something an individual does on a particular occasion because sex with a specific person at that time is something she desires on that occasion; consent is not something an accused imagines because he desires it or imagines she is the type of woman to consent or because she consented to the accused or to a third party on a prior occasion. The law also specifies what follows from this definition: no, in law, means no; third parties may not grant anyone access to another's body; consent at one time or to one act with the accused or with another individual may not, in law, be construed as a grant of perpetual consent; consent may be revoked; women incapable of voluntarily agreeing to anything because they are heavily medicated or intoxicated or asleep are, in law, sexually inaccessible. This focus on the actual communications between two people respects women as full persons entitled to security of the person and to sexual self-determination. If belatedly, the law since 1992 has ceased excusing those men who presume the right to define and control women's sexual desires or abdicate responsibility to control their own.

By enumerating interactions which will not be recognized as "voluntary agreement" in law, Bill C-49 converted self-serving or ignorant reliance on common rape myths and rationalizations from so-called "honest" mistakes previously capable of exculpating those who in fact sexually violated others, into errors of law of which ignorance is no excuse. Men who prefer to consult stereotypes or fantasies about women rather than the actual wishes of the actual woman in front of them are no longer innocent in the eyes of the law if they impose sex on an unwilling partner. In itself, this is a momentous step toward treating women as full persons before and under the law. But by outlawing myth- or stereotype-based mistakes and focusing sexual assault trials on the actual interactions between two people on a specific occasion, Bill C-49 sought to and should have dramatically narrowed the range of possible circumstances in which a complainant's past sexual history with others or with the accused should ever be even arguably relevant to the fact-finding which should be the focus of trial proceedings.

Bill C-49 clarified the scope of the defence of "honest mistake" which follows from its positive definition of consent. Unless an accused takes "reasonable steps" to ascertain whether a self-determining woman voluntarily agreed to sex with him at the relevant time, he may not excuse proceeding to have sex on the basis that he mistakenly imagined her to be consenting. An accused's past sexual history with the complainant, a complainant's prior sexual choices concerning men other than the accused and "propensities" projected on a complainant by an accused on the basis of any discriminatory stereotypes about "women" or particular "types" of women may no longer be an acceptable legal proxy for communicating directly with an actual individual on a single occasion. This being so, a complainant's past history should have little, if any, logical bearing on the innocence or guilt of an accused.

Finally, through s. 276.1-276.5, Bill C-49 codified specific purposes for which evidence of sexual history is not admissible. It then set out a procedure and constitutionally-driven and highly detailed list of factors judges must consider before admitting any sexual history evidence not precluded on those specified impermissible grounds. These provisions correct for *Seaboyer* by specifically requiring judges to weigh complainants' constitutional rights and anti-discrimination principles along with accuseds' fair trial rights when determining the admissibility of sexual history evidence. Parliament recognized that not all judges are as bias-free as imagined by the *Seaboyer* majority. Systemic inequalities shape the world-views, value-judgments and "common sense" of everyone in our society, however unconsciously. Bill C-49's admissibility guidelines correct for unconscious bias by directing judges to put their minds to the ways inegalitarian assumptions, myths or stereotypes might be operating when they exercise their discretion. Put differently, the guidelines require judges to make admissibility determinations mindful of and consistent with all, not just some, *Charter* guarantees. They also seeks to inject some consistency and, hence predictability into the law.

ENDNOTES

1. For an overview of these inegalitarian rules, see Christine Boyle, *Sexual Assault*, (Toronto: Carswell), 1984, Chapter 1.

2. *Pleas of the Crown* (Vol. 1, 1678 at 635).

3. Julian Roberts, *Criminal Justice Processing of Sexual Assault Cases* (1994), 14:7 Juristat 1. The reasons women gave for not reporting sexual attacks were: incident too minor (28 per cent); did not think the police would do anything (14%); wanted to keep the incident private (17%); shame or embarrassment (15%); dealt with through other channels (12%); did not want involvement with police or courts (12%); felt they would not be believed (8%); fear of the perpetrator (6%); and did not want him arrested or jailed (3%): see Table 4. (Figures do not add up to 100% because multiple reasons offered by respondents).

4. See Roberts and Grossman, "Changing Definitions of Sexual Assault: An Analysis of Police Statistics" in Roberts and Mohr, eds. *Confronting Sexual Assault: A Decade of Legal and Social Change* (Toronto, 1991) 57 at 59-60 and Gunn and Linden, "The Processing of Child Sexual Abuse Cases" also in Roberts and Mohr, at 95; and Andrias, "Rape Myths: A Persistent Problem in Defining and Prosecuting Rape" (1992), *Crim. J.* 2 3-4.

5. *R. v. Seaboyer* [1991] 2 S.C.R. 650.

6. Ministry of the Solicitor General, *Canadian Urban Victimization Survey,* "Female Victims of Crime" (Ottawa, 1985) 2; *Report of the Committee on Sexual Offence Against Children and Youth* [The Badgley Report], Vol. 1 (Ottawa 1984) at 196.98; and Burt, "Rape Myths and Acquaintance Rape" in Parrot & Bechhofer, eds. *Acquaintance Rape* (1991).

7. Reprisals may include actual or threatened deportation, demotion or discharge, placement in foster care, denial of letters of academic or professional references, loss of athletic scholarships or advancement and police harassment. Statistics Canada found 6% of victims did not report due to fear of the perpetrator. A 1985 report of the Solicitor General, "The Canadian Urban Victimization Survey: Reported and Unreported Crimes," found fear of revenge from the offender was a factor in 33% of reported sexual offences, (at 10).

8. *Andrews v. Law Society of British Columbia*, [1989] 1 S.C.R. 143, per McIntyre, J. 171.

9. *R. v. Osolin* [1993] 4 S.C.R. 669

10. *Janzen v. Playt Enterprises Ltd.* [1989], 1285.

11. The Badgley Report, *supra* note 26 at 1-2, 196-98 and 213-15, and *The Violence Against Women Survey* (Ottawa: Statistics Canada, Nov. 18, 1993).

12. Sobsey, "Patterns of Sexual Abuse and Assault" (1991), 9 *Sexuality and Disability* 243, 248-49; and Sobsey, "Sexual Offences and Disabled Victims: Research and Practical Implications," (1988) Vol. 6, No. 2, *Vis a Vis: A National Newsletter on Family Violence*, 1.

13. Shirley Masuda, *Meeting Our Needs: Access for Transition Houses,* (Disabled Women's Network. 1992) asp., 3-35.

14. Ontario Native Women's Association, *Breaking Free: A Proposal for Change to Aboriginal Family Violence* (December 1989).

15. Hamilton and Sinclair, Report of the Aboriginal Juice Inquiry of Manitoba, Vol. 1, *The Justice System and Aboriginal People*, (1991), 478 and 481-82, Assembly of First Nations, *Breaking the Silence: An Interpretive Study of Residential School Impact and Healing as Illustrated by the Stories of First Nations Individuals*, 1994, 1-16, and 167.

16. Hamilton and Sinclair, *ibid.,* Vol. 2, *The Deaths of Helen Betty Osborne and John Joseph Harper*, 52.

17. See Nightengale, "Judicial Attitudes and Differential Treatment: Native Women in Sexual Assault Cases" (1991), 23 *Ottawa L. Rev. 71*; Nahanee, "Sexual Assault of Inuit Females: A Comment on 'Cultural Bias'" in Roberts and Mohr, eds., *supra* note 20, 192.

18. See, e.g.. Schafran, "Writing and Reading About Rape: A Primer" (1993), 66 *St. John's L Rev. 979*, 1004; Torrey, "When Will We Be Believed? Rape Myths and the Idea of a Fair Trial in Rape Prosecutions" (1991), 24 U. *Cal. Davis L. Rev.* 1001 at 1053.

19. Courts overtly resisted the statutory amendment eliminating the corroboration requirement; converted 1976 amendments designed to restrict irrelevant questioning of complainants about their past sexual history into a vehicle that actually expended defence lawyers' opportunities to cross-examine complainants on such history; finessed the abrogation of the "recent complaint" rule by readmitting evidence of a prompt complaint through *res gestae* principles; and found creative ways to admit sexual history evidence formally barred by the 1983 amendments. See Boyle, *supra,* note 20 and Boyle *et al.*, *A Feminist Review of Criminal Law* (Ottawa: Ministry of Supply and Services, 1985), 96-100.

20. See, e.g., *Seaboyer, supra* at 604 and 630; *R. v. M.L M. supra* and *R. v. W(R)*, [1992] 2 S.C.R. 122 at 136.

21. See the analysis of Lamer, C.J.C. In *R. v. O'Connor* [1995] 4 S.C.R. (at paragraphs 26 and 29) and the five judge majority in *R. v. Carosella* [1997] 15 C.R. (at paragraph 46). For the questionable pedigree of the birth of this "syndrome" and its in scientifically unproven and unrecognized status, see Enns, McNeilly, Corkery and Gilbert, "The Debate about Delayed Memories of Child Sexual Abuse: A Feminist Perspective" (1995), 23 The *Counselling Psychologist* 185. Because the phenomenon of repressed and recovered memory is little understood and because there is no consensus within the scientific community that such a thing as "false memory syndrome" exists, courts may not, as a matter of law, take judicial notice of this so-called "syndrome," far less build legal doctrine upon it.

22. See, Busby, "Discriminatory Uses of Personal Records in Sexual Violence Cases" (1997), 9 *C.J.W.L.* 150, text accompanying notes, 75-84; and Vella, "False Memory Syndrome: Therapists are the target in new sexual assault defence theory," *National Lawyer*, January-February 1994, 36.

23. Busby, *Ibid.,* in text accompanying note 102.

LOOKING THROUGH A FEMINIST LENS

Canadian Panel on
Violence Against Women

Introduction

Every day in this country women are maligned, humiliated, shunned, screamed at, pushed, kicked, punched, assaulted, beaten, raped, physically disfigured, tortured, threatened with weapons and murdered. Some women are indeed more vulnerable than others, but all women, simply by virtue of their gender, are potential victims of violence. Moreover, the violence is often directed at them by those whom they have been encouraged to trust, those whom they are taught to respect, those whom they love. Violence against women cuts across all racial, social, cultural, economic, political and religious spectrums. While there is no question that violence may be conditioned by these factors, the fact remains that all women are at risk.

The voices of women throughout this report are a sample of what we heard during our consultations across the country. Their words—unadorned, unedited—tell the story more effectively than volumes of explanation, exhortation and interpretation. The message is direct and urgent, carried by quotes throughout the text—voices of women of all ages, faiths, colour and class who have been there, are still there.

We know that Canadians have a sense that violence against women exists and that many women live with violence on a daily basis. However, we also know that Canadians do not have a real perception of the enduring repercussions of violence and how the experience and fear of violence affect the daily existence of women. There is no better way for people to appreciate these conditions than through the words of the women who have survived them.

This chapter begins by defining violence and its various dimensions, both subjects of a great deal of debate. This report emphasizes that violence must be understood as a continuum that ranges from verbal insults through physical blows to murder. The voices we heard, the submissions we received and extensive research demonstrate the many dimensions of violence against women—physical, sexual, psychological, financial and spiritual. For many women, all these are part of their experience of violence.

This chapter also looks at the severe human costs of violence against women, the driving force for us as panel members. Yet, we also know that there are monetary costs, practically impossible to calculate accurately, but nevertheless an issue for all Canadians.

Each individual experience of violence must be seen in a larger social context. An effective analysis of violence against women requires a framework, or a way of thinking about the issue which emphasizes that acts of violence are socially structured. Our approach rests on the premise that although individual men make individual choices to be, or not be, violent toward women, explanations that focus solely on individual characteristics and traits cannot account for the scope, proportion and dimensions of violence against women today and throughout history.

We call this focus a feminist lens through which violence against women is seen as the consequence of social, economic and political inequality built into the structure of society and reinforced through assumptions expressed in the language and ideologies of sexism, racism and class.[sic] We see this framework as an essential first step in working toward the goals of our National Action Plan.

While an examination and critique of gender inequality are often seen as the hallmarks of feminist thinking, a feminist approach also emphasizes the importance of recognizing women, not only as women, but as women of a particular class and race. These realities condition the lives of women in important and complex ways. A feminist analysis, if it is to be truly successful, must take the variations and the similarities among women into account. Our framework rests on the belief that violence is linked not only to the sexist nature of society, but also to the racism and class inequality upon which our society is based....

Women live in a social milieu textured by inequality, a reality that leaves them vulnerable to violence. As long as women have unequal access to choice and freedom, as long as women live with the fear of violence, their options will be restricted, their movements curtailed and their lives vitally affected....

Violence Against Women

Myths and misinformation surround violence against women. One of the most pervasive is the myth that places responsibility for violence on the victim rather than on the perpetrator: women provoke, tease and taunt men, invite their sexual advances and then push them away. Women annoy, disobey and confront, thus leading or contributing to the violence they encounter. They were wearing the wrong clothing, drank too much alcohol, walked alone at night, etc.

We flatly reject any analyses that place any degree of responsibility for violence on the women themselves no matter what their actions, appearance, demeanour or behaviour. Such assumptions detract from useful work and from the formulation of solutions. When Canadians realize the staggering levels of violence against women across this country, they too will reject individualized or specious explanations.

Defining Violence

A shared definition of exactly what constitutes violence is crucial to the understanding of the sources and consequences of that violence. Although there has been a certain amount of debate on the subject, a proposed United Nations Declaration defines violence against women as:

> ... any act of gender-based violence that results in, or is likely to result in, physical, sexual or psychological harm or suffering to women, including threats of such acts, coercion or arbitrary deprivation of liberty whether occurring in public or private life.[1]

The Declaration describes the persistence of violence against women as

> ... a manifestation of historically unequal power relations between men and women, which have led to domination over and discrimination against women by men and which have prevented women's full advancement. Violence against women is one of the crucial social mechanisms by which women are forced into a subordinate position compared to men. [2]

That violence against women is socially structured is the main tenet of this report. It is our belief that all social institutions, from the family through to the legal-judicial system, are characterized by unequal power relations between men and women. "Violence surpasses all other forms of abuse suffered by women. It occurs in private (families) and in public (pornography) and is the expression of the extreme limit of male dominance."[3] In the family, these power imbalances may express themselves in various ways, from an unequal division of household work or child care, to violent verbal, psychological, physical or sexual attacks. In the legal-judicial system, gender inequality is written into laws and manifests itself in charging policies and sentencing practices that fail to hold men accountable for their violent actions toward women.

While we recognize the extent to which violence against women is the outcome of inequality we also believe that individual acts of violence against women are individually willed.

> A man who exhibits violence verbally, psychologically, physically, sexually or financially toward his partner is not losing self-control; on the contrary, he is affirming his power, which he wants to preserve at all costs and which makes him neither monstrous nor sick. If he abuses his wife, it is because he has the privilege and the means to do so.[4]

Men who are violent bear sole responsibility for their violent actions by systematically using power and control to override the will of their victims; they make conscious choices including their choice of victim, the places and circumstances of their violence and the degree of force they use. Abusive behaviour cannot be explained away by loss of control or unfavourable circumstances. Problems within relationships, stress, alcohol, anxiety, depression and unemployment may contribute to violence against women, but they are neither acceptable excuses nor root causes. Other people under the same circumstances choose not to harm women. Removing these conditions alone will not end male violence against women.

In a society whose very structure condones male violence, all men, whether or not they are violent, derive substantial benefit from its institutionalization. The advantage may be as meagre as receiving preferential treatment in a group discussion, or as grand as avoiding competition with women for a job. The threat of violence also keeps women in unwanted relationships with men, defines the social situations and locations that women frequent, restricts women's activities in the workplace and undermines their potential for self-expression and self-confidence. All women pay the price of male violence: while not every woman has directly experienced violence, there are few who do not fear it and whose lives are not in some way affected and restricted by its pervasive presence in our society.[5]

Naming Violence Against Women

All forms of male violence against women we refer to as woman abuse. The term "family violence" was widely used in both research literature and service delivery in the 1970s and 1980s to describe what actually constitutes abuse of women—not family. Although the home may be the most dangerous place for girls and women, the term is misleading and inaccurate.

The term "family violence" is a euphemism for violence against women and children, and it works to protect men .... Men's abuse is a social problem—they don't change because they don't have to.

Like many of the people from whom we heard, we choose to name the violence accurately. Using the term family violence to describe what is overwhelmingly violence against women obscures the facts. Further, we feel that the term "family violence" masks the huge spectrum of violence that women encounter outside their intimate relationships or families. We focus on the damage violence does to women and not its effects on the family institution.

Identifying Dimensions of Violence

For the purposes of analysis, we have divided violence against women into five dimensions, all discussed in detail later in this report: physical, sexual, psychological, financial and spiritual. In an intimate relationship, these dimensions may be experienced as a progression. In other cases, the experience may be of a single direction of violence, or a combination of several. For these reasons, when enumerating the different dimensions, we have chosen to illustrate both the random and the escalating nature of violence.

Physical violence, the most obvious, can range from pushing and shoving, to hitting, beating, torture and murder. Sexual violence—i.e., any form of non-consensual sexual activity, ranging from unwanted sexual touching to rape—must be clearly distinguished from intimate sexual contact which is mutual and consensual in nature. Because sexual violence often takes place within socially sanctioned relationships—marriage, dating, live-in partnerships as well as familial, parental and work relationships—its identification and disclosure are more difficult.

Psychological violence encompasses various tactics to undermine a woman's self-confidence, such as taunts, jeers, insults, abusive language, threats of physical violence or isolation. The deliberate withholding of various forms of emotional support may also be used. In relationships where children are present, men may also taunt women regarding their suitability as mothers or feed lies to the children to undermine their love and attachment to their mother. The panel heard many instances of men spreading lies about their partners at their places of work, in the community, and in social groups or denying them the use of the car and telephone and monitoring their mail. Some men use various emotional and psychological tactics to ensure that a woman cuts ties with her nuclear and extended families. Such actions erode and eventually destroy a woman's social relationships, leaving her isolated and vulnerable.

Women are also the victims of financial violence. Male partners and/or family members may deny women access to employment opportunities outside the home or to other avenues for gaining some financial independence, such as part-time work or taking care of children in their own homes. Men may withhold or maintain control over all or substantial amounts of money. Women are sometimes cheated out of their inheritance, employment or other income. This may involve denying women access to financial records and knowledge about investments, income or debt. Senior women are often the victims of financial abuse.

Spiritual abuse erodes or destroys an individual's cultural or religious beliefs through ridicule or punishment. Perhaps one of the most heinous examples of such abuse was the establishment of the residential school system which resulted in the uprooting of Aboriginal children to be "educated" in the white educational system. Such education was founded upon the destruction of Aboriginal languages, traditions and beliefs in favour of the dominant culture. Residential schools provide a striking example of the interrelationships between racism, sexism and violence. Another example of spiritual violence is the exclusion of women from key positions in some religious institutions.

Categorizing dimensions of violence is helpful for discussion purposes and to underscore the breadth and depth of brutality women have endured and continue to endure. It is not so cut-and-dried in real life. The reality is that in many instances the violence women suffer entails a combination of all these dimensions. A woman who has been battered by her partner may have been raped by him, verbally maligned, psychologically scarred and financially deprived as well.

Prevalence of Violence Against Women in Canada

Almost daily, newspapers, and radio and television broadcasts carry chilling reports of women harassed, women terrorized, women raped, women shot, women bludgeoned, women killed—almost always by men. So prevalent are these events that they have been described by one parliamentary committee as a "war against women."[6] And the accounts that reach the media are only a fraction of the events that never get reported, that remain invisible.

Despite a wealth of research in the area, we have only educated estimates of the prevalence of violence against women in Canada today. No matter what methodology is used, the figures are consistently alarming and, most researchers point out, underestimate the incidence of violence.

This is not likely to change because for many women, there are good reasons not to disclose their experiences of violence. Fear of reprisal is the principal one: they keep silent often knowing from past experience that they will pay a painful price if they speak out. Another reason for silence is shame. Many women feel degraded by the abuse and cannot bear to talk about the violence they survive with family, friends or even strangers.

Some women have come to believe that they are somehow responsible for the violence. Their self-esteem has been so eroded that they consider themselves failures for not achieving the "domestic bliss" for which women are held responsible. The risk of being judged by those around them is often intolerable. Other women fear having to leave the relationship if they disclose its violent nature. Some are still hoping for change in the man they love; others know they cannot manage to support themselves and their children if they do leave.

Another major reason some women will not tell is that they know they will not be believed. Too often this has been reinforced by denial among friends and family members who have seen the signs of abuse and have done nothing to help. And tragically, some women cannot tell because they cannot remember. To survive they have blocked out memories too painful to recall. The best and most scientific methods of data collection cannot overcome these enforced silences.

Current research is also limited by its exclusion of many Canadian women. In particular, very little is specifically focused on the experiences of Inuit and Aboriginal women, women of colour, immigrant and refugee women, rural, poor or homeless women, women with disabilities, women with low literacy skills and lesbians. Also, much research is carried out in French and/or English, thereby excluding women who do not understand or speak these languages....

HIGHLIGHTS OF THE FINDINGS OF THE WOMEN'S SAFETY PROJECT

The following information is based on 420 in-depth interviews with women between the ages of 18 and 64.

Sexual Abuse of Girls (Age 16 and under)

- More than one half (54 percent) of the women had experienced some form of unwanted or intrusive sexual experience before reaching the age of 16.
- 24 percent of the cases of sexual abuse were at the level of forced or attempted forced sexual intercourse.
- 17 percent of women reported at least one experience of incest before age 16.
- 34 percent of women had been sexually abused by a non-relative before age 16.
- 43 percent of women reported at least one experience of incest and/or extrafamilial sexual abuse before age 16.
- 96 percent of perpetrators of child sexual abuse were men.

Sexual Abuse of Women (Age 16 and over)

- 51 percent of women have been the victim of rape or attempted rape.
- 40 percent of women reported at least one experience of rape.
- 31 percent of women reported at least one experience of attempted rape.
- Using the Canadian Criminal Code definition of sexual assault (this includes sexual touching): two out of three women have experienced what is legally recognized to be sexual assault.
- 81 percent of sexual assault cases at the level of rape or attempted rape reported by women were perpetrated by men who were known to the women.

Physical Assault in Intimate Relationships

- 27 percent of women have experienced a physical assault in an intimate relationship.
- In 25 percent of the cases, women who were physically assaulted reported that their partners explicitly threatened to kill them.
- In 36 percent of the cases, women reporting physical assault also reported that they feared they would be killed by their male intimate. Typically, women reported that the fury and violence exhibited during attacks made them fear for their lives.
- 50 percent of the women reporting physical assault also experienced sexual assault in the context of the same relationship.
- All of the physical assaults on women were perpetrated by male intimates.

Looking Through a Feminist Lens

The analysis in this report draws on a specific way of thinking about violence against women. Rather than focusing on the violent actions of individual men, our approach looks at the problem in a much broader social context. We are asking: What is it about our present and past social organization that fosters and supports violent actions on the part of men toward women?

Our approach is not new. We have taken a feminist approach reflecting work already done at the grass-roots level. In the pages which follow we will demonstrate how looking through a feminist lens enables us to see how gender, race and class oppress women and how these forms of oppression are interrelated and interconnected.

Two central tenets of feminism are the socially structured nature of gender inequality and the requirement for political action to overturn the power imbalance between men and women. Feminism redefined politics and placed issues previously defined as personal squarely on the political agenda. These include child care, birth control, sexual assault, housework, women's unequal wage levels and safe living environments. No longer, feminists asserted, was it acceptable to ignore women's inequality. Neither was it acceptable to attribute women's inequality to "bad choices" or "mistakes" made by women, their biology or a host of individual actions or decisions.

Patriarchy and Violence

Violence against women, both now and in the past, is the outcome of social, economic, political and cultural inequality. This inequality takes many forms, but its most familiar form is economic.[7]

Day-to-day economic inequality, unequal political power, unequal protection under the law and unequal access to justice for women are all supported and perpetuated at the level of ideas. Language, myths, symbols, notions and beliefs about the superiority of men over women bolster the existing social structure and maintain women's inequality.

Understanding the concept of patriarchy is essential to our analysis of the nature of gender inequality and its impact on the vulnerability of women to violence, and of our society's tolerance of male violence against women.

The Patriarchal Society

Patriarchy in its wider meaning is:

> The manifestation and institutionalization of male dominance over women and children in the family and the extension of male dominance over women in society in general. It implies that men hold power in all the important institutions in society and that women are deprived of access to such power. It does not imply that women are either totally powerless or totally deprived of rights, influence and resources, but certainly women as a group have less power, less influence and fewer resources than men.[8]

In the social structures and dynamics of society, women and men have gender-specific roles in the power structure which, among other things, legitimizes men's authority to be violent toward women.[9] Some men consider domination and control of women as their right; using violence when they see fit is not challenged. This in turn leads to widespread tolerance of male violence at both the individual and institutional levels.

DIMENSIONS OF INEQUALITY

Canada ranks second among nations (to Japan) on the Human Development Index compiled by the United Nations.[10] However, when the Index is adjusted for gender disparities, Canada drops to 11th place overall. While the statistical bases upon which the UN compiles its Human Development Index is open to debate the following statistics illustrate the objective realities of gender inequality Canadian women face every day.

1. The average annual wage of women full-time workers in 1991 was $26,842. For men it was $38,567.[11]

2. The average wage of women increased by 14% in the decade of the 1980s, while that of men remained consent. However by 1990, despite a decade of employment equity and increased educational attainment and work experience among women, women's earnings were still just 60.3% those of men.[12]

3. Three out of four earners in the 10 lowest paying occupations are women. Eight out of ten earners in the highest paying occupations are men.[13]

4. The lowest average employment income in 1990 was for child care occupations at $13,518.[14]

5. The average income for female lone parent families in 1990 was $26,500. For male lone parent families it was $40,792. There were 165,245 male lone parent families and 788,400 female lone parent families in 1990.[15]

6. In 1989, only 7% of all full professors at Canadian universities were women. In engineering and applied sciences women accounted for only 15% of lecturers and instructors and just 1% of full professors. Even in education faculties, only 15% of full professors were women.[16]

7. 11% of women in 2 parent families with pre-school children missed work in 1991 for family reasons. Only 2% of men in these families had absences from work for family reasons.[17]

8. On average, women who work outside the home for pay spend almost an hour and a half more per day on unpaid household work, including domestic work, primary child care and shopping, than do men—3.2 hours per day on average over a 7-day week compared with 1.8 hours per day for men.

9. Four times as many women as men reported that 4 out of 5 domestic responsibilities were mostly theirs. Women said they had the main responsibility for household shopping, cleaning inside the home, looking after ill children and taking children to activities. Men said they had primary responsibility only for "cleaning outside the home."[18]

10. 42% of women household maintainers (i.e. the person responsible for mortgages, rent, taxes and upkeep) own their dwelling, compared with 70% of male household maintainers.[19]

11. Elderly unattached women are among the poorest Canadians. But, while the percentage of these women living in poverty has gone down since 1980, an increasing proportion of all low income elderly people are women.[20]

---

12. In 1991-92, all levels of government expended $1.876 billion on adult correctional services. On an average day, there were 25,712 prisoners serving a custodial sentence. Women accounted for just 1,254 or 9% of all provincial prisoners, and only 354 or 3% of all federal inmates.[21]

13. Women account for 10% of all persons charged with violent crimes and 20% of those charged with property crimes.[22]

14. Breast cancer is the leading cause of death for Canadian women aged 35-54 and the leading cause of death from cancer for women aged 30-74. Less that 1% of health care research funds are spend on breast cancer.[23]

The treatment of women, their labour, their reproductive capacity and their sexuality as commodities is certainly not just a product of modern industrial and capitalist society; it has been that way since long before the creation of Western civilization. Over time, women became a resource and a form of property acquired and controlled by men....

Heterosexism

Heterosexism is the assumption that a woman's life will be organized around and defined in relation to a man. It falsely presumes that all women will marry and have children, and that all worthy paths for women lead to marriage and motherhood. Opposition to heterosexism is often unfairly cast as an attack on the institutions of marriage and motherhood. In reality, opposition to heterosexism supports women's equality. It upholds a woman's right to be defined as an autonomous, independent person rather than being defined only in relation to men and children. It recognizes the diverse roles a woman plays in life and frees her to attach priorities to these roles as she sees fit. It supports a woman's right to choose her love partner with freedom, and it calls for a transformation of societal structures that support all freely chosen relationships.

Canadian society is organized around compulsory heterosexuality. Our culture and societal institutions function as if the primary role for women is that of wife and mother caring for her husband and bearing and nurturing children. In the ideal, she is the archetypal madonna: demure, slight, beautiful, chaste, deferential, passive, co-operative, alluring and servile. These feminine attributes prepare her to marry and be relegated to the private domain of the family. Her greatest assigned values are her reproductive capacity and her commitment to her family. Her domestic labour remains unpaid; her paid work remains underpaid.

In antithesis to the ideal woman, the ideal man is the protector and the breadwinner. He is seen to be best equipped for that role if he is bold, strong, powerful, active, competitive, virile and in command. These masculine characteristics have high value in the private realm of the family where he is seen to be the head of the household, and in the public spheres of commerce, law and politics. He is presumed to be a careerist first and a husband second. His masculine qualities are valued highly and are well rewarded in the marketplace. He carries these qualities with him into the public world where they become the core philosophy and where structures are crafted to suit the male experience.

We continue to live with the legacy of these archetypes. Despite modern reality, our institutions and social conventions are all constructed in a manner that limits choices for women in an effort to force them to conform to the role of wife and mother. Families, religion, politics, media and education are all organized around the concept of heterosexism and consistently reinforce and re-create the ideal by rewarding those who most closely conform to it and by punishing those who dare to be different. Hence the tomboy is tamed, the outspoken woman is silenced, the prostitute is cast out. Heterosexism is evident in worries about appearance, eating disorders, reluctance to participate in sports and hiding academic achievements to avoid appearing too smart or too successful....

The imbalance of power inherent in the masculine and feminine sex roles takes on greater significance when we look at the dynamics of male violence against women. Generally men are in control and women are controlled by them. Men are independent; women are dependent on them. When men choose violence as a means to control women, women have little power to withstand the violence. Even men who do not actively use violence against women often tolerate it by other men....

On the surface, women who live within heterosexist boundaries seem better off. Many, without doubt, garner privileges, such as access to male resources, a husband's protection from other men and legitimacy for children born of the relationship. But these are all derivative benefits. The man continues to be the primary source of support, defines the terms of protection and gives the children his name. Power is his to wield as he wishes. In this arrangement the woman remains in a state of dependency on the man, vulnerable to his will.

If women choose to speak out against heterosexism and its inherent inequality, to resist it, to expose the male violence it supports, they are considered "shrill" and unwomanly and often face violence for doing so. Heterosexism is one of patriarchy's strongest and most insidious tools. It allows society to cast aside women's experience and construct a society on models of what patriarchy wants her to be, not who she really is or could be....

It is ironic that, while separate and distinct from the public world of work and politics, the family is a private realm where men still dominate and exercise the same control they wield in the public arena. Traditional family relations also confer certain "conjugal rights" upon men. Exclusive and unlimited sexual access to women by men has been a cornerstone of the family, a right often interpreted by some men to extend to their daughters, nieces and granddaughters. It was not until 1983 that a woman could charge her husband with rape in Canada. Until then, men had the legal right to rape their wives without fear of reprisal.[24]...

Even after marriages break down, some men continue to exercise what they believe to be their proprietary rights to their wives and children. The best evidence we have of this belief in ownership is the incidence of "intimate femicide," murder of a woman by someone close to her. It is estimated that women who are separated from their spouses are five times more likely to be killed by their intimate partners than are other women. Male anger and rage over the loss of their wives/property apparently have no obvious counterpart in killings of men by female intimate partners. "If I can't have her, no one will have her" is the ultimate expression of the patriarchal family ideology....

We are taught, encouraged, moulded by and lulled into accepting a range of false notions about the family. As the source of some of our most profound experiences, it continues to be such an integral part of our emotional lives that it appears beyond criticism. Yet hiding from the truth of family life leaves women and children vulnerable. Many of us, including policy makers, legislators, law enforcement personnel, judicial officials, doctors and religious leaders, are afraid to examine the reality of power relations within the home. Many are quick to dismiss disclosures of psychological, physical or sexual abuse because such events depart so profoundly from our idealized images of family life. For many it is difficult to reconcile the conflicting images of father/husband as protector and father/husband as perpetrator of violence. As difficult as this process is, it is important that we confront the potential dangers of family life for women and children....

Ultimately, patriarchal society is synonymous with the political, social, cultural and economic inequality of women. Unequal political power is exemplified by the current representation of women in political office and by the predominance of a male political culture that operates along lines of male privilege. Unequal sexual freedom sees women as objects of consumption in pornographic magazines and sees females taking almost total responsibility for birth control and being denied access to full choice around issues of childbearing. Unequal legal power is manifested in laws that do not adequately protect women and children as survivors of abuse and in regulations that discriminate against women in the determination of their immigrant and refugee status. Unequal social power keeps women silent, even in the midst of abusive treatment by partners, employers, doctors, social workers and clergy.

The action plan proposed by this panel stresses the importance of eliminating the conditions that support patriarchy by emphasizing that gender equality and freedom from violence are equal and concurrent goals. However, we recognize that the experiences and the degree of violence are different for women of colour, for women of different races and different cultural and ethnic backgrounds, for poor and elderly women, for lesbians and for disabled women. Their particular experiences of inequality, and of violence are the outcome of a society which devalues, marginalizes and discriminates against them. It is not the race, ethnicity, colour, age, physical ability or sexual orientation which make the lives of these women so different; it is how individuals and various sectors in the social structure react to the reality of these women that compounds their experiences of violence and inequality....

Patriarchy is not fully revealed solely in terms of gender and class power differentials. Race power relations are involved as well. Just as Canadian ideologies, policies and social practices are structured around male and elite values and experiences, they are also rooted in the belief that white people have the right to dominate. Canadians are generally presumed to be white and this is the central reference point of all social institutions. Therefore racism is structural in nature and cannot be explained as the product of bad communication among individuals.

> ... racism is [not] merely a misunderstanding among people, a question of interpersonal relations, or an unchanging part of human nature. Racism, like sexism, is an integral part of the political and economic system under which we live. This system uses racism and sexism to divide us and to exploit our labour for super-profits and gives some women privilege.[25]

In much the same way that men benefit from the inequality of women, both white men and white women benefit from the perpetuation of racism. For example, many white women and men in North America benefit from the conditions that drive women of colour out of their own countries in search of work alternatives in North America.

White middle class families employ "nannies" from the Philippines, Malaysia and the Caribbean at lower wages than would be paid other workers in Canada....

For women of colour, race, gender and class issues intersect very clearly in the labour market. Women are already seen as a secondary source of labour. Added to this are racist ideologies that "justify" low wages for women of colour and racist hiring practices that force many women of colour into low status jobs with poor working conditions. It is easy to see how two oppressions, gender and race, interlock in a way that forces class oppression into play. This is not simply a layering of three separate oppressions but a complex interplay of oppressions that results in compounded social inequality.

When a woman of colour experiences violence she experiences it as a simultaneous attack on both her gender and her race. From experience she knows that anger and hatred directed at both these aspects of her identity are real. When she calls upon systems to respond she cannot trust the response because she knows that she is calling upon systems that do not understand, value or incorporate her experience either as a woman or as a person of colour.

The feminist lens reveals that while all women are at risk of male violence because of gender, their experiences of that violence are essentially informed by their race and class. So are the responses to their experiences. Building alliances across the issues that divide women will have to be given priority in the struggle to end violence against women. Patriarchy thrives on fragmentation and divisions. The existence of one oppression creates fertile conditions for the others. That is why all oppressions must be resisted together.

A strong coalition to end male violence against women is only possible if the differences among women are recognized, fully appreciated and equally applied to all endeavours to overcome patriarchy and end violence....

ENDNOTES

1. United Nations, *Declaration on the Elimination of Violence Against Women*, 6. The U.N. Commission on the Status of Women approved the draft in March 1993.

2. *Ibid.*

3. G. Larouche, *Agir contre la violence* (Montreal: éditions La pleine June, 1987), 32.

4. Dominique Bilodeau "L'approche féministe en masion d'hébergement: quand la patrique enrichit la théories," *Nouvelles pratiques sociales*, Vol. 3, No. 2, (1990), 48.

5. Barbara Hart, *Safety For Women: Monitoring Batterers' Programs* (Harrisburg: Pennsylvania Coalition Against Domestic Violence, 1988), 18.

6. Sub-Committee on the Status of Women, *The War Against Women: Report of the Standing Committee on Health and Welfare, Social Affairs, Seniors and the Status of Women* (Ottawa: House of Commons, June 1991).

7. Louise Vandelac, Diane Bélisle, Anne Gauthier and Yolande Pinard, *Du travail et de l'amour* (Montreal: Saint Martin, 1986), passim.

8. G. Lerner, *The Creation of Patriarchy* (New York: Oxford University Press, 1986), 239.

9. Ginette Larouche, *Agir contre la violence* (Montreal: Editions La Pleine June 1987), 35.

10. United Nations Development Program, *Human Development Report 1992* (New York: Oxford University Press, 1993).

11. Statistics Canada, "Earnings of Men and Women," in *The Daily*, January 14th, 1993, 3.

12. Abdul Rashid, "Seven Decades of Wage Changes," in *Perspectives on Labour and Income*, Volume 5, No. 2. Summer 1993, 13 & 18.

13. Statistics Canada, "1991 Census: Highlights," in *The Daily*, April 13th, 1993, 1.

14. *Ibid.,* 1

15. *Ibid.,* 3

16. Statistics Canada, "Women in Academia—A Growing Minority," in *The Daily*, March 11th, 1993, 3.

17. Nancy Zukewich Graham, "Women in the Workplace," in *Canadian Social Trends*, No. 28, Spring 1993, 6.

18. Canada Health Monitor, "Highlights Report Survey #6," January 1992. Price Waterhouse and Earl Berger, Toronto 1992, 3.

19. Statistics Canada, *Women in Canada—A Statistical Report*, Minister of Supply and Services, Ottawa, 1990, 27.

20. *Ibid.,* 108-109.

21. Canadian Centre for Justice Statistics, "Correctional Expenditures and Personnel in Canada," in *Juristat*, Vol. 12, No. 22, November 30th, 1992, 1, and Statistics Canada, *Adult Correctional Services in Canada—1991-92*, Ottawa 1992.

22. Statistics Canada, *Women in Canada—A Statistical Report*, op. cit., 147.

23. National Action Committee on the Status of Women, "Review of the Situation of Women in Canada—1992," Toronto, May 1992, 12.

24. Department of Justice Canada, Research Section, *Sexual Assault Legislation in Canada: An Evaluation: Overview* (Report No. 5) (Ottawa, 1990), 13-14.

25. C. Allen and J. Persaud, "Fighting Racism and Sexism Together," as cited in N.L. Adamson et al., *ibid.,* 106.

A CRITICAL LOOK AT STATE DISCOURSE ON "VIOLENCE AGAINST WOMEN"

Lise Gotell

Deconstructing the Narrative of the Report: A Story of Victimization

Informing the Canadian Panel *Report* is a construction of sexuality as uniformly oppressive. The narrative underscored in the *Report* is as follows. Violence is a tool of male power and a purposeful outgrowth of that power. Violence is rooted in male domination. As the *Report* argues, the context of "violence against women" is gender power; in this sense violence is the result of inequality. But if violence is the result of inequality, it is also the primary mechanism for enforcing that inequality— "women will not be free of violence until there is equality, and equality cannot be achieved until the violence and the threat of violence is removed from all women's lives" (Canadian Panel on Violence against Women 1993a, xiii). The *Report* does not simply represent a recognition of the contextual and structural character of women's victimization through male violence; it does far more than this. In the discursive web woven by the Panel, violence is raised to an ontological status; it becomes the beginning, the middle, and the end of gender power. Enclosed within the Panel's narrative are three specific components: first, an open-ended and virtually unrestrained conception of violence; second, a construction of all women as thoroughly victimized; third, a new basis for the claim to social entitlement—that is, women's victimization.

As we have seen, the *Report* endorses an extremely broad conception of violence. While the breadth of this definition is in some respects positive, it is also perhaps so broad as to be "politically and epistemologically imprecise" (Pidduck 1994, 8). According to the narrative presented in the *Report*, violence becomes the endpoint of a range of systemic practices. The opening words of Canadian Panel *Report* express the notion of gender domination as a continuum of violence—"Every day in this country, women are maligned, humiliated, shunned, screamed at, pushed, kicked, punched, assaulted, beaten, raped, physically disfigured, tortured, threatened with weapons and murdered" (*Ibid.*, 1). As Pidduck observes, this description "functions rhetorically through hyperbole" (Pidduck 1994, 8). It creates a series of intensifying forms of abuse and presents a barely indistinguishable field of activities from discrimination to violence. In this manner, violence comes to stand in for and becomes the logical conclusion of gender domination. As a result, the concept of violence takes on an irrepressible quality, subsuming many complex and specific aspects of gender relations. In the *Report*, a whole range of practices are simply poured into the category "violence against women." As the Panel contends, for example, "[v]iolence thrives on but is not unique to poverty, ... poverty is abusive in itself" (Canadian Panel on Violence Against Women 1993a, 63). If poverty is constructed as violence, so too are many other complex practices. Ignoring significant controversies within feminism, for example, pornography and reproductive technology are considered in the *Report* under the heading "Underacknowledged Forms of Violence" (*Ibid.*, 49-51, 53). By constructing these practices as undeniably "violent" the Panel ignores that just as pornography and reproductive technology may be sites of power against women, so too may they be sites of power for women (Gotell 1996; McCormack 1996).

The consequences of defining violence as the essence of gender relations are complex and very troubling. On a conceptual level, the impact of this construction is to deny the specificity of "violence against women." As Vega argues, when violence is presented as undifferentiated from other aspects of gender power, the concept becomes redundant; in order to make sense, the concept must derive its meaning from specific contexts (Vega 1988, 85). On a political level, the project of constructing appropriate strategies for combating violence becomes very difficult as violence extends beyond coercion. However, and perhaps even more troubling, when violence is conflated with gender domination, to address violence is to appear to be addressing women's inequality. This conflation, of course, can be happily assimilated by governmental actors. As we have seen, federal attention to violence has coincided with resistance to the broader agenda of Canadian feminism. If violence rhetorically represents women's oppression, the contradictory implications of the state's violence agenda fade into obscurity.

A second and related element of the *Report*'s narrative is the construction of all women as potential victims of violence and its flip side, the creation of all men as potential perpetrators. The allegory of women's victimization through male violence is, in fact, the most recurrent story presented in the *Report*. In part, this is an effect of the Panel's mandate and its methodology. The Panel was directed to "identify and define violence from the perspective of women's experience" (Canadian Panel on Violence Against Women 1993b, 4; Health and Welfare Canada 1991, 111). Its process emphasized the telling of women's experiences of abuse and the *Report* edits these stories, weaves them throughout its exploration of violence, and uses them to legitimate its claims. Personal testimony, as Smart has suggested, is increasingly deployed instrumentally as a feminist strategy and it functions as a highly legitimate claim to "truth"—"As a form of political intervention, the personal testimony can have the authority denied the theorist, statistician or demographer" (Smart 1992, 189). Nevertheless, as Smart and others have emphasized, the meaning attached to personal testimony is only revealed in the context of the discourse into which it is inserted. When inserted within a narrative emphasizing violence as all encompassing, the experience that becomes meaningful is that of victimization. The *Report*, through a careful selection and editing of "testimony," constructs a picture of women's inescapable victimization, despite its claims to the contrary. Approximately 100 quotes weave through the *Report*; all present horrifying stories of women's immobilization through male violence; very few depict women's resistance and subversion in the face of these practices. Moreover, while the *Report* occasionally uses the phrase "survivor" to refer to women who have experienced "violence," by far the most recurring depiction is "the victim." In these ways, then, the

Panel constitutes women as victims. It is not simply that the Panel recognizes the significant social fact that many women have been victimized. Instead, it transforms all women into victims, actual and potential. This is not a transitory state, nor even a critical event shaping women's condition. Rather it becomes a permanent identity.

What is immediately striking about this construction of women as victims is how closely it resembles the image of women lurking at the foundations of government law and order discourse. In both cases, women are represented as helpless and in need of protection. Both discourses emphasize, and in fact produce, a gendered "fearscape." Stressing victimization, and denying women's spaces of resistance, these discourses carry the tendency to frighten women out of their wits (Pidduck 1994, 6). Loseke, for example, contends that fear and victimization tend to go hand in hand; fear is a generalizable characteristic that "immobilizes (victims), rules their actions, their decisions, their very lives" (Loseke 1992, 25-26). The effect of both discourses is to produce a disempowered female object and to justify state protectionism, since in the final analysis this person requires help (*ibid.*).

The implications of the construct "women as victims" are profound. First, the Panel's emphasis on women's victimization can have the effect of confirming government's efforts to squeeze the problem of "violence against women" into an agenda narrowly focussed on criminalization. While it is true that the Panel's proposal for a broad strategy of action may work to resist such a narrowing, the unprioritized and grab-bag nature of its recommendations also allows federal actors to pick and choose. Moreover, the *Report* does contain a strong call for enhanced criminal protection of women victims. It recommends a range of criminal law reforms, creating new crimes (the abuse of women in pornography, for example), more punitive sanctions for violent crimes, and new forms of compensation for "victims" (Canadian Panel on Violence Against Women 1993a, part 5, 56-58). Given the federal emphasis on law and order policy, a trend that continues under the new Liberal government there is a real potential for these recommendations to be taken out of context.

Second, and related to the theme of protectionism, the narrative of victimization functions to deny women's political agency. While feminist activists have also deployed the metaphor of victimization to mobilize public support and government action, the emphasis of much feminist violence activism has been the necessity and the potential of women's empowerment (Snider 1990). To this end, feminists have sought to help women who have experienced violence to help themselves. This effort has taken a variety of forms, including establishing self-help, peer support, and consciousness-raising groups, counselling programmes, and shelters. The *Report*'s emphasis on "disempowerment" by contrast, denies the efficacy of these spaces of resistance—it creates "victims" as primarily in need of "help." It is also the case that the narrative of victimization functions to delegitimize feminist representation. As an effect of the feminist boycott, the Panel's *Report* was robbed of feminist support. But through constructing women as victims, the representative claims of the Panel are bolstered. Relying on personal testimony and unmediated by feminist groups (those boycotting and those excluded), the Panel can claim to speak directly on behalf of women victims, those silenced through violence. In this manner, the importance of feminist knowledge and activism on the terrain of violence is discounted. When set within the context of state efforts to challenge feminism's representative claims, this becomes particularly worrying.

The third and final element of the Panel's narrative represents a combination of the first two elements—that is, violence as uncontainable and women as "victims." The fusion of gender equality with the struggle to end violence could result in the potential narrowing of claims for social entitlement. If gender inequality is violence, then perhaps the identity victim could become the new prerequisite for making demands on the state. This danger is raised by Loseke who also criticizes the exaggeration of "victimization" informing many contemporary constructions of "violence against women." As she asks,

> "[will] women need to buy their way into emergency social services by proving themselves as "victims"? [Will] women need to show their broken bones to receive public sympathy? [Will] women need to be a battered woman—a poor defenseless helpless creature—in order to secure needed housing?" (Loseke 1992, 10).

There is little to reassure us that the Panel's analysis could not be taken in this way. The *Report* does indeed recommend a broad social policy agenda as a prerequisite for ending violence. Nevertheless, the call for enhanced social supports is framed as a necessary response to "victims," rather than a necessary response to disadvantage and inequality. As the *Report* states, the government should "direct special attention, in the provision of social assistance, social services, education, training and employment, to the needs of female victims of violence" (Canadian Panel on Violence Against Women 1993a, part 5, 17). In a context marked by government efforts to reform social programmes and target benefits to the needy, the discourse of "victimization" could provide a new justification for the erosion of entitlement.

In sum, there is much in the *Report* that could be used to legitimize current trends and discourses in state policy, including the denial of feminist claims to represent women. In this sense, the *Report*, as an emergent state discourse, may constitute more an appropriation than a recognition of feminist claims on "violence against women." The former Conservative government's reaction to the *Report* was in many ways predictable. It embraced the thrust of this document, including its call for "zero tolerance" but refused to commit any new budgetary resources to the battle against violence (Levan 1996, 348). In other words, the former federal government rejected the Panel's call to action but did not reject its discourse.

ENDNOTE

Essay excerpt from "Deconstructing the Narrative of the Report: A Story of Victimization" by Lise Gotell, taken from: *Women and Political Representation in Canada*, by Caroline Andrew and Manon Tremblay, eds., 1998, pp. 39-84. Ottawa: Ottawa University Press.

OUR STORY

Canadian Panel on
Violence Against Women
(Aboriginal Panel),
Final Report, Ottawa, 1993

Aboriginal women held a position of authority in the family, clan and nation. Traditional societies universally recognized the power of women to bear life. It was believed that women shared the same spirit as Mother Earth, the bearer of all life, and she was revered as such.

By virtue of her unique status, the Aboriginal woman had an equal share of power in all spheres. In some traditional societies, such as the Six Nations of the Iroquois Confederacy, the clan mother held the esteemed position of appointing and deposing the chiefs or heads of clans. In other societies, such as the Montagnais, decision making was shared equally between women and men.

One common misconception held by Europeans, and perpetuated by their general ignorance of traditional Aboriginal societies and their own patriarchal structures, is that Aboriginal women were subservient to men. In fact, early European explorers and fur traders depended heavily on the innate abilities and survival skills of Aboriginal women for their survival in the "New World."

The early years of French and British colonization in Canada brought extensive change for the Aboriginal people of this land. Their economic infrastructures, sustained by vast natural resources, were perceived as uncivilized by early colonists who were unacquainted with the Aboriginal people's non-materialistic culture.

During the fur trade, colonists used Aboriginal people for their hunting and trapping abilities to exploit Canada's natural resources for commercial gain. Early land exploration and subsequent treaty making—the foundation of the colonization process—were largely dependent on the survival skills and communication abilities of Aboriginal guides and interpreters. Aboriginal nations were also sought as military allies during the colonial wars between the French and the British and between the British and the Americans as well as during the American Civil War.

It was also during the fur trade, when Aboriginal women first came into contact with Europeans, that the Métis nation was born. Métis women walked in two worlds. Their language was a blend of European and Aboriginal languages. Their way of life embraced both Aboriginal and white customs, enriched by the bringing together of two cultures and passed on to their children. The Métis nation was born from the strength of Aboriginal women, and their nation's survival depended on them.

With the coming of European colonists, the long and systematic devolution of the

Aboriginal woman's inherent rights, her equality and her unique status began. It eventually eroded and undermined her valued position among her people. The Aboriginal woman was denied any formal leadership role during the treaty-making process between the European and Aboriginal nations. Her role as a wife, mother and grandmother diminished as European attitudes and values toward women were gradually adopted by Aboriginal society.

Pre-Confederation policy involved the converting of Aboriginal people to European religions and the reform of existing Aboriginal social, economic and political structures to reflect the European institutions of the day. Family-oriented social structures were gradually replaced with the European class system; communal economies in which Aboriginal women enjoyed economic and social equality were exchanged for the barter-and-trade economy dominated by Aboriginal and European men; and Aboriginal women lost their status when the traditional matriarchal societies were displaced by the European patriarchy which considered women and children to be men's property.

Following Confederation, the *Indian Act* was legislated in 1876 to "govern Indians in Canada." This Act was to become the government's most effective tool in the abolition of Aboriginal women's rights, status and identity, and it left in its wake a path of cultural and social destruction. The lines that separated Aboriginal women—Status from non-Status and Métis—were clearly drawn. The law separated Aboriginal people through classification and created a new social order that would eventually divide nations, clans and families.

The *Indian Act* was to "continue until there is not a single Indian in Canada that has not been absorbed into the body politic, and there is no Indian question and no Indian Department."[1] This goal was pursued by outlawing spiritual practices, severing Aboriginal peoples' connection with the land, destroying traditional Aboriginal economies, indoctrinating Aboriginal people into the dominant culture by force through church or state-run residential schools and through legally denying Status to all women who married non-Status or non-Aboriginal men and their children.

Aboriginal peoples who wished to acquire a university or professional education, leave the reserve for extended periods or send their children to public rather than residential schools, in addition to women who married non-Status men, were forced to give up their rights under the *Indian Act* and join white society.

> I was married for 42 years. You work together, have joint goals and talk about our work and lives peacefully. Kids today who form relationships through alcohol have nothing to talk about. In the past, drum dances and tea dances were held to celebrate the end of hard work. Now when elders see the younger people carry on these ceremonies, they are happy. But for some reason, the women don't dance any more.

The *Indian Act* prohibited three or more Indians from taking organized action against civil servants. A pass system was introduced in 1885 to prevent organized political activities and to keep parents from visiting their children in residential schools. Spiritual practices and gatherings such as the Sun Dance, the Thirst Dance and the potlatch were outlawed, as were wearing traditional dress and dancing of any form, to sever spiritual connections. The pass system fell into disuse in the early 20th century, despite aggressive attempts at enforcement by the Department of Indian Affairs.

Local political structures comprised male chiefs and councils, as set out in the *Indian Act*, but they were administered and controlled by Indian agents. Also, local by-laws had to be approved by the federal government. Indian agents had full control over daily life, and as the justices of the peace, they had authority over the administration of "justice."

Local economies were destroyed by preventing the sale of produce off reserve, and reserve lands could not be mortgaged to finance the purchase of farm implements which were needed to develop an agricultural economic base. Aboriginal peoples were restricted to cultivating an area of land that could be maintained by personal labour and were restricted to using "simple implements as he would likely be able to command if entirely thrown upon his own resources, rather than to encourage farming on a scale to necessitate the employment of expensive labour-saving machinery."[2] Converting Aboriginal peoples from nomadic hunters and gatherers to sedentary farmers was seen as the most economical and humanitarian approach. As one historical source stated: "they had to make up their mind to one of three policies ... to help the Indians to farm and raise stock, to feed them or to fight them."[3]

At home, on land "reserved" by treaty, Aboriginal women faced new challenges. In most southern regions, the traditional economy of hunting, fishing and gathering was displaced by agriculture. Aboriginal women worked along with their mates, learning new skills, but they also maintained traditional economic activities, wherever resources allowed, to supplement their meagre existence. They continued to practise midwifery, herbalism and ceremonies long after these activities were outlawed by the *Indian Act*.

In spite of the daily hardships, Aboriginal peoples endured, often by faith and prayer alone. Many converted to Christianity, surrendering traditional beliefs in favour of the white man's religion, while others clung fiercely to their traditional ceremonies, forced underground by Canadian law.

The *Indian Act* determined who was entitled to be registered as an "Indian" under Canadian law. Section 12 (1)(b) of the *Indian Act* stripped Aboriginal women of their Status rights upon marriage to a non-Status Aboriginal or non-Aboriginal man. Over the next century, many Aboriginal women, their children and grandchildren were dispossessed of their inherent rights. It was illegal for them to own, reside on or be buried on "Indian" lands, and they were denied any monetary benefits resulting from treaties. These laws were in direct contravention of the existing unwritten laws of the traditional Aboriginal societies.

The human rights violations suffered by Aboriginal women were second only to the multiple horrors and abuse that their children were subject to throughout the residential school era. The residential school system cut to the very soul of Aboriginal women by stealing their most valued and vital roles of mother and grandmother, along with their children.

The children returned from the residential schools to their homes and communities, unfamiliar with the language and culture of their people. Traditionally, elders, grandmothers and grandfathers were the first teachers of Aboriginal children; they passed on their knowledge, values and skills to the children by way of stories and legends. This oral tradition was dependent on trust, which was nurtured over time, between children and grandparents. In many cases, the residential school experience permanently severed this tie between child and elder, altering the values and identity of the child and traditional Aboriginal society forever.

The residential school era marked a turning point for Aboriginal women in Canada. Their rights, status and identity were now fading into near obscurity. Once fiercely proud and independent, Aboriginal women now struggled daily for survival, amid the turmoil of violence and abuse that had become a new reality.

For Aboriginal women, living in post-Confederation Canada meant living in two worlds—the white world and the Aboriginal world. Many were forced to give up their Status rights upon marrying a non-Status or non-Aboriginal man. Without the support of family and community, the cities became new homelands for these women. Here, Aboriginal women were domestic labourers, cleaners, cooks, factory workers. For Aboriginal women, higher education was not likely. Despite social and economic inequities, Aboriginal women worked diligently and survived.

Poverty became a way of life. Substandard housing, social welfare and lack of medical care were the Aboriginal woman's lot in the post-World War II era. While the country flourished with new-found vigour and resolve, her fragile world was crumbling beneath her feet.

Social conditions worsened with the introduction of the welfare system to the Aboriginal community. Traditional systems of family and communal support crumbled, and in time they were replaced by a growing dependency on "relief." Many Aboriginal families became second-, third- or fourth-generation "welfare families."

Historically, alcohol had been present in Aboriginal communities since contact was established with European colonists. Status Indians, however, were prohibited by law to purchase or consume alcohol, so alcohol consumption was limited to bootleg or homebrew. In 1954, the law was amended to permit alcohol consumption by Aboriginal people, and within four decades alcohol had made an indelible mark on the lives of Aboriginal men, women and children.

The strain began to take its toll on Aboriginal women, partially because of their loss of power and weakened status under the *Indian Act.* Aboriginal women fell victim to multiple abuses, which were inflicted on them as children, wives, mothers and elders, often at the hands of those most trusted. The abuse was kept hidden. Untreated, it spread to epidemic proportions. Most cases of abuse could be traced to the residential school, from where victims often carried the abuse back to their homes and communities.

After extensive hearings, the *Indian Act* was amended in 1951, but Indian agents retained their control over daily life and continued to serve as justices of the peace. In addition to the provisions of the *Indian Act*, provincial laws were applied to reserves "to involve provincial governments more actively in daily life and to reduce the unique legal status that reserves had enjoyed previously."[4]

One of the most significant consequences of the imposition of provincial laws was the enforcement of child welfare legislation and the accompanying imposition of urban middle-class standards. Thousands of Aboriginal children were deemed to be in need of protection and were removed from their homes in "the Sixties Scoop."[5] "Combined with the residential school system, it meant that generations of children were not raised within their families or communities, thereby never learning their traditional culture or patterns of parenting."[6]

In 1969, a white paper proposed the abandonment of treaties and treaty rights and the transformation of reserves into communities in the interest of equality.[7] Aboriginal leaders and activists entered the battle for Aboriginal rights, and Aboriginal peoples, united as nations, defeated the policy. After the "disastrous failure"[8] of the paper, the federal government was forced to abandon previous blatant paternalistic policies and attitudes and to seek the opinion of Aboriginal peoples. The federal government provided funding for regional and national Aboriginal organizations and transferred some administrative functions from the Department of Indian Affairs to local, predominantly male chiefs and councils. Women's cries for justice and equality, however, went unheard, and Aboriginal women's rights were rejected by their own Aboriginal leaders.

After a long and courageous campaign, Bill C-31 was passed in 1985 to amend the Indian Act "with the explicit objective of bringing it into line with the equality provision of the *Charter of Rights and Freedoms*."[9] Bill C-31 amended section 12(1)(b) of the *Indian Act*, which forced enfranchisement on Aboriginal women, and introduced legislation to restore Status rights to women who had married non-Status or non-Aboriginal men and to their children. The Bill also contained limited self-government provisions giving bands authority to develop their own membership codes.

Under the provisions of Bill C-31, by 1990, the Status population increased by 115,000.[10] Fifty-eight percent of those individuals reinstated under Bill C-31 were Aboriginal women.[11] It is significant to note that the majority of those seeking reinstatement (86 percent) cited as the reason for their application: personal identity, culture or a sense of belonging, correction of injustice or Aboriginal rights.[12]

Although separate funds for housing, education and other rights were designated by the federal government for the women and their families reinstated under Bill C-31, the funds were inadequate. A false perception exists that women and their children who were reinstated under Bill C-31 receive preferential treatment in the allocation of band resources. Families who had long been on waiting lists for housing, for example, saw families returning under the provisions of the Bill receive houses, built with those specially allocated funds, while they were forced to continue to live in often overcrowded and substandard housing.

Under Bill C-31, bands can determine their own membership. Since many chiefs and councils are opposed to the provisions of the legislation, Aboriginal women continue to be effectively denied their rights under Bill C-31.

Bill C-31 has been interpreted by some as a means of cultural genocide that will lead to the eventual extinction of Aboriginal peoples in Canada. This "ethnic cleansing" aspect of the Bill is clearly explained in the *Report of the Aboriginal Justice Inquiry of Manitoba*:

> The continuing discrimination enters the picture in terms of the differential treatment between the sexes regarding the children of Status Indians. This is an extremely convoluted registration scheme in which the discrimination is not readily apparent on the surface. It requires an examination of how the Act treats people to detect the fundamental unfairness. Examples are necessary to make this more obvious.
>
> Joan and John, a brother and sister, were both registered Indians. Joan married a Métis man before 1985 so she lost her Indian status under section 12(1)(b) of the former Act. John married a white woman before 1985 and she automatically became a Status Indian. Both John and Joan have had children over the years. Joan is now eligible to regain her Status under section 6(1)(c) and her children will qualify under section 6(2). They are treated as having only one eligible parent, their mother, although both parents are Aboriginal. John's children gained Status at birth as both parents were Indians legally, even though only one was an Aboriginal person.
>
> Joan's children can pass on status to their offspring only if they also marry registered Indians. If they marry unregistered Aboriginal people or non-Aboriginal people, then no Status will pass to their grandchildren. All John's grandchildren will be Status Indians regardless of who his children marry.
>
> Thus, entitlement to registration for the second generation has nothing to do with racial or cultural characteristics. The Act has eliminated the discrimination faced by those who lost Status, but has passed it on to the next generation.... Not only does the *Indian Act* maintain improper and probably illegal forms of sexual discrimination, but it also threatens the long-term survival of Indians.

The current regime has a de facto form of a "one-quarter blood" rule. As shown in the previous example, intermarriage between registered Indians and others over two successive generations results in descendants who are not entitled at law to be status Indians. This may threaten the very existence of First Nations in the not too distant future, especially small communities who have considerable interaction with neighbouring Métis or non-Aboriginal communities.

In our view, discriminating against Indian people by virtue of such provisions imposed by Parliament should cease.[13]

Bill C-31 will cause more Aboriginal people to lose or not qualify for Status rights than the *Indian Act*. Although on the surface Bill C-31 appeared to eliminate sex discrimination against Aboriginal women, it has created a new social order among Aboriginal peoples which continues to have a far-reaching impact on the lives of those reinstated under the legislation.[14]

While Aboriginal leaders have mounted political campaigns for self-government and constitutional reform, Aboriginal women have been at the forefront of a social revolution, demanding better housing, child welfare, education and health care.

The colonization process and the *Indian Act* have dispossessed Aboriginal women of their inherent role as leaders in their own nation and have created a serious imbalance in Aboriginal society that accords Aboriginal men greater political, social and economic influence and opportunity than Aboriginal women.

This balance must be restored, with Aboriginal women assuming their rightful position as full and equal partners in the shaping of their own destinies.

Aboriginal Women's View of Violence

Violence against Aboriginal women must be seen through the eyes of Aboriginal women. Aboriginal women do not share the same world as their non-Aboriginal sisters. Aboriginal women must engage in two simultaneous struggles—to restore equality with Aboriginal men and to strive to attain equality with non-Aboriginal women. It has been said that violence in Aboriginal families and communities is a "reaction against systems of domination, disrespect and bureaucratic control."[15] ...

These differences must be acknowledged and respected. In Aboriginal society, the family is the heart of the community, an entity made powerful by human spirit. Families are linked to one another through kinship on the mother's or father's side, or on both. These extended families are representative of the traditional clan system of their ancestors. Many of them are matriarchal, with elderly women presiding as the head. Aboriginal communities are devoid of the non-Aboriginal "class" structure, and individual family standing is not measured by material possessions or accumulated wealth. Instead, a family is often valued by the contribution of its extended family to the community, its ability to get along with others and the strength and character of its members.

The ties that bind the Aboriginal family have been held sacred for many generations. Often this dependency on one's family has been the only means of social and economic survival, and Aboriginal women have been taught to uphold the tradition of family, sometimes at the expense of their own safety.

The extended family tradition in Aboriginal communities has been called both "a blessing and a curse," for the tradition that provides nurturing, love and protection to children and women can also cause the destruction of the family affected by violence. For a victim of violence in an Aboriginal community, disclosing her abuse would publicly shame her family and could result in being ostracized by the family, her only means of support.

Women stay in violent relationships through fear, threats, intimidation, pressure from the community leadership, the destruction of self-esteem and the imposed belief that survival outside the relationship or family is impossible. Also, these women may feel that no one would believe and/or help them.

One of Aboriginal women's greatest fears in disclosing violence in the home is that their children may be taken from them by provincial, or white authorities or by Aboriginal child welfare workers who may report to chiefs and councils. This fear is largely based on the historical relationship between child welfare agencies and the Aboriginal community. Many Aboriginal women will stay in an abusive relationship to keep the family together, and the perceived threat of losing their children keeps them silent. These women carry the pain of their abuse alone and in silence, sometimes for a lifetime.

The dignity and safety of Aboriginal women and their families must be preserved and protected when disclosing violence. Violence against Aboriginal women must be viewed from the perspective of Aboriginal women living within their culture and must be considered in terms of the reality of their situation. Some Aboriginal women may be prevented from reporting violence because of cultural values of kindness, reconciliation and family cohesiveness.[16]

Generally, Aboriginal women do not view themselves and their needs as separate from the needs of their children and families. Their roles as mothers, grandmothers and caregivers of their nation are still widely recognized and honoured by Aboriginal women today.

Some Aboriginal women do not relate to non-Aboriginal feminist philosophy and terminology because historically and culturally Aboriginal women were not subject to the European social structures that oppressed non-Aboriginal women. Aboriginal women have been subjected to extreme sexism and racism since contact was made with European colonists.

Violence in the home and in the community has severe consequences for Aboriginal women. In a study on federally imprisoned Aboriginal women,[17] the women prisoners reported victimization throughout their life. The violence they experienced was generally at the hands of men.

> The Canadian Panel on Violence Against Women must be aware that the approach to the problem of violence is perceived differently in Native communities. Please do not change our perspective and ideas and solutions. Respect what people tell you. The problem is being dealt with through a holistic approach; we look at all aspects at the same time—sexual abuse, battered women, drug and alcohol abuse. We also involve men, we identify the problem as a family [problem].

For many Aboriginal women seeking to resolve their experiences of abuse, traditional methods of healing have gained widespread acceptance and respect. Women's healing circles and informal support groups have begun in many Aboriginal communities. These initiatives, which operate with little or no outside funding, reflect the commitment of Aboriginal women to restore the balance and well-being of their communities.

Aboriginal women have become leaders in the struggle against violence in their communities. A grass-roots movement by Aboriginal women who are seeking personal healing and healing for their families has increased awareness of the issue of abuse in the Aboriginal community.

Aboriginal leaders, however, have been slow to react. Most regional and national political organizations, grappling with self-government issues, have made little more than a verbal commitment to healing the violence in Aboriginal communities. Local Aboriginal governments, struggling for economic survival, are reluctant to commit their already meagre resources to concrete initiatives.

Both Aboriginal and non-Aboriginal governments must be active participants in this healing process. Governmental support must entail more than verbal commitments. The goals of "zero violence" for Aboriginal communities and the safety of Aboriginal women and children must be reflected in the actions of government at all levels—local, regional and national. These actions must include developing immediate and long-term initiatives to match the diverse needs and aspirations of Aboriginal women and the communities to help the healing process continue.

As Aboriginal women assume greater leadership roles, the priorities of national Aboriginal agendas are beginning to shift. National Aboriginal women's advocacy groups, such as the Native Women's Association of Canada, Aboriginal Nurses Association of Canada and Pauktuutit, the Inuit Women's Association, have become Aboriginal women's strongest allies in their struggle against violence.

There are many social, economic and political factors that have contributed to the oppressions that victimize Aboriginal women, and no single solution can meet all their needs. However, to guarantee that these needs are addressed with expediency and efficiency, Aboriginal women must regain their rightful place as full and equal partners within their families, their communities and their nations. The involvement of Aboriginal women is vital, and their participation must be an integral component in all healing initiatives.

For Aboriginal women, the Zero Tolerance Policy must be implemented in a culturally relevant manner. It must encompass individual, family and community healing, restore community standards which place equal value on women and men, and provide adequate public and private enforcement and response to end all violence against women in the home, the community and society as a whole.

ENDNOTES

1. Province of Manitoba, *Report of the Aboriginal Justice of Manitoba* (Winnipeg, 1991), 73.

2. *Ibid.,* 71.

3. J.R. Miller "Owen Glendower, Hotspur and Canadian Indian Policy," in *Sweet Promises: A Reader on Indian-White Relations in Canada*, ed. J.R. Miller, 326.

4. Province of Manitoba, *Aboriginal Justice Inquiry, op. cit.*, 79.

5. *Ibid.,* 79.

6. *Ibid.,* 79.

7. Statement of the Government of Canada on Indian Policy, cited in *Report of the Aboriginal Justice Inquiry*, Province of Manitoba (Winnipeg, 1991), 79.

8. Province of Manitoba, *Aboriginal Justice Inquiry*, op. cit., 80.

9. *Ibid.,* 201.

10. House of Commons, *Minutes of Proceedings and Evidence of the Standing Committee on*

Aboriginal Affairs, Issue 12, 12:8.

11. Department of Indian Affairs and Northern Development, *Impact of the 1985 Amendments to the Indian Act (Bill C-31): Summary Report* (Ottawa, 1990), ii.

12. *Ibid.,* 15.

13. Province of Manitoba, *Aboriginal Justice Inquiry, op. cit.*, 204.

14. C. Saulis, National Association of Friendship Centres, telephone interview, April 20, 1993.

15. Ontario Native Women's Association, *Breaking Free: A Proposal for Change to Aboriginal Family Violence* (Thunder Bay, Ontario, 1989), 8.

16. "Squamish Family Violence Prevention and Treatment Model Project." cited in *Violence Against Aboriginal Women*, by T. Nahanee (Research paper prepared for the Canadian Panel on Violence Against Women, Ottawa, 1993).

17. *Survey of Federally Sentenced Aboriginal Women in the Community*, cited in *Creating Choices: The Report of the Task Force on Federally Sentenced Women*, (Solicitor General of Canada: Ottawa, 1990), 16.

BIBLIOGRAPHY

Acheson, T.W. 1985. *Saint John: The Making of a Colonial Urban Community*. Toronto: University of Toronto Press.

Adachi, Ken. 1976. *The Enemy That Never Was*. Toronto: McClelland & Stewart.

Adamson, Nancy, Linda Briskin, and Margaret McPhail. 1988. *Feminists Organizing for Change: The Contemporary Women's Movement in Canada*. Toronto: Oxford University Press.

Agnew, Vijay. 1993a. "Canadian Feminism and Women of Colour," *Women's International Studies Forum* 16(3): 217-27.

Akyeampong, Ernest. 1989. "Working for Minimum Wage," *Perspectives on Labour and Income* 3, 8-20.

Albrecht, Lisa, and Rose Brewer, eds. 1990. *Bridges of Power: Women's Multicultural Alliances*. Philadelphia: New Society.

Allen, Paula Gunn. 1986. *The Sacred Hoop*. Boston: Beacon Press.

American Psychiatric Association. 1987. "Diagnostic Criteria for 302.50, Transsexualism," *Diagnostic and Statistical Manual of Mental Disorders*. 4th edition, revised. Washington: American Psychiatric Association.

Andrews, Caroline. 1984. "Women and the Welfare State 27(4)," *Canadian Journal of Political Science*, 667-83.

Anzalda, Gloria. 1990. "Bridge, Drawbridge, Sandbar or Island: Lesbians of Colour." In *Bridges of Power: Women's Multicultural Alliances*, ed., L. Albrecht and R. Brewer. Philadelphia: New Society, 216-33.

Armstrong, Pat, and Hugh Armstrong. 1996. *Wasting Away: The Undermining of Canadian Health Care*. Toronto: Oxford.

Armstrong, Pat. 1996. "Unravelling the Safety Net: Transformations in Health Care and the Impact on Women." In *Women and Canadian Public Policy*, ed., Janine Brodie. Toronto: Harcourt Brace, 129-50.

Armstrong, Pat. 1995. "The Feminization of the Labour Force: Harmonizing Down in a Global Economy." In *Invisible Issues in Women's Occupational Health*, eds., Karen Messing, Barbara Neis, and Lucie Dumais. Charlottetown: Gynergy Books, 368-92.

Armstrong, Pat. 1994. *The Double Ghetto*. Toronto: McClelland & Stewart.

Armstrong, Pat. 1994. "Closer to Home: More Work for Women." In *Take Care: Warning Signals for Canada's Health System*, eds., Pat Armstrong, Hugh Armstrong, Jacqueline Choiniere, Gina Feldberg, and Jerry White. Toronto: Garamond, 95-110.

Armstrong, Pat. 1988. "Taking Women into Account: Redefining and Intensifying Employment in Canada." In *Feminization of the Labour Force: Paradoxes and Promises*, eds., Elizabeth Hagen, Jane Jenson, and Trudi Kozol. New York: Oxford, 65-84.

Aronowitz, Stanley. 1984. "When the New Left was New." In Sohnya Sayres, Anders Stephanson, and Frederic Jameson, eds., *The 60s Without Apology*. Minneapolis: University of Minnesota Press, 11-43.

Balancing Act: The Post-Deficit Mandate. Toronto: Oxford University Press, 1998.

Bannon, Sharleen. 1975. "The Women's Bureau Is 21," *Labour Gazette*, Anniversary Issue, 629-31.

Barber, Marilyn. 1986. "In Search of a Better Life: A Scottish Domestic in Rural Ontario," *Polyphony* 8(1-2): 13-16.

Bashevkin, Sylvia. 1985. *Toeing the Lines: Women and Party Politics in English Canada*. Toronto: University of Toronto Press.

Benditt, Theodore. 1983. "Surrogate Gestation: Law and Morality." In *Biomedical Ethics Review*, eds., James M. Humber and Robert F. Almeder. Clifton, New Jersey: Humana.

Benson, Margaret and Pat Davit. 1975. "Women Invent Society," *Canadian Dimension*, 10(2).

Benston, Maggie. 1993. In conversation with Ursula Franklin, "Complexity and Management," *Canadian Woman Studies/les cahiers de la femmes,* 66.

Benston, Margaret. 1969. "The Political Economy of Women's Liberation," *Monthly Review*, vol. 24, no. 4.

Berkowitz, Jonathan. 1993. *Where Are the Children? An Overview of Child Care Arrangements in Canada*. Ottawa: Health and Welfare Canada (cat. no. 89-527E).

Bhasin, Kamla. 1990. "Asian Women Against Mal-development," (Keynote address to the Third International Interdisciplinary Congress of Women, Dublin, Ireland, 1987). Fenix no. 00:22-26.

Bhavnani, Kum Kum, and Margaret Coulson. 1986. "Transforming Socialist-Feminism: The Challenge of Racism," *Feminist Review* 23: 81-92.

Bird, Florence. 1974. *Anne Francis: An Autobiography*. Toronto: Clark Irwin.

Black, Naomi. 1988. "The Canadian Women's Movement: The Second Wave." In *Changing Patterns: Women in Canada*, eds., S. Burt, L. Code, and L. Dorney. Toronto: McClelland & Stewart, 80-102.

Black, Robert C. 1981. "Legal Problems of Surrogate Motherhood," *New England Law Review*, 16:3, 373-395.

Bornstein, Kate. 1994. *Gender Outlaw: On Men, Women, and the Rest of Us*. New York: Routledge.

Bourgeault, Ron G. 1991. "Race, Class and Gender: Colonial Domination of Indian Women." In *Race, Class, Gender: Bonds and Barriers*, ed., Jesse Vorst et al. Toronto: Society of Socialist Studies and Garamond.

Bowes, Nancy. 1990. *Telling our Secrets: Abortion Stories from Nova Scotia*. Halifax: CARAL.

Boyd, Susan B. 1994. "Expanding the Family in Family Law: Recent Ontario Proposals on Same Sex Relationships," *Canadian Journal of Women and the Law* 7(2), 545-63.

Brand, Dionne. 1991. *No Burden to Carry: Narratives of Black Working Women in Ontario, 1920s to 1950s.* Toronto: Women's Press.

———. 1992. *Canada's Women*. Ottawa: Minister of Industry, Science and Technology (cat. no. 71-205).

Brand, Dionne. 1988. "A Conceptual Analysis of How Gender Roles Are Racially Constructed: Black Women," M.A. Thesis, University of Toronto.

Bristow, Peggy et al., 1994. *We're Rooted Here and They Can't Pull Us Up: Essays in African Canadian Women's History*. Toronto: University of Toronto Press.

Brodie, Janine. 1985a. "From Waffles to Grits: A Decade in the Life of the New Democratic Party." In *Party Politics in Canada*. 5th ed., Hugh C. Thorburn, ed., Scarborough: Prentice-Hall Canada.

Brodie, Janine, and Jill McCalla Vickers. 1982. *Canadian Women in Politics: An Overview*. CRIAW paper no. 2. Ottawa: CRIAW.

Brodie, Janine. 1985b. *Women and Politics in Canada*. Toronto: McGraw Hill-Ryerson.

Buchignani, Norman L., and Doreen Indra. 1985. *Continuous Journey*. Toronto: McClelland & Stewart.

Bunch, Charlotte. 1987. *Passionate Politics, Feminist Theory in Action: Essays, 1968–1986*. New York: St. Martin Press.

Bunch, Charlotte. 1990. "Making Common Cause: Diversity and Coalitions." In *Bridges of Power: Women Multicultural Alliances*, ed. L. Albrecht and R. Brewer. Philadelphia: New Society, 49-57.

Burt, Sandra. 1986a. "Difference Democracies? A Preliminary Examination of the Political Worlds of Canadian Men and Women," *Women and Politics* 6(4) (Winter): 57-79.

Burt, Sandra. 1986b. "Women's Issues and the Women's Movement in Canada since 1970." In *The Politics of Gender, Ethnicity, and Language in Canada*, eds., Alan Cairns and Cynthia Williams. Toronto: University of Toronto Press, 111-169.

Califia, Pat. 1997. *Sex Changes: The Politics of Transgenderism*. San Francisco: Cleis Press.

Calliste, Agnes. 1991. "Canada's Immigration Policy and Domestics from the Caribbean: The Second Domestic Scheme." In *Race, Class, Gender: Bonds and Barriers*, ed., Jesse Vorst et al. Toronto: Society for Socialist Studies and Garamond.

Canada Health and Welfare. 1991. "New Family Violence Initiative Underway," *Canadian Women's Studies* 12(1): 111.

Canada, Statistics Canada. 1995c. *Earnings of Men and Women 1993*. Ottawa: Minister of Industry, Science and Technology (cat. no. 13-217).

Canada, Statistics Canada. 1994b. *Labour Force Annual Averages 1993*. Ottawa: Minister of Industry, Science and Technology (cat. no. 71-220).

Canada, Statistics Canada. 1994a. *Women in the Labour Force 1994*. Ottawa: Minister of Industry, Science and Technology (cat. no. 75-507E).

Canada, Statistics Canada. 1990. *Women in Canada*. 2nd ed. Ottawa: Minister of Supply and Services Canada (cat. no. 89-503E).

Canadian Educational Women's Press. 1972. *Women Unite!* Toronto: Canadian Educational Women's Press.

Canadian Panel on Violence against Women. 1993a. *Changing the Landscape: Ending Violence—Achieving Equality, Final Report.* Ottawa: Minister of Supply and Services.

Canadian Research Institute for the Advancement of Women (CRIAW). 1987. *Women's Involvement in Political Life.* CRIAW papers no. 16-17. Prepared for UNESCO Division of Human Rights and Peace. Ottawa: CRIAW.

Carty, Linda. 1994. "African Canadian Women and the State: 'Labour Only, Please,'" CASNP (Canadian Association in Support of Native Peoples). 1978. Bulletin 18(4): 34-35.

Chan, Anthony B. 1983. *The Gold Mountain. The Chinese in the New World.* Vancouver: New Star Books.

Cherfas, Jeremy and John Gribbin. 1984. *The Redundant Male.* London: The Bodley Head.

Christiansen, Juliette M., Anne Thornley-Brown, and Jean A. Robinson. n.d. *West Indians in Toronto.* Toronto: Family Services Association of Metro Toronto.

Code, Lorraine. 1993. "Feminist Theory." In *Changing Patterns: Women in Canada*, eds., Sandra Burt, Lorraine Code and L. Dorney. Toronto: McClelland & Stewart, 19-57.

Conway, Shelagh. 1992. *The Faraway Hills are Green: Voices of Irish Women in Canada.* Toronto: Women's Press.

Corrigan, Philip, ed. 1980. *Capitalism, State Formation and Marxist Theory.* London: Quarter Books.

Coulson, Margaret, Branka Magas, and Hilary Wainwright. 1975. "The Housewife and Her Labour Under Capitalism—a Critique," *New Left Review*, no. 89, 59-71.

Court of Canada, *Canadian Journal of Women and the Law* 4(2), 407-39.

Crosbie, Lynn. 1999. "Agitprop for 'REAL' Women: Dannielle Crittenden's Book on the 'Failure' of Feminism is a Stew of Other, More Original Ideas," *Globe and Mail*, February 20, D11.

Daenzer, Patricia. 1991. "Ideology and the Formation of Migration Policy: The Case of Immigrant Domestic Workers," 1940-90. PhD diss., University of Toronto.

Das Gupta, Tania. 1994. "Political Economy of Gender, Race and Class: Looking at South Asian Immigrant Women in Canada," *Canadian Ethics Studies* 26:1, 59-64.

———. 1993. *Equal Pay for Work of Equal Value.* Report prepared for the Public Service Alliance of Canada in Canadian Postal Workers v. Canada Post. Canadian Human Rights Commission.

Das Gupta, Tania. 1986. *Learning from Our History: Community Development by Immigrant Women in Canada, 1958-86: A Tool for Action.* Toronto: Cross Cultural Communication Centre.

Dewar, Elaine. 1993. "Wrongful Dismissal: Angry Anti-racists Drove June Callwood From Nellie's, The Shelter for Women She Created, Because She Couldn't Share her 'White-Skinned Privilege,'" *Toronto Life* (March): 32-47.

Diamond, Irene, and Gloria Feman Orenstein, Eds. 1990. *Reweaving the World: The Emergence of Ecofeminism.* San Francisco: Sierra Club Books.

Dill, Bonnie Thorton. 1992. "Our Mothers' Grief: Racial Ethnic Women and the Maintenance of Families." In *Race, Class and Gender: An Anthology*, eds., Margaret L. Anderson and Patricia Hill Collins. Belmont, Cal.: Wadsworth, 215-238.

Dixon, Marlene. 1972. "Ideology, Class and Liberation." In *Mother Was Not A Person*, ed., Margaret Anderson. Montreal: Our Generation Press, 227-41.

Dixon, Marlene. 1971. "Where Are We Going?" In *From Feminism to Liberation*, ed., Edith Altbach. London: Schenkman Publishing Company.

Djao, Angela W. and Roxana Ng. 1987. "Structured Isolation: Immigrant Women in Saskatchewan." In *Women: Isolation and Bonding. The Ecology of Gender*, 141-158, ed., Kathleen Storrie. Toronto: Methuen.

Doman, Mahinder. 1984. "A Note on Asian Indian Women in British Columbia 1900-1935." In *Not Just Pin Money: Selected Essays on the History of Women's Work in British Columbia*, eds., Barbara K. Latham and Roberta J. Pazdro. Victoria: Camosun College.

Draper, Hal. 1972. "Marx and Engels on Women's Liberation." In *Female Liberation*, ed., Roberta Salper. New York: Alfred A. Knopf, 83-107.

Duckworth, Muriel, and Peggy Hope-Simpson. 1981. 'Voice of Women Dialogue.' *Atlantis* 6/2 (Spring): 168-76.

Dunphy, Cathy. 1987. "Canadian History of Chinese Women," *Toronto Star*, July 14, G1.

Egan, Carolyn, Linda Gardner, and Judy Persad. 1988. "The Politics of Transformation: Struggles with Race, Class, and Sexuality in the March 8th Coalition." In *Social Movements/Social Change: The Politics and Practice of Organizing*, ed., F. Cunningham et al. Toronto: Between the Lines, 22-47.

Eichler, Margrit. 1988. "New Reproductive Technologies." In *Families in Canada Today: Recent Changes and Their Policy Consequences*. 2nd enlarged and revised edition. Toronto: Gage, 280-310.

Eisenstein, H. 1983. *Contemporary Feminist Thought*. Boston: G.K. Hall.

Estable, Alma, and Mechtild Meyer. 1989. *A Discussion Paper on Settlement Needs of Immigrant Women in Ontario*. Ottawa: Immigrant Settlement and Adaptation Program.

Estable, Alma. 1986. "Immigrant Women in Canada. Current Issues." A Background Paper prepared for the Canadian Advisory Council on the Status of Women.

Feinberg, Leslie. 1996. *Transgender Warriors: Making History from Joan of Arc to Ru Paul*. Boston: Beacon Press.

Findlay, Sue. 1987. "Facing the State: The Politics of the Women's Movement Reconsidered." In *Feminism and Political Economy*, eds., Heather Jon Maroney and Meg Luxton. Toronto: Methuen, 31-50.

Firestone, Shulamith. 1970. *The Dialectic of Sex*. New York: Morrow.

Fireweed 16 (Spring 1983).

Ford, Clellan Stearns. 1964. *A Comparative Study of Human Reproduction*. Reprinted by Human Relations Area Files Press. Yale University: New Haven.

Franklin, Ursela. 1990. *The Real World of Technology*. Toronto: Anansi Press.

Freeman, Jo. 1983. *The Politics of Women's Liberation*. 2nd edition. New York: Longman.

Frenken, Hubert, and Karen Master. 1992. "Employer-Sponsored Pension Plans—Who Is Covered?," *Perspective on Labour and Income* 4(4): 27-34.

Freud, Sigmund. 1964. *New Introductory Lectures on Psychoanalysis*. New York: W.W. Norton.

Frideres, James S. 1987. "Native Peoples and Canadian Education." In *The Political Economy of Canadian Schooling*, ed., Terry Wotherspoon. Toronto: Methuen, 275-290.

Fudge, Judy, and Patricia McDermott, eds. 1991. *Just Wages: A Feminist Assessment.*

Gabriel, Chris, and Katherine Scott. 1993. "The Women's Press at Twenty: The Politics of Feminist Publishing." In *And Still We Rise*, ed. Linda Carty. Toronto: Women's Press, 25-52.

Gandhi, Nandita, and Vasantha Kannabiran. 1989. "Feminism." In *South Asian Workshop on Women and Development*, 12-15.

Garland, Anne Witte. 1988. *Women Activists Challenging the Abuse of Power*. New York: Feminist Press.

Gelb, Joyce. 1989. *Feminism and Politics: A Comparative Perspective*. Berkeley: University of California Press.

George, Margaret. 1973. "From Good Wife to Mistress: The Transformation of the Female in Bourgeois Culture," *Science and Society*, 152-77.

Goelman, Hillel, Alan Pence, Donna Lero, Lois Brockman, Ned Glick, and Linda J. Gordon. 1987. "Reproductive Rights for Today," *Nation*, Sept. 12, 230-2.

Gotell, Lise. 1996. "Policing Desire: Obscenity Law, Pornography Politics, and Feminism in Canada." In *Women and Public Policy in Canada*, ed., Janine Brodie. Toronto: Harcourt Brace, 279-317.

Greaves, Lorraine. 1991. "Reorganizing the National Action Committee on the Status of Women, 1986–1988." In *Women and Social Change: Feminism Activism in Canada*, eds., J. Dawn Wine and J. Ristock, 101-16. Toronto: James Lorimer.

Greer, Germaine. 1970. *The Female Eunuch*. London: MacGibbon and Kee.

Hall, Martha. 1985. "Rights and the Problems of Surrogate Parenting," *The Philosophical Quarterly*, 35:141.

Hawthurst, Donna, and Sue Morrow. 1984. *Living Our Visions: Building Feminist Community*. Arizona: Temple University Press.

Henry, Frances, Carol Tator, Winston Mattis, and Tim Rees, 1995. *Colour of Democracy*. Toronto: Harcourt Brace.

Hollinger, Joan Heifetz. 1985. "From Coitus to Commerce: Legal and Social Consequences of Noncoital Reproduction," *Journal of Law Reform*. 18: 865-932.

hooks, bell. 1997. "Black Women and Feminism." In *Feminisms*, eds., Sandra Kemp and Judith Squires. Oxford University Press, 227-228.

hooks, bell. 1984. *Feminist Theory from Margin to Center*. Boston: South End Press.

Hudson, Pete, and Brad McKenzie. 1981. "Child Welfare and Native People: The Extension of Colonialism." *The Social Worker* 49(2): 63-88.

Hunt, Judith. 1975. "Women and Liberation," *Marxism Today* 19(11): 326-37.

Hunt, Judith, and Alan Hunt. 1974. "Marxism and the Family." *Marxism Today* 18(2), 59-61.

Immigrant and Visible-Minority Women. 1985. Brief from Immigrant and Visible-Minority Women to Flora McDonald, Minister of Employment and Immigration. Unpublished.

Ince, Susan. 1984. "Inside the Surrogate Industry." In *Test Tube Women. What Future for Motherhood?*, eds., Rita Arditti, Renate Duelli Klein and Shelley Minden. London: Pandora, 99-116.

Instructions on Respect for Human Life in its Origin and on the Dignity of Procreation: Replies to Certain Questions of the Day. 1987.

International Women's Day Celebrations. 1986. *Newsletter.*

Jamieson, Kathleen. 1981. *Indian Women and the Law in Canada: Citizens Minus*. Ottawa: Advisory Council on the Status of Women and Indian Rights for Indian Women, April 1978.

Johnson, Graham E. 1983. "Chinese Family and Community in Canada: Tradition and Change." In *Two Nations, Many Cultures: Ethnic Groups in Canada*, ed., Jean Leonard Elliot. Scarborough: Prentice-Hall, 393-411.

Johnston, Patrick. 1983. *Native Children and the Child Welfare System*. Toronto: Canadian Council on Social Development.

Juteau-Lee, Danielle and Barbara Roberts. "Ethnicity and Femininity," *Canadian Ethnic Studies* 13(1).

Katz, Avi. 1986. "Surrogate Motherhood and the Baby Selling Laws," *Columbia Journal of Law and Social Problems*, 20:1:1-53.

Kemp, Sandra, and Judith Squires. 1997. "Introduction." In *Feminisms*. Oxford: Oxford University Press, 3-12.

Kinsmen, Gary. 1987. *The Regulation of Desire. Sexuality in Canada*. Montreal: Black Rose Books.

Kline, Marlee. 1989b. "Women's Oppression and Racism: A Critique of the 'Feminist Standpoint.'" In Race, Class, and Gender: Bonds and Barriers, ed., J. Vorst et al. Toronto: Between the Lines, 37-64.

Kobayashi, Cassandra. 1978. "Sexual Slavery in Canada: Our History," *The Asianadian* 1(3): 63-88.

Koedt, Anne. 1973. "The Myth of the Vaginal Orgasm". In *Radical Feminism*, ed., Anne Koedt, Ellen Levine and Anita Rapone. New York: Quadrangle/The New York Times Book Co., 198-207.

Koedt, Anne, Ellen Levine, and Anita Rapone, eds. 1973. *Radical Feminism*. New York: Quadrangle.

Kome, Penney. 1985. Women of Influence: Canadian Women and Politics. Toronto: Doubleday Canada.

Kostash, Myrna. 1980. *Long Way from Home*. Toronto: James Lorimer and Company.

LaMarsh, Judy. 1969. *Memoirs of a Bird in a Gilded Cage*. Toronto: McClelland & Stewart.

Lamoureaux, Diane. 1987. "Nationalism and Feminism in Québec: An Impossible Attraction." In *Feminism and Political Economy: Women's Work, Women's Struggles*, eds., Heather Jon Maroney and Meg Luxton. Toronto: Methuen, 51-68.

Latham, Barbara K., and Roberta J. Pazdro, eds. 1984. *Not Just Pin Money: Selected Essays on the History of Women's Work in British Columbia*. Victoria: Camosun College.

Laxer, James. 1960. "The Americanization of the Canadian Student Movement." In *Close the 49th Parallel*, ed., Ian Lumsden. Toronto: University of Toronto Press.

Lay, Jackie. 1980. "The Columbia on the Tynemouth: The Emigration of Single Women and Girls in 1862." In *In Her Own Right: Selected Essays on Women's History in B.C.*, eds., Barbara Latham and Cathy Kess. Victoria: Camosun College, 19-42.

Leila Khalid Collective. 1970. Position paper. Available from Toronto Women's Movement Archives.

Li, Peter S., and B. Singh Bolaria. 1983. *Racial Minorities in Multicultural Canada*. Toronto: Garamond.

Lindsay, Colin. 1992. *Lone-Parent Families in Canada*. Ottawa: Minister of Industry, Science and Technology (cat. no. 89-522E).

Lindstrom-Best, Varpu. 1986. "Going to Work in America: Finnish Maids, 1911-1930," *Polyphony* 8(1–2): 17-20.

Lipset, Seymour Martin. 1990. *Continental Divide*. New York: Routledge.

Locust, Carol. 1990. "Discrimination Against American Indian Families in Child Abuse Cases," *Indian Child Welfare Digest*, (Feb.-March): 7-9.

Loney, Martin. 1977. "A Political Economy of Citizen Participation." In *The Canadian State: Political Economy and Political Power,* ed., Leo Panitch. Toronto: University of Toronto Press.

Loseke, Donileen. 1992. *The Battered Women and Shelters: The Social Construction of Wife Abuse*. Albany: State University of New York Press.

Lovenduski, Joni. 1986. *Women and European Politics: Contemporary Feminism and Public Policy*. Amherst, MA: University of Massachusetts Press.

Lygre, David G. 1979. *Life Manipulation*. New York: Walker.

MacDonald, Marilyn. 1987. Private conversation.

MacKinnon, Catharine. 1991. "From Practice to Theory, or What is a White Woman Anyway?" *Yale Journal of Law and Feminism* 4: 13-22.

MacKinnon, Catherine. 1989. *Toward a Feminist Theory of the State*. Cambridge: Harvard University Press.

Macpherson, Kay, and Meg Sears. 1976. "The Voice of Women: A History." In *Women in the Canadian Mosaic*, ed., Gwen Matheson. Toronto: Peter Martin, 71-89.

Macpherson, Kay. 1975. "The Seeds of the Seventies," *Canadian Dimensions* 10(8): 39-41.

Mady, Theresa. 1981. "Surrogate Mothers: The Legal Issues," *American Journal of Law and Medicine*, 7:3, 323-352.

Manley, John. 1980. "Women and the Left in the 1930s: The Case of the Toronto CCF Women's Joint Committee," *Atlantis* 5(2), 100-119.

Maroney, Heather Jon and Meg Luxton. "From Feminism and Political Economy to Feminist Political Economy." In *Feminism and Political Economy*, eds., Heather Jon Maroney and Meg Luxton. Toronto: Methuen, 5-28.

Marsh, Leonard. 1975. *Report on Social Security for Canada 1943*. Toronto: University of Toronto Press.

Martin, Brendon. 1993. *In the Public Interest*. London: Zed Press.

Marx, Karl. 1906. *Capital. A Critique of Political Economy*. Vol. I, Chicago: Charles H. Kerr.

Mawdsley, Ralph D. 1983. "Surrogate Parenthood: A Need for Legislative Direction." *Illinois Bar Journal*, 412-417.

Maykovich, Minako K. 1980. "Acculturation versus Familialism in Three Generations of Japanese Canadians." In *Canadian Families: Ethnic Variations*, ed., K. Ishwaran. Toronto: McGraw-Hill Ryerson, 65-83.

McAdam, Doug. 1988. "Gender Implications of the Traditional Academic Conception of the Political." In *Changing Our Minds: Feminist Transformations of Knowledge*, eds., Susan Hardy Aiken et al. Albany: State University of New York Press, 59-76.

McCormack, Thelma. 1996. "Reproductive Technologies: Rights, Choices, and Coercion." In *Women and Public Policy in Canada*, ed., Janine Brodie. Toronto: Harcourt Brace, 199-221.

McCormack, Thelma. 1975. "Toward a Non-Sexist Perspective on Social and Political Change." In *Another Voice*, eds., M. Millman and R. Kanter. New York: Doubleday, 1-33.

McDonald, Lynn. 1979. "The Evolution of the Women's Movement in Canada," Parts I, 2. *Branching Out* 6 (I): 32-5, 6 (2): 39-43.

McIntosh, Mary. 1978. "The State and the Oppression of Women." In *Feminism and Materialism, Women and Modes of Production*, 254-289, eds., Annette Kuhn and Ann Marie Wolpe. London: Routledge and Kegan Paul.

Menzies, Heather. 1989. *Fastforward and Out of Control*. Toronto: MacMillan of Canada.

Mies, Maria and Vandana Shiva. 1993. *Ecofeminism*. London: Zed.

Miles, Angela. 1982. "Ideological Hegemony in Political Discourse: Women's Specificity and Equality." In *Feminism in Canada: From Pressure to Politics*, eds., Angela Miles and Geraldine Finn. Montreal: Black Rose Books, 213-227.

Minh-ha, Trinh T. 1989. *Women, Native, Other*. Bloomington: Indiana University Press.

Mitchell, Juliet. 1971. *Women's Estate*. Harmondsworth: Penguin Books.

Morissette, Rene, John Myles, and W.G. Picot. 1993. *What Is Happening to Earnings Inequality in Canada?* Ottawa: Statistics Canada.

Morris, Cerise. 1982. "No More Than Simple Justice." PhD diss., McGill University.

Morton, Peggy. 1972. "Women's Work is Never Done." In *Women Unite!* Toronto: Women's Educational Press, 46-68.

Mossman, Mary Jane. 1994. "Running Hard to Stand Still: The Paradox of Family Law Reform," *Dalhousie Law Journal* 17, 5-33.

Narayan, Uma. 1990. "The Project of Feminist Epistemology: Perspectives from a Nonwestern Feminist." In *Gender/Body/Knowledge: Feminist Reconstruction of Being and Knowing* eds., A.M. Jaggar and S.R. Bordo. New Brunswick: Rutgers University Press, 256-72.

Nataf, Zachary. 1996. *Lesbians Talk Transgender*. London: Scarlet Press.

National Action Committee on the Status of Women. 1986. Presentation to the Standing Committee of the Secretary of State.

National Council of Welfare. 1990. *Women and Poverty Revisited*. Ottawa: National Council of Welfare.

NCFS (Native Child and Family Services of Toronto). 1991. *Annual General Report*.

Nelson, E.D. and Robinson, B.W. 1995. *Gender in the 1990's: Images, Realities and Issues*. Toronto: Nelson Canada.

Nett, Emily M. 1988. *Canadian Families: Past and Present*. Toronto: Butterworths.

Newman, Lucile F. 1972. *Birth Control: An Anthropoligal View*. An Addison-Wesley Module in Anthropology, No. 27.

Newton, Lisa H. 1983. "Surrogate Motherhood. The Ethical Implications." In *Biomedical Ethics Review*, eds., James M. Humber and Robert F. Almeder. Clifton, New Jersey: Humana.

Ng, Roxana. 1988a. *The Politics of Community Service*. Toronto: Garamond.

Ng, Roxana, and Tania Das Gupta. 1981. "Nation Builders? The Captive Labour Force of Non-English Speaking Immigrant Women," *Canadian Women's Studies* 3(1): 83-85.

Ng, Roxana and Judith Ramirez. 1981. *Immigrant Housewives in Canada*. Toronto: Immigrant Women's Centre.

Normand, J. 1995. "Education of Women in Canada," *Canadian Social Trends* 39, Winter 1995: 17-21.

Ontario Law Reform Commission. 1985. *Report on Human Artificial Reproduction and Related Matters*. Vol. I and II.

Ontario Women's Directorate. 1987. *Report on the 1987 Community Workshops with Visible Minority and Immigrant Women*. Toronto: The Directorate.

Open letters to Catharine MacKinnon. 1991. *Yale Journal of Law and Feminism* 4: 177-90.

Ornstein, Michael, and Tony Haddad. 1991. *About Time: Analysis of a 1986 Survey of Canadians*. Toronto: Institute for Social Research and Department of Sociology, York University, 1993.

Overall, Christine. 1987. *Ethics and Human Reproduction: A Feminist Analysis*. Boston: Allen & Unwin.

Panitch, Leo, ed. 1977. *The Canadian State: Political Economy and Political Power*. Toronto: University of Toronto Press.

Parker, Philip J. 1983. "Motivation of Surrogate Mothers: Initial Findings," *American Journal of Psychiatry*, 140: 1.

Parmar, Pratibha. 1986. "Gender, Race, and Class: Asian Women in Resistance." In *The Empire Strikes Back: Race and Racism in 70s Britain*. ed., Centre for Contemporary Cultural Studies. London: Hutchinson, 236-75.

Parsons, Talcott, and Robert F. Bales. 1955. *Family, Socialization and Interaction Process*. USA: The Free Press of Glencoe.

Perpitan, Soledad. 1993. "Peace: A Breakaway from Patriarch," Paper presented to the Fifth International Interdisciplinary Congress on Women, San José, Costa Rica, 22-26 February.

Peter, Karl. 1981. "The Myth of Multiculturalism and Other Political Fables." In *Ethnicity Power and Politics in Canada*, eds., J. Dahlie and T. Fernando. Toronto: Methuen, 56-67.

Pidduck, Julianne. 1994. "Feminist Rhetoric of 'Violence against Women' and the Production of Everyday Fear," Paper presented at the York University Feminist Political Science Conference, North York.

Pink, Peter. 1973. "Marxism and the family," *Marxism Today*, 284-86.

Piven, Frances Fox. 1984. "Women and the State: Ideology, Power, and the Welfare State." *Socialist Review* 74:4, 11-19.

Plant, Judith, ed. 1989. *Healing the Wounds: The Promise of Ecofeminism*. Philadelphia: New Society Publishers.

Pold, Henry. 1994. "Jobs! Jobs! Jobs!" *Perspectives on Labour and Income* 6(3), 14-17.

Porter, Marion, John Porter, and Bernard Blishen. 1973. *Does Money Matter?* Toronto: York University, Institute for Behavioural Research.

Poyen, Bernard, Jean-Claude Penochet, André Mattei and Michèle Choux. 1980. "Is There a Right AID?" In *Human Artificial Insemination and Semen Preservation*, eds., David Georges and Wendel S. Price. New York: Plenum, 413-418.

Prentice, Alison, Paula Bourne, Gail Cuthbert Brandt, Beth Light, Wendy Mitchinson, and Naomi Black. *Canadian Women: A History*. Toronto: Harcourt Brace Jovanovich, 1988.

Primera, May. 1992. "The Discrimination Against Third World Housekeepers," *The Philippines Reporter*, Feb. 1-15, 12.

Ramazanoglu, Caroline. 1989. *Feminism and the Contradictions of Oppression*. London: Routledge.

Rauhala, Ann. 1987. "Despite Dangers, 1.5 million Canadians Take Birth-Control Pills," *The Globe and Mail*, Oct. 13.

Raymond, Janice. 1979. *The Transsexual Empire: The Making of the She-Male*. Boston: Beacon Press.

Reed, Evelyn. 1972. *Is Biology Woman's Destiny?* New York: Pathfinder Press.

Reiff, Philip. 1961. *Freud: The Mind of the Moralist*. Garden City, New York: Doubleday.

Reiter, Rayna, ed. 1975. *Toward an Anthropology of Women*. New York: Monthly Review Press.

Rennie, Susan. 1993. "Breast cancer prevention: Diet vs. Drugs," *Ms. Magazine* 3(6): 38-46.

Ribes, Bruno. 1978. *Biology and Ethics*. Paris: UNESCO.

Richardson, Joan. 1983. "The Structure of Organizational Instability: The Women's Movement in Montreal, 1974-1977," PhD diss., New School for Social Research, New York.

Ricks, Francie, George Matheson, and Sandra Pyke. 1972. "Women's Liberation: A Case Study of Organizations for Social Change," *Canadian Psychologist* 13(1): 30-39.

Ristock, Janice. 1991. "Feminist Collectives: The Struggles and Contradictions in our Quest for a 'Uniquely Feminist Structure.'" In *Women and Social Change: Feminist Activism in Canada*, eds., J. Dawn Wine and J. Ristock. Toronto: James Lorimer, 41-55.

Roberts, Barbara. 1990. "Ladies, Women and the State: Managing Female Immigration, 1880-1920." In *Community Organization and the Canadian State*, eds., Roxana Ng, Gillian Walker and Jacob Muller. Toronto: Garamond Press, 108-130.

Rooke, P.T. and R.I. Schnell. 1987. *No Bleeding Heart: A. Charlotte Whitton, A Feminist on the Right*. Vancouver: University of British Columbia Press.

Rothschild, Joan. 1983. *Machina Ex Dea*. New York: Pergamon.

Rowbotham, Sheila. 1973. *Woman's Consciousness, Man's World*. Harmondsmith: Pelican Books.

Rowbotham, Sheila. 1972. *Women, Resistance and Revolution*. New York: Vintage Books.

Rushing, Beth and Suzanne Onorato. 1987. "Feminist Theories and the New Reproductive Technologies," Paper presented at 1987 annual meetings of the Southern Sociological Society.

Russo, Ann. 1991. "We Cannot Live Without our Lives: White Women, Antiracism, and Feminism." In *Third-World Women and the Politics of Feminism*, eds., C. Mohanty, A. Russo, and L. Torres. Bloomington: Indiana University Press, 297-313.

Sangster, Joan. 1989. *Dreams of Equality: Women on the Canadian Left, 1920-1950*. Toronto: McClelland & Stewart.

Satzewich, Vic, ed. 1992. *Deconstructing a Nation*. Halifax: Fernwood.

Scott, Joan Wallach, ed. 1997. "Women's Studies on the Edge," (special issue) *Differences*, Vol. 9.

Seccombe, Wally. 1975. "Domestic Labour: A Reply to Critics," *New Left Review* 94: 85-96.

Segal, Lynn. 1987. *Is the Future Female? Troubled Thoughts on Contemporary Feminism*. London: Virago.

Sherwin, Susan. 1984-85. "A Feminist Approach to Ethics," *Dalhousie Review* 64(4): 704-713.

Shiva, Vandana. 1989. *Staying Alive: Women, Ecology, and Development*. London: Zed.

Singh Bolaria, B., and Peter S. Li. 1988. *Racial Oppression in Canada*. 2nd ed. Toronto: Garamond.

Smith Dorothy E. 1985a. "Women, Class and Family." In *Women, Class, Family and the State*, eds., Varda Burstyn and Dorothy E. Smith. Toronto: Garamond Press, 1-44.

Smith, Dorothy E. 1977. "Some Implications of A Sociology of Women." In *Women in a Man-made World*, eds., Nona Glazer, and Helen Youngelson Waehrer. Chicago: Rand McNally.

Snider, Lauren. 1993. "Criminalization: Panacea for Sexual Assaulted but Anathema for Corporate Criminals?," Paper presented at Social Inequality and Social Justice Conference.

Snowden, R. and G.D. Mitchell. 1981. *The Artificial Family*. London: Allen & Unwin.

Spelman, Elizabeth V. 1988. Inessential Woman: Problems of Exclusion in Feminist Thought. Boston: Beacon.

Statistics Canada. 1995b. *Women in Canada*. 3rd ed. Ottawa: Minister of Industry (cat. no. 89-503E).

Statistics Canada. 1993. *Violence Against Women: A National Survey*. Ottawa.

Steinem, Gloria. 1983. *Outrageous Acts and Everyday Rebellions*. New York: Holt, Rinehart and Winston.

Stumpf, Andrea E. 1986. "Redefining Mother: A Legal Matrix for New Reproductive Technologies." *Yale Law Journal* 96(1): 187-208.

Task Force on Child Care. 1986. *Report*. Ottawa: Status of Women Canada.

Teghtsoonian, Katherine. 1997. "Who Pays for the Family: Public Policy and the Devaluation of Women's Work." In *Challenging the Public-Private Divide: Feminism, Law and Public Policy*, ed., Susan Boyd. Toronto: University of Toronto, 113-143.

Thornhill, Esmeralda. 1991. "Focus on Black Women!" In *Race, Class, and Gender: Bonds and Barriers*, eds., Jesse Vorst et al. Toronto: Society for Socialist Studies and Garamond, 26-36.

Toronto Coalition for a Just Refugee and Immigration Policy. 1987. *Borders and Barriers. An Education Kit: Canada's Policy on Refugee/Family Reunification*.

Trotsky, Leon. 1970. *Women and the Family*. New York: Pathfinder Press.

Turritin, Jane Sawyer. 1983. "We Don't Look for Prejudice." In Jean Leonard Elliot, ed., *Two Nations, Many Cultures: Ethnic Groups in Canada*. Scarborough: Prentice-Hall.

Van Dieren, Karen. 1984. "The Response of the WMS to the Immigration of Asian Women, 1888-1942." In *Not Just Pin Money: Selected Essays on the History of Women's Work in British Columbia*, eds., Barbara K. Latham and Roberta J. Pazdro. Victoria: Camosun College.

Vega, Judith. 1988. "Coercion and Consent: Classic Liberal Concepts on Sexual Violence," *International Journal of the Sociology of Law* 16(1): 75-89.

Vickers, Jill. 1991. "Bending the Iron Law of Oligarchy: Debates On the Feminization of Organization and the Political Process in the English Canadian Women's Movement." In *Women and Social Change: Feminist Activism in Canada*, eds., J. Wine and J. Ristock. Toronto: James Lorimer, 75-95.

Vickers, Jill. 1989. "Feminist Approaches to Politics." In *Beyond the Vote: Canadian Women and Politics*, eds., Linda Kealey and John Sangster. Toronto: University of Toronto Press, 16-36.

———. n.d. "Feminist Ethics and In-Vitro Fertilization" (mimeo)

———. and Hugh Armstrong. 1996. *Wasting Away: The Undermining of Canadian Health Care*. Toronto: Oxford.

Vickers, Jill. 1988. "Politics as if Women Mattered. The Institutionalization of the Canadian Women's Movement and its Impact on Federal Politics, 1965-1988." Paper presented at ACSNAZ, Canberra.

Vickers, Jill. 1988a. *Getting Things Done: Women's Views of Their Involvement in Political Life*. Ottawa/Paris: CRIAW and UNESCO.

Vickers, Jill McCalla. 1986. "Equality-Seeking in a Cold Climate." In *Righting the Balance: Canada's New Equality Rights*, ed., Lynn Smyth. Saskatoon: Canadian Human Rights Reporter.

Vickers, Jill. 1984. "Integrative Feminism," *Fireweed: A Feminist Quarterly* 19: 54-81.

Vickers, Jill McCalla, and Janine Brodie. 1981. "Canada." In *The Politics of the Second Electorate*, eds., Joni Lovenduski and Jill Hills. London: Routledge, 52-82.

Vickers, Jill. 1975. "Women's Liberation: Opening Chapter Two," *Canadian Dimension* 10(8): 56-68.

Vorst, Jesse, et al. 1991. *Race, Class, Gender: Bonds and Barriers*. Toronto: Society for Socialist Studies and Garamond.

Warren, Mary Anne. 1985. *Gendercide: The Implications of Sex Selection*. Totowa, New Jersey: Rowman & Allanheld.

Wikler, Norma Juliet. 1986. "Society's Response to the New Reproductive Technologies: The Feminist Perspectives," *Southern California Law Review* 59(4): 1043-57.

Wollheim, Richard. 1975. "Psychoanalysis and Feminism," *New Left Review* 93: 61-9.

Women Working with Immigrant Women. 1985-86. *Annual Report*. N.P.

World Health Organization (WHO) (1975) *The Epidemiology of Infertility*. Technical Report No. 582. Geneva.

World Women's Congress for a Healthy Planet. 1992. *Official Report, Including Women's Action Agenda 21 and Findings of the Tribunals*. New York: Women's Environment and Development Organization (WEDO).

Yalnizyan, Armine. 1994. "Creating Canadian Social Policy." In *Shifting Time*, eds., Armine Yalnizyan, T. Ron Ide, and Arthur J. Cordell. Toronto: Between the Lines, 17-72.

Yawney, Carol. 1983. "To Grow a Daughter: Cultural Liberation and the Dynamics of Oppression in Jamaica." In *Feminism in Canada*, eds., Angela Miles and G. Finn. Montreal: Black Rose, 177-202.

Yee, Shirley. 1977. "The 'Women' in Women's Studies." In *Differences* 9:46-64 (special issue). *Women's Studies on the Edge*, ed., Joan Wallach Scott.

York, Geoffrey. 1989. *The Dispossessed: Life and Death in Native Canada*. Toronto: Lester and Orpen Dennys.

Zaretsky, Eli. 1973. "Capitalism, Family and Personal Life," *Socialist Revolution* 13-14: 69-125.

Zimmerman, Shirley L. 1982. "Alternatives in Human Reproductions for Involuntary Childless Couples," *Family Relations*, 31.

INDEX